The Social Movements Reader

BLACKWELL READERS IN SOCIOLOGY

Each volume in this authoritative series aims to provide students and scholars with comprehensive collections of classic and contemporary readings for all the major sub-fields of sociology. They are designed to complement single-authored works, or to be used as stand-alone textbooks for courses. The selected readings sample the most important works that students should read and are framed by informed editorial introductions. The series aims to reflect the state of the discipline by providing collections not only on standard topics but also on cutting-edge subjects in sociology to provide future directions in teaching and research.

The Social Movements Reader

Cases and Concepts

Edited by

Jeff Goodwin and James M. Jasper

Blackwell
Publishing

Editorial material and organization © 2003 by Jeff Goodwin and James M. Jasper

BLACKWELL PUBLISHING
350 Main Street, Malden, MA 02148-5020, USA
108 Cowley Road, Oxford OX4 1JF, UK
550 Swanston Street, Carlton, Victoria 3053, Australia

First published 2003 by Blackwell Publishing Ltd
Reprinted 2004 (twice)

Library of Congress Cataloging-in-Publication Data

The social movements reader : cases and concepts / edited by Jeff Goodwin and James
M. Jasper.
    p. cm.—(Blackwell readers in sociology ; 12)
    Includes bibliographical references and index.
    ISBN 0-631-22195-6 (alk. paper)—ISBN 0-631-22196-4 (pbk. : alk. paper)
    1. Social movements.　2. Social movements—Case studies.　I. Goodwin, Jeff.　II.
Jasper, James M., 1957–　III. Series.
    HM881.S64　2003
    303.48′4—dc21

                                               2002074758

A catalogue record for this title is available from the British Library.

Set in 10/12 pt Sabon
by Kolam Information Services Pvt. Ltd, Pondicherry, India
Printed and bound in the United Kingdom
by TJ International Ltd, Padstow, Cornwall

The publisher's policy is to use permanent paper from mills that operate a
sustainable forestry policy, and which has been manufactured from pulp
processed using acid-free and elementary chlorine-free practices. Furthermore,
the publisher ensures that the text paper and cover board used have met
acceptable environmental accreditation standards.

For further information on
Blackwell Publishing, visit our website:
http://www.blackwellpublishing.com

Contents

Key Concepts

Key concepts are defined by the editors and appear in boxes throughout the readings.

Acknowledgments

Aho, J. A., 1990, extracts from *The Politics of Righteousness: Idaho Christian Patriotism*. Reproduced by permission of the University of Washington Press.

Alinsky, Saul D., extract from *Rules for Radicals*, copyright © 1971 by Saul D. Alinsky. Reproduced by permission of Random House Inc.

Amenta, E., Dunleavy, K., and Mary Bernstein, "Stolen Thunder? Huey Long's Share Our Wealth, Political Mediation, and the Second New Deal," from *American Sociological Review* 59 (1994) pp. 678–702. Reproduced by permission of the American Sociological Association and the author.

Bernstein, M., "Celebration and Suppression: The Strategic Uses of Identity by the Lesbian and Gay Movement," from *American Journal of Sociology* 103 (3) pp. 531–65. Reproduced by permission of the University of Chicago Press and the author.

Blumberg, R. L., 1984, extract from *Civil Rights: The 1960s Freedom Struggle*. Reproduced by permission of Twayne Publishers, pp. 17–36.

Clemens, E. S., "Organizational Repertoires and Institutional Change: Women's Groups and the Transformation of U.S. Politics, 1890–1920," from *American Journal of Sociology* 98 (4) pp. 755–98. Reproduced by permission of the University of Chicago Press and the author.

Cotgrove, S. and Duff, A., 1980, "Environmentalism, Middle-Class Radicalism and Politics," from *Sociological Review* 28 (2) pp. 333–49. Reproduced by permission of Blackwell Publishing and the author.

D'Emilio, John, 1983, "The Gay Liberation Movement," from *Sexual Politics, Sexual Communities*. Reproduced by permission of the University of Chicago Press, and the author.

Epstein, Barbara, "What Happened to the Women's Movement?" from *Monthly Review* 53 (1) (May 2001). Reproduced by permission of the *Monthly Review* and the author.

Eyerman, R. and Jamison, A., 1998, extract from *Music and Social Movements*. Reproduced by permission of Cambridge University Press and the authors.

Finnegan, William, 2000, "After Seattle," from *The New Yorker*, April 17, pp. 40–51. Reproduced by permission of the Condé Nast Group.

Freeman, Jo, "The Origins of the Women's Liberation Movement" from *American Journal of Sociology* 78 (4) pp. 792–811. Reproduced by permission of the author.

Gamson, J., 1995, "Must Identity Movements Self-Destruct? A Queer Dilemma," from *Social Problems* 42 (3) pp. 390–407. Reproduced by permission of the University of California Press journals and the author.

Gamson, W. A., 1990, extract from *The Strategy of Social Protest*. Reproduced by permission of the author.

Ganz, Marshall, "Resources and Resourcefulness," from *American Journal of Sociology* 105 (4) pp. 1003–62. Reproduced by permission of the University of Chicago Press and the author.

Gitlin, T., 1980, extract from *The Whole World is Watching*. Copyright © 1980 The Regents of the University of California. Reproduced by permission of the University of California Press.

Hirsch, E. L., "Sacrifice for the Cause: Group Processes, Recruitment, and Commitment in a Student Social Movement," from *American Sociological Review* 55 (Apr.) pp. 243–54. Reproduced by permission of the American Sociological Association and the author.

Inglehart, R., 1977, extract from *The Silent Revolution*. Reproduced by permission of Princeton University Press.

Jasper, James M., 1998, "The Emotions of Protest," from *Sociological Forum* 13 (3). Reproduced by permission of Kluwer Academic/Plenum Press and the author.

Jenkins J. C. and Perrow, C., "Insurgency of the Powerless," from *American Sociological Review* 42 (Apr.) pp. 248–68. Reproduced by permission of the American Sociological Association and the author.

Katzenstein, M. F., 1998, extract from *Faithful and Fearless: Moving Feminist Protest Inside the Church and Military*. Reproduced by permission of Princeton University Press.

Klandermans, B., 1997, extracts from *The Social Psychology of Protest*. Reproduced by permission of Blackwell Publishing.

Kurzman, Charles, "Structural and Perceived Opportunity: The Iranian Revolution of 1979," from *American Sociological Review* 61 (Feb.) pp. 153–70. Reproduced by permission of the American Sociological Association and the author.

Luker, K., 1984, extract from *Abortion and the Politics of Motherhood*. Copyright © 1984 The Regents of the University of California. Reproduced by permission of the University of California Press.

McAdam, D., 1988, extracts from *Freedom Summer*. Reproduced by permission of Oxford University Press, New York.

McCarthy John D. and Zald, Mayer N., "Resource Mobilization and Social Movements: A Partial Theory," from *American Journal of Sociology* 82 (6) pp.

1212–41. Reproduced by permission of the University of Chicago Press and the authors.

Mansbridge, J. J., 1986, "Ideological Purity in the Women's Movement," from *Why We Lost the ERA*. Reproduced by permission of the University of Chicago Press and the author.

Meyer, David S., 1990, extract from *A Winter of Discontent*. Reproduced by permission of the Greenwood Publishing Group, Inc., Westport, CT.

Morris, A. D., 1984, extract from *The Origins of the Civil Rights Movement*. Reproduced by permission of Simon and Schuster Inc.

Sexton, P. C., 1991, extract from *The War on Labor and the Left*. Reproduced by permission of the Perseus Books Group.

Wapner, Paul, "Politics Beyond the State: Environmental Activism and World Civic Politics," from *World Politics* 47: (3). Copyright © Center for International Studies, Princeton University. Reprinted by permission of the Johns Hopkins University Press.

Whittier, N., 1995, extract from *Feminist Generations*. Reproduced by permission of Temple University Press.

Part I

Introduction

1 Editors' Introduction

Jeff Goodwin and James M. Jasper

Throughout history, humans have complained about the things they disliked. Sometimes they do more than complain; they band together with others to change things. In modern societies, more than

> **Political or Social Protest** Protest refers to the act of challenging, resisting, or making demands upon authorities, powerholders, and/or cultural beliefs and practices by some individual or group.

ever before, people have organized themselves to pursue a dizzying array of goals. There are the strikes, pickets, and rallies of the labor movement, aimed at unionization but also at political goals. In the early nineteenth century the Luddites broke into early British factories and smashed new machines. There have been dozens of revolutions like those in France, Russia, China, Cuba, and Iran. We have seen Earth Day and organizations like the Union of Concerned Scientists and the Natural Resources Defense Council. Animal rights activists have broken into labs and "liberated" experimental animals. The women's movement has tried to change family life and gender relations. There have been plenty of right-wing movements as well, from Americans opposed to immigrants in the 1840s to those who fought federally mandated busing in the 1970s to those who have bombed abortion clinics in more recent years.

Some of these movements have looked for opportunities to claim new rights while others have responded to threats or violence. Some have sought political and economic emancipation and gains, while others have fought lifestyle choices they disliked or feared. Some have created formal

> **Social Movement** A social movement is a collective, organized, sustained, and noninstitutional challenge to authorities, powerholders, or cultural beliefs and practices. A **revolutionary movement** is a social movement that seeks, at minimum, to overthrow the government or state.

organizations, others have relied upon informal networks, and still others have used more spontaneous actions such as riots. Movements have regularly had to choose between violent and nonviolent activities, illegal and legal ones, disruption and education, extremism and moderation.

Social movements are conscious, concerted, and sustained efforts by ordinary people to change some aspect of their society by using extra-institutional means. They are more conscious and organized than fads and fashions. They last longer than a single protest or riot. There is more to them than formal organizations, although such organizations usually play a part. They are composed mainly of ordinary people as opposed to army officers, politicians, or economic elites. They need not be explicitly political, but many are. They are protesting against something, either explicitly as in antiwar movements or implicitly as in the back-to-the-land movement that is disgusted with modern urban and suburban life.

* * *

Why study social movements? First, you might be interested in them for their own sake, as a common and dramatic part of the world around you. You might simply wish to understand protestors and their points of view, especially when they seem to want things that to you seem undesirable. Why do some people think animals have rights? Others that the United Nations is part of a sinister conspiracy? Understanding social movements is a good way to comprehend human diversity.

But there are other reasons for studying social movements, which are windows onto a number of aspects of social life. You might study social movements if you are interested in politics, as movements are a main source of political conflict and change. They are often the first to articulate *new* political issues and ideas. As people become attuned to some social problem they want solved, they typically form some kind of movement to push for a solution. Political parties and their leaders are rarely asking the most interesting questions, or raising new issues; bureaucracy sets in, and politicians spend their time in routines. It is typically movements outside the political system that force insiders to recognize new fears and desires.

You might also study social movements because you are interested in human action more generally, or in social theory. Scholars of social movements ask why and how people do the things they do, especially why they do things together: this is also the question that drives sociology in general, especially social theory. Social movements raise the famous Hobbesian problem of social order: why do people cooperate with each other when they might get as many or more benefits by acting selfishly or alone? The study of social movements makes the question more manageable: if we can see why people will voluntarily cooperate in social movements, we can understand why they cooperate in general. Political action is a paradigm of social action that sheds light on action in other spheres of life. It gets at the heart of human motivation. For example, do people act to maximize their material interests? Do they act out rituals that express their beliefs about the world, or simply reaffirm their place in that world? What is the balance between symbolic and "instrumental" action? Between selfish and altruistic action?

You will also benefit from the study of social movements if you are interested in social change. This might be a theoretical interest in why change occurs, or it might be a practical interest in encouraging or preventing change. Social movements are one central source of social change. Other sources include those formal organizations, especially corporations, that are out to make a profit: they invent new technologies that change our ways of working and interacting. Corporations are always inventing new ways of extracting profits from workers, and inventing new products to market. These changes typically disrupt people's ways of life: a new machine makes people work harder, or toxic wastes have to be disposed of near a school. People react to these changes, and resist them, by forming social movements.

But while formal organizations are the main source of technical change, they are rarely a source of change in values, in social arrangements. Why? In modern societies with tightly knit political and economic systems, the big bureaucracies demand economic and political control, stability. So they try to routinize everything in order to prevent the unexpected. They resist changes in property relations, for example, which are one of the key components of capitalism.

So innovation in values and political beliefs often arises from the discussions and efforts of social movements. Why don't societies just endlessly reproduce themselves intact? It is often social movements that develop new ways of seeing society and new ways of directing it. They are a central part of what has been called "civil society" or the "public sphere," in which groups and individuals debate their own futures.

If you have a *practical* interest in spreading democracy or changing society, there are tricks to learn, techniques of organizing, mobilizing, influencing the media. There have been a lot of social movements around for the last forty years, and people in those movements have accumulated a lot of know-how about how to run movements. This is not the main focus of this reader, but we hope there are a few practical lessons to be learned from it.

Finally, you might want to study social movements if you have an interest in the moral basis of society. Social movements are a bit like art: they are efforts to express sensibilities that have not yet been well articulated, that journalists haven't yet written about, that lawmakers have not yet addressed. We all have moral sensibilities – including unspoken intuitions as well as articulated principles and rules – that guide our action, or at least make us uneasy when they are violated. Social movements are good ways to understand these moral sensibilities.

Social movements play a crucial role in contemporary societies. We learn about the world around us through them. They encourage us to figure out how we feel about government policies and social trends and new technologies. In some cases they even inspire the invention of new technologies or new ways of using old technologies. Most of all, they are one means by which we work out our moral visions, transforming vague intuitions into principles and political demands.

Civil rights mvmt changed way scholars viewed social mvmts.

***

Research on social movements has changed enormously over time. Until the 1960s, most scholars who studied social movements were frightened of them. They saw them as dangerous mobs who acted irrationally, blindly following demagogues who sprang up in their midst. In the nineteenth century, the crowds that attracted the most attention were those that periodically appeared in the cities of Europe demanding better conditions for workers, the right to vote, and other conditions we now take for granted. Most elites, including university professors, had little sympathy for them. Crowds were thought to whip up emotions that made people do things they otherwise would not do, would not want to do, and should not do. They transformed people into unthinking automatons, according to scholars of the time. The last hurrah of this line of thinking was in the 1950s, as scholars analyzed the Nazis in the same way they had crowds: as people who were fooled by their leaders, whom they followed blindly and stupidly. For more than one hundred years, most scholars feared political action outside of normal, institutionalized channels.

These attitudes changed in the 1960s, when for one of the first times in history large numbers of privileged people (those in college and with college educations) had considerable sympathy for the efforts of those at the bottom of society to demand freedoms and material improvements. The civil rights movement was the main reason views changed, as Americans outside the South learned what conditions of repression Southern blacks faced. It was hard to dismiss civil rights demonstrators as misguided, immature, or irrational. As a result, scholars began to see aspects of social movements they had overlooked when they had used the lens of an angry mob. There were several conceptual changes or "turns" made in social movement theories.

First was an economic turn. In 1965 an economist named Mancur Olson wrote a book, *The Logic of Collective Action*, in which he asked when and why individuals would protest if they were purely rational, in the sense of carefully weighing the costs and benefits of their choices. Although Olson portrayed people as overly individualistic (caring only about the costs and benefits to them individually, not to broader groups), he at least recognized that rational people could engage in protest. Within a few years, John McCarthy and Mayer Zald worked out another economic vision of protest, taking formal organizations as the core of social movements and showing that these social movement organizations (SMOs, for short) act a lot like firms: they try to accumulate resources, hire staff whose interests might diverge from constituents', and "sell" their point of view to potential contributors. SMOs even compete against one another for contributions; together they add up to a "social movement industry." Because of their emphasis on SMOs' mobilization of time and money, they came to be known as "resource mobilization" theorists. Just as Olson saw individuals as rational, so McCarthy and Zald saw their organizations as rational. Protestors were no longer dismissed as silly or dangerous.

Around the same time, scholars also discovered the explicitly political dimension of social movements. Most older social movements, like the labor or the civil rights movements, were making demands directly of the state. Foremost were claims for new rights, especially voting rights. Thus the state was involved as not only the target but also the adjudicator of grievances. In this view, which came to be known as "political process" theory, social movements were also seen as eminently rational; indeed, they were little more than normal politics that used extra-institutional means. As in the economic models of mobilization theories, protestors were seen as normal people pursuing their interests as best they could. By highlighting social movements' interactions with the state, these process theories have focused on conflict and the external environments of social movements, to the extent that they even explain the emergence of social movements as resulting from "opportunities" provided by the state (such as a lessening of repression or a division among economic and political elites).

In the late 1980s, yet another dimension of social movements came to be appreciated: their cultural side. Whereas the economic and political "turns" had both featured protestors as straightforwardly rational and instrumental, scholars now saw the work that goes into creating symbols, convincing people that they have grievances, and establishing a feeling of solidarity among participants. Two cultural components have been studied more than others. The processes by which organizers "frame" their issues in a way that resonates with or makes sense to potential recruits and the broader public is one such component. The other is the "collective identity" that organizers can either use or create in arousing interest in and loyalty to their cause. Most fortunate are those activists who can politicize an existing identity, as when black college students in the South around 1960 began to feel as though it was up to them to lead the civil rights movement into a more militant phase. Other activists may try to create an identity based on membership of the movement itself, as communists did for much of the twentieth century.

Recently scholars have begun to recognize and study even more aspects of social movements. For example, many movements have a global reach, tying together protest groups across many countries or having international organizations. The environmental movement, or the protest against the World Trade Organization and the unregulated globalization of trade, are examples. Yet most of our models still assume a national movement interacting with a single national state.

The emotions of protest are also being rediscovered. A variety of complex emotions accompany all social life, but they are especially clear in social movements. Organizers must arouse anger and outrage and compassion, often by playing on fears and anxieties. Sometimes these fears and anxieties need to be mitigated before people will protest. Typically, organizers must also offer certain joys and excitements to participants in order to get them to remain in the movement. These represent some of the future directions that research on social movements seems likely to take in coming years.

Our understanding of social movements has grown as these movements themselves have changed. Like everyone else, scholars of social movements are influenced by what they see happening around them. Much protest of the nineteenth century took the form of urban riots, so it was natural to focus on the nature of the crowd. In the 1950s, it was important to understand how the Nazis could have taken hold of an otherwise civilized nation, so "mass society" theories were developed to explain this. Scholars who have examined the labor movement and the American civil rights movement recognized that claims of new rights necessarily involve the state, so it was natural for them to focus on the political dimensions of protest. Social scientists who came of age in the 1960s and after were often favorably disposed toward the social movements around them, and so portrayed protestors as reasonable people. Many of the movements of the 1960s and after were not about rights for oppressed groups, but about lifestyles and cultural meanings, so it was inevitable that scholars sooner or later would turn to this dimension of protest. Likewise in recent years, several important social movements have become more global in scope. Many movements are also interested in changing our emotional cultures, especially movements influenced by the women's movement, which argued that women were disadvantaged by the ways in which different emotions were thought appropriate for men and for women.

Research on social movements will undoubtedly continue to evolve as social movements themselves evolve.

* * *

Scholars and activists themselves have asked a number of questions about social movements. We have grouped the readings in this volume around nine main questions. Foremost, of course, why do social movements form, and why do they form when they do? Who joins and supports them? What determines how long a person stays in a social movement: who stays and who drops out? What kinds of things do participants think, want, and feel? How are movements organized? What do they do? In other words, how do they decide what tactics to deploy? How are they affected by the media? By the state and elites? What happens to them over time? Why and how do they decline or end? What changes do they bring about? The pages that follow give a variety of answers to each of these questions.

So that students can learn something about specific movements as well as theoretical questions and hypotheses, we have chosen a disproportionate number of readings about several movements in the United States, especially civil rights, the women's movement, environmentalism, and the gay and lesbian movement. Although we apologize to non-American readers for this emphasis, we felt these cases would interest a large number of curious students. Movements with these concerns, of course, have also arisen outside the United States.

Part II

When and Why Do Social Movements Occur?

Introduction

The most frequently asked question about social movements is why they emerge when they do. Not only does this process come first in time for a movement, but it is also basic in a logical sense as well. Until a movement takes shape, there is not much else we can ask about it. Where we think a movement comes from will color the way we view its other aspects too: its goals, personnel, tactics, and outcomes. In general, theories of movement origins have focused either on the characteristics of participants or on conditions in the broader environment which the movement faces. Only in recent years have cultural approaches tried to link these two questions.

Theorists before the 1960s addressed the question of origins to the exclusion of almost all others, for they frequently saw movements as mistakes that were best avoided! For them, the urgent political issue was how to prevent them, and to do this you needed to know why they appeared. "Mass society" theorists, for instance, argued that social movements occurred when a society had lost other, "intermediary" organizations that discontented individuals could join (Kornhauser, 1959). These might be trade unions, community groups, churches – or any other organization that could mediate between the individual and government, aggregating individual preferences and providing outlets for letting off steam. These "regular" organizations were thought to be stable and normal and healthy, unlike social movements. Other theorists emphasized the kind of people they thought likely to join movements, which would form when enough people were "alienated" from the world around them, or had infantile psychological needs that absorption in a movement might satisfy (Hoffer, 1951). In general, early theorists saw movements as a function of discontent in a society, and they saw discontent as something unusual. Today, scholars see social movements as a normal part of politics, and so these early theories are no longer taken very seriously.

In the 1960s and 1970s, a group of researchers known as the "resource mobilization" school noticed that social movements usually consisted of formal organizations (McCarthy and Zald, 1977, excerpted in part VI). And one prerequisite for any organization was a certain level of resources, especially money, to sustain it. They argued that there were always enough discontented people in society to fill a protest movement, but what varied over time – and so explained the emergence of movements – was the resources available to nourish it. They accordingly focused on how movement leaders raise funds, sometimes by appealing to elites, sometimes through direct-mail fundraising from thousands of regular citizens. As a society grows wealthier, moreover, citizens have more discretionary money to contribute to social movement organizations, and so there are more movements than ever before. With this point of view, the focus shifted decisively away from the kinds of individuals who might join a movement and toward the infrastructure necessary to sustain a movement. Today, scholars still consider resources an important part of any explanation of movement emergence.

The paradigm that has concentrated most on movement emergence is the "political process" approach (Jenkins and Perrow, 1977; McAdam, 1982; Tarrow, 1998). In this view, economic and political shifts occur, usually independently of protestors' own efforts, that open up a space for the movement. Because they perceive movements as primarily political, making demands of the state and asking for changes in laws and policies, they see changes in the state as the most important opportunity a movement needs. Most often, this consists of a slackening in the repression that organizers are otherwise assumed to face, perhaps because political elites are divided (the movement may have found some allies within the government), or because political and economic elites have divergent interests. There may be a general crisis in the government, perhaps as a result of losing a foreign war, that distracts leaders (Skocpol, 1979). In many versions, the same factors are seen as explaining the rise of the movement and its relative success (e.g., Kitschelt, 1986).

Rhoda Blumberg's description of the preconditions of the American civil rights movement (taken from her book, *Civil Rights*) reflects the process perspective, although it adds a few other factors as well. The migration of African-Americans out of the rural South provided more resources and denser social ties, a church and organizational infrastructure through which money could be channeled to civil rights work, as well as an entirely new cultural outlook. These in turn allowed a greater degree of mobilization, especially through the NAACP, which in turn won inspiring legal victories (especially *Brown v. Board of Education* in 1954). Resources, organization, the emotions of raised expectations, and a sense of new opportunities all encouraged the civil rights movement that grew rapidly beginning in 1955.

Alongside mobilization and process approaches, a number of scholars have emphasized the social networks through which people are mobilized into social movements. Although networks have been used primarily to explain *who* is recruited (as we will see in part III), the very existence of social ties among potential recruits is seen as a prerequisite for the emergence of a social movement. If most process theorists emphasize conditions in the external world (especially the state) that allow a movement to emerge, network theorists look at the structural conditions within the community or population of those who might be recruited. Those with "dense" ties, or preexisting formal organizations, will find it easier to mobilize supporters, and build a movement.

Jo Freeman's article, "The Origins of the Women's Liberation Movement," was one of the first accounts of a movement to place networks front and center. She was arguing against early theorists who saw discontented and unorganized masses as spontaneously appearing in the streets. (Freeman herself was one of the founders of the younger branch of the movement in Chicago.) Freeman asserts that, if spontaneous uprisings exist at all, they remain small and local unless they have preexisting organizations and social ties. Those networks are important for communication, vital to the spread of a movement. Like most network theorists, however, she does not discuss the emotions that are the real life blood of networks: people respond to the information they receive through networks because of affective ties to those in the network. She also admits that organizers can set about building a new network suited to their own purposes, an activity that takes longer than mobilizing or coopting an existing network.

John D'Emilio's account of the 1969 Stonewall rebellion in New York City and subsequent development of a militant gay and lesbian movement also emphasizes the critical importance of social networks. This apparently spontaneous eruption of gay militancy in fact marked the public emergence of a long-repressed, covert urban subculture. D'Emilio points out that the movement was also able to draw upon preexisting networks of activists in the radical movements then current among American youth. The "gay liberation" movement recruited from the ranks of both the New Left and the women's movement. It also borrowed its confrontational tactics from these movements. Many lesbians and gay men, D'Emilio notes, had already been radicalized and educated in the arts of protest by the feminist and antiwar movements.

These structural approaches redefined somewhat the central question of movement emergence. Scholars began to see movements as closely linked to one another, because leaders and participants shifted from one to the other, or shared social networks, or because the same political conditions encouraged many movements to form at the same time. So researchers began to ask what caused entire waves of social movements to emerge, rather than asking about the origins of single movements (Tarrow, 1998:ch. 9). In this structural view, all movements are equivalent.

In the cultural approach that has arisen in recent years, not all movements are seen as structurally similar. In one version, movements are linked to broad historical developments, especially the shift from an industrial or manufacturing society to a postindustrial or knowledge society, in which fewer people process physical goods and more deal with symbols and other forms of knowledge (Touraine, 1977). Social movements are seen as efforts to control the direction of social change largely by controlling a society's symbols and self-understandings. This often involves shaping or creating their own collective identities as social movements (Melucci, 1996).

In cultural approaches, the goals and intentions of protestors are taken seriously. For instance, the origin of the animal protection movement has been linked to broad changes in sensibilities of the last two hundred years that have allowed citizens of the industrial world to recognize the suffering of nonhuman species – and to worry about it (Jasper and Nelkin, 1992). Such concerns would simply not have been possible in a society where most people worked on farms and used animals both as living tools (horses, dogs, dairy cows) and as raw materials (food, leather, etc.). The point is to observe or ask protestors themselves about their perceptions and desires and fantasies, without having a theory of history that predicts in advance what protestors will think and feel. Perceptions are crucial in this view.

From this perspective, Charles Kurzman's article, excerpted below, helped change the way scholars think about political opportunities. Process theorists had insisted that these were objective changes, independent of protestors' perceptions, but for the case of the Iranian Revolution, Kurzman shows that the perceptions matter more than some underlying "reality." A movement can sometimes succeed merely because it thinks it can. In other words, cultural perceptions can play as important a role as changes in state structure. Process theorists had apparently not tested their model in cases where perceptions and objective realities diverged. We are tempted to go even further than Kurzman does: the objective shifts in repression, elite alliances, and so on (the "opportunities" of process theorists) may only have an effect if they are perceived as such. In other words, perceptions, rhetoric, symbols, and emotions matter as much or more than structural shifts in the state.

Structural and cultural approaches disagree in part because they have examined different kinds of social movements (on the conflict between these two views, see Goodwin and Jasper, 2003). Most process theorists have focused on movements of groups who have been systematically excluded from political power and legal rights, in other words groups who are demanding the full rights of citizenship. Cultural approaches have been more likely to examine movements of those who already have the formal rights of citizens – who can vote, pressure legislators, run for office – but who nonetheless feel they must step outside normal political channels to have a greater impact (such as the so-called new social movements). In a related difference, structural theorists usually assume that groups of people know what they want already, and merely need an opportunity to go after it; culturalists recognize that in many cases people need to figure out what they want, often because organizers persuade them of it (e.g., that animals can suffer as much as humans, that marijuana is a danger to respectable society, that the U.S. government is the tool of Satan).

There are a number of factors to look for in explaining why a movement emerges when and where it does, drawn from all these perspectives: political factors such as divisions among elites, lessened repression from the police and army; economic conditions such as increased discretionary income, especially among those sympathetic to a movement's cause; organizational conditions such as social-network ties or formal organizations among aggrieved populations; demographic conditions such as the increased population density that comes with industrialization (if you live a mile from your nearest neighbor, it is hard to organize collectively); cultural factors such as moral intuitions or sensibilities that support the movement's cause. And in many cases, potential protestors must frame and understand many of these factors as opportunities before they can take advantage of them.

Culturalists have reasserted the importance of perceptions, ideas, emotions, and grievances, all of which mobilization and process theorists once thought did not matter or could simply be taken for granted. But these are examined today in the context of broader social and political changes, not in isolation from them. It is not as though people develop goals, then decide to go out and form movements to pursue them; there is an interaction between ideas, mobilization, and the broader environment. But some people hold ideas that others do not, so that the question of the origins of a social movement begins to overlap with that of who is recruited to it.

Discussion Questions

1 In what ways might the *Brown v. Board of Education* decision of 1954 have encouraged the civil rights movement? (Think about emotional dynamics as well as cognitive ones.)
2 What were the two branches of the women's movement of the late 1960s and how do they differ?
3 In what ways did the New Left and women's movement spur the development of the gay liberation movement?
4 What is the relationship between "objective" political opportunities and people's perceptions of them? What effect does each have?
5 What are the competing sets of factors that might explain popular participation in the Iranian Revolution of 1979? Which does Kurzman favor?

2 The Civil Rights Movement

Rhoda Lois Blumberg

Trends and events in the first half of the twentieth century significantly affected black people and provided the necessary conditions for the successful take-off of the civil rights movement. Militant free and ex-slave black leaders had come forward prior to the Civil War; whites as well as blacks had struggled in the abolitionist movement. Yet by the end of the nineteenth century, the main spokesperson for the race was the accommodationist leader, Booker T. Washington, who espoused gradual change rather than political action.

Poverty, segregation, and violence were rampant when Washington came to prominence. Most former slaves had been deprived of their newly won right to vote and were still members of a rural peasantry in the South. Washington advised adjustment to the biracial situation and to disenfranchisement. He stressed self-help, racial solidarity, economic accumulation, and industrial education. His polite, conciliatory stance toward whites was coupled with the premise that black folk should take responsibility for their own advancement – to prove themselves worthy of the rights many thought they had already won.

Washington's 1895 speech at the Cotton States and International Exposition in Atlanta was hailed by whites. He gained the financial backing of foundations and controlled, through the "Tuskegee machine," important governmental appointments of black individuals during the Theodore Roosevelt and Taft administrations.

Protest had not entirely died out, however. The Afro-American Council, in existence from 1890 to 1908, had a militant outlook. Antilynching crusader Ida Wells-Barnet and William Monroe Trotter, editor of the outspoken *Boston Guardian*, lashed out against Washington. W. E. B. Du Bois gradually made public his growing disagreements with Washington, and through his role as editor of *Crisis* magazine, Du Bois renewed the move toward integration and equal rights. But until his death in 1915, and despite some erosion of his power, Booker T. Washington probably remained the most influential political figure of the race.

What happened to move a people from accommodation to protest? The most important interacting events that made the transition possible included:

1. A mass migration of black peasantry out of the South, eventuating in their transformation to a predominantly urban group
2. White violence against the black urban newcomers which demanded response
3. Two world wars and an economic depression
4. Years of litigation culminating in important legal victories
5. The development of community institutions and organizations in the cities
6. The rise of leaders who utilized opportunities for protest and were able to mobilize potential participants
7. A changed international climate confronting American racism

[...]

World War II stimulated another major migration to the North, so that by 1950 almost one-third of all black people lived outside the South. Over 20 million people, more than 4 million of them black, were forced to leave the land after 1940.

A Chronology of the U.S. Civil Rights Movement

1896: Supreme Court upholds "separate but equal" doctrine in *Plessy v. Ferguson*

1905: W. E. B. Du Bois and others form the Niagara Movement, demanding abolition of racially discriminatory laws

1909: The National Association for the Advancement of Colored People (NAACP) is formed

1941: Labor leader A. Philip Randolph threatens massive march on Washington; President Roosevelt orders the end of racial discrimination in war industries and government

1948: President Truman ends segregation in the armed forces

1954: Supreme Court, in *Brown v. Board of Education of Topeka*, rules that segregated public schools are unconstitutional

1955: Emmett Till is lynched in Mississippi; Rosa Parks is arrested for violating the bus segregation ordinance in Montgomery, Alabama; the Montgomery bus boycott begins

1956: Supreme Court rules that segregation on public buses is unconstitutional

1957: Southern Christian Leadership Conference (SCLC) is formed with Martin Luther King, Jr., as president; President Eisenhower sends paratroopers to Little Rock, Arkansas, to enforce school integration

1960: Sit-ins at segregated lunch counters begin in Greensboro, North Carolina, Nashville, Tennessee, and elsewhere; student activists form the Student Nonviolent Coordinating Committee (SNCC, pronounced "Snick")

1961: "Freedom Riders" expose illegal segregation in bus terminals

1963: Major demonstrations are begun by the SCLC in Birmingham, Alabama, to protest segregation; Medgar Evers, head of the Mississippi NAACP, is assassinated; the March on Washington attracts hundreds of thousands of demonstrators to Washington, DC; four black girls are killed by a bomb at Birmingham's Sixteenth Street Baptist Church

1964: Hundreds of white college students participate in Freedom Summer, a Mississippi voter registration project; three civil rights workers are murdered near Philadelphia, Mississippi; the Civil Rights Act of 1964, banning discrimination in voting and public accommodations, is passed; the Mississippi Freedom Democratic Party challenges the state's all-white delegation to the Democratic national convention in Atlantic City, NJ; Martin Luther King, Jr., receives the Nobel Peace Prize

1965: Malcolm X is assassinated in New York City; police brutally attack a planned march in Selma, Alabama; a massive march takes place from Selma to Montgomery after a U.S. District Court rules that protestors have the right to march; President Johnson signs the Voting Rights Bill into law; riot in the Watts section of Los Angeles is the largest race riot in U.S. history up to that time

1966: SNCC leader Stokely Carmichael popularizes the slogan, "Black power"; the Black Panther Party is formed in Oakland, CA; riots occur in major cities, continuing through 1967; SNCC votes to exclude white members

1968: Martin Luther King, Jr., is assassinated in Memphis; riots occur in more than 100 cities; Richard Nixon is elected president

Although the federal government subsidized farmers to take land out of production in order to reduce agricultural surpluses at the end of the war, few sharecroppers received their share of the subsidies. Vastly increased mechanization made much human labor power obsolete. The result was the loss of 1 million farms between 1950 and 1969, with only the larger ones remaining. By 1960, 73 percent of black people were urban and by 1965, the figure had risen to 80 percent. Another important fact was that, by 1960, about half of the black population lived outside of the most repressive areas – the old slave states.

The movement to the cities resulted in conditions favorable to protest: the amassing of large numbers of people with similar grievances, a slight economic improvement over rural poverty so that folks could be less concerned about their daily bread, a nucleus of organizations through which communication and mobilization could occur, and a cultural support system for black pride and militancy. The segregated black world contained contradictions, from which both problems and strengths derived. Among the latter was the possibility of high population concentrations creating a rich, varied, all-black group life. On the other hand, urban conditions were crowded, dangerous, and unhealthy, and the black population was subject to exploitation. There also came to be vested interests in preserving segregation.

Even during slavery, free African Americans had gravitated to cities, finding relatively more freedom there to seek their rights. They acquired property, created schools and churches, met in conventions, petitioned state legislatures, and protested segregation. As abolitionists, they were largely responsible for the escape route to the North and Canada – the underground railroad. Denmark Vesey, the leader of a major slave revolt in Charleston, South Carolina, in 1822 was a freeman and a successful carpenter. These urban-dwelling free Negroes and former slaves became the nucleus of a more educated class. Within the black communities, a vast network of organizations grew – churches, fraternal orders, and lodges. Many local and state organizations – some temporary and some long-lived – provided forums for the working out of survival and protest strategies.

Mass migration to northern cities in the twentieth century provided an even stronger base for dealing with racism. Unlike the white immigrants who preceded them, ghetto blacks found no escape route to "better," more healthful neighborhoods. Housing segregation became increasingly rigid; neighborhood businesses continued to be controlled by whites. The separate black world came to share a sense of oppression and a sense of community. The black press grew and became a vital source of communication, supplementing white newspapers with race news – full coverage of black problems, issues, personalities, and cultural life. Through their own publications, leaders publicly and heatedly debated the correct course of action for their people. Fiery critics, such as Marcus Garvey and Malcolm X after him, seemed best able to capture the imaginations of urban blacks and to verbalize their smoldering resentment.

These large concentrations of people had ready access to one another and to the mass communication media. They were voters or potential voters; by the early 1940s, New York's Harlemites were able to elect one of their own, the young minister and race leader Adam Clayton Powell, Jr., to the city council. In 1945, black urbanites of the new 18th Congressional District started sending him to Congress. A vocal advocate for equal rights, Powell had followed his father as pastor of the Abyssinian Baptist Church. Although most African Americans were concentrated in unskilled or semiskilled jobs, some found additional avenues of employment and status. The city became the center of intellectual thought and cultural development. It placed black protest leaders in contact with white liberals and radicals and created the possibility of a northern support system for the southern-based civil rights movement of the 1960s.

Harlem, the mecca of African American culture, began to take shape and character as a Negro community around 1910. The Harlem Renaissance, a creative outburst of talent and nationalism, was led by black poets like Langston Hughes, Countee Cullen, and Claude McKay. Black theater and black music became popular.

Many of the writings of the 1930s projected themes of protest. Richard Wright's works, such as *Native Son*, gained him recognition as a major American writer. This literary movement accelerated, with such giants as Ralph Ellison and James Baldwin incisively examining the effects of white racism on black life. Another cultural renaissance would mark the transition from the civil rights movement to the black power movement in the 1960s. The growth of a literature of protest provided ideological and emotional impetus for the movement and gave sympathetic whites a greater understanding of black life.

White liberals had supported the Harlem Renaissance. Without an adequate economic base, black artists were often dependent on white sponsors and white patronage. Critics, such as Harold Cruse (1967), say that white patrons influenced the directions of black artistic expression, preventing it from fully achieving its promise. Others view this cultural era as significantly fostering black pride and black consciousness. Always there would be this debate about the influence of white liberals. They brought black interests to the attention of the public, but, it was argued, they did so in a patronizing fashion that would have to lead, eventually, to rejection. A somewhat different criticism would be made intermittently of white Communists, who also focused public attention on black issues. They were frequently accused of using racial issues for their own purposes. The question of whether or not to work with white leftists would plague black organizations; paradoxically some of the most anticommunist black organizations would be accused of being reds by their white enemies....

Relative Deprivation The poor are not always the most rebellious people in a society, nor do people always protest during the worst of times. Rather, people typically become angry and feel that their situation is unjust when there is a significant difference between the conditions of their lives and their expectations. In other words, people judge the fairness of their social situation and of the society in which they live not against some absolute standard, but relative to the expectations that they've come to hold about themselves or their society. Such relative deprivation may be found among quite comfortably-off and even privileged people. Relative deprivation may also become widespread when a long period of prosperity is followed by an abrupt economic downturn (the J-curve theory). When this happens, people cannot quickly or easily adjust their expectations to fit their new situation; instead, they may feel that something is badly wrong with the society in which they live. See Gurr (1970) and Gurney and Tierney (1982).

As World War II approached, black leaders remembered the bitter experiences of World War I – the segregated units, the struggle to be allowed into combat, the difficulty in gaining access to any but the lowest of assignments, and the Red Summer of 1919. Two issues loomed large – continued segregation in the armed forces and the inability of blacks to work in defense industries. As whites began to profit from these burgeoning industries, African Americans were once more being discriminated against. They were blocked from entering training for some of the newly available jobs. The 1940 statistics on the employment of blacks in war industries showed that only a tiny proportion had been hired. The armed forces were strongly racist: the Selective Service System operated under discriminatory quotas; the navy restricted blacks to messmen and other menial positions; the army segregated them. As national rhetoric proclaimed the contrast between the free and totalitarian worlds, black leadership initiated a "double V" campaign – victory abroad and victory over racism at home.

Black anger was growing. Leaders attempted to negotiate with the national government. In September 1940, the executive secretary of the NAACP, Walter White, along with Randolph and other prominent blacks, met with President Roosevelt to protest segregation in the armed forces. This effort proved futile, despite the fact that the black vote had helped FDR gain a second term. Not only did the president reaffirm the policy of segregation in the armed forces, but his press statement seemed to imply that the black leaders had gone along with it. This they immediately denied. The NAACP held a national protest day, January 26, 1941, calling it "National Defense Day." African American newspapers, firmly supported by the black public (as shown in polls), unanimously called for an end to racial discrimination during the national emergency. In contrast, the white press ignored the grievances of blacks, confining itself to the usual reporting of black crimes.

It was in this context that Randolph, who had tried so hard to move organized labor from within, took bolder action. He created the March on Washington Movement (MOWM), threatening a mass protest demonstration of 100,000 black people in Washington on the first of July 1941. The black press fully supported the proposed march, the aims of which were to secure the admission of blacks into defense industries on a nondiscriminatory basis and to end segregation in the armed forces. After first resisting the demands, FDR became convinced that he could not deter the leaders. At the last moment, on June 25, 1941, he created the first national Fair Employment Practices Commission through Executive Order 8802. Thus only the threat of a major demonstration, combined with a situation perceived as a national emergency, could move the federal government into the area of employment discrimination.

A student of the first March on Washington action ranks it as a high point in black protest and sees it as the best example of pressure unanimously and militantly applied against a president up to that point. A short-lived but extremely significant event, the MOWM incorporated several elements that would reappear in the civil rights movement of the 1960s. Randolph tried to build mass participation and recognized the importance of black consciousness in the development of a racial protest movement. Besides his belief in the need to mobilize the black masses, Randolph had become distrustful of white allies. The CP opposed the planned march until close to its deadline, when an event abroad led it to reverse its position – the Nazi attack on the Soviet Union in June 1941. Randolph planned an all-black march. Integrationist in orientation, the NAACP was lukewarm about it, providing little coverage in its official publications. But much grass-roots recruiting took place, with the formation of neighborhood committees, speaking tours by leaders, and huge outdoor meetings.

The NAACP and the Urban League had become the main bastions of black leadership following the demise of Garvey. Yet for a year and a half, from the inception of the MOWM until its decline, A. Philip Randolph was the major black leader in America. A member of the board of directors of the NAACP, Randolph was never averse to starting a new organization when he thought one was needed. This strong leader met tremendous opposition from white unionists and received little of the acknowledgment from other white Americans that King later would.

Shortly after the first FEPC hearing, the Japanese bombed Pearl Harbor and the United States became formally involved in the shooting war. Black leaders persisted in seeking equality during the war but were unable to achieve desegregation in the armed forces. That would not occur until President Truman signed an executive order in 1948. Nevertheless, the mood of black people during the war is probably accurately reflected in this statement by Ottley in a book published in 1943:

> Tradition must be overturned, and democracy extended to the Negro.... The color problem has become a world-wide issue to be settled here and now. Should tomorrow the Axis surrender unconditionally, Negroes say, the capitulation would provide only a brief interlude of peace.... There is nothing mystical about the Negro's aggressive attitude. The noisy espousal of democracy in the last war gave stimulus to the Negro's cause, and set the race implacably in motion. By advancing it in this war, democracy has become an immediate goal to the Negro. His rumblings for equality in every phase of American life will reverberate into a mighty roar in the days to come. (344)

Ottley's dramatic projection into the future was based not only on internal developments within the United States but also on a changing international environment. During the war, black soldiers went abroad again in the name of democracy, experienced segregation in the armed forces and their recreational facilities, and met Europeans who were far less prejudiced than white Americans. Racial clashes between white and black servicemen occurred. But the aftermath of World War II would differ from that of the first war. White supremacy in Africa and Asia was in decline: between 1945 and 1960, forty new independent nation-states were formed. The impact on the United States was considerable. Says Isaacs, "The downfall of the white-supremacy system in the rest of the world made its survival in the United States suddenly and painfully conspicuous. It became our most exposed feature and in the swift unfolding of the world's affairs, our most vulnerable weakness" (1963, 6–7).

The United States competed for the friendship of the newly independent nations, but reports of American segregation and discrimination interfered. The Soviet Union, engaged in a cold war with the United States, could point to this country's hypocrisy. The CP-USA publicized cases of racial injustice and championed the victims. The foreign press gave full coverage to America's racial disgraces, such as the 1955 murder of the teenager Emmett Till in Mississippi. Battles over school desegregation following the 1954 Supreme Court decision also made headlines. In particular, a famous incident at Little Rock, Arkansas, gained national attention. A reluctant President Eisenhower was forced to send in airborne troops to enforce a federal desegregation order and escort nine black students into high school. Vivid pictures showing angry adults screaming at black students were flashed around the world. The incident so embarrassed the president that he went on television and radio to criticize the actions of the governor of the state and justify his own.

Other incidents, involving ambassadors or citizens of new African or Asian states, were causing the country acute chagrin. A number of them were refused service or segregated in restaurants and motels along U.S. Route 40, which leads into Washington, D.C. Sometimes official apologies were necessary. Of course, Washington itself, the nation's capital, discriminated against dark-skinned peoples. Route 40 would become the target of demonstrations by CORE, intended to test desegregation laws. But meanwhile, the NAACP was continuing its pursuit of desegregation through the courts.

Another area of discrimination was the world of sports, from which blacks had been almost totally excluded. In the fight ring, where they could compete, Joe Louis reigned as world heavyweight champion. The color barrier in baseball was finally breached when Jackie Robinson was hired by the Brooklyn Dodgers in 1945, which some saw as a hopeful sign.

The end of World War II did not see a resurgence of race riots for several reasons. Labor shortages provided some employment gains for blacks, and the country did not experience a severe recession. Larger numbers of black people now lived in the North, where they could vote and did. The 1948 Democratic party convention adopted a strong civil rights plank, but was challenged by a separate Dixiecrat candidate drawing off party voters. Against this rival and Progressive and Republican party candidates, Harry S. Truman pulled off his surprising victory. In the same year, black citizens received their reward for support – Truman's executive order ending segregation in the armed forces. Black voters were beginning to play a pivotal role in national elections. . . .

A final but major precondition to the modern civil rights movement was the continuing battle in the nation's courts. The NAACP had taken as a mission the investigation of cases where justice had been mishandled in the courts as well as in the streets. It fought and finally won a number of cases against segregation in graduate and professional education, successfully demonstrating the inferiority of schools for blacks.

As early as the 1930s, the Supreme Court had begun to reverse its post-Civil War negativity to the black cause. A 1938 Missouri case was decided favorably, with the Court insisting that equal educational opportunities had to be made available to black students. Two important cases followed. In *Sweatt v. Painter*, the Court ruled that the state law school set up in Texas for blacks was not comparable to the white school. The following year the Court went even further in *McLaurin v. Oklahoma*. By maintaining segregation in the classroom, cafeteria, and library, the University of Oklahoma was judged to have deprived a black student of the equality guaranteed by the Fourth Amendment. By the fall of 1953, blacks had been integrated, in a token manner, into twenty-three publicly supported colleges in southern or border states at the graduate level. There was even a small amount of integration at the undergraduate level. But in the five states of the lower South, the public schools were totally segregated, and data showed that black schools were vastly unequal in resources and in the education they offered. Many of the southern states made a last ditch effort to try to improve black schools. Cautious at first, the NAACP decided to attack the principle of segregation itself. Five cases challenging the constitutionality of school segregation were moving up to the Supreme Court from South Carolina, Virginia, Kansas, Delaware, and the District of Columbia. In December 1952, the Supreme Court ordered the litigants to submit briefs on a list of questions for a new hearing in the case of *Oliver Brown et al. v. Board of Education of Topeka, Kansas*.

The unanimous ruling of the Court under Chief Justice Earl Warren favored the black plaintiffs. In often-quoted words, the Court declared that segregation has a detrimental effect upon colored children because it "generates a feeling of inferiority as to their status in the community that may affect their hearts and minds in a way unlikely ever to be undone" (Woodward 1974, 147). These victories of the litigation phase were crucial developments.

The Supreme Court decision was greeted with hope by black Americans, who did not realize at the time how long and hard a struggle lay ahead. Soon they would turn to nonviolent action to protest the much-hated, humiliating segregation in public transportation. Courts and law were not abandoned as an avenue of redress, but more and more it was felt that mass action was necessary to supplement the legal process. Beginning in 1955, nonviolent protest spread significantly, backed by a clearly enunciated ideology. The proliferation of leaders and escalation of involvement lasted over most of the 1960s and was popularly called – at the time – the civil rights movement.

References

Cruse, Harold 1967 *The Crisis of the Negro Intellectual*. London: W. H. Allen.

Isaacs, Harold R. 1963 *The New World of Negro Americans*. London: Phoenix House.

Ottley, Roi 1943 '*New World A-Coming*': *Inside Black America*. Boston: Houghton Mifflin.

Woodward, C. Vann 1974 *The Stange Career of Jim Crow*. 3rd edn. New York: Oxford University Press.

Biography

A brief biography of Martin Luther King, Jr., written by the editors of this volume, can be found on page 370

3 The Women's Movement

Jo Freeman

The emergence in the last few years of a feminist movement caught most thoughtful observers by surprise. Women had "come a long way," had they not? What could they want to be liberated from? The new movement generated much speculation about the sources of female discontent and why it was articulated at this particular time. But these speculators usually asked the wrong questions. Most attempts to analyze the sources of social strain have had to conclude with Ferriss (1971, p. 1) that, "from the close perspective of 1970, events of the past decade provide evidence of no compelling cause of the rise of the new feminist movement." His examination of time-series data over the previous 20 years did not reveal any significant changes in socioeconomic variables which could account for the emergence of a women's movement at the time it was created. From such strain indicators, one could surmise that any time in the last two decades was as conducive as any other to movement formation.

[...]

An investigation into a movement's origins must be concerned with the microstructural preconditions for the emergence of such a movement center. From where do the people come who make up the initial, organizing cadre of a movement? How do they come together, and how do they come to share a similar view of the world in circumstances which compel them to political action? In what ways does the nature of the original center affect the future development of the movement?

Most movements have very inconspicuous beginnings. The significant elements of their origins are usually forgotten or distorted by the time a trained observer seeks to trace them out, making retroactive analyses difficult. Thus, a detailed investigation of a single movement at the time it is forming can add much to what little is known about movement origins. Such an examination cannot uncover all of the conditions and ingredients of movement formation, but it can aptly illustrate both weaknesses in the theoretical literature and new directions for research. During the formative period of the women's liberation movement, I had many opportunities to observe, log, and interview most of the principals involved in the early movement. The descriptive material below is based on that data. This analysis, supplemented by five other origin studies made by me, would support the following three propositions:

Proposition 1: The need for a preexisting communications network or infrastructure within the social base of a movement is a primary prerequisite for "spontaneous" activity. Masses alone don't form movements, however discontented they may be. Groups of previously unorganized individuals may spontaneously form into small local associations – usually along the lines of informal social networks – in response to a specific strain or crisis, but, if they are not linked in some manner, the protest does not become generalized: it remains a local irritant or dissolves completely. If a movement is to spread rapidly, the communications network must already exist. If only the rudiments of one exist, movement formation requires a high input of "organizing" activity.

Proposition 2: Not just any communications network will do. It must be a network that is *co-optable* to the new ideas of the incipient movement. To be co-optable, it

A chronology of the U.S. women's movement

1961: President Kennedy forms President's Commission on the Status of Women, chaired by Esther Peterson and Eleanor Roosevelt; only 3.6 percent of law students are women

1963: Betty Friedan's book, *The Feminine Mystique*, becomes a best-seller; the Equal Pay Act is signed into law

1964: The Civil Rights Act of 1964 is signed into law; Title VII of the Act bars sex discrimination in employment; Mary King and Casey Hayden write a paper decrying the treatment of women in the Student Nonviolent Coordination Committee (SNCC)

1965: The U.S. Supreme Court, in *Griswold v. Connecticut*, bans laws that prohibit the use of, or the dissemination of information about, birth control; King and Hayden's paper on "Sex and Caste" is circulated widely (and published in the journal *Liberation* in 1966).

1966: National Organization of Women (NOW) founded with Betty Friedan as president

1967: Women's consciousness-raising (CR) groups formed in Berkeley and elsewhere; CR groups proliferate, especially during 1968 and 1969

1968: Protests are staged against the Miss America Pageant in Atlantic City; Shirley Chisholm becomes the first African-American woman elected to Congress; women are hissed and thrown out of a convention of Students for a Democratic Society (SDS) for demanding a women's liberation plank in the group's platform

1969: Feminist activists disrupt Senate hearings on the birth control pill for excluding testimony about its dangerous side-effects

1970: Tens of thousands participate in the Women's Equality March in New York City; much feminist work is published, including Kate Millett's *Sexual Politics*, Shulamith Firestone's *The Dialectic of Sex*, *The Black Woman*, edited by Toni Cade Bambara, and *Sisterhood is Powerful*, edited by Robin Morgan; the Feminist Press is founded; Rita Mae Brown spurs the "Lavender Menace" protest in favor of including lesbian rights as part of the women's movement; lesbian feminist CR groups proliferate during 1970 and 1971; the U.S. House passes the Equal Rights Amendment (ERA); four states, including New York, pass liberal abortion laws

1971: The first courses in women's history and literature are offered at many colleges; the National Women's Political Caucus is founded by Bella Abzug, Shirley Chisholm, Betty Friedan, and Gloria Steinem, among others

1972: Title IX of the 1972 education bill prohibits sex discrimination in educational programs (including sports programs) that receive federal assistance; 12 percent of law students are now women; Shirley Chisholm runs for the Democratic nomination for president; the first rape crisis and battered women's shelters open; *Ms.* magazine begins publishing

1973: Supreme Court, in *Roe v. Wade*, eliminates restrictions on first-trimester abortions; the National Black Feminist Organization is formed

1974: The Equal Opportunity Act forbids discrimination on the basis of sex or marital status; the Coalition of Labor Union Women is founded; the Combahee River Collective of Black Women begins meeting in Boston; eleven women are ordained as Episcopal priests in violation of church law

1978: The first "Take Back the Night March" is held in Boston

1979: The Moral Majority is founded by Rev. Jerry Falwell, opposing the ERA, abortion, and gay rights

Early 1980s: The women's movement is divided over the issue of pornography

1982: The ERA is defeated, falling three states short of the thirty-eight needed for ratification

must be composed of like-minded people whose background, experiences, or location in the social structure make them receptive to the ideas of a specific new movement.

Proposition 3: Given the existence of a co-optable communications network, or at least the rudimentary development of a potential one, and a situation of strain, one or more precipitants are required. Here, two distinct patterns emerge that often overlap. In one, a crisis galvanizes the network into spontaneous action in a new direction. In the other, one or more persons begin organizing a new organization or disseminating a new idea. For spontaneous action to occur, the communications network must be well formed or the initial protest will not survive the incipient stage. If it is not well formed, organizing efforts must occur; that is, one or more persons must specifically attempt to construct a movement. To be successful, organizers must be skilled and must have a fertile field in which to work. If no communications network already exists, there must at least be emerging spontaneous groups which are acutely atuned to the issue, albeit uncoordinated. To sum up, if a co-optable communications network is already established, a crisis is all that is necessary to galvanize it. If it is rudimentary, an organizing cadre of one or more persons is necessary. Such a cadre is superfluous if the former conditions fully exist, but it is essential if they do not.

Before examining these propositions in detail, let us look at the structure and origins of the women's liberation movement.

The women's liberation movement manifests itself in an almost infinite variety of groups, styles, and organizations. Yet, this diversity has sprung from only two distinct origins whose numerous offspring remain clustered largely around these two sources. The two branches are often called "reform" and "radical," or, as the sole authoritative book on the movement describes them, "women's rights" and "women's liberation" (Hole and Levine 1971). Unfortunately, these terms actually tell us very little, since feminists do not fit into the traditional Left/ Right spectrum. In fact, if an ideological typography were possible, it would show minimal consistency with any other characteristic. Structure and style rather than ideology more accurately differentiate the two branches, and, even here, there has been much borrowing on both sides.

I prefer simpler designations: the first of the branches will be referred to as the older branch of the movement, partly because it began first and partly because the median age of its activists is higher. It contains numerous organizations, including the lobbyist group (Women's Equity Action League), a legal foundation (Human Rights for Women), over 20 caucuses in professional organizations, and separate organizations of women in the professions and other occupations. Its most prominent "core group" is the National Organization for Women (NOW), which was also the first to be formed.

While the written programs and aims of the older branch span a wide spectrum, their activities tend to be concentrated on legal and economic problems. These groups are primarily made up of women – and men – who work, and they are substantially concerned with the problems of working women. The style of organization of the older branch tends to be traditionally formal, with elected officers, boards of directors, bylaws, and the other trappings of democratic procedure. All started as top-down national organizations, lacking in a mass base. Some have subsequently developed a mass base, some have not yet done so, and others do not want to.

Conversely, the younger branch consists of innumerable small groups – engaged in a variety of activities – whose contact with each other is, at best, tenuous. Contrary to popular myth, it did not begin on the campus nor was it started by the Students for a Democratic Society (SDS). However, its activators were, to be trite, on the other side of the generation gap. While few were students, all were "under 30" and had received their political education as participants or concerned observers of the social action projects

---

Cognitive Liberation People will not usually rebel against the status quo, no matter how wretched they are, unless they feel that it is unjust or illegitimate (as opposed to natural or inevitable) and that they have the capacity to change it for the better. Together, these feelings of injustice and efficacy constitute what Doug McAdam (1982) has called "cognitive liberation." Of course, it is possible that people only develop or discover a sense of efficacy or empowerment *after* they have begun protesting with others. At first, and sometimes for a long time, people may be uncertain as to whether their protests will actually make a difference. In this sense, cognitive liberation is sometimes a product rather than a cause of protest.

of the last decade. Many came direct from New Left and civil rights organizations. Others had attended various courses on women in the multitude of free universities springing up around the country during those years.

The expansion of these groups has appeared more amoebic than organized, because the younger branch of the movement prides itself on its lack of organization. From its radical roots, it inherited the idea that structures were always conservative and confining, and leaders, isolated and elitist. Thus, eschewing structure and damning the idea of leadership, it has carried the concept of "everyone doing her own thing" to the point where communication is haphazard and coordination is almost nonexistent. The thousands of sister chapters around the country are virtually independent of each other, linked only by numerous underground papers, journals, newsletters, and cross-country travelers. A national conference was held over Thanksgiving in 1968 but, although considered successful, has not yet been repeated. Before the 1968 conference, the movement did not have the sense of national unity which emerged after the conference. Since then, young feminists have made no attempt to call another national conference. There have been a few regional conferences, but no permanent consequences resulted. At most, some cities have a coordinating committee which attempts to maintain communication among local groups and to channel newcomers into appropriate ones, but these committees have no power over any group's activities, let alone its ideas. Even local activists do not know how big the movement is in their own city. While it cannot be said to have no organization at all, this branch of the movement has informally adopted a general policy of "structurelessness."

Despite a lack of a formal policy encouraging it, there is a great deal of homogeneity within the younger branch of the movement. Like the older branch, it tends to be predominantly white, middle class, and college educated. But it is much more homogenous and,

unlike the older branch, has been unable to diversify. This is largely because most small groups tend to form among friendship networks. Most groups have no requirements for membership (other than female sex), no dues, no written and agreed-upon structure, and no elected leaders. Because of this lack of structure, it is often easier for an individual to form a new group than to find and join an older one. This encourages group formation but discourages individual diversification. Even contacts among groups tend to be along friendship lines.

In general, the different style and organization of the two branches was largely derived from the different kind of political education and experiences of each group of women. Women of the older branch were trained in and had used the traditional forms of political action, while the younger branch has inherited the loose, flexible, person-oriented attitude of the youth and student movements. The different structures that have evolved from these two distinctly different kinds of experience have, in turn, largely determined the strategy of the two branches, irrespective of any conscious intentions of their participants. These different structures and strategies have each posed different problems and possibilities. Intramovement differences are often perceived by the participants as conflicting, but it is their essential complementarity which has been one of the strengths of the movement.

Despite the multitude of differences, there are very strong similarities in the way the two branches came into being. These similarities serve to illuminate some of the microsociological factors involved in movement formation. The forces which led to NOW's formation were first set in motion in 1961 when President Kennedy established the President's Commission on the Status of Women at the behest of Esther Petersen, to be chaired by Eleanor Roosevelt. Operating under a broad mandate, its 1963 report (*American Women*) and subsequent committee publications documented just how thoroughly women are still denied many rights and opportunities. The most concrete response to the activity of the president's commission was the eventual establishment of 50 state commissions to do similar research on a state level. These commissions were often urged by politically active women and were composed primarily of women. Nonetheless, many believe the main stimulus behind their formation was the alleged view of the governors that the commissions were excellent opportunities to pay political debts without giving women more influential positions.

The activity of the federal and state commissions laid the groundwork for the future movement in three significant ways: (1) it brought together many knowledgeable, politically active women who otherwise would not have worked together around matters of direct concern to women; (2) the investigations unearthed ample evidence of women's unequal status, especially their legal and economic difficulties, in the process convincing many previously uninterested women that something should be done; (3) the reports created a climate of expectations that something would be done. The women of the federal and state commissions who were exposed to these influences exchanged visits, correspondence, and staff and met with each other at an annual commission convention. Thus, they were in a position to share and mutually reinforce their growing awareness and concern over women's issues. These commissions thus created an embryonic communications network among people with similar concerns.

During this time, two other events of significance occurred. The first was the publication of Betty Friedan's (1963) book, *The Feminine Mystique*. An immediate best seller, it stimulated many women to question the status quo and some to suggest to Friedan that a new organization be formed to attack their problems. The second event was the addition of "sex" to Title VII of the 1964 Civil Rights Act. Many men thought the "sex" provision was a joke. The Equal Employment Opportunity Commission (EEOC) certainly treated it as one and refused to adequately enforce it. The first EEOC executive director even stated publicly that the provision was a "fluke" that was "conceived out of wedlock." But, within the EEOC, there was a "pro-woman" coterie which argued that "sex" would be taken more seriously if there were "some sort of NAACP for women" to put pressure on the government. As government employees, they couldn't organize such a group, but they spoke privately with those whom they thought might be able to do so. One who shared their views was Rep. Martha Griffiths of Michigan. She blasted the EEOC's attitude in a June 20, 1966 speech on the House floor declaring that the agency had "started out by casting disrespect and ridicule on the law" but that their "wholly negative attitude had changed – for the worse."

On June 30, 1966, these three strands of incipient feminism were knotted together to form NOW. The occasion was the last day of the Third National Conference of Commissions on the Status of Women, ironically titled "Targets for Action." The participants had all received copies of Rep. Griffith's remarks. The opportunity came with a refusal by conference officials to bring to the floor a proposed resolution that urged the EEOC to give equal enforcement to the sex provision of Title VII as was given to the race provision. Despite the fact that these state commissions were not federal agencies, officials replied that one government agency could not be allowed to pressure another. The small group of women who had desired the resolution had met the night before in Friedan's hotel room to discuss the possibility of a civil rights organization for women. Not convinced of its need, they chose instead to propose the resolution. When the resolution was vetoed, the women held a whispered conversation over lunch and agreed to form an action organization "to bring women into full participation in the mainstream of American society now, assuming all the privileges and responsibilities thereof in truly equal partnership with men." The name NOW was coined by Friedan, who was at the conference researching her second book. Before the day was over, 28 women paid $5.00 each to join.

By the time the organizing conference was held the following October 29–30, over 300 men and women had become charter members. It is impossible to do a breakdown on the composition of the charter membership, but one of the first officers and board is possible. Such a breakdown accurately reflected NOW's origins. Friedan was president, two former EEOC commissioners were vice-presidents, a representative of the United Auto Workers Women's Committee was secretary-treasurer, and there were seven past and present members of the State Commissions on the Status of Women on the 20-member board. Of the charter members, 126 were Wisconsin residents – and Wisconsin had the most active state commission. Occupationally, the board and officers were primarily from the professions, labor, government, and the communications industry. Of these, only those from labor had any experience in organizing, and they resigned a year later in a dispute over support of the Equal Rights Amendment. Instead of organizational expertise, what the early NOW members had was media experience, and it was here that their early efforts were aimed.

As a result, NOW often gave the impression of being larger than it was. It was highly successful in getting publicity, much less so in bringing about concrete changes or organizing itself. Thus, it was not until 1969, when several national news media simultaneously decided to do major stories on the women's liberation movement, that NOW's membership increased significantly. Even today, there are only 8,000 members, and the chapters are still in an incipient stage of development.

In the meantime, unaware of and unknown to NOW, the EEOC, or to the state commissions, younger women began forming their own movement. Here, too, the groundwork had been laid some years before. Social action projects of recent years had attracted many women, who were quickly shunted into traditional roles and faced with the self-evident contradiction of working in a "freedom movement" without being very free. No single "youth movement" activity or organization is responsible for the younger branch of the women's liberation movement; together they created a "radical community" in which like-minded people continually interacted with each other. This community consisted largely of those who had participated in one or more of the many protest activities of the sixties and had established its own ethos and its own institutions. Thus, the women in it thought of themselves as "movement people" and had incorporated the adjective "radical" into their personal identities. The values of their radical identity and the style to which they had been trained by their movement participation directed them to approach most problems as political ones which could be solved by organizing. What remained was to translate their individual feelings of "unfreedom" into a collective consciousness. Thus, the radical community provided not only the necessary network of communication; its radical ideas formed the framework of analysis which "explained" the dismal situation in which radical women found themselves.

Papers had been circulated on women, and temporary women's caucuses had been held as early as 1964, when Stokely Carmichael made his infamous remark that "the only position for women in SNCC is prone." But it was not until late 1967 and 1968 that the groups developed a determined, if cautious, continuity and began to consciously expand themselves. At least five groups in five different cities (Chicago, Toronto, Detroit, Seattle, and Gainesville, Florida) formed spontaneously, independent of each other. They came at a very auspicious moment. The year 1967 was the one in which the blacks kicked the whites out of the civil rights movement, student power had been discredited by SDS, and the organized New Left was on the wane. Only draft-resistance activities were on the increase, and this movement more than any other exemplified the social inequities of the sexes. Men could resist the draft; women could only counsel resistance.

What was significant about this point in time was that there was a lack of available opportunities for political work. Some women fit well into the "secondary role" of draft counseling. Many did not. For years, their complaints of unfair treatment had been ignored by movement men with the dictum that those things could wait until after the revolution. Now these movement women found time on their hands, but the men would still not listen.

A typical example was the event which precipitated the formation of the Chicago group, the first independent group in this country. At the August 1967 National Conference for New Politics convention, a women's caucus met for days but was told its resolution wasn't significant enough to merit a floor discussion. By threatening to tie up the convention with procedural motions, the women succeeded in having their statement tacked to the end of the agenda. It was never discussed. The chair refused to recognize any of the many women standing by the microphone, their hands straining upward. When he instead called on someone to speak on "the forgotten American, the American Indian," five women rushed the podium to demand an explanation. But the chairman just patted one of them on the head (literally) and told her, "Cool down little girl. We have more important things to talk about than women's problems."

The "little girl" was Shulamith Firestone, future author of *The Dialectic of Sex* (1971), and she didn't cool down. Instead, she joined with another Chicago woman, who had been trying to organize a women's group that summer, to call a meeting of those women who had half-heartedly attended the summer meetings. Telling their stories to those women, they stimulated sufficient rage to carry the group for three months, and by that time it was a permanent institution.

Another somewhat similar event occurred in Seattle the following winter. At the University of Washington, an SDS organizer was explaining to a large meeting how white college youth established rapport with the poor whites with whom they were working. "He noted that sometimes after analyzing societal ills, the men shared leisure time by 'balling a chick together.' He pointed out that such activities did much to enhance the political consciousness of the poor white youth. A woman in the audience asked, 'And what did it do for the consciousness of the chick?'" (Hole and Levine 1971, p. 120). After the meeting, a handful of enraged women formed Seattle's first group.

Groups subsequent to the initial five were largely organized rather than emerging spontaneously out of recent events. In particular, the Chicago group was responsible for the creation of many new groups in that city and elsewhere and started the first national newsletter. The 1968 conference was organized by the Washington D.C. group from resources provided by the Center for Policy Studies (CPS), a radical research organization. Using CPS facilities, this group subsequently became a main literature-distribution center. Although New York groups organized early and were featured in the 1969–70 media blitz, New York was not a source of early organizers.

Unlike NOW, the women in the first groups had had years of experience as local-level organizers. They did not have the resources, or the desire, to form a national organization, but they knew how to utilize the infrastructure of the radical community, the underground press, and the free universities to disseminate ideas on women's liberation. Chicago, as a center of New Left activity, had the largest number of politically conscious organizers. Many traveled widely to Left conferences and demonstrations, and most used the opportunity to talk with other women about the new movement. In spite of public derision by radical men, or perhaps because of it, young women steadily formed new groups around the country.

Initially, the new movement found it hard to organize on the campus, but, as a major congregating area of women and, in particular, of women with political awareness, campus women's liberation groups eventually became ubiquitous. While the younger branch of the movement never formed any organization larger or more extensive than a city-wide co-ordinating committee, it would be fair to say that it has a larger "participationship" than NOW and the other older branch organizations. While the members of the older branch knew how to use the media and how to form national structures, the women of the younger branch were skilled in local community organizing.

From this description, there appear to be four essential elements contributing to the emergence of the women's liberation movement in the mid-sixties: (1) the growth of a preexisting communications network which was (2) co-optable to the ideas of the new movement; (3) a series of crises that galvanized into action people involved in this network, and/or (4) subsequent organizing effort to weld the spontaneous groups together into a movement. To further understand these factors, let us examine them in detail with reference to other relevant studies.

1. Both the Commissions on the Status of Women and the "radical community" created a communications network through which those women initially interested in creating an organization could easily reach others. Such a network had not previously existed among women. Historically tied to the family and isolated from their own kind, women are perhaps the most organizationally underdeveloped social category in Western civilization. By 1950, the 19th-century organizations which had been the basis of the suffrage movement – the Women's Trade Union League, the General Federation of Women's Clubs, the Women's Christian Temperance Union, the National American Women's Suffrage Association – were all either dead or a pale shadow of their former selves. The closest exception was the National Women's Party (NWP), which has remained dedicated to feminist concerns since its inception in 1916. However, since 1923, it has been essentially a lobbying

group for the Equal Rights Amendment. The NWP, having always believed that a small group of women concentrating their efforts in the right places was more effective than a mass appeal, was not appalled that, as late as 1969, even the majority of avowed feminists in this country had never heard of the NWP or the ERA.

[...]

Other evidence also attests to the role of previously organized networks in the rise and spread of a social movement. According to Buck (1920, pp. 43–44), the Grange established a degree of organization among American farmers in the 19th century which greatly facilitated the spread of future farmers' protests. In Saskatchewan, Lipset (1959) has asserted, "The rapid acceptance of new ideas and movements ... can be attributed mainly to the high degree of organization. ... The role of the social structure of the western wheat belt in facilitating the rise of new movements has never been sufficiently appreciated by historians and sociologists. Repeated challenges and crises forced the western farmers to create many more community institutions ... than are necessary in a more stable area. These groups in turn provided a structural basis for immediate action in critical situations. [Therefore] though it was a new radical party, the C.C.F. did not have to build up an organization from scratch." More recently, the civil rights movement was built upon the infrastructure of the Southern black church (King 1958), and early SDS organizers made ready use of the National Student Association (Kissinger and Ross 1968, p. 16).

[...]

The development of the women's liberation movement highlights the salience of such a network precisely because the conditions for a movement existed *before* a network came into being, but the movement didn't exist until afterward. Socioeconomic strain did not change for women significantly during a 20-year period. It was as great in 1955 as in 1965. What changed was the organizational situation. It was not until a communications network developed among like-minded people beyond local boundaries that the movement could emerge and develop past the point of occasional, spontaneous uprising.

2. However, not just any network would do; it had to be one which was co-optable by the incipient movement because it linked like-minded people likely to be predisposed to the new ideas of the movement. The 180,000-member Federation of Business and Professional Women's (BPW) Clubs would appear to be a likely base for a new feminist movement but in fact was unable to assume this role. It had steadily lobbied for legislation of importance to women, yet as late as "1966 BPW rejected a number of suggestions that it redefine... goals and tactics and become a kind of 'NAACP for women'...out of fear of being labeled 'feminist'" (Hole and Levine 1971, p. 81). While its membership has become a recruiting ground for feminism, it could not initially overcome the ideological barrier to a new type of political action.

On the other hand, the women of the President's and State Commissions on the Status of Women and the feminist coterie of the EEOC were co-optable, largely because their immersion into the facts of female status and the details of sex-discrimination cases made them very conscious of the need for change. Likewise, the young women of the "radical community" lived in an atmosphere of questioning, confrontation, and change. They absorbed an ideology of "freedom" and "liberation" far more potent than any latent "antifeminism" might have been. The repeated contradictions between these ideas and the actions of their male colleagues created a compulsion for action which only required an opportunity to erupt. This was provided by the "vacuum of political activity" of 1967–68.

[...]

A co-optable network, therefore, is one whose members have had common experiences which predispose them to be receptive to the particular new ideas of the incipient movement and who are not faced with structural or ideological barriers to action. If the new movement as an "innovation" can interpret these experiences and perceptions in ways that point out channels for social action, then participation in social movement becomes the logical thing to do.

3. As our examples have illustrated, these similar perceptions must be translated into action. This is the role of the "crisis." For women of the older branch of the movement, the impetus to organize was the refusal of the EEOC to enforce the sex provision of Title VII, precipitated by the concomitant refusal of federal officials at the conference to allow a supportive resolution. For younger women, there were a series of minor crises. Such precipitating events are common to most movements. They serve to crystallize and focus discontent. From their own experiences, directly and concretely, people feel the need for change in a situation that allows for an exchange of feelings with others, mutual validation, and a subsequent reinforcement of innovative interpretation. Perception of an immediate need for change is a major factor in predisposing people to accept new ideas. Nothing makes desire for change more acute than a crisis. If the strain is great enough, such a crisis need not be a major one; it need only embody symbolically collective discontent.

4. However, a crisis will only catalyze a well-formed communications network. If such networks are only embryonically developed or only partially co-optable, the potentially active individuals in them must be linked together by someone. As Jackson et al. (1960, p. 37) stated, "Some protest may persist where the source of trouble is constantly present. But interest ordinarily cannot be maintained unless there is a welding of spontaneous groups into some stable organization." In other words, people must be organized. Social movements do not simply occur.

The role of the organizer in movement formation is another neglected aspect of the theoretical literature. There has been great concern with leadership, but the two roles are distinct and not always performed by the same individual. In the early stages of a movement, it is the organizer much more than any "leader" who is important, and such an individual or cadre must often operate behind the scenes. Certainly, the "organizing cadre" that young women in the radical community came to be was key to the growth of that branch of the women's liberation movement, despite the fact that no "leaders" were produced (and were actively discouraged). The existence of many leaders but no organizers in the older branch of the women's liberation movement and its subsequent slow development would tend to substantiate this hypothesis.

The crucial function of the organizer has been explored indirectly in other areas of sociology. Rogers (1962) devotes many pages to the "change agent" who, while he does not necessarily weld a group together or "construct" a movement, does do many of the same things for agricultural innovation that an organizer does for political change. Mass-society theory makes reference to the "agitator" but fails to do so in any kind of truly informative way. A study of farmer's movements indicates that many core organizations were organized by a single individual before the spontaneous aspects of the movement predominated. Further, many other core groups were subsidized by older organizations, federal and state governments, and even by local businessmen. These organizations often served as training centers for organizers and sources of material support to aid in the formation of new interest groups and movements.

Similarly, the civil rights movement provided the training for many another movement's organizers, including the young women of the women's liberation movement. It would appear that the art of "constructing" a social movement is something that requires considerable skill and experience. Even in the supposedly spontaneous social movement, the professional is more valuable than the amateur.

[. . .]

References

Buck, Solon J. *The Agrarian Crusade.* 1920. New Haven, Conn.: Yale University Press.

Ferriss, Abbott L. 1971. *Indicators of Trends in the Status of American Women.* New York: Russell Sage.

Firestone, Shulamith. 1971 *The Dialectic of Sex.* New York: Morrow.

Friedan, Betty, 1963. *The Feminine Mystique.* New York: Dell.

Hole, Judith, and Ellen Levine. 1971. *Rebirth of Feminism.* New York: Quadrangle.

Jackson, Maurice, Eleanora Petersen, James Bull, Sverre Monsen, and Patricia Richmond. 1960. "The Failure of an Incipient Social Movement." *Pacific Sociological Review 3*, no. 1 (Spring): 40.

King, Martin Luther, Jr. 1958. *Stride toward Freedom.* New York: Harper.

Kissinger, C. Clark, and Bob Ross. 1968. "Starting in '60: Or From SLID to Resistance." *New Left Notes*, June 10.

Lipset, Seymour M. *Agrarian Socialism.* Berkeley: University of California Press, 1959.

Rogers, Everett M. 1962. *Diffusion of Innovations.* New York: Free Press.

Biography

A brief biography of Betty Friedan, written by the editors of this volume, can be found on page 371.

4   The Gay Liberation Movement

John D'Emilio

On Friday, June 27, 1969, shortly before midnight, two detectives from Manhattan's Sixth Precinct set off with a few other officers to raid the Stonewall Inn, a gay bar on Christopher Street in the heart of Greenwich Village. They must have expected it to be a routine raid. New York was in the midst of a mayoral campaign – always a bad time for the city's homosexuals – and John Lindsay, the incumbent who had recently lost his party's primary, had reason to agree to a police cleanup. Moreover, a few weeks earlier the Sixth Precinct had received a new commanding officer who marked his entry into the position by initiating a series of raids on gay bars. The Stonewall Inn was an especially inviting target. Operating without a liquor license, reputed to have ties with organized crime, and offering scantily clad go-go boys as entertainment, it brought an "unruly" element to Sheridan Square, a busy Village intersection. Patrons of the Stonewall tended to be young and nonwhite. Many were drag queens, and many came from the burgeoning ghetto of runaways living across town in the East Village.

However, the customers at the Stonewall that night responded in any but the usual fashion. As the police released them one by one from inside the bar, a crowd accumulated on the street. Jeers and catcalls arose from the onlookers when a paddy wagon departed with the bartender, the Stonewall's bouncer, and three drag queens. A few minutes later, an officer attempted to steer the last of the patrons, a lesbian, through the bystanders to a nearby patrol car. "She put up a struggle," the *Village Voice* (July 3, 1969, p. 18) reported, "from car to door to car again." At that moment,

the scene became explosive. Limp wrists were forgotten. Beer cans and bottles were heaved at the windows and a rain of coins descended on the cops.... Almost by signal the crowd erupted into cobblestone and bottle heaving.... From nowhere came an uprooted parking meter – used as a battering ram on the Stonewall door. I heard several cries of "let's get some gas," but the blaze of flame which soon appeared in the window of the Stonewall was still a shock.

Reinforcements rescued the shaken officers from the torched bar, but their work had barely started. Rioting continued far into the night, with Puerto Rican transvestites and young street people leading charges against rows of uniformed police officers and then withdrawing to regroup in Village alleys and side streets.

By the following night, graffiti calling for "Gay Power" had appeared along Christopher Street. Knots of young gays – effeminate, according to most reports – gathered on corners, angry and restless. Someone heaved a sack of wet garbage through the window of a patrol car. On nearby Waverly Place, a concrete block landed on the hood of another police car that was quickly surrounded by dozens of men, pounding on its doors and dancing on its hood. Helmeted officers from the tactical patrol force arrived on the scene and dispersed with swinging clubs an impromptu chorus line of gay men in the middle of a full kick. At the intersection of Greenwich Avenue and Christopher Street, several dozen queens screaming "Save Our Sister!" rushed a group of officers who were clubbing a young man and dragged him to safety. For the next few hours, trash fires blazed, bottles and stones flew through the air, and cries of "Gay Power!" rang in the streets as the police, numbering over 400, did battle with a crowd estimated at more than 2,000.

After the second night of disturbances, the anger that had erupted into street fighting was channeled into intense discussion of what many had begun to memorialize as the first gay riot in history. Allen Ginsberg's stature in the 1960s had risen almost to that of guru for many counterculture youth. When he arrived at the Stonewall on Sunday evening, he commented on the change that had already taken place. "You know, the guys there were so beautiful," he told a reporter. "They've lost that wounded look that fags all had ten years ago." The New York Mattachine Society hastily assembled a special riot edition of its newsletter that characterized the events, with camp humor, as "The Hairpin Drop Heard Round the World." It scarcely exaggerated. Before the end of July, women and men in New York had formed the Gay Liberation Front, a self-proclaimed revolutionary organization in the style of the New Left. Word of the Stonewall riot and GLF spread rapidly among the networks of young radicals scattered across the country, and within a year gay liberation groups had sprung into existence on college campuses and in cities around the nation.

The Stonewall riot was able to spark a nationwide grassroots "liberation" effort among gay men and women in large part because of the radical movements that had so inflamed much of American youth during the 1960s. Gay liberation used the demonstrations of the New Left as recruiting grounds and appropriated the tactics of confrontational politics for its own ends. The ideas that suffused youth protest found their way into gay liberation, where they were modified and adapted to describe the oppression of homosexuals and lesbians. The apocalyptic rhetoric and the sense of impending revolution that surrounded the Movement by the end of the decade gave to its newest participants an audacious

daring that made the dangers of a public avowal of their sexuality seem insignificant.

In order to make their existence known, gay liberationists took advantage of the almost daily political events that young radicals were staging across the country. New York's Gay Liberation Front had a contingent at the antiwar march held in the city on October 15, 1969, and was present in even larger numbers at the November moratorium weekend in Washington, where almost half a million activists rallied against American involvement in Southeast Asia. Gay radicals in Berkeley performed guerrilla theater on the campus during orientation that fall and carried banners at the November antiwar rally in San Francisco. In November 1969 and again the following May, lesbians from GLF converged on the Congress to Unite Women, which brought to New York women's liberationists from around the East. Gay activists ran workshops at the 1969 annual convention of the National Student Association. In May 1970 a GLF member addressed the rally in New Haven in support of Bobby Seale and Ericka Huggins, the imprisoned Black Panther leaders. A large contingent of lesbians and gay men attended the national gathering called by the Panthers in the fall of 1970, and the next year a gay "tribe" took part in the May Day protests in Washington against the war. In raising the banner of gay liberation at these and other local demonstrations, radical gays reached closeted homosexuals and lesbians in the Movement who already had a commitment to militant confrontational politics. Their message traveled quickly through the networks of activists created by the New Left, thus allowing gay liberation to spread with amazing rapidity.

The first gay liberationists attracted so many other young radicals not only because of a common sexual identity but because they shared a similar political perspective. Gay liberationists spoke in the hyperbolic phrases of the New Left. They talked of liberation from oppression, resisting genocide, and making a revolution against "imperialist Amerika." GLF's statement of purpose, printed in the New Left newspaper *RAT* (August 12, 1969), sounded like many of the documents produced by radicals in the late 1960s, except that it was written by and about homosexuals:

> We are a revolutionary group of men and women formed with the realization that complete sexual liberation for all people cannot come about unless existing social institutions are abolished. We reject society's attempt to impose sexual roles and definitions of our nature. We are stepping outside these roles and simplistic myths. We are going to be who we are. At the same time, we are creating new social forms and relations, that is, relations based upon brotherhood, cooperation, human love, and uninhibited sexuality. Babylon has forced us to commit ourselves to one thing – revolution!

Gay liberation groups saw themselves as one component of the decade's radicalism and regularly addressed the other issues that were mobilizing American youth. The Berkeley GLF, for instance, passed a resolution on the Vietnam War and the draft demanding that "all troops be brought home at once" and that homosexuals in the armed forces "be given Honorable discharges immediately." Its Los Angeles counterpart declared its "unity with and support for all oppressed minorities who fight for their freedom" and expressed its intention "to build a new, free and loving Gay counter-culture." Positions such as these made it relatively easy for previously closeted but already radicalized homosexuals and lesbians to join or form gay liberation organizations, and the new movement quickly won their allegiance.

Gay liberationists targeted the same institutions as homophile militants, but their disaffection from American society impelled them to use tactics that their predecessors would never have adopted. Bar raids and street arrests of gay men in New York City during August 1970 provoked a march by several thousand men and women from Times Square to Greenwich Village, where rioting broke out. Articles hostile to gays in the *Village Voice* and in *Harper's* led to the occupation of publishers' offices. In San Francisco a demonstration against the *Examiner* erupted into a bloody confrontation with the police. Chicago Gay Liberation invaded the 1970 convention of the American Medical Association, while its counterpart in San Francisco disrupted the annual meeting of the American Psychiatric Association. At a session there on homosexuality a young bearded gay man danced around the auditorium in a red dress, while other homosexuals and lesbians scattered in the audience shouted "Genocide!" and "Torture!" during the reading of a paper on aversion therapy. Politicians campaigning for office found themselves hounded by scruffy gay militants who at any moment might race across the stage where they were speaking or jump in front of a television camera to demand that they speak out against the oppression of homosexuals. The confrontational tactics and flamboyant behavior thrust gay liberationists into the public spotlight. Although their actions may have alienated some homosexuals and lesbians, they inspired many others to join the movement's ranks.

As a political force, the New Left went into eclipse soon after gay liberation appeared on the scene, but the movement of lesbians and gay men continued to thrive throughout the 1970s. Two features of gay liberation accounted for its ability to avoid the decline that most of the other mass movements of the 1960s experienced. One was the new definition that post-Stonewall activists gave to "coming out," which doubled both as ends and means for young gay radicals. The second was the emergence of a strong lesbian liberation movement.

From its beginning, gay liberation transformed the meaning of "coming out." Previously coming out had signified the private decision to accept one's homosexual desires and to acknowledge one's sexual identity to other gay men and women. Throughout the 1950s and 1960s, leaders of the homophile cause had in effect extended their coming out to the public sphere through their work in the movement. But only rarely did they counsel lesbians and homosexuals at large to follow their example, and when they did, homophile activists presented it as a selfless step taken for the benefit of others. Gay liberationists, on the other hand, recast coming out as a profoundly political act that could offer enormous personal benefits to an individual. The open avowal of one's sexual identity, whether at work, at school, at home, or before television cameras, symbolized the shedding of the self-hatred that gay men and women internalized, and consequently it promised an immediate improvement in one's life. To come out of the "closet" quintessentially expressed the fusion of the personal and the political that the radicalism of the late 1960s exalted.

Coming out also posed as the key strategy for building a movement. Its impact on an individual was often cathartic. The exhilaration and anger that surfaced when men and women stepped through the fear of discovery propelled them into political activity. Moreover, when lesbians and homosexuals came out, they crossed a critical dividing line. They relinquished their invisibility, made themselves vulnerable to attack, and acquired an investment in the success of the movement in a way that mere adherence to a political line could never accomplish. Visible lesbians and gay men also served as magnets that drew others to them. Furthermore, once out of the closet, they could not easily fade back in. Coming out provided gay liberation with an army of permanent enlistees.

A second critical feature of the post-Stonewall era was the appearance of a strong lesbian liberation movement. Lesbians had always been a tiny fraction of the homophile movement. But the almost simultaneous birth of women's liberation and gay liberation propelled large numbers of them into radical sexual politics. Lesbians were active in both early gay liberation groups and feminist organizations. Frustrated and angered by the chauvinism they experienced in gay groups and the hostility they found in the women's movement, many lesbians opted to create their own separatist organizations. Groups such as Radicalesbians in New York, the Furies Collective in Washington, D.C., and Gay Women's Liberation in San Francisco carved out a distinctive lesbian-feminist politics. They too spoke in the radical phrases of the New Left, but with an accent on the special revolutionary role that lesbians filled because of their dual oppression as women and as homosexuals. Moreover, as other lesbians made their way into gay and women's groups, their encounters with the chauvinism of gay men and the hostility of heterosexual feminists provided lesbian liberation with ever more recruits.

Although gay liberation and women's liberation both contributed to the growth of a lesbian-feminist movement, the latter exerted a greater influence. The feminist movement offered the psychic space for many women to come to a self-definition as lesbian. Women's liberation was in its origins a separatist movement, with an ideology that defined men as the problem and with organizational forms from consciousness-raising groups to action-oriented collectives that placed a premium on female solidarity. As women explored their oppression together, it became easier to acknowledge their love for other women. The seeming contradiction between an ideology that focused criticism on men per se and the ties of heterosexual feminists to males often provoked a crisis of identity. Lesbian-feminists played upon this contradiction. "A lesbian is the rage of all women condensed to the point of explosion," wrote New York Radicalesbians in "The Woman-Identified Woman," one of the most influential essays of the sexual liberation movements:

> Lesbian is the word, the label, the condition that holds women in line.... Lesbian is a label invented by the man to throw at any woman who dares to be his equal, who dares to challenge his prerogatives, who dares to assert the primacy of her own needs.... As long as women's liberation tries to free women without facing the basic heterosexual structure that binds us in one-to-one relationships with our own

oppressors, tremendous energies will continue to flow into trying to straighten up each particular relationship with a man.... It is the primacy of women relating to women, of women creating a new consciousness of and with each other which is at the heart of women's liberation, and the basis for the cultural revolution.

Under these circumstances many heterosexual women reevaluated their sexuality and resolved the contradiction between politics and personal life by coming out as lesbians. Lesbian-feminist organizations were filled with women who came not from the urban subculture of lesbian bars but from the heterosexual world, with the women's liberation movement as a way station. As opponents of feminism were quick to charge, the women's movement was something of a "breeding ground" for lesbianism.

Besides the encouragement it provided for women to come out, women's liberation served lesbians – and gay men – in another way. The feminist movement continued to thrive during the 1970s. Its ideas permeated the country, its agenda worked itself into the political process, and it effected deep-seated changes in the lives of tens of millions of women and men. Feminism's attack upon traditional sex roles and the affirmation of a nonreproductive sexuality that was implicit in such demands as unrestricted access to abortion paved a smoother road for lesbians and homosexuals who were also challenging rigid male and female stereotypes and championing an eroticism that by its nature did not lead to procreation. Moreover, lesbians served as a bridge between the women's movement and gay liberation, at the very least guaranteeing that sectors of each remained amenable to the goals and perspectives of the other. Feminism helped to remove gay life and gay politics from the margins of American society.

By any standard of measurement, post-Stonewall gay liberation dwarfed its homophile predecessor. In June 1970 between 5,000 and 10,000 men and women commemorated the first anniversary of the riot with a march from Greenwich Village to Central Park. By the second half of the decade, Gay Freedom Day events were occurring in dozens of cities, and total participation exceeded half a million individuals. The fifty homophile organizations that had existed in 1969 mushroomed into more than 800 only four years later; as the 1970s ended, the number reached into the thousands. In a relatively short time, gay liberation achieved the goal that had eluded homophile leaders for two decades – the active involvement of large numbers of homosexuals and lesbians in their own emancipation effort.

Numerical strength allowed the new breed of liberationists to compile a list of achievements that could only have elicited awe from homophile activists. In 1973 the American Psychiatric Association altered a position it had held for almost a century by removing homosexuality from its list of mental disorders. During the 1970s more than half the states repealed their sodomy laws, the Civil Service Commission eliminated its ban on the employment of lesbians and homosexuals, and several dozen municipalities passed antidiscrimination statutes. Politicians of national stature came out in favor of gay rights. Activists were invited to the White House to discuss their grievances, and in 1980 the Democratic party platform included a gay rights plank.

The stress gay liberation placed upon coming out also gave the movement leverage of another kind. Not only did men and women join groups that campaigned for equality from outside American institutions; they also came out within their professions, their communities, and other institutions to which they belonged. Gay Catholics, for instance, formed Dignity, and gay Episcopalians, Integrity. In some denominations gay men and women sought not only acceptance but also ordination as ministers. Military personnel announced their homosexuality and fought for the right to remain in the service. Lesbian and gay male academicians, school teachers, social workers, doctors, nurses, psychologists, and others created caucuses in their professions to sensitize their peers to the needs of the gay community and to combat discrimination. Openly gay journalists and television reporters brought an insider's perspective to their coverage of gay-related news. The visibility of lesbians and gay men in so many varied settings helped make homosexuality seem less of a strange, threatening phenomenon and more like an integral part of the social fabric.

Finally, the post-Stonewall era witnessed a significant shift in the self-definition of gay men and women. As pressure from gay liberationists made police harassment the exception rather than the rule in many American cities, the gay subculture flourished as never before. The relative freedom from danger, along with the emphasis the movement placed on gay pride, led not only to an expansion of the bar world but also to the creation of a range of "community" institutions. Gay men and lesbians formed their own churches, health clinics, counseling services, social centers, professional associations, and amateur sports leagues. Male and female entrepreneurs built record companies, publishing houses, travel agencies, and vacation resorts. Newspapers, magazines, literary journals, theater companies, and film collectives gave expression to a distinctive cultural experience. The subculture of homosexual men and women became less exclusively erotic. Gayness and lesbianism began to encompass an identity that for many included a wide array of private and public activities.

Stonewall thus marked a critical divide in the politics and consciousness of homosexuals and lesbians. A small, thinly spread reform effort suddenly grew into a large, grassroots movement for liberation. The quality of gay life in America was permanently altered as a furtive subculture moved aggressively into the open.

Reference

Radicalesbians, 1992 "The Woman-Identified Woman," in Karla Jay and Allen Young *Out of the Closets,* New York: Douglas Book Corp, pp. 172–7.

5 The Iranian Revolution

Charles Kurzman

"When a people which has put up with an oppressive rule over a long period without protest suddenly finds the government relaxing its pressure, it takes up arms against it."

—*Tocqueville 1955: 176*

Alexis de Tocqueville's famous dictum is based on two observations about the French Revolution. On one hand, the government undercut and alienated its bases of support through ill-conceived efforts at reform. On the other hand, the populace perceived a lessening of "pressure" and rose up to take advantage. The strength of Tocqueville's analysis lies in its combination of objective and subjective factors. It is not only the structural weakness of the state that precipitates revolution in Tocqueville's model, or the subjective sentiments of collective efficacy, but the combination of the two.

Social-movement theory has recently revived this combined approach after years of veering between structuralist and subjectivist extremes. McAdam's (1982) oft-cited book, *Political Process and the Development of Black Insurgency*, may be the model for contemporary social-movement theorizing on structure and consciousness. McAdam argues that the "structure of political opportunities" is one of two major determinants of political protest, the other being organizational strength: "The opportunities for a challenger to engage in successful collective action...vary greatly over time. And it is these variations that are held to be related to the ebb and flow of movement activity" (pp. 40–41). The "crucial point," he states, is that the political system can be more open or

less open to challenge at different times (p. 41). But structural conditions, McAdam argues, do not automatically translate into protest: They are mediated by "cognitive liberation," an oppressed people's ability to break out of pessimistic and quiescent patterns of thought and begin to do something about their situation (pp. 48–51).

> **Political Opportunities** Some groups are eager and sufficiently organized to protest, yet are fearful that they will be ignored or even repressed if they do. These groups may not engage in protest, accordingly, until (1) they have at least some access to authorities, or they see signs that (2) repression is declining, (3) elites are divided, or (4) elites or other influential groups are willing to support them. Such shifts in the political environment diminish the risks associated with protest and amplify the political influence of protesters. The appearance or "expansion" of these types of "political opportunities" may be a necessary precondition for – and may explain the precise timing of – the emergence of a protest movement. The same political opportunities, whether or not their participants are even aware of them, may also help movements to change laws and public policies. Of course, when they are willing to take sufficient risks, movements sometimes create opportunities for themselves, rather than simply waiting for changes among elites.

McAdam's (1982) analysis shows the tight fit between subjective perceptions and the structure of opportunities. The optimism of African Americans in the 1930s (pp. 108–10) and early 1960s (pp. 161–63) reflected structural shifts in Federal policies (pp. 83–86, 156–60). Conversely, in the late 1960s, perceptions of diminishing opportunities reflected the actual diminishing of opportunities (p. 202). State structure and subjective perceptions are treated as closely correlated.

Structural opportunities generally coincide with perceived opportunities in other recent studies in the Tocquevillean tradition. Tarrow (1994), for instance, recognizes the interplay between the macro-and micro-levels of analysis. He notes that "early risers" – protest groups at the beginning stages of a cycle of widespread protest activity – may make opportunities visible that had not been evident, and their actions may change the structure of opportunities (pp. 96–97). However, over most of the protest cycle, perceptions closely follow the opening and closing of objective opportunities (pp. 85–96, 99). "The main argument of this study," Tarrow emphasizes, "is that people join in social movements in response to political opportunities" (p. 17).

[...]

These Tocquevillean analyses recognize that structural opportunities and perceived opportunities may not always match. Cognitive liberation is a distinct variable that is not reducible to political opportunity structure, according to McAdam; "early risers" may protest despite unfavorable structural conditions in Tarrow's model; not all state crises lead to revolution, Goldstone (1991a) notes. The Tocquevillean tradition, however, has focused on cases in which the opportunity structure and perceptions agree, and has not examined mismatches.

[...]

I explore this latter possibility through an examination of the Iranian Revolution of 1979. Protestors *were* concerned with prospects for success – they did not participate in large numbers until they felt success was at hand. However, most Iranians did not feel that the state had weakened or that structural opportunities had opened up. Indeed, I argue that the state was *not*, by several objective measures, particularly vulnerable in 1978 when widespread protest emerged. Instead, Iranians seem to have based their assessment of the opportunities for protest on the perceived strength of the opposition. In other words, Iranians believed the bal-

ance of forces shifted, not because of a changing state structure, but because of a changing opposition movement.

Unlike the Tocquevillean cases, then, structural opportunities and perceived opportunities may have been at odds. Thus, the Iranian Revolution may constitute a "deviant" case for social-movement theory, one that allows a comparison between the relative effects of structural versus subjective factors. This is a historic issue in sociological theory, and far too weighty for the imperfectly documented Iranian case. However, the case at least raises the historic issue in a new guise for social-movement theory. In addition to researching the links between the structural and subjective levels of analysis, as social-movement theory has attempted to do in recent years, the case suggests that conflicts and disjunctures between these levels are also worth examining.

[...]

Because I do not proceed chronologically, a brief summary of the events leading to the fall of the Iranian monarchy in February 1979 is in order. The revolutionary movement is generally dated from mid-1977, when liberal oppositionists began to speak out publicly for reforms in the Iranian monarchy. Late in 1977, some of Iran's Islamic leaders called for the removal of Shâh Muhammad Rizâ Pahlavî, and their followers embarked on a series of small demonstrations that the regime suppressed with force. Casualties at each incident generated a cycle of mourning demonstrations throughout the first half of 1978. The bulk of Iran's population, however, did not participate in these events. The revolutionary movement attracted a large following only in September 1978, following a suspicious theater fire and a massacre of peaceful demonstrators; both events persuaded many Iranians that the Pahlavî regime must fall. Beginning in September 1978, strikes began to shake the country and built up to a virtual general strike that lasted until the revolution's success in February 1979. By the end of 1978, the shah was actively seeking a reformist prime minister. When he finally found an oppositionist willing to take the position and left for a "vacation" in mid-January, the country had become ungovernable. Exiled religious leader Imâm Rûhullah Khumeinî returned to Iran to great acclaim at the end of January and named his own prime minister. Two weeks later, a mutiny in one of the air force barracks in Tehran sparked an unplanned citywide uprising. Within 40 hours, the military declared its "neutrality" and allowed the revolutionaries to take power.

Charisma   Some political or religious leaders are popular not simply because of their ideas, but also because they are viewed as possessing some extraordinary personal quality, a "gift" of superhuman power, which requires loyalty and obedience even in the face of great risks. Indeed, people are willing and even eager to sacrifice their lives for charismatic leaders. (If they are not, then the leader is not charismatic.) People seem to attribute or "project" magical or prophetic powers upon certain exemplary leaders during times of political chaos or uncertainty, when people have become frustrated with politics-as-usual and are looking for someone or something to lead them to a more glorious future. (Note: Many people now incorrectly use the word "charismatic" as a synonym for "popular.") Notable charismatic leaders include Adolf Hitler and the Ayatollah Khomeini.

The Structure of Political Opportunity

Scholars of the Iranian Revolution have generally characterized the Pahlavî regime as highly susceptible to collapse. Four structural weaknesses are often cited as constituting a structure of political opportunities conducive to revolution.

Monarchy's Social Support Undermined by Reforms

One alleged weakness of the state is the undermining of the state's social support, particularly by the elite, as a result of the monarchy's vigorous efforts at reform. This argument takes different forms depending

on the affected group. For instance, the shah's land reforms of the 1960s threw the landed oligarchy into the opposition. The shah's industrialization policies and punitive price-control measures threw the traditional *bazaari* sector into the opposition. Harsh labor repression threw workers into the opposition. The overheated oil-boom economy led to the inflation of urban housing prices, throwing poor migrants into the opposition. Political repression threw intellectuals and the middle classes into the opposition. Secularizing reforms threw religious leaders into the opposition. In sum, the state "destroyed its traditional class base while failing to generate a new class base of support" (Moshiri 1991:121).

There are three problems with this argument. First, the affected groups were not entirely oppositional. Second, even as reforms created enemies for the state, they also created new allies. Third, the shah needed relatively little internal support because of the state's oil revenues and international support, and this internal autonomy may have strengthened rather than weakened the state.

The most affected elite group was the Islamic clerics. State reforms took away their longstanding judicial roles, limited their educational roles, and challenged their role in welfare distribution. Clerics had the clearest reason to resent the Pahlavî state. Yet prior to the revolution, relatively few clerics favored Khumeinî's revolutionary proposals. During the revolutionary movement, senior clerics tried to dissuade protestors from confronting the state, and one cleric even met secretly with government representatives to seek a compromise.

Similarly, leading oppositionist *bazaaris* and intellectuals opposed the revolutionary tide; they favored reforming the monarchy, not ousting it. Workers' demands centered on workplace gains and only switched to revolutionary demands in the fall of 1978, months after the revolutionary movement began. Urban migrants who suffered the most from the state's policies did not participate in large numbers in the revolutionary movement. Indeed, strikers at one factory blamed recent urban migrants for being too apolitical. In sum, the extent to which the shah's reform policies undermined his popular support should not be exaggerated.

Meanwhile, the state created new classes dependent on state patronage and therefore inclined to support the shah. The most important of these was the military, which expanded greatly during the shah's decades in power. The loyalty of the military remained largely unshaken to the end (see below). Another class created by state fiat was the industrial bourgeoisie, which emerged through credit subsidies and royal patronage. This class allegedly abandoned the shah by transferring its assets overseas and then emigrating at the first hint of trouble. Certainly rumors to this effect were circulating during the fall of 1978. But evidence suggests that some of the bourgeoisie stayed and actively supported the shah to the end. Groups of industrialists met in November 1978 and January 1979 to determine common solutions to strikes and money shortages; representatives worked with the prime minister on these matters. Thus, the shah was not totally abandoned by his allies.

In any case, the shah's access to oil revenues and foreign support made internal support less important than it was for most regimes. On theoretical grounds, it is difficult to say whether this is a sign of state weakness or strength. While reliance on foreign powers may create an image of a puppet regime, state autonomy is often identified as a strength, as the state can impose collective solutions on recalcitrant social groups. If the basis for autonomy breaks down, of course, the state is left without a reed to lean on. However, the shah retained international support during the revolutionary movement.

International Pressure on the Monarchy

The second alleged weakness of the state is the widespread impression that international constraints stayed the monarchy's hand and prevented the crackdown that would have crushed the protest movement. Many academic analyses have applied Skocpol's (1979) structural model to the Iranian Revolution, arguing that international pressures weakened the state and made it vulnerable to revolution (Ashraf and Banuazizi 1985:19–20; Liu 1988:202–203; Milani 1988:30–31). However, none of these analysts presents evidence of such pressure.

Jimmy Carter campaigned for President in 1976 on a platform that included the consideration of human rights in U.S. foreign policy, and he threatened to weaken U.S. support for the shah. But this threat never materialized. When the shah visited Washington in November 1977, Carter's meetings with him barely touched the subject of human rights. A month later, Carter made his famous New Year's toast to the shah in Tehran: "Iran, because of the great leadership of the Shah, is an island of stability in one of the more troubled areas of the world. This is a great tribute to you, Your Majesty, and to your leadership and to the respect and the admiration and love which your people give to you" (*Weekly Compilation of Presidential Documents*, January 2, 1978, p. 1975).

As the revolutionary movement grew during 1978, the shah received no international complaints about his handling of Iranian protests, even when his troops shot hundreds, perhaps thousands, of unarmed demonstrators in Tehran on September 8. In fact, Carter telephoned the shah from Camp David two days later to express his continuing support. When the shah installed a military government on November 6, U.S. officials voiced their full approval (*New York Times*, November 7, 1978, p. 14). National Security Advisor Zbigniew Brzezinski had telephoned the shah several days earlier to encourage him to be firm. Riot-control equipment, blocked for months on human-rights grounds, was then shipped to Iran (*Newsweek*, November 20, 1978, p. 43). As late as December 28, 1978, the U.S. Secretary of State cabled to his ambassador in Tehran the firm statement "that U.S. support is steady and that it is essential, repeat essential, to terminate the continuing uncertainty."

Throughout the fall of 1978, the shah met regularly with the U.S. ambassador, William Sullivan. The shah's final autobiography notes that "the only word I ever received from Mr. Sullivan was reiteration of Washington's complete support for my rule" (Pahlavi 1980: 161). In fact, according to Sullivan (1981), "the Shah himself in due course told me he was somewhat embarrassed by the constant reiteration of our public support, saying it made him look like a puppet" (p. 204).

The shah was apparently unaware of divisions within the U.S. administration. Carter's cabinet was split into hostile camps over the extent of force the shah should use, the advisability of a coup d'état, and the desirability of a nonmonarchical government in Iran – in short, how to respond to the Iranian revolutionary movement. This debate was never resolved. As a result, Washington never sent detailed recommendations to Iran. Ambassador Sullivan in Tehran repeatedly told the shah that he had "no instructions" from his superiors.

This lack of instructions may have deepened the shah's suspicions about the United States' true intentions. The head of the French secret service insisted to the shah that the United States was secretly planning his ouster, and the shah asked visitors on several occasions whether the United States had abandoned him. Offhand public remarks by U.S. officials suggesting that the United States was considering various contingencies in Iran reached the shah and worried him, despite official denials and reassurances.

In sum, the United States continued to pledge its support, although the shah did not entirely believe it. But there is no evidence of international pressure constraining the monarchy's response to protest.

Overcentralization and Paralysis of the State

A third alleged weakness focuses on the structure of the Iranian state. According to this argument, a concerted crackdown would have worked, but the state lacked the will to carry it out. At its basest, this explanation accuses individual officeholders of treason. At its most theoretical, this analysis argues that the Iranian state was structurally susceptible to paralysis because of its overcentralization around the person of the shah. Fatemi's (1982) analysis is perhaps the most succinct: "Since the *raison d'être* of this organizational structure was mostly to protect the shah and his throne from potential threats, such as military *coups d'état* and strong political rivals" (p. 49), the state demanded loyalty to the monarch, arranged overlapping responsibilities and rivalries, and forbade lateral communication. "To operate this system the shah had effectively made himself the sole decision-making authority in every significant phase of Iran's political affairs" (p. 49). Therefore, the system depended for its operation on a fully functioning shah. In 1978, however, the shah was ill with cancer. According to this thesis, the state was thereby paralyzed in its response to the protest movement.

There is abundant evidence of the centralization of the state around the person of the shah. There is also evidence of the shah's illness. He was under medication and appeared at times to be depressed or listless and not his usual decisive self. But evidence of paralysis is much less convincing. To be sure, the shah repeatedly stated his unwillingness to massacre his subjects in order to save his throne. "The instructions I gave were always the same: 'Do the impossible to avoid bloodshed'" (Pahlavi 1980:168). One general allegedly offered to kill a hundred thousand protestors to quell the disturbances. Another supposedly proposed to bomb the holy city of Qum. The head of a neighboring country suggested the execution of 700 mullahs. The shah vetoed all these plans.

However, the refusal to authorize slaughter does not necessarily indicate lack of will or structural paralysis. Less extreme measures were vigorously pursued. Throughout the fall of 1978, security forces routinely broke up protests at gunpoint. They arrested virtually every prominent oppositionist in the country at least once. At one time or another they occupied virtually all key economic and governmental institutions and forced striking personnel back to work in the oil fields, power stations, airlines, customs offices, and telecommunications centers. Plans began to be drawn up for a possible pro-shah military coup.

Moreover, the Pahlavî regime – despite its pretensions – was a Third World state and not overly efficient in the best of times: Iran's intelligence service was hardly more than a glorified police force, according to the head of the French secret service; Tehran had no sewage system; and industry suffered frequent power shortages. The flurry of state actions in response to the revolutionary movement hardly represents paralysis.

State Vacillation

A fourth possible weakness concerns the state's "vacillating" (Abrahamian 1982:518); or "inconsistent" (Arjomand 1988:115) responses to the protest movement. The combination of concession and repression is said to have encouraged protestors while providing them with new reasons to protest. Because of this vacillation, according to these analyses, the Iranian revolution grew from a small and sporadic movement into a massive and continuous upheaval. The implication is that a more one-sided policy – either reform *or* crackdown – would have been more effective in stifling protest.

Such a conclusion goes against the advice of numerous royal advisors. In ancient India, Kautilîya (1972:414) instructed kings on how to deal with revolts: "Make use of conciliation, gifts, dissension and force." In eleventh-century Persia, Nizam al-Mulk (1960, chaps. 40, 44) urged caliphs to imitate the mercy and liberality of Harun ar-Rashid, but also the deviousness and repression of Nushirwan. In sixteenth-century Italy, Machiavelli advised princes to gain both the fear of the people and the love of the people, combining punishment and reward, cruelty and clemency. [...] On theoretical grounds, then, it is not clear whether a combined state response constitutes vacillation and vulnerability, or carrot-and-stick and co-optation.

In any case, the shah had used a similar strategy for years. The two major pre-revolutionary studies of the Iranian political system make this point repeatedly. Zonis (1971) notes that co-operation of the opposition had become routine, to the extent that the shah told one foreign visitor not to worry about youthful subversives. "We know just who those young men are and will be offering them high-level jobs as appropriate" (pp. 331–32). Bill (1972:100) describes the state's "three-pronged strategy of intimidation, bribery, and selected concessions" toward student oppositionists. Both authors view the shah's repression and his co-optive concessions as complementary parts of a single coherent system of political opportunities.

This combined approach continued through 1978. At several crucial junctures, the shah cracked down on protestors, but at the same time offered minor concessions and promised future reforms. In mid-May, soldiers opened fire on a demonstration in Tehran, but troops were removed from the seminary city of Qum and a ban was announced on pornographic films, clearly gestures toward religious oppositionists. In early August, the shah announced that free elections were going to be held, but soon placed the city of Isfahan under martial law. In late August, the shah placed 11 cities under martial law, but also granted various concessions, including freedom of the press, and appointed a new prime minister thought to be more acceptable to the religious opposition. In November, the shah installed a military government that flooded Tehran with armored vehicles and cracked down on the oilfield strikes. At the same time, the shah made an apologetic televised speech and promulgated limits on the royal family's business activities.

There was a definite logic to these state responses. The government sent protestors a mixed but consistent message: Continue protesting and you'll be killed; stop protesting and you'll get reforms. The combination of crackdowns with promises of future reforms was intended to defuse the short-term situation while reaffirming the long-term commitment to liberalization. The shah stuck to the structure of political opportunities he had maintained for decades, one that was conducive to co-optive political participation and inimical to revolutionary street protests.

The Perception of Political Opportunity

Perceptions of the State's Coercive Power

Casualties increased as the protest movement progressed. Moreover, the Iranian people recognized that street protests were dangerous, including the large demonstrations that were legal, well-organized, and rarely repressed. For instance, marches on the religious holidays of Tâsû'â and 'Âshûrâ in December 1978 were certain to attract millions of participants, but they still inspired fear. The leading cleric in Shiraz warned on the eve of the demonstrations: "Maybe we'll be killed tomorrow. We're facing guns, rifles and tanks. Whoever is afraid shouldn't come" (Hegland 1986:683).
  [. . .]
But recognition of the state's coercive power did not translate into obedience. Frequently, repression led to increased militancy. In late August, after the immolation of several hundred moviegoers in Abadan – a tragedy many Iranians blamed on the state – protests increased from several thousand participants to hundreds of thousands. In early September, the day after hundreds and perhaps thousands of peaceful demonstrators were gunned down in Tehran's Zhâlih Square, wildcat strikes spread across the country. In early November, within weeks of the installation of a military government, the opposition denounced the government as illegal and began planning for huge con-

frontations during the Shi'i holy month of Muharram.
On an individual level, acts of repression that hit close to home were a major source of revolutionary zeal. An anthropologist who spent much of the revolutionary period in a village near Shiraz reports that this response was called "*az khud guzashtih*" or "*az jân guzashtih*" (literally, "abandoning oneself" or "abandoning life"):

> People felt this emotion and gained this attitude through hearing about or participating in events in which government forces treated people with violence and injustice.... Villagers reported to me their horror, fury, and frustration upon hearing about such events, as well as their resolve that they would never rest until the shah and the government that did such inhuman things to their fellow Iranians no longer existed. (Hegland 1983:233–34)

Repression was such a mobilizing force that the opposition circulated a hoax audio cassette, along with other opposition cassettes, on which an indistinct voice resembling the shah's was heard giving his generals formal orders to shoot demonstrators in the streets. If scare tactics of this sort were revolutionary propaganda, and not counterrevolutionary propaganda, then something was clearly amiss with the shah's carrot-and-stick strategy.

Perceptions of the Opposition's Power

What was amiss, I propose, was the Iranian people's perception of political opportunities. Iranians continued to recognize and fear the state's coercive powers. However, they felt that these powers were insignificant compared with the strength of the revolutionary movement. [. . .]Popular perceptions are difficult to identify, particularly during a period of repression and unrest. But this is no excuse for leaving popular perceptions unexamined. The bits of evidence that exist show consistently that Iranians considered the strength of the protest movement to be

a decisive factor in their decisions to participate.

At the first mass demonstration of the
protest movement, on September 4 in
Tehran, journalists reported a sense of
euphoria among the protestors: "'The shah
is finished,' they cry above all" (Brière and
Blanchet 1979:46). This judgment was premature, but the sentiment seems genuine.
Protestors felt that revolution was not only
possible, but practically inevitable.

[. . .]

On a smaller scale, it appears that Iranians preferred to participate in a particular
protest only if they had assurances that
others would protest as well. U.S. diplomats
in Tehran noted during the strike day of
October 16, 1978:

> Most shops have closed during [the] morn-
> ing, however, as shopkeepers evaluated
> [the] local situation: no one wants to have
> the only open shop on the block. . . . Every-
> one knew of Khomeini's appeal [to strike],
> yet [the] vast majority came to work, they
> decided to stay or return based on what
> neighbors were doing. (National Security
> Archive 1989: Document 1594)

At its margins, this desire to go with the
flow shaded into fear of persecution for nonparticipation. "I could not go to [the] office
against the will of my employees," said the
managing director of a state agency that was
on strike. "Besides, anything could happen
to me" (Farazmand 1989:172). The owner
of a tiny shop in central Tehran expressed a
similar opinion:

> He explained candidly that he had put a
> photograph of the Ayatollah, whom he
> said he respected, in his store window
> because he feared it would be smashed
> otherwise. "Most of the people want an Is-
> lamic Republic," he said wearily. "And I
> want anything that most of the people
> want." (*New York Times*, February 2,
> 1979, p. A9)

The fear of violence should not be over-
estimated, however, despite the dark suspicions of several foreign observers – notably
British Ambassador Anthony Parsons, U.S.
military envoy Robert Huyser and U.S. diplomats. The Iranian Revolution exhibited
remarkably little retribution against back-
sliders, especially when compared with the
revolutionary violence reported in South
Africa, Palestine, and the Sikh independence
movement in India.

Rather, the fear of violence should probably be considered part of the overall "bandwagon effect" (Hirsch 1986:382), whereby
individuals' willingness to participate in a
protest is correlated with their expectations
of the size and success of the protest. [. . .]

Perhaps the best evidence of the bandwagon effect comes from the reformist
oppositionists who opposed outright revolution. These liberals are more fully represented than are other social groups in the
government, journalistic, and oral-history
sources available for this research. Liberals
were highly sensitive to the structure of
opportunities – they had begun to speak
out publicly for reform in 1977 when the
shah allowed such opposition to be voiced.
In late 1977, when the shah clamped down
again after his cordial meetings with Carter,
liberals muted their protests. In the summer
of 1978, when the shah made a few concessions and promised to hold free elections,
liberals were elated and rushed to take
advantage of the new freedoms. During the
fall of 1978, liberals began to sense that
the opposition movement was larger than
they had imagined, and "out of our
hands." This sense crystallized for some on
September 4, when liberal *bazaar* oppositionists chased in vain after a massive revolutionary demonstration, trying to disperse
the crowd and reminding people that they
were not supposed to be demonstrating.

In the following months, liberals joined the
revolutionary movement, not because they
now favored revolution, but because
they felt the revolutionary movement was
too strong to oppose. [. . .]In a memorandum
dated December 8, 1978, a U.S. diplomat
reported asking a moderate Iranian religious
leader if he and other clerics would approve

a constitutional settlement to the crisis and go against Khumeinî. The cleric, "perhaps not wanting his followers to understand, replied in broken English, 'That would be dangerous and very difficult'" (*Asnâd-i Lânih-yi Jâsûsî* 1980–1991, vol. 26, p. 61). By the end of 1978, when the shah was casting about for a prime minister, a series of liberal oppositionists turned down the position. Several months earlier they would have considered the appointment a dream come true – now they considered it futile.

Perception Versus Structure

Confident of the revolution's ultimate victory, millions of Iranians participated in mass protests against the shah in the final months of 1978. Yet, at the end of the year, the shah's military remained largely intact. The two sides faced a potentially cataclysmic confrontation. But as protestors' perception of political opportunities clashed with the state's structural position, the structure of the state gave way.

As late as early December 1978, top generals still thought they could subdue the protest movement. Thus, the collapse of the military followed, rather than preceded, mass mobilization of the protest movement. Like the broad state-breakdown argument, this suggests that military breakdown may be an outcome of mobilization rather than a necessary precondition.

During demonstrations, protestors handed flowers to soldiers and chanted slogans such as: "Brother soldier, why do you kill your brothers?" and "The army is part of the nation" (Kamalî 1979). On several occasions, large throngs of protestors persuaded soldiers to give up their arms, throw off their uniforms, and join the demonstration. On other occasions, protestors attacked security personnel and even military bases.

Nonetheless, the effectiveness of popular pressure on the military is unclear. Even in mid-January 1979, as the shah was about to leave Iran, desertions remained relatively

low, only about a thousand a day out of several hundred thousand troops, according to the Iranian chief of staff. However, authorized leaves may have been increasing dramatically as soldiers requested furloughs to check on their families and property after riots and other disturbances. (In a Crisis Meeting on January 23, the chief of staff estimated that the armed forces were only at 55 percent of their strength, although the tone of his comments suggests that this figure was picked more for effect than for accuracy.) Small mutinies increased. [...]

Whether or not popular pressure was effective, however, military leaders were clearly worried about it. This concern prevented the military from being used to its full capacity because each military operation exposed the troops to fraternization and further appeals from protestors. On January 15, 1979, the head of the ground forces proposed keeping the soldiers away from this nefarious influence:

> We should round up the units and send them someplace where [the demonstrators] won't have any contact with the soldiers. Because yesterday they came and put a flower in the end of a rifle barrel, and another on the [military] vehicle.... The soldiers' morale just disappears. (*Misl-i Barf* 1987:50)

During the largest demonstrations, military commanders kept their troops well away from the march routes, guarding "key" sites and neighborhoods. On a few occasions they ordered the military back to barracks, twice as a direct result of defections.

[...]

But several hundred thousand troops could not be held in their barracks for long. A number of soldiers, even officers, slipped out and joined protests – out of uniform, of course, because a uniform would attract dangerous attention from protestors and security forces that remained loyal. In early February of 1979 when whole units of troops began to demonstrate in uniform against the shah, the military's disintegration was imminent. After only a day and a half of street fighting, the chiefs of staff declared the military's "neutrality" and allowed the revolutionaries to take power.

Implications for Social-Movement Theory

I have argued that the Iranian state was not particularly vulnerable to revolution in 1978, according to several indicators. The Pahlavî regime's domestic support had not withered away, nor had its international support. State centralization and the shah's illness did not prevent the state from responding actively to the revolutionary movement, combining carrot and stick, cracking down on opposition activities while promising future reforms, as it had done for decades.

In terms of popular perceptions, the Iranian people considered the coercive power of the state to be intact right up to the end. At the same time, however, evidence suggests that the Iranian people considered political opportunities to have increased as a result of the growth of the opposition. The strength of the revolutionary movement induced even non-revolutionary liberals to join in. Acting on this perception of opposition strength, Iranians altered the structure of opportunities by fraternizing with the military and making it partially unusable as a coercive force.

In more theoretical terms, there was a mismatch between the structure of political opportunities and popular perceptions of political opportunities. Rather than calculate opportunities solely on the basis of changes in the state, as Tocquevillean theory suggests, Iranians appear to have calculated opportunities on the basis of changes in the opposition. Ultimately, their perceptions proved self-fulfilling: The balance of forces had indeed tilted toward the opposition, and perceptions proved stronger than the state structure.

This finding suggests that social-movement theory should reconsider the relation between "objective" and "subjective" definitions of political opportunity. If opportunity is like a door, then social-movement theory generally examines cases in which people realize the door is open and walk on through. The Iranian Revolution may be a case in which people saw that the door was closed, but felt that the opposition was powerful enough to open it. These people were not millenarians, masochists, fanatics, or martyrs – the case is not dismissed so easily. It turns out that Iranians were able to open the door on their own.

[...]

References

Abrahamian, Ervand. 1982. *Iran Between Two Revolutions*. Princeton, NJ: Princeton University Press.

Arjomand, Said Amir. 1988. *The Turban for the Crown: The Islamic Revolution in Iran*. New York: Oxford University Press.

Ashraf, Ahmad and Ali Banuazizi. 1985. "The State, Classes, and Modes of Mobilization in the Iranian Revolution." *State, Culture, and Society* 1:3–40.

Bill, James A. 1972. *The Politics of Iran*. Columbus, OH: Charles E. Merrill.

Blumer, Herbert. 1969. "Collective Behavior." Pp. 65–121 in *Principles of Sociology*, 3rd. ed., edited by A. M. Lee. New York: Barnes and Noble Books.

Brière, Claire and Pierre Blanchet. 1979. *L'Iran: La Révolution au Nom de Dieu* (The Revolution in the Name of God). Paris, France.

Farazmand, Ali. 1989. *The State, Bureaucracy, and Revolution in Modern Iran: Agrarian Reforms and Regime Politics*. New York: Praeger.

Fatemi, Khosrow. 1982. "Leadership by Distrust: The Shah's *Modus Operandi*." *Middle East Journal* 36: 48–61.

Goldstone, Jack A. 1991a. "Ideology, Cultural Frameworks, and the Process of Revolution." *Theory and Society* 20:405–53.

——1991b. *Rebellion and Revolution in the Early Modern World*. Berkeley, CA: University of California Press.

——1994. "Is Revolution Really Rational?" *Rationality and Society* 6:139–66.

Gramsci, Antonio. 1971. *Selections From the Prison Notebooks*. Translated by Q. Hoare and G. N. Smith. New York: International Publishers.

Granovetter, Mark. 1978. "Threshold Models of Collective Behavior." *American Journal of Sociology* 83:1420–43.

Hegland, Mary Elaine. 1983. "Two Images of Husain." Pp. 218–35 in *Religion and Politics in Iran*, edited by Nikki R. Keddie. New Haven, CT: Yale University Press.

—— 1986. "Imam Khomaini's Village: Recruitment to Revolution." Ph.D. dissertation. Department of Anthropology, State University of New York, Binghamton, NY.

Hirsch, Eric L. 1986. "The Creation of Political Solidarity in Social Movement Organizations." *The Sociological Quarterly* 27:373–87.

Kamalî, Alî. 1979. *Inqilâb* (Revolution). Tehran, Iran: Massoud Publishing House.

Kautilîya. 1972. *The Kautilîya Arthaśâstra*. Pt. 2, 2nd ed. Edited by R. P. Kangle. Bombay, India: University of Bombay.

Khalîlî. Akbar. 1981. *Gâm bih Gâm bâ Inqilâb* (Step by Step with the Revolution). Tehran, Iran: Surûsh.

Kuran, Timur, 1989. "Sparks and Prairie Fires: A Theory of Unanticipated Political Revolution." *Public Choice* 61:41–74.

Lichbach, Mark I. 1994. "Rethinking Rationality and Rebellion: Theories of Collective Action and Problems of Collective Dissent." *Rationality and Society* 6:8–39.

Liu, Michael Tien-Lung. 1988. "States and Urban Revolutions: Explaining the Revolutionary Outcomes in Iran and Poland." *Theory and Society* 17:179–209.

Marwell, Gerald and Pamela Oliver. 1993. *The Critical Mass In Collective Action: A Micro-Social Theory*. Cambridge, England: Cambridge University Press.

McAdam, Doug. 1982. *Political Process and the Development of Black Insurgency, 1930–1970*. Chicago, IL: University of Chicago Press.

Milani, Mohsen. 1988. *The Making of Iran's Islamic Revolution: From Monarchy to Islamic Republic*. Boulder, CO: Westview Press.

Misl-i Barf Âb Khwâhîm Shud: Muzâkirât-i "Shûrâ-yi Farmândihân-i Artish" (Dey-Bahman 1357) (We Will Melt Like Snow:

Conversations of the "Council of the Army Commanders" [January 1979]). 1987. 3rd printing. Tehran, Iran: Nashr-i Ney.

Moshiri, Farrokh. 1991. "Iran: Islamic Revolution Against Westernization." Pp. 116–35 in *Revolutions of the Late Twentieth Century*, edited by Jack A. Goldstone, Ted Robert Gurr, and Farrokh Moshiri. Boulder, CO: Westview Press.

National Security Archive. 1989. *Iran: The Making of U.S. Policy, 1977–1980*. Microfiche Collection, Index, and Guide. Alexandria, VA: Chadwyck-Healey.

Nizam al-Mulk. 1960. *The Book of Government*. London, England: Routledge and Kegan Paul.

Oberschall, Anthony R. 1994. "Rational Choice in Collective Protests." *Rationality and Society* 6:79–100.

Olson, Mancur. 1965. *The Logic of Collective Action*. Cambridge, MA: Harvard University Press.

Pahlavi, Mohammad Reza. 1980. *Answer to History*. New York: Stein and Day.

Pîshtâzân-i Shahâdat dar Inqilâb-i Sivvum (The Front Ranks of Martyrdom in the Third Revolution). 1981. Qum, Iran: Daftar-i Intishârât-i Islâmî.

Schelling, Thomas C. 1978. *Micromotives and Macrobehavior*. New York: Norton.

Skocpol, Theda. 1979. *States and Social Revolutions*. Cambridge, England: Cambridge University Press.

—— 1982. "Rentier State and Shi'a Islam in the Iranian Revolution." *Theory and Society* 11:265–83.

Sullivan, William. 1981. *Mission to Iran*. New York: W.W. Norton.

Tarrow, Sidney. 1994. *Power in Movement: Social Movements, Collective Action and Politics*. Cambridge, England: Cambridge University Press.

Tocqueville, Alexis de. 1955. *The Old Regime and the French Revolution*. Translated by S. Gilbert. Garden City, NY: Doubleday Anchor.

Tullock, Gordon. 1971. "The Paradox of Revolution." *Public Choice* 11:89–99.

Zonis, Marvin. 1971. *The Political Elite of Iran*. Princeton, NJ: Princeton University Press.

Part III

Who Joins or Supports Movements?

Introduction

Once initial activists in a social movement form groups and begin to think of themselves as a movement, their next step is usually to try to expand their movement by recruiting others to their cause. Like theories of movement origins, theories of recruitment have evolved through several stages, from an emphasis on individual traits to one on structural availability, and finally toward a synthesis of these dimensions.

Before the 1960s, researchers tended to see protestors as swept up in crowds, acting in abnormal and sometimes irrational ways because of frustration with their individual circumstances. In some theories marginal and alienated members of society were seen as most likely to join social movements (Kornhauser, 1959); in others it was those who were insecure or dogmatic (Adorno et al., 1950; Hoffer, 1951). Such claims were usually demeaning to protestors, who were thought to be compensating for some sort of personal inadequacy, and subsequent empirical research did not generally support the image of protestors as more angry or alienated than others.

Problems like these helped inspire the resource mobilization paradigm, which shifted attention from what kinds of *people* protested to what kinds of *structural conditions* facilitated protest. Attitudes were summarily dismissed as unimportant or at least insufficient, for many people had the right attitudes but did not participate. As part of this new agenda, "biographical availability" was seen as necessary for participation (McCarthy and Zald, 1973; McAdam, 1986). More importantly, researchers found that the best predictor of who will join is whether a person knows someone else already in the movement (Snow, Zurcher and Ekland-Olson, 1980). In many movements, a majority of participants are recruited this way. Social networks were seen as a precondition for the emergence of a movement as well as the explanation for who was recruited. In the extreme case of "bloc recruitment" organizers bring a social network almost intact into a movement (Oberschall, 1973).

Different kinds of social networks can be used for recruitment. They may not be political in origin or intent. Black churches were crucial to the Southern civil rights movement in the 1950s (Morris, 1984); fundamentalist churches helped defeat the Equal Rights Amendment (Mansbridge, 1986); and mosques facilitated the Iranian Revolution (Snow and Marshall, 1984). Networks developed for earlier political activities can also aid recruitment into a new movement – one reason that a history of previous activism makes someone more likely to be recruited (McAdam, 1988). The clustering of movements in waves makes this mutual support especially important, as one movement feeds into the next (Tarrow, 1998). Because of these networks, prior activism and organizational memberships help predict who will be recruited (and who will not be).

This view of recruitment is summed up in the excerpt included in this volume from Doug McAdam's book on "Freedom Summer" of 1964, when hundreds of mostly white college students went South to help in voter registration drives. McAdam's methodological strategy is to look first at the students who applied to the project (compared implicitly to college students generally), then at those who actually participated (as opposed to those who were accepted but did not show up). He finds three factors important in explaining who applied: biographical availability, ideological compatibility, and social-network ties. In explaining those who showed up and those who did not, the first two factors drop out and the third factor becomes crucial. Those who knew others who were going were the most likely to follow through on their plans.

Recent work on recruitment has criticized the mechanical image of networks in much of the earlier research. Without denying the importance of personal contacts, this work has examined the cultural messages transmitted across these networks. Edward Walsh (1981), for example, described "suddenly imposed grievances": dramatic and unexpected events that highlight some social problem. In his case the Three Mile Island accident in 1979 alerted people to the risks of nuclear energy, giving a big boost to the antinuclear movement. Recruitment involves a cognitive shift for participants. McAdam (1982) called this "cognitive liberation," when potential participants begin to think they may have a chance of success.

In this view, direct personal contacts are seen as important because they allow organizers and potential participants to "align" their "frames," to achieve a common definition of a social problem and a common prescription for solving it (see Snow et al. 1986). In successful recruitment, organizers offer ways of seeing a social problem that resonate with the views and experiences of potential recruits. Networks are important *because* of the cultural meanings they transmit. Networks and meanings are not rival explanations; they work together.

Snow and Benford (1988) distinguish three successive types of framing necessary for successful recruitment: *diagnostic*, in which a movement convinces potential converts that a problem needs to be addressed; *prognostic*, in which it convinces them of appropriate strategies,

> **Framing and Frame Alignment** In order to attract people to join and remain committed to a movement, its issues must be presented or "framed" so that they fit or resonate with the beliefs, feelings, and desires of potential recruits. Like a picture-frame that highlights what is in the frame but excludes everything outside it, frames are simplifying devices that help us understand and organize the complexities of the world; they are the filtering lenses, so to speak, through which we make sense of this world. Frames may take the form of appealing stories, powerful clusters of symbols, slogans and catch words, or attributions of blame for social problems. Social-movement leaders and recruiters work hard to find the right frames, ones "aligned" with the understandings of potential recruits. Framing is thus one of the principal activities in which movement activists participate, and activists are often involved in framing contests or "framing wars" with their opponents in an attempt to win the "hearts and minds" of the public. See Snow et al. (1986) and Snow and Benford (1992).

tactics and targets; and *motivational*, in which it exhorts them to get involved in these activities (this last seems primarily about arousing the right emotions). They argue that frames are more likely to be accepted if they fit well with the existing beliefs of potential recruits, if they involve empirically credible claims, if they are compatible with the life experiences of the audiences, and if they fit with the stories or narratives the audiences tell about their lives. Frames, in other words, must resonate with the salient beliefs of potential recruits.

Collective identity is another concept used to get at the mental worlds of participants that might help explain participation: in order to devote time and effort to protest, people must usually feel part of a larger group they think they can help (Melucci, 1996). (On collective identity, read also the selection by Mary Bernstein in Part VII, where she shows how different kinds of identity claims can be important strategic moves.) Pieces of culture such as frames and identities have audiences outside the movement as well as inside it.

This emphasis on culture challenges the arguments of many structuralists who promoted the idea that individual characteristics do not help explain who will be recruited to a social movement, an idea that is a kind of half-truth. The structuralists concentrated on arguing against personality traits as a predictor – without ever gathering serious evidence about personality traits (Klandermans, 1983, 1989). But they also rejected attitudes and grievances as part of an explanation, in favor of structural traits (Gurney and Tierney, 1982; Useem, 1980; Klandermans and Oegema, 1987). But this kind of argument went to ridiculous extremes: bigots don't join civil rights campaigns just because they are in the right network; leftists don't join right-wing movements because a "bloc" of their fellow parishioners do. The fact that not *everyone* with a set of beliefs or personality traits gets recruited does not mean that supportive ideas or other traits are not a necessary condition. They are just not sufficient.

Our other readings on this topic take a cultural approach even broader than that of frame alignment, showing how attitudes and worldviews matter. Political scientist Ronald Inglehart has done more than anyone else to analyze the values and beliefs that individuals hold in the kind of society that has emerged in the advanced industrial nations since the 1960s. Through most of human history, in his view, people have been forced to worry about basic material needs such as food, shelter, and security, but since World War II the advanced industrial world has been largely spared traditional privations. Those born after World War II (especially the college-educated and affluent middle class) were "freed" to pursue "higher" goals such as control over their lives, environmental protection, and satisfying work, rather than worrying primarily about their paychecks. The spread of mass communications and higher education contributed to the same trends. Together, the result has been less emphasis on economic redistribution, class-based political organizations, or the pursuit of political power. Instead we have seen movements critical of large bureaucracies, complex technologies, and many different forms of oppression. Inglehart refers to this as "post-material" politics.

Stephen Cotgrove and Andrew Duff try to explain who is likely to support the environmental movement, depending on their relationship to industrial production. In doing so, they elaborate on the concept of post-material politics articulated by Inglehart. They show how a movement can have a middle-class social base, even though it is not pursuing the economic interests of this class. So the growth of a post-industrial sector of the economy can help explain not only changes over time (Inglehart's interest) but different sympathies across parts of the population at any given time.

In the final excerpt, James Aho looks at the extreme right, the "patriot" movement of Christian fundamentalists in Idaho. Aho criticizes early explanations of right-wing extremism as a kind of confused "displacement" of discontent among social groups losing their economic power, who then looked around for scapegoats who had nothing to do with the causes of their problems (for example, blaming their problems on an international Jewish conspiracy). Instead, Aho takes the activists' theology seriously, as a kind of lens through which they view the world. Through this lens, a number of groups and trends in the modern world look evil. We may not share this vision, but we cannot simply dismiss it as irrational. We all hold beliefs that cannot be disproven – in other words on faith – and act on the basis of them.

Recruitment involves more than cognitive beliefs about how the world works. Its moral and emotional dimensions are equally important. All the key concepts used to explain recruitment depend heavily on their emotional dynamics. The term "moral shock" is meant to incorporate some of these other dimensions, as events or information raise such a sense of outrage in people that they become inclined toward political action, with or without a network of contacts (Jasper and Poulsen, 1995; Jasper, 1997). Social networks are also grounded in the emotional bonds among their members: we pay attention to people in our networks because we are fond of them or trust them.

The new synthesis pays more attention to what goes on inside people's heads (and hearts). Protest is no longer seen as a compensation for some lack, but part of an effort to impose cognitive meaning on the world, to forge a personal and collective identity, to define and pursue collective interests, and to create or reinforce affective bonds with others. These are things that all humans desire and pursue. There is today considerable consensus that structural positions in networks and cultural (including cognitive, moral, and emotional) orientations and transformations are equally important in recruitment. But there are also cases in which cultural messages can be used to recruit people in the absence of social networks, relying on moral shocks instead of personal contacts. For virtually all social movements, only a small fraction of potential recruits actually join, and it takes all the factors we have considered to understand who does and who does not sign up.

"Moral Shocks" and Self-Recruitment

Sometimes in the course of daily life something happens to us that distresses, surprises, and outrages us. A loved one may be killed by a drunk driver. Our boss may ask us for sexual favors. Construction on a nuclear power plant may begin down the street. Sometimes we are shocked by information we receive (perhaps from a newspaper or political pamphlet) rather than by personal experience. We learn that cosmetics are tested by being put into the eyes of rabbits, or that NATO is deploying a new type of nuclear missile throughout Europe. These "moral shocks" are often strong enough to propel us into trying to do something. We may seek out a social movement organization if we know one exists. We may even try to found our own. Although people who join a social movement typically know someone involved in it, a moral shock may still be the trigger that gets them to join. In some cases it can even push us into participation when we do not know anyone at all in the movement. In such cases, we see a process of "self-recruitment" to a movement: people actively seek out a movement or movement organization in which they can participate, as opposed to being recruited by the movement itself.

Discussion Questions

1   What is the role of daily life in affecting one's likelihood of joining a social movement, even a movement one is sympathetic to?
2   Why must social-movement organizers take care how they "frame" their arguments and choose their symbols in trying to recruit members?
3   What are post-material values? Who is most likely to have them and why?
4   What kinds of people are more likely to sympathize with the environmental movement? Does this mean they will join it?
5   What are the beliefs of the Christian far-right that might lead them to join the "Patriot" movement?
6   How do individual traits and structural conditions interact in recruitment to social movements?

6 Recruits to Civil Rights Activism

Doug McAdam

The roots of the Summer Project are to be found in the strategic stalemate that confronted SNCC's Mississippi operation in the fall of 1963. For all the courage, hard work, and sacrifice its field workers had expended in the state since 1961, the organization had achieved few concrete victories. They had been able to persuade only a small number of prospective voters to try registering, and had succeeded in registering only a fraction of these. Three factors had combined to limit the effectiveness of SNCC's campaign in Mississippi. The first was simply the state's intransigence to any form of racial equality. The second was the absence of any aggressive federal presence in the state that might have blunted the effectiveness of state resistance. The third was SNCC's inability to generate the type of publicity that Martin Luther King, Jr. had used so effectively elsewhere in coercing supportive federal action.

[...]

At a loss as to how to counter these obstacles, the SNCC braintrust grasped at a straw of a plan offered it by Allard Lowenstein. Lowenstein, a peripatetic Democratic Party activist and sometime college administrator, had come to Mississippi in July of 1963 to investigate the racial situation. Never one to wait for a formal invitation, Lowenstein had made himself welcome in the SNCC office in Jackson, and in the course of discussion there had offered up a suggestion that spoke to the strategic impasse SNCC found itself facing. With the state's gubernatorial election scheduled for the fall, Lowenstein proposed a protest vote to demonstrate the desire of blacks to participate in the electoral process. In the con-

text of the dilemma confronting SNCC, the plan offered much that was attractive. There was the distinct possibility that such a campaign might generate the kind of national publicity that had thus far eluded SNCC. Second, the very effort of coordinating a statewide campaign promised to strengthen SNCC's organizational presence throughout Mississippi. Finally, the symbolic nature of the project was likely to forestall the type of violent opposition that had undermined virtually all of SNCC's previous campaigns in the state.

With few workable alternatives before them, SNCC's Mississippi staff opted for the plan. The basic idea called for SNCC fieldworkers to conduct a mock gubernatorial election among Mississippi's black population. The first step in the process took place in August with the casting of protest votes in the regular state Democratic primary. In all, some 1,000 blacks cast votes in the election, principally in Greenwood and Jackson. Encouraged by the success of the primary campaign, SNCC, under the direction of Bob Moses, set about planning for the regular gubernatorial election in November. Two changes were proposed and approved for the fall campaign. First, blacks would be asked to vote, not in the regular election, but in a parallel "Freedom Vote" designed to minimize the potential for violence, and thereby insure maximum voter turnout. To give Mississippi's black population someone to vote for, a slate of "freedom" candidates was selected, headed by Aaron Henry, the president of the Mississippi NAACP, and Tougaloo College's white chaplain, Ed King. Finally, to offset the increased need for staff during the

"Freedom Vote" campaign, the decision was made to import Northern college students for the duration of the project. This decision was reached partly in response to Lowenstein's assurance that he could supply as many students as the project required. Lowenstein made good on his promise. Drawing upon contacts established during earlier administrative stints at Stanford and Yale, Lowenstein was able to recruit some 100 students to come South to help with the vote.

Most arrived late in October and stayed through the November 4 conclusion of the campaign. During that time, the volunteers worked with SNCC staffers in all phases of the project, from canvassing black neighborhoods and registering black voters to staging the actual election. In all, nearly 80,000 blacks cast votes in the election, testament both to SNCC's organizing skills and the electoral willingness of Mississippi's black minority.

SNCC insiders, most important, Bob Moses, deemed the project and the use of the white volunteers a success. While the presence of so many upper-middle-class whites had exacerbated racial tensions on the project, these new volunteers had also contributed a great deal of valuable labor to the effort. Moreover, their presence had also insured a great deal of favorable publicity for SNCC as well as the campaign itself. Then too, the attention lavished on the volunteers helped popularize Southern civil rights work among Northern college students. [...]

Back in Mississippi, Bob Moses wasted little time in proposing an ambitious extension of the Freedom Vote campaign. At SNCC's November 14–16 staff meeting in Greenville, Mississippi, the idea of bringing an even larger, though unspecified, number of white students to Mississippi for the summer of 1964 was raised. Debate on the proposed plan was heated. Opponents used the occasion to raise the whole issue of white participation in the movement. Citing the Freedom Vote campaign as an example, several black staffers warned of the tendency of white students to appropriate leadership roles. This tendency, they argued, retarded the development of indigenous black leadership while also reinforcing traditional patterns of racial dominance and submission within the movement. Overall, though, sentiment at the Greenville meeting seemed to favor the plan.

[...]

Finally, there was the little matter of recruiting volunteers. How was SNCC to get word of the project to prospective applicants? How were applications to be handled? Who was to produce and distribute the forms? Who would select the volunteers? What criteria would guide the selection process? These and hundreds of other details of the recruitment process were still to be worked out. In one sense, though, the underlying rationale for the project had long since resolved the most important issue of all, that being the basic aim of the recruiting process. The fundamental goal of the project was to focus national attention on Mississippi as a means of forcing federal intervention in the state. For the project to be successful, then, it had to attract national media attention. What better way to do so than by recruiting the sons and daughters of upper-middle-class white America to join the effort? Their experiences during the Freedom Vote campaign had convinced the SNCC high command that nothing attracted the media quite like scenes of white college kids helping "the downtrodden Negroes of Mississippi." The SNCC veterans had also learned that the presence of well-heeled white students insured the conspicuous presence of federal law enforcement officials. Describing the Freedom Vote campaign, SNCC veteran, Lawrence Guyot, said:

> Wherever those white volunteers went FBI agents followed. It was really a problem to count the number of FBI agents who were there to protect the [Yale and Stanford] students. It was just that gross. So then we said, "Well, now, why don't we invite lots of whites ... to come and serve as volunteers in the state of Mississippi?" (Quoted in Raines, 1983: 287).

In a 1964 interview, Bob Moses (quoted in Atwater, 1964) put the matter a bit more obliquely when he remarked that "these students bring the rest of the country with them. They're from good schools and their parents are influential. The interest of the country is awakened and when that happens, the government responds to that issue." Or as James Forman, SNCC's Executive Director at the time of the Summer Project, put it more recently, "we made a conscious attempt...to recruit from some of the Ivy League schools...you know, a lot of us knew...what we were up against. So that we were, in fact, trying to consciously recruit a counter power-elite."

The financial straits SNCC found itself in on the eve of the project served to reinforce the strategic decision to recruit at elite colleges and universities. The organization simply lacked the resources to subsidize the participation of the summer volunteers.[...]

Faced with such severe financial constraints, SNCC would have been hard pressed to pay the volunteers even had strategic considerations argued for doing so. In the end, the strategic and financial imperatives of the project combined to convince project organizers to pitch their recruiting appeals to those who could bear the costs of a summer in Mississippi. Practically, this translated into a recruitment campaign geared to the nation's elite colleges and universities. Schools, such as Stanford, Harvard, and Princeton, offered project recruiters large numbers of students who not only could pay their own way, but whose social and political connections fit the public relations aims of the project.

[...]

The Applicants: A Profile

The information from the applications provides a broad-brush portrait of the Freedom Summer applicants. There are three components to this portrait: the applicants' background characteristics, motives for applying, and what might be called their "social relationship" to the Summer Project.

Background Characteristics

No doubt the single most salient characteristic of the Freedom Summer applicants is the comfortable, if not elite backgrounds from which they were drawn. [...] That meant that some of the least privileged persons in America were to play host to the offspring of some of the most privileged. This clash of class backgrounds was to produce some of the most poignant and eye-opening moments of the summer for both volunteers and residents alike.

The privileged character of the applicants makes sense, given two features of SNCC's recruiting efforts. First, SNCC's policy requiring the volunteers to be self-supporting encouraged the class bias noted above. Secondly, SNCC's stress on recruiting at elite colleges and universities also favored the well-to-do over the average student. Again, the figures show clearly just how much emphasis SNCC placed on recruiting at high-status colleges and universities. While 233 schools contributed applicants, the majority of students who applied came from the top thirty or so schools in the country. Elite private universities, such as Harvard, Yale, Stanford, and Princeton, accounted for nearly 40 percent of the total. In fact, those four schools alone contributed 123 of the 736 students who applied to work on the project. An additional 145 applicants were drawn from among the dozen most prestigious state universities – including Berkeley, Wisconsin, Michigan – in the country. All told, then, students from the nation's highest ranking public and private colleges and universities made up 57 percent of the total applicant pool.

The class advantages that account for the elite educational backgrounds of the volunteers may also help to explain the relatively small numbers of blacks who applied to the project. Less than 10 percent of the applicants were black. [...]

A bit more surprising is the relatively large number of women who applied to the project. Forty-one percent of all applicants were female. This represents a slight overrepresentation of women among the applicants when compared to their proportion among all college students. In 1964, women comprised only 39 percent of all undergraduates. Then, too, it must be remembered that the women applicants had come of age during one of the more romanticized and traditional eras of gender socialization in this country's history. For them to have even applied required a level of rejection of traditional sex roles not demanded of the male applicants.

[...]

Taken together, these various bits and pieces of information yield a reasonably coherent portrait of the applicants. The central theme of that portrait is one of biographical availability. For all the social-psychological interpretations that have been proposed to account for the conspicuous role of students in social protest there may be a far more mundane explanation. Students, especially those drawn from privileged classes, are simply free, to a unique degree, of constraints that tend to make activism too time consuming or risky for other groups to engage in. Often freed from the demands of family, marriage, and full-time employment, students are uniquely available to express their political values through action. Certainly, this view is consistent with the information we have on the applicants. Only 22 percent of those who applied held full-time jobs, and nearly 70 percent of this group were teachers out of school for the summer. The rest of the applicants were spared the need to work during the summer by virtue of their advantaged class backgrounds. The same story applies on a personal level. Barely 10 percent of the applicants were married, more often than not to another applicant. Less than 2 percent were parents.

Attitudes and Values

[...]

The applicants were exactly who we would have expected them to be, given the era in which they were raised and the class advantages most of them enjoyed. To the extent that they were drawn from that privileged segment of the American middle and upper-middle classes who came of age in postwar America, they shared in the generalized optimism, idealism, and sense of potency that was the subjective heritage of their class and generation.

[...] The following excerpts capture the dominant tone of the applications:

> As Peter Countryman said at the Conference on Racial Equality held at Pomona in February, "The only thing necessary for the triumph of evil is for the good men to do nothing."...I have always known that discrimination was wrong and that *now* is the time to overcome these obstacles....Until we do, all that we stand for in democracy and Christianity is negated, mocked while such oppression exists....I can not sit by idly, knowing that there is discrimination and injustice, knowing that there is terror and fear, while I do nothing.

> I want to work in Mississippi this summer because...there is a great deal of work to be done and...just as great [a] need for workers....But more than that, I feel that I *must* help. There is so much to do, so many barriers between men to be broken, so much hate to be overcome. I think that this is most acutely true of Mississippi, where barriers of ignorance, fear and hate are only now beginning to be effectively attacked. I want to contribute what I can to the effort so that we might at long last build a truly colorblind [*sic*] society "with liberty and justice for all."

[...]

What strikes the reader first about these statements is the depths of idealism they express. Indeed, that idealism is so passionately stated that it occasionally sounds naive and a bit romanticized. That it does may tell us as much about the lack of idealism in contemporary America as it does about any lack of sophistication on the part of the applicants. In any case, what is more important than *our* reaction to the statements is, first, the consistency with which these views were expressed, and second, what they tell us about the applicants. These were deeply idealistic individuals, dedicated to achieving equal rights and human dignity for all. What sets the applicants apart from a good many others who espouse similar values was their optimism that these values could be realized through a kind of generational mission in which they shared. Wrote one applicant:

I no longer can escape the tension, the spirit, the anxiety that fills my heart and mind concerning the movement in the South. It is impossible for me to deny the fact that the fight against racial prejudice, intolerance, ignorance – the fight for Civil Rights – is the most significant challenge and the most crucial war my generation will ever be called to fight.

[...]

So the applicants' idealism was informed by a sense of generational potency that made them extremely optimistic about the prospects for social change. One even referred to the need "to solve the racial question, so we can move on to eliminate hunger and poverty in America." Never let it be said that the applicants lacked either imagination or confidence!

These quotes also say something about the ideological diversity of the applicants on the eve of the Summer Project. Clearly, their perceptions of the world were not being filtered through a single dominant interpretive frame. Their narrative statements predate the emergence of the mass New Left and the dissemination of its political perspective throughout mainstream youth culture. So unlike activists in the late Sixties, for whom the "correct" *political* analysis became de rigueur, the Freedom Summer applicants display a remarkably eclectic mix of world views and reasons for wanting to go to Mississippi. In fact, many of the answers on the applications make no mention of larger political issues or motivations. As Elinor Tideman Aurthur told me in the course of her interview:

[D]uring that period [prior to Freedom Summer] I was...apolitical...I was into

the humanities, and culture...and literature. I was kind of impatient with my father and his involvement with social causes. I felt that was dead...I wanted to write...I didn't have the confidence to write but I saw myself as a writer, and I did not do anything political.

[...]

Those applicants whose statements evidence the least political orientation to the project fall into one of two groups. The first are teachers or education majors whose primary motivation for applying represents a simple extension of their occupational roles or future career plans.

[...]

The second group of "nonpolitical" applicants consists of persons whose reasons for applying appear to be primarily religious. For them the project represented an extension of the social gospel in action or, reflecting the existential theology of the day, an opportunity to bear "personal witness" to the idea of Christian brotherhood. One applicant put it this way: "Christ called us to *act* in the service of brotherhood, not just talk about it. I'm tired of talking. Mississippi is my opportunity to act."

The widespread salience of religious motives among the applicants may surprise some readers unfamiliar with America's long-standing tradition of church-based activism. From religious pacifists to Quaker abolitionists to Catholic settlement workers, much of America's activist history has had deep roots in the church. With its ministerial leadership and strong ideological ties to Southern black theology, the civil rights movement merely continued this tradition. It is hardly surprising, then, to find religious sentiments being voiced by many of the volunteers.

Among the more political applicants, a kind of conventional patriotic rhetoric was more often invoked than a radical leftist analysis. Many applicants cited a desire to "honor the memory" or "carry out the legacy of John F. Kennedy" as their principal reason for applying. Another sounded particularly Kennedyesque when he said that he was attracted to the project "by a desire to enhance the image of the United States abroad, thereby undercutting Communist influence among the underdeveloped nations of the world."

[...]

The impression that one gets from reading the applications, then, is one of healthy ideological diversity. All of the groups identified here seem to have been present in roughly equal numbers in the ranks of the applicants. What is interesting is that these ideological differences mask a common source of inspiration for whatever values the applicants espouse. Regardless of ideological stripe, the vast majority of applicants credit their parents with being the models for their actions. [...]

This, then, is one case in which the popular view of the Sixties activist is *not* consistent with the evidence. Far from using Freedom Summer as a vehicle for rebellion against parents, the applicants simply seem to be acting in accord with values learned at home. This finding is consistent with most previous research on the roots of student activism.

Social Relationship to the Project

Were freedom from adult responsibilities and sympathetic attitudes enough to account for the applicant's decision to apply to the project? Or were there ways in which concrete social ties served to "pull" people into the project? The answer to this last question would appear to be "yes." The image of the activist as a lone individual driven only by the force of his or her conscience applies to very few of the applicants. Rather, their involvement in the project seems to have been mediated through some combination of personal relationships and/or organizational ties.

Organizationally the applicants were a very active group. Only 15 percent of the prospective volunteers reported no group memberships, while 62 percent list two or more. The percentage of volunteers listing various types of organizations is shown below:

Civil rights organization	48%
Student club or social group	21
Church or religious group	21
Socialist or other leftist organization	14
Democrat or Republican party affiliate	13
Academic club or organization	13
Teachers organization	10

Not surprisingly, the highest percentage of memberships are to civil rights groups. Within this category, CORE or Friends of SNCC chapters account for better than half of all the affiliations. Given that SNCC and CORE supplied 100 percent of the field staff for the Summer Project, it seems reasonable to assume that membership in one of their chapters would have insured a certain knowledge of and loyalty to the project.

The remaining organizational categories mirror the ideological diversity touched on above. Each of the informal divisions discussed in the previous section correspond to one of the next six largest organizational categories. [...]

The real importance of these organizations lies not so much in the ideological divisions they reflect as in the role they played in drawing the applicants into civil rights activity *before* Freedom Summer. One volunteer described her initiation into the Movement in this way:

> [The] Church was very important to me. I was studying to be a minister at the time that I went to Mississippi and actually that is how I got involved in it [Freedom Summer] because I went to Beaver College which was an all female institution, wanting to be a missionary eventually, got involved in the YWCA there and was sent on a voter registration drive, which Al Lowenstein headed, in Raleigh, North Carolina... he... told us about the Mississippi summer project and after having my eyes opened by the whole Raleigh experience I knew I wanted to go.

[...]

For the vast majority of applicants, then, Freedom Summer did *not* mark their initial foray into the civil rights movement. Instead, through a variety of sponsoring organizations, some 90 percent of the applicants had already participated in various forms of activism. Not that the nature of their involvements was in all cases terribly significant. Most of the applicants had confined their activities to such safe forms of participation as "on-campus civil rights organizing" (36 percent) or fund-raising (10 percent). But it is not the intensity of these earlier involvements as much as the fact that they took place that is significant. Extremely risky, time-consuming involvements such as Freedom Summer are almost always preceded by a series of safer, less demanding instances of activism. In effect, people commit themselves to movements in stages, each activity preparing the way for the next. The case of the volunteer, who engaged in voter registration work in Raleigh, North Carolina, prior to Freedom Summer, illustrates the process. While in Raleigh, three very important things happened to her. First, she met activists she had not known previously, thus broadening her range of movement contacts. Second, talking with these activists and confronting segregation firsthand clearly deepened the volunteer's understanding of and commitment to the movement. Finally, at the level of identity, the week in Raleigh allowed her to "play at" and grow more comfortable with the role of activist. As the research on identity transformation suggests, it is precisely such tentative forays into new roles that pave the way for more thoroughgoing identity change. Playing at being an activist is usually the first step in becoming one. As a result, the volunteer left Raleigh knowing more people in the movement and more ideologically and personally disposed toward participation in the Summer Project. As she herself said, "the trip to Raleigh really laid the foundation for Mississippi ... I don't think I would have even applied to the project otherwise."

So most of the applicants were already linked to the civil rights movement either through the organizations to which they belonged or their own modest histories of civil rights activism. But what about their links to one another? How extensive were the ties *between* prospective volunteers on the eve of the summer? The presumption, of course, is that an individual would have found it easier to apply had they known someone else who had done so.

Fortunately, one question on the application allows for a very conservative estimate of the extent of such ties. That question asked the applicant to "list at least ten persons who ... would be interested in receiving information about your [summer] activities." These names were gathered in an effort to mobilize a well-heeled, Northern, liberal constituency who might lobby Washington on behalf of protection for civil rights workers as well as other changes in civil rights policy. Judging from the names they listed, most of the applicants seem to have been well aware of this goal. The names most often provided by the applicants were those of parents, parents' friends, professors, ministers, or other noteworthy or influential *adults* with whom they had contact. On occasion, however, the applicant also included another applicant in their list of names. Just how often was surprising.

Exactly a fourth of the applicants listed at least one other prospective volunteer on their applications. What makes this figure impressive is the fact that the intent of the question was not to have the applicants identify other applicants. That 25 percent did so suggests that the personal ties between the applicants were extensive. Interviews with the applicants confirm this impression. Forty-nine of the eighty applicants said they knew at least one other applicant in advance of the summer. And their accounts make it clear that these ties were important in their decision to apply to the project. Several even described their decision to apply as more a group than an individual process. As one volunteer put it:

[T]he group that went down to Raleigh ... were from Cornell, Dartmouth, Amherst, BU [Boston University], Yale ... and I just felt that I was with a very special group of people and I wanted to be with them for as long as I could and we would sit up at night talking about whether we would go down [to Mississippi] and [then] we communicated with each other after that Raleigh experience . . . [and] talked each other into going.

Together, the bits and pieces of information presented above yield a fairly coherent portrait of the Freedom Summer applicants. The central themes embodied in this portrait are those of "biographical availability," "attitudinal affinity" and "social integration." Raised by parents who espoused values consistent with the project, the applicants found themselves disposed to participate on attitudinal grounds. Then too, their freedom from family and employment responsibilities (the latter owing largely to their privileged class backgrounds) made it possible for them to act on their attitudes and values. Finally, a combination of organizational ties, personal links to other applicants, and their own histories of activism served to pull the applicants into the project even as their values were pushing them in that direction. [. . .]

The Survivors: Distinguishing Volunteers from No-Shows

Confronted by various hurdles, roughly a quarter of the applicants fell by the wayside prior to the start of the project. Can these no-shows be distinguished from those who did make it to Mississippi? Are there specific factors that account for the different courses of action taken by those in each group? The answer is yes. Expressed in terms of the three broad factors touched on earlier in the chapter, it appears that going or not going to Mississippi had more to do with the applicants' biographical availability and social links to the project than to any apparent differences in attitude between the volunteers and the no-shows. What is more, it would seem that the impact of these factors is closely related to the three major hurdles – staff rejection, parental opposition, and applicant fears – already noted.

[. . .]

Biographical Availability   Many people are deterred or prevented from protesting by the responsibilities and constraints of daily life which are imposed by work, parents, spouses or partners, children, or friends. Not everyone, in other words, is "biographically available" for protest, even if they are sympathetic to the cause. Of course, some people try to work around these constraints, or try to change them, if they are especially motivated to protest. In other words, people sometimes *make* themselves biographically available for protest. See McAdam (1988).

Together, the findings reported here offer a consistent picture of the Freedom Summer volunteers. Stated simply, the volunteers enjoyed much stronger social links to the Summer Project than did the no-shows. They were more likely to be members of civil rights (or allied) groups, have friends involved in the movement, and have more extensive histories of civil rights activity prior to the summer. The practical effect of this greater "proximity" to the movement would have been to place the volunteer at considerable "risk" of being drawn into the project via the application process. Having applied, the volunteer's close ties to the civil rights community would then have served another function. Given the extended time commitment expected of Freedom Summer volunteers and the highly publicized dangers of the campaign, it seems reasonable to assume that individual applicants – even highly committed ones – would have considered withdrawing from the campaign prior to the summer. What might have discouraged applicants from acting on these fears was the presence of strong *social* constraints discouraging withdrawal. If one acted alone in applying to the project and remained isolated in the months leading up to the campaign, the social costs of withdrawing from the project would not have been great. On the other hand, the individual who applied in consort with friends or as a movement veteran undoubtedly risked considerable social disapproval for withdrawal. One can also stress a more positive interpretation of the same process. In the months leading up to the summer, well-integrated applicants were no doubt encouraged to make good on their commitment through the reinforcement and sense of strength they derived from other applicants. As one volunteer explained, his relationship with another applicant was "probably the key to me making it to Mississippi...[he] and I just sort of egged each other on...I'm pretty sure I wouldn't have made it without him and probably that was true for him too." Whichever interpretation one chooses, it is clear from the data that participants *do* differ significantly from no-shows in the extent and strength of their social links to the project.

Those applicants who finally made it to Mississippi, then, were an interesting and very special group. They were independent both by temperament and by virtue of their class advantages and relative freedom from adult responsibilities. They were not children, however, but young adults whose slightly older age granted them an immunity from parental control not enjoyed by the no-shows. Owing to the formidable obstacles the female applicants faced, the volunteers were disproportionately male. Academically, they numbered among "the best and the brightest" of their generation, both in the levels of education they had obtained and the prestige of the colleges and universities they were attending. Reflecting their privileged class backgrounds as much as the prevailing mood of the era, the volunteers

held to an enormously idealistic and optimistic view of the world. More important, perhaps, they shared a sense of efficacy about their own actions. The arrogance of youth and the privileges of class combined with the mood of the era to give the volunteers an inflated sense of their own specialness and generational potency. This message was generally reinforced at home by parents who subscribed to values consistent with those of the project. Finally, the volunteers were already linked to the civil rights community. Whether these links took the form of organizational memberships, prior activism, or ties to other applicants, the volunteers benefited from greater "social proximity" to the project than did the no-shows. In fact, nothing distinguishes the two groups more clearly than this contrast. Biographical availability and attitudinal affinity may have been necessary prerequisites for applying, but it was the strength of one's links to the project that seems to have finally determined whether one got to Mississippi or not.

References

Atwater, James 1964 "'If we can crack Mississippi...'." *Saturday Evening Post*, July 25, p. 16.

Raines, Howell 1983 *My Soul Is Rested*. New York: Penguin Books.

7 Changing Values in Post-Industrial Societies

Ronald Inglehart

Introduction

The values of Western publics have been shifting from an overwhelming emphasis on material well-being and physical security toward greater emphasis on the quality of life. The causes and implications of this shift are complex, but the basic principle might be stated very simply: people tend to be more concerned with immediate needs or threats than with things that seem remote or non-threatening. Thus, a desire for beauty may be more or less universal, but hungry people are more likely to seek food than aesthetic satisfaction. Today, an unprecedentedly large portion of Western populations have been raised under conditions of exceptional economic security. Economic and physical security continue to be valued positively, but their relative priority is lower than in the past.

We hypothesize that a significant shift is also taking place in the distribution of political skills. An increasingly large proportion of the public is coming to have sufficient interest and understanding of national and international politics to participate in decision-making at this level. Mass publics have played a role in national politics for a long time, of course, through the ballot and in other ways. Current changes enable them to play an increasingly active role in formulating policy, and to engage in what might be called "elite-challenging" as opposed to "elite-directed" activities. Elite-directed political participation is largely a matter of elites mobilizing mass support through established organizations such as political parties, labor unions, religious institutions, and so on. The newer "elite-challenging" style of politics gives the public an increasingly important role in making specific *decisions*, not just a choice between two or more sets of decision-makers. One of the most important elements contributing to this change is the fact that potential counter-elites are distributed more widely among the public than ever before.

The two processes of change reinforce each other. One aspect of the change in values, we believe, is a decline in the legitimacy of hierarchical authority, patriotism, religion, and so on, which leads to declining confidence in institutions. At the same time, the political expression of new values is facilitated by a shift in the balance of political skills between elites and mass. Certain basic values and skills seem to be changing in a gradual but deeply rooted fashion. Undoubtedly there will be counter-trends that will slow the process of change and even reverse it for given periods of time. But the principal evolutionary drift is the result of structural changes taking place in advanced industrial societies and is unlikely to be changed unless there are major alterations in the very nature of those societies.

This book will focus on these two changes, moving both backward and forward from them: backward along the causal chain to seek the *sources* of these changes; and forward in an attempt to analyze their likely *consequences*. How we will do this is suggested by figure 7.1 which provides an overview of the book. The remaining sections of this chapter will briefly discuss each of the variables shown in the diagram and in doing so, lay out the argument more explicitly. Our analysis moves from the system level to the individual level and

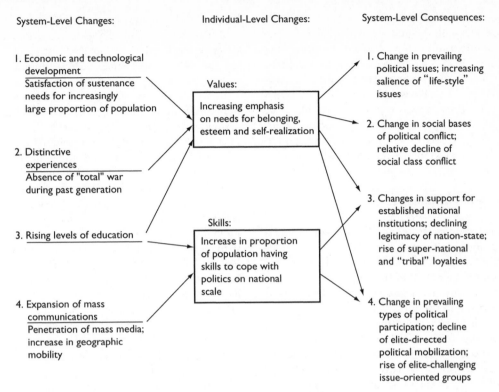

Figure 7.1   Overview: The process of change examined in this book

back again. It starts with events in given societies, turns to their impact on what people think, and finally examines the consequences these intrapersonal events may have on a society. The values and skills of individuals are at the center of the diagram, and they will be the central concern – for relatively little is known about them. Yet we must never lose sight of the setting in which an individual lives. If we devote less attention to the economic, social, and political structures of given countries, it is not because we consider them unimportant: their role is crucial. But a number of excellent studies of these aspects of given societies are already available. The present work is intended to supplement them, providing insight into a relatively unexplored set of influences on Western politics. The central focus is on things that exist within individuals, and these things can best be measured with survey data. But we trace their causes to changes in a society as a whole; and we are

interested in their eventual impact on the political system. The linkages between the individual and the system are complex. We cannot take it for granted that if increasing numbers of people hold given values, their political system will automatically adopt policies which reflect those values. It depends partly on how politically skilled those people are. And it depends at least equally on the political institutions of the given country. What the people get is conditioned not only by what the people want, but by whether they have one dominant party or several competitive political parties; a Presidential system or a Parliamentary system; a free press or a controlled press; and numerous other institutional factors. It depends, in short, on their country's political structure.

While certain changes in values and skills seem to be more or less universal among advanced industrial societies, political institutions are not. They differ profoundly from nation to nation. A country's political structure must be kept in mind at every stage of our analysis, and we will refer to it frequently, for it can facilitate or hinder values and skills from having an impact on politics.

Thus, not two but three variables are crucial to the analysis: values, skills, and structure. These three types of variables, we believe, largely determine the pace of political change. Now let us turn our attention to the socio-economic roots of change.

Sources of Change

Before undertaking an exploration of social change, we need to ask a simple but fundamental question: *is* change, in fact, taking place? A prevailing stereotype in comparative politics used to depict the Third World as being in the process of rapid change and development, while the West was assumed to have reached some sort of end state.

It seems that in many ways, the industrialized world is actually undergoing change which is more rapid and more genuinely new than what is occurring in the New Nations. But change in the industrialized world is far harder to grasp, harder to conceptualize. One tends to use familiar images because we have no model of the future. The notion that the Third World countries would come to resemble the contemporary West may have been an illusion, but it at least provided a concrete picture of where they were headed. Change in highly industrialized nations is even more of a leap into the unknown. In a confused way, one senses change in all directions – in sex roles, morals, life-styles, fashions, in the ecology, the economy, and politics. Finally, one is tempted to fall back on the past, in search of solid ground.

Is change taking place? On one level, we can give an unequivocal yes. Reliable time series data demonstrate clearly that massive change *is* taking place in the infrastructure of advanced industrial society. These system-level changes might well alter individual-level values, beliefs, and behavior. Among the many forces for change are eco-nomic development, expansion of secondary and higher education, the growing size and diversity of the mass media, and discontinuities in the life experiences of large numbers of people.

Statistics on income, education, mass communications, and foreign travel all tell a similar story. In the United States the rate of access to higher education doubled from 1950 to 1965. It more than doubled in West Germany during that period, and more than tripled in France. In the electorate that participated in the 1952 American Presidential election, people whose education was limited to grade school outnumbered people with any college education by nearly three to one. In 1972, people who had been to college outnumbered the grade school educated by more than two to one. Secondary and university-level education are now far more widely distributed among Western populations than ever before, and this change has had a particularly heavy impact on the younger age-cohorts.

Television and foreign travel have become a part of the common man's experience in the post-war era. In 1963, only a third of the households in France and Italy had television sets; by 1970, TV was present in more than 70 percent of the households of those countries. Foreign travel is no longer limited to the very top and bottom of the economic scale. Before World War II, only a tiny minority of native-born Americans had ever visited Europe; in the last twenty years, higher incomes and charter flights have enabled millions of Americans to cross the Atlantic. Similarly, by 1970 most Western Europeans had visited at least one foreign country; indeed proportionately more Germans visited Italy than Americans visited Florida that year.

Technological Innovation – The thread of technological innovation ties these changes together. Technology has made possible the unprecedented productivity that underpins advanced industrial society; it renders expanded educational opportunities both necessary and possible; it has created the contemporary mass media; and it involves men and women in drastic shifts in personal environment that uproot them from previous patterns.

Changes in Occupational Structure – Daniel Bell has emphasized the importance of changes in occupational structure probably more than any other recent writer. Indeed, they are the basis of his definition of "Post-Industrial Society." Bell foresees a society in which the creation and utilization of knowledge provides the axis along which a new stratification system is emerging. He anticipates a continuing displacement of industrial employment into the tertiary sector, especially into what is often called the knowledge industry. This emerging society values most highly those elites who possess theoretical knowledge, followed by technicians and administrators of knowledge industries. In addition, Bell emphasizes the importance of new industries that exploit technological innovation. He predicts a growing divergence of outlook between the new elites oriented toward scientific and professional goals and older elites attached to profits, economic growth, and their own particular firms or bureaucracies. The dynamics of organizations in Post-Industrial societies reinforce these tendencies, Bell argues. As professionalization increases in an organization, members become more and more oriented toward external points of reference such as their own professional group's norms of behavior and universalistic rather than particularistic concerns.

Technology is creating the Post-Industrial society just as it created the Industrial society. Innovations in agricultural production already have enabled a very few people to feed the rest. Now industrial innovation is reducing the proportion of the population needed to produce an increasing quantity of manufactured goods. In the United States only a minority of the labor force is engaged in the agricultural and industrial sectors, and other Western countries are approaching or are already at the point of having 50 percent of the work force in the tertiary or service sector. In France, for example, 37 percent of the population was still employed in the primary sector as recently as 1946; this had declined to a mere 12 percent in 1970. Within a few years, a majority of the French work force will be employed in the tertiary sector. The United States passed this milestone in 1956, becoming the world's first "Post-Industrial" society. But by 1980, most Western European countries will also be "Post-Industrial."

In a sense, Bell's analysis may give an exaggerated impression of the growth of the middle class. His figures are accurate, but much of the growth of the tertiary sector reflects the increasing employment of women, most of whom have non-manual jobs. In 1972, 58 percent of non-agriculturally employed American males still had manual jobs. In many households the principal wage earner was a manually employed male, with a secondary income from a female having a clerical or sales occupation. At the risk of being sexist, one might argue that such households remained primarily oriented toward the industrial sector. Still, there is no question that the trend Bell describes does exist: there has been a substantial decline in the share of the work force having manual occupations, even if we consider males exclusively. Thus, it seems more than likely that this change has important implications for the outlook and behavior of Western populations.

Economic Growth – Income levels have shown equally impressive change: real income per capita is now at least double the highest level attained before World War II in virtually all Western countries, and in many it has tripled or even quadrupled economic and physical security, as higher incomes and welfare programs reduce the economic deprivations previously felt by most of the population. Never before have the sustenance needs been secure for such a large share of the population. Although economic growth came to a halt with the Recession of 1973–1975, real income remained at unprecedentedly high levels.

Expansion of Education – Changes in income and occupation are closely tied in with the expansion of higher education.

Numerous studies have demonstrated the impact that higher education has on the development of political consciousness and the development of cognitive skills. Indeed, education turns out to be one of the most important variables in almost any cross-national analysis. Summarizing studies of the impact of college, Feldman and Newcomb conclude that college makes students more liberal, less authoritarian, less dogmatic, less ethnocentric, and more interested in political matters. But it is equally true that students enter college already well ahead of the general population on these dimensions.

The fact that the better-educated emphasize certain kinds of values may seem intuitively understandable. But education is an extremely complex variable. We must distinguish between education as an indicator of affluence, education as an indicator of cognitive development, and education as an indicator of integration into a specific communications network. Differences in values and behavior *could* simply reflect differential exposure to given communications networks.

In the recent past, students have been particularly active exponents of new values and political styles: one wonders to what extent this simply reflects the influence of their own particular milieu. The period of maximum isolation of the youth culture, from late high school through college, corresponds with the development of higher cognitive skills and, in Mannheim's words, "political cultural consciousness." At this stage youth has passed the stage of maximum family influence and is groping toward an intellectual justification of beliefs and behavioral predispositions. It seems significant that today this stage tends to be spent in a milieu that minimizes the impact of the larger society.

Development of Mass Communications – The mass media are undoubtedly among the major sources of change, but it is not easy to specify how the influence process works. Information from communications media is filtered through numerous mediating factors and influences and is processed in ways that are not yet thoroughly understood. The expansion of the communications networks of advanced societies has been made possible by technological innovation. The result has been to make information networks national and even international, and to communicate information very rapidly from anywhere in the world or even from outer space. But such innovation has also made possible a growing diversity of mass communications networks, extending across great distances but reaching specialized audiences.

The pockets of traditionalism within industrialized nations continue to shrink. Even if the adults are not greatly affected in their belief systems by what they see and hear, it undoubtedly will be more difficult than in the past for traditionally oriented adults to pass on their values to the young in an unaltered form. For even when the media are controlled and consciously programmed to reflect the dominant values of a society, their coverage of news leads them to transmit information that is often threatening to existing values. This fact is clearly grasped by protestors, who plan their activities so as to maximize their publicity value. The mass media consequently are a force for change, since they communicate dissatisfaction, alternative life-styles, and dissonant signals, even when they are directly controlled by the "Establishment."

Thus, the role of the mass media is mixed. On the one hand, they serve to incorporate more and more people into larger communication networks. They undoubtedly have increased the knowledge and sophistication of the population, especially through their impact on the young. They probably have a stereotyping and conventionalizing effect in many areas of life. Yet, at the same time, they communicate a great deal of opposition to conventional values, particularly when they are tailored to specialized audiences.

Distinctive Cohort Experiences – Practically all of the factors just mentioned have contributed to the fact that the younger generation in Western countries has been brought up in a quite different world from the one which shaped their parents or grandparents. They have grown up in relatively affluent, communications-rich societies. Numerous other factors make their experience distinctive, but one is of such importance that it will be singled out for special mention: although the older generations have experienced total war in one form or another, the younger generation in these countries has never experienced invasion of their homeland by hostile forces. For them, war has been something that happens in other countries.

[...]

Some Consequences of Change Among Western Publics

If change is occurring, what impact is it likely to have on the politics of Western nations? Moving from the left-hand side of figure 7.1 to the right, several topics are outlined.

Political Issues – Change in individual values affects one's orientation toward political issues. If material concerns lessen in relative importance, there may be a decline in the importance of issues that reflect the stratification system of industrial society; ideology, ethnicity, life-style, and so on may assume greater importance. Class politics may decline in favor of status or cultural or "ideal" politics.

We see the outlines of some consequences of change in current demands for participation in decisions that affect one's life, whether it is in schools, universities, welfare agencies, offices, factories, or church. If these demands are successful, they will bring great changes in a wide variety of institutions.

Along with demands for participation, other types of issues are brought into the political arena – issues that derive more from differences in life-style than from economic needs. For example, one can point to such things as protection of the environment, the quality of life, the role of women, the redefinition of morality, drug usage, and broader public participation in both political and non-political decision-making. Few of

these issues are completely new. What is changing is their quantitative importance. Conservation of natural resources has been a subject of political controversy for many decades; and students have been politically active for almost as long as there have been students. But it is difficult to find a previous instance of the triumph of environmental interests over major economic interests that is comparable in magnitude to the rejection of the proposed American supersonic transport; or the persisting opposition to offshore oil drilling and strip-mined coal, in face of an energy shortage. Likewise, it is difficult to find a precedent for the fact that students now make up a larger proportion of the American population than does organized labor.

Changes in Social Bases of Politics – The emergence of these new issues presents the existing political parties with a dilemma. If they realign themselves to appeal to the new groups, they risk losing their existing constituencies. The "new politics" often clash with strongly held traditional values and norms. This has resulted in pressures toward the formation of new political parties and attempts by spokesmen for the new values to influence and capture existing parties.

In the early phases of industrial society, the population tended to be divided between a large mass of poorly paid workers and a relatively small number of owners and managers having much higher incomes and a radically different life-style. In advanced industrial societies, the ranks of the middle class are greatly increased by growth in the number of people in managerial, technical, clerical and sales occupations; the relative number of manual workers diminishes but their income levels rise and the amount of leisure time at their disposal increases, with the result that many of them are able to adopt a life-style relatively close to conventional middle class standards. A number of analysts, representing various perspectives, have argued that we are likely to witness a shift in social conflict, with a portion of the middle class becoming radical while most of the working class and lower-middle class become increasingly conservative. Data on the relationship between party preference and occupation, income, education, and labor union membership make it clear that the industrial pattern of political cleavage has by no means disappeared. Nevertheless, the evidence indicates that a gradual decline in class voting has been occurring. In the future, new support for parties of the Left may be increasingly recruited from middle-class sources, while status quo parties may draw their support more and more from an embourgeoisified working class.

Support for National Institutions – Apparently, nationalistic sentiments are not being transmitted to the young with the same fidelity as in the past. Governments traditionally have exploited patriotic symbols as sources of legitimacy for their actions. As popular support of these symbols declines, governments can no longer draw so easily on this resource.

Changes in individual value priorities may partially account for the decline in satisfaction with governmental outputs and national institutions that has been documented in surveys of American politics over the past decade. The political and economic systems continue to produce outputs that respond relatively well to traditional demands, but they do not seem to provide adequate satisfaction for other needs and demands that are increasingly important among certain segments of the population. Changing values combine with a growing sense of the inadequacy of existing institutions to encourage the use of new and different political inputs, including protest activity and the formation of new political movements and organizations. These innovations are facilitated by the shift in the distribution of education: political skills are no longer concentrated largely among the holders of official and corporate roles, and formerly peripheral groups are able to act as participants with an unprecedented degree of organizational skill.

At the same time, other groups oppose changing what they see as the rules of the game in which they have come to believe. They are unhappy with existing institutions, but unhappy because they do not function as they used to rather than because they need to be changed. Hence the stage is set for a new polarization.

As expectations of mass publics change, their perceptions of the adequacy of institutional arrangements also change. Key American institutions from the business corporation to the government itself seem to be undergoing a crisis of legitimacy. Many short-run factors undoubtedly intervene to affect confidence, such as progress or lack of it in ending war and racism and specific political scandals, and we certainly do not anticipate a permanent decline in trust. But with changing values and political skills and, consequently, a more involved and critical public, the downward trend in support for national institutions seems to be one symptom of a long-range transformation of Western publics.

One result of this transformation can be an increased openness to international integration. But the search for social identity can also move in the opposite direction. There has been a resurgence of interest in ethnic ties in the United States and demands for autonomy based on language and culture in Belgium and Great Britain. These trends do not simply reflect a reawakened parochialism. Surprisingly enough, a relative emphasis on *both* supranational and subnational ties often exists in the same individuals.

Changing Styles of Political Participation – The politics of classical industrial society were based on mass parties and associated movements such as trade unions and church-related organizations that were generally bureaucratic and oligarchical in structure. Emerging cultural values emphasize spontaneity and individual self-expression. Furthermore, the expansion of education means that increasing numbers of people are available with political skills that enable them to play roles previously limited to a small political elite. For both objective and subjective reasons the old parties are being challenged by new forces that seem less and less amenable to an elite-directed type of organization.

Insofar as these demands of newly articulate groups cannot be accommodated within existing structures, support for governmental institutions may erode. Governments face the same dilemma as the parties: to the extent that governing elites reorient themselves along the new lines they risk suffering a backlash from groups imbued with traditional values. Governments can no longer rely on appeals to nationalism and patriotism as much as in the past. Rising skill levels have been accompanied by a declining emphasis on such values as national security, which traditionally justified the existence of a strong nation-state.

There may be no more dissatisfaction among mass publics today than at various times in the past. But there is reason to believe that the *types* of dissatisfaction now most likely to lead to political action have different roots from those of the past. If this is true, it poses difficult problems for the policy-makers of these societies.

A decade ago, it could still be taken for granted that the fundamental test of a society's leadership was the extent to which it achieved economic growth regardless of long-term consequences. And it could still be assumed that leadership which passed this test had gone a long way toward establishing its legitimacy among the general public. These comfortable assumptions are no longer tenable. The public's goals seem to be shifting. Insofar as policy-makers seek to promote the general welfare, they will need to take subjective aspects of well-being more and more into account. An increasingly articulate and politically sophisticated public may leave them little choice.

The late 1960's and early 1970's were a period of ferment for advanced industrial societies. In the United States, the combination of the civil rights movement and widespread opposition to the war in Vietnam aroused segments of the population that previously had only sporadically been involved in public affairs. Political action took new and more militant forms with widespread challenges to existing institutions such as schools, parties, churches, and the military. The violent phase seems to have passed. Ghetto riots and university disruptions came to a halt, and with the end of the war in Vietnam there was a decline in the ability of militants to attract active support from broader segments of the population.

Despite the decline in dramatic forms of protest, surveys indicate a continuing withdrawal of support from key institutions. The American public's feelings of trust for the national government have been measured repeatedly for a number of years. In 1958, a representative sample of the American public gave overwhelmingly positive responses; only 28 percent showed predominantly distrustful attitudes. By the mid-1970's, a clear majority of the public gave distrustful responses. A similar pattern of decline can be seen in public attitudes toward political parties. This decline obviously reflects the impact of short-term events such as the Watergate scandals, but it may also be a symptom of a long-term transformation which is rooted in the formative experiences of given generations and progressively revealed as one generation replaces another. For these changes are not merely American. Decline in patriotism and support for key national institutions can be found among the young of virtually all advanced industrial countries.

8 Middle-Class Radicalism and Environmentalism

Stephen Cotgrove and Andrew Duff

There has been increasing interest in recent years in the possibility of fundamental changes in the political system, with the emergence of new social groups, new interests and new values which cut across traditional class-based alignments and cleavages. Moreover, in recent decades, there has been a marked increase in direct action, and the growth of outsider politics, a decline in partisan support for the traditional parties, and other indications of a loss of legitimacy. Such indications of strain and stress take on a special significance with the possibility that industrial societies, which have relied so heavily on policies of sustained and rapid economic growth for maintaining a broad spectrum of consensus and support, may be facing special challenges with intransigent problems of unemployment and inflation, exacerbated by increasing shortages of materials and energy.

The environmentalist movement provides an important case study and focus for exploring such issues. In the last decade the awareness of environmental problems has not only increased dramatically, but has taken on a new political significance. Environmentalist groups have been at the centre of protest, locally and nationally, against motorways, airports and dams, and have vigorously opposed the nuclear programme in a number of countries. And in the last few years, newly formed 'ecology parties' have captured a sizeable proportion of the votes at elections. The significance of the environment has shifted from a preoccupation with the preservation of the countryside, historic buildings and local amenities, to become the focus for radical protest. Above all, environmentalists have challenged the central values and ideology of industrial society. It is with this dimension of the environmentalist movement that this analysis is concerned. Is environmental protest indicative of a fundamental change in social values, and if so, what strains and problems will this generate for the political system? What are the sources of support? Is there a potentially larger political constituency?

In order to clarify the analysis, it is necessary first to emphasise the heterogeneous character of those who come under the broad umbrella of environmentalists. On the one hand there are those who are mainly interested in protecting wildlife, preserving the countryside, and our national heritage of buildings. They wish simply to give a higher priority to the protection of the environment. But at the other extreme there are those who argue that the problem requires more than simply a shift in priorities, and that fundamental changes are essential if we are to survive growing threats to the environment and the exhaustion of materials which result from a high-growth, energy-consuming and environmentally-damaging way of life. It is environmentalists in this 'strong' sense, and who have joined associations which promote such policies, who are the object of this analysis.

Environmental Awareness and Beliefs

The most plausible explanation for environmental activism is that those who join such

A Chronology of the U.S. Environmental Movement

1845: Henry David Thoreau moves to Walden Pond, where he stays for two years, and writes one of a series of careful observations of the New England environment which he made throughout his life.

1872: U.S. Congress creates the first national park, Yellowstone, but also passes legislation (still in effect today) allowing private individuals and companies to stake mining claims in public lands for a nominal fee.

1891: Forest Reserve Act allows the President to set aside public lands with only restricted uses.

1892: The Sierra Club is founded by outdoorsmen to conserve California's wilderness, with John Muir as its first president.

1913: After long controversy, Congress passes a law to allow the damming of California's Hetch Hetchy, a dramatic and beautiful valley much like Yosemite. The conflict pitted pragmatic conservationists like Gifford Pinchot, who favored the dam for the electric power it would produce, against more radical preservationists like John Muir.

1949: Aldo Leopold publishes *The Sand Country Almanac*, which argues that all life (human and nonhuman) is connected through its presence in balanced habitats. We all benefit, he said, from the biological diversity of ecosystems.

1962: Marine biologist Rachel Carson publishes *Silent Spring* in serial form in *The New Yorker*, on the unintended effects of DDT and other chemical pesticides.

1964: President Johnson signs the Wilderness Act, which allows large tracts of land to be protected from development.

1966: Victor Yannacone and others sue to stop the spraying of DDT on Long Island; a year later they form the Environmental Defense Fund (EDF). The Ford Foundation provides startup grants to several legally oriented environmental groups, including EDF, the Natural Resources Defense Council, and the Sierra Club Legal Defense Fund.

1968: Paul Ehrlich publishes *The Population Bomb*, warning of the many risks of rapid population growth around the world.

1969: David Brower, dynamic head of the Sierra Club who has radicalized that organization, is forced out and founds the Friends of the Earth. When he is later ousted from that group, he will form the Earth Island Institute.

1970: On January 1, President Nixon signs the National Environmental Policy Act; within a decade two dozen other environmental acts will be passed, creating among other things the Environmental Protection Agency and the Occupational Safety and Health Administration.

1970: Twenty million Americans participate in the first Earth Day, April 22, aiming to spread awareness of environmental problems and solutions. This is probably the largest single show of support for any cause in U.S. history.

Mid-1970s: Within several years, a number of direct-action ecology groups are founded, including Greenpeace, the Environmental Policy Institute, and the Sea Shepherd Conservation Society.

Late 1970s: Ecology movement helps inspire antinuclear movement against civilian nuclear reactors.

1978: Love Canal makes headlines and places toxic waste at the top of environmental agenda; thousands of local environmental groups (sometimes called "NIMBYs" for "Not In My BackYard") are formed.

1980: Led by Dave Foreman, former lobbyist for the Wilderness Society, Earth First! is founded on the principle of sabotage against logging, mining, and other incursions into wilderness areas.

1981: President Reagan appoints James Watt of Wyoming as Secretary Interior as part of the "sagebrush rebellion" of western businesses and politicians against federal intervention to protect the environment or slow down commercial exploitation; millions join the major environmental groups in response.

1990: A conference in Michigan and a book, *Dumping in Dixie* by Robert Bullard, help create the environmental justice movement, which emphasizes that poor communities are the biggest victims of pollution and hazards.

associations are particularly aware of the problems. To test this we asked a series of questions about environmental issues. The questionnaire was distributed to three target groups: environmentalists (members of Friends of the Earth and the Conservation Society), leading industrialists (drawn from *Business Who's Who* and *Who's Who in British Engineering*), and a sample of the general public from Bath and Swindon. The results were surprising. On items testing awareness of environmental damage such as 'Rivers and waterways are seriously threatened by pollution' and 'Some animals and plants are being threatened with extinction', both environmentalists and the public generally agreed that the environment was being damaged, although the strength of agreement was greater for environmentalists. On a cluster of items testing awareness of shortages, such as 'There are likely to be serious and disruptive shortages of essential raw materials if things go on as they are', there was still substantial agreement about the threat of shortages. So it is clear that awareness of environmental dangers can only account in part for membership of the more activist environmental groups.

It is when we turn to an exploration of the significance and meaning of beliefs about the environment in the context of wider systems of belief and action that larger differences between environmentalists and others begin to emerge. Firstly, environmentalists see environmental dangers and problems to be much more serious: 93 per cent define them as extremely serious or very serious, compared with 56 per cent of the general public. Environmentalists differed too in their attitude toward science and technology. In answer to items such as 'Science and technology can solve our problems by finding new sources of energy, materials, and ways of increasing food production' and 'We attach too much importance to reason and science to the neglect of our intuition', it was the environmentalists who showed their lack of confidence in, and even hostility to science and technology by contrast with the public. And on a scale of opposition to the

institutions of industrial society environmentalists were significantly more opposed than members of the general public. Substantial differences in values and ideals between the two groups also emerged. Using a modified form of Inglehart's scale for measuring 'material' and 'post-material' values, we found a marked polarization between environmentalists and the public, the former scoring higher on items indicating support for post-material values, and much lower on material items. Support for material values was indicated by high priority given to items such as 'Maintaining a high rate of economic growth' and 'Maintaining a stable economy'. By contrast, the environmentalists gave high priority to 'Progressing toward a less impersonal, more humane society', and 'Progressing toward a society where ideas are more important than money'.

The second source of empirical evidence is more complex. Our study of environmentalists' literature pointed to the probability that environmentalists held strongly negative views about many features of industrial society. In order to explore this, we devised a series of items to enable respondents to indicate their preferences for the kind of society they would like to see.[...]

At the top of the list for the general public was preference for a society with more emphasis on law and order, followed by satisfying work, economic growth, differentials, and rewards for achievement. By contrast, environmentalists want a society which above all attaches more importance to humanly satisfying work, in which production is selective rather than aiming to satisfy the demand for consumer goods, which sets limits to economic growth, and emphasizes participation, as against the influence of experts.

Environments at Risk

What differentiates the environmentalists then from the general public is not primarily their awareness of environmental dangers. Rather, it is the use to which they have put environmental beliefs which distinguishes them. They are opposed to the dominant values and institutions of industrial society, and want to change them. Now such a challenge faces enormous odds. But the environment has provided ammunition for their case. Beliefs about environmental dangers have been harnessed and put to work to support their challenge to the dominant values and ideology. What they are saying is that the society we have got is bad: that the way we behave is against Nature, our children will suffer, and time is running out. They are adopting a practice which is widespread in human societies. In the words of Mary Douglas, 'Time, money, God and Nature are the universal trump cards plunked down to win an argument'. So, she says, the 'laws of nature are dragged in to sanction the moral code: this kind of disease is caught by adultery, that by incest; this meteorological disaster is the effect of political disloyalty, that the effect of impiety'. In advanced industrial societies too, the environment has become a doom-point: a trump card thrown down by the environmentalists to win a moral argument. Nuclear power stations in particular have come to have a deep symbolic significance: centralized, technologically complex and hazardous, and reinforcing all those trends in society which environmentalists most fear and dislike – the increasing domination of experts, threatening the freedom of the individual, and reinforcing totalitarian tendencies. Opposition to nuclear power is seen for many as a key issue on which to take a stand against the further advance of an alliance between state power and commercial interests. For the objectors, the material advantages from nuclear power cannot justify the risks involved.

As was stressed earlier, environmentalists are far from being a homogeneous group. This raises problems in testing ideas about the political significance of the environmentalists' movement. Some members of the environment associations do not share such radical views, nor wish to harness environment beliefs to challenging the dominant

values. Their main concern is rather with the protection of the countryside. Indeed, a significant minority of our sample support both material values and 'economic individualism'. The most important distinguishing factor was position on the political spectrum. Those on the left had less confidence in science, higher scores on the anti-industrial society scale, higher post-material scores, and were more opposed to economic individualism. And despite the fact that their perceptions of environmental damage and shortages did not differ from those on the right, it was this group who were most likely to rate environmental dangers as extremely or very serious. Such evidence lends even stronger support to the view that it is the use to which environmental beliefs are put which is the key to the political significance of the environmentalist movement.

Competing Paradigms

The environmentalist movement then has provided a vehicle for harnessing beliefs about environmental dangers to support an attack on the central values and beliefs of industrial capitalism – the hegemony of economic goals and values, and the rational and systematic orientation of action to these ends. In industrial societies economic criteria become the bench-mark by which a wide range of individual and social action is judged and evaluated. And belief in the market and market mechanisms is quite central. Clustering round this core belief is the conviction that enterprise flourishes best in a system of risks and rewards, that differentials are necessary incentives to maximize effort and to call forth talent and achievement, and in the necessity for some form of division of labour, and a hierarchy of skills and expertise. In particular, there is a belief in the competence of experts in general and of scientists in particular. More than this, scientific knowledge and the scientific method enjoy a special epistemological status as superior ways of knowing, so that statements of the form 'it is a scientific fact that...' are treated with special deference. And as a corollary, there is an emphasis on quantification. In short, it is possible to identify a dominant social paradigm – a set of beliefs about the nature of society which provides both a guide to action and a legitimation of policies.

The alternative environmental paradigm polarizes on almost every issue. The first and most obvious point of difference is the environmentalists' opposition to the dominant value attached to economic growth. This in turn rests on beliefs that the earth's resources are finite – a view encapsulated in Boulding's telling metaphor 'space ship earth'. But their disagreement with the central values and beliefs of the dominant social paradigm runs deeper than this. Not only do they challenge the importance attached to material and economic goals, they by contrast give much higher priority to the realization of non-material values – to social relationships and community, to the exercise of human skills and capacities, and to increased participation in decisions that affect our daily lives. They disagree too with the beliefs of the dominant social paradigm about the way society works. They have little confidence in science and technology to come up with a technical fix to solve the problems of material and energy shortages. And this is in part rooted in a different view of nature which stresses the delicate balance of ecological systems and possibly irreversible damage which may result from the interventions of high technology. They question whether the market is the best way to supply people with the things they want, and the importance of differentials as rewards for skill and achievement. They hold a completely different world-view, with different beliefs about the way society works, and about what should be the values and goals guiding policy and the criteria of choice. It is, in short, a counter-paradigm.

What is being argued then is that what differentiates environmentalists is a complex of beliefs about the nature of industrial society, about both the effectiveness and desir-ability of many of its core institutions and values. Their world-view differs markedly from the dominant view. It constitutes an alternative paradigm, with different beliefs about nature and man's relations with his environment, about how the economy can best be organized, about politics and about the nature of society (figure 8.1).

Middle-Class Radicalism

How then can we explain the existence of a group within industrial societies which rejects the dominant social paradigm? The most plausible explanation is to be found when we look at the occupations of environmentalists. What is particularly striking is the high proportion of environmentalists in our sample occupying roles in the non-productive service sector: doctors, social workers, teachers, and the creative arts (table 8.1). In short, it will be argued, environmentalists are drawn predominantly from a specific fraction of the middle class whose interests and values diverge markedly from other groups in industrial societies. Firstly, environmentalism is an expression of the interests of those whose class position in the non-productive sector locates them at the periphery of the institutions and processes of industrial capitalist societies. Hence, their concern to win greater participation and influence and thus to strengthen the political role of their members. It is a protest against alienation from the processes of decision making, and the depoliticization of issues through the usurpation of policy decisions by experts, operating within the dominant economic values. It is the political dimension of their role which goes far to account for their particular form of dissent. Their sense of being political outsiders is reflected especially in the attitudes of environmentalists towards working through the existing political parties. As many as 17 per cent rejected the left-right dimension in political beliefs, compared with 4.7 per cent of the industrial sample. And 64 per cent would

	Dominant Social Paradigm	Alternative Environmental Paradigm
CORE VALUES	Material (economic growth)	Non-material (self-actualization)
	Natural environment valued as resource	Natural environment intrinsically valued
	Domination over nature	Harmony with nature
ECONOMY	Market forces	Public interest
	Risk and reward	Safety
	Rewards for achievement	Incomes related to need
	Differentials	Egalitarian
	Individual self-help	Collective/social provision
POLITY	Authoritative structures (experts influential)	Participative structures (citizen/worker involvement)
	Hierarchical	Non-hierarchical
	Law and order	Liberation
SOCIETY	Centralized	Decentralized
	Large-scale	Small-scale
	Associational	Communal
	Ordered	Flexible
NATURE	Ample reserves	Earth's resources limited
	Nature hostile/neutral	Nature benign
	Environment controllable	Nature delicately balanced
KNOWLEDGE	Confidence in science and technology	Limits to science
	Rationality of means	Rationality of ends
	Separation of fact/value, thought/feeling	Integration of fact/value, thought/feeling

Figure 8.1 Competing social paradigms

support direct action to influence government decisions on environmental issues, compared with 60 per cent of the industrial sample who were opposed.

But this is only part of the answer. Their attack is not simply rooted in their subordinate position. It is also a challenge to the goals and values of the dominant class, and the structures and institutions through which these are realized. Environmentalists' rejection of beliefs in the efficacy of the market, risk-taking and rewards for achievement, and of the overriding goal of economic growth and of economic criteria is a challenge to the hegemonic ideology which legitimates the institutions and politics of industrial capitalism. Central to the operation of such societies is the role of the market. It is the relation between individuals and those subsystems of society which operate either within or largely outside the market which we will argue is the clue to

the clash of value systems and social paradigms.

If this explanation is correct, then we would expect support for the dominant social paradigm to be strongest in precisely those occupations which are the polar opposite of the environmentalists – among those who occupy dominant positions in the market sector. Support for the dominant social paradigm is markedly stronger amongst our industrial sample. It is here that we find overwhelming support for economic individualism; for differentials, rewards for achievement, for a society in which market forces and private interests predominate and for managerial authority.

What we are arguing then is that the clue to understanding the quite different values and beliefs of environmentalists and 'industrialists' is to be found in part in their relations to the core economic institutions of society. It is

Table 8.1   Occupations of environmentalists and public

	Environmentalists %	Public %
Commerce and industry		
— professional and supervisory	14.3	13.6
— clerical	5.6	12.2
Self-employed	9.6	4.8
Service, welfare, creative	38.4	12.2
Manual	5.4	28.2
Retired	9.1	7.8
Housewife	8.0	18.0
Unemployed	1.6	1.7
Student	8.0	1.4
	100.0	99.9
	(N = 427)	(N = 294)

class position and the interests and values which this generates to which we now turn.

The New Middle Class

Analyses of class in industrial societies, especially those in the Marxist tradition, have been overwhelmingly preoccupied with the way in which the capitalist relations of production generate antagonisms and conflicts of interest within societies in which the production of goods and services is the dominant activity. Such a model has faced considerable difficulty in relating a 'middle' class of managers, technicians, and service workers, to the two main antagonistic classes. What is notable is the almost complete omission of any extended discussion of the particular fraction of the middle class which has been identified in this analysis: those operating in those subsystems in industrial societies concerned with the pursuit of non-economic values, and functioning outside the market, and in this sense, non-capitalistic elements persisting within capitalist societies.

The central question raised by this analysis is the extent of any relative autonomy of such subsystems within the framework of the dominant institutions of industrial capitalism. The Marxist tradition sees the institutions of health and welfare as functionally necessary

for the reproduction of labour, thus serving the interests of a capitalist class. Now while this may possibly explain state support for 'non-productive' sectors, such an explanation does not offer a satisfactory account of either the interests or values of those who work in the personal service, intellectual, and artistic sectors. Our evidence demonstrates that many such hold values and beliefs which are sharply antagonistic to the dominant ideology.

The precise connection between occupation and values is problematic, though there are strong grounds for concluding that values are a major factor influencing occupational choice. What our evidence does is to draw attention to the relationship between opposition to the dominant ideology and occupational role. Non-productive sub-systems functioning outside the market, orientated to non-economic goals and values persist in all industrial societies. Those who work in them resist in varying degrees the intrusion of market values and processes (the commercialization of art, the vocationalizing of all education and learning). To the extent that schools, hospitals and welfare agencies operate outside the market-place, and those who work in them are dedicated to maximizing non-economic values, they constitute non-industrial enclaves within industrial societies and are the carriers of alternative non-economic values. And they may well provide a more congenial environment for those for whom the values and ideology of industrial capitalism do not win unqualified enthusiasm and unquestioning support. In short, those who reject the ideology and values of industrial capitalism are likely to choose careers outside the marketplace. Moreover, such occupations can offer a substantial degree of personal autonomy for those who have little taste for a subordinate role in the predominantly hierarchical structures of industrial society.

Discussion: Ideologies, Paradigms, and Political Legitimacy

It is not being suggested that the traditional antagonisms of capital and labour are no longer relevant. Conflicts of power and interest deriving from the ownership and control of production persist. But such conflicts tend to be focused primarily around economic values. What the new politics brings to the surface and feeds in to the political system are demands stemming from non-economic values. These have always constituted an element in left-wing politics, which has never lent support to unbridled economism, and whose dream of a new Jerusalem has gone beyond material goals, however important these have been for those suffering material deprivation and inequality. Any attempt to assimilate the ideology of this particular fraction of the middle class to that of either the bourgeosie or the proletariat flies in the face of the evidence. Nor can their values and beliefs be explained away as 'false consciousness', being firmly rooted in their structural position. But although the new politics cuts across the trade union economism which dominates Labour Party policies, the new dimension is much closer to the left than it is to the right with its strong commitment to the dominant social paradigm. The radicalism located in this particular fraction of the middle class is then much more than an emotional satisfaction derived from the expression of personal values in

action, as Parkin argued from his study of the C.N.D. movement, and has much more radical potential than most theorists have recognized. Although position on the political spectrum accounted for much of the variance in scores on post-materialism and economic individualism, environmentalists had significantly higher post-material scores and were more strongly anti-economic individualism than the general public with the same political affiliations.

[...]

Now it is not being suggested that environmentalists are about to man the barricades. Nevertheless, environmental issues have provided a focus for direct action – ranging from the disruption of inquiries on motorways, the massive protests against nuclear power sites in Germany and France, our own Windscale inquiry, to the violent opposition to the opening of Tokyo airport and even the strong reaction against the culling of grey seals. But more important, the dominant social paradigm provides not only a set of beliefs about how society works, and taken-for-granted assumptions about goals and criteria: it functions also as an ideology, legitimating and justifying the dominant political institutions and processes. And it is at the level of legitimacy that the environmentalist movement may provide its greatest challenge to the political system. Because of its taken-for-granted character, the dominant social paradigm can systematically repress the articulation of alternative viewpoints. Given support for economic values and growth, confidence in experts, and in the power of science and technology to come up with answers, then the conclusions of Mr. Justice Parker at Windscale can be seen to be not only reasonable but right. Given the acceptance of the dominant goals and values of society, problems are seen to be essentially questions of means, soluble by harnessing knowledge and expertise to the political process. Rationality is defined in narrowly technical or instrumental terms. What are properly political questions involving conflicts of values and interest are de-politicized and treated as technical questions. This, it is argued, is precisely what happened at Windscale. It is under such conditions that political institutions distort communications and there is no genuine dialogue. There is little doubt that alternative social paradigms generate major problems of communication and understanding. Hence the charges and counter-charges of unreason and irrationality between environmentalists and supporters of the status quo. From the environmentalist perspective, it is modern industrial societies dominated by the value of 'technology–organization–efficiency–growth–progress...' whose sanity is called into question: '... only such single-valued mindlessness would cut down the last redwoods, pollute the most beautiful beaches, invent machines to injure and destroy plant and human life. To have only one value, is, in human terms, to be mad. It is to be a machine'. And from the industrialists' perspective, environmentalist policies look silly, utopian, or plain mad.

Those who seek to promote alternative goals and values look with exasperation at the failure of the main parties to grasp the essential issues, and to formulate appropriate policies. The traditional left-right polarization is seen to be no longer relevant. The normal channels for feeding interests and demands into the system are clogged by incomprehension: the hegemony of the dominant taken-for-granted values and beliefs of liberal capitalism blocks off meaningful dialogue and communication. The charges and counter-charges of unreason are rooted in the failure to grasp that what is at stake is competing world-views and ideologies. The debate about environmental issues becomes a dialogue of the blind talking to the deaf. It is such experiences which, it can be argued, contribute to the decline in political legitimacy, a falling-off in support for traditional political parties and processes, and an increase in direct action.

This analysis suggests that many prescriptions for increasing the rationality of the environmentalist debate fail to penetrate to the heart of the problem. Its 'irrational' character is generally diagnosed as being due to a failure to settle crucial scientific and technical issues. Opposition to nuclear energy is seen to be irrational, because the scientific evidence demonstrates it to be safer than windmills. A more sophisticated version recognises that the evidence of those who have an interest in an issue may be partial or distorted. So, it is argued, the way to ensure a rational debate for the inquiry on fast-breeder reactors is to set up more broad-based machinery which would not be dependent on those institutionally committed to official options, but would be able to initiate, conduct or commission independent research. In short, the problem of achieving rationality is seen to be fundamentally one of getting the facts right, and of discovering the right technical and organizational solutions. Such an approach fails to recognise the problems of communication and understanding rooted in alternative paradigms. What is not appreciated is the existence of what may be described as an anthropological problem of competing cultures and meaning systems. If this is correct, then the 'new' politics will present a serious challenge to the parties of the left to come to grips with conflicts of values and beliefs which run deeper than simply a reordering of priorities. Such conflicts have always been evident in the left. But any decisive generational shift away from the overriding materialism and economism of industrial societies, reinforced by intransigent economic problems of 'stagflation' and material and energy shortages, could place new strains on any tenuous consensus.

Biography

A brief biography of Lois Gibbs, written by the editors of this volume, can be found on page 375.

9 "Christian Patriots"

James A. Aho

The subjects of this book know themselves as Christians and patriots. As Christians, the patriots assent to faith in Jesus Christ as savior (either through His example or His sacrifice), to the promise of salvation for all men (although there is debate among the patriots concerning what constitutes a human being capable of faith), and to the exclusive monopoly of Christianity over the means of eternal life.

The sample subjects consider their religion to be far more than an adjunct to life celebrated one hour weekly. On the contrary, they feel themselves duty bound to go into the world to reform it (and themselves) in a manner pleasing to the Lord. *The Politics of Righteousness* is my term. It encompasses both the reformist orientation of Christian patriotism and its abiding sense of guiltlessness and rightness in the Lord. It stands for all the tactics, from oral persuasion to outright violence, advocated and used by Christian patriots, in certain knowledge of their divine election, to establish God's rule on earth.

A Christian patriot minister, presently under police surveillance for alleged anti-Semitism, has described the politics of righteousness in these bitterly ironic words: "You too, can experience [the] honor... [of being] listed in a Jewish Hate Movement Report [as he did in 1987].... All you need to do is believe in and obey the Lord Jesus Christ,... desire and work for a Christian America as well as a Christian world,... acknowledge His Law as perfect... and expose the anti-Christ actions and hatred of modern-day Talmudic Jewry."

Christian patriots distinguish between Law and legality, Morality and legalese.

The former of these pairs is determined, respectively, by their readings of the so-called organic Constitution (the original Articles of Constitution plus the Bill of Rights) and selected edicts from the Pentateuch (the first five books of the Bible). They believe they have little, if any, *moral* obligation to obey legal statutes inconsistent with Law or Morality.

Naturally, as students of the Bible, Christian patriots are well aware of scriptural injunctions to submit themselves to public authority (cf. Romans 13:1–7; I Peter 2:13–16; and Titus 3:1). But they believe that with increasing frequency state regulations interfere with and even contradict biblical and constitutional law: Pastors are imprisoned for having Christian schools out of compliance with what they consider "satanic" curriculum guidelines. Pastors are fined for holding church services in areas not properly zoned for such activity. Store owners are forced to remove Christian banners from their flagpoles because they fail to meet sign ordinances. To negotiate these apparent contradictions, patriot casuists differentiate between secular *authority* and secular *power*. Truly authoritative enactments either derive directly from God (as read in the Bible) or are in accordance with His will discerned by the Founding Fathers. These enactments alone are binding upon the Christian citizen. Ordinances more or less than this may be enforced by state power, but they have no authority to command the voluntary compliance of the patriot. To quote the same patriot minister cited above:

You see county mounties with 357's on the hip and a badge on the chest, with back-ups on the way and the blessings of the county commissioners...but that doesn't in itself make them the higher... authority described in Romans 13. Just because someone sets themselves up in a position of power...be it OSHA [Occupational Safety and Health Administration] or a dog catcher – that doesn't make them the authorities of Romans 13.

There is a good bit of debate among patriots over which specific state regulations are authoritative and which merely tyrannical. To some, virtually the entire government, to which they afix the ominous title "ZOG" (Zionist Occupation Government), is biblically and constitutionally illegitimate, worthy only of armed resistance. To the less radical, the detested object may be a particular legal statute, a zoning law, a local tax, or the closing of a Forest Service trail to motorized travel. Some patriots conscientiously disobey the statute in question. Others fight it with legal means.

The politics of righteousness is pictured by Christian patriots as a battle against a satanic cabal that has insidiously infiltrated the dominant institutions of society, especially the mass media, public schools, established churches, and state agencies like the Internal Revenue Service. The goal of this cabal is to subvert God's will (i.e., Law and Morality, as understood above) by promoting, among other things, equal rights for "unqualified" ethnic and racial minorities, non-Christian religions such as "secular humanism," and moral perversion – pornography, homosexuality, abortion, crime, and usury. God tolerates "neither fornicators, nor idolaters, nor adulterers, nor effeminates, nor homosexuals, nor thieves, nor the covetous, nor drunkards, nor revilers, nor swindlers" (I Corinthians 6:9–11). Neither should the Christian patriot who does His will.

The *end* of Christian patriotism is the preservation of "Christian values" and "Americanism," as the patriots understand them. In this sense it may be taken as, and indeed sometimes calls itself, "conservative." However, it is even more typical for the

people studied here to disassociate themselves from conservatism, which they equate with institutionalized uncharitableness, a bluff and swagger do-nothing foreign policy, and appeasement of the liberal status quo. Furthermore, and more to the point, the patriots in the sample are not averse to advocating the use of revolutionary *means* to achieve their ends. For this reason, I systematically avoid the use of "conservative" in this volume. Instead, when I wish to avoid repetitious overuse of "Christian patriotism," where appropriate I substitute for it the words "far right," "right-wing extremism," or "rightist." These substitutes are not meant to imply anything more than the word they replace.

"Leftist" and "rightist" are terms used in political oratory to pre-judge and attack one's opponents. It should be clear that this is not my intention. Furthermore, a few patriots will object to being classified in these pages as rightists. Some sample subjects place themselves in the very center of the political spectrum, the titles of their groups – e.g., "Golden Mean Society" – reflecting this image of themselves. John Birchers, for example, consider themselves the only authentic centrists in America. They place Posse Comitatus to their right and call it a form of "right-wing anarchy." Nazism (national socialism), meanwhile, they group with liberalism and Communism as promoting "left-wing totalitarianism."

Similar confusion has long surrounded the proper classification of anti-elitist Populist Party adherents, members of Liberty Lobby, and the so-called crypto-fascists such as Huey Long and Father Coughlin. Furthermore, not every member of the groups I deal with here assents to Christian patriotism as depicted above. Nationwide, there is a smattering of Jewish Birchers; in some eastern states national socialists worship pagan Nordic gods; and some American Nazi and Klan splinter groups can boast of Jewish members. It is even alleged that ADL operatives once posed as neo-Nazis in a television documentary entitled "Armies of the Right." Indeed, I know of an Idaho Klan group that inadvertently designated a black railroad laborer as its Grand Titan. (He simply sent in the required application form on a lark – absent his racial identity – and found himself so honored.) But in the greater Idaho region these exceptions prove the rule: There is virtual unanimity of religious confession and racial type among Gem State radical patriots.

To summarize, then, as used in this book "Christian patriot" refers to a person who:

- Assents to faith in Jesus Christ as savior, either through His example or through His sacrifice.
- Believes that the promise of salvation has been given to all "human beings."
- Believes that only through Jesus Christ can one be saved.
- Feels duty-bound to reform the world after God's will, as discerned in the Bible and as manifested in the organic Constitution.
- Has a moral obligation to submit to secular authority that rules according to God's will, as understood above.
- Believes a secret satanic conspiracy has infiltrated America's major institutions to subvert God's will.
- Believes that the actions and policies of these subverted institutions must be battled by means of a politics of righteousness.

[...]

While sociological theory seems to account for why some people are likely to join the patriot cause, intellectually it is not completely satisfying. It is a bit like trying to explain widespread earthquake damage by pointing to negligent building codes. The account may be true enough, but the question still remains: Why the massive terrestrial movement in the first place? The two-step theory of mobilization tells us why, once they are aroused, some people are inclined to express their grievances in the politics of righteousness. The choice of expressive strategy is largely a product of the opportunity structure within which (largely by chance) they happen to find themselves. But the primary question is still unanswered: What is it that arouses a population in the first place? What is the historical context that has produced and nourished radical patriot groups in Idaho in the late 1970s and 1980s? This is the "big picture" of Idaho Christian patriotism.

In the following pages I will not be concerned with the factors inducing individuals to join patriot groups as such. Instead I will inquire into the social conditions behind the emergence of the groups themselves. These are the political and economic circumstances independent of, prior to, and historically associated with, periods of right-wing resurgence in America.

We begin by placing before us the award-winning account of American political extremism by sociologist Seymour Martin Lipset and his collaborator Earl Raab, *The Politics of Unreason* (1973). [...]

It will be impossible to do little more than briefly brush in broad strokes the basic tenets of Lipset and Raab's theory. In so doing, the actual complexity and sophistication of their views must of necessity be ignored. However, I am confident that the general tone of their views can be faithfully rendered in few words.

To Lipset and Raab the distinguishing mark of right-wing movements is their preservative, backlash character. Right-wingers look nostalgically on the (sometimes imaginary) past, whereas left-wing groups look hopefully to an often equally fanciful future. This is because while left-wing movements are engineered by people experiencing upward mobility, the right wing attracts those whose status in the world is threatened with displacement.

Lipset and Raab go on to say that the displacement of some groups by others has been an enduring fact of American history. Hence, this country has been more prone to extremisms of preservatism than to their opposite. This also explains why extremism in America typically takes symbolic or expressive forms, emphasizing sexual mores, dress standards, religious preferences, and race. Those whose class position and power in society are threatened have little else with which to dramatize their superiority but their lifestyle. Right-wingers shore up their sagging esteem by inflicting their morality on others.

The ranks of extremist movements are not filled with basically evil types, Lipset and Raab remind the reader, but with ordinary people caught in certain kinds of stress: the terrifying specter of losing their position in the world. The disconcerting elements of right-wing ideology—Manichaeistic dualism, conspiratorialism, historical simplism, moralistic advocacy of violence, and bigotry – are less neurotic symptoms than the "cultural baggage," as Lipset calls it, that *any* American political group must adopt if its commodity is to be marketed successfully. The broader culture from which this baggage is drawn is an uneasy combination of classical liberalism (antielitism, egalitarianism, and *laissez-faire* economics) with Arminian Christianity (self-improvement, social reform, moralism, hard work, and hygiene).

Lipset and Raab appreciate that this "baggage" can have a dynamic of its own, but as the word implies, it is to them clearly subsidiary material taken along by people already politically disembarked for altogether different reasons. The following quotations give the flavor of the book's emphasis:

In speaking of American Protection Association activism in the 1890s, the authors say "Protestantism, fundamentalism, manners, and morals are often less the motivation [i.e., the cause] than the excuse for nativist bigotry – its 'cultural baggage' rather than its engine."

When addressing Klan insurgency in the 1920s, the authors recognize that two-thirds of the national Klan leaders were fundamentalist preachers, but then they insist that "the congruence of Protestant fundamentalism and moralism is largely an historical accident....Moralism does not create right-wing extremism. Desperately preservative movements require a moralistic stance, and will find it somewhere." During the 1920s

religious energies were "invoked" after the fact to serve the goal of preserving the faltering status of America's southern, white, rural, Protestant citizenry.

Similar reasoning is used to account for the over-representation of fundamentalists among George Wallace's supporters in his campaign for President in 1968. In short: "[R]eligious fundamentalism and fanaticism is seen [by the authors] primarily as the specific symbolic content of lost-group status...rather than as a kind of intellectual mind-set which is the direct source of right-wing extremism."

One weakness of the Lipset-Raab theory is that "status displacement" is never explicitly defined. Indeed the authors admit as much, claiming that the comprehensiveness of their model "defies...any particularistic definition." In the final chapters of the book they substitute for it the all-embracing subjective concept "Quondam Complex," a psychological attachment to and stake in the past. The reader can sympathize with the authors; historical reality rarely fits into narrow sociological categories. Nevertheless, this maneuver opens Lipset and Raab to the criticism of circular reasoning, for without an explicit definition to the contrary, virtually anything can be taken as an indicator of the Quondam mind-set.

Some of these indicators do seem to have face validity. For example, in explaining the rise of anti-Illuminati hysteria around 1800 among New England mercantilists, the authors point to the emerging political threat to the Federalist Party posed by populist farmers on the Northeast frontier. To explain the popularity of the American Protection Association in the 1890s among skilled Protestant laborers, the authors cite the influx of Catholic immigrants into American cities, the subsequent industrialization of work, and corrupt machine politics. (The statistics used by the authors do not support their own contentions, however. American Protection Association membership was in fact not highest in the native urban middle class, but in the Rocky Mountain and western states, where skilled workers were still in great demand at the turn of the century and machine politics was minimal.)

But many more of the authors' attempts to fit extremists into the Quondam Complex seem overly clever. For example, Lipset and Raab admit that in the 1930s, Father Coughlin's National Union for Social Justice appealed mostly to lower-class, urban Catholics, a stratum which can only with difficulty be said to have lost its already rock-bottom status during the Great Depression. The authors are therefore forced to introduce a new concept, "anomic status preservatism." Unemployed Catholics were not actually threatened with the loss of social position, say Lipset and Raab, but with the loss of their attachments to the larger community. At this point they invoke William Kornhauser and his mass theory of political extremism, taking it (incorrectly) as a specific case of their overall position.

Again, the early 1950s was a time of "unprecedented" and widespread prosperity in America, when one might expect status threats to be relatively muted and therefore right-wing extremism to have little public sympathy. But, in fact, this was the high-point of postwar anti-Communist hysteria. Lipset and Raab handle this evident incongruity by arguing that the new wealth of the postwar period produced new status anxieties: "With the possession of status comes the fear of dispossession." To this they add status anxiety over America's postwar foreign policy reversals. My point is not that what the authors say is necessarily untrue, although they never do provide concrete evidence of status insecurity for any of the movements they study. It is rather that the concept is so vaguely posed that virtually nothing is excluded.

Does the theory of status politics account for the Christian patriot movement of the 1980s? In a 1981 *Commentary* article, Lipset and Raab reply in the affirmative. The social status of the evangelicals, they say, was increasingly threatened by "aspects of modernity" appearing in the turbulent 1960s and 1970s: gay rights, women's rights, porn-

ography, and sexual promiscuity. This is to say nothing of sky-rocketing inflation and the oil crisis. (Again, observe the inherently malleable nature of the concept of status displacement.) This anxiety finally culminated in election booth support for the Reagan Revolution.

In a piece composed that same year, sociologist John H. Simpson blasted the Lipset-Raab account as a misreading of recent American religious history. Members of evangelical and fundamentalist churches had occupied the most marginal positions in America's status hierarchy for more than fifty years. The sexual experimentation and drug use of the 1960s did nothing to change this. To suggest anything else is to ignore the devastating symbolic impact to fundamentalists of the repeal of the Prohibition Amendment in 1933, the public ridicule of fundamentalist champion William Jennings Bryan in the infamous "Monkey" trial of 1925, and the longstanding cultural relegation of fundamentalism to a sideshow menagerie of teetotaling loudmouths by urban sophisticates like H. L. Mencken. If the Lipset-Raab theory is valid, then the evangelical political response should have come fifty years earlier than it did.

Simpson fails to articulate fully an alternative explanation for the rise of the new Christian right, but he suggests that far from declining in status, evangelical/fundamentalist Protestants have, since 1975, been quickly advancing themselves. It is the forces and proponents of modernism who are beating a hasty retreat. In the intellectual and moral disarray of liberal modernism, evangelicals have sensed an opportunity to enhance their own political and social status. What I have called the politics of righteousness is not, at least according to Simpson, the fearful reaction of losers but the expression of growing confidence by a rising stratum. If anything, the new Christian right confirms the theory of rising expectations.

Figure 9.1 illustrates the relationship between economic cycles and periods of right-wing resurgence in America from 1795 to 1985. It may be taken as a very limited test

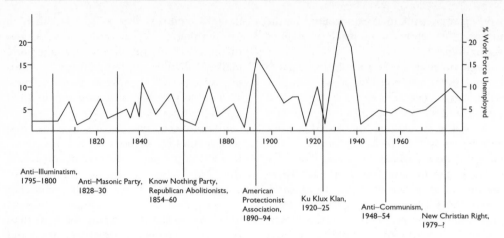

Figure 9.1   Unemployment and right-wing extremism, America 1795–1985
Source: Unemployment cycles estimated from data in Walter B. Smith and Arthur Cole, *Fluctuations in American Business: 1792–1860* (Cambridge, Mass.: Harvard University Press, 1935), pp. 12–21, 59–69, 93–101; Paul Ringenbach, *Tramps and Reformers: 1873–1916* (Westport, Conn.: Greenwood Press Inc., 1973), p. 24; Charles Hoffman, *The Depression of the Nineties* (Westport, Conn.: (Greenwood Press, 1970), pp. 106, 107, 109–10, and from *Long-Term Economic Growth: 1860–1965* (Washington D.C.: U.S. Dept. of Commerce, 1966), p. 40.

of the theory that status displacement is historically associated with right-wing extremism. I say "very limited" because this interpretation is subject to the proviso that economic booms are times of enhanced opportunity for most people, while busts magnify threats to established status. If this assumption is true, then economic recessions should be temporally associated with increases in right-wing activism.

Because nationwide employment and business statistics were not kept until around 1900, the comparative heights of the unemployment cycles on the graph must be read as little more than pedagogical suggestions. Furthermore, the table is not intended to give the impression that there has ever been a time in American history without right-wing activity. There have, however, been what appear to be seven distinct apogees of right-wing rabidity in this country since its founding. Only one of these seems to have taken place during a bonafide depression: the American Protection Association which, according to its own record-keepers, grew to 2.5 million members by 1893–94. The recession of 1982–83, following the implementation of Reagan adminis-

tration monetary policy, may be considered more a consequence than a cause of the fanaticism of this period.

Mine is not a novel observation. Even Lipset and Raab agree that "most of the previous right-wing extremist movements in America had their genesis and often their greatest strength during times of economic growth and prosperity." To their minds this does not confute the theory of status displacement, but proves that during economic booms, rising social groups threaten relatively privileged segments of the population. An equally plausible hypothesis, however, is that people can afford moralistic politics when they prosper economically. Without working definitions of either status insecurity or prosperity, both of which are subjective experiences, there is no way of ascertaining the truth of these conjectures.

I have an alternative theoretical interpretation of the periodicity of right-wing resurgences in America. This interpretation is consistent both with the information gathered in the previous chapters and also with the bewildering variety of alleged status threats cited by Lipset and Raab. It is presented here not as a fully documented proposition but as a hypothesis for further research. Furthermore, it should be emphasized that, as a sociological rather than a psychological theory, it makes no claim to explain individual cases of extremism. Like the theory of status politics itself, it is intended only to account for general political trends in American history.

I begin with a confession by Richard Hofstadter, who in 1955 invented the theory of status politics in an attempt to explain the outrages of the Ku Klux Klan and the anti-Communist hysteria of his own time. If the article were rewritten in light of what he knew just seven years later, Hofstadter says, a factor he originally overlooked would "now loom large indeed." The factor is Christian fundamentalism. "To understand the Manichaean style of thought, the apocalyptic tendencies, the love of mystification, the intolerance of compromise that are observable in the right-wing mind, we need to understand the history of fundamentalism." In place of the concept of status politics, which he now sees as "inadequate," Hofstadter proposes a theory of "projective politics." Right-wing extremism, he says, "involves the projection of interests and concerns, not only private but essentially pathological, into the public scene."

Without an *a priori* devaluation of the projections as sick or pathological, the hypothesis presented here is the theory of projective politics that Hofstadter calls for. It takes religion (as mediated by one's intermediate social networks) as an independent correlate of right-wing extremism. Theology, in this view, is not mere "baggage" acquired after the fact to justify aggression toward groups that threaten people's worlds. On the contrary, right-wing radicals sense certain events as threats to their worlds because these events are filtered through religiously tinted lenses. This assumption rests on a fundamental axiom in sociology: Things defined as real become real in their consequences. The people, events, and objects enumerated below are experienced as dangerous because they are *defined* as wicked and harmful, not because they are objective threats. To deter-

mine why Jews, liberals, public school teachers, Dungeons and Dragons, Oriental mysticism, and illicit drugs, "pornography," and sex are so judged we must inquire less into the things themselves than into the frames of reference of the definers.

It is not without irony that Lipset and Raab are forced to concede the validity of the theory of projective politics in their account of the abolitionist movement during the 1850s. At first they attribute abolitionist sentiment to "New England leadership which had become increasingly frustrated over [its] ... lost ... influence on the country." New England WASPs had become a "downgraded" elite, "an elite without function, a displaced class in American society." But within a page the authors are admitting that "the extreme moral fervor poured into the abolitionist movement cannot be attributed solely or even primarily, to the ... reaction of displaced groups. The moralistic concerns were stimulated by the direct line to evangelical Protestantism and its commitment to oppose sinful behavior." Once men and women are led to "define" (the word is theirs) certain things as evil, they work actively to eliminate them.

What, then, are the projective lenses through which right-wing activists view reality and pronounce judgments on it? To summarize the discussion:

First and preeminently, dualism. Relative to the doctrine of divine transcendence, of a perfected, spiritualized (male) Creator residing in distant heavens, the material (that is, feminine) world is profanity, unconsciousness, and death. Among the images of this fallen world are the "curse" of matriarchy, "bull-dyke" women and ladylike men; actions alleged to be associated with them – sex education, birth control, sloth, drunkenness, pornography, drug addiction, raucous music, gluttony, revelry, dance, and provocative dress; policies that presumably promote these – passivity, pacifism, communalism, and moral "dissolution" as expressed in the practices of profit without productivity, pay without work, crime without punishment, seizure without compensation, purchase without cash, and its inexorable accessory, usury; knee-jerk tolerance; the promiscuous mixing of "distinct" things – creeds, nations, species, races, classes, and roles; philosophies of hazed vision, blurred edges, and relativity; games of chance, ouija boards, the I Ching, astrology, and other New Age "satanic" technologies; and promoters of these policies – secular humanist educators, the liberal media, "politicians" (by which is meant those who aggrandize themselves by compromising with all of the above), the "Soviet-controlled" National Council of Churches, "socialist" bureaucrats, and the chief conspirator himself, the archetypal "Jew."

Once again, these things are not evil in themselves, nor are they judged evil because they constitute status threats in the narrow way depicted by Lipset and Raab. Even less are they annexed after the fact to more fundamental occasions of status insecurity. Rather, ignoring their modern variants, they are the traditional vices in orthodox Christianity. For they represent, among other things, the assertion of the feminine principle and the loss of masculine control, sensibility, creativity, consciousness, aggressiveness, and rationality.

A second element in the projections of those called to Christian patriotism is conspiratorialism – the psychologizing of history and the reduction of historical events to the conscious intentions of omniscient and all-powerful Benefactors and Malefactors. The search for the ultimate causes of social decline invariably ends in the quest for whom to blame and whom to eliminate.

Third and finally, there is a pervading conviction of cosmic exigency, that the world and thus life itself is in dire emergency, and that the Second Coming is imminent. This is the *criterion definiendum* of fundamentalism, dispensationalism and its never-ending search for signs of the Apocalypse and the Last Dispensation.

Part IV

Who Remains In Movements, and Who Drops Out?

Introduction

Recruiting activists and supporters is one obvious challenge that movements confront. Keeping these recruits active within the movement is quite another. Meeting this challenge is important because movements typically need to work for many years or even decades to bring about desired changes. A movement that constantly needs to replace recruits who have dropped out is not likely to be very effective. And, of course, if too many people drop out and cannot be replaced, then the movement will decline or disappear altogether, an issue we take up more directly in Part IX.

The reasons that people remain active in movements may be very different from the reasons they became involved in the first place. Recruits may greatly enjoy (or come to dislike!) their lives with other activists or movement supporters. The movement or movement organization may head in a direction that supporters either applaud or reject. Why people remain committed to a movement for some significant period of time, then, is a different question than asking why they joined in the first place; likewise, why some people drop out of movements is a different question than asking why some never joined in the first place.

> **Free-Rider Problem** People who would benefit from a social movement may not in fact protest but rather "free ride" on the efforts of others. Such people calculate that their own contribution to the movement (assuming that its constituency is large) is likely to be minimal and that they will enjoy the achievements of the movement anyway. So why should they bother to protest? Of course, this problem assumes that (and only arises when) people are rather narrowly self-interested. But many people protest because they feel morally obligated to do so, or because they derive pleasures or benefits from protesting (e.g., new friends) whether or not they think it will succeed. See Olson (1965).

Despite their importance, these questions have received much less attention from scholars than the recruitment issue, but they have not been neglected altogether. The issue of commitment to a cause was taken up many years ago by Rosabeth Moss Kanter (1972) in her study of nineteenth-century communes like Brook Farm and Oneida – communities that share a number of characteristics with social movements, including voluntary membership, idealism, and a rejection of certain aspects of the larger society (see also Hall, 1988). Kanter emphasizes that commitment to a cause or group is simultaneously cognitive, affective, and moral – it involves people's beliefs, feelings, and moral judgments. Kanter catalogues a variety of "commitment mechanisms" that helped to keep people in the communes she studied, some of which lasted for many decades. Communes were more successful, for example, when they did not have to compete for their members' loyalties. The opportunities and temptations of the "outside world" would often pull people out of communes (just as they pull people out of movements), so they tried to insulate themselves in various ways, sometimes geographically. Radical movement groups, which generally demand a lot from their members, also typically try to limit members' relationships with outsiders. Of course, the heavy time commitment that some such groups require of their members has the same practical effect, although activists notoriously "burn out" if too much is demanded of them for too long.

Another threat to commitment which Kanter found came from within the communes themselves, namely, the possibility that members would spend too much time with family, friends, or people to whom they were romantically or sexually attracted, neglecting their obligations to the larger group. To prevent this, communes often separated family members, raised children communally, and prohibited monogamous marriages. Movements also face the potential threat of "dyadic withdrawal," as when movement activists meet, fall in love, and gradually withdraw from public activities for the pleasures of a more private life (see Goodwin, 1997).

Kanter also found that communes lasted longer the more they engaged in collective activities that forged a strong group identity and *esprit de corps*. Working, eating, singing, playing, praying, and making decisions together – all of these activities, which movements have also practiced, helped to develop strong affective bonds among commune members as well as a strong moral commitment to their common enterprise. The excerpt included in this volume by Eric L. Hirsch similarly emphasizes how collective "consciousness-raising" discussions and collective decision making helped to build solidarity among members of a student movement opposed to university investments in South Africa.

> **Mass Society**   Before the 1960s, most scholars took a dim view of protest. They preferred politics within normal institutional channels. They usually argued that people protested because they were swept up in irrational crowds, or because they had personality flaws for which they were trying to compensate. One popular theory claimed that people joined social movements when they had lost other organized contacts with the main institutions of their society, like clubs or churches. In "mass society" people watch television as individuals, the argument goes, rather than going out and joining bowling leagues and volunteer groups. This makes them susceptible to demagogues like Lenin or Hitler. (The theory was heavily influenced by fears of communism and fascism.) Today, few scholars accept this argument, having shown that protestors are usually well integrated into their communities and social networks. See Kornhauser (1959).

(Consciousness-raising groups were first popularized by the women's movement, especially its more radical wing, during the late 1960s and early 1970s.) Hirsch also argues that polarization and the escalation of conflict may build group solidarity as outside threats induce members to turn inward for mutual support and protection (intellectual, moral, and sometimes physical). The resulting "ideological purity" binds activists together, although it may also prevent them from understanding potential allies or making compromises (see the excerpt by Jane Mansbridge in Part V).

The reading by Nancy Whittier explores how some women in Columbus, Ohio, continue to identify themselves as radical feminists, and remain committed to radical feminist principles, despite the fact that the women's movement as a whole has been in decline. Their radical feminist identity is sustained by a number of factors that overlap with those stressed by Hirsch: collective activities, including consciousness-raising groups and protest itself; interactions among a dense network of like-minded friends and acquaintances; the use of feminist language; and, interestingly, the ritual telling of "cautionary tales" about women who have "sold out" their feminist principles. These and other factors establish group boundaries between radical feminists and others. Whittier suggests, however, that while group boundaries often become rigidified and exclusive when movements are in decline, the boundaries drawn by the radical feminists whom she studied have generally become more permeable. Radical feminists are more accepting of and emotionally open to non-feminists and men, especially gay men.

Finally, the excerpt by Bert Klandermans explores why people disengage from movements, whether passively and unobtrusively or actively and loudly. Again, a variety of factors may push people to disengage, depending upon the movement they are in and their level of commitment to it. Unlike Hirsch, Klandermans suggests that polarization can lead people to pull out of a movement, rather than deepening their commitment to it. Sometimes people receive negative reactions from their "significant others" about their political commitments. (This is why communes and some movements try to limit contact with such people.) Disengagement often results from bad relationships – or few contacts at all – with fellow members. Activists often "burn out" from time-consuming and stressful work. People may withdraw from a movement organization when its strategy and tactics seem ill advised, although some then may jump to another group with a different strategy or tactics. Changes in the political environment may convince people that their enthusiasm for certain causes was misplaced or unrealistic.

Social scientists still have a lot to learn about why people stay in or pull out of movements, but the readings in this section make a good start.

Discussion Questions

1   What type of collective activities might help to sustain commitment to a particular movement? Might some such activities seem too demanding?
2   How might the escalation of a conflict between a movement and its opponents reinforce the solidarity of that movement? When might an escalating conflict lead people to disengage from a movement?
3   How do people sustain their commitment to a cause that has fallen upon hard times?
4   Why do activists "burn out"? What might movements do to prevent this?

10 Generating Commitment Among Students

Eric L. Hirsch

[...] This article develops an alternative perspective on recruitment and commitment to protest movements; it emphasizes the importance of the development of *political solidarity*, that is, support for a group cause and its tactics. Mobilization can then be explained by analyzing how group-based political processes, such as *consciousness-raising*, *collective empowerment*, *polarization*, and *group decision-making*, induce movement participants to sacrifice their personal welfare for the group cause. Empirical support for this perspective comes from a detailed analysis of a Columbia University student movement that demanded that the university divest itself of stock in companies doing business in South Africa.
[...]

Impact of Group Processes

[...]

> **Affective Ties**   Social relationships based on friendship or sexual attraction are often important in recruiting people to protest events and social movements, and these relationships also help to keep people in a group or movement once they have joined. (It is alleged, for example, that many young men became involved in the Reverend Jim Lawson's civil disobedience workshops in Nashville in order to be close to Diane Nash.) Such affective ties are thus an important component of "indigenous organization." These ties, however, may also hurt movements. Strong affective ties to people outside a movement may prevent one from joining that movement or developing a strong commitment to it; such ties, in other words, may make one biographically *unavailable* for protest. And people may meet in a movement, fall in love, and drop out, a phenomenon known as "dyadic withdrawal." See Goodwin (1997).

Consciousness-Raising

Potential recruits are not likely to join a protest movement unless they develop an ideological commitment to the group cause and believe that only non-institutional means can further that cause. Consciousness-raising involves a group discussion where such beliefs are created or reinforced. It may occur among members of an emerging movement who realize they face a problem of common concern that cannot be solved through routine political processes. Or it may happen in an ongoing movement, when movement activists try to convince potential recruits that their cause is just, that institutional means of influence have been unsuccessful, and that morally committed individuals must fight for the cause. Effective consciousness-raising is a difficult task because protest tactics usually challenge acknowledged authority relationships. Predisposing factors, such as prior political socialization, may make certain individuals susceptible to some appeals and unsympathetic to others.

Consciousness-raising is not likely to take place among socially marginal individuals because such isolation implies difficulty in communicating ideas to others. And it is not likely to happen among a group of rational calculators because the evaluation of society and of the chances for change is often influenced more by commitment to political or moral values than by self-interest calculations (Fireman and Gamson 1979; Ferree and Miller 1985). Consciousness-raising is facilitated in non-hierarchical, loosely structured, face-to-face settings that are isolated from persons in power; in such *havens*

(Hirsch 1989), people can easily express concerns, become aware of common problems, and begin to question the legitimacy of institutions that deny them the means for resolving those problems.

Collective Empowerment

The recruitment and commitment of participants in a protest movement may also be affected by a group process called collective empowerment. While recruits may gain a sense of the potential power of a movement in consciousness-raising sessions, the real test for the movement comes at the actual protest site where all involved see how many are willing to take the risks associated with challenging authority. If large numbers are willing to sacrifice themselves for the movement, the chances for success seem greater; a "bandwagon effect" (Hirsch 1986) convinces people to participate in this particular protest because of its presumed ability to accomplish the movement goal. Tactics are more easily viewed as powerful if they are highly visible, dramatic, and disrupt normal institutional routines.

Polarization

A third important group process is polarization. Protest challenges authority in a way that institutional tactics do not because it automatically questions the rules of the decision-making game. The use of non-routine methods of influence also means that there is always uncertainty about the target's response. For these reasons, one common result of a protest is unpredictable escalating conflict. Each side sees the battle in black and white terms, uses increasingly coercive tactics, and develops high levels of distrust and anger toward the opponent.

Polarization is often seen as a problem since it convinces each side that their position is right and the opponent's is wrong; this makes compromise and negotiation less likely. Since it leads each side to develop the

independent goal of harming the opponent, movement participants may lose sight of their original goal. Finally, escalation of coercive tactics by those in power can result in demobilization of the movement as individual participants assess the potential negative consequences of continued participation.

But if other group processes, such as consciousness-raising and collective empowerment, have created sufficient group identification, the protesters will respond to threats as a powerful, angry group rather than as isolated, frightened individuals. Under these circumstances, polarization can have a strong positive impact on participation (Coser 1956, 1967; Edelman 1971). The sense of crisis that develops in such conflicts strengthens participants' belief that their fate is tied to that of the group. They develop a willingness to continue to participate despite the personal risks because they believe the costs of protest should be collectively shared. Greater consensus on group goals develops because the importance of social factors in perception increases in an ambiguous conflict; protesters become more likely to accept the arguments of their loved fellow activists and less likely to accept those of their hated enemy. Because of the need to act quickly in a crisis, participants also become willing to submerge their differences with respect to the group's tactical choices.

Collective Decision-Making

Finally, collective decision-making often plays an important role in motivating the continuing commitment of movement participants. Movements often have group discussions about whether to initiate, continue, or end a given protest. Committed protesters may feel bound by group decisions made during such discussions, even when those decisions are contrary to their personal preferences. Participation in a protest movement is often the result of a complex group decision-making process, and not the consequence of many isolated, rational individual decisions.

The Columbia Divestment Campaign: A Case Study

The importance of these four group processes – consciousness-raising, collective empowerment, polarization, and group decision-making – in recruitment and commitment in a protest movement is illustrated by the Columbia University divestment protest. In April of 1985, several hundred Columbia University and Barnard College students sat down in front of the chained doors of the main Columbia College classroom and administrative building, Hamilton Hall, and stated that they would not leave until the university divested itself of stock in companies doing business in South Africa. Many students remained on this "blockade" for three weeks. This was a particularly good case for the analysis of movement recruitment and commitment because the majority of the participants in the protest had not been active previously in the divestment or other campus protest movements.

Protest actions of this kind can create problems for researchers because the organizers' need for secrecy often prevents the researcher from knowing of the event in advance. The best solution is to use as many diverse research methods as possible to study the movement after it has begun. I spent many hours at the protest site each day observing the activities of the protesters and their opponent, the Columbia administration. I also discussed the demonstration with participants and non-participants at the protest site, in classrooms, and other campus settings; and examined the many leaflets, position papers, and press reports on the demonstration.

During the summer of 1985, I completed 19 extended interviews, averaging one and one-half hours each, with blockaders and members of the steering committee of the Coalition for a Free South Africa (CFSA), the group that organized and led the protest. The interviews covered the protester's political background, previous experience in politics and protest movements, her/his

experiences during the three weeks of the protest, and feelings about the personal consequences of participation. All quotes are taken from transcripts of these interviews.

[...]

Consciousness-Raising

The Coalition for a Free South Africa (CFSA) was founded in 1981 to promote Columbia University's divestment of stock in companies doing business in South Africa. It was a loosely structured group with a predominantly black steering committee of about a dozen individuals who made decisions by consensus, and a less active circle of about fifty students who attended meetings and the group's protests and educational events. The group was non-hierarchical, non-bureaucratic, and had few resources other than its members' labor. The CFSA tried to convince Columbia and Barnard students that blacks faced injustice under apartheid, that U.S. corporations with investments in South Africa profited from the low wages paid to blacks, that Columbia was an accomplice in apartheid because it invested in the stock of these companies, and that divestment would advance the anti-apartheid movement by putting economic and political pressure on the white regime of South Africa.

This consciousness-raising was done in a variety of small group settings, including dormitory rap sessions, forums, and teach-ins. Coverage of the CFSA's activities in the Columbia student newspaper and television reports on the violent repression of the anti-apartheid movement in South Africa increased student consciousness of apartheid and encouraged many students to support divestment.

Even in this early period, conflict between the CFSA and the Columbia administration affected the views of potential movement recruits. At first, the CFSA tried to achieve divestment by using traditional avenues of influence. In 1983, the organization was able to gain a unanimous vote for divestment by administration, faculty, and student representatives in the University Senate, but Columbia's Board of Trustees rejected the resolution. As one protester pointed out, that action was interpreted by many students as an indication that traditional means of influence could not achieve divestment:

> I remember in '83 when the Senate voted to divest. I was convinced that students had voiced their opinion and had been able to convince the minority of administrators that what they wanted was a moral thing. It hadn't been a bunch of radical youths taking buildings and burning things down, to destroy. But rather, going through the system, and it seemed to me that for the first time in a really long time the system was going to work. And then I found out that it hadn't worked, and that just reaffirmed my feelings about how the system at Columbia really did work.

The result of CFSA's extensive organizing work was that many students were aware of the oppressed state of blacks in South Africa, the call for divestment by anti-apartheid activists, and the intransigence of the university President and Trustees in the face of a unanimous vote for divestment by the representative democratic body at the university.

Collective Empowerment: The Initiation of the Blockade

In the next phase of the movement, the CFSA sponsored rallies and vigils to call attention to the intransigence of the Trustees. Few students attended these demonstrations, probably because few supporters believed they would result in divestment. Deciding that more militant tactics were necessary, the CFSA steering committee began to plan a fast by steering committee members and a takeover of a campus building. The plan called for chaining shut the doors of the building and blocking the entrance with protesters; this, it was assumed, would lead to a symbolic arrest of a few dozen steering committee members and other hard-core supporters of divestment. The intent was to draw media coverage to dramatize the continuing fight for divestment.

Because they had worked hard on publicity, the steering committee of CFSA expected a large turnout for their initial rally, but fewer than 200 students gathered at the Sundial in the center of campus on the morning of April 4. Speeches were made by a local political official, a representative of the African National Congress, several black South African students, and members of the CFSA steering committee. Many of those interviewed had been at the rally, but none felt that the speeches were any more or less inspiring than speeches they had heard at previous CFSA events.

At the conclusion of the speeches, nearly all of those present agreed to follow one of the CFSA steering committee members on a march around campus. Most expected to chant a few anti-apartheid and pro-divestment slogans and return to the Sundial for a short wrap-up speech. Instead, they were led to the steps in front of the already-chained doors at Hamilton Hall. The protesters did not understand at first why they had been led to this spot, and few noticed the chained doors.

The steering committee member then revealed the day's plan, stating that this group of protesters would not leave the steps until the university divested itself of stock in companies doing business in South Africa. At least 150 students remained where they were; no one recalls a significant number of defections. Within two hours, the group on the steps grew to over 250.

Why did so many students agree to participate in this militant protest? The CFSA steering committee did not have an answer. Student participation in their relatively safe rallies and vigils had been minimal, so they certainly did not expect hundreds to join a much riskier act of civil disobedience. According to one steering committee member:

> Needless to say, I was quite startled by the events of April 4. By noon, there must have

been hundreds more people than I expected there would be. I was hoping for 50 people, including the hard core. We would all get carted off, and whatever obstacles were blockading the door would be cut, removed, or thrown up. That's what everyone was expecting. We would have a story written and the press would report that we had done this. Jesus Christ, what happened that day was absolutely mind boggling! I still haven't gotten over it.

It was hard for anyone to predict the high level of mobilization based on the prior actions and attitudes of the participants because so few had been active in the divestment movement prior to April 4. Only 9 percent of the random sample of students reported that they had been at least somewhat active in the divestment movement, yet 37 percent participated in blockade rallies and/or slept overnight on the steps of Hamilton Hall. In fact, these students did not know that they would join this militant protest until it was actually initiated.

It is unlikely that the decision to participate was due to a narrow individual cost/benefit analysis including such costs as the time involved and the definite possibilities of arrest and/or disciplinary action by the university. Regarding personal benefits, it is hard to see how any Columbia student could gain from the divestment of South Africa-related stock.

Rather, participation was due to a belief in the cause and the conviction that this protest might work where previous CFSA actions had failed. Consciousness-raising had convinced these students of the importance of divestment, but they had not participated in the movement because they did not believe its tactics would work. Once several hundred were in front of the doors, many demonstrators felt that such a large group using a dramatic tactic would have the power to call attention to the evils of apartheid and cause the university to seriously consider divestment:

Often when I would see a rally, I'd think that here was a bunch of people huffing

and puffing about an issue who are going to be ignored and things are going to go on just as they were before this rally. The fact that there were a couple of hundred people out there with the purpose of altering the way the University does business gave me the feeling that this would be noticed, that people would pay attention.

The belief in the potential power of the tactic was reinforced by the willingness of several leaders of the movement to sacrifice their individual interests to achieve divestment. Two black South African students who spoke at the rally faced the possibility of exile or arrest and imprisonment upon their return home. About half a dozen CFSA steering committee members had fasted for nearly two weeks simply to get a meeting with the university President and Trustees; two of these students were eventually hospitalized. As one blockader testified:

The fasters were doing something that personally took a lot of willpower for them, and that gave you a little extra willpower. To have to go into the hospital because you were off food for fifteen days, and the Trustees won't even speak to you. It really made me angry at the Trustees, so I was determined that this was not something that was just going to wimper off. At least I was going to be there, and I know others felt the same way.

The leaders of the protest recruited participants by taking personal risks that demonstrated their own commitment to the cause and to this particular tactic; other students in the blockade ignored individual interests in favor of the cause as well.

I do think it has something to do with the support of peers, just seeing that there were people who were willing to extend themselves and put their own asses on the line. I guess it's the self-sacrifice aspect of it that appealed to me, that really drew my attention. These people were willing to sacrifice their own personal interests in a big way, or a larger way than usual. That's something that hit a chord with me. It was the degree to which people were willing to give up self-interest.

Another factor influencing participation may have been the fact that the protesters were not forced to decide to join the protest at all. Instead, they were led as a group to a position in front of the doors, unaware that this was an act of civil disobedience; the only decision to be made was whether or not to leave the protest. Although this was done because CFSA did not want to reveal its plans to campus security prematurely, the unintended consequence was to maximize participation; it was difficult for demonstrators to leave the steps because of the public example of self-sacrificing black South Africans and the fasters.

Of course, each protester had many less public opportunities to leave the protest during the three weeks after April 4th. Most stayed, partly because of growing evidence of the power of this tactic. The protest soon gained the public support of a variety of groups locally and nationally, including Harlem community groups and churches, the Columbia faculty, unions on and off the campus, the African National Congress, and the United Nations. Students on other campuses engaged in similar protests. This support made the blockaders believe that their challenge to the authority of the Columbia administration was moral, necessary, and powerful. One blockader described this as being "part of something that was much larger than myself." Another suggested:

> One thing I believe now is that people in a grassroots movement can actually have an impact, that we're not all completely helpless. I guess it was that sense of power that I didn't have before.

Polarization and Increased Commitment

Because the blockade was an unconventional attempt to gain political influence, the steering committee of CFSA was unable to predict how many would participate. For the same reason, they were unable to predict their opponent's reaction to their tactic. Based on the information they had on recent South African consulate and embassy protests, they assumed they would be arrested soon after the doors of Hamilton Hall were chained. As these expectations of a mostly symbolic arrest were communicated to the less politically experienced blockaders, a consensus developed that the blockade would be short-lived.

However, the administration did not order the arrest of the protesters. Instead, Columbia's President sent a letter to everyone at the university arguing that the students were "disruptive" and "coercive," and that they were trying to impose their will on the rest of the university. He suggested that "countless avenues of free speech" in the university community were open to them and that what they were doing was illegal, that divestment would probably hurt rather than help blacks in South Africa, and that the university was doing all it could to fight apartheid.

University officials began to videotape the protesters in order to prosecute them under university regulations on obstructing university buildings and disrupting university functions. They sent letters threatening suspension or expulsion to the members of the CFSA steering committee and a few others. Guarantees were given that those who reported for individual disciplinary hearings would be treated more leniently than those who did not. They also obtained a court order calling on participants in the blockade to cease and desist.

By threatening suspensions and expulsions, the administration had raised the stakes; the protesters felt much more threatened by these academic penalties than by symbolic arrests. There were other costs associated with participating in this protest, including dealing with the cold and freezing rain; missing classes, exams, and study time; and losing close relationships with nonblockaders. Ignoring these costs, the steering committee members who received letters refused to go to the disciplinary hearings, suggested that the administration was engaging in unfair selective prosecution, and reiterated their determination to remain in front of Hamilton Hall until the university divested.

Such actions were to be expected from the strongly committed CFSA steering committee. The surprise was that the less experienced majority of protesters also refused to be intimidated and remained on the blockade. They did so in part because of an example of self-sacrifice by one of their own. One of the politically inexperienced students, a senior with three weeks to go before graduation, received a letter threatening him with expulsion. Initially, he was scared:

> I was petrified, especially since Columbia has not been fun for me but rather painful. I really wanted to get out of here, and I was horrified by the thought that I would either have to come back to Columbia or go somewhere else and lose credits by transfering. My reaction was, "Why do they have to pick me? Why do I have to be the focal point of this whole thing?"

But he decided not to report for disciplinary action. He felt that he could not give in to his fears in the face of the sacrifices being made by the fasters and South African students.

> Listening to the commitment on the part of the steering committee people who had received letters made me feel bad that I even considered leaving the blockade. One other factor was the fasters, the fact that there were South Africans involved in it, and that these people had more on the line than I did. I felt like I could not let these people down. I also felt that I was a sort of representative of a lot of people on the blockade and I felt I could not set a precedent by leaving and backing down.

His example was extremely important for the maintenance of commitment by the other inexperienced blockaders:

> They threatened (the blockader) with expulsion. It was sobering in a way. But it

helped bond us together. It was stupid to do that because it just made people more furious, and it made people more resolved to stay. We just said we're not going to let him be expelled. We're all going to stick together in this.

The protesters responded as a group to administration threats, not as isolated individuals. Individual concerns about disciplinary actions were now secondary; each blockader saw her or his welfare as tied to the group fate. Paradoxically, the potential for high personal costs became a reason for participation; protesters wanted to be part of an important and powerful movement and they did not want fellow activists to face the wrath of the authorities alone. The night the threat of arrest was assumed to be greatest, Easter Sunday, was also the one night out of twenty-one with the greatest number sleeping out on the blockade. Soon after this, 500 students signed a statement accepting personal responsibility for the blockade.

Collective Decision-Making and the End of the Blockade

Another group process which influenced participation in this protest was collective decision-making. Open-ended rap sessions among the blockaders, lasting up to four or five hours, were begun after administration representatives delivered the first disciplinary letters to the protesters. In all cases, a serious attempt was made to reach consensus among all those on the steps; votes were held on only a few occasions. One of the main questions was whether to continue the protest. This discussion was initiated by members of the CFSA steering committee because of their commitment to democratic decision-making, and because they understood that the blockaders would be more likely to continue the protest if they participated in a collective decision to do so. During the first two weeks of the protest, the consensus was to continue the blockade.

By the third week, though, some of the protesters began to feel that the protest should be ended. The sense of crisis had been dulled by the lack of action by the administration to back up their threats. It was now clear that there were no plans to call in the police to make arrests. As one blockader put it, the "university's policy of waiting it out was becoming effective." Also, an event can be news for only so long, and the image of Columbia students sitting on some steps became commonplace. Diminishing television and print coverage reduced the collective belief in the power of this particular tactic. As one protester suggested:

> It was during the third week that I started spending nights at home and coming up in the morning. During the last week I probably spent three nights out [on the steps] and four nights at home. During that third week a kind of mood of lethargy hit, and it became a chorelike atmosphere. There was a lot of feeling that it was kind of futile to stay out there.

In the face of declining participation, long and heated discussions were held about ending the protest. Proponents of continuing the action argued that protesters ought to honor their commitment to stay in front of the doors until Columbia divested. Those who advocated ending the protest argued that divestment was not imminent and that the blockade was no longer effective. As one protester put it:

> The blockade ended because a very thoughtful and carefully planned decision was made. It was a question of what we could do that would be most effective for divestment. We decided that the blockade had done a lot, but at this point other things would be better, seeing how the administration was willing to sit us out.

On the 25th of April, the blockade officially ended with a march into Harlem to a rally at a Baptist Church. Five months later, the Columbia Trustees divested.

[...]

Conclusion

[...]

Years of well-organized activities by the CFSA were crucial in raising consciousness about the apartheid issue and on the need for noninstitutional means of influence to achieve divestment. The blockade itself was initiated only after two months of careful planning by the CFSA steering committee.

The blockaders were not just isolated individuals with preferences for divestment nor a set of confused, insecure people; rather, they were people who had been convinced by CFSA meetings that apartheid was evil, that divestment would help South African blacks, and that divestment could be achieved through protest. They joined the blockade on April 4th because it appeared to offer a powerful alternative to previously impotent demonstrations and because of the example of self-sacrificing CFSA leaders. The solidarity of the group increased after the administration's escalation of the conflict because group identification among the protesters was already strong enough so that they responded to the threat as a powerful group rather than as powerless individuals. Protesters remained at this long and risky protest partly because of the democratic decision-making processes used by the group.

This analysis of the 1985 Columbia University divestment protest indicates that useful theories of movement mobilization must include insights about how individual protesters are convinced by group-level processes to sacrifice themselves for the cause. This means asking new kinds of questions in movement research: What kinds of arguments in what kinds of settings convince people to support a political cause? Why do potential recruits decide that noninstitutional means of influence are justified and necessary? Under what circumstances is the example of leaders sacrificing for the cause likely to induce people to join a risky protest? Why do some tactics appear to offer a greater chance of success than others? Under what conditions do threats or actual repression by authorities create greater internal solidarity in a protest group? Under what conditions do threats or repression result in the demobilization of protest? What kinds of group decision-making processes are likely to convince people to continue to participate in a protest movement?

Generalizing from case studies is always difficult. Some aspects of student movements make them unusual, especially the ability of organizers to take advantage of the physical concentration of students on campuses. But the important impact of group processes on movement recruitment and commitment is not unique to the 1985 Columbia anti-apartheid movement. The development of solidarity based on a sense of collective power and polarization was also found in a Chicago community organization (Hirsch 1986). And these same group processes were crucial in the mobilization and development of the Southern civil rights movement of the 1950s and 1960s. Consciousness-raising occurred in black churches and colleges. The collective power of protest was evident to those who participated in bus boycotts, sit-ins, freedom rides, and in Freedom Summer. The movement relied heavily on the creation of polarized conflict between the white Southern segregationist elite and black protesters to recruit participants, to gain national media attention, and ultimately to force federal intervention to redress the social and political grievances of Southern blacks (McAdam 1982; Morris 1984).

References

Coser, Lewis. 1956. *The Functions of Social Conflict*. New York: Free Press.

———. 1967. *Continuities in the Study of Social Conflict*. New York: Free Press.

Edelman, Murray. 1971. *Politics and Symbolic Action*. New York: Academic.

Ferree, Myra Marx and Frederick D. Miller. 1985. "Mobilization and Meaning: Toward an Integration of Social Psychological and Resource Perspectives on Social Movements." *Sociological Inquiry* 55: 38–61.

Fireman, Bruce and William Gamson. 1979. "Utilitarian Logic in the Resource Mobilization Perspective." Pp. 8–44 in *The Dynamics of Social Movements*, edited by Mayer N. Zald and John D. McCarthy. Cambridge: Winthrop.

Hirsch, Eric L. 1986. "The Creation of Political Solidarity in Social Movement Organizations." *Sociological Quarterly* 27: 373–87.

———. 1989. *Urban Revolt: Ethnic Politics in the Nineteenth Century Chicago Labor Movement*. Berkeley, Cal.: University of California Press.

McAdam, Douglas. 1982. *Political Process and the Development of Black Insurgency*. Chicago: University of Chicago.

Morris, Aldon. 1984. *The Origins of the Civil Rights Movement*. New York: Free Press.

11 Sustaining Commitment Among Radical Feminists

Nancy Whittier

Remaining Radical Feminists

What does it mean to say that a political generation has retained a radical feminist collective identity? In terms of practices – women's real lives – it means that participants have kept in touch with each other, believe they have things in common that they do not share with others, hold fast to central tenets of feminist ideology, and think of themselves as "radical feminist" and therefore different from the mainstream. Virtually all the women I interviewed continue to identify with the term "feminist" and most with "radical feminist," and this identification remains important to them. "If someone asks me, 'Who are you?' I'm a radical feminist," declared a woman who now works for a public interest organization. "And I see radical feminism as my life's work, even though I'm spending most of my days, most of my weeks, most of my years, doing something else." Seeing oneself this way still sets women apart from the majority of the population. As one woman succinctly put it, "Like most radical feminists, I'm really odd wherever I go." This "oddness" stems from her beliefs or consciousness and from her membership in a distinct group of women's movement veterans. Radical feminists' political consciousness about the world and their construction of group boundaries both set them apart from others and bind them together. I will first discuss consciousness and how it has changed, then turn to group boundaries and their changes.

Feminist Consciousness

Developing feminist consciousness was, and is, a central task of the radical women's

> **Collective Identity** Before members of any group can present "their" demands to authorities or strategize about how "they" can best bring about desired changes, they need to know who "they" are. In whose name do activists speak? Feeling part of a broader group can be exhilarating, providing a major incentive for collective action. Some collective identities are widely accepted, and activists can take them for granted. Martin Luther King, Jr., for example, did not have to persuade African-Americans who lived in Birmingham in 1955 that they faced discrimination by virtue of their skin color. Under other circumstances, however, activists have to work hard to get a certain category of people to think of themselves as belonging to a group with distinctive problems and interests. Collective identities such as "Hispanic" or "gay" (or "queer") do not always come naturally to people (that is, they do not always result from ordinary, everyday interactions). These identities may have to be consciously created, and in fact they are often as much a result as a cause of protest. Some collective identities, in fact, are based solely on participation in a movement, such as "animal protectionist" or "human rights activist." Even a favored tactic can provide an identity, as with those who espouse nonviolent "direct action." And membership in an organization is also a potential basis for collective identity.

movement. Most movements possess a formal body of writings and scholarship that communicate interpretive frameworks and explain the group's position in the social structure, and members also interweave political understandings into their daily life and interactions. The radical women's movement of the 1970s took the meshing of politics and everyday life to a new height. In consciousness-raising groups and other settings, women discussed their experiences and politics with the aim of rethinking their understandings of the world. From this work grew elaborate theoretical frameworks that explained women's oppression, male dominance, and patriarchy, and politicized all aspects of life with the notion of the personal as political.

In the late 1970s, WAC's (Women's Action Collective, a radical feminist group in Columbus, Ohio, founded in 1971) orientation sessions were a political education for many women that included analyzing their own experiences through a feminist framework and constructing and learning theoretical analyses. As one woman explained, "It taught me everything I know about feminism, racism, classism." Whether individuals experienced "consciousness raising" through a consciousness-raising group, in the course of protest, or through a political orientation session, these transforming experiences forever changed the way a generation of feminist activists looked at the world. As one succinctly put it, "It's like once you realize that the world is round, you can never again believe that it's flat."

Most women I interviewed were emphatic that the beliefs they formed during the women's movement had endured, although they were aware of the popular stereotype of 1960s radicals selling out. A woman who has not remained active in feminist organizations maintained that her feminist principles still exist, saying, "We continued to believe that a better world is possible, that we do need a creation of a new culture." Another woman, who became part of WAC in the mid-1970s, explained that the women's movement had a lasting and profound effect on how she looks at the world despite her belief that feminism is now in "the doldrums."

It helped me learn how to construct principles....And that was in a sense the beginning of a real life for me, of choosing to live a principled life.... And so, even if the doldrums continue forever and ever, I am light years ahead of them, personally.

Participating in consciousness-raising groups, activist organizations, and political actions such as boycotts or pickets gave women a new interpretation of themselves and the events around them. A former member of WAC explained how her feminist framework grew from consciousness-raising groups.

Everything that happens in the world, I have a framework for understanding it. And that framework comes from the consciousness raising first, and understanding women's common experiences and my own experiences and the validity of that, and then seeing the rest of that through that validity.... If I didn't have a feminist framework to look at the world, I'd be, like most people, kind of adrift.

The women's movement developed highly complex interpretive frameworks. Feminist theory analyzes the sources and operation of patriarchy and male dominance, women's economic and social oppression, violence against women, the links between sexism and racism and classism, the role of homophobia in perpetuating female subordination, and a variety of other phenomena. Such analyses are widespread in written works but are not limited to the printed page. Women's movement organizations in Columbus and elsewhere discussed and refined feminist theory as part of their daily operation, and activists were sufficiently well-versed in feminist analysis to explain the reasons for a demonstration to the press, argue with each other, and interpret their own lives in light of feminist theory in consciousness-raising groups. The large number of discussion groups that emerged in the late 1970s around specific issues such as women and economics, the workplace, radical feminism, and white supremacy are a testimonial to the importance of theory to the women's movement. An antirape activist explained the centrality of theory development to WAC strategy during the 1970s.

In the [Women's Action] Collective when we were doing theory [we used the process of] trying to figure out what you are doing by starting with your metaprinciples, and then going down to your principles, and then your objectives, and your goals, and then your strategies, and then your tactics. Everything relates back up to your metaprinciple, which in the case of rape prevention was respect for persons. The easiest way to get rid of rape would be to kill all the men, but that's not respectful of persons, therefore you can't do it. You have to keep going up and down this, to try to figure out. Whatever you do is going to be principled.

Theory remained important. Many respondents reported forming discussion groups in the late 1980s and early 1990s on topics including feminist theory, women and economics, feminist art criticism, and "How do we keep hanging on?" in hard times.

Despite the complexity of feminist theory, the lasting beliefs that respondents attributed to their participation in the women's movement were a general ethic of personal responsibility, egalitarianism, skepticism, freedom, and a policy of treating others well. Just over half of the women I talked to spontaneously mentioned the Golden Rule ("Do unto others as you would have them do unto you") as part of their core values. Although the Golden Rule was part of feminist ideology earlier in the century, its biblical origins make it widely known and consistent with mainstream culture. Yet longtime feminists translated it into a radical political context. The following statements by three different women illustrate the broad definitions of feminist principles.

Just nonsexist, nonracist, nonclassist, treating people fairly, nonhomophobic, all those -isms.... Mostly, I just try to use the Golden Rule, I guess. I just try to treat people the same way I would want them to treat me.

That ethic of the sixties is very egalitarian, political, and realizing there's politics in everything personal. And not always believing what your government says, and questioning everything. And questioning authority above all.

I still have the same idealism. I'd still like people to be free to do what they want, and I'd still like people to have choices, and I'd like us all to be working on important issues. Bringing peace to the world, ending war.

Respondents have not forgotten or disregarded the more specific and complex elements of feminist consciousness over the years. Rather, they take for granted the application of feminist theory to specific topics. Feminist analyses of rape, for example, as an act of violence rather than sex, of sexual harassment, and of sexism in advertising, have become so intrinsic to participants' views of the world that they did not articulate them when I asked about their feminist principles.

Most respondents thought that their feminist beliefs have been a positive force in their lives, even in the 1980s and 1990s, when support for radical feminism made them increasingly politically marginal. One activist described the far-reaching effects.

I think it's made me stronger. I think it's made me really clear about who I am. It's made me very clear about what the problems are that women face in society. ... I almost feel like my life has a theme. It's not just like I'm this little ant out there living and working with all the other ants on the anthill. There are things that I care really, really deeply about, and that sort of infuses my whole life with meaning. And I've retained that, and I think I always will.

Attributing the difficulties in one's life to structural rather than personal causes (seeing the personal as political) is an important component of oppositional consciousness and helps motivate people to participate in collective action aimed at changing their circumstances. It also makes daily life easier for respondents and motivates activism, as one woman who is now a professor explained.

If you really understand that the problems are out there, instead of blaming yourself, it makes you willing to take more risks. It makes you more motivated to fight the motherfuckers!...If I didn't have that base to latch onto, I would just go nuts.

A few respondents, however, felt that their feminist beliefs, although accurate, made their lives more difficult. As one woman who has not remained active in feminist organizations explained:

> From becoming active in the women's movement...I've gotten a different perspective on politics and how government is conducted, how business is conducted, almost everything that goes on in our society. And I don't like a lot of what I see. Much of what I see is extremely disturbing. Some of it frightens me or depresses me or angers me. And there are times that I wish I had never joined that first women's CR group and learned to look at the world differently.

Despite her regrets, she, too, has been changed irrevocably. Yet there have been some important changes in feminist consciousness as well as continuities over the past two decades.

Changes in Consciousness

Reflecting changes in the larger women's movement, respondents reported that they have become less concerned with "political correctness," or taking a strict political line on everything. Instead, they criticize some features of the 1960s–1970s movement, view feminism as broader and encompassing a variety of social reform issues, and are more aware of race and class differences. One woman articulated the declining significance of political correctness, commenting, "I don't look at life now in terms of feminism and what's politically correct and what's not." This remark must be placed in the larger social context of the 1990s, where a backlash against multiculturalism has taken the form of attacks on so-called mandated political correctness within universities. It has become unfashionable and perhaps pol-

itically dangerous to appear to be overly concerned with language use, subtle forms of discrimination, verbal harassment, and the like.

Nevertheless, many participants reacted against what they perceived as the excess and mistakes of the women's movement in the 1970s. Many singled out collective structure as an experiment they did not want to repeat. One former member of WAC proclaimed that she no longer believed in the collective process.

> To be honest, we got really sick of consensual decision making...Some of us feel like, I wouldn't go to a meeting if that was the way it was going to be! I don't want to be part of it, I have no patience with it.

Another WAC veteran commented in a similar vein:

> We did a lot of experimentation with the collective process, thinking that was the ideal structure, and found out that it wasn't. And now, I wouldn't be involved in a collective if you paid me a million bucks. Absolutely not!

Participants' reactions against perceived errors in the women's movement of the 1970s have led not only to disillusionment but to new and perhaps more effective organizational structures as well. "I've got to have radicals [on the board of directors] who at this point are so mellow on their own stuff that they're going to say to me, 'It's your vision, do what you want. Run with it...,'" explained a woman who founded a feminist organization in the 1980s. "I wanted some way to counter the fact that we got so bound up by the end of the seventies. We've got to give women the chance in their lifetimes to fly, and this is mine." Further, some women commented that they simply wanted their lives to be less serious than in the 1970s. "We had some fun in the seventies, but we were also quite grim a lot of the time," commented one woman about her changing approach to activism. "And I want to have some good times for the rest of my life. I want to do some fun things."

A second major change in the women's movement in the 1980s and 1990s has been an increase in attention to differences among women, particularly to issues of race and class. Sustainers and others began discussing race and class in the late 1970s. These discussions and feminist writings by women of color changed the outlook of the entire political generation. Longtime feminists reported a growing awareness that women are not an undifferentiated group and reflected critically on the race and class homogeneity of the women's movement in the 1960s and 1970s. One woman described the changes in her consciousness as follows:

> Back in the Ohio days I would have described myself as a radical feminist and since then I'd describe myself as a socialist feminist... [In the early 1980s] we started wondering why we were all white, and what was wrong... So I had a heavy infusion of thinking about race and class. It means that instead of viewing women as this undifferentiated group that are oppressed more or less equally by men, there are differences of class as well as race.

Only three of the women I interviewed reported that their identification had changed from radical to socialist feminist, but most reported an increasing concern with race and class.

A third change is a broadening of the goals and analyses of feminism. The women I interviewed increasingly define feminism as encompassing other struggles such as peace, environmental protection, animal rights, humanism, lesbian and gay freedom, socialism, and human rights. One woman who has become involved with the movement for recovery from addictions articulated the shift in her consciousness this way:

> I haven't forgotten the women's movement. But to me it's a piece of this larger issue, in which we need to think about how all people can be empowered, as who they

are. It's the feminist criticism, I think, that has expanded our consciousness to the point where we can even see that there's a problem. But I guess I don't see feminism as my guiding call anymore. It's sort of part of the whole picture.

[...]

The broadening of concerns and the increasing incorporation of race and class issues do not signify a drastic or discontinuous shift in feminist consciousness for this generation. Rather, respondents are applying the basic principles of feminist consciousness to additional issues. In addition, women who came to the women's movement from the New Left are returning to some of their earlier concerns and examining them in a feminist light. When asked if her beliefs or view of the world had changed over the past twenty years, almost every interviewee first answered, "No," and then described some shifts. In other words, the core of feminist consciousness has remained consistent for this generation although there have been modifications. As one woman said, "I still retain my feminist principles absolutely, although they have evolved and changed."

Group Boundaries

Although participants construct their consciousness interactively in a movement context, individuals internalize it. Much of the foregoing evidence addresses this individual level. But collective identity is about far more than consciousness. At root it is about seeing oneself as part of a group, a collectivity. The mechanism by which this is accomplished is the construction of group boundaries, or symbolic and material distinctions between members of the collectivity and others. Participants establish group boundaries through a symbolic system and by constructing an alternative culture or network that serves as a "world apart" from the dominant society. These manifestations of collective identity are visible in interactions among group members and in the actions of individuals; they are not limited to the attitudes or beliefs of individuals.

The notion of group boundaries may imply rigid delineation of who is permitted to be a feminist. But in fact it refers to a much more ambiguous process by which people try to make sense of their lives and of their similarities to and differences from others. Group boundaries can be rigid or permeable and vary in their importance. For longtime feminist activists, boundaries between themselves and others became less important in the 1980s even as their sense of self remained inextricably linked to feminism. Boundaries have both persisted and been transformed between feminists and nonfeminists, women and men, and different political generations. A network of relationships among feminist veterans helps them to maintain their collective identity.

Distinguishing feminists from nonfeminists. Despite rhetoric of sisterhood, the "we" defined by radical feminists twenty-five years ago did not include all women. The labels "feminist" and "radical feminist" distinguished between women who adopted such labels and those who did not. For participants, a transformed individual identity as a woman meant seeing oneself as a member of the collectivity "feminists"; adopting "feminist" or "radical feminist" as a public identity signified membership in the group of women who had experienced such a transformation.

Despite the continuing importance of feminism for self-definition, the distinction between feminists and nonfeminists has become less significant in two ways. First, many women I interviewed said that they are less likely to form negative impressions of people who do not identify publicly as feminists. As one woman who now leads workshops on sexual harassment put it:

> I'm much kinder to women who aren't feminists and who are deferring to men when it's clearly against their best interests. I'm much better in discussing it with her and helping her overcome that than I

would have been five years ago. Fifteen years ago I would have kind of jumped down her throat, and she would have had to avoid me. [*Laughs*]

Another woman, now a lawyer, remarked that she, too, is less critical of those who differ politically from her.

> I used to size people up in two minutes concerning their politics, and if their politics weren't right, I didn't have any use for them. I would cast them aside and be on my way...And that was stupid, and I've stopped doing that.

In other words, the boundary between feminists and nonfeminists has become more permeable, and feminists are willing to cooperate more with those outside the group.

Second, many longtime feminists reported that they are less likely to see themselves as part of a common group with someone simply because she calls herself a feminist. As one professor of women's studies declared:

> One thing I know now is that just because someone calls herself, or himself, a feminist does not mean that person's values or behavior or way of operating in the world is going to be something that I identify with...So I'm much less influenced by someone marching up to me and announcing they're a feminist. I'm much more wanting to watch how that person operates before I make a decision about whether I'm really in league with them.

[...]

Language use is an additional marker of the boundary between feminists and nonfeminists. The women's movement developed a sweeping critique of sexism in language that brought about substantial change in language use. Derogatory terms used to refer to women – chick, cunt, bitch, girl, and so forth – were a special target of feminists in the initial years of the movement and have remained so since then. Like the label "feminist," the use of language remains an important boundary marker, but, as one woman indicated, failure to conform to feminist terminology (indicating "outsider" status) carries fewer consequences than it did during the 1970s.

> I paid too much attention to language [in the 1970s] as a means to assess politics. I think language is important, and to this day I'd have real problems having a close personal friendship with somebody who referred to women as chicks. But it got to be so crazy, and if people didn't use your exact terminology they were an enemy.

Other feminists suggested that even their own use of language has changed to include terms that would previously have been used only by outsiders, as this lawyer commented:

> I can remember the time that my tongue would have rotted in my cheeks before I would have said the word "girl" in relation to a woman at all. And at least now I've gotten to the point where I can joke with some of my friends and at least use the word. But I can't even imagine being in a meeting and talking about a young woman as being a girl. That still would really make me nuts.

In short, what would previously have been a fairly serious boundary violation has become acceptable, but only within limits and in certain settings.

Distinguishing women from men. Another means by which radical feminists established boundaries in the 1970s was by emphasizing women's difference from men and denigrating many masculine traits. Some feminists made this argument in essentialist terms – the view that the differences between women and men reflected the sexes' innate natures. Many others, however, viewed the differences as a socially constructed product of socialization and structural position. One woman explained how being a feminist kept her from forming close relationships with men during the 1970s.

> It made it impossible to be close to men anymore, because...I was entering a universe that [they] couldn't come into...All men became aliens when I realized that I didn't have to live as though I approved of patriarchy. They just can't relate.

Most feminist veterans reported that their close friendships and their political alliances are still primarily with women. Like other boundary markers, however, the division between women and men has lessened. Many lesbians reported increasing political work and a feeling of commonality with gay men. Both lesbian and heterosexual participants indicated a tension between a continuing view of men as untrustworthy and different from themselves and increasing cooperative contact with men. This woman's comment illustrates the ambivalence.

> I have to deal with men on a day-by-day basis, so I do deal with them. I'm not sure that I like them or I trust them any more than I did twenty years ago. But I've also learned that there are really some very, very good men out there who do try and are very supportive. And I don't think when I was truly involved with the women's movement that I would have admitted that, at all.

Like the distinction between feminists and nonfeminists, the boundary between women and men is more permeable than it was ten years ago.

Two kinds of changes can occur in how challenging groups construct their boundaries when their social movement falls on hard times. One model is illustrated by the National Woman's Party in the 1950s, which developed an elite-sustained structure. Boundaries become rigidified, increasing the commitment of a small cadre of activists but keeping out new recruits and allies. The second possibility, which has occurred in the Columbus women's movement, is that boundaries may become more permeable and differences less salient. Although members still see radical feminists as a distinct group, they are more willing to cross the boundaries between their group and others, opening up the possibility for the coalitions that have developed in the 1980s.

Accompanying this development is a reframing of emotions, from anger to acceptance or openness. Almost everyone I interviewed said she felt an increasing "mellowness," more tolerance for people with different political views or lifestyles, less stridency, a growth in spirituality, and an increasing reluctance to be motivated by anger. One woman's comments were typical.

> In the early seventies, when I was eating and breathing and sleeping feminist activity, I was so angry! I was really fueled by fury a lot of the time. And at this point in my life, to be angry is too hard. I just can't do it. It doesn't feel good to be angry, and I also had the realization that I didn't like the way things went for me when I was angry. When you're angry, other people are intimidated and they don't want to do what you want them to do. It really sets up an opposition.

Relationships among feminists, once stormy, calmed somewhat for these women. "Now I'm much more into why can't we all get along, and getting people to deal more on a one-to-one or in small groups of people," explained one. Many women saw their changed attitudes as a function of age, as this woman did.

> When you reach your thirties and forties, you have a more overall view of life. I don't in any way think that I have become less radical or that I have mellowed, I think that's not a proper use of your greater age. It's just that I have a wider view of things and I'm more tolerant of other people because I'm more compassionate now than I was then.

It is difficult to know how much of this change is actually due to age, but "mellowing" in political attitudes is not biologically determined. Years of experience and the need for unity in a hostile environment made feminists less angry and more willing to compromise.

Generational boundaries. Unlike the differences between feminists and nonfeminists and between women and men, which have been socially reconstructed and minimized, the women I interviewed perceived a variety of differences between themselves and people who did not share their experiences in the women's movement of the 1960s and 1970s because of age or politics. One woman who was very active in lesbian feminist protest during the mid- to late 1970s described her perception of younger lesbians who had not shared her experience in the women's movement.

> When I am involved with women who have not been through the experience I've been through, I feel a little bit sad for them. I feel that they have lost a major part of what it is to be a feminist, and to be a lesbian.... And it's hard to convey to them what feminism is, let alone what lesbian feminism is, in the sense that I learned it, and how encompassing it is.

Another veteran of the earliest days of WL, who now works in a mainstream corporation, felt that her social movement participation set her apart from people of different ages.

> I talk to some of these young kids at work, and it's like they don't know anything about the politics in El Salvador, they don't know anything about anything. They've just been yuppified. And they don't see the big political picture. Or people that are ten or fifteen years older. It's like [they say], "What's wrong with you?" when I start ranting about politics, or Bush, or Reagan.

Movement veterans symbolically underscore the importance of remaining true to one's political commitments by telling "cautionary tales" about women who were formerly radical feminists and have "sold out" in the 1980s and 1990s. One woman, who is employed by a nonprofit organization and owns a modest house, told such a tale.

I'm not a big consumer or a real high materialist. But I know some women who went the other way. I know one woman who makes a lot of money, well over a hundred thousand dollars a year. And she used to be in WAC.... And now she's just very different.

Another told a similar story about a woman who "went from being a radical lesbian to being a Reagan Republican who wanted to get rich." A variation on this theme concerns a rumored social group for professional lesbians, including former radical feminists, that limits membership to women above a certain income. A sense of identity and commonality is reinforced by those who are different. Thus, stories of women who have sold out serve to support others' status as "dedicated feminists" and symbolically underscore the boundary between those who have retained commitment and those who have abandoned it.

Lesbian feminist identity. Throughout the 1970s lesbians became more visible in the radical women's movement; lesbian feminist ideology developed, and in practice activists often conflated the categories "lesbian" and "radical feminist." By the end of the decade, heterosexual women were a shrinking minority in radical feminist groups at the same time that a lesbian feminist subculture was growing. Large women's movement organizations embraced lesbian issues, but animosities remained between heterosexual and lesbian women. The new source of conflict was some heterosexual women's charge that lesbians dominated the movement. "I think that straight women have been pushed out of the women's movement by lesbian women," complained one heterosexual respondent, "and it's been pretty ugly.... The women's movement is the only place in the world where women have to come out of the closet as a heterosexual." Most of the heterosexual women I interviewed did not share this sentiment, but many felt left out of a predominantly lesbian movement. During the 1970s, the celebration of womanhood had made

heterosexual women welcome as part of the mostly lesbian "women's community." But by the 1980s and 1990s, lesbians were increasingly unwilling to soft-pedal either their sexuality or their political demands. Both lesbian and heterosexual identity became more salient in the radical women's movement as a result.

At the same time, divisions among lesbians diminished. In the early and mid-1970s, lesbian feminists were often critical of longtime lesbians for "mimicking heterosexuality" in butch–fem roles, viewing women as sex objects, and not participating in feminist activities. For example, a fundraising talent show in Columbus attempted to bring the bar and political worlds together. A humorous skit in which a woman adopted a "ditzy" feminine character, enjoyed by bar women, was loudly protested by political women, who disrupted the performance arguing that it parodied women. The talent show ended prematurely, and the alliance between the two groups stalled. By the late 1970s and early 1980s, however, the local lesbian bar, Summit Station (commonly known as "Jack's"), sometimes hosted feminist fundraisers and became more of a hangout for lesbian feminists. At the same time feminists softened critiques of traditional butch–fem relationships and subculture and increasingly recognized political resistance by lesbians outside the formal women's movement. One longtime lesbian activist described the changes in relations between lesbian feminists and other groups of lesbians.

[In the 1970s] the community was fairly well segregated, so that the political community was separate from the softball community and was separate from the community of teachers.... Over time those sort of walls came down, among those groups at least, as women aged.... [Now] there's a great deal of mix and less separation between and among those women that define themselves variously.

[...]

In addition to the lessening of distinctions among lesbians, the division between lesbians and gay men has become more per-meable in the 1980s, particularly with the rise of acquired immune-deficiency syndrome (AIDS) and lesbians' extensive participation in the AIDS movement. One woman who had been part of Lesbian Peer Support commented that she had become involved with a local AIDS organization because

> for the first time I identified that this is happening to my tribe. These are my people, and I need to stand with them now, because this is important.

"My people" means lesbians and gay men for her now, whereas in the 1970s it meant women.

[...]

Another woman who has been active on gay and lesbian issues since the 1970s explained her continuing identification with gay men.

> It doesn't have to do as much with an identity of being a woman as of being a gay and lesbian sort of outcast.... That's more direct and more related to my own set of things than other kinds of issues like childcare or abortion.

Seeing lesbianism, rather than womanhood, as the defining element of her identity is a significant change.

A final notable pattern is illustrated by three participants who identified as lesbian but reported having sexual relationships with men in the 1980s for the first time in two decades. Two of the three continued to identify themselves as lesbians, whereas the third identified as bisexual. One lesbian, who described her affair with a man as "totally peculiar," saw affairs with men as a widespread phenomenon, commenting that she has "discovered since that a whole lot of us, lesbians, went through a phase like that." This "phase" occurred as lesbian feminist identity became more fluid, permitting sexual experimentation without the stigma of political betrayal. At the same time, it may be that as the feminist community weakened in the early 1980s, the ideal of being "woman-identified" came to seem less real

and more difficult to maintain. In the early 1990s the counterintuitive notion of "lesbians who sleep with men" spread: The lesbian writer Jan Clausen published an article in a gay publication about her relationship with a man, singer Holly Near wrote in her autobiography about being a lesbian but having sex with men, and students at OSU (Ohio State University) formed a support group for "lesbians who just happen to be in relationships with politically correct men." Most of the women I interviewed still believed that sexuality was linked to politics and that the political implications of being a lesbian who slept with men were different from those of being a lesbian who did not. But the borders between lesbians and nonlesbians were undeniably blurred. The debate over whether one can identify as a lesbian and still be sexually involved with men is, at core, about collective identity: What behavior must one exhibit (or refrain from) in order to be considered a lesbian? A feminist?

The feminist network.   Veterans of the Columbus women's movement have maintained an elaborate and meaningful network that makes them more than an abstract political generation; they are a community. The network is a material embodiment of group boundaries. Many participants kept in touch with each other, and even when they had not been in touch, often kept tabs on each other's locations and activities. One woman, for example, told me that each year she checked the new phone book listing for another activist to make sure that she was still at the same address, although they had not talked in years. Of course, not all women who were active in the Columbus radical women's movement have kept in touch with each other. More peripheral members, those who have become conservative, former lesbians, and those who were "trashed out" are all less likely to have retained contacts with others. But even though the network is partial and has many broken links, many women are integrated into it in some way.

In part, the network exists because women's political commitments still make them inclined to work together on social change issues. One woman who recently ran for political office noted that a former member of the Women's Caucus at OSU was the first person to send a contribution to her campaign. Another woman contacted a fellow activist who had established a new feminist organization and took publicity about the new organization to a local conference. A national feminist organization founded in the 1980s by a veteran of the Columbus women's movement now has a board of directors that includes several women who participated in feminist organizations together in the 1970s.

In addition, the network remains important because of the emotional and intellectual closeness that grows from sharing a common important experience. Many longtime feminists reported that friendships they formed in the women's movement of the 1970s have remained important in the 1980s and 1990s. One woman explained the quality of such relationships.

> Some of these people, I've known them for so long now that we can refer back to a certain event or series of events with just a word or two. It's that kind of communication you can have with someone you've known for a long time, so that we don't really discuss it, we know what we mean. And we get that kind of good feeling that you have with people that you've been through a lot with and you've known for so long.

Another woman described formalizing important relationships through the creation of what she terms "chosen kinship."

> I've been working on my own chosen family...[and] I run workshops for women on kinship and chosen kinship.... At this point, I have a ritual and I take people in only if they seem to be really staying powers in my life. I don't do this lightly.

Although her chosen family is not limited to women with whom she was active in the 1970s, several such women are part of her network. The formality of the notion of chosen kinship emphasizes the importance of a network for establishing group boundaries.

Such relationships serve to sustain commitment to feminist politics and collective identity. One woman who works in a non-feminist setting explained that in order to retain feminist commitment when social pressures urge her to be absorbed into the political mainstream, "I surround myself with all my friends...people that I think still have a political world ethic about them." Another woman who is in a committed relationship with a woman she met in the Columbus women's movement of the 1970s said simply:

> Without each other I don't know how we'd be surviving.... One of the things we are for each other more than anything else is a reality check. Without the reality check, we could fall off the edge. In the 1980s, I certainly could have fallen off the edge if [she] hadn't been here.

Perhaps, in the end, the "reality check" is the most important contribution of the network: the reminder that, despite opposition and sometimes invisibility, feminists are neither crazy nor alone.

The women who were the furthest removed from the organized women's movement and whose feminist identity was the least important to them were those who had lost contact with the feminist network. One woman, who had formerly identified as a lesbian and had later married a man, reported that her resulting loss of membership in the lesbian community made it difficult to remain a feminist activist at the same level. Three other women who had moved to conservative parts of the country similarly found it difficult to remain active feminists because of the loss of a feminist network.

Because the lesbian feminist movement remained vibrant and large in the 1980s and 1990s and built a social movement community and political culture, lesbians often were able to maintain their commitment more easily than heterosexual women. The lesbian feminist community has aided lesbians in maintaining a feminist collective identity and has provided support and opportunities for practicing political principles in daily life and mobilizing collective action. As a result, fewer of the lesbians than the heterosexual women I interviewed moved into mainstream careers or lifestyles, and more lesbians have continued to participate in organized collective efforts for social change. The four women I interviewed who have remained fulltime radical feminist activists are all lesbians. Even for lesbians, however, the highly politicized activist community of the 1970s no longer exists.

The loss of community that accompanied the decline of organized feminism in the early 1980s left all participants feeling a sense of loss, alienation, and nostalgia, and deprived them of the networks and culture that supported their collective identity and translated it into mobilization. Male participants in the civil rights and student movements of the 1960s described similar feelings of dislocation. Both in terms of the friendships they developed and the sense of shared political mission in life, participants felt that their experience in the women's movement of the 1970s in Columbus differed sharply from the communities of the 1990s. One woman expressed her nostalgia for the friendships she formed in the 1970s.

> I have never had the friendships, the significance, the meaning, everything that you could want in relationships, since then.... We saw ourselves as family. And I have never had that kind of family since, and I don't think I ever will.

Another woman compared the ease of making friends in a social movement culture with the difficulty she faces now.

> I find it very difficult to keep friends these days, because I don't run into anybody

naturally. Like I used to just every day go into work [at WAC], you'd see all these people. You'd make plans to do things; it was just part of the flow. Now it's like you never see anybody, and you've got to call somebody up and make plans, it's this big effort.

The close-knit nature of women's movement culture fostered conflict, but it was nevertheless an important source of strength and continuing commitment for members, as this participant in WAC commented:

> We lived and worked together, literally.... It was just too much. You couldn't get away from anybody. And yet, the closeness of it was just not replicable.

Even in the absence of that "closeness," longtime feminists continued to rely on their connections to one another in the 1980s.

The clearest examples of how networks establish group boundaries come from separatist movements or those with separatist elements, such as utopian communes of the 1800s or the black nationalist movement of the 1960s. In such cases, movements create "a world apart" from the dominant culture in which participants can redefine their group. Feminists of the 1960s and 1970s have not created such a world apart in the present. Rather, they have dispersed, holding jobs where they may be one of only a few feminists. Yet friendship ties, political cooperation, and a sense of shared past bind them together.

The Survival of Feminist Commitment

The antifeminist backlash affected how longtime feminists understand themselves and their group. Changes in the external environment have not *determined* changes in feminist collective identity. They have, however, provided the context and events that feminists try to understand and interpret. Despite the hostility and opposition they encounter, the women's movement of the 1960s and 1970s forever marked participants' understanding of the world and their own place in it. Of course, not every participant in the women's movement has retained her radical feminist identity and beliefs to the same degree. A few women repudiate their earlier beliefs, and others vary in how much their outlooks have changed over the years.

Regardless of how women think of themselves and what they believe is true about the world, their daily lives have changed greatly.

It is the conflict between this generation's enduring radical feminism and their limited opportunities for action in a constricting economy and hostile political climate that shaped feminist actions in the 1980s and early 1990s. This loss of political community, for most women, made it more difficult to continue externally oriented activism. Faced with the loss of the community that had sustained their activism, they turned to their jobs and their families, attempting to continue living their lives in a political way.

12 Disengaging from Movements

Bert Klandermans

Maintaining Movement Commitment

Movement commitment does not last by itself. It must be maintained via interaction with the movement and any measure that makes that interaction gratifying helps to maintain commitment. Downton and Wehr (1991) discuss mechanisms of social bonding which movements apply to maintain commitment. Leadership, ideology, organization, rituals, and social relations which make up a friendship network each contribute to sustaining commitment and the most effective is, of course, a combination of all five. These authors refer to the 'common devotion' that results from shared leadership; to group pressure as the primary means of maintaining a social movement's ideology; to 'taking on a role within the organization itself' as a way of increasing people's investment in the organization; to rituals as patterns of behaviour that are repeated over time to strengthen core beliefs of the movement; and to circles of friends that strengthen and maintain individual commitment by putting an individual's beliefs and behaviour under greater scrutiny and social control.

Although not all of them are equally well researched, each of these five mechanisms are known from the literature on union and movement participation as factors which foster people's attachment to movements. For example, it is known from research on union participation that involving members in decision-making processes increases commitment to a union (Klandermans 1986; 1992). For such different groups as the lesbian movement groups (Taylor and Whittier 1995) and a group called Victims of Child Abuse Laws (Fine 1995) it was demonstrated how rituals strengthen the membership's bond to the movement. Unions and other movement organizations have developed all kind of services for their members to make membership more attractive. Selective incentives may seldom be sufficient reasons to participate in a movement, but they do increase commitment.

It is important to emphasize, that at least theoretically, affective, continuance and normative commitment have different sets of determinants. Empirical support for these assumptions may not yet be conclusive, but certainly points in the hypothesized direction. To recapitulate, affective commitment relates to how gratifying the exchange relationship is between a movement and a participant; continuance commitment to the stakes someone has in a movement and the attractiveness of alternatives; and normative commitment refers to a congruence between one's values and those of the movement. Affective commitment more than the other two dimensions seems to be dependent on interactions with the organization one is a member of. The more satisfactory these interactions are, the stronger the affective commitment. Therefore, attempts to make contacts with the movement more satisfactory are instrumental to the maintenance of affective commitment. Continuance commitment is dependent on investments made and the perceived attractiveness of alternatives: the more members have invested and the less attractive alternatives appear to them the stronger their continuance commitment will be. Therefore, sacrifices required from members or other attempts to increase members' investments, derogation of alternatives, and attempts to convince members of the superiority of their own organization are ways to maintain continuance commitment. Normative commitment depends on long term processes of socialization. There is little a movement organization can do in terms of influencing processes of long term socialization, but through frame alignment (Snow et al. 1986) it can try to increase the degree of congruence between the values of the organization and those of the individual.

Despite its efforts, and with the possible exception of some religious sects and underground organizations, it is unlikely for a movement organization to be able to prevent participants from leaving the organization if they are determined to do so. Turnover of supporters is, thus, part and parcel of the life of every movement. Although it is hardly possible to estimate turnover rates in movements, because movements do not carry membership administrations, many movement organizations do administer their membership. In the Netherlands among organizations such as labour unions, Amnesty International, and Greenpeace annual turnover rates of 10 per cent are not unusual. Maintaining commitment may be an important resource to keep people within the movement, but there is of course more. Leaving – like joining – is a process which is controlled by a complex set of determinants and again there is reason to assume that the process will not be identical for various forms of participation. In an attempt to explain why people leave a social movement, I will in the next part of this chapter discuss evidence we collected in the context of research among former participants of the labour movement and the peace movement. What made them decide to leave?

Disengagement

Disengagement can take different forms and not every kind of participation can be discontinued in the same way. Sometimes it is enough to just stay away, sometimes disaffiliation requires some action, and some-times an individual chooses to combine exit and voice and leave the organization in a highly vocal way. For example, those supporters of the Dutch peace movement who in June 1985 stated to our interviewers that they were prepared to sign the petition against cruise missiles the peace movement had announced to organize that fall, but changed their minds needed not to take any action, it sufficed to just refrain from signing (Oegema and Klandermans 1994). On the other hand, those members of IKV-groups who were so disappointed after the Dutch government had decided in November 1985 to deploy cruise missiles, that they wanted to quit the movement, had to actually inform their fellow-activists that they were going to give up and may have encountered some attempts to make them stay. But with the movement being on the wane as witnessed, for example, by an increasing number of people who felt that the movement was declining (Oegema 1993), little of that kind may have occurred and groups may even have collapsed as a whole. Indeed, with some simplification one could say that two years after the government's decision, one third of the local peace groups had collapsed, and, of those groups that were still alive one third of the members had left, while the activity level was down to not even one third of what it had been before. Members of such organizations as Amnesty International, Greenpeace or a union, however, must formally resign by writing a letter to the organization and volunteers in these kind of organizations tend to be looked at almost as personnel with periods of advanced notice if they want to resign. And finally, in a chemical company where we conducted some research for the union, a working-group announced publicly that they were going to change to another union collectively because they disagreed with their union's stand in the negotiations, thus actually turning their defection into an act of protest.

Disengagement need not restrict itself to enduring forms of participation. In fact, movement participation often concerns taking part in a string of events (attending a meeting, taking part in a demonstration, signing a petition). In that context, defection can simply take the form of staying away, or as one could call it *passive defection* or *neglect*. Obviously, this is the form disaffiliation usually takes in the case of once-only activities. In the case of enduring forms of participation, however, disengagement requires explicit steps. Therefore, one could call it *active defection* or *exit*.

What makes people defect? Insufficient gratification in combination with lack of commitment seems the answer. For example, more than 70 per cent of the workers who left their unions did so because they were dissatisfied, frustrated or felt that they weren't treated well by their union (van de Putte 1995). But discontent is not a sufficient condition. Obviously, movement commitment must also decline. Indeed, Moreland and Levine (1982) hypothesized that the level of commitment of those members who eventually leave a group develops in a cyclical way. Initially, it increases until some peak level is reached, then it declines until the level is reached at which people decide to quit.

That raises, of course, the questions of what causes insufficient gratification, and of why commitment declines? Psychologically speaking, it is too simple to assume that disengagement is the opposite of engagement, if only because, in the course of participation, a certain level of commitment develops which interacts with levels of gratification. Moreover, the three forms of commitment do not necessarily reach the same degree. Similarly, they may decline at different rates and for different reasons. Taking the results with regard to union commitment into account, normative commitment presumably is the most stable of the three. Seeing that its roots are in long term socialization processes, this is what one would expect. Continuance commitment seems to be the next in terms of stability. Investments, of course, are made in the past and cannot be changed anymore, but new alternatives may appear and existing alternatives may become more attractive so that continuance commit-

ment may decline. Affective commitment is the most variable of the three. It declines when interaction with the movement or its members becomes less gratifying. Note that under such circumstances the two other forms of commitment may restrain someone from quitting. Affective commitment, continuance commitment and normative commitment balance each other out; and thus the more stable forms of commitment may compensate for a decline in those that are less stable. If a person sees no attractive alternatives, has invested heavily in the organization, and is truly committed to the values and goals of the movement, he or she may decide, that all things considered, he or she would rather continue to share the burden and make the necessary sacrifices than leave.

Thus disengagement, passive and active alike, results from the interaction of insufficient levels of gratification and commitment. In the next few sections, I will further elaborate on this assumption with the help of evidence from our research on the Dutch peace movement and labour movement.

Neglect: Erosion of Support

Neglect is difficult to observe. How to assess how many people could have been at an event staged by a movement? And then, far from all the no-shows are people who have turned away from the movement. Indeed, as I have argued in the previous chapter there are all kinds of reasons why sympathizers end up being no-shows, which have nothing to do with defection. Yet sometimes people who initially support a movement change their minds and become unwilling to support the movement any longer. In this case, the problem isn't that sympathy is not converted into action, but rather that sympathy disappears. *Erosion of support*, as we defined it (Oegema and Klandermans 1994) is the nonparticipation of individuals who, though once prepared to participate, have changed their minds and lost their readiness to take action. Erosion, we hypothesized, occurs when individuals perceive the ratio of costs to benefits as *becoming* less favourable over time, and/or their grievances are no longer pressing, and/or their sympathy for the movement wanes.

Erosion of support occurs in the context of movement decline, changes in public opinion, and issue attention cycles. These settings have to do with the macro-context of movement participation. In fact, resignation in those contexts is most of the time not so much deliberate decisions to withdraw, but natural attrition. Erosion of support, however, can also occur in the context of action mobilization campaigns, as a reverse effect of mobilization. In that context erosion is not so much an additional symptom of movement decline, but a well-considered refusal to participate any longer. In the context of disaffiliation, it is this kind of erosion that I am interested in.

Mobilization campaigns polarize a population – cognitively and socially. *Cognitive* polarization takes place because, in the context of action mobilization, the mobilizing organization's features become especially distinct: goals and means become pronounced, rhetoric changes, and interactions with opponents become confrontational. Opposing parties argue, previously mild debates sharpen, and latitudes of indifference become smaller and smaller. Opponents and countermovement organizations are often extremely skilled in creating caricatures of the movement and sowing doubt in the hearts of half-hearted sympathizers. In other words, action mobilization forces a shift in public discourse: In the media and in informal conversations among citizens, public discourse becomes increasingly focused on campaign issues. As a result, individual citizens and societal actors are forced to take sides.

Action mobilization implies *social* polarization, for it rearranges an individual's social environment into proponents and opponents of the movement. Most individuals live in a fairly homogeneous social environment and will find themselves unambiguously in one camp or the other, but some

may discover that groups, organizations, or parties with which they identify are suddenly in their enemy's camp or that groups and people with whom they feel little affinity have become allies. If they don't like the social identity implied by these new arrangements, they may choose to detach themselves from the movement. In the context of election campaigns, Lazarsfeld, Berelson, and Gaudet (1948: 56–64) referred to this process of conflicting identifications as 'cross pressure' (see also Lane 1964: 197–203). Nothing can illustrate this argument about cross pressure put on individuals better than the following data from the petition-campaign of the peace movement in the Netherlands.

Peace Movement Sympathizers Under Cross Pressure

Close to one-fifth of those interviewees who were prepared to sign the People's Petition against the deployment of cruise missiles changed their minds and indicated that they no longer wanted to sign (I refer to these respondents as 'switchers'). They were predominantly sympathizers who identified with one of the two political parties in power in the government (Christian Democrats and Conservatives), that is to say, the government that was about to decide to deploy the missiles. These individuals reported that their social environments became less supportive during the anti-missile campaign, and because their support was only lukewarm to begin with, the increasingly negative environment undermined their motivation to sign (as shown by a less positive evaluation of the peace movement and less strong rejection of cruise missiles). Interestingly, these individuals reported an increase in the number of their personal conversations about cruise missiles. This increase and the fact that their decision *not* to sign evoked supportive reactions from significant others are evidence of social pressure. I must emphasize, however, that it is the *combined* impact of these factors that accounts for erosion. Identification with one of the two parties in government was not in itself sufficient to produce erosion – after all, a fair proportion of those who identified with one of the parties had wanted to sign and did indeed sign. Rather, the turnabout from sympathizer to switcher was the result of a combination of factors: identification with one of the two parties; the perception that one's environment did not support the movement; plus, initially, the expectation, and later, the experience, of negative reactions from significant others, which weakened an already halfhearted motivation. Comparison of the four communities where we conducted our research, furthermore, highlights the impact of countercampaigns in this regard: As indicated in the previous chapter an intense countercampaign in one community produced high levels of erosion. But on the basis of our current discussion we may add now that apparently, countercampaigns have this effect especially in a context of a nonsupportive social environment.

Important for my argument on the interaction of insufficient gratification and commitment is the observation that during the campaign the initially relatively positive feelings among switchers toward the people in the movement changed into strongly negative ones: by November switchers no longer felt any sympathy for the people in the movement. This factor, together with their already less than positive feelings toward other aspects of the peace movement, contributed to their change of mind.

Exit: Resigning as a Participant

In 1991 we interviewed some 3 000 union members. Twenty months later 195 (6.5 per cent) of them had left their union; in that same period 25 (14 per cent) of the union activists stopped being activists. Resigning one's membership or quitting as a volunteer is different from erosion, if only because one must have entered the organization to begin with to be able to exit it – as a member of a group, a paid-up member of a movement organization, a volunteer, a paid official, and so on. Moreover, resignation is active withdrawal and therefore much more than passive defection or neglect seen as an evaluative move. Why do people resign from a movement that they entered more or less enthusiastically some longer or shorter time ago?

Disappointment, stressful experiences, burnout, attractive alternatives, changed life stage, or simply lost motivation, all may account for resignation. Depending on the position a person is exiting some of these processes and experiences may be more or less important. In this section I will draw from our research among ex-union members, ex-union activists, and ex-peace activists. How do their experiences differ from those who stayed? Although the process of resignation may be different for different movements, I do believe that understanding resignation from a labour union or the peace movement is informative in a more general sense.

Resigning one's union membership. In the Netherlands, union membership is voluntary and so is resigning as a member. As a consequence, being a union member is an individual choice determined by belief in unionism and in the instrumentality of a union membership, and a pro-union climate in one's company (van Rij 1994, 1995; van Rijn 1995). Most workers become union members within five years of entering the labour market. Chances that workers become members further on in their careers are much lower. Half of the new members have left the organization again within five years (van de Putte 1995). Doubts about the instrumentality of union membership, disappointing experiences with the union as a service-organization, and a change in career (becoming unemployed or disabled or changing jobs) were the main reasons given for their resignation. There appear to be two patterns of resignation: (a) 40 per cent of the members who had quit had already been considering leaving the union when we interviewed them a year and a half before. At the time when they still had been members, people who considered leaving had significantly lower levels of commitment than those who did not. Yet, only one-fifth of those who considered leaving, did eventually leave. (b) The remaining 60 per cent had no intention whatsoever of leaving the organization at the time of our first interview, but nevertheless resigned in the period between our two interviews. What happened in that period to both groups? Lack of contact seems to be the main cause of resignation among the first group. Nobody in the organization prevented them from carrying out their intentions. One of our interviewees complained that when he resigned nobody in the organization tried to persuade him to stay. Lack of contact or negatively experienced contacts seemed the main reasons for the second group. In sum, then, disappointment in the organization and low levels of commitment prepare people to resign, but negatively experienced contacts or lack of positively experienced contacts make them actually decide to leave. This evokes the spiral image of mutually reinforcing levels of commitment and participation. Low levels of commitment are, inter alia, caused by lack of positive contacts with the organization. Once levels of commitment are lowering and doubt is sown in the hearts, then, when gratifying contacts still fail to occur the step to resign as a member is easily taken.

Religious sects but also underground organizations are very much aware of these mechanisms, and therefore make serious efforts to maintain both levels of commitment and contacts with the organization very high (Richardson, van der Lans and Derks, 1986; della Porta 1992b). Thus Richardson et al. observe that voluntary disaffiliation in communal religious groups is usually much more difficult for the individual than in noncommunal groups (p. 105; see also Robbins 1988).

Resigning as a union activist. Becoming a union activist requires higher than average

levels of union commitment (Barling et al. 1992), more frequent contact with the union, belief in unionism, feelings of responsibility, and a highly supportive social environment (Nandram 1995; Hoekstra 1994). Unlike their fellow-members, members who become activists find union activism an attractive job to take on. Indeed, many of them are activists for an extended period of time – up to ten years or more. Yet some 35 per cent considered quitting activism and 14 per cent actually did so. The question, of course, is why?

Being a union activist is a time-consuming job. On average activists spend 4 hours per week (half of it of their free time, half of it their working time) on their union, and a fair proportion even 5–10 hours a week. It is not only a time-consuming job, it is also stressful. Union activists can get caught between many fires, company management, union officials, members, colleagues, spouses. As a consequence, many of them report overload and role conflicts. One-third to half of the activists feel that they have more tasks than they can manage. Half to two-thirds report conflicting expectations from their employers and their unions. A quarter to one-third experience contradictory demands from their colleagues, fellow-activists, or constituencies. Yet interestingly, these are not sufficient reason to quit. But, for some activists such stressful experiences produce burnout and burnout *is* a reason to step down, especially in the context of an unsupportive environment (colleagues and/or family members who discourage continuation).

Burnout is a stress reaction typical of people who work with people. It is an overarching concept which covers loss of motivation, cynicism and depersonalization (Maslach 1982). Burnout is typically observed among idealistically motivated volunteers, who start their job with unrealistically high expectations. The question remains, of course, why some activists experience burnout and quit while others don't and remain active. In fact, we do not know much about that subject. But our own research among union activists and peace activists and a modest but interesting study by Gomes and Maslach (1991) suggest some of the answers, that could perhaps stimulate more research into the dynamics underlying long-term commitment to activism.

Research in our own group suggests that a fair proportion of both union activists and peace movement activists experience burn-out – up to 50 per cent if a loose measure of loss of motivation is used and some 10 per cent if a more elaborated but strict measure of burnout is used (Nandram 1995; Struik 1991). Interestingly, it is not so much the costs and tensions associated with participation that produce burnout. That at least is not what the scant research leads one to suspect. Costs, tensions, risks and the like seem to be part of the game in the eyes of the participants. The results presented by both Gomes and Maslach and Struik, seem to suggest that it is high costs or high levels of psychological tension *in combination* with high levels of commitment that produce burnout. It is the inability to be flexible about their work as an activist and to take time to relax that seems to do the damage. In the words of one of Gomes and Maslach's (1991, p. 6) interviewees: 'You keep pushing yourself. There's no limit. It's like an anorexic getting thin – you're never quite thin enough. When you're an activist you're never working hard enough. So you're exhausted and feel like you've got nothing left to give.' Such observations have important implications. Activists are by definition the more committed members of a movement who feel a moral obligation to actively support the movement. In a way this makes them more vulnerable to burnout than other supporters. If on the top of that they are part of a movement culture which conveys the message that no periods of low motivation can be permitted, the already existing susceptibility to burnout is easily carried through. Indeed, Gomes and Maslach suggest that unreasonably high standards of unwavering commitment often backfires, leading eventually to complete withdrawal and that by living a more flexible life activists can increase their overall effectiveness

and function as role models for other activists and enjoy their lives more along the way.

But movement organizations can have a salutary impact. From social psychology we know that social support plays a vital role in people's efforts to cope with stress (Lazarus and Folkman 1984). Our research among union activists suggests that the extent to which stress results in loss of motivation (burnout) also depends on the amount of social support activists experience that they receive from their unions (Hoekstra and Klandermans 1995). Being an activist *is* on many an occasion a taxing experience. Seeing that your movement organization appreciates your hardship and is prepared to support you in your efforts to cope with it, apparently makes a real difference.

Persisters, shifters and terminators. Not every activist who leaves a movement is burned out, however. It is not uncommon to see movements lose momentum, whereupon certain categories of activist start to evacuate the arena. This process has been demonstrated time and again in accounts of movement decline (see for example Oberschall 1978 on the Students for a Democratic Society; Duffhues and Felling 1989 on the Dutch Catholic Movement; or Silverman 1991 on the Canadian Peace Movement). But, to my knowledge our study of defection among activists of the Dutch peace movement in its period of decline was the first attempt to map and understand who left at different times and who stayed and where those who left did go. We called them persisters, shifters and terminators depending on their careers over the six years we investigated. *Persisters* were those who stayed behind as prophetic minorities to maintain the abeyance structure (Taylor 1989) of the peace movement. *Shifters* were those who left the peace movement to become active in another movement and *terminators* were those who gave up political activism altogether.

In 1991, six years after we interviewed our activists for the first time, 87.5 per cent were no longer active in the peace movement. The majority of those who quit did so in the years since our previous interviews in 1987. At that point 28 per cent of the people interviewed had left their group since our interviews in 1985, and 43 per cent of those who stayed had considered leaving. Who were the people who left and why did they leave? First of all, 16 per cent were members of groups that had ceased to exist and so discontinuation of participation in their case was not active defection. The remaining 44 per cent chose to quit while the group was still functioning. Some of them had already left the movement in 1987, while others quit between 1987 and 1991. In both cases we may rightly ask why.

But let me contextualize these dates a little bit first. The year 1985 was the year of the petitionnement against the cruise missiles. The activists had worked themselves to a standstill for the petition, and the total disregard of the outcome by the government was a major blow to many of them, although paradoxically very few had expected a different outcome. Yet, what kept many of them going were the coming elections in 1987 and the confident expectation that the parties in government (Christian Democrats and Conservatives) would be punished for the stand they had taken on cruise missiles. To their dismay nothing of the kind took place and worse perhaps the IKV (the Interdenominational Peace Council, the core organization of the Dutch peace movement in those days) decided not to campaign against the parties in government because it did not want to estrange the churches any further by campaigning against the Christian Democratic Party.

Two blows in a row forced many activists to reconsider their participation in the peace movement. Yet there is no single answer to the question of why they eventually left or stayed. Some of those who left were marginal members to begin with: they had spent relatively little time in activism in 1985, they were less committed to the movement, and had already considered leaving the movement in 1985. Some of those who left were burned out, had lost their faith or felt estranged from the other people in the movement. Others radicalized when the movement refused to adopt more militant strategies. Again others shifted to other movements. And finally, some left for reasons which had nothing to do with any of these factors, but because of personal reasons (family responsibilities, studies, jobs, moved to another city and so on).

Note that none of these explain movement decline. These are reasons why people leave movements, but movement decline is the outcome of both exiting and entering. Indeed, movement decline results from the movement's inability to keep participants *and* its inability to attract new participants to replace those who leave (Cornfield 1986). There are always people leaving movements. Even in 1985 at the Dutch peace movement's peak, activists were leaving, but more activists were joining so the net result was growth. It was only in the years after 1985, after the movement's failure to have an impact on the government and after the start of the talks between Reagan and Gorbachev that the movement lost its attraction and that those quitting outnumbered those joining.

Unlike those who left, *persisters* consisted of activists who were somewhat older, politically less radical, more often active members of church organizations. For most of them the peace movement had been the first movement they had joined in their lives. They spent a relatively large amount of time in the movement and occupied formal positions. When asked why they remained active in the peace movement they referred predominantly to commitment to the group they were part of and the people in that group.

Those who left had lost much of their commitment to the movement when they did so and especially to the IKV, the movement organization they were members of. In their eyes the movement had lost much of its vitality and had little to offer any more. Among those who left, however, *shifters* and *terminators* were of two different kinds and left for different reasons and with different destinations. Shifters had been active in other movements more often than terminators before they engaged in the peace movement. The movements mentioned were movements such as the anti-nuclear power movement, the anti-Vietnam war movement, the environmental movement, the student movement, third world support groups, the women's movement, and so on. Moreover, shifters had more often participated in more militant protests like blockades and site-occupations. Unlike the terminators, the shifters left the movement because they opted for more militant strategies against the policy of the IKV. Shifters spent the most hours a week on the movement, even more than persisters; terminators spent the least. Among shifters being an activist seems to have been a central part of their identity, whereas among terminators activism was a more external affair – though certainly more active than the average citizen, activism did not occupy their lives completely. Among those who stopped because their group ceased to exist, those who quit activism altogether reported feelings of burnout, unlike those who shifted to other movements.

In sum, *persisters* had no history in social movement participation. The peace movement was the first movement they had joined in their lives. They spent a relatively large amount of time in the movement, occupied formal positions in the movement, and continued to be active. They were more often committed to a church than the other types. Of the three they identified most strongly with the peace movement. *Shifters*, on the other hand, have a lifelong history as activists. They were active in other movements before they entered the peace movement and they continued to be active in other movements after they had left the peace movement. Of the three types they had spent the most time on movement activities in the past and in the present. They were active on a broad range of activities, which adds to their image as activists 'pur sang'. *Terminators* who had finally left a still existing group, had a more marginal position

in their groups compared to the others. They spent less time, took less responsibility and identified less with the movement. Those who had stopped because their group had broken up however, quit political activism altogether because of feelings of burnout.

As an epilogue, the international peace movement attempted in 1991 to remobilize to protest the Gulf War, in the Netherlands with surprisingly little success. Persisters, shifters and terminators among the former activists alike took an extremely negative stand on the military intervention, much more so than the general population in the Netherlands. However, while 63 per cent of the persisters took part in actions against the war, this held for only 32 per cent of the shifters and 22 per cent of the terminators. Apparently chances were low that the latter two – disconnected from the peace movement networks as they were – were targeted and mobilized. This was evidenced by the fact that shifters and terminators not only were asked to participate less often, but hardly spoke about the war with any other person still active in the peace movement.

Radicalization.   Our findings regarding the Dutch peace movement draw our attention to the fact that becoming inactive is not the only response to movement decline. Indeed, radicalization has been described as an alternative response to movement decline by several authors (cf. della Porta and Tarrow 1986; Kriesi, Koopmans, Duyvendak and Giugni 1995). Some of the peace activists we interviewed were young, militant and frustrated by the movement's failure and its unwillingness to turn to more militant strategies. They joined other more militant groups of the peace movement or left the peace movement altogether and joined some other more radical protest movement such as the antifascism movement. It is important to note that these activists were already more radical when, at the time, they entered the movement. Most of them joined the movement at its peak as what has been called the 'second generation' of activists. As such they seem to have followed the more general route to radicalization described in the literature on underground organizations (della Porta 1992b). According to this literature 'radicals' in a movement are more militant from the outset. They enter the movement at a later point in the cycle and, then, when the government becomes less responsive or even repressive they further radicalize.

Important for our discussion on sustained participation and defection is the observation that sustained participation can take the form of radicalization. Evidence collected thus far points to the vital role of social networks in this regard (see della Porta 1992a for a compilation). Loyalty to the peer group is an important motive as activists move towards ever-deepening political commitment and make the transition from non-militant groups to the underground. Yet it is important to emphasize that radicalization is not a self-induced process but a response to something, be it movement failure, decline or institutionalization, or state repression. The point is, however, that as a rule only a minority within the larger political subculture responds to such a course of events with radicalization. In della Porta's words, it is 'the second generation of activists, which was socialized to politics after violence has become accepted in larger or smaller wings of the social movement sector, [which] thus accepted radical action as routine' (p. 23). [...] Donatella della Porta (1992b) emphasizes that most participants in underground organizations started their movement careers with more moderate forms of movement participation. Underground organizations evolve when protest repertoires gradually escalate toward violence, because more moderate strategies are deemed to be ineffective or because state repression impresses people as 'absolute injustice'. Kriesi et al. (1995) make the interesting observation that institutionalization of a movement and radicalization often coincide. As movement organizations are co-opted by state agencies or become more moderate, more radical factions break away from the alliance and stage militant forms of

protest. Movement cycles as Tarrow (1989a and b) argued, are triggered by tactical innovation. As long as authorities do not yet know the answer to the new tactics these innovations offset the balance of power between challengers and authorities with movement successes as the result. It is these early successes which not only make for rapid diffusion of protest but for a 'second generation' of activists flocking into the movement organizations associated with the initial successful strategy. As long as the strategy pays off, more militant activists are willing to abide by it, but as the novelty wanes and the authorities learn how to respond, the coalition of moderates and militants breaks down. The militants plead for more radical directions which the moderates are unwilling to take. The militants may then take over the organization and force the moderate majority out – as, for example, the Weathermen did in the case of SDS (Braungart and Braungart 1992) or leave the organization and establish separate groups that stage radical and sometimes violent protest – a process described for the Italian protest cycle of the late sixties and early seventies by della Porta and Tarrow (1986) and for the Dutch and German protest cycles in the seventies and eighties by Kriesi et al. (1995).

The Dutch peace movement provides a typical example of this dynamic. When the movement was in the upswing militant activists flocked into its ranks. This was not always to the enchantment of the original more moderate activists, who often felt overruled by this 'second generation.' As long as the moderate strategy of the movement seemed to be successful in mobilizing mass support the extremes could be held together, but once it became clear that the Dutch government was not impressed at all and key movement organizations such as the IKV were unwilling to resort to more militant strategies the militants started to abandon the ranks again (Klandermans 1994). For a short period they staged more confrontational protest events, but then the talks between Reagan and Gorbachev and the

INF-treaty resulting from it meant the end of the Dutch peace movement as a manifest movement (Oegema 1991).

[…]

References

Barling, Julian, Clive Fullagar and Kevin E. Kelloway. 1992. *The Union and Its Members. A Psychological Approach*. New York/Oxford: Oxford University Press.

Braungart, Richard and Margaret M. Braungart. 1992. 'From Protest to Terrorism: The Case of SDS and the Weathermen.' Pp. 45–78 in della Porta, Donatella (ed.). 'Social Movements and Violence: Participation in Underground Organizations.' *International Social Movement Research*, Vol. 4. Greenwich, Conn.: JAI-Press.

Cornfield, Daniel B. 1986. 'Declining Union Membership in the Post World War II Era: The United Furniture Workers, 1939–1982', *American Journal of Sociology*.

Della Porta, Donatella (ed.). 1992a. 'Social Movements and Violence: Participation in Underground Organizations.' *International Social Movement Research*. Vol. 4. Greenwich, CT: JAI-Press.

Della Porta, Donatella. 1992b. 'Political Socialization in Left-Wing Underground Organizations: Biographies of Italian and German Militants.' Pp. 259–290 in della Porta, Donatella (ed.). 'Social Movements and Violence: Participation in Underground Organizations.' *International Social Movement Research*, Vol. 4. Greenwich, Conn.: JAI-Press.

Della Porta, Donatella and Sidney Tarrow. 1986. 'Unwanted Children: Political Violence and the Cycle of Protest in Italy: 1966–1973.' *European Journal of Political Research*, 14: 607–632.

Downton, James V. and Paul Wehr. 1991. 'Peace Movements: The Role of Commitment and Community in Sustaining Member Participation.' *Research in Social Movements, Conflicts and Change*. Vol. 13: 113–134.

Duffhues, Ton and Albert Felling. 1989. 'The Development, Change, and Decline of the Dutch Catholic Movement.' Pp. 95–117 in Organizing for Change: Social Movement Organizations in Europe and the United States. *International Social Movement Research*, Vol. 2. edited by Bert Klandermans, Greenwich, Conn.: JAI-Press.

Fine, Gary Alan. 1995. 'Public Narration and Group Culture: Discerning Discourse in Social Movements.' Pp. 127–143 in *Social Movements and Culture*, edited by Hank Johnston and Bert Klandermans, Minneapolis/London: University of Minnesota Press/UCL Press.

Gomes, Mary E. and Christina Maslach. 1991. Commitment and Burnout among Political Activists: An In-depth Study. Paper presented at the 14th Annual Meeting of the International Society of Political Psychology. Helsinki, Finland.

Hoekstra, Manon. 1994. CNV-kaderleden: Recrutering en ondersteuning. Amsterdam, Vrije Universiteit.

Hoekstra, Manon and Bert Klandermans. 1995. Role Conflicts of Union Activists: How Social Support Can Help. Paper presented at the Second International Conference on Emerging Union Structures. Stockholm, Sweden.

Klandermans, Bert. 1986. 'Psychology and Trade Union Participation: Joining, Acting, Quitting.' *Journal of Occupational Psychology*, 59: 189–204.

Klandermans, Bert. 1992. 'The Social Construction of Protest and Multi-organizational Fields.' In Aldon Morris and Carol Mueller (eds.) *Frontiers in Social Movement Theory*. New Haven, CT: Yale University Press.

Klandermans, Bert. 1994. 'Transient Identities? Membership Patterns in the Dutch Peace Movement.' Pp. 168–184 in *New Social Movements. From Ideology to Identity*, edited by Enrique Larana, Hank Johnston and Joseph R. Gusfield. Philadelphia: Temple University Press.

Kriesi, Hanspeter, Ruud Koopmans, Jan-Willem Duyvendak and Marco G. Giugni. 1995. *The Politics of New Social Movements in Western Europe. A Comparative Analysis*. Minneapolis/London: University of Minnesota Press/UCL Press.

Lane, Robert E. 1964. *Political Life. Why and How People Get Involved in Politics*. New York: Free Press.

Lazarsfeld, Paul F., Bernard B. Berelson, and Hazel Gaudet. 1948. *The People's Choice*. New York: Columbia University Press.

Lazarus, R.S. and S. Folkman. 1984. *Stress Appraisal and Coping*. New York: Springer.

Maslach, C. 1982. *Burn-out. The Costs of Caring*. Englewood Cliffs: Prentice Hall.

Moreland, Richard L. and John Levine. 1982. 'Socialization in Small Groups: Temporal Changes in Individual-Group Relations', *Advances in Experimental Social Psychology*, 15: 137–192.

Nandram, Sharda. 1995. Het beredeneerd aan – en afmelden als kaderlid. Een studie naar het vrijwilligerswerk binnen de vakbond. Unpublished dissertation, Vrije Universiteit, Amsterdam.

Oberschall, Anthony. 1978. 'The Decline of the 1960's Social Movements,' *Research in Social Movements, Conflict and Change*, Vol. I, Greenwich, Conn.: JAI Press.

Oegema, Dirk. 1991. 'The Dutch Peace Movement, 1977 to 1987.' Pp. 93–149 in *Peace Movements in Western Europe and the United States International Social Movement Research*, Vol. 3 edited by Bert Klandermans. Greenwich, Conn.: JAI-Press.

Oegema, Dirk. 1993. *Tussen petitie en perestroika. De nadagen van de Nederlandse vredesbeweging*. Dissertatie Vrije Universiteit.

Oegema, Dirk and Bert Klandermans. 1994. 'Why Social Movement Sympathizers Don't Participate: Erosion and Non-conversion of Support.' *American Sociological Review*, 59: 703–722.

Richardson, James T., Jan van der Lans and Frans Derks. 1986. 'Leaving and Labeling: Voluntary and Coerced Disaffiliation from Religious Social Movements.' *Research in Social Movements, Conflicts and Change*, 9: 97–126.

Robbins, Thomas. 1988. *Cults, Converts and Charisma*. London: Sage.

Snow, David A., Rochford E. Burke Jr., Steve K. Worden and Robert D. Benford. 1986. 'Frame Alignment Processes, Micro-mobilization and Movement Participation.' *American Sociological Review*, 51: 464–481.

Struik, Anne-Margriet. 1991. Stoppen of doorgaan? Redenen om te stoppen of door te gaan met participeren in de lokale afdelingen van de vredesbeweging. Unpublished thesis, Vrije Universiteit, Amsterdam.

Tarrow, Sidney. 1989a. *Struggle, Politics and Reform: Collective Action, Social Movements and Cycles of Protest*. Cornell University, Western Societies Paper No. 21.

Tarrow, Sidney. 1989b. *Democracy and Disorder; Protest and Politics in Italy. 1965–1975*. Oxford: Oxford University Press.

Taylor, Verta. 1989. Social Movement Continuity: The Women's Movement in Abeyance.' *American Sociological Review*, 54: 761–775.

Taylor, Verta and Nancy E. Whittier. 1995. 'Analytical Approaches to Social Movement Culture: The Culture of the Women's Movement.' Pp. 163–187 in *Social Movements and Culture*, edited by Hank Johnston and Bert Klandermans. Minneapolis/London: University of Minnesota Press/UCL Press.

Van de Putte, Bas. 1995. 'Uit de bond: Bedanken als vakbondslid.' Pp. 87–112 in *De vakbeweging na de welvaartsstaat*. Edited by Bert Klandermans en Jelle Visser, Assen: van Gorcum.

Van Rij, Coen. 1994. To Join or Not to Join. An Event-History Analysis of Trade-Union Membership in the Netherlands. Unpublished Dissertion, Amsterdam: Nimmo.

Van Rij. Coen. 1995. 'Naar de bond: Vakbondsloopbanen en beroepsloopbanen.' Pp. 67–86 in *De vakbeweging na de welvaartsstaat*, edited by Bert Klandermans and Jelle Visser. Assen: van Gorcum.

Van Rijn, Ingrid. 1995. Why Workers Join Unions – and Leave Them. Matters of Money and Mind. Unpublished Dissertation, Free University, Amsterdam.

Part V

What Do Movement Participants Think and Feel?

Introduction

To a non-sociologist, the point of view of movement participants would seem to be the most important issue in understanding social movements. What do they want to accomplish? What do they demand? What kinds of emotions propel or draw them into the street? What goes through their minds? Are these people like the rest of us, or somehow different? In this chapter we try to get inside the heads – but also the hearts – of protestors, to see the world from their point of view. In the end, we all care about something deeply enough that, under the right circumstances, we could be drawn into a movement that addresses it.

One hundred years of scholarship thought this was an important goal, but unfortunately the same scholars assumed they knew what was inside protestors' heads without doing much empirical research to see if they were right. To them protest was such an unusual activity that protestors had to be either immature, mistaken, or irrational. For some of these early theorists, people could be driven mad by crowds, swept up into the motion of the crowd and led to do things they otherwise would not (LeBon, 1895). Others assumed that people must be alienated from their societies in order to engage in such deviant behavior. Still others thought there must be some kind of strange psychological dynamics at work: people joined because they felt personally inadequate and wished to become part of something larger than themselves (Hoffer, 1951); or young people used protest as a way to rebel against their fathers in an Oedipal dynamic (Smelser, 1968). These theories were so dismissive of social movements that a new generation of scholars in the 1960s, who were sympathetic to many of the movements they saw around them, and sometimes participated in, virtually abandoned the effort to look inside the heads of protestors.

The mobilization and then process theorists simply assumed that protestors had rational goals, primarily the pursuit of their own economic, political, and legal interests. By assuming this, they did not have to investigate protestors' points of view any more than their predecessors had. To them, the idea that protestors had strong emotions seemed to admit that protestors were not rational; the idea that protestors needed to do some cultural work to "construct" their grievances and goals seemed to make these less important, more arbitrary. Besides, if a group's interests were structurally determined – by their economic class position, say, or by racism in the laws – it was easy to concentrate on the mobilization of resources and other opportunities for action that most interested these theorists. They assumed the willingness to protest was already there, and only needed an opportunity for expression.

But even at the height of these structural approaches, not all social scientists were willing to give up on the minds of protestors. Kristin Luker was one of these. The chapter of her book, *Abortion and the Politics of Motherhood*, that you will find excerpted below, masterfully lays out the crux of the abortion debate: those on each side see the world in very different ways. They make conflicting assumptions about what mother-hood means, about what a woman's life should be like, about what can be left to chance and what is a valid area for human planning and control. They live in different worlds, and are shocked and outraged when they find out about the other side's world. Luker describes the worldviews of the two sides in largely cognitive terms, but she is also trying to explain the emotional reactions – surprise, outrage, vindictiveness – that result. She does not explicitly theorize about emotions, perhaps afraid that this might make the protestors seem less rational. Her main contribution is to show that both sides are acting reasonably given their visions of the world. (Because of space limitations, we have only reproduced her analysis of the anti-abortion activists.)

In many debates, people on the two sides simply live in different social and cultural worlds, with contrasting experiences, moral values, and beliefs. Neither side is altogether irrational, although each may make claims or hold beliefs that can be tested – and potentially disproved – through scientific evidence. In the years since Luker wrote her book, there has been an explosion of research on the mental worlds of protestors. Frame alignment deals with different ways of viewing the world, different ways of cutting it up in order to put some aspects in the frame and leave others out of it. Collective identity is another tool for dividing up the world in a way that may spur action.

This cultural "constructionist" approach does not suggest that protestors are ir-rational, as mobilization and process theorists sometimes assume. But protestors some-times make mistakes, such as constructing visions of the world that hurt their own cause. These are strategic errors, from which they usually try to learn, rather than a form of irrationality. Jane Mansbridge examines one such malfunction in her chapter on the women's movement. Efforts to pass the ERA (Equal Rights Amendment) depended on volunteers who were there because of their strong beliefs and feelings. As a result they tended to divide the world into "us" (inside the movement) and "them" (everyone else). This is a common temptation for social movements (it was even stronger, Mansbridge says, among the ERA's opponents), but it encourages extreme claims out of touch with the broader public and legislators. It is a common cause of radicalization in movements. This is a dilemma for most movements: whether to rely on exclusivity, purity, and homogeneity in order to reach in, or whether to "water down" the message in order to reach out. Both strategies have their advantages and disadvantages.

Almost all scholars now admit that cultural meanings are an important dimension of social movements, that we need to look at how protestors view the world, and the kind of rhetoric they use to present this vision to others. There are still two large gaps in the literature, however. For all the process theorists' emphasis on the state and other players in a movement's environment, they have done little work to understand these other people's points of view. State bureaucrats, politicians, and police officers also have distinctive worldviews, and also try to persuade others that their arguments and perspec-tives are valid. Few scholars have approached these others from a cultural point of view (for one exception, see Jasper, 1990). This has been left to neighboring fields of research such as that on moral panics (e.g. Goode and Ben-Yehuda, 1994).

Another big gap has been the emotions of protestors. Almost all the cultural work on social movements has been about their cognitive beliefs and moral principles, but an equally important part of culture consists of their feelings about the world, themselves, and each other. A variety of emotions are apparent in Luker's and Mansbridge's selec-tions, as thoughts and feelings are not easily separated.

James Jasper has tried to outline the importance of emotions, especially arguing that many standard explanatory concepts in social-movement research have emotions hidden inside them, unexamined and untheorized. It is often these emotions that are doing the causal work for the concepts, as when "opportunities" provide, most of all, emotional inspiration for protestors. Some emotions, he argues, have to do with people's long-term feelings toward each other, while others are more immediate reactions to events and information. Social movements work hard to shape both of these. Jasper argues that emotions are a part of culture, just like beliefs and moral values. (For more on emotions, see Jasper, 1997; and Goodwin, Jasper, and Polletta, 2001).

As Mansbridge shows, the views and feelings that maintain the enthusiasm of members may not advance a movement's cause with the external world: these are two very different audiences for a social movement's words and actions. In Part VII we will examine the strategic uses of words and images, in other words, how movements employ words and images to attain their goals. There may be tradeoffs between their external effectiveness and their internal solidarity, enthusiasm, and ability to recruit new members.

Discussion Questions

1 What are the core elements of the anti-abortion worldview?
2 What is the tradeoff between reaching in and reaching out, as Mansbridge describes it?
3 What are reactive and affective emotions? What is the relationship between them?
4 Can you think of other examples of the role of emotions in social movements?

13 World Views of Pro- and Anti-Abortion Activists

Kristin Luker

[...] Different beliefs about the roles of the sexes, about the meaning of parenthood, and about human nature are all called into play when the issue is abortion. Abortion, therefore, gives us a rare opportunity to examine closely a set of values that are almost never directly discussed. Because these values apply to spheres of life that are very private (sex) or very diffuse (morality), most people never look at the patterns they form. For this reason the abortion debate has become something that illuminates our deepest, and sometimes our dearest, beliefs.

At the same time, precisely because these values are so rarely discussed overtly, when they are called into question, as they are by the abortion debate, individuals feel that an entire *world view* is under assault. An interesting characteristic of a world view, however, is that the values located within it are so deep and so dear to us that we find it hard to imagine that we even have a "world view" – to us it is just reality – or that anyone else could not share it. By definition, those areas covered by a "world view" are those parts of life we take for granted, never imagine questioning, and cannot envision decent, moral people not sharing.

When an event such as the abortion controversy occurs, which makes it clear that one's world view is not the only one, it is immediately apparent why surprise, outrage, and vindictiveness are the order of the day. Individuals are surprised because for most of them this is the first time their deepest values have been brought to explicit consciousness, much less challenged. They are outraged because these values are so taken for granted that people have no vocabulary with which to discuss the fact that what is at odds is a fundamental view of reality. And they are vindictive because denying that one's opponents are decent, honorable people is one way of distancing oneself from the unsettling thought that there could be legitimate differences of opinion on one's most cherished beliefs.

In the course of our interviews, it became apparent that each side of the abortion debate has an internally coherent and mutually shared view of the world that is tacit, never fully articulated, and, most importantly, completely at odds with the world view held by their opponents. This chapter will examine in turn the world views of first the pro-life activists, then the pro-choice activists to demonstrate the truth of what many of the activists we interviewed asserted: that abortion is just "the tip of the iceberg." To be sure, not every single one of those interrelated values that I have called a "world view" characterized each and every pro-life or pro-choice person interviewed. It is well within the realm of possibility that an activist might find some individual areas where he or she would feel more akin to the values expressed by their opponents than by those on their own side. But taken as a whole, there was enough consistency in the way people on each side talked about the world to warrant the conclusion that each side has its own particular "world view," that these world views tend to be isolated from competing world views, and that forced to choose, most activists would find far more in common with the world view of their side than that of their opponents.

Pro-Life Views of the World

To begin with, pro-life activists believe that men and women are intrinsically different, and this is both a cause and a product of the fact that they have different roles in life. Here are some representative comments from the interviews:

The question is, what is natural for human life and what will make people happy? Now I deplore the oppression of any people, and so I would ipso facto deplore the oppression of women but a lot of things are being interpreted as oppression simply [out of] restless agitation against a natural order that should really be allowed to prevail. The feminist movement has wanted to, as it were, really turn women into men or to kind of de-sex them, and they [feminists] pretend that there are no important differences between men and women. Now when it comes to a woman doing a job, a woman being paid the same rate that a man gets for the same job, I'm very much in favor of all that. [What] I find so disturbing [about] the whole abortion mentality is the idea that family duties – rearing children, managing a home, loving and caring for a husband – are somehow degrading to women. And that's an idea which is very current in our society – that women are not going to find fulfillment until they get out there and start competing for a livelihood with men and talking like men, cursing and whatever, although not all men curse. I don't mean that to sound . . . maybe that's beginning to have an emotional overtone that I didn't want it to have.

[. . .]

[Men and women] were created differently and we're meant to complement each other, and when you get away from our [proper] roles as such, you start obscuring them. That's another part of the confusion that's going on now, people don't know where they stand, they don't know how to act, they don't know where they're coming from, so your psychiatrists' couches are filled with lost souls, with lost people that for a long time now have been gradually led into confusion and don't even know it.

[. . .]

Movement Culture Social movements often have, and self-consciously cultivate, an internal culture that is different from the larger culture in which they are embedded. In other words, participants in movements often share beliefs, norms, ways of working together, forms of decision-making, emotional styles, sexual practices, musical, literary, and sartorial tastes, etc., that are distinct from those of the larger culture. Sometimes movement cultures are warm, jovial, and inviting; sometimes they are austere, serious, and even intimidating. Some are cultivated to attract the greatest number of people; some are intended to attract, or produce, a relatively small number of highly committed people. Distinctive types of movement culture may prove politically effective in certain contexts, yet quite ineffectual in others.

Pro-life activists agree that men and women, as a result of these intrinsic differences, have different roles to play: men are best suited to the public world of work, and women are best suited to rear children, manage homes, and love and care for husbands. Most pro-life activists believe that motherhood – the raising of children and families – is the most fulfilling role that women can have. To be sure, they live in a country where over half of all women work, and they do acknowledge that some women are employed. But when they say (as almost all of them do) that women who work should get equal pay for equal work, they do not mean that women *should* work. On the contrary, they subscribe quite strongly to the traditional belief that women should be wives and mothers *first*. Mothering, in their view, is so demanding that it is a full-time job, and any woman who cannot commit herself fully to it should avoid it entirely.

Well, if that's what you've decided in life, I don't feel that there's anything wrong with not being a wife or mother. If someone wants a career, that's fine. But if you are a mother I think you have an important job to do. I think you're responsible for your home, and I think you're responsible for the children you bring into the world, and you're responsible, as far as you possibly can be, for educating and teaching them; obviously you have to teach them what you believe is right – moral values and responsibilities and rights.... It's a huge job, and you never know how well you're doing until it's too late.

Because pro-life activists see having a family as an emotionally demanding, labor-intensive project, they find it hard to imagine that a woman could put forty hours a week into an outside job and still have time for her husband and children. Equally important, they feel that different kinds of emotional "sets" are called for in the work world and in the home.

[...]

For a woman to shift gears from her emotional role in the home to a competitive role in the office is not only difficult, they argue, but damaging to both men and women, and to their children.

These views on the different nature of men and women and the roles appropriate to each combine to make abortion look wrong three times over. First, it is intrinsically wrong because it takes a human life and what makes women special is their ability to nourish life. Second, it is wrong because *by giving women control over their fertility*, it breaks up an intricate set of social relationships between men and women that has traditionally surrounded (and in the ideal case protected) women and children. Third and finally, abortion is wrong because it fosters and supports a world view that de-emphasizes (and therefore *downgrades*) the traditional roles of men and women. Because these roles have been satisfying ones for pro-life people and because they believe this emotional and social division of labor is both "appropriate and natural," the act of abortion is wrong because it plays havoc with this arrangement of the world. For example, because abortion formally dimin-

ishes male decision-making power, it also diminishes male responsibility. Thus, far from liberating women, pro-life people argue, abortion oppresses them.

[...]

I think I like men enough to know that men still want women to be a little bit feminine and all the rest of it, and I think [pro-choice people] have helped destroy that, I think they've made women into something like the same as men, and we're not. I think we're totally different. I don't think that means that we can't do some jobs they do, but I think we're totally different. I think that they've helped destroy the family because they want to make it so free for the woman to go to work, like with the childcare centers and all the rest of it. You know, now, evidently they're thinking up Social Security for the woman who works in the home and all the rest of it, and I just think that's ridiculous.

Because pro-life people see the world as inherently divided both emotionally and socially into a male sphere and a female sphere, they see the loss of the female sphere as a very deep one indeed. They see tenderness, morality, caring, emotionality, and self-sacrifice as the exclusive province of women; and if women cease to be traditional women, who will do the caring, who will offer the tenderness? A pro-life doctor argued that although women may have suffered from the softening influence they provided for men and for the society as a whole, they had much to gain as well.

I think women's lib is on the wrong track. I think they've got every [possible] gripe and they've always been that way. The women have been the superior people. They're more civilized, they're more unselfish by nature, but now they want to compete with men at being selfish. And so there's nobody to give an example, and what happens is that men become *more* selfish. See, the women used to be an example and they had to take it on the chin for that... but they also benefited from it because we don't want to go back to the cavemen, where you drag the woman around and treat her like nothing. Women were to be protected, respected, and treated like something important.

In this view, everyone loses when traditional roles are lost. Men lose the nurturing that women offer, the nurturing that gently encourages them to give up their potentially destructive and aggressive urges. Women lose the protection and cherishing that men offer. And children lose full-time loving by at least one parent, as well as clear models for their own futures.

These different views about the intrinsic nature of men and women also shape pro-life views about sex. The nineteenth century introduced new terms to describe the two faces of sexual activity, distinguishing between "procreative love," whose goal is reproduction, and "amative love," whose goal is sensual pleasure and mutual enjoyment. [...]

For the pro-life people we talked with, the relative worth of procreative sex and amative sex was clear. In part this is because many of them, being Catholic, accept a natural law doctrine of sex, which holds that a body part is destined to be used for its physiological function. As one man put it: "You're not just given arms and legs for no purpose.... There must be some cause [for sex] and you begin to think, well, it must be for procreation ultimately, and certainly procreation in addition to fostering a loving relationship with your spouse."

In terms of this view, the meaning of sexual experiences is distorted whenever procreation is not intended. Contraception, premarital sex, and infidelity are wrong not only because of their social consequences but also because they strip sexual experience of its meaning. The man just quoted continued to spell out the implications of this position:

Most pro-lifers think that people, regardless of their station in life, ought to be chaste – this means chaste also for married people....I think this is because [pro-lifers], much more than pro-abortion people, are in reverence of sexuality and believe it literally to be a sacred thing. I really think pro-abortion people have a hard time arguing that they think that. [But] if you do think this way, [sex is] something very special, it's the means by which two people can express their union with one another, spiritual and physical. Then you see that it must be protected somehow, by certain forms and conventions, including marriage. [...]

[...]

Because many pro-life people see sex as literally sacred, they are disturbed by values that seem to secularize and profane it. The whole constellation of values that supports amative (or "recreational") sex is seen by them as doing just that. Values that define sexuality as a wholesome physical activity, as healthy as volleyball but somewhat more fun, call into question everything that pro-life people believe in. Sex is sacred because in their world view it has the capacity to be something transcendent – to bring into existence another human life. To routinely eradicate that capacity through premarital sex (in which very few people seek to bring a new life into existence) or through contraception or abortion is to turn the world upside down.

As implied by our discussion so far, the attitudes of pro-life people toward contraception are rooted in their views about the inherent differences between men and women and about the nature and purpose of sexuality. Although the activists we interviewed often pointed out that the pro-life movement is officially neutral on the topic of contraception, this statement does not fully capture the complexity of their views and feelings. Virtually all of them felt very strongly that the pill and the IUD are abortifacients (they may cause the death of a very young embryo) and that passage of a human life law against abortion would also ban the pill and the IUD. Most of them, furthermore, refused to use traditional contraceptives on moral grounds. As a pro-life doctor said:

I think it's quite clear that the IUD is abortifacient 100 percent of the time and the pill is sometimes an abortifacient – it's hard to know just when, so I think we need to treat it as an abortifacient. It's not really that much of an issue with me, [but] I think there's respect for germinal life that is equivalent to a respect for individual life, and if one doesn't respect one's [own] generative capacity, I think one will not respect one's own life or the progeny that one has. So I think there's a spectrum there that begins with one's self and one's generative capacity.

Their stance toward other people's use of contraception is therefore ambivalent. They disapprove of "artificial" contraception, by which they mean use of the condom, the diaphragm, and vaginal spermicides. Many of them feel that the only acceptable "natural" method of birth control is natural family planning (NFP), the modern version of the rhythm method. As one woman said:

I know that some Catholics are split on the contraceptive issue, but I feel contraception is a stopping of the consequences of a natural act, so therefore I don't believe in it. And I have a certain faith [that] if the Lord has sent this problem, He'll send a solution, and so [here is] this natural family planning thing which is beginning to be perfected – well, it's just like I was telling a priest who was beginning to believe in contraceptives, I said there's going to be an answer through natural law.

Developed in large part by Drs. John and Evelyn Billings of Australia, NFP improves upon the older rhythm method by teaching couples to recognize changes in the woman's body that signal the onset of ovulation. NFP is morally acceptable to Catholics because, at least in the original formulation of the method, individuals abstain from sex right before, during, and right after ovulation. Pro-life people who practice NFP argue that it has secular benefits as well. Here is what one woman [...] had to say:

It's really a whole new way of life for a married couple because it demands very close communication, to have to communicate with one another every day about their fertility. I think that's so beautiful. They both learn about one another's bodies, and it creates a tremendous closeness, and I think it demands a very mature love. Because, you know, a husband sees that he can't just demand love from his wife if she is not feeling good, if she is sick. So the same thing applies if she's fertile and they just can't afford to have another child right then. They have to postpone...making love in that fashion during those few days of the cycle....It creates a completely new closeness and respect for one another, and devotion, and they live very much closer and happier, with much more love in their lives.

[...]

Again, several factors interact to reinforce the belief that "artificial" contraception is wrong. To begin with, if the goal of sex is procreation, then contraceptives are by nature wrong, and this is the starting point for many pro-life people. But it is important to remember that this is a personal choice for them, not a matter of unquestioning obedience to doctrine. Many will say that they do not use contraception because their church does not approve; but, in fact, Catholics are increasingly using contraception in patterns similar to those of non-Catholics, and their families (and family ideals) are becoming increasingly hard to distinguish from those of the population at large. Moreover, some data suggest that the most direct representative of the church, the parish priest, is also likely to be tacitly in favor of birth control. Most pro-life people are therefore part of an institution that proclaims a value that most of its members and some of its officials ignore.

When pro-life people use NFP as a form of fertility control, they have not only a different moral rationale but also a different goal than pro-choice people have when they use contraception. They are using it *to time the arrival of children, not to foreclose entirely the possibility of having them.* For them, the risk of pregnancy while using NFP is not only *not a* drawback, it is a positive force that can enhance the marriage. As one man said:

> I'll tell you, when you're using a so-called natural method...you can be incredibly perceptive as to when the fertile period is. But you're not going to be so perceptive that you're going to shut off every pregnancy. You know, there are a lot of things that people just simply do not understand because they've had no experience with them. It's like people who eat in restaurants all the time and have never been on the farm and had a natural meal – you know, where the food comes from the freshly killed animals the same day, from the fields. They don't have any concept of what a natural meal is like, and I think the same thing is true in the sexual area. I think that when you take the step of cutting off all possibility of conception indefinitely, it puts emotional and physical restraints on a relationship that remove some of its most beautiful values....The frame of mind in which you know there might be a conception in the midst of a sex act is quite different from that in which you know there could not be a conception....I don't think that people who are constantly using physical, chemical means of contraception really ever experience the sex act in all of its beauty.

Thus the one thing we commonly assume that everyone wants from a contraceptive – that it be 100 percent reliable and effective – is precisely what pro-life people do *not* want from their method of fertility control.

Pro-life values on the issue of abortion – and by extension on motherhood – are intimately tied to the values we have just illustrated. But they also draw more directly on notions of motherhood (and fatherhood) that are not shared by pro-choice people. This might seem obvious from the fact that pro-life people often account for their own activism by referring to the notion that babies are being murdered in their mothers' wombs. But pro-life feelings about the nature of parenthood draw on other more subtle beliefs as well.

Pro-life people believe that one becomes a parent by *being* a parent; parenthood is for them a "natural" rather than a social role. One is a parent by virtue of having a child, and the values implied by the in-vogue term *parenting* (as in *parenting classes*) are alien to them. The financial and educational preparations for parenthood that pro-choice people see as necessary are seen by pro-life people as a serious distortion of values. Pro-life people fear that when one focuses on job achievement, home owning, and getting money in the bank *before* one has children, children will be seen as barriers to these things. As one pro-life woman put it:

> There has been a very strong attitude that the child represents an obstacle to achievement. Not just that the child is something desirable that you add further down the line...but that the child is an obstacle to a lifestyle that will include the yacht and weekend skiing....A great many couples are opting not to have any children at all because of the portrayal of the child as an obstacle, especially to a woman's career and a two-salary family.

It is worth noting, in this context, that several pro-life women said that few people actually *enjoy* the state of being pregnant. [...]

> I think it's a normal thing [not to enjoy pregnancy]. I think it's also kind of built into the system because everything changes in your body and very often you're sick and...you kind of hate the thought that things are changing, but after you start feeling a little better, you start looking forward to the baby. [But] a lot of the abortions are already done by that time.

> I never wanted to have a baby, I never planned to have five children, I never felt the total joy that comes from being pregnant. I mean I was *sick* for nine months. I mean my general attitude was, "Hell, I'm pregnant again." But I thought pregnancy was a natural part of marriage, and I believed so much in the word *natural*, and so

I loved the babies when they were born. I realized that a lot of women have abortions in that first trimester out of the... physical and psychological fear that they experience, and the depression.... A lot of them will regret having that abortion later on. They work too fast, the doctors advise them too fast. They can outgrow that feeling of fear if they give themselves a chance.

[...]

Clearly, pro-life activists are concerned about the fact that women may seek abortions before they have had a chance to accommodate themselves to the admittedly unpleasant reality of being pregnant.

Pro-life people tacitly assume that the way to upgrade motherhood is to make it an *inclusive* category, that all married people should be (or be willing to be) parents. In particular, women who choose to be in the public world of work should eschew the role of wife and mother, or, if they marry, should be prepared to put the public world of work second to their role as wife and mother. If a man or woman is to be sexually active, they feel, he or she should be married. And if married, one should be prepared to welcome a child whenever it arrives, however inopportune it may seem at the time. In their view, to try to balance a number of competing commitments – especially when parenthood gets shuffled into second or fourth place – is both morally wrong and personally threatening.

Pro-life people also feel very strongly that there is an anti-child sentiment abroad in our society and that this is expressed in the strong cultural norm that families should have only two children.

Well, I think there's always been a problem with kids. But it doesn't seem to me that they're looked on as positively as they used to be. People look down on someone who wants to have more than two kids. Kids are looked on as a burden, [as] work. And they are. [People aren't] looking at the fun side of it and the nice side of it.

[...]

Since one out of every five pro-life activists in this study had six or more children, it is easy to see how these values can seem threatening. In the course of our interviews, a surprising number of activists said they did not feel discriminated against because of their pro-life activities, including their opposition to abortion, but that they did feel socially stigmatized because they had large families. As one woman with several children said: "[My husband,] being a scientist, gets a lot [of questions]. You know, having a large family, it's just for the poor uneducated person, but if you have a doctor's degree and you have a large family, what's wrong with you?" The pro-choice argument that parents must plan their families in order to give their children the best emotional and financial resources therefore sounds like an attack on people with large families. "[People think] children can't possibly make it and be successful if they come from a large family... because you can't give them all the time and energy that they need. Well, first of all, I'm here [at home], I'm not out working, which adds to the amount of time that I can give."

Pro-life values on children therefore represent an intersection of several values we have already discussed. Because pro-life people believe that the purpose of sexuality is to have children, they also believe that one should not plan the exact number and timing of children too carefully, for it is both wrong and foolish to make detailed life plans that depend upon exact control of fertility. Because children will influence life plans more than life plans will influence the number of children, it is also wrong to value one's planned accomplishments – primarily the acquisition of the things money can buy – over the intangible benefits that children can bring. Thus, reasoning backwards, pro-life people object to every step of the pro-choice logic. If one values material things too highly, one will be tempted to try to make detailed plans for acquiring them. If one tries to plan too thoroughly, one will be tempted to use highly effective contraception, which removes the potential of childbearing from a marriage. Once the potential for children is eliminated, the sexual act is distorted (and for religious people, morally wrong), and husbands and wives lose an important bond between them. Finally, when marriage partners who have accepted the logic of these previous steps find that contraception has failed, they are ready and willing to resort to abortion in order to achieve their goals.

This is not to say that pro-life people do not approve of planning. They do. But because of their world view (and their religious faith) they see human planning as having very concrete limits. To them it is a matter of priorities: if individuals want fame, money, and worldly success, then they have every right to pursue them. But if they are sexually active (and married, as they should be if they are sexually active), they have an obligation to subordinate other parts of life to the responsibilities they have taken on by virtue of that activity.

These views about the nature of parenthood and the purpose of sexuality also come together to shape attitudes about premarital sex, particularly among teenagers. Not surprisingly, people who feel that sex should be procreative find premarital sex disturbing. Since the purpose of sex is procreation (or at least "being open to the gift of a new life"), people who are sexually active before marriage are by definition not actively seeking procreation; and in the case of teenagers, they are seldom financially and emotionally prepared to become parents. So for pro-life people, premarital sex is both morally and socially wrong. As one man put it:

> One of my pet peeves is the words *sexually active young person* because I don't equate being sexually active with having sex – that's not my value system. "Sexually active" [sounds like what] any nice Christian teen-aged girl and guy ought to be. I trust that my sexuality is broader than the act of sex.... I want young people to be reinforced so they don't think of themselves as some kind of neuter because [they are not having sex]. And that's what we're doing with sex.

Although they agree that there is a very real problem with teen-aged pregnancy in the United States today, pro-life people believe that the availability of contraception is what encourages teens to have sex in the first place, so they feel that sex education and contraception simply add fuel to the fire.

> I don't think that we would have as many sexually active teenagers, first of all, if contraception weren't readily available and acceptable. And when they use the term *responsible sex*, they don't mean the same thing I do, or that many of us do. *Responsible sex* to people who are in the contraceptive world means use contraception so you don't get pregnant [or catch a] venereal disease, which I've been reading is a false security they've been given.... So there's possibly more of a temptation to participate in sex than we had when we were young, aside from morality, because you just knew that if you were sexually active you might well get pregnant.

[...]

For most pro-life people, the answer to the problems of teen-aged sexuality is *moral* rather than practical: teenagers should be taught that sex before marriage is wrong. For example: "There is really only going to be one way to avoid the tremendous increase in teen-age pregnancies, abortion, unwed mothers, and venereal disease. And that is to try very hard to promote and go back to an ethic that makes a strong standard of abstinence for the unwed – I guess I can't just say teens."

Providing contraception (and abortion) services for teenagers represents a clear threat to pro-life views. A series of legal and policy decisions in the United States as a whole have put teenagers in a rather peculiar situation. A person under the age of eighteen, as a minor, cannot have medical treatment without parental consent, but there are three exceptions to this doctrine. Teenagers may seek contraceptive services, may have an abortion, and may seek treatment for venereal disease without parental consent. As a matter of public policy, the social benefits to these treatments are considered to outweigh the social benefits of requiring parental consent.

Pro-life people believe that this policy acts to cut off parental support and resources precisely when children need them most. They feel that children underestimate how accepting and supportive parents will be and therefore make hasty (and irrevocable) decisions alone. They also think the policy serves to loosen the ties between parent and child. They argue that families have enough pressures on them anyway and that this policy in effect gives children permission to engage in activities whose consequences they cannot fully appreciate – and more to the point, activities their parents disapprove of.

Equally important, pro-life people see public policy in this realm as intruding the state into areas where it does not belong, namely, within the family. From their point of view, the family is both beleaguered and sacred, and any policy that seeks to address the members of a family as separate entities, rather than as an organic whole, is a priori harmful. As one woman put it:

> Even this...family planning is sexual education. It's planned downtown with Planned Parenthood, it's not planned with the parents. So [under] the laws which exist now, the children get contraceptives without parental consent. What it's doing is [creating] a gap in family relationships. And the home and the family...should be the primary source of moral values. Well, if some parents don't take responsibility, then I think it's the responsibility of education *to encourage parents to do it, rather than take it away from them* – which is what has happened [emphasis added].

This pro-life opposition to sex education, however, springs from feelings that are even deeper than a concern about the state intruding itself between members of a family. Their opposition draws on certain strongly felt but rarely articulated beliefs about the nature of morality. Pro-life people as a group subscribe to explicit and well-articulated moral codes. (After all, many of them are veterans of childhood ethics and religion classes.) Morality, for them, is a straightforward and unambiguous set of rules that specify what is moral behavior. Since they believe that these rules originate in a Divine Plan, they see them as transcendent principles, eternally valid regardless of time, cultural setting, and individual belief. "Thou shalt not kill," they argue, is as valid now as it was 2,000 years ago, and the cases to which it applies are still the same. They tend to locate their morality in traditional, ancient codes such as the Ten Commandments and the "Judeo-Christian" law, which have stood the test of time and exist as external standards against which behavior should be judged.

Thus, abortion offends the deepest moral convictions of pro-life people in several ways. To begin with, it breaks a divine law. The Commandment says "Thou shalt not kill." The embryo is human (it is not a member of another species) and alive (it is not dead). Thus, according to the reasoning by syllogism they learned in childhood religion classes, the embryo is a "human life," and taking it clearly breaks one of the Commandments.

Moreover, the logic used by pro-choice advocates (and the Supreme Court) to justify abortion affronts the moral reasoning of pro-life people. For them, either the embryo is a human life or it is not; the concept of an intermediate category – a *potential* human life – seems simply inadmissible. Further, the argument that individuals should arrive at a *personal* decision about the moral status of this intermediate category is as strange to most of them as arguing that individual soldiers in wartime should act according to their own judgment of the wisdom of the army's battle plan.

A professed unwillingness to deviate from a strict moral code naturally has its repercussions in private life. Pro-life people, their rhetoric notwithstanding, do have abortions. Among pro-choice people who were associated with organizations that arrange abortions, it was something of a cliché that pro-life people were believers only until they found themselves with an unwanted pregnancy, which made them more than willing to seek an abortion. When pressed for proof, however, these pro-choice activists retreated behind medical ethics, claiming they could not invade a patient's privacy by actually naming names. Later in the study, however, more persuasive evidence was offered by pro-life people active in Life Centers. These centers, staffed and funded by the pro-life movement, are located in hospitals or other medical settings and offer free pregnancy tests and pregnancy counseling should the pregnancy test prove positive. Although counselors in Life Centers actively encourage women to continue their pregnancies, they do not openly advertise their pro-life stand; they explain only that they provide free pregnancy tests and counseling. But since most places that offer free tests and counseling are also abortion referral centers, many women come to Life Centers in order to get such a referral. Life Center counselors estimate that as many as a third of the women they see go on to have an abortion, even after having had pro-life counseling. Since Life Centers are by definition pro-life, when people who work in them say that pro-life members (and in particular the children of pro-life members) have come into their centers seeking abortions, we can probably believe them. After all, they have nothing to gain by admitting that their own members (and their own children), like the rest of us, sometimes have trouble living up to their ideals.

Thus, pro-life people, like the pro-choice people we will examine shortly, have a consistent, coherent view of the world, notwithstanding the fact that like anyone else, they cannot always bring their behavior in line with their highest ideals. The very coherence of their world view, however, makes clear that abortion, and all it represents, is profoundly unsettling to them. By the same token, the values that pro-life people bring to bear on the abortion issue are deeply threatening to those people active in the pro-choice movement.

[...]

World Views

All these different issues that divide pro-life and pro-choice activists from one another – their views on men and women, sexuality, contraception, and morality – in turn reflect the fact that the two sides have two very different orientations to the world and that these orientations in turn revolve around two very different moral centers. The pro-life world view, notwithstanding the occasional atheist or agnostic attracted to it, is at the core one that centers around God: pro-life activists are on the whole deeply committed to their religious faith and deeply involved with it. A number of important consequences follow.

Because most pro-life people have a deep faith in God, they also believe in the rightness of His plan for the world. They are therefore skeptical about the ability of individual humans to understand, much less control, events that unfold according to a divine, rather than human, blueprint. From their point of view, human attempts at control are simply arrogance, an unwillingness to admit that larger forces than human will determine human fate. One woman made the point clearly: "God is the Creator of life, and I think all sexual activity should be open to that [creation]. That does not mean that you have to have a certain number of children or anything, but it should be open to Him and His will. The contraceptive mentality denies his will, 'It's my will, not your will.' And here again, the selfishness comes in."

This comment grew out of a discussion on contraception, but it also reveals values about human efficacy and its role in a larger world. While individuals can and should control their lives, pro-life people believe they should do so with a humility that understands that a force greater than themselves exists and, furthermore, that unpredicted things can be valuable. A woman who lost two children early in life to a rare genetic defect makes the point: "I didn't plan my son, my third child, and only because I was rather frightened that I might have a problem with another child. But I was certainly delighted when I became pregnant and had him. That's what I mean, I guess I feel that you can't plan everything in life. Some of the nicest things that have happened to me have certainly been the unplanned." Another woman went further: "I think people are foolish to worry about things in the future. The future takes care of itself."

Consequently, from the pro-life point of view, the contemporary movement away from the religious stand, what they see as the "secularization" of society, is at least one part of the troubles of contemporary society. By this they mean at least two things. First, there is the decline in religious commitment, which they feel keenly. But, second, they are also talking about a decline of a common community, a collective sense of what is right and wrong. From their viewpoint, once morality is no longer codified in some central set of rules that all accept and that finds its ultimate justification in the belief in a Supreme Being, then morality becomes a variation of "do your own thing."

For pro-life people, once the belief in a Supreme Being (and by definition a common sense of culture) is lost, a set of consequences emerge that not only creates abortion per se but creates a climate where phenomena such as abortion can flourish. For example, once one no longer believes in an afterlife, then one becomes more this-worldly. As a consequence, one becomes more interested in material goods and develops a world view that evaluates things (and, more importantly, people) in terms of what Marxists would call their "use value." Further, people come to live in the "here-and-now" rather than thinking of this life – and in particular the pain and disappointments of this life – as spiritual training for the next life. When the belief in God (and in an afterlife) are lost, pro-life people feel that human life becomes selfish, unbearably painful, and meaningless.

I think basically a secular nature of our society, that we basically lost our notion of God as being important in our lives... it's hard at times to see that suffering can

make you a better person, so people don't want any part of it.

I think there's a decline in our civilization. Bracken, Dr. Julius Bracken, said that the problem used to be why does God allow suffering or pain or things like that, and now the problem is man's own existence, you know, man believes that he's in a circle of nothingness and therefore there is no such thing as a moral or immoral act.

One of the harshest criticisms pro-life people make about pro-choice people, therefore, which encapsulates their feeling that pro-choice people are too focused on a short-term pragmatic view of the present world rather than on the long-term view of a transcendent world, is that pro-choice people are "utilitarian."

In part, pro-life people are right: the pro-choice world view is not centered around a Divine Being, but rather around a belief in the highest abilities of human beings. For them, reason – the human capacity to use intelligence, rather than faith, to understand and alter the environment – is at the core of their world; for many of them, therefore, religious or spiritual beliefs are restricted only to those areas over which humans have not yet established either knowledge or control: the origin of the universe, the meaning of life, etc. As one pro-choice activist, speaking of her own spiritual beliefs, noted: "What should I call it? Destiny? A Supreme Being? I don't know. I don't worship anything, I don't go anyplace and do anything about it, it's just an awareness that there's a whole area that might be arranging something for me, that I am not arranging myself – though every day I do more about arranging things myself."

Whatever religious values pro-choice people have are subordinated to a belief that individuals live in the here and now and must therefore make decisions in the present about the present. Few pro-choice people expressed clear beliefs in an afterlife so that their time frame includes only the worldly dimension of life. Thus, the entire articulation of their world view focuses them once again on human – rather than divine – capacities and, in particular, on the capacity for reason.

There are important implications to the fact that reason is the centerpiece of the pro-choice universe. First, they are, as their opponents claim, "utilitarian." Without explicitly claiming the heritage of the Scottish moralists, utilitarianism is consonant with many of the pro-choice side's vaguely Protestant beliefs and, more to the point, with their value of rationality and its extensions: control, planning, and fairness. Second, as this heritage implies, they are interventionists. From their point of view, the fact of being the only animal gifted with intellect means that humans should use that intellect to solve the problems of human existence. What the pro-life people see as a humility in the face of a God whose ways are unknowable to mere humans, pro-choice people see as a fatalistic reliance upon a Creator whom humans wishfully endow with magical powers. These same values lead pro-choice people to be skeptical of the claim that certain areas are, or should be, sacrosanct, beyond the reach of human intervention. *Sacred* to them is too close to *sacred cow*, and religion can merge imperceptibly into dogma, where the church could persecute Galileo because science was too threatening both to an old way of thinking of things and an established power structure. Truth, for pro-choice people, must always take precedence over faith.

Because of their faith in the human ability to discover truth, pro-choice people are on the whole optimistic about "human nature." While in their more despairing moments they can agree with the pro-life diagnosis of malaise in contemporary American life – that "things fall apart and the center does not hold" in Yeats' terms – they emphatically disagree upon the solution. Rather than advocate what they see as a retreat from the present, an attempt to re-create idealized images of the past, they would argue that "the Lord helps those who help themselves" and that people should rally to the task of applying human ingenuity to the problems that surround us.

In consequence, pro-choice people do not see suffering as either ennobling or as spiritual discipline. In fact, they see it as stupid, as a waste, and as a failure, particularly when technology exists to eliminate it. While some problems are not at present amenable to human control, pro-choice people will admit, they are sure to fall to the march of human progress. Thus, not only can humans "play God," it is, in an ironic sort of way, what they owe their Creator, if they have one: given the ability to alter Nature, it is immoral not to do so, especially when those activities will diminish human pain.

All of these values come home for pro-choice people when they talk about the *quality of life*. By this term they mean a number of things. In part they use this phrase as a short-hand way of indicating that they think of *life* as consisting of social as well as biological dimensions. The embryo, for example, is only a potential person to them in large part because it has not yet begun to have a social dimension to its life, only a physical one. In corollary, a pregnant woman's rights, being both social and physical, transcend those of the embryo. This view is rooted in their values about reason: biological life is physical and of the body. Humans share physical life with all other living beings, but reason is the gift of humans alone. Thus social life, which exists only by virtue of the human capacity for reason, is the more valuable dimension of life for pro-choice people. (This viewpoint explains in part why many pro-choice people find unfathomable the question of "when does life begin?" For them it is obvious: physical life began only once, most probably when the "cosmic soup" yielded its first complex amino acids, the forerunners of DNA; social life begins at "viability" when the embryo can live – and begin to form social relationships – outside of the womb.)

But for pro-life people, this line of reasoning is ominous. If social life is more important than physical life, it then follows that people may be ranked by the value of their social contributions, thus making invidious distinctions among individuals. In contrast, if physical life is valued because it is a gift from the Creator, then no mere human can make claim to evaluate among the gifts with which various individuals are born. A view that the physical or genetic dimension of life is paramount – that all who are born genetically human are, a priori, persons – means that at some level all are equal. A hopelessly damaged newborn is, on this level, as equally deserving of social resources as anyone else. What pro-life people fear is that if the pro-choice view of the world is adopted, then those who are less socially *productive* may be deemed less socially *valuable*. For pro-life people, many of whom have situational reasons to fear how pro-choice people would assign them a social price tag, such a prospect is a nightmare.

The phrase *quality of life* evokes for pro-choice people a pleasing vista of the human intellect directed to resolving the complicated problems of life – the urge for knowledge used to tame sickness, poverty, inequality, and other ills of humankind. To pro-life people, in contrast, precisely because it is focused on the here and now and actively rejects the sacred and the transcendent, it evokes the image of Nazi Germany where the "devalued" weak are sacrificed to enlarge the comfort of the powerful.

Thus, in similar ways, both pro-life and pro-choice world views founder on the same rock, that of assuming that others do (or must or should) share the same values. Pro-life people assume that all good people should follow God's teachings, and moreover they assume that most good-minded people would agree in the main as to what God's teachings actually are. (This conveniently overlooks such things as wars of religion, which are usually caused by differences of opinion on just such matters.) Pro-choice people, in their turn, because they value reason, assume that most reasonable people will come to similar solutions when confronted with similar problems. The paradox of utilitarianism, that one person's good may be another person's evil, as in the case of the pro-life belief that a too-effective contraceptive is a bad thing, is not something they can easily envisage, much less confront.

What neither of these points of view fully appreciates is that neither religion nor reason is static, self-evident, or "out there." Reasonable people who are located in very different parts of the social world find themselves differentially exposed to diverse realities, and this differential exposure leads each of them to come up with different – but often equally reasonable – constructions of the world. Similarly, even deeply devout religious people, because they too are located in different parts of the social world and, furthermore, come from different religious and cultural traditions, can disagree about what God's will is in any particular situation. When combined with the fact that attitudes toward abortion rest on these deep, rarely examined notions about the world, it is unambiguously clear why the abortion debate is so heated and why the chances for rational discussion, reasoned arguments, and mutual accommodation are so slim.

Biography

A brief biography of Joan Andrews, written by the editors of this volume, can be found on page 376.

14 Ideological Purity in the Women's Movement

Jane J. Mansbridge

Like all social movements, both American feminism and Schlafly's brand of political fundamentalism faced a basic tension between reaching out and reaching in. To change the world, a movement must include as many people as possible. But to attract devoted activists, a movement must often promote a sense of exclusivity – "we few, we happy few, we band of brothers."

If many forces in the ERA movement promoted inclusivity, other forces promoted the separatism, concern with purity, and homogeneity of thought associated with exclusivity. Despite their inclusive ideals, activists working for the ERA tended to maintain their own morale by dividing the world into "us" and "them," seeking doctrinal purity, and rejecting interpretations of reality that did not fit their preconceptions. The fundamentalist churches were, if anything, even more subject to this kind of tension, since they believed that impurity could lead not just to social exclusion but to personal damnation.

Us Against Them

Rosabeth Moss Kanter's study of nineteenth-century communes found that when communes institutionalized exclusivity they were more likely to survive. The most successful communes discouraged relationships outside the group through geographic isolation, economic self-sufficiency, a special language and style of dress, and rules that controlled members' and outsiders' movements across the boundaries of the community. Three-quarters of Kanter's successful communes did not recognize the traditional

American patriotic holidays. Half read no outside newspapers. More than a quarter specifically characterized the outside world as wicked.

Although social movements are usually inclusive in their conscious aims, building an organization on belief in a principle can, when the world refuses to go along with that principle, produce a deep sense of "us" against "them." When two movements organized with ideological incentives are pitted against each other, reality will provide plenty of temptations to see the opposition as evil incarnate. For an opponent of the ERA, a photograph of two lesbians in cut-off shorts embracing in the middle of an ERA demonstration triggered the perception of evil. For proponents, a legislator's characterization of them as "bra-less, brain-less broads," patronizingly repeated time after time, called forth equally intense hatred. Opponents' images of "libbers" and an "East Coast Establishment media blitz," and proponents' images of "right-wing crazies" or legislators conniving to kill the ERA in "smoke-filled rooms" all had elements of truth in them. The process of struggle accentuated the gulf. As a proponent, I found it impossible to sit in a legislative gallery, hear even a few legislators joke as they voted down equal rights for women, and not hate. And I have rarely seen such concentrated hate as I saw on the faces of some women in red when I stepped into an elevator in the state capitol on lobbying day wearing my green "ERA YES" button.

Like nationalism and some forms of religious conversion, some kinds of political activity engender a transformation of self that requires reconfiguring the world into camps of enemies and friends. Running for office or campaigning for social legislation is likely to have this effect. Other kinds of political activity, like holding political office, require people to break down such boundaries, or at least make them more subtle. The movements for and against the ERA had the same effects on participants as most struggles over social legislation, solidifying in-group ties without creating lines of dialogue with the "other." Political comradeship within the groups arose from mutual dependence and mutual respect, as proponents worked together late into the night preparing testimony or opponents piled into rented vans at 6:00 in the morning to nego-

tiate icy roads to the state capitol. Both sides also demanded sacrifice. The conviction that "if I don't do this, the cause may fail" brought many women for the first time in their lives to write out checks for fifty, one hundred, five hundred, or even a thousand dollars for a political cause. The people who experienced that solidarity and made that sacrifice often began to think of themselves as political beings, helping produce – not simply consume – the politics that affected them. But this admirable result frequently depended on a Manichaean vision of "us" and "them" to bring it about.

Doctrinal Purity

Once the necessary distinction has been made between "us" and "them," it follows that the less you are like "them," the more you are one of "us." Becoming "us" involves purifying your beliefs. The dynamic that binds activists to the movement entails idealism, radicalism, and exclusion. It works against the inclusive policy of accommodation and reform.

In organizations that have chosen ideological exclusivity as a means for building community, leaders are likely to be even more radical than their followers, for the leaders now serve not as intermediaries and ambassadors to the outside world but as moral exemplars whose function is inspiration. While traditional organizational theory predicts that leaders will grow more conservative than the rank and file, both Ellie Smeal of NOW and Phyllis Schlafly of STOP ERA – although undoubtedly less radical than some of their most active volunteers – were almost certainly further apart in their views than were the majority of people who gave time or money to their respective movements.

Neither the pro- nor the anti-ERA movement seems to have pushed its adherents strongly toward internal disputes over purity, but some pressures were there on both sides. Among the proponents, for example, these pressures came out in the lawyers' decisions on combat and abortion.

> **Cross-Cutting Ties** In some social contexts (institutions, cities, countries), people who belong to one social group (e.g., an economic class, ethnicity, religion, gender, etc.) have ongoing and even intimate social ties or connections with people in other types of groups. Irish-Americans, for example, may have friends, lovers, co-workers, roommates, and so forth who are Italian-American, African-American, etc. Their social ties, in other words, "cut across" two or more groups or categories of people. Other things being equal, these cross-cutting ties tend to reduce the likelihood that incompatible or contradictory identities, ideas, values, or interests will form among the groups in question; these ties thereby reduce the likelihood of group conflict. It is difficult (although not impossible) to feel that a group of people with whom you regularly and intimately associate are your enemies; you may have disagreements with such people, but you are likely to feel that such disagreements can be resolved through dialogue and compromise. By contrast, when no such cross-cutting ties exist, and religious groups (for example) only associate "with their own kind," then distinctive identities, ideas, values, and interests are more likely to emerge among such religious groups, with the result that sectarian conflict is also more likely. Groups with whom one seldom if ever associates are likely to seem more different, foreign, and inscrutable. In extreme cases, some groups may not even be considered human beings by others. In such instances, obviously, disagreements are likely to result in open conflict and even violence.

Homogeneity

In groups that are building a sense of community, like attracts like, and potential deviants try to suppress their differences in order to belong. The internal homogeneity that the members create binds them to one another more fully.

The very inclusivity of a social movement paradoxically accentuates homogeneity. A social movement, unlike an organization, has no formal entrance requirements or certification of membership; its members define themselves and identify themselves to one another solely in terms of their ideology. You are a member of a movement to the degree that you believe what the other people in the movement believe. Once you stop so believing you are, by definition, no longer "in" the movement. All members know this, at least subconsciously. They also know that they have "joined" the movement in part to have the support of like-minded people – to make and keep friends. If deviating too far from the movement's current ideology will cause you to lose your friends, you will only move in this direction when you already feel estranged, or when you feel you have "no choice."

Among proponents, the pressure to conform was probably strongest in the radical women's movement, where "betraying the women's movement" by not taking the correct ideological line could be "as terrifying as betrayal of your family, your closest friends." But even in the most conservative branch of the ERA movement in Illinois, ERA Illinois, I felt nervous about suggesting that we include in our 1982 testimony before the Illinois legislature a statement supporting the "deferential" interpretation on the military, which I had just discovered. As it turned out, the board of directors had no problem with my suggestion. My nervousness came from self-censorship and from fantasies of rejection, not from an accurate projection of what would happen. But inchoate fears of this kind are common among those whose particular access to information or experience leads them to contemplate deviations from "the party line." I have no direct evidence regarding such pressures among opponents, but it is hard to imagine that they were not equally intense. Indeed, since active opponents were by and large more rooted in small communities where they expected to spend the rest of their lives, and many were often more committed to their churches than feminists were to "the movement," the costs of challenging their co-workers were probably even higher.

Turning Inward: An Iron Law?

If social movements cannot reward their members materially, and if the activists must find their rewards in ideology and solidarity, we might expect such movements to follow an "iron law of involution," by which "every social movement tends to splinter into sects, unless it wins quickly, in which case it turns into a collection of institutions."

The socialist movement in America illustrates this iron law. As Daniel Bell argues, it foundered on the tension between inclusion and exclusion. The labor movement turned into an institution, while the Communist party turned into a sect. The party became ideologically exclusive, the very commitment of its members stemming in part from "that inward dread of not proving sufficiently revolutionary which hounds us all." Its members also became social isolates, cut off from others, not only because others ostracized them but also because they needed isolation to avoid confronting the wide gap between their revolutionary expectations and their actual achievements. Their intense political commitment left little room for their jobs or families, and they felt uncomfortable with people who did not share their mission. Said one member,

When you are in the party for many years, as I have been, you develop warm bonds with your comrades. I have had a few friends outside the party, but they can never be as close friends. They can't be friends at all if they are hostile to the party. You never feel as comfortable with an outsider as you do with your comrades.

All committed activists sense that their political commitment sets them apart from the great majority of citizens. The extreme case occurs when activism requires illegal action – as in Resist, a draft resistance group founded in 1967–1968, whose members had all committed the illegal act of burning or turning in a draft card. With that one act the resisters became outlaws. But processes more common to all activists intensified their estrangement from the outside world. The resisters tended to feel both moral superiority and anger at having risked a great deal for the welfare of others without personally receiving anything in return. As politics took up more of their identities, ideological disagreements with their former friends became harder to stand. Finally, their decreasing interest in nonpolitical activities slowly eroded any ties outside the movement world, while they built up an almost religious sense of community within.

In the Black Power movement, activists struggled over the extent to which blacks should work with whites; in the Pentecostal movement, religious groups struggled over "whether or not a 'Spirit-filled' Christian should come out of the 'whore of Babylon' or remain within and try to redeem her." In the women's movement, one activist concluded sadly of another group, "We saw them as not being as pure as we. They still exist, and we don't."

The strengths of exclusivity are the strengths of a committed cadre. Exclusivity can produce a personal life that is intense, deep, and meaningful. Shared commitment and assumptions can also engender penetrating intellectual discourse, for the very intensity of the commitment urges one beyond both platitude and party line. Organizationally, an exclusive group can count on its members to do what needs doing.

By contrast, the strength of inclusivity is "the strength of weak ties." Personally, a loose and inclusive organization makes possible the ego-strengthening retreat into apolitical sanctuaries like the family. Intellectually, it allows friendships that run the "whole gamut of political views." Organizationally, it allows a host of different ties to the larger community. William Kornhauser, comparing the political and personal lives of liberal political activists affiliated with Americans for Democratic Action to those of Communist party members, concludes that "a liberal group finds strength in the multiple ties its members establish in the community." Mark Granovetter, comparing two communities resisting urban renewal – one a tightly knit Italian neighborhood of long standing, the other a more loosely organized aggregation – argues that one reason the loose aggregation succeeded while the tightly knit community failed may have been that members of less exclusive and less tightly knit neighborhoods could use their many weak contacts with diverse organizations and individuals outside the neighborhood to further the neighborhood's interests. As with contacts, so with information. Granovetter demonstrates that there is a

> structural tendency for those to whom one is only *weakly* tied, to have better access to…information one does not already have. Acquaintances, as compared to close friends, are more prone to move in different circles than one's self. Those to whom one is closest are likely to have the greatest overlap in contact with those one already knows, so that the information to which they are privy is likely to be much the same as that which one already has.

So too with thinking itself. Acquaintances with different views and different structural roles can force us to articulate our hidden expectations and understandings, and even, on occasion, to negotiate, reflect, and make choices – all processes central to thinking well.

Escaping the Iron Law

What conditions tend to turn a movement into a sect? Or, if we assume that the dynamics of recruiting are such as to turn every movement inward, what conditions impede this natural tendency toward exclusivity? The history of the ERA movement suggests three conditions: the likelihood of winning, the dependence of the movement on actors in different structural roles, and an explicitly inclusive ideology.

The ERA came extremely close to being ratified. Although no state ratified after 1977, the votes came so close in several states between 1977 and 1982 that even the sponsors were not able to predict beforehand which way the legislature would go. These conditions should have maximized the impact of political realism, by reducing both overconfidence and the temptation of the loser to retreat to purity. Because the goal of this particular social movement was to ratify a U.S. constitutional amendment, which requires a supermajority, the usual pressures for inclusivity – and therefore heterogeneity – in membership were increased.

The decentralized nature of the ERA movement also led to a division of labor between different states, between different communities within each state and between different constituencies on both the local and state levels. One organization within the movement would attract a more conservative membership, another a more radical one. Internally, this decentralization let members of each group feel more comfortable with one another. Externally, the division of labor made possible a "Mutt and Jeff" (or "good cop/bad cop") act, in which the more conservative organization could tell relevant power holders that if certain concessions were not forthcoming it could not hold back the radicals much longer. But most important, the division of labor fostered distinctive perspectives that had the effect of undermining any unifying ideology. "Hydra-headed" organizationally, the movement was also "fly-eyed." It depended on many different kinds of individual actors – homemakers, secretaries, executives, writers, lawyers, academics, and politicians – almost all of whom remained in their other roles while working for the ERA. The dis-

tinctive incentives and exposures of their other roles gave these different members of the movement slightly different views of the common struggle, and these views produced different insights.

Finally, the ideology of the women's movement itself is inclusive, stressing the sisterhood of women of differing classes, ethnicities, regions, and traditional politics. That ideology requires women to listen to one another, on the grounds that each woman's story has its own validity and right to be heard. The first, simple statement of that ideology is that all women are sisters and fundamentally "on the same side." They are on the same side no matter what their class, their upbringing, or their politics, because structurally they have similar relationships to the world, and particularly to men. The "consciousness-raising group" of the women's movement typically did its work by allowing women who habitually sorted themselves by class, mores, and politics to see their similarities as women. It allowed each woman to hear other women talking about their lives as they had lived them, and to feel compassion for scenes never lived through, joy for memories mutually held but previously thought trivial, and the anger of recognition at events not shared until that moment. The movement's assertion that the "personal is political" means, among other things, that when women speak of what is important to them, those experiences often derive from common experiences in a world where men have most of the power. This means that it is a mistake not to listen and try to make sense of what other women say, even when one disagrees with them. In the ERA movement, no matter how involved any particular set of activists became with trying to persuade a legislator, organize a demonstration, or write a brief, the inclusive ideology of the broader women's movement was always there to push, gently, toward a strategy of listening to what other women – even in the opposition – had to say.

These forces in the ERA movement meant that if any movement could escape the iron law of involution, this would have been the one. That it did not fully escape means that no organization based on voluntary membership is likely to do so.

Social movements become "movements" only by building on common values and common dreams. They may hope to include everyone someday, but they cannot, by definition, do so today. To survive, they must balance the conflicting claims of pragmatism and purity, reaching out and turning in. Perhaps no social movement can maintain this balance for long, which may be why social movements are usually transitory. But some certainly maintain it longer than others, and exert more influence as a result. While the feminist movement that began in the late 1960s was often out of touch with middle-of-the-road legislators and with the millions of Americans whom they represented, it maintained a far better balance between reaching out and turning in than any of the other movements that began in the 1960s. This may help explain its longevity. Whether the conservative antifeminist movement of the 1970s and 1980s, with its renewed emphasis on traditional family values and sexual behavior, will prove equally resilient remains to be seen.

15 The Emotions of Protest

James M. Jasper

Emotions have disappeared from models of protest. When crowds and collective behavior, not social movements and collective action, were the lens for studying protest, emotions were central. Frustration, anger, alienation, and anomie were not merely an incidental characteristic but the motivation and explanation of protest. Such images were displaced 30 years ago by metaphors of rational economic calculators and purposive formal organizations, for whom social movements were just one more means of pursuing desired ends. In the last 15 years, these instrumental metaphors have themselves been challenged from a cultural perspective in which protestors have a variety of reasons for pursuing a range of goals, not all of them material advantages for individuals or groups. Goals, interests, even strategies and political opportunities are increasingly viewed as embedded in and defined by cultural meanings and practices.

In this wave of culturally oriented research, considerable respect has still been paid to the rationality of protestors. They know what they want, varied though this may be, and they set out to get it. This respect may be the reason that most cultural researchers, although harking back to collective-behavior traditions in some ways, have avoided the issue of emotions. A variety of key cultural concepts – identity, injustice frames, cognitive liberation, and others – have been treated as though they were entirely cognitive, as though their highly charged emotional dimensions hardly mattered. If protestors are emotional, does that make them irrational? Recent researchers seem to fear – wrongly – that it does.

Emotions pervade all social life, social movements included. The most prosaic daily routines, seemingly neutral, can provoke violent emotional responses when interrupted. Unusual actions probably involve even more, and more complex, feelings. Not only are emotions part of our responses to events, but they also – in the form of deep affective attachments – shape the goals of our actions. There are positive emotions and negative ones, admirable and despicable ones, public and hidden ones. Without them, there might be no social action at all. To categorize them as rational or irrational (much less to dismiss them all as interferences with rationality) is deeply wrongheaded. We can categorize protestors' actions, usually *post hoc*, as strategically effective or mistaken, but rarely as irrational or rational. Even the proverbial Southern sheriff who flies into a rage and hits a peaceful civil rights demonstrator, although acting upon hateful and extreme emotions, has probably made a strategic error (at least when caught on camera) more than he has acted irrationally.

Emotion Management Political activists typically try hard to induce emotions that they think are good for their movement or cause and to prevent emotions or moods that they think are bad. At their planning meetings and at protest events themselves, activists often work hard at generating such emotions as outrage, excitement, joy, guilt, hope for the future, solidarity, and/or commitment to the cause. Emotion management may also involve attempts to mitigate fear, depression, hopelessness, and boredom. Activists may also try to calm down especially angry people, whose behavior may cause problems for the movement, especially if it professes nonviolent principles.

Emotions are as much a part of culture as cognitive understandings and moral visions are, and all social life occurs in and through culture. We are socialized (or not socialized) into appropriate feelings in the same way we learn or do not learn our local culture's beliefs and values. There is some individual variation in all three aspects of culture, and we recognize deviant emotional reactions and attachments as readily as deviant beliefs. As with the rest of culture, there is tension between the public, systematic expectations concerning emotional expression, and the individual innovations and idiosyncrasies that diverge from them. Emotions are learned and controlled through social interaction, although never with complete effectiveness.

In what follows, I argue for the centrality of emotions for understanding one corner of social life: the collective, concerted efforts to change some aspect of a society that we label social movements. I first discuss what emotions are, in particular the degree to which they are defined by context and culture in the same way that cognitive meanings are. I distinguish emotions that are transitory responses to external events and new information (such as anger, indignation, or fear) from underlying positive and negative affects (such as loyalties to or fears of groups, individuals, places, symbols, and moral principles) that help shape these responses. Then I distinguish emotions according to the social context that creates and shapes them, especially between those that form outside an organized movement and those that occur inside it. The former group primarily includes emotions that might lead individuals to join or even found protest groups; the latter, emotions that spur action, maintain the group, or lead to its demise.

[...]

What Are Emotions?

Emotions do not merely accompany our deepest desires and satisfactions, they constitute them, permeating our ideas, identities, and interests. They are, in Collins' words (1990:28), "the 'glue' of solidarity – and what mobilizes conflict." Recently, sociologists have rediscovered emotions, although they have yet to integrate them into much empirical research outside of social psychology. One aspect of this renewal has been an emphasis on how emotions are culturally constructed (and hence linked to cognitive appraisals) rather than being automatic somatic responses (and hence potentially less controllable, or less "rational"). To the extent that emotions depend on cognitions, they more clearly allow learning and adaptation to one's environment, i.e., rationality.

Older schools of thought viewed emotions as natural sensations – "feelings" – originating in the body, beyond the control of those experiencing them. In common parlance, people are said to be "seized by emotion," to be "in the grip" of passions such as jealousy or anger. The irrefutable bodily symptoms of emotions, whether increased adrenaline or redness in the face, are taken to be the emotions themselves, to which we then attach names. Emotions, in this view, thwart our wiser intentions and prevent effective actions. No doubt this sometimes happens, as in the case of the Southern sheriff. But people make cognitive mistakes as easily as emotional ones, and more strategic battles have been lost, in all likelihood, by mistaken cognitions than by mistaken emotions. Mistakes, furthermore, are not necessarily irrational, just mistaken.

Constructionists respond by pointing to the considerable interpretation that our bodily states require as well as to the cross-cultural diversity of emotions. Rather than being a simple set of inner sensations (are the physical sensations that accompany annoyance and indignation, for example, distinguishable?), an emotion is an action or state of mind that makes sense only in particular circumstances. Averill (1980:308) describes emotions as transitory social roles, which he in turn defines as "a socially prescribed set of responses to be followed by a person in a given situation." The rules governing the response consist of "social norms or shared expectations regarding appropriate behavior."

In the constructionist view, then, emotions are constituted more by shared social meanings than automatic physiological states. Some theorists argue that bodily changes are there, but must be interpreted before they can become emotions; others take the more extreme view that bodies change only in response to cultural settings associated with particular emotions. Evidence of the many cross-cultural differences in emotions seems to support the latter position. Nonetheless, the apparent existence of several universals, especially facial expressions of surprise, anger, and fear, suggests a weaker constructionist model in which, while some or most of any emotion is socially constructed, there is some natural expression involved as well. Thoits (1989:320) distinguishes a strong version of constructionism – there are no basic, universal emotions – from a weaker version – basic emotions may exist but explain little. Primary emotions such as anger and surprise may be more universal and tied directly to bodily states, whereas complex secondary ones such as compassion or shame may depend more on cultural context. It is possible as well that primary emotions are more important in face-to-face settings – of the kind many symbolic interactionists study – than in ongoing political processes, where secondary emotions such as outrage or pride may be more influential.

Both the strong and the weak forms of constructionism tie emotions to cognition in several ways. Emotions involve beliefs and assumptions open to cognitive persuasion. We often can be talked out of our anger on the grounds that it is too extreme a response, or that we are misinformed. The plots of many plays or novels, from Shakespeare to Hardy, depend on "mistaken" emotions derived from incorrect information. Because emotions normally have objects (we are afraid *of* something), they depend at least partly on cognitive understandings and appraisals of those objects.

This allows learning and adaptation. If emotions are tied to beliefs and contexts, they are also partly open to debate as to whether they are appropriate or not at a given time. Because there are cultural rules governing them, emotions can usually be labeled as normal or deviant. Even our gut-level emotions, if they exist, are conditioned by our expectations, which in turn are derived from knowledge about appropriate conditions in the world.

Emotions are also tied to moral values, often arising from perceived infractions of moral rules. According to Harré (1986:6), "the study of emotions like envy (and jealousy) will require careful attention to the details of local systems of rights and obligations, of criteria of value and so on. In short, these emotions cannot seriously be studied without attention to the local moral order." One context in which emotions unfold is that of common human narratives, or what de Sousa (1987) calls "paradigm scenarios." Just as the death of a friend leads one through several predictable emotional stages, other unexpected and unpleasant events – such as a proposal for a nearby nuclear power plant – may lead to surprise, sadness, anger, then outrage. Solomon (1976) even describes the roles that accompany these plots: with anger, you are the judge and the other person is the defendant; with contempt, you are pure and blameless while the other person is vile and despicable. Each emotion implies a family of terms to hurl at your opponent. A social movement organizer deploys different language and arouses different emotions in her listeners if she paints her opponents as inherently malevolent or well-meaning but ignorant.

Most constructionists focus on emotions that represent temporary responses to events and information, since these are so clearly tied to cognition. But emotions also cover more permanent feelings of the type normally labeled affect or sentiment: love for one's family and other selected individuals; a sense of identification with a group and loyalty to its members; fondness for places and objects, perhaps based on memories;

positive responses to symbols of various kinds; and negative versions of each of these. To Heise (1979), affect is a central component of social life: all actions, actors, and settings have an affective component, involving not only a good-bad dimension but a potency dimension and a dimension capturing level of activity (lively–quiet). Humans act, according to Heise, in order to confirm their underlying sentiments. If "neighborhood" has positive connotations of safety and quiet, Heise's affect control theory would predict that a resident would fight to keep her neighborhood that way. Much political activity, no doubt, involves the reference to or creation of positive and negative affects toward groups, policies, and activities.

Trust and respect are examples of affects with an enormous impact on political action. We have deep tendencies to trust certain individuals, groups, and institutions but not others, and many of our allegiances, alliances, and choices follow from this pattern. Past experience or observation, agreement over goals or values or styles, collective identities, maybe even abstract deductions from principles: all these affect whom we trust. We tend to trust those we agree with and agree with those we trust. Generalized trust in the political system, furthermore, affects political behavior, usually dampening protest because of an assumption that the government will fix things without public pressure.

Affects and reactive emotions are two ends of a continuum with a grey area in the middle. At one end, love for a parent or loyalty to a country are usually strong and abiding affects, in the context of which many specific emotional reactions can come and go. Anger over a decision, at the other extreme, is usually a short-term response. In between are cases such as respect for a political leader, which can be an ongoing affect or a response to a particular action or a combination of the two. Fear, for instance, can slide along the continuum, depending on whether it is fear of abstract entities such as war or radiation or it is fear of more concrete embodiments such as a specific war or proposed

nuclear reactor. Also in the middle are what are frequently labeled "moods": chronic or recurring feelings that do not always have a direct object. They may begin as, and are shaped by, reactions, but they linger.

General affects and specific emotions are a part of all social life as surely as cognitive meanings and moral values are. What is more, they are relatively predictable, not accidental eruptions of the irrational. The transitory emotional responses, it seems to me, are a function of both external context (or, more precisely, interpreted information about that context) and deeper affective states, for the latter help explain why people respond differently to the same information. Those who feel positively about their neighborhood, for instance, may respond with greater outrage to proposals to change it. Parallel loyalties to professional ethics might determine who becomes a whistleblower when asked by one's boss to break certain rules (Bernstein and Jasper, 1996). The affects help shape the responses.

The relationship between these two kinds of emotions varies, perhaps, also along a continuum. At one extreme, rigid affective loyalties dominate all responses, potentially leading to paranoia or rigid ideologies. At the other extreme, these affects are flexible or weak, and emotional responses are dominated more by immediate context. The responses might themselves be weaker as a result, or they might simply consist of the kind of reaction that almost anyone would have in the same situation.

At stake in the constructionist debate is the rationality of emotions: to the extent that they are collectively shaped, depend on context, and are based on cognitions (themselves changeable through learning), they do not appear irrational. The dismissal of emotions as irrational comes in part from the tendency of Freudian psychological theories, especially earlier in the 20th century, to explain emotions through personality, in other words as a result of individual idiosyncrasies fixed early in life rather than as responses to changing cultural contexts. Works such as Lasswell's *Psychopathology and Politics*

(1930) were filled with discussions of narcissism, latent homosexuality, oral dependence, and anal retention – often aimed at showing protest participation to be an immature activity. Freudians emphasized processes of ego-defense, which Greenstein (1987:3) defines as "the means through which individuals, often without realizing it, adapt their behavior to the need to manage their inner conflicts." According to Greenstein, the development in the 1960s of a post-Freudian ego psychology, which stressed the cognitive strengths and adaptive resources of the ego, discouraged the view that political participation arose from psychopathologies. The ego was adapting to external realities, not simply projecting internal conflicts.

The apparent threat to rationality remains, though, in any model of the unconscious. Conflicts, urges, or affects that we cannot understand or control, may prevent us from learning or adapting to new circumstances – processes that might be thought of as a minimal requirement for rationality. Such psychodynamics certainly exist. But it may be unfair to label them as emotions, in contrast to cognition, for they encompass both. They are part of the many limits on human reasoning power, with emotional limits alongside the many cognitive limitations documented by psychologists and others. Neurotic patterns derived from childhood interfere with our processing of cognitive information as much as they do with our emotional responses. Paranoia, for instance, is largely a problem of giving too much credence to irrelevant cognitive cues.

There is a difference between emotions as transitory social roles, which are publicly defined and shaped as much as cognitive meanings are, and the emotions attendant to individual idiosyncrasies, personalities, and affective loyalties. The latter may occasionally thwart the well-defined emotional expectations of those around one. But the issue here is not that of emotions, but of how individuals relate to social expectations. There is always some individual variation in behavior, cognition, and emotional responses. This makes social-scientific generalizations difficult, but no more so for emotions than for other aspects of social life. We recognize structured systems of cognitive meanings that, like language, can be defined independently of individuals. That some individuals use these improperly or substitute their own meanings on occasion does not invalidate the systems or ruin their explanatory power. The same is true for emotions. There are systematic pressures to have well-defined emotional responses and affective ties in certain contexts. When individuals fail to meet these expectations, we can explain why without questioning the logic of the emotional system. Even patterns of affect have rules.

Beliefs can be mistaken, emotions inappropriate. But irrational? Either beliefs or emotions can be irrational if they cause actions that consistently lead to a deterioration in one's resources or strategic position or if they prevent learning and improvement. Affective loyalties such as love might blind us in this way, for they are more likely to frame the interpretation of new information than to change in response to that information, making us less adaptable and thus perhaps less rational. But since these affects are very close to moral values and basic goals, a commitment to them is hard to dismiss simply as irrational. They make nonsense of the very means/ends distinction that allows us to judge actions as ineffective for certain goals. Shorter term emotional responses, such as the sheriff's anger, can hurt one's strategic position, but learning and improvement are possible even here. One learns, as other angry sheriffs have, not to strike peaceful protestors. Or not to strike them when cameras are rolling. If a fear of irrationality has prevented students of social movements from incorporating emotions into their models, the time has come to rethink this stance.

Emotions in Protest

As an integral part of all social action, affective and reactive emotions enter into protest activities at every stage. Some help explain why individuals join protest events or groups, ranging from emotional responses they can have as individuals to those that recruiters can stir in them. Others are generated during protest activities, including both affective ties among fellow members and feelings toward institutions, people, and practices outside the movement and its constituent groups. These affect whether a movement continues or declines, and when. In all stages, there are both preexisting affects and shorter term emotional responses to events, discoveries, and decisions.

Our world is patterned by affect. Our relationships with other humans, even fleeting ones, are charged with emotions. Those intimates whom we know well are wrapped in a complex web of emotions that we can never fully sort out. Affection or resentment toward our parents gives many activities associated with them (even symbolically) a positive or negative affective charge; we may protest in order to shock them, gain their respect, or replicate some childhood dynamic. Admiration for others also influences our choices, as we follow their examples or strive for their approval. We also have many emotional attachments to places and fight fiercely when we feel certain locales are threatened. We often have simple feelings even about strangers: attraction or repulsion, for example. Sexual desire, fulfilled or merely aroused, affects many of our choices of how to spend our time – or more precisely, with whom. Through group stereotypes, we also have emotions toward those we have never met.

But that is not all. On top of these affects, and often based on them, we have transitory feelings about all our activities. As Harold Garfinkel showed, even relatively thoughtless habits, when disrupted, release a torrent of emotions. We have feelings about our lives, whether boredom or excitement, about politics, no matter how remote it sometimes seems, even about events on the other side of the globe. There would be no social movements if we did not have emotional responses to developments near and far. Sometimes emotional responses are strong enough that people search out protest groups on their own. It is affects and emotional responses that political organizers appeal to, arouse, manipulate, and sustain to recruit and retain members. Table 15.1 lists some of the emotions that help lead people into social movements, keep them there, and drive them away. Some are primarily affects, others mostly reactive emotions, still others share aspects of each. In this latter category are the emotions often labeled "moods." In many cases, the same emotions – in different contexts, or with different objects – that lead people into social movements can lead them out again.

Just to list these emotions should suggest their prevalence in social movements, but we can categorize them further. Table 15.2 provides examples of emotions according to the two basic distinctions I have mentioned: affects vs. reactive emotions, and the social settings where they are developed and sustained. It is the interaction between the affects and responses outside the movement that may propel someone to join an organization, participate in an event, contribute money, or be receptive to a recruiter's plea. The right side of the table suggests a number of internal movement dynamics: affects about one's fellow members may lead to either continued allegiance or defection; responses to the decisions and actions of other players in a conflict help explain strategic choices, including whether to continue or not. Although many emotions can only fall in the right-hand column or in the left, many others can be created or sustained in either setting; most of the affects and reactive emotions that would draw someone to a movement would also help keep her there.

Every extensive study of a social movement is filled with emotions like those that fill these tables, but they almost never receive theoretical attention or even appear in indices [...]. There seem to be two main exceptions, in which scholars have addressed the emotions of social movements.

Certain social movements aim at changing the broader culture of their society, including

Table 15.1   Some emotions potentially relevant to protest

Primarily affective

Hatred, Hostility, Loathing: Powerful step in the creation of outrage and the fixing of blame. Can alter goals from practical results to punishment of opponents.

Love: One can have erotic and other attachments to people already in a movement; love also shapes one's affective map of the world.

Solidarity, Loyalty: Positive feelings toward others can lead to action on behalf of that group or category.

Suspicion, Paranoia: Often lead to indignation and articulation of blame.

Trust, Respect: Basic positive affects that influence other emotional and cognitive responses, patterns of alliances, and credibility.

Primarily reactive

Anger: Can have many sources, and can be channeled in many directions, including both rage and outrage. Can interfere with effective strategies.

Grief, Loss, Sorrow: Loss, especially of a loved one, can bring on life passage and raise issues of the meaning of life.

Outrage, Indignation: These build on other emotions, largely by providing a target for analysis.

Shame: Can lead to anger and aggressive reactions.

Moods and others in between

Compassion, Sympathy, Pity: One can imagine the plight of others and develop a desire to help them.

Cynicism, Depression: They discourage protest by dampening hopes for change.

Defiance: Stance that encourages resistance.

Enthusiasm, Pride: Positive emotions that protest leaders try to encourage: enthusiasm for the movement and cause, pride in the associated collective identity, as in Black Power, gay and lesbian rights.

Envy, Resentment: Exaggerated by early crowd theorists, these are emotions that few admit to and which usually lead to actions other than protest; yet they may also appear among protestors.

Fear, Dread: These can arise from a sense of threat to one's daily routines or moral beliefs. They can paralyze but also be developed into outrage.

Joy, Hope: One can be attracted by the joys of empowerment, a sense of "flow" in protest and politics, or the anticipation of a better state of affairs in the future.

Resignation: Like cynicism, can dampen perceived possibility for change.

Table 15.2   Examples of emotions by social setting

Types	Settings where developed and sustained	
	Outside movement	*Inside movement*
Ongoing affects, loyalties	Love for family members. Fondness for neighborhood. Reassuring security of home. Fears of radiation, war. Trust in certain public figures, mistrust of others. Racial or other prejudices.	Love, attraction to other members. Loyalty to shared symbols, identity. Respect, trust for leaders. Jealousy of leaders, others. Trust or mistrust of allies. Trust or mistrust of government officials, politicians.
Responses to events, information	Shock at loved one's death. Anger at government decision. Outrage at plans for nuclear plant. Indignation over siting of waste dump. Resignation over government inaction.	Anger, outrage, indignation over government actions, reactions to movement demands, responses of media.

the acceptability and display of certain emotions. These are often movements fighting against the stigmatization of some group. And since emotions are often defined as "women's work," such efforts have frequently been part of the women's movement. In the late 1960s thousands of consciousness-raising groups helped women learn to feel less guilty about their resentment toward husbands, fathers, employers, and other men. Anger was not only considered positive, it was almost a requirement for membership, argues Hochschild (1975:298), who continues, "Social movements for change make 'bad' feelings okay, and they make them useful. Depending on one's point of view, they make bad feelings 'rational.' They also make them visible." According to Taylor and Whittier (1995), women's groups regularly try to transform the negative feelings many women have because of their structural positions, including depression, fear, and guilt. Taylor (1996) has examined self-help groups for mothers suffering from postpartum depression, an emotion widely stigmatized as "inappropriate," not part of the mother role. In this paper I do not examine such cases, where changes in emotions are among a movement's explicit goals, but rather I examine emotions as part of a movement's own dynamics.

The other exception is the collective-behavior approach, which traditionally acknowledged the importance of emotions – but by linking the anger of organized protestors to the fears of panics. For example John Lofland (1985:32), in describing the joys of crowds, recognizes the problematic emotions emphasized in the collective-behavior tradition, summed up in the image of a crowd: "with all the emotional baggage of irrationality, irritability, excess, fickleness, and violence." Lofland seems to imply that negative emotions such as fear and anger are closer to irrationality than positive ones such as joy. And organized social movements, as opposed to crowds, still appear free from emotions. There is still a taint or suspicion of irrationality surrounding most emotions.

[...]

Movements are themselves a distinct setting in which emotions can be created or reinforced. In contrast to emotions that grow out of existing moral frameworks such as religious systems or professional ethics, the emotions created within social movements are attempts, often explicit, to elaborate intuitive visions into explicit ideologies and proposals. The anger of a farmer living near a proposed site for a nuclear plant is the intuition that the antinuclear movement tries to build into a systematic ideology of opposition. What the farmer sees first as "meddlesome outsiders" develops into "technocracy"; fear develops into outrage. Each cognitive shift is accompanied by emotional ones.

Some of the emotions generated within a social movement – call them *reciprocal* – concern participants' ongoing feelings toward each other. These are the close, affective ties of friendship, love, solidarity, and loyalty, and the more specific emotions they give rise to. Together they create what Goodwin (1997) calls the "libidinal economy" of a movement, yielding many of the pleasures of protest, including erotic pleasures. Other emotions – call them *shared* – are consciously held by a group at the same time, but they do not have the other group members as their objects. The group nurtures anger toward outsiders, or outrage over government policies. Reciprocal and shared emotions, although distinct, reinforce each other – thereby building a movement's culture. Each measure of shared outrage against a nuclear plant reinforces the reciprocal emotion of fondness for others precisely because they feel the same way. They are like us; they understand. Conversely, mutual affection is one context in which new shared emotions are easily created. Because you are fond of others, you want to adopt their feelings. Both kinds of collective emotion foster solidarity within a protest group. They are key sources of identification with a movement.

Collective emotions, the reciprocal ones especially, are linked to the pleasures of protest. Most obvious are the pleasures of being with people one likes, in any number of ways. Other pleasures arise from the joys of collective activities, such as losing oneself in collective motion or song. This can be satisfying even when done with strangers – who of course no longer feel like strangers. And articulating one's moral principles is always a source of joy, pride, and fulfilment – even when it is also painful.

Emotions are one of the products of collective action, especially internal rituals. Collective rites remind participants of their basic moral commitments, stir up strong emotions, and reinforce a sense of solidarity with the group, a "we-ness." Rituals are symbolic embodiments, at salient times and places, of the beliefs and feelings of a group. Singing and dancing are two activities often found in rituals, providing the requisite emotional charge through music, coordinated physical activity, and bodily contact (McNeill, 1995). Since Durkheim first described "collective effervescence," it has been clear that these activities were crucial in creating it, by transporting participants onto another plane, into what they feel is a more ethereal, or at any rate different, reality. In many ways, singing and dancing are the kernel of truth in older crowd theories, the one moment when a large group can attain a certain coordination and unity, can silence the small groups talking among themselves, can concentrate the attention of all. Of course, this coordination does not emerge spontaneously, since participants must know the dances and the lyrics. And it is hard to imagine *all* participants joining in (McPhail, 1991). But Durkheim was pointing to important processes that reinforce emotions in predictable ways.

Singing was especially important to the civil rights movement (Morris, 1984). Lyrics such as "Onward Christian Soldiers," "There's a great day coming," and "We shall overcome" lent biblical authority to the campaign with specific references to fundamental beliefs and narratives (Watters, 1971). Deliverance through a great leader – Moses, Jesus, Martin Luther King, Jr. – was

a reassuring emotional message. Extensive religious training meant that almost all African American participants knew the music, loudly generating a moving feeling of solidarity. Lyrics are a form of shared knowledge that helps one feel like an insider. Morris (1984:47) quotes King: "The opening hymn was the old familiar 'Onward Christian Soldiers,' and when that mammoth audience stood to sing, the voices outside (the church building could not accommodate the large gatherings) swelling the chorus in the church, there was a mighty ring like the glad echo of heaven itself.... The enthusiasm of these thousands of people swept everything along like an onrushing tidal wave." It is hard to imagine more powerful emotional materials.

[...]

References

Averill, James R. 1980 "A constructivist view of emotion." In Robert Plutchik and Henry Kellerman (eds.), *Emotion: Theory, Research, and Experience, vol. 1: Theories of Emotion*. New York: Academic Press.

Bernstein, Mary and James M. Jasper 1996 "Interests and credibility: Whistle-blowers in technological conflicts." *Social Science Information* 35:565–589.

Collins, Randall 1990 "Stratification, emotional energy, and the transient emotions." In Theodore D. Kemper (ed.), *Research Agendas in the Sociology of Emotions*. Albany: SUNY Press.

de Sousa, Ronald 1987 *The Rationality of Emotion*. Cambridge: MIT Press.

Goodwin, Jeff 1997 "The libidinal constitution of a high-risk social movement. Affectual ties and solidarity in the Huk Rebellion." *American Sociological Review*, 62:53–69.

Greenstein, Fred I. 1987 Personality and Politics, new ed. Princeton: Princeton University Press.

Harré, Rom 1986 "An outline of the social constructionist viewpoint." In Rom Harré (ed.), *The Social Construction of Emotions*. Oxford: Basil Blackwell.

Heise, David R. 1979 *Understanding Events*. Cambridge: Cambridge University Press.

Hochschild, Arlie Russell 1975 "The sociology of feeling and emotion: Selected possibilities." In Marcia Millman and Rosabeth Moss Kanter (eds.), *Another Voice*. Garden City NY: Anchor Books.

Lasswell, Harold D. 1930 *Psychopathology and Politics*. Chicago: University of Chicago Press.

Lofland, John 1985 *Protest*. New Brunswick, NJ: Transaction Publishers.

McNeill, William H. 1995 *Keeping Together in Time: Dance and Drill in Human History*. Cambridge, MA: Harvard University Press.

McPhail, Clark 1991 *The Myth of the Madding Crowd*. New York: Aldine de Gruyter.

Morris, Aldon D. 1984 *The Origins of the Civil Rights Movement*. New York: Free Press.

Solomon, Robert C. 1976 *The Passions*. New York: Doubleday-Anchor.

Taylor, Verta 1996 *Rock-a-by Baby*. New York: Routledge.

Taylor, Verta and Nancy Whittier 1995 "Analytical approaches to social movement culture: The culture of the women's movement." In Hank Johnston and Bert Klandermans (eds.), *Social Movements and Culture*. Minneapolis: University of Minnesota Press.

Thoits, Peggy A. 1989 "The sociology of the emotions." *Annual Review of Sociology* 15:317–342.

Watters, Pat 1971 *Down to Now*. New York: Pantheon.

Part VI

How Are Movements Organized?

Introduction

Forty years ago, social movements were thought to be extremely disorganized affairs. Individuals were believed to drift into them for personal rather than political reasons; crowds were thought to be irrational and shifting in their focus. This is why movements were categorized as a form of "collective behavior," which implies less purpose and intention than the term collective "action." If politics occurred outside normal institutional channels such as parties and voting, then it was thought not to have any form of organization at all.

Perhaps the biggest breakthrough in the field of social movements beginning in the late 1960s was to show that social movements are thoroughly organized, both formally and informally. The informal organization consists of social networks through which individuals are recruited: it turns out they are not isolated and alienated but well integrated into society (see part III). Networks like these also shape what movements can do once they emerge. On the formal dimension, movements usually create, even consist of, formal organizations, which are often legal entities recognized by the state. This section examines these formal organizations (usually dubbed "SMOs" for social movement organizations) and the way they are related to each other in a social movement.

> **Indigenous Organization** In order to sustain protest, people need to communicate with one another, strategize, advertise, recruit new protestors, and generally coordinate their activities. It often helps, accordingly, if would-be protestors already belong to the same (or linked) political or social organizations, churches, friendship networks, schools, sports clubs, work places, neighborhoods, and so on. Sometimes entire organizations or networks are recruited into a movement, a process known as **bloc recruitment**. If such "indigenous organization" (sometimes called **mobilizing structures**), whether formal or informal, does not already exist, would-be protestors have to create their own protest organizations. Self-organization or self-recruitment to movements, in other words, is sometimes as important as pre-existing organization. These connections are helpful not only for coordinating action and spreading information, but also for building affective ties and loyalties.

SMOs vary enormously. Some have a great deal of formal structure and rules, while others have nothing but informal traditions and habits. Some are centralized and hierarchical, others decentralized and egalitarian. Some require a lot of money to function and survive, while others subsist on nothing more than the hours contributed by volunteers. They also differ in their sources of funding: some get grants from philanthropic foundations, others from broad direct-mail efforts; members themselves support some, governments actually support others. There are great differences as well in the commitment required of members. For revolutionary cells, protest is a full-time job that usually entails cutting ties with non-members. Other protest groups require nothing more than a Saturday afternoon every few months – or even just an occasional contribution (many SMOs have different kinds of members, ranging from financial supporters to those who volunteer their labor to full-time staff).

Most of the "new" social movements that began to emerge in the 1960s, including student movements, the New Left, and later environmental, feminist, and antinuclear movements, thought it important to avoid bureaucratic organizations. They preferred egalitarian groups that encouraged everyone to participate in decision making. Joyce Rothschild and Allen Whitt (1986) described these alternative organizations as avoiding the traditional trappings of bureaucracy: paid staff, experts, hierarchy, impersonal rules, and a permanent division of labor. In other words, organizational forms are one area in which many protestors have tried to change the way their societies do things, in anticipation of the kind of future they envision (Breines, 1982; Polletta, 2002). One of the purposes of avoiding traditional bureaucracy is to foster "free spaces" in which creative alternatives to mainstream practices can be imagined, discussed, and tried out (Evans and Boyte, 1986).

Social movements also vary in how many component organizations they have, and in how these are related to each other. At one extreme there may be a single organization that directs the movement, as with some revolutionary movements. At the other there may be many organizations with little coordination among them: each may be reassured by the existence of others but have little direct need for them. Most movements fall somewhere between these extremes. No matter how many SMOs they contain, movements still vary in the degree of coordination among them. Gerlach and Hine (1970) once described social movements as segmented, polycephalous, and reticulate: each group is relatively autonomous from the others, there is no definite head, and yet they have loose links among the parts.

John McCarthy and Mayer Zald, in a famous article excerpted in this section (1977), looked at social movement organizations as though they were like business firms in a market. If an SMO is like a firm, then a movement is like an industry. The important implication is that SMOs may have to compete with each other over the same volunteers and contributors, even when they are in the same movement and thus have the same goals. The economic metaphor focuses our attention on the financing of SMOs, including the many different kinds of relationships they can have with contributors – who are not necessarily the beneficiaries. Paid staff, the "entrepreneurs" who put SMOs together, are crucial. This emphasis on resources helped create the "resource mobilization" approach to social movements. Their approach seems to work well in understanding moderate, well-behaved groups, such as mainstream environmental organizations, that employ professional staffs and raise most of their funds through direct-mail solicitations.

Another tradition of research, exemplified by Charles Tilly (1978), used political rather than economic metaphors to understand social movement organizations. Research on labor unions and other groups that pursued economic and political benefits at the same time helped inspire what has come to be called the "political process" school. Researchers in this tradition view protest groups as like political parties, except operating outside the electoral system. SMOs are a normal part of politics, whatever form they take. They are instrumental vehicles for the pursuit of group interests.

The weakness of these traditions emphasizing formal organizations was to depict protestors as invariably self-interested and indeed selfish. Having rejected the psychology of older traditions, these scholars inadvertently embedded the assumptions of neoclassical economics in their models: people were rational pursuers of their own narrow interests. These scholars ignored one of the central issues of social movements: how people come to perceive a shared grievance or interest, especially in something remote from their daily lives, such as global warming, nuclear energy, or human rights abuses in distant lands. There are many emotional and cognitive processes that go into the construction of movement goals. We can't lose sight of what people want from their protest organizations.

We can go further. Organizations themselves are more than instruments for attaining goals. They also carry symbolic messages in their very structures. Protestors want to attain their goals, to be sure, but they also want to show that they are certain kinds of people (e.g., compassionate, objective, outraged, maybe even dangerous). With certain kinds of organizational forms, they can show they mean business, or that they are radically different from existing organizations. A school of thought called the "new institutionalism" has arisen in organizational theory to show that organizational structures are never simply the most efficient means to given ends, but also reflect their surrounding cultures' assumptions about the world. An organization's structure often reflects cultural fads popular at the time of its founding.

Elisabeth Clemens, in an article excerpted below, applies this school of thought to social movement organizations. Focusing on women's groups, she suggests that marginalized populations typically adapt culturally familiar forms of organization (e.g., clubs, unions, parliaments, even armies) for political purposes. The "repertoire" or models of organization available to a population shape the ways in which it may organize itself for collective action. When choosing a model from this organizational repertoire, moreover, normative considerations are typically more important than efficiency.

The excerpt by Paul Wapner argues that many movements, including the environmental and human rights movements, increasingly organize across national boundaries. Transnational forms of organization, of course, make sense in an increasingly integrated world. Many contemporary social problems simply cannot be addressed at a national level. In this sense, transnational organization is a response to "globalization." Transnational environmental activist groups (TEAGs, as Wapner calls them) pressure governments, but they do much more than this. They have been instrumental in disseminating an ecological sensibility to new groups, pressuring multinational corporations, and empowering local communities. Thus, they are an important component of an emerging "world civic politics" or "global civil society" that is independent of national states.

As movements have taken on global issues, paradoxically, some have drawn upon small-scale, face-to-face forms of organization. In his examination of the movement against corporate-led globalization, William Finnegan discusses the "affinity-group model" of organization, which has some similarities with anarchism, including a distaste for all forms of hierarchy. Affinity groups are small, semi-independent groups of like-minded activists (they may live in the same neighborhood or have similar political or aesthetic tastes) which typically coordinate their actions with other, similar affinity groups. Coalitions based on affinity groups typically display a great deal of tactical flexibility, but they are inherently more difficult to direct and control than more centralized forms of organization.

There have been debates over the effects of formal organization on social movements. William Gamson (1990) found that social movements with more bureaucratic organizations were more successful. They are certainly likely to survive longer, as the point of rules and formality is to persist. However, Frances Fox Piven and Richard Cloward (1979), looking at a number of poor people's movements, argued that the most powerful tool of the oppressed is their ability to disrupt things. Bureaucratization usually interferes with this, as bureaucrats begin to develop an interest in maintaining their organizations. This debate continues.

Discussion Questions

1   In what ways do SMOs differ from each other?
2   When would SMOs have an advantage in being formal, when informal? When hierarchical, when egalitarian?
3   What are some of the symbolic messages that SMOs might wish to convey through their formal structures? To whom?
4   If you joined a movement, what type of organization would you find appealing? What would turn you off?
5   In what ways is transnational or cross-border organizing easier than it might have been, say, one hundred years ago? What are some of the difficulties involved in organizing a transnational movement?
6   What are the advantages of the affinity-group model of organization? What are its disadvantages?

16 Social Movement Organizations

John D. McCarthy and Mayer N. Zald

For quite some time a hiatus existed in the study of social movements in the United States. In the course of activism leaders of movements here and abroad attempted to enunciate general principles concerning movement tactics and strategy and the dilemmas that arise in overcoming hostile environments. Such leaders as Mao, Lenin, Saul Alinsky, and Martin Luther King attempted in turn to develop principles and guidelines for action. The theories of activists stress problems of mobilization, the manufacture of discontent, tactical choices, and the infrastructure of society and movements necessary for success. At the same time sociologists, with their emphasis upon structural strain, generalized belief, and deprivation, largely have ignored the ongoing problems and strategic dilemmas of social movements.

Recently a number of social scientists have begun to articulate an approach to social movements, here called the resource mobilization approach, which begins to take seriously many of the questions that have concerned social movement leaders and practical theorists. Without attempting to produce handbooks for social change (or its suppression), the new approach deals in general terms with the dynamics and tactics of social movement growth, decline, and change. As such, it provides a corrective to the practical theorists, who naturally are most concerned with justifying their own tactical choices, and it also adds realism, power, and depth to the truncated research on and analysis of social movements offered by many social scientists.

The resource mobilization approach emphasizes both societal support and constraint of social movement phenomena. It examines the variety of resources that must be mobilized, the linkages of social movements to other groups, the dependence of movements upon external support for success, and the tactics used by authorities to control or incorporate movements. The shift in emphasis is evident in much of the work published recently in this area (J. Wilson 1973; Tilly 1973, 1975; Tilly, Tilly, and Tilly 1975; Gamson 1975; Oberschall 1973; Lipsky 1968; Downs 1972; McCarthy and Zald 1973). The new approach depends more upon political, sociological and economic theories than upon the social psychology of collective behavior.

This paper presents a set of concepts and propositions that articulate the resource mobilization approach. It is a partial theory because it takes as given, as constants, certain components of a complete theory. The propositions are heavily based upon the American case, so that the impact of societal differences in development and political structure on social movements is unexplored, as are differences in levels and types of mass communication. Further, we rely heavily upon case material concerning organizations of the left, ignoring, for the most part, organizations of the right.

The main body of the paper defines our central concepts and presents illustrative hypotheses about the social movement sector (SMS), social movement industries (SMI), and social movement organizations (SMO).

However, since we view this approach as a departure from the main tradition in social movement analysis, it will be useful first to clarify what we see as the limits of that tradition.

Perspectives Emphasizing Deprivation and Beliefs

Without question the three most influential approaches to an understanding of social movement phenomena for American sociologists during the past decade are those of Gurr (1970), Turner and Killian (1972), and Smelser (1963). They differ in a number of respects. But, most important, they have in common strong assumptions that shared grievances and generalized beliefs (loose ideologies) about the causes and possible means of reducing grievances are important preconditions for the emergence of a social movement in a collectivity. An increase in the extent or intensity of grievances or deprivation and the development of ideology occur prior to the emergence of social movement phenomena. Each of these perspectives holds that discontent produced by some combination of structural conditions is a necessary if not sufficient condition to an account of the rise of any specific social movement phenomenon. Each, as well, holds that before collective action is possible within a collectivity a generalized belief (or ideological justification) is necessary concerning at least the causes of the discontent and, under certain conditions, the modes of redress. Much of the empirical work which has followed and drawn upon these perspectives has emphasized even more heavily the importance of understanding the grievances and deprivation of participants. (Indeed, scholars following Gurr, Smelser, and Turner and Killian often ignore structural factors, even though the authors mentioned have been sensitive to broader structural and societal influences, as have some others.)

Recent empirical work, however, has led us to doubt the assumption of a close link between preexisting discontent and generalized beliefs in the rise of social movement phenomena. A number of studies have shown little or no support for expected relationships between objective or subjective deprivation and the outbreak of movement phenomena and willingness to participate in collective action (Snyder and Tilly 1972; Mueller 1972; Bowen et al. 1968; Crawford and Naditch 1970). Other studies have failed to support the expectation of a generalized belief prior to outbreaks of collective behavior episodes or initial movement involvement (Quarantelli and Hundley 1975; Marx 1970; Stallings 1973). Partially as a result of such evidence, in discussing revolution and collective violence Charles Tilly is led to argue that these phenomena flow directly out of a population's central political processes instead of expressing momentarily heightened diffuse strains and discontents within a population (Tilly 1973).

Moreover, the heavy focus upon the psychological state of the mass of potential movement supporters within a collectivity has been accompanied by a lack of emphasis upon the processes by which persons and institutions from outside of the collectivity under consideration become involved; for instance, Northern white liberals in the Southern civil rights movement, or Russians and Cubans in Angola. Although earlier perspectives do not exclude the possibilities of such involvement on the part of outsiders, they do not include such processes as central and enduring phenomena to be used in accounting for social movement behavior.

The ambiguous evidence of some of the research on deprivation, relative deprivation, and generalized belief has led us to search for a perspective and a set of assumptions that lessen the prevailing emphasis upon grievances. We want to move from a strong assumption about the centrality of deprivation and grievances to a weak one, which makes them a component, indeed, sometimes a secondary component in the generation of social movements.

We are willing to assume (Turner and Killian [1972] call the assumption extreme)

"... that there is always enough discontent in any society to supply the grass-roots support for a movement if the movement is effectively organized and has at its disposal the power and resources of some established elite group" (p. 251). For some purposes we go even further: grievances and discontent may be defined, created, and manipulated by issue entrepreneurs and organizations.

We adopt a weak assumption not only because of the negative evidence (already mentioned) concerning the stronger one but also because in some cases recent experience supports the weaker one. For instance, the senior citizens who were mobilized into groups to lobby for Medicare were brought into groups only after legislation was before Congress and the American Medical Association had claimed that senior citizens were not complaining about the medical care available to them (Rose 1967). Senior citizens were organized into groups through the efforts of a lobbying group created by the AFL-CIO. No doubt the elderly needed money for medical care. However, what is important is that the organization did not develop directly from that grievance but very indirectly through the moves of actors in the political system. Entertaining a weak assumption leads directly to an emphasis upon mobilization processes. Our concern is the search for analytic tools to account adequately for the processes.

Resources To sustain themselves over time, social movements need resources: money and the physical or professional capacities it can buy. Today, organizers need telephones, FAX machines, computers, direct-mail fundraising services, paid lobbyists, photocopiers, and postage. They need to rent offices and hire staff. They devote considerable time to raising the funds for such purposes. Some resources are "lumpy": you don't need a second bullhorn if your first works fine. And in all cases, there needs to be the know-how to put physical capacities to work. What is more, resources are not fixed in amount: activists work hard to mobilize more resources, to see their existing capacities in new and imaginative ways, and to find ways to protest that are within their means.

Resource Mobilization

The resource mobilization perspective adopts as one of its underlying problems Olson's (1965) challenge: since social movements deliver collective goods, few individuals will "on their own" bear the costs of working to obtain them. Explaining collective behavior requires detailed attention to the selection of incentives, cost-reducing mechanisms or structures, and career benefits that lead to collective behavior (see, especially, Oberschall 1973).

Several emphases are central to the perspective as it has developed. First, study of the aggregation of resources (money and labor) is crucial to an understanding of social movement activity. Because resources are necessary for engagement in social conflict, they must be aggregated for collective purposes. Second, resource aggregation requires some minimal form of organization, and hence, implicitly or explicitly, we focus more directly upon social movement organizations than do those working within the traditional perspective. Third, in accounting for a movement's successes and failures there is an explicit recognition of the crucial importance of involvement on the part of individuals and organizations from outside the collectivity which a social movement represents. Fourth, an explicit, if crude, supply and demand model is sometimes applied to the flow of resources toward and away from specific social movements. Finally, there is a sensitivity to the importance of costs and rewards in explaining individual and organizational involvement in social movement activity. Costs and rewards are centrally affected by the structure of society and the activities of authorities.

We can summarize the emerging perspective by contrasting it with the traditional one as follows:

1. Support base
   A. Traditional. Social movements are based upon aggrieved populations which provide the necessary resources and labor. Although case

studies may mention external supports, they are not incorporated as central analytic components.

B. Resource mobilization. Social movements may or may not be based upon the grievances of the presumed beneficiaries. Conscience constituents, individual and organizational, may provide major sources of support. And in some cases supporters – those who provide money, facilities, and even labor – may have no commitment to the values that underlie specific movements.

2. Strategy and tactics

A. Traditional. Social movement leaders use bargaining, persuasion, or violence to influence authorities to change. Choices of tactics depend upon prior history of relations with authorities, relative success of previous encounters, and ideology. Tactics are also influenced by the oligarchization and institutionalization of organizational life.

B. Resource mobilization. The concern with interaction between movements and authorities is accepted, but it is also noted that social movement organizations have a number of strategic tasks. These include mobilizing supporters, neutralizing and/or transforming mass and elite publics into sympathizers, achieving change in targets. Dilemmas occur in the choice of tactics, since what may achieve one aim may conflict with behavior aimed at achieving another. Moreover, tactics are influenced by interorganizational competition and cooperation.

3. Relation to larger society

A. Traditional. Case studies have emphasized the effects of the environment upon movement organizations, especially with respect to goal change, but have ignored, for the most part, ways in which such movement organizations can utilize the environment for their own purposes (see Perrow 1972). This has probably been largely a result of the lack of comparative organizational focus inherent in case studies. In analytical studies emphasis is upon the extent of hostility or toleration in the larger society. Society and culture are treated as descriptive, historical context.

B. Resource mobilization. Society provides the infrastructure which social movement industries and other industries utilize. The aspects utilized include communication media and expense, levels of affluence, degree of access to institutional centers, pre-existing networks, and occupational structure and growth.

Theoretical Elements

Having sketched the emerging perspective, our task now is to present a more precise statement of it. In this section we offer our most general concepts and definitions. Concepts of narrower range are presented in following sections.

A *social movement* is a set of opinions and beliefs in a population which represents preferences for changing some elements of the social structure and/or reward distribution of a society. A *countermovement* is a set of opinions and beliefs in a population opposed to a social movement. As is clear, we view social movements as nothing more than preference structures directed toward social change, very similar to what political sociologists would term issue cleavages. (Indeed, the process we are exploring resembles what political scientists term interest aggregation, except that we are concerned with the margins of the political system rather than with existing party structures.)

The distribution of preference structures can be approached in several ways. Who holds the beliefs? How intensely are they held? In order to predict the likelihood of preferences being translated into collective action, the mobilization perspective focuses upon the preexisting organization and integration of those segments of a population which share preferences. Oberschall (1973) has presented an important synthesis of past work on the preexisting organization of preference structures, emphasizing the opportunities and costs for expression of preferences for movement leaders and followers. Social movements whose related populations are highly organized internally (either communally or associationally) are more likely than are others to spawn organized forms.

Social Movement Organizations (SMOs) Some analysts have studied social movements as though they were composed primarily of formal organizations that act much as businesses do. This is partly just a metaphor and partly a reflection of the fact that many social movements are indeed composed largely of formal organizations. This means that one of their main activities is raising funds (or "mobilizing resources") to keep themselves afloat and their staffs paid. They compete with each other for contributions, especially from those who support the movement in no way other than financially. This development reflects modern laws governing nonprofit organizations, the affluence of societies in which many people have discretionary income to contribute to their favorite causes, and the ability of activists to find professional careers in social change organizations. In addition to social movement organizations (often abbreviated SMOs), scholars have also analyzed "social-movement industries," in which different SMOs compete for resources and attention, as well as the entire "social-movement sector" of societies.

A *social movement organization* (SMO) is a complex, or formal, organization which identifies its goals with the preferences of a social movement or a countermovement and attempts to implement those goals. If we think of the recent civil rights movement in these terms, the social movement contained a large portion of the population which held preferences for change aimed at "justice for black Americans" and a number of SMOs such as the Student Non-Violent Coordinating Committee (SNCC), the Congress of Racial Equality (CORE), the National Asso-

ciation for the Advancement of Colored People (NAACP), and Southern Christian Leadership Conference (SCLC). These SMOs represented and shaped the broadly held preferences and diverse subpreferences of the social movement.

All SMOs that have as their goal the attainment of the broadest preferences of a social movement constitute a *social movement industry* (SMI) – the organizational analogue of a social movement. A conception paralleling that of SMI, used by Von Eschen, Kirk, and Pinard (1971), the "organizational substructure of disorderly politics," has aided them in analyzing the civil rights movement in Baltimore. They demonstrate that many of the participants in a 1961 demonstration sponsored by the local chapter of CORE were also involved in NAACP, SCLC, the Americans for Democratic Action (ADA), or the Young People's Socialist Alliance (YPSA). These organizations either were primarily concerned with goals similar to those of CORE or included such goals as subsets of broader ranges of social change goals. (The concept employed by Von Eschen et al. is somewhat broader than ours, however, as will be seen below.)

Definitions of the central term, social movement (SM), typically have included both elements of preference and organized action for change. Analytically separating these components by distinguishing between an SM and an SMI has several advantages. First, it emphasizes that SMs are never fully mobilized. Second, it focuses explicitly upon the organizational component of activity. Third, it recognizes explicitly that SMs are typically represented by more than one SMO. Finally, the distinction allows the possibility of an account of the rise and fall of SMIs that is not fully dependent on the size of an SM or the intensity of the preferences within it.

Our definitions of SM, SMI, and SMO are intended to be inclusive of the phenomena which analysts have included in the past. The SMs can encompass narrow or broad preferences, millenarian and evangelistic preferences, and withdrawal preferences.

Organizations may represent any of these preferences.

The definition of SMI parallels the concept of industry in economics. Note that economists, too, are confronted with the difficulty of selecting broader or narrower criteria for including firms (SMOs) within an industry (SMI). For example, one may define a furniture industry, a sitting-furniture industry, or a chair industry. Close substitutability of product usage and, therefore, demand interdependence is the theoretical basis for defining industry boundaries. Economists use the *Census of Manufacturers* classifications, which are not strictly based on demand interdependence. For instance, on the one hand various types of steel are treated as one industry, though the types (rolled, flat, wire) are not substitutable. On the other hand, some products are classified separately (e.g., beet sugar, cane sugar) when they are almost completely substitutable (Bain 1959, pp. 111–18).

Given our task, the question becomes how to group SMOs into SMIs. This is a difficult problem because particular SMOs may be broad or narrow in stated target goals. In any set of empirical circumstances the analyst must decide how narrowly to define industry boundaries. For instance, one may speak of the SMI which aims at liberalized alterations in laws, practices, and public opinion concerning abortion. This SMI would include a number of SMOs. But these SMOs may also be considered part of the broader SMI which is commonly referred to as the "women's liberation movement" or they could be part of the "population control movement." In the same way, the pre-1965 civil rights movement could be considered part of the broader civil liberties movement.

Economists have dealt with this difficulty by developing categories of broader inclusiveness, sometimes called sectors. Even this convention, however, does not confront the difficulties of allocating firms (SMOs) which are conglomerates, those which produce products across industries and even across sectors. In modern America there are a number of SMOs which may be thought of as conglomerates in that they span, in their goals, more narrowly defined SMIs. Common Cause, the American Friends Service Committee (AFSC), and the Fellowship of Reconciliation (FOR) are best treated in these terms as each pursues a wide variety of organizational goals which can only with difficulty be contained within even broadly defined SMIs. The *social movement sector* (SMS) consists of all SMIs in a society no matter to which SM they are attached. (The importance of this distinction will become apparent below.)

Let us now return to the resource mobilization task of an SMO. Each SMO has a set of *target goals*, a set of preferred changes toward which it claims to be working. Such goals may be broad or narrow, and they are the characteristics of SMOs which link them conceptually with particular SMs and SMIs. The SMOs must possess resources, however few and of whatever type, in order to work toward goal achievement. Individuals and other organizations control resources, which can include legitimacy, money, facilities, and labor.

Although similar organizations vary tremendously in the efficiency with which they translate resources into action, the amount of activity directed toward goal accomplishment is crudely a function of the resources controlled by an organization. Some organizations may depend heavily upon volunteer labor, while others may depend upon purchased labor. In any case, resources must be controlled or mobilized before action is possible.

From the point of view of a SMO the individuals and organizations which exist in a society may be categorized along a number of dimensions. For the appropriate SM there are adherents and nonadherents. *Adherents* are those individuals and organizations that believe in the goals of the movement. The *constituents* of a SMO are those providing resources for it.

At one level the resource mobilization task is primarily that of converting adherents into constituents and maintaining constituent involvement. However, at another level the task may be seen as turning nonadherents into adherents. Ralph Turner (1970) uses the term bystander public to denote those nonadherents who are not opponents of the SM and its SMOs but who merely witness social movement activity. It is useful to distinguish constituents, adherents, bystander publics, and opponents along several other dimensions. One refers to the size of the resource pool controlled, and we shall use the terms mass and elite to describe crudely this dimension. Mass constituents, adherents, bystander publics, and opponents are those individuals and groups controlling very limited resource pools. The most limited resource pool which individuals can control is their own time and labor. Elites are those who control larger resource pools.

Each of these groups may also be distinguished by whether or not they will benefit directly from the accomplishment of SMO goals. Some bystander publics, for instance, may benefit directly from the accomplishment of organizational goals, even though they are not adherents of the appropriate SM. To mention a specific example, women who oppose the preferences of the women's liberation movement or have no relevant preferences might benefit from expanded job opportunities for women pursued by women's groups. Those who would benefit directly from SMO goal accomplishment we shall call *potential beneficiaries*.

In approaching the task of mobilizing resources a SMO may focus its attention upon adherents who are potential beneficiaries and/or attempt to convert bystander publics who are potential beneficiaries into adherents. It may also expand its target goals in order to enlarge its potential beneficiary group. Many SMOs attempt to present their goal accomplishments in terms of broader potential benefits for ever-wider groupings of citizens through notions of a better society, etc. (secondary benefits). Finally, a SMO may attempt to mobilize as adherents those who are not potential beneficiaries. *Conscience adherents* are individuals and groups who are part of the appropriate SM but do not stand to benefit directly from SMO goal accomplishment. *Conscience constituents* are direct supporters of a SMO who do not stand to benefit directly from its success in goal accomplishment.

William Gamson (1975) makes essentially the same distinction, calling groups with goals aimed at helping nonconstituents universalistic and those whose beneficiaries and constituents are identical, nonuniversalistic. Gamson concludes, however, that this distinction is not theoretically important, since SMOs with either type of constituents have identical problems in binding them to the organization. It is not more "irrational," in Olson's sense, to seek change in someone else's behalf than in one's own, and in both cases commitment must be gained by other means than purposive incentives. The evidence presented by Gamson suggests that this dimension does not bear much relationship to SMO success in goal accomplishment or in the attainment of legitimacy. We argue below, however, that the distinction should be maintained: it summarizes important attachments and social characteristics of constituents. The problems of SMOs with regard to binding beneficiary and conscience constituents to the organization are different, not with regard to the stakes of individual involvement relative to goal accomplishment (the Olson problem) but with regard to the way constituents are linked to each other and to other SMOs, organizations, and social institutions.

A SMO's potential for resource mobilization is also affected by authorities and the delegated agents of social control (e.g., police). While authorities and agents of control groups do not typically become constituents of SMOs, their ability to frustrate (normally termed social control) or to enable resource mobilization is of crucial importance. Their action affects the readiness of bystanders, adherents, and constituents to alter their own status and commitment. And they themselves may become adherents and constituents. Because they do not always act in concert, Marx (1974) makes a strong case that authorities and delegated agents of control need to be analyzed separately.

The partitioning of groups into mass or elite and conscience or beneficiary bystander publics, adherents, constituents, and opponents allows us to describe more systematically the resource mobilization styles and dilemmas of specific SMOs. It may be, of course, to the advantage of a SMO to turn bystander publics into adherents. But since SMO resources are normally quite limited, decisions must be made concerning the allocation of these resources, and converting bystander publics may not aid in the development of additional resources. Such choices have implications for the internal organization of a SMO and the potential size of the resource pool which can be ultimately mobilized. For instance, a SMO which has a mass beneficiary base and concentrates its resource mobilization efforts toward mass beneficiary adherents is likely to restrict severely the amount of resources it can raise. Elsewhere (McCarthy and Zald 1973) we have termed a SMO focusing upon beneficiary adherents for resources a classical SMO. Organizations which direct resource appeals primarily toward conscience adherents tend to utilize few constituents for organizational labor, and we have termed such organizations professional SMOs.

Another pattern of resource mobilization and goal accomplishment can be identified from the writings of Lipsky (1968) and Bailis (1974). It depends upon the interactions among beneficiary constituency, conscience adherents, and authorities. Typical of this pattern is a SMO with a mass beneficiary constituency which would profit from goal accomplishment (for instance, the Massachusetts Welfare Rights Organization) but which has few resources. Protest strategies draw attention and resources from conscience adherents to the SMO fighting on behalf of such mass groups and may also lead conscience elites to legitimate the SMO to authorities. As a result of a similar pattern, migrant farmworkers benefited

from the transformation of authorities into adherents.

But a SMO does not have complete freedom of choice in making the sorts of decisions to which we have alluded. Such choices are constrained by a number of factors including the preexisting organization of various segments of the SM, the size and diversity of the SMI of which it is a part, and the competitive position of the SMS. Also, of course, the ability of any SMO to garner resources is shaped by important events such as war, broad economic trends, and natural disasters.

The Elements Applied: Illustrative Hypotheses

Let us proceed to state hypotheses about the interrelations among the social structure, the SMS, SMIs, and SMOs. Occasionally, we introduce specifying concepts. Because the levels of analysis overlap, the subheadings below should be viewed as rough organizing devices rather than analytic categories.

Resources, the SMS, and the Growth of SMIs

Over time, the relative size of the SMS in any society may vary significantly. In general it will bear a relationship to the amount of wealth in a society. Hence, hypothesis 1: *As the amount of discretionary resources of mass and elite publics increases, the absolute and relative amount of resources available to the SMS increases.* This hypothesis is more of an orienting postulate than a directly testable hypothesis, but it is central to our perspective. And some related supporting evidence can be given.

By discretionary resources we mean time and money which can easily be reallocated, the opposite of fixed and enduring commitments of time and money. In any society the SMS must compete with other sectors and industries for the resources of the population. For most of the population the allocation of resources to SMOs is of lower priority than allocation to basic material needs such as food and shelter. It is well known that the proportion of income going to food and shelter is higher for low-income families, while the proportion of income going to savings and recreation increases among high-income families. The SMOs compete for resources with entertainment, voluntary associations, and organized religion and politics.

There is cross-sectional evidence that the higher the income the larger the average gift to charitable activities and the greater the proportion of total income given (see Morgan, Dye, and Hybels 1975). Moreover, Morgan et al. (1975) show that (1) the higher the education the more likely the giving of time, and (2) people who give more time to volunteer activities also give more money. As the total amount of resources increases, the total amount available to the SMS can be expected to increase, even if the sector does not increase its relative share of the resource pool. However, as discretionary resources increase relative to total societal resources, the SMS can be expected to gain a larger proportional share. This argument is based upon our belief that, except in times of crisis, the SMS is a low-priority competitor for available resources – it benefits from the satiation of other wants.

Of course, the validity of this hypothesis depends upon a *ceteris paribus* proviso. What might the other factors be? First, the existing infrastructure, what Smelser (1963) terms structural conduciveness, should affect the total growth of the SMS. Means of communication, transportation, political freedoms, and the extent of repression by agents of social control, all of which may affect the costs for any individual or organization allocating resources to the SMS, serve as constraints on or facilitators of the use of resources for social movement purposes. Also, the technologies available for resource accumulation should affect the ability of SMOs within the sector to mobilize resources. For instance, the advent of mass-mailing techniques in the United States has dramatically affected the ability of the SMS to compete with local advertising in offering a product to consumers. The organization of the SMIs will support or hinder the growth of the sector as additional resources become available. The greater the range of SMOs, the more different "taste" preferences can be transformed into constituents.

Hypothesis 2: *The greater the absolute amount of resources available to the SMS the greater the likelihood that new SMIs and SMOs will develop to compete for these resources.* This and the previous proposition contain the essence of our earlier analysis (McCarthy and Zald 1973). That study accounts in part for the proliferation in SMOs and SMIs in the 1960s in the United States by demonstrating both the relative and the absolute increases of resources available to the SMS. The major sources of increase in financial resources were charitable giving among mass and elite adherents and government, church, foundation, and business giving among organizational adherents.

These two propositions attempt to account for the total growth of the SMS. They ignore variations in the taste for change over time. They imply nothing about which SMI will reap the benefits of sector expansion. Nor do they imply what types of SMOs will lead the growth of an expanding SMI. They explicitly ignore the relationship between the size of the SMS and the intensities of preferences within a SM.

Parallel hypotheses could be stated for the relationship of resources amongst different categories of SM adherents and SM growth. For instance, hypothesis 3: *Regardless of the resources available to potential beneficiary adherents, the larger the amount of resources available to conscience adherents the more likely is the development of SMOs and SMIs that respond to preferences for change.* The importance of this hypothesis in our scheme hinges upon the growing role of conscience constituents in American social movements. First, the greater the discretionary wealth controlled by individuals and organizations the more likely it is that some of that wealth will be made available to causes beyond the direct self-interest of the contributor. An individual (or an organization) with large amounts of discretionary resources may allocate resources to personal comfort and to the advancement of some group of which he or she is not a member. Second, those who control the largest share of discretionary resources in any society are also those least likely to feel discontentment concerning their own personal circumstances.

In a sense, hypothesis 3 turns Olson (1965) on his head. Though it may be individually irrational for any individual to join a SMO which already fights on behalf of his preferences, the existence of a SM made up of well-heeled adherents calls out to the entrepreneur of the cause to attempt to form a viable organization. To the extent to which SM beneficiary adherents lack resources, SMO support, if it can be mobilized, is likely to become heavily dependent upon conscience constituents.

This argument is also important in understanding the critique of interest group pluralism as a valid description of modern America. Many collectivities with serious objective deprivations, and even with preexisting preferences for change, have been highly underrepresented by social movement organizations. These SMs tend to be very limited in their control of discretionary resources. It is only when resources can be garnered from conscience adherents that viable SMOs can be fielded to shape and represent the preferences of such collectivities.

Organization Structure and Resource Mobilization

How do the competitive position of the SMS, processes within a SMI, and the structure of a SMO influence the task of resource mobilization? Some aspects of these questions have been treated by Zald and Ash (1966). To discuss SMOs in detail we need to introduce assumptions about relevant SMO processes and structures.

Assume that SMOs operate much like any other organization (J. Q. Wilson 1973), and consequently, once formed, they operate as though organizational survival were the primary goal. Only if survival is insured can other goals be pursued. Second, assume that the costs and rewards of involvement can account for individual participation in SMOs and that, especially, selective incentives are important since they tend to raise the rewards for involvement. Gamson (1975) and Bailis (1974) provide impressive evidence that selective material incentives operate to bind individuals to SMOs and, hence, serve to provide continuous involvement and thus resource mobilization.

For a number of reasons the term member has been avoided here. Most important, membership implies very different levels of organizational involvement in different SMOs. The distinction between inclusive and exclusive SMOs has been utilized in the past to indicate intensity of organizational involvement (Zald and Ash 1966), but intensity of involvement actually includes several dimensions, usefully separated. Let us attempt to partition constituent involvement in any SMO. First there is the *cadre*, the individuals who are involved in the decision-making processes of the organization. Cadre members may devote most of their time to matters of the organization or only part of their time. Those who receive compensation, however meager, and devote full time to the organization, we term professional cadre; those who devote full time to the organization, but are not involved in central decision making processes, we term professional staff; those who intermittently give time to organizational tasks, not at the cadre level, we term workers. (Remember, constituents are those who give time *or* money.)

A *transitory team* is composed of workers assembled for a specific task, short in duration. Transitory teams are typically led by cadre members. Members of transitory teams and cadre have more extensive involvement than other segments of a SMO constituency. What distinguishes these constituents from others is that they are directly linked to the organization through tasks – they are involved directly in the affairs of the SMO. Since involvement of this sort occurs in small face-to-face groups, workers, whether through transitory teams or through continuous task involvement, can be expected to receive solidary incentives from such involvement – selective benefits of a nonmaterial sort.

Federated and Isolated Structure

A SMO which desires to pursue its goals in more than a local environment may attempt to mobilize resources directly from adherents or to develop federated chapters in different local areas. Federation serves to organize constituents into small local units. The SMOs which develop in this manner may deal with constituents directly as well as through chapters or only through chapters. But many SMOs do not develop chapters. These deal directly with constituents, usually through the mails or through traveling field staff. The important point is that constituents in nonfederated SMOs do not normally meet in face-to-face interaction with other constituents and hence cannot be bound to the SMOs through solidary selective incentives. We term these constituents, isolated constituents.

Federation may occur in two ways. One strategy assigns professional staff the task of developing chapters out of isolated adherents or constituents. To some extent SDS and CORE utilized this approach during the 1960s. Common Cause seems to have used it recently. Another strategy relies upon preexisting nonmovement local groups which have heavy concentrations of adherents or isolated constituents. This latter style, termed group mobilization by Oberschall (1973), was typical of several waves of recruitment by the Ku Klux Klan. Federation developing out of preexisting groups can occur quite rapidly, while organizing unattached individuals probably requires more time and resources. To the

extent that it utilized mass involvement in the South, SCLC operated through preexisting groups. We have argued elsewhere (McCarthy and Zald 1973) that nonfederated SMOs dealing with isolated constituents accounted for much of the SMS growth during the burst of SMO activity during the decade of the 1960s.

Empirically, SMOs will combine elements of the two major organizational forms we have identified here. The manner in which the organization garners the bulk of its resources should be used to characterize it during any time period. For instance, CORE would be deemed federated until the early 1960s, nonfederated at its peak during the early 1960s, and then federated again. It maintained a set of federated chapters during this entire period, but during the interim period its major resource flow was provided by isolated conscience constituents.

Hypothesis 4: *The more a SMO is dependent upon isolated constituents the less stable will be the flow of resources to the SMO.* Because isolated constituents are little involved in the affairs of the SMO, support from them depends far more upon industry and organizational (and counter-industry and counterorganizational) advertising than does support from constituents who are involved on a face-to-face basis with others. Advertising and media attention provide information about the dire consequences stemming from failure to attain target goals, the extent of goal accomplishment, and the importance of the particular SMO for such accomplishment.

Strickland and Johnston's (1970) analysis of issue elasticity is useful in understanding isolated constituent involvement in SM activities. At any time a number of target goals are offered to isolated adherents to any SM by one or more SMOs (and by other SMIs). Isolated adherents may choose to become constituents by allocating resources to one or another SMO based upon the goals propounded. The SMOs within any SMI will tend to compete with one another for the resources of these isolated adherents. If they allocate resources, but remain isolated, their ties to the SMO remain tenuous. To the extent that any individual is an adherent to more than one SM, various SMIs will also be competing for these resources.

Treating SMO target goals as products, then, and adherence as demand, we can apply a simple economic model to this competitive process. Demand may be elastic, and its elasticity is likely to be heavily dependent upon SMO advertising. Products may be substitutable across SMIs. For example, while various SMOs may compete for resources from isolated adherents to the "justice for black Americans" SM, SMOs representing the "justice for American women" SM may be competing for the same resources (to the extent that these two SMs have overlapping adherent pools). Some adherents may have a high and inelastic demand curve for a SMO or SMI, others' demand curves may show great elasticity.

This suggests that effective advertising campaigns may convince isolated adherents with high-issue elasticity to switch SMOs and/or SMIs. Issue elasticity relates to what Downs (1972) terms "issue attention cycles." These apparent cycles, he observes, include the stages of a problem discovered, dramatic increases in adherence as advertising alerts potential adherents, attempts at problem solution, lack of success of such attempts, and a rapid decline in adherence and advertising. Isolated adherents may purchase a target goal product when offered but can be expected to base decisions about future purchases upon their conception of product quality. Tullock (1966) has argued that the consumption of such products is vicarious, not direct; thus, perceived product quality is not necessarily related to actual goal accomplishment. Much publicity is dependent upon a SMO's ability to induce the media to give free attention, as most SMOs cannot actually afford the high costs of national advertising. They do, however, use direct-mail advertising. The point is that the media mediate in large measure between isolated constituents and SMOs.

Perceived lack of success in goal accomplishment by a SMO may lead an individual to switch to SMOs with alternative strategies or, to the extent that products are substitutable, to switch to those with other target goals. It must be noted, however, that there is also an element of product loyalty in this process. Some isolated constituents may continue to purchase the product (to support a SMO) unaware of how effective or ineffective it may be.

One could treat individual SMO loyalty in the same way as political party loyalty is treated by political sociologists, but most SMOs do not command such stable loyalties from large numbers of people. Certain long-lasting SMOs, the NAACP and the AFSC, for instance, may command stable loyalties, and the process of socializing youth into SMO loyalty could be expected to be similar to that of socialization into party loyalty. This process, however, most probably occurs not among isolated constituents, but among those who are linked in more direct fashion to SMOs.

Advertising by SMOs recognizes that isolated constituents have no direct way of evaluating the product purchased; therefore it may stress the amount of goal accomplishment available to the isolated constituent for each dollar expended. The AFSC, for instance, informs isolated potential constituents in its mass mailings that its overhead costs are among the lowest of any comparable organization, and hence the proportion of each donation used for goal accomplishment is higher. Within an industry SMO products are normally differentiated by conceptions of the extremity of solutions required (Killian 1972) and by strategies of goal accomplishment (passive resistance, strikes, etc.). When products are not differentiated in either of these ways, we can expect differentiation in terms of efficiency.

These considerations lead to a subsidiary hypothesis, 4a: *The more dependent a SMO is upon isolated constituents the greater the share of its resources which will be allocated to advertising.* As indicated, SMO advertising can take the form of mailed material which demonstrates the good works of the organization. Media bargaining (Lipsky 1968) can also be conceptualized as SMO advertising. By staging events which will possibly be "newsworthy," by attending to the needs of news organizations, and by cultivating representatives of the media, SMOs may manipulate media coverage of their activities more or less successfully. Some kind of information flow to isolated constituents including positive evaluation is absolutely essential for SMOs dependent upon them.

The foregoing reasoning, combined with hypotheses 1 and 2, leads us to hypothesis 4b: *The more a SMO depends upon isolated constituents to maintain a resource flow the more its shifts in resource flow resemble the patterns of consumer expenditures for expendable and marginal goods.* Stated differently, if a SMO is linked to its major source of constituent financial support through the advertising of its products, isolated constituents will balance off their contributions with other marginal expenditures. Time of year, state of the checkbook, mood, and product arousal value will influence such decision making.

The more attractive the target goal (product) upon which such a solicitation is based, the more likely that isolated adherents will become isolated constituents. Consequently, SMOs depending heavily upon such resource mobilization techniques must resort to slick packaging and convoluted appeal to self-interest in order to make their products more attractive. This should be especially true within competitive SMIs. The behavior in the early 1970s of environmental groups, which depend heavily upon isolated constituents, appears to illustrate this point. Many of those SMOs took credit for stalling the Alaskan pipeline and attempted to link that issue to personal self-interest and preferences in their direct-mail advertising. Slick packaging is evident in the high quality of printing and the heavy use of photogravure.

Another technique advertisers utilize to appeal to isolated adherents is the linking of names of important people to the organ-

ization, thereby developing and maintaining an image of credibility. In the same way that famous actors, sports heroes, and retired politicians endorse consumer products, other well-known personalities are called upon to endorse SMO products: Jane Fonda and Dr. Spock were to the peace movement and Robert Redford is to the environmental movement what Joe Namath is to pantyhose and what William Miller is to American Express Company credit cards.

The development of local chapters helps bind constituents to SMOs through networks of friendships and interpersonal control. But, hypothesis 5: *A SMO which attempts to link both conscience and beneficiary constituents to the organization through federated chapter structures, and hence solidary incentives, is likely to have high levels of tension and conflict.* Social movement analysts who have focused upon what we have termed conscience constituency participation normally call it outsider involvement. Von Eschen et al. (1971), for instance, show that for a local direct action civil rights organization involvement on the part of geographical outsiders (both conscience and beneficiary) created pronounced internal conflict in the organization. Marx and Useem (1971) have examined the record of the recent civil rights movement, the abolitionist movement, and the movement to abolish untouchability in India. In these movements, "...outsiders were much more prone to be active in other causes or to shift their allegiances from movement to movement" (p. 102). Ross (1975) has argued the importance of friendship ties based upon geographical and generational lines to the internal conflict of SDS. The more unlike one another workers are, the less likely there is to be organizational unity, and the more likely it is that separate clique structures will form. If conscience constituents are more likely to be active in other SMOs and to be adherents of more than one SM, we would expect their involvement to be less continuous.

Now we can combine our earlier discussion of conscience and beneficiary constituents with our analysis of SMI and SMO processes. First, conscience constituents are more likely to control larger resource pools. Individuals with more resources exhibit concerns less directly connected with their own material interests. Consequently, conscience constituents are more likely to be adherents to more than one SMO and more than one SMI. Though they may provide the resources for an SMO at some point, they are likely to have conflicting loyalties.

This provides an account for why SMO leaders have been skeptical of the involvement of conscience constituents – intellectuals in labor unions, males in the women's liberation movement, whites in the civil rights movements. Conscience constituents are fickle because they have wide-ranging concerns. They may be even more fickle if they are isolated constituents – they are less likely to violate personal loyalties by switching priority concerns. But organizations which attempt to involve them in face-to-face efforts may have to suffer the consequences of the differences in backgrounds and outside involvements from those of beneficiary constituents. On the one hand, involving only conscience constituents in federated chapters, which might be a method of avoiding such conflict, forces the SMO to pay the price of legitimacy – how can a SMO speak for a beneficiary group when it does not have any beneficiary constituents? On the other hand, depending exclusively upon mass beneficiary constituents reduces the potential size of the resource pool which can be used for goal accomplishment.

Not only may the involvement of conscience and beneficiary constituents lead to interpersonal tensions, it also leads to tactical dilemmas. Meier and Rudwick (1976) document the extent to which the question of whether the NAACP should use black or white lawyers to fight its legal battles has been a continuous one. Especially in the early days, the symbolic value of using black lawyers conflicted sharply with the better training and court room effectiveness of white lawyers. W. E. B. Du Bois came out on the side of court room effectiveness.

Rates of Resource Fluctuation and SMO Adaptation

We have focused thus far upon the development of resource flows to SMOs, primarily in terms of how they link themselves to their constituents and the size of the resource pool controlled by constituents. What are the implications of larger or smaller resource flows for the fate of SMOs, for careers in social movements, and for the use of different types of constituencies?

An interesting question concerns the staying power of new and older entries into a SMI. Hypothesis 6: *Older, established SMOs are more likely than newer SMOs to persist throughout the cycle of SMI growth and decline*. This is similar to the advantage of early entry for a firm in an industry: A structure in place when demand increases improves the likelihood of capturing a share of the market. Stinchcombe (1965, p. 148) points out that "as a general rule, a higher proportion of new organizations fail than old. This is particularly true of new organizational *forms*, so that *if an alternative requires new organization*, it has to be much more beneficial than the old before the flow of benefits compensates for the relative weakness of the newer social structure." All the liabilities of new organizational forms which Stinchcombe elaborates – new roles to be learned, temporary inefficiency of structuring, heavy reliance upon social relations among strangers, and the lack of stable ties to those who might use the organization's services – beset new organizations of established forms as well, if to a lesser degree. Moreover, a history of accomplishment is an important asset, and, as Gamson (1975) shows for his sample of SMOs, longevity provides an edge in the attainment of legitimacy. Older organizations have available higher degrees of professional sophistication, existing ties to constituents, and experience in fund-raising procedures. Thus, as factors conducive to action based upon SM preferences develop, older SMOs are more able to use advertising to reach isolated adherents, even though new SMOs may of course benefit from the experience of older ones. The NAACP, for instance, already had a fund-raising structure aimed at isolated adherents before the increase in demand for civil rights goals increased in the 1960s. And CORE had the advantage of a professional staff member who was committed to the development of such techniques, but it took time for him to convince the decision makers of the organization to pursue such resource mobilization tactics (Meier and Rudwick 1973). Newer SMOs may capture a share of the isolated constituent market, but they will be disadvantaged at least until they establish a clear image of themselves and a structure to capitalize upon it. J. Q. Wilson (1973) cogently argues that competition between SMOs for resources occurs between organizations offering the most similar products, not between those for which competition in goal accomplishment produces conflict. Since SMOs within the same SMI compete with one another for resources, they are led to differentiate themselves from one another. The prior existence of skilled personnel and preexisting images are advantages in this process. In the same way that name recognition is useful to political candidates it is useful to SMOs when issue campaigns occur.

Hypothesis 7: *The more competitive a SMI (a function of the number and size of the existing SMOs) the more likely it is that new SMOs will offer narrow goals and strategies.* We have alluded to the process of product differentiation. As the competition within any SMI increases, the pressure to specialize intensifies. The decision of George Wiley to present the National Welfare Rights Organization as an organization aimed at winning rights for black welfare recipients was apparently made partially as a result of the preexisting turf understandings of other civil rights organizations.

Hypothesis 8: *The larger the income flow to a SMO the more likely that cadre and staff are professional and the larger are these groups.* This proposition flows directly from an economic support model. It is obvi-

ous that the more money is available to an organization, the more full-time personnel it will be able to hire. Though this is not a necessary outcome, we assume that SMOs will be confronted with the diverse problems of organizational maintenance, and as resource flows increase these will become more complex. As in any large organization, task complexity requires specialization. Specialization is especially necessary in modern America, where the legal requirements of functioning necessitate experienced technicians at a number of points in both resource mobilization and attempts to bring influence to bear. The need for skills in lobbying, accounting, and fund raising leads to professionalization.

It is not that SMOs with small resource flows do not recognize the importance of diverse organizational tasks. In them, a small professional cadre may be required to fulfill a diverse range of tasks such as liaison work with other organizations, advertising, accounting, and membership service. Large resource flows allow these functions to be treated as specialties, though organizations of moderate size may have problems of premature specialization. Economies of scale should be reached only at appropriate levels of growth. In CORE we have a good example of this process: early specialization required constant organizational reshuffling in order to combine functions and staff members in what seemed to be the most efficient manner (Meier and Rudwick 1973).

Hypothesis 9: *The larger the SMS and the larger the specific SMIs the more likely it is that SM careers will develop.* A SM career is a sequence of professional staff and cadre positions held by adherents in a number of SMOs and/or supportive institutions. Such a career need not require continuous connection with a SMI, though the larger the SMI the more likely such continuous involvement ought to be. Supportive institutions might be universities, church bodies, labor unions, governmental agencies and the like (Zald and McCarthy 1975). Moreover, target institutions sometimes develop positions for SM cadre, such as human-relation councils in local governments. Corporations have affirmative-action offices and antitrust lawyers.

When the SMI is large, the likelihood of SMI careers is greater simply because the opportunity for continuous employment is greater, regardless of the success or failure of any specific SMO. Though many of the skills developed by individuals in such careers (public relations, for instance) may be usefully applied in different SMIs, our impression is that individuals typically move between SMIs which have similar goals and hence have overlapping constituencies. While we might find individuals moving between civil rights and labor SMOs, we would be unlikely to find movement from civil rights SMOs to fundamentalist, anticommunist ones. (But it should be remembered that communists have become anticommunists, and that an antiwar activist such as Rennie Davis later took an active role in the transcendental meditation movement.) The relevant base for SMO careers, then, is usually SMIs or interrelated SMIs.

Funding strategies affect not only careers but also the use of beneficiary constituents as workers. Hypothesis 10: *The more a SMO is funded by isolated constituents the more likely that beneficiary constituent workers are recruited for strategic purposes rather than for organizational work.* This proposition is central to the strategy of the professional SMO. It leads to considering the mobilization of beneficiary constituent workers as a rational tool for attempts to wield influence, rather than as an important source of organizational resources. Earlier we mentioned the creation of senior citizen groups for purposes of bargaining by the AFL-CIO in the Medicare fight. The use of some poor people for strategic purposes by the Hunger Commission, a professional SMO, also illustrates the point. Also germane is the fact that of the groups in Gamson's study (1975) none that were heavily dependent upon outside sponsors provided selective material incentives for constituents. Binding beneficiary constituents to a SMO with incentives is not so important to an organization which does not need them in order to maintain a resource flow.

Much of our discussion has been framed in terms of discretionary money, but discretionary time is also of importance.

[...]

Conclusion

The resource mobilization model we have described here emphasizes the interaction between resource availability, the preexisting organization of preference structures, and entrepreneurial attempts to meet preference demand. We have emphasized how these processes seem to operate in the modern American context. Different historical circumstances and patterns of preexisting infrastructures of adherency will affect the strategies of SMO entrepreneurial activity in other times and places. Our emphasis, however, seems to be useful in accounting for parallel activity in different historical contexts, including peasant societies, and in explaining the processes of growth and decline in withdrawal movements as well.

The history of the Bolshevik SMO (Wolfe 1955) shows how important stable resource flows are to the competitive position of a SMO. The Bolsheviks captured the resource flow to the Russian Social Revolutionary movement and, at certain points in their history, depended heavily upon isolated conscience constituents. Free media are probably necessary to mass isolated constituent involvement in resource flows, so isolated adherents with control over large resource pools are probably more important to SMI growth in societies without mass media. Leites and Wolf (1970) make a similar analysis of the revolutionary SMI in its relationship to the constant rewards of participation by the peasants in Vietnam. Of course, the extent of discretionary resources varies considerably between that case and the modern American case, but so did the ability of authorities to intervene in the manipulation of costs and rewards of individual involvement in the revolutionary

SMO. The flow of resources from outside South Vietnam was important in the SMO's ability to manipulate these costs and rewards. Extranational involvement in the American SMS seems almost nonexistent.

Moreover, Oberschall (1973) has shown how important communal associations may be for facilitating mobilization in tribal and peasant societies. Although the number of SMOs and hence the size of the SMI may be smaller in peasant societies, resource mobilization and SM facilitation by societal infrastructure issues are just as important.

Withdrawal movements are typically characterized primarily by the way in which constituents are bound to the SMO (Kanter 1972). But SMOs in withdrawal SMs also encounter difficulties in developing stable resource flows, and they use a variety of strategies similar to those of other SMOs in response to their difficulties. The recent behavior of the Unification Church of America (led by the Rev. Sun Myung Moon) in the United States illustrates processes close to those we have focused upon for modern reform movements: heavy use of advertising and emphasis upon stable resource flows in order to augment the development of federated constituencies. The Father Divine Peace Mission (Cantril 1941) utilized rather different strategies of resource mobilization, including a heavier dependence upon the constituents themselves, but the importance of maintaining flows for continued viability was recognized in both of these withdrawal movements.

Our attempt has been to develop a partial theory; we have only alluded to, or treated as constant, important variables – the interaction of authorities, SMOs, and bystander publics; the dynamics of media involvement; the relationship between SMO workers and authorities; the impact of industry structure; the dilemmas of tactics. Yet, in spite of the limitations of our brief statement of the resource mobilization perspective, we believe it offers important new insights into the understanding of social movement phenomena and can be applied more generally.

References

Bailis, L. 1974. *Bread or Justice*. Springfield, Mass.: Heath-Lexington.

Bain, J. S. 1959. *Industrial Organization*. New York: Wiley.

Bowen, D., E. Bowen, S. Gawiser, and L. Masotti. 1968. "Deprivation Mobility, and Orientation toward Protest of the Urban Poor." Pp. 187–200 in *Riots and Rebellion: Civil Violence in the Urban Community*, edited by L. Masotti and D. Bowen. Beverly Hills, Calif.: Sage.

Cantril, H. 1941. *The Psychology of Social Movements*. New York: Wiley.

——. 1965. *The Pattern of Human Concern*. New Brunswick, N. J.: Rutgers University Press.

Crawford, T. J., and M. Naditch. 1970. "Relative Deprivation, Powerlessness and Militancy: The Psychology of Social Protest." *Psychiatry* 33 (May): 208–23.

Critical Mass Bulletin. 1973–74. Vol. 1. University of Tennessee.

Downs, A. 1972. "Up and Down with Ecology – the Issue Attention Cycle." *Public Interest* 28 (Summer): 38–50.

Gamson, W. A. 1975. *The Strategy of Protest*. Homewood, Ill.: Dorsey.

Gurr, T. R. 1970. *Why Men Rebel*. Princeton, N. J.: Princeton University Press.

Harrington, M. 1968. *Toward a Democratic Left: A Radical Program for a New Majority*. New York: Macmillan.

Kanter, R. M. 1972. *Commitment and Community: Communes and Utopias in Sociological Perspective*. Cambridge, Mass.: Harvard University Press.

Killian, L. 1972. "The Significance of Extremism in the Black Revolution." *Social Forces* 20 (Summer): 41–48.

Leites, N., and C. Wolf, Jr. 1970. *Rebellion and Authority*. Chicago: Markham.

Lipsky, M. 1968. "Protest as a Political Resource." *American Political Science Review* 62:1144–58.

Lowi, T. J. 1971. *The Politics of Disorder*. New York: Basic.

McCarthy, J. D., and M. N. Zald. 1973. *The Trend of Social Movements in America: Professionalization and Resource Mobilization*. Morristown, N. J.: General Learning Press.

Marx, G. T. 1970. "Issueless Riots." *Annals* 391 (September): 21–33.

Marx, G. T. 1974. "Thoughts on a Neglected Category of Social Movement Participant: The Agent Provocateur and the Informant." *American Journal of Sociology* 80 (September): 402–42.

Marx, G. T., and M. Useem. 1971. "Majority Involvement in Minority Movements: Civil Rights, Abolition, Untouchability." *Journal of Social Issues* 27 (January): 81–104.

Meier, A., and E. Rudwick. 1973 *CORE: A Study in the Civil Rights Movement, 1942–1968*. New York: Oxford University Press.

———. 1976. "Attorneys Black and White. A Case Study of Race Relations within the NAACP." *Journal of American History* 62 (March): 913–46.

Morgan, J. N., R. F. Dye and J. H. Hybels. 1975. *A Survey of Giving Behavior and Attitudes: A Report to Respondents*. Ann Arbor, Mich.: Institute for Social Research.

Mueller, E. 1972. "A Test of a Partial Theory of Potential for Political Violence." *American Political Science Review* 66 (September): 928–59.

Oberschall, A. 1973. *Social Conflict and Social Movements*. Englewood Cliffs, N. J.: Prentice-Hall.

Olson, M., Jr. 1965. *The Logic of Collective Action*. Cambridge, Mass.: Harvard University Press.

Perrow, C. 1972. *Complex Organizations: A Critical Essay*. Glenview, Ill.: Scott, Foresman.

Quarantelli, E. L., and J. R. Hundley. 1975. "A Test of Some Propositions about Crowd Formation and Behavior." Pp. 317–86 in *Readings in Collective Behavior*, edited by R. R. Evans. 2d ed. Chicago: Rand McNally.

Rose, A. 1967. *The Power Structure*. New York: Oxford University Press.

Ross, R. 1975. "Generational Change and Primary Groups in a Social Movement." Unpublished paper. Clark University, Worcester, Mass.

Smelser, N. 1963. *Theory of Collective Behavior*. New York: Free Press.

Snyder, D., and C. Tilly. 1972. "Hardship and Collective Violence in France." *American Sociological Review* 37 (October): 520–32.

Stallings, R. A. 1973. "Patterns of Belief in Social Movements: Clarifications from Analysis of Environmental Groups." *Sociological Quarterly* 14 (Autumn): 465–80.

Stinchcombe, A. L. 1965. "Social Structure and Organizations." Pp. 142–93 in *Handbook of Organizations*, edited by James March. Chicago: Rand-McNally.

Strickland, D. A., and A. E. Johnston. 1970. "Issue Elasticity in Political Systems." *Journal of Political Economy* 78 (September/October): 1069–92.

Tilly, C. 1973. "Does Modernization Breed Revolution?" *Comparative Politics* 5 (April): 425–47.

———. 1975. "Revolution and Collective Violence." Pp. 483–555 in *Handbook of Political Science*, edited by F. Greenstein and N. Polsky. Vol. 3. *Macro Political Theory*. Reading, Mass.: Addison-Wesley.

Tilly, C., L. Tilly, and R. Tilly. 1975. *The Rebellious Century: 1830–1930*. Cambridge, Mass.: Harvard University Press.

Tullock, G. 1966. "Information without Profit." Pp. 141–60 in *Papers on Non-Market Decision Making*, edited by G. Tullock. Charlottesville: University of Virginia, Thomas Jefferson Center for Political Economy.

Turner, R. H. 1970. "Determinants of Social Movement Strategies." Pp. 145–64 in *Human Nature and Collective Behavior: Papers in Honor of Herbert Blumer*, edited by Tamotsu Shibutani. Englewood Cliffs, N. J.: Prentice-Hall.

Turner, R. N., and L. Killian. 1972. *Collective Behavior*. 2d ed. Englewood Cliffs, N. J.: Prentice-Hall.

Von Eschen, D., J. Kirk, and M. Pinard. 1971. "The Organizational Sub-Structure of Disorderly Politics." *Social Forces* 49 (June): 529–43.

Wilkinson, P. 1971. *Social Movements*. New York: Praeger.

Wilson, J. 1973. *Introduction to Social Movements*. New York: Basic.

Wilson, J. Q. 1973. *Political Organizations*. New York: Basic.

Wolfe, B. 1955. *Three Who Made a Revolution*. Boston: Beacon.

Wootton, G. 1970. *Interest Groups*. Englewood Cliffs, N. J.: Prentice-Hall.

Zald, M. N., and R. Ash. 1966. "Social Movement Organizations: Growth, Decline and Change." *Social Forces* 44 (March): 327–40.

Zald, M. N. and J. D. McCarthy 1975. "Organizational Intellectuals and the Criticism of Society." *Social Service Review* 49 (September): 344–62.

17 Organizational Repertoires

Elisabeth S. Clemens

Although we commonly think of social movements as agents of change, the dominant accounts of the relation of movements to politics lead to the opposite conclusion. While movements are often credited with limited substantive achievements – the passage of legislation or the defeat of a particular politician – at an organizational level we have come to expect co-optation, conservative goal transformation, and the "iron law of oligarchy," all operating to minimize differences between a challenging social movement and existing political institutions (Jenkins 1977; Michels [1911] 1962). Even in the case of social revolution, as Tocqueville ([1856] 1955) argued, insurgent movements may only intensify already emergent patterns of state authority. In each of these contests between established political institutions and oppositional social movements, the existing institutions endure even if the substance of policy is altered. But analytically, we are left with the question of how political institutions change. What accounts for transformations in the basic models or conventions that inform political organization and action?

Such a broad question is most easily approached in a specific context. In the decades immediately before and after the turn of the century, the institutions of American politics underwent "one of the more significant governmental transformations in American history – the emergence of meaningful regulatory and administrative policies" along with "a series of lasting changes in the nature and structure of political participation; party voting declined and interest-group politics became more important" (McCormick 1986, p. 83). These changes in the basic models of political participation came in the wake of efforts by agrarian groups and organized labor to secure greater leverage in a polity where the formal equality of white male citizens seemed increasingly irrelevant. At the same time, women mobilized to secure the vote for the one half of the adult population that was formally disenfranchised. But the connections between changing political institutions and the wave of popular political mobilization remain unclear.

In the scholarly division of labor, these two problems have been addressed by separate literatures: the study of social movements and the history of party systems or electoral regimes. Of late, however, women's historians have questioned this partitioning of inquiry, arguing that as more "is learned of the magnitude and centrality of women's contributions in these years, the more likely it seems that understanding them will provide a basis for the comprehensive analysis of progressivism that has eluded historians until now" (DuBois 1991, pp. 162–63). In order to arrive at such an analysis, however, two theoretical assumptions that have led us to discount social movements as sources of change must be reconsidered.

First, some movement organizations may be comparatively immune to pressures to adapt to the existing institutional environment. To establish this possibility, I will identify the logics of political incorporation implicit in the classic models of political sociology – specifically those of Robert Michels and Max Weber – and then apply them to a set of social movement groups known collectively as the "woman movement" of the late 19th and early 20th centuries in the

United States. This movement was rooted in the antebellum proliferation of female benevolent societies and abolitionist activities. When the Civil War amendments failed to provide for their enfranchisement, women gradually regrouped around the causes of temperance and woman suffrage, while constructing an impressive network of nationwide, federated women's organizations (Scott 1991). By the 1880s, women's organizations and causes were established alongside, but largely apart from, the nation's formal political institutions. The next decades saw increasing political mobilization of women as well as a series of legislative gains that compared favorably not only with the successes of women in other nations but also with the victories of labor and agrarian insurgents in the United States (Clemens 1990; Skocpol and Ritter 1991). The ability of women's groups to enter the political arena without being fully co-opted suggests that processes of conservative organizational transformation are conditioned by both the social identity of those organized and the character of existing political institutions.

Second, at least some of the interactions between social movements and existing political institutions must be capable of producing changes in those conventions that inform political action and organization. After presenting an alternative model of the interaction of movements and institutions, I will argue that the organizational dynamics of the American woman movement help to explain one of the most important institutional changes in U.S. political history: the shift from the 19th-century "state of courts and parties" to a political regime grounded in legislative activity and interest-group bargaining (Skowronek 1982; McCormick 1986). While internal struggles and electoral tactics were central forces in the decline of the parties and the preeminent position of electoral politics (McGerr 1986; Shefter 1983), voluntary associations played a key role in elaborating a new style of politics focused on specific issues, interests, and legislative responses. A rapidly growing literature now documents the widespread involvement of women's groups in a political project that moved from the "municipal housekeeping" of the 1890s to the development of formidable state and national lobbies during the 1910s and the 1920s. While rarely producing a pure expression of womanhood, these efforts did span lines of race, ethnicity, class, and region (Baker 1991; Frankel and Dye 1991; Muncy 1991; Scott 1991). Women's groups were not alone in this organizational innovation, but because of their marginal position with respect to electoral politics, their efforts to create an institutional alternative are particularly clear.

The central point, then, is to replace the focus on bureaucratization that characterizes work in the Michels-Weber tradition with a recognition that the social world offers multiple models of organization as well as conventions concerning who may use what models for what purposes. Models of organization comprise both templates for arranging relationships within an organization and sets of scripts for action culturally associated with that type of organization. Thus, models may be thought of as being intermediate to abstract dimensions of organizational form (e.g., degree of hierarchy) and to examples of specific organizations. Models can refer to "organizations of that type" or to "organizations that do that type of thing." Mention of either an attribute or an action may invoke a shared model or form of organizing.

Women's groups, along with others, were politically successful insofar as they adapted existing nonpolitical models of organization for political purposes. Rather than adopting a single bureaucratic form, these groups made use of multiple models of organization – unions, clubs, parliaments, and corporations – each of which articulated in different ways with existing political institutions. This finding requires that the scope of the standard Michels-Weber account of social movement development be delimited by a more elaborated analysis of social organization. Drawing on current debates in organization theory, I will argue that our understanding of the relation of social movements to political change has been handicapped by the twin assumptions that the choice of organizational form is governed primarily by considerations of efficacy and that classic bureaucratic hierarchies are the most effective form for achieving political goals. The choice of organizational models may also be governed by "logics of appropriateness" (March and Olsen 1989, pp. 23–24) or institutional norms (DiMaggio and Powell 1983) and, given variations in environment, composition, and organizational goals, bureaucratic forms may well prove less effective than network arrangements, solidary groups, or other conceivable alternatives (Powell 1990). Finally, when deployed in novel ways by unfamiliar groups, even the most familiar organizational models can have unsettling consequences for political institutions.

The set of organizational models that are culturally or experientially available may be thought of as an "organizational repertoire." This concept integrates the theoretical vocabulary of organization theorists sensitive to diversity of form with the cognitive or cultural framework of "repertoires of collective action" put forward by social movement scholars attuned to historical variation (Tilly 1978, 1986). As in social constructionist accounts, institutionalization, and by extension institutional change, is understood as the product of habitualization, the self-reproduction (or failure thereof) of a particular social pattern (Jepperson 1991). But rather than focusing on a "shared history" of interaction as the primary source of reciprocal typifications (Berger and Luckmann 1966, pp. 53–67), this analysis argues that consensus may also result as actors make use of a common, culturally available (rather than situationally constituted) repertoire of alternative models for interpreting a situation or acting in it. By deploying multiple organizational models in diverse institutional fields, social movements can be a source of institutional change even if they themselves undergo transformations of a more or less conservative nature.

In developing a model of institutional change, this argument draws on contemporary organization theory while requiring a shift in focus away from the centers of institutionalized organizational fields and toward their peripheries. Rather than attributing the disruption of organizational fields to various exogenous shocks, this account suggests that strategic political action as well as the search for collective identities produces migrations of organizational models and, potentially, the disruption of organized fields of action. The institutions of modern society are understood to be "potentially contradictory and hence make multiple logics available to individuals and organizations" (Friedland and Alford 1991, p. 232). These movements of organizational models are patterned in at least two ways: by the distribution of multiple memberships in organizational fields – the Simmelian web of group affiliations – and by the cultural logics informing the deployment of organizational repertoires. In developing a theory of organizational choice, James March pointed to the role of imitation as a component of "sensible foolishness," arguing that "in order for imitation to be normatively attractive we need a better theory of who should be imitated" (1979, pp. 75–76). Earlier generations of political actors found just such a theory embedded in their repertoires of organization, the cultural understandings linking organizational models to actors and purposes.

The Woman Movement: Scope and Sources

The potential of social movements or voluntary associations to transform institutional politics is evident in a striking – although, until recently, underappreciated – case of political organization by a comparatively disadvantaged group. The American "woman movement" of the late 19th and early 20th centuries drew together women who were relatively privileged in terms of economic standing and education (Blair 1980; Sklar 1985), yet suffered from formal and informal exclusionary practices that limited their ability to cultivate political skills or to exercise those skills if they were somehow acquired. Notwithstanding their formal disenfranchisement in much of the nation (the Nineteenth Amendment was not ratified until 1920), middle-class and upper-middle-class women constructed an impressive array of voluntary associations that were a significant force in the public life of the nation. Eighteen years after its founding in 1874, the Women's Christian Temperance Union (WCTU) numbered 150,000 members (Bordin 1981, pp. 3–4) and exerted influence on legislation ranging from temperance to woman suffrage. The General Federation of Women's Clubs (GFWC) was founded in 1890 and had perhaps 500,000 members by 1905 and over 1 million by the end of the decade. In addition to these groups, associated charities, civic clubs, auxiliaries to fraternal orders, and suffrage associations filled out a dense network of women's organizations. As a key element of the era's social reform constituency, these groups contributed to the founding of America's distinctively "maternalist" welfare state, a policy regime emphasizing programs such as mothers' pensions rather than unemployment and old age insurance (Gordon 1990; Skocpol 1992).

At an institutional level, women's groups were central to a broader reworking of the organizational framework of American politics: the decline of competitive political parties and electoral mass mobilization followed by the emergence of a governing system centered on administration, regulation, lobbying, and legislative politics. This change involved the invention of new models of political participation outside the established parties and the articulation of interests and demands that could be addressed by legislation and the active intervention of state agencies. Although the invention of modern interest-group politics may not have been intended by women activists, it was one of the most important consequences of this period of experimentation with political organization.

Although women's organizations of the period realized that some form of political action would be needed to advance many of their causes, politics as usual was out of the question. In addition to their formal exclusion from electoral activity, women's associations joined in a broader cultural attack on political methods. According to Mrs. Croly, the first president of the GFWC: "If I were to state what seems to me to be the great hindrance to club life and growth, it would be the employment of political methods, of political machinery and wire-pulling to bring about results. Politics can never be purified until its methods are changed, while its introduction into our club life subverts the whole intention and aims of club organization" (Croly 1898, p. 128).

Politics itself was not rejected, only the existing forms of political organization, the models of the electoral party and patronage machines. To construct an alternative, women's groups drew on models of organization that were culturally or experientially available in other areas of social life. Borrowing from this broader repertoire of social organization, these groups helped transform the repertoire of political action in the Progressive Era.

[...]

Focusing on repertoires of organization, the analysis seeks to establish mechanisms for such changes by locating the interaction of social movements and politics within a broader social system that embraces alternative models of organization and multiple institutions that may promote organizational conformity or isomorphism (DiMaggio and Powell 1983). While applications of the neo-institutionalist model that examine a single focal institution (usually the state or the professions) tend to emphasize how isomorphic processes promote stability and homogeneity, the opposite outcome is also possible. When familiar organizational forms are deployed in unfamiliar ways, insurgent groups may well destabilize existing institutions and ultimately contribute to the institutionalization of new conventions for political action. Organizational heterogeneity is reflected in the repertoires of organization; this is an account of cultural "tool kits" whose potential to create change flows from the complex organization of modern societies rather than from "unsettled" times (Swidler 1986). Rather than rejecting the classic Michels-Weber model, I will use the case of the woman movement to identify scope conditions for that model and, by extension, to provide criteria for identifying the types of movements most likely to contribute to significant institutional change in the political arena.

The Iron Law Reconsidered

Political organization can have profoundly ironic effects. As Robert Michels argued in his classic study of the Social Democratic Party in Wilhelmine Germany, "Organization is the weapon of the weak in the struggle with the strong." But this leverage is gained at a high price: "Organization is . . . the source from which the conservative currents flow over the plain of democracy, occasioning there disastrous floods and rendering the plain unrecognizable" ([1911] 1962, pp. 61–62). Hierarchical bureaucratic organization is necessary to compete effectively in the formal political arena, yet the processes of competition and organization distance the leadership from the interests of their followers and from the organization's initial commitment to the transformation of the political system.

Although the inevitability of such conservative transformations has been challenged within the literature on social movements, immunity is associated with forms of insulation – economic independence, membership exclusivity, and ideological or professional purity (Jenkins 1977; Selznick 1960, pp. 23, 77, 153; Zald and Ash 1966). Furthermore, these studies have tended to focus on the internal dynamics of voluntary organizations rather than on their interactions with political institutions. For Michels, however, these may well be the exceptions that prove the rule. In his original analysis, ongoing

interaction of radical political organizations with the institutions of formal politics and the economic environment was the primary engine of conservative transformation. Thus, we are left with a paradox, one that has been central to critiques of political pluralism (McAdam 1982, pp. 5–6, 18–19). To the extent that organized groups committed to political change seek to secure change through political processes – the give-and-take of coalition building and electoral mobilization – they seem doomed to fail as their goals of social change are sacrificed to the constraints of political process.

In this article, my central claim is that turn-of-the-century women's organizations – along with other associations – did cause substantial changes within American politics. Therefore, my first task must be to explain why women's organizations were comparatively immune from the logics of conservative transformation described in Michels's analysis. In *Union Democracy* (1956), the famous deviant case analysis of the International Typographical Union, Lipset, Trow, and Coleman argued that the "internal politics" of the union (the organization of work, the strength of locals, and a distinctive history of political conflict) contributed to its relative immunity from Michels's iron law. To understand the transformative potential of the women's groups of the Progressive Era, however, three aspects of external politics must be examined. The first two concern the relation of an organizational model to broader social structures. Michels's argument builds on two distinctive logics of incorporation – economic and political – that assume an organizational membership of enfranchised heads of households. Consequently, the effects of organization may vary with the social identity of those who are organized. The third point involves the symbolic rather than instrumental aspects of organizational models; the appropriation of an established model by marginal groups may have consequences that are less than entirely conservative. Given the economic and political situations of their members, women's groups were less likely to be drawn into established forms of political organization. Insofar as they did adopt these established models, however, heightened contradiction rather than effective co-optation was often the result.

The Logic of Economic Incorporation

One of the rules of investigative journalism is to follow the money. This rule also plays an important part in political sociology, receiving its classical form in Weber's analysis of the routinization of charismatic authority. The "administrative staff" of a movement or organization have: "an interest in continuing it in such a way that both from an ideal and a material point of view, their own position is put on a stable everyday basis. This means, above all, making it possible to participate in normal family relationships or at least to enjoy a secure social position in place of the kind of discipleship which is cut off from ordinary worldly connections, notably in the family and in economic relationships" (Weber 1978, p. 246).

This familiar passage identifies two distinct mechanisms by which economic imperatives shape the relation of the administrative staff to the organization: the interest in the continuation of the organization itself and the assurance of their own economic situation "making it possible to participate in normal family relations." Both of these imperatives play a prominent role in Michels's account of the iron law of oligarchy. The administrative staff will be unwilling to challenge the leadership from within: "Financial dependence upon the party, that is to say upon the leaders who represent the majority, enshackles the organization as with iron chains" (Michels 1962, pp. 140, 138). The status of party officials as breadwinners for their families also pushes the organization's goals in a conservative direction. For that fraction of the bourgeoisie who cast their lot with the working class, "no backward path is open. They are enchained by their own past. They have a family, and this family must be fed" (Michels

1962, p. 208). Family responsibilities and social position produce similar effects on leaders recruited from among the workers, who will be reluctant to abandon their improved status as officials of a labor organization (1962, p. 259). This account is generalizable, therefore, only to the extent that alternative forms of organizational support (e.g., personal or institutional patronage, see Jenkins [1977]) are unavailable and that staff or members are responsible for their own economic well-being and that of their dependents.

These dynamics continue to figure prominently in contemporary discussions of social movements, although a conservative outcome is no longer assumed to be inevitable. Analyses of funding stress the dangers of co-optation posed by a reliance on outside funding or patronage, while noting the limitations of resources within various communities marginalized by established political institutions (Jenkins 1977; McAdam, McCarthy, and Zald 1988). The constraints of everyday life have also been recognized in less narrowly economic terms as "biographical availability" (McAdam 1986); career and family responsibilities may constrain one's ability or inclination to participate in politics.

As I will argue below, the impact of these resource constraints is mediated by the form of organization. The more obvious point, however, is that the Michels-Weber account overlooks the gendered division of labor within households. Many of the leading figures in the woman movement were subject to a different set of constraints. At the most general level, changes in the division of labor and the growth of a market for consumer commodities left middle-class and upper-middle-class women of the late 19th century with increasing amounts of time free from household responsibilities (Wood 1912, pp. 24–25). Among those most active in the women's associations, many were supported financially by their husbands, and others came from families of considerable wealth and education (Blair 1980; Sklar 1985). The imperatives of the breadwinner, so central to both Weber and Michels, were clearly less relevant for these groups. For the less privileged, the women's groups themselves might provide a community – such as the settlement houses (Deegan 1988, pp. 40–45) – or activist careers might be funded by either broad constituencies or prominent patrons. The fact that many educated women remained single or childless – along with many mothers active in these associations having the help of a household staff – lessened the constraints of biographical availability.

The Logic of Political Incorporation

Just as the logic of economic incorporation is mediated by the forms of social organization and family life, the logic of political incorporation is structured by specific institutions. In Michels's terms, political participation leads to the conservative transformation of oppositional organizations by way of the system of electoral competition and the identification of movement leaders with the political establishment. Foreshadowing Anthony Downs's analysis of party systems (1957), Michels argued that by competing in elections, oppositional parties would be drawn toward the political center and, thereby, moderate their radical goals (1962, pp. 334–35). But if electoral competition does not produce favorable outcomes, even formal political parties may adopt alternative organizational models and strategies that emphasize ideological purity or solidary incentives rather than electoral advantage (Kitschelt 1989, p. 41). Furthermore, sheer numbers are less closely linked to victory in other systems of political contestation. For a revolutionary party, the requirements of training cadres may well outweigh the advantages of a large membership. For lobbying groups, as for all those engaged in "symbolic politics," resources, status, and style may matter more than numbers.

Women's formal disenfranchisement obviously distanced them from the logic of elect-oral incorporation. Although their groups frequently sought to persuade male voters to support woman suffrage or temperance or some other cause – and often moderated the radicalism of these claims for strategic ends – these efforts were only loosely coupled to the internal life of most women's associations. Barred from efforts to mobilize members directly as a voting bloc – with the consequent need to acquire majority, if not unanimous, consent to the organization's goals – women's associations typically developed internal "departmental" structures that allowed individual members to focus their efforts on a variety of goals, from visiting the sick to agitating for social legislation. Combined with a political mission summed up in the WCTU motto "Do Everything!" the departmental structure allowed factions or local organizations to experiment in advance of any consensus by the national membership. The organizational arrangements of the woman movement often freed it from the conservative consequences of consensual decision making (Baker 1991, pp. 20–21); when the Woman's Joint Congressional Committee was established in 1920, "procedure held that whenever three of the WJCC's organizations voted to support or oppose a piece of legislation, they formed a subcommittee to do their lobbying" (Muncy 1991, p. 103). Such systems of "loose coupling" (Thompson 1967) provided an additional source of insulation, buffering the internal life of the organization from both environmental constraints that might favor centralized bureaucratic forms directed toward discrete instrumental goals and from the veto of conservative factions within a given group.

The Instrumental Claim for Bureaucratic Organization

The claim for the efficacy of hierarchical bureaucratic organization was the first substantive argument made by Michels (1962) and remains widely accepted, even among his critics:

It is indisputable that the oligarchical and bureaucratic tendency of party organization is a matter of technical and practical necessity. It is the inevitable product of the very principle of organization. Not even the most radical wing of the various socialist parties raises any objection to this retrogressive evolution, the contention being that democracy is only a form of organization and that where it ceases to be possible to harmonize democracy with organization, it is better to abandon the former than the latter. Organization, since it is the only means of attaining the ends of socialism, is considered to comprise within itself the revolutionary content of the party, and this essential content must never be sacrificed for the sake of form. [p. 72]

While it is possible to imagine circumstances in which oppositional groups will be immune from the economic and political logics of conservative incorporation, this claim is the bedrock of Michels's assertion that "who says organization says oligarchy" and, by extension, that organization entails both internal and external conservative transformations. In its most simple form, the argument runs as follows: (1) hierarchical, centralized bureaucracies are the most effective form of organization; (2) consequently, existing political parties and institutions have adopted this form of organization; (3) in the course of pursuing their ends, oppositional parties will adopt the same organizational form for strategic reasons, even at the expense of their ideological commitments; (4) therefore, growing organizational isomorphism will lead oppositional parties to become like established political groups, precluding the possibility of meaningful political change.

This argument may be challenged on at least two points. I will discuss the first, the assumption that there is a single form of bureaucratic hierarchy toward which all organizations evolve in the pursuit of efficacy, in the context of an alternative model to be developed below. The second, however, concerns the assumption that the adoption of existing organizational forms by an oppositional group necessarily has a conservative or moderating influence on its critical stance toward existing political institutions and endangers "internal" democracy. Since politics is structured by intersecting rules – how to organize, who should organize, and for what – it is possible that the adoption of conventional organizational models may be destabilizing as it exposes contradictions within the existing system.

Many early efforts by politically active women accepted both the institutionalized models of American politics and the traditional cultural division of the social world into "separate spheres" for men and women. Yet this borrowing revealed incompatibilities between the organizational systems of politics and gender. Attempts by women to use recognizably political methods eventually necessitated a denial of the dual system of separate spheres. Initially, women's political institutions were largely self-directed. In 1848 the Women's Rights Convention at Seneca Falls issued a formal "Declaration of Principles" and Elizabeth Cady Stanton declared that "woman herself must do this work; for woman alone can understand the height, the depth, the length, the breadth of her degradation" (quoted in Flexner 1970, p. 77). By the second half of the century, women's organizations were promoting "Women's Parliaments" as forums in which women could debate and publicize their views. Through the rest of the 19th century, women drew on this model of separate polities parallel to the separate spheres. In 1892, for example, the Southern California Womans Parliament met for "the full and free discussion of reforms necessary to the progress of women's work in the church, home and society" (1892, p. 1). Women's work was redefined in public terms rather than traditional religious terms, but retained its identity as a distinct feminine realm. Yet by the end of the century, the appeal of this form of political organization had been undermined, in part by its own success. By establishing a common ground for public involvement and domestic ideals, the parliaments helped to make the idea of political involvement by women more widely acceptable. But because the parliaments were so easily linked with the highly contentious issue of woman suffrage, women frequently faced less opposition when they pursued their goals through organizational models that were not derived directly from the existing political system.

But what would such organizational models be like? For women's associations, and for the suffrage organizations in particular, the immediate dilemma was that any instrumental advantages of hierarchical, centralized bureaucratic form counted against one of the central goals of these groups: the demonstration that women were capable of being independent citizens rather than subject to undue direction by priests, husbands, or other authorities. Consequently, it was not enough to replace hierarchical organizations headed by men with bureaucratic voluntary associations led by elite women. From the level of local parlor meetings to national conventions, attention was paid to the form – if not always the substance – of participatory organization and proper procedure. In San Francisco, the Richelieu club was "mostly composed of the presidents of other clubs.... The club's aim is to carry on the drill of parliamentary usage with a view of having a more accurate knowledge of one's rights upon the floor and one's duty in the chair of an assembly" (*Club Life*, October 1902, p. 3). Women's papers regularly featured drills on parliamentary procedure. Although some organizations were dominated by a single national figure (such as the WCTU under Frances Willard), the GFWC regularly elected new presidents and, in almost all cases, the federated structure and complex departmental divisions of these associations provided for considerable opportunity and flexible participation within the woman movement. Although an organizational chart of any of the major women's groups would possess many traits of a classical bureaucracy, individual careers rarely involved a regular progression

through a hierarchy of offices, suggesting that these groups accommodated the shifting familial and economic obligations of activists (Clemens and Ledger 1992). While embracing the internal specialization of the modern corporation, women were much more ambivalent about establishing a clear hierarchy of authority. Although studies of interest-group politics and social movements have both viewed organization in terms of its contribution to instrumental goals of policy change and legislation, the advantages of centralization and specialization may be tempered by the meanings attributed to organizational models and the differing ability of organizational forms to sustain involvement.

This brief overview of women's organizations does, however, establish the premises upon which an alternative account of political organization and institutional change must be fashioned. The first point is that the choice of organizational models is not governed solely by instrumental considerations. Cultures have rules about who should organize in what way and for what purposes; consequently, the choice of a conventional model by an unconventional group may produce neither the efficacy nor the conservative transformations suggested by Michels's analysis. Second, complex societies present many possible models of organization – multiple combinations of hierarchy, centralization, authority, and exchange – which may be simultaneously "legitimate" and incompatible. Americans of the late 19th century were familiar with both the centralized hierarchical forms of the patronage party and the modern corporation, yet the period's politics are often portrayed as a conflict between these two models of organizing public life. To the extent that a challenging group is immune to the processes of incorporation discussed above, both its potential to cause institutional change and the character of that change will reflect the range of alternative models available in its members' repertoires of organization.

Repertoires of Organization: An Alternative Approach

For much of political sociology, organizations matter as resources; they make coordinated action possible and success more likely. The role of organizations in blocking action has also been demonstrated; prior commitments and established networks can make new patterns of mobilization difficult (Connell and Voss 1990). But organization has consequences beyond the process of mobilization itself. As a group organizes in a particular way, adopts a specific model of organization, it signals its identity both to its own members and to others. Models of organization are part of the cultural tool kit of any society and serve expressive or communicative as well as instrumental functions. In addition, the adoption of a particular organizational form influences the ties that an organized group forms with other organizations. The chosen model of collective action shapes alliances with other groups and relations with political institutions. At both cultural and institutional levels, models of organization and collective activity are central mechanisms in the transformation of political systems. Once organizational form is viewed as being simultaneously a statement of identity and constitutive of broader institutional fields, social movements appear as not only vehicles of preexisting interests and causes of specific political outcomes, but as critical sources of institutional change.

In order to make sense of such change, the language of cultural analysis is helpful. If a society's cultural heritage constitutes a set of "models of" and "models for" action (Geertz 1973), an organizational repertoire, the appropriation of each of these possible models is not equally probable. Instead, certain models are privileged by the existing distributions of power, status, and wealth as well as by established institutional arrangements. At the most basic level, there are certain advantages to familiarity: "Even government officials and industrial managers of our own time generally behave as though they pre-

ferred demonstrations and strikes to utterly unconventional forms of collective action" (Tilly 1986, p. 391). Organization theorists have emphasized this process, exploring the ways in which conformity to institutional rules produces increasing homogeneity within organizational fields (DiMaggio and Powell 1983; Meyer and Rowan 1977). But if one recognizes an established *repertoire* of acceptable forms instead of a single institutional rule, processes of institutional isomorphism can also promote change within a social system.

Consider the following possibilities. A group finds itself in a situation where the established models of organization and paths of action are inadequate. This may occur for many reasons: existing models may be tactically or culturally discredited (as wire-pulling and other "methods of politics" were for Mrs. Croly); existing models may be unavailable or off-limits (as electoral politics were for most American women); or no established models of action may be associated with that situation (e.g., methods of holding legislators accountable for specific votes prior to the development of preelection pledges and legislative roll-call reporting). Confronted with analogous situations, organization and decision theorists have developed accounts of search procedures. These accounts typically establish some relation – either purposive or stochastic – between an environment that provides multiple potential "solutions" and some selection criteria or procedures (e.g., Heclo 1974; Kingdon 1984; March and Olsen 1989; Meyer and Rowan 1977). Once selected, the choice of a particular solution or organizational model then has consequences for both the environment and the system of relations among organizations. Certain choices may produce organizations that make sufficient demands on their environment to induce new organizations to form (Westney 1987). At the same time, the choice of a model may draw an organization closer to some groups while weakening other interorganizational ties. For example, teachers may choose to affiliate with an occupational group based on the model of the labor union or one modeled on the professions. This difference, in turn, sets up distinctive alliance patterns with other organizations such as the AFL-CIO or the American Medical Association (Hess 1990).

Applied to the study of political change, this account highlights the significance of the available set of organizational models and the process of selection. The repertoire of organization both reflects and helps to shape patterns of social organization. As it is mastered by any given individual or group, a repertoire is largely constituted through experience or awareness of existing forms of social organization. We know what it is to be part of a committee or a commune or a platoon because we have participated in, observed, or heard of these different forms of organization. Similarly, we know what different organizational models signify with respect to the expectations and behaviors of members as well as the collective identity presented to others. Thus, the initial use of familiar forms by unfamiliar groups will have a destabilizing effect on existing conventions of organization. For example, the clubwomen, now quaint and moderate figures, named themselves in violation of established feminine conventions. While the term "club" was rejected by some as a "masculine" label, more daring groups such as the New England Women's Club "deliberately chose *club* to indicate a break with tradition; it did not want to be associated with good-works societies" (Martin 1987, p. 63; emphasis in source; see also Ruddy 1906, p. 24). For outsiders, organizational form was a signal of these groups' novel qualities and aims. "'What is the object?' was the first question asked of any organization of women, and if it was not the making of garments, or the collection of funds for a church, or philanthropic purpose, it was considered unworthy of attention, or injurious doubts were thrown upon its motives" (Croly 1898, p. 9).

By distancing themselves from religious associations and charitable societies, women's clubs constituted themselves as "absolutely a new thing under the sun" (Wood 1912, p. 188). And in defining itself through the appropriation of organizational models not traditionally associated with female groups, the women's club movement is a clear example of innovation grounded in the materials at hand. This process of organizational change through the rearrangement of existing repertoires characterized the woman movement as a whole.

Once one group has pioneered the use of an organizational model in a new arena, that model may then be adopted for use by other groups. Although the rationale for adoption may flow from momentary strategic advantages, widespread adoption is a source of fundamental change in the organizing categories of the political system. Returning to the specific case of political change in the United States, I argue that the shift from the electoral regime of highly competitive parties to the legislative and administrative focus of interest-group bargaining can be understood by examining the organizational experiments of groups that were comparatively disadvantaged under the first of these regimes. The subsequent shift in the available repertoire of organization – the recognized set of political options – then gave way to a system in which this form of mobilization became part of the taken-for-granted. Writing in 1907, John R. Commons, a prominent economist and social reformer, observed that "there is no movement of the past twenty years more quiet nor more potent than the organization of private interests. No other country in the world presents so interesting a spectacle" ([1907] 1967, p. 359). With respect to the conventions of political action and organization, this new system entailed a focus on legislative rather than electoral politics and a consequent organization on the basis of stakes in particular issues rather than broad political philosophies. As one commentator complained by the 1920s:

The present unionized era of leagues, societies, alliances, clubs, combines and cliques offers confederation for mutual support of almost any interest conceivable except for the diversified interests of the humble in the application of general law. With united front the bankers, the brokers, the dairy men, the detectives, the sportsmen, the motorists, the innkeepers, the barbers, the mintgrowers, the Swiss bell ringers, *et al.*, may and do present their complaints to the legislature for adjustment. [Wismer 1928, p. 172]

Although manufacturers organized non-partisan trade associations in both the United States and Europe, only in the United States did "interest" – rather than party, class, language, or religion – become the primary idiom of political life, a *legitimate* if not necessarily welcome form of political organization (see also Clemens 1990; Maier 1981; McCormick 1986; Reddy 1987; Rodgers 1987). The making of specific claims on legislatures was not in itself new, but previously took the form of petitions, private bills directed at individuals, or the considerable bribery of the Gilded Age (Thompson 1985). What was new was the exertion of issue-specific pressure through political education, public opinion, expert testimony, and the increasingly sophisticated legislative tactics of issue- or constituency-based organizations.

This new system of political organization grew out of an eclectic process of reorganization. Rather than accepting a single model for political action, groups drew on both traditional models and the most modern good government groups as well as imitating what worked for their frequent opponents, the corporations and political machines. By the 1890s, for example, temperance associations and women's groups had set up their own precinct organizations and departmental organizations to exert focused pressure on specific government institutions (Bordin 1981; Kerr 1980). In California, the Women's Christian Temperance Union "exerted an influence out of proportion to its size, because of its strong church support, its unique ability to cooperate easily with all other temperance organizations, and because, unlike the fraternal societies, it de-

voted its energies almost entirely to agitation and reform work. On the model of the national W.C.T.U. the state organization set up many departments, thirty in all, each concentrating on a separate phase of temperance work" (Ostrander 1957, p. 58).

Recognizing the need to create a political counterweight and a vehicle for shaping public opinion, the liquor industry responded by appropriating an organizational model then unfamiliar in business politics: "The liquor dealers formed an organization which, to outward appearances at least, was based on an idea new to California. They formed what was publicized as a liquor-men's temperance association. Following the example of many temperance organizations before them, the liquor dealers patterned themselves after Masonic design. The new organization was called the Knights of the Royal Arch, and in April, 1902, the Grand Lodge of the Knights of the Royal Arch was formed in San Francisco" (Ostrander 1957, p. 100).

Complete with exotically titled officials, and, no doubt, secret handshakes, this innovation by the liquor interests appears retrograde, a move away from the modern politics of interest based on public opinion and expertise rather than fraternal solidarity. But to conceive of institutional change as the product of novel applications of existing organizational repertoires is not to claim that all such applications will be effective. If California's liquor dealers engaged in a retrospective form of organizational borrowing, temperance advocates and especially women's groups helped to transform the meaning of corporate political models such as the lobby. In the process, a model that had been associated with corrupt practices was now transformed and legitimated as a taken-for-granted component of political action.

This account of changes in the forms of political organization generates a series of propositions quite different from those associated with the Michels-Weber model. *First*, rather than identifying a unilinear trend toward hierarchical, bureaucratic forms, this alternative account suggests that we should expect to find a lot of cultural work around the questions of What kind of group are we? and What do groups like us do? The links between organizational and cultural analysis are clear; models of organization are not only conventions for coordinating action but also statements of what it means for certain people to organize in certain ways for certain purposes (Kanter 1972). *Second,* we should expect that both the substance of these debates and the subsequent patterns of mobilization should vary by the set of organizational models that are culturally and experientially available to a given group at a particular point in time. *Third,* patterns of organization in response to novel or ambiguous situations should be shaped by a group's existing or desired ties to other groups committed to a particular model of organization. The selection of a specific organizational form should then strengthen ties between some organizations while weakening others.

[. . .]

References

Baker, Paula. 1991. *The Moral Frameworks of Public Life: Gender, Politics, and the State in Rural New York, 1870–1930.* New York: Oxford University Press.

Berger, Peter L., and Thomas Luckmann. 1966. *The Social Construction of Reality: A Treatise in the Sociology of Knowledge.* Garden City, N.Y.: Anchor.

Blair, Karen J. 1980. *The Clubwoman as Feminist: True Womanhood Redefined, 1868–1914.* New York: Holmes & Meier.

Bordin, Ruth. 1981. *Woman and Temperance: The Quest for Power and Liberty, 1873–1900.* Philadelphia: Temple University Press.

Braude, Ann. 1989. *Radical Spirits: Spiritualism and Women's Rights in Nineteenth-Century America.* Boston: Beacon.

Clemens, Elisabeth S. 1990. "Organizing as Interests: The Transformation of Social Politics in the United States, 1890–1920." Ph.D. dissertation. University of Chicago, Department of Sociology.

Clemens, Elisabeth S., and Patrick Ledger. 1992. "Careers of Activism in the Woman Suffrage Movement." Paper presented at the meetings of the American Sociological Association, Pittsburgh.

Commons, John R. (1907) 1967. *Proportional Representation.* New York: Augustus M. Kelley.

Connell, Carol, and Kim Voss. 1990. "Formal Organization and the Fate of Social Movements: Craft Association and Class Alliance in the Knights of Labor." *American Sociological Review* 55 (2): 255–69.

Croly, Mrs. J. C. 1898. *The History of the Women's Club Movement in America.* New York: Henry G. Allen.

Deegan, Mary Jo. 1988. *Jane Addams and the Men of the Chicago School, 1892–1918.* New Brunswick, N.J.: Transaction.

DiMaggio, Paul, and Walter W. Powell. 1983. "The Iron Cage Revisited: Institutional Isomorphism and Collective Rationality in Organizational Fields." *American Sociological Review* 48 (2): 147–60.

——. 1991. Introduction to *The New Institutionalism in Organizational Analysis,* edited by Walter W. Powell and Paul DiMaggio. Chicago: University of Chicago Press.

Downs, Anthony. 1957. *An Economic Theory of Democracy.* New York: Harper & Row.

DuBois, Ellen C. 1991. "Harriot Stanton Blatch and the Transformation of Class Relations among Woman Suffragists." Pp. 162–79 in *Gender, Class, Race, and Reform in the Progressive Era,* edited by Noralee Frankel and Nancy S. Dye. Lexington: University Press of Kentucky.

Flexner, Eleanor. 1970. *Century of Struggle: The Woman's Rights Movement in the United States.* New York: Atheneum.

Frankel, Noralee, and Dye, Nancy S., eds. 1991. *Gender, Class, Race and Reform in the Progressive Era.* Lexington: University Press of Kentucky.

Friedland, Roger, and Robert R. Alford. 1991. "Bringing Society Back In: Symbols, Practices, and Institutional Contradictions." Pp. 232–63 in *The New Institutionalism in Organizational Analysis,* edited by Walter W. Powell and Paul DiMaggio. Chicago: University of Chicago Press.

Geertz, Clifford. 1973. *The Interpretation of Cultures.* New York: Basic.

Gordon, Linda, ed. 1990. *Women, the State, and Welfare*. Madison: University of Wisconsin Press.

Hannan, Michael T., and John Freeman. 1986. "Where Do Organizational Forms Come From?" *Sociological Forum* 1 (1): 50–72.

Heclo, Hugh. 1974. *Modern Social Politics in Britain and Sweden*. New Haven, Conn.: Yale University Press.

Hess, Carla. 1990. "The Construction of Boundaries and Divisions of Labor: Teachers, Workers, and Professionals." Paper presented at the annual meetings of the American Political Science Association, San Francisco.

Jenkins, J. Craig. 1977. "Radical Transformation of Organizational Goals." *Administrative Science Quarterly* 22 (4): 568–86.

Jepperson, Ronald L. 1991. "Institutions, Institutional Effects, and Institutionalism." Pp. 143–63 in *The New Institutionalism in Organizational Analysis*, edited by Walter W. Powell and Paul DiMaggio. Chicago: University of Chicago Press.

Kanter, Rosabeth Moss. 1972. *Commitment and Community: Communes and Utopias in Sociological Perspective*. Cambridge, Mass.: Harvard University Press.

Kerr, K. Austin. 1980. "Organizing for Reform: The Anti-Saloon League and Innovation in Politics." *American Quarterly* 32 (1): 37–53.

Kingdon, John W. 1984. *Agendas, Alternatives, and Public Policies*. Boston: Little, Brown.

Kitschelt, Herbert. 1989. *The Logics of Party Formation: Ecological Politics in Belgium and West Germany*. Ithaca, N.Y.: Cornell University Press.

Lipset, Seymour Martin, Martin A. Trow, and James S. Coleman. 1956. *Union Democracy: The Internal Politics of the International Typographical Union*. Glencoe, Ill.: Free Press.

Maier, Charles S. 1981. "'Fictitious bonds...of wealth and law': On the Theory and Practice of Interest Representation." Pp. 27–61 in *Organizing Interests in Western Europe: Pluralism, Corporatism, and the Transformation of Politics*, edited by Suzanne Berger. New York: Cambridge University Press.

March, James G. 1979. "The Technology of Foolishness." Pp. 69–81 in *Ambiguity and Choice in Organizations*, 2d ed. Edited by J. G. March and J. P. Olsen. Bergen: Universitetsforlaget.

March, James G., and Johan P. Olsen. 1989. *Rediscovering Institutions: The Organizational Basis of Politics*. New York: Free Press.

Martin, Theodora Penny. 1987. *The Sound of Our Own Voices: Women's Study Clubs, 1860–1910*. Boston: Beacon.

McAdam, Doug. 1982. *Political Process and the Development of Black Insurgency, 1930–1970*. Chicago: University of Chicago Press.

———. 1986. "Recruitment to High-Risk Activism: The Case of Freedom Summer." *American Journal of Sociology* 92:64–90.

McAdam, Doug, John McCarthy, and Mayer Zald. 1988. "Social Movements." Pp. 695–737 in *Handbook of Sociology*, edited by Neil Smelser. Newbury Park, Calif.: Sage.

McCormick, Richard P. 1986. *The Party Period and Public Policy: American Politics from the Age of Jackson to the Progressive Era*. New York: Oxford University Press.

McGerr, Michael. 1986. *The Decline of Popular Politics: The American North, 1865–1928*. New York: Oxford University Press.

Meyer, John W., and Bryan Rowan. 1977. "Institutionalized Organizations: Formal Structure as Myth and Ceremony." *American Journal of Sociology* 83 (2): 340–63.

Michels, Robert. (1911) 1962. *Political Parties: A Sociological Study of the Oligarchical Tendencies of Modern Democracy*. New York: Free Press.

Muncy, Robyn. 1991. *Creating a Female Dominion in American Reform, 1890–1935*. New York: Oxford University Press.

Ostrander, Gilman M. 1957. "The Prohibition Movement in California, 1848–1933." *University of California Publications in History*, vol. 57. Berkeley: University of California Press.

Perry, Lewis. 1973. *Radical Abolitionism: Anarchy and the Government of God in Antislavery Thought*. Ithaca, N.Y.: Cornell University Press.

Powell, Walter W. 1990. "Neither Market nor Hierarchy: Network Forms of Organization." *Research in Organizational Behavior* 12:295–336.

Reddy, William M. 1987. *Money and Liberty in Modern Europe: A Critique of Historical Understanding*. New York: Cambridge University Press.

Rodgers, Daniel. 1987. *Contested Truths: Keywords in American Politics since Independence*. New York: Basic Books.

Ruddy, Ella Giles, ed. 1906. *The Mother of Clubs, Caroline M. Seymour Severance: An Estimate and Appreciation*. Los Angeles: Baumgardt.

Scott, Anne Firor. 1991. *Natural Allies: Women's Associations in American History.* Urbana: University of Illinois Press.

Selznick, Philip. 1960. *The Organizational Weapon: A Study of Bolshevik Strategy and Tactics.* Glencoe, Ill.: Free Press.

Shefter, Michael. 1983. "Regional Receptivity to Reform: The Legacy of the Progressive Era." *Political Science Quarterly* 98 (3): 459–83.

Shepsle, Kenneth A., and Barry R. Weingast. 1987. "The Institutional Foundations of Committee Power." *American Political Science Review* 81 (1): 85–104.

Sklar, Kathryn Kish. 1985. "Hull House in the 1890s: A Community of Women Reformers." *Signs* 10:658–77.

Skocpol, Theda. 1992. *Protecting Soldiers and Mothers: The Politics of Social Provision in the United States, 1870s–1920s.* Cambridge, Mass.: Harvard University Press, Belknap.

Skocpol, Theda, and Gretchen Ritter. 1991. "Gender and the Origins of Modern Social Policies in Britain and the United States." *Studies in American Political Development* 5 (1): 36–93.

Skowronek, Stephen. 1982. *Building a New American State: The Expansion of National Administrative Capacities, 1877–1920.* New York: Cambridge University Press.

Swidler, Ann. 1986. "Culture in Action: Symbols and Strategies." *American Sociological Review* 51 (2): 273–86.

Thompson, James. 1967. *Organizations in Action.* New York: McGraw-Hill.

Thompson, Margaret. 1985. *The "Spider Web": Congress and Lobbying in the Age of Grant.* Ithaca: N.Y.: Cornell University Press.

Tilly, Charles. 1978. *From Mobilization to Revolution.* Reading, Mass.: Addison-Wesley.

——. 1986. *The Contentious French.* Cambridge, Mass.: Harvard University Press, Belknap.

Tocqueville, Alexis de. (1856) 1955. *The Old Regime and the French Revolution,* translated by Stuart Gilbert. New York: Anchor.

Van Voris, Jacqueline. 1987. *Carrie Chapman Catt: A Public Life.* New York: Feminist Press.

Weber, Max. 1978. *Economy and Society,* edited by Guenther Roth and Claus Wittich. Berkeley: University of California Press.

Westney, D. Eleanor. 1987. *Imitation and Innovation: The Transfer of Western Organizational Patterns to Meiji Japan.* Cambridge, Mass.: Harvard University Press.

Williamson, Oliver E. 1985. *The Economic Institutions of Capitalism.* New York: Free Press.

Wismer, Otto G. 1928. "Legal Aid Organizations: 'Lobbyists for the Poor.'" *Annals of the American Academy of Political and Social Science* 136 (March): 172–76.

Wood, Mary I. 1912. *The History of the General Federation of Women's Clubs: For the First Twenty-Two Years of Its Organization.* New York: General Federation of Women's Clubs.

Zald, Mayer N., and Roberta Ash. 1966. "Social Movement Organizations: Growth, Decay and Change." *Social Forces* 44:327–41.

18 Transnational Environmental Activism

Paul Wapner

Transnational Advocacy Network (TAN) Some activists live in different societies and yet collaborate and assist one another across borders. These activists share common beliefs and concerns (e.g., the environment, human rights, international trade and investment), and they exchange information and resources in pursuit of common goals. Transnational networks of activists and organizations sometimes arise because certain problems can only be addressed at a transnational level. In some cases, these networks arise because activists or organizations in one society reach out to those in other societies who have more resources or more political clout. See Keck and Sikkink (1998).

Interest in transnational activist groups such as Greenpeace, European Nuclear Disarmament (END), and Amnesty International has been surging. [...] Recent scholarship demonstrates that Amnesty International and Human Rights Watch have changed state human rights practices in particular countries. Other studies have shown that environmental groups have influenced negotiations over environmental protection of the oceans, the ozone layer, and Antarctica and that they have helped enforce national compliance with international mandates. Still others have shown that peace groups helped shape nuclear policy regarding deployments in Europe during the cold war and influenced Soviet perceptions in a way that allowed for eventual superpower accommodation. This work is important, especially insofar as it establishes the increasing influence of transnational nongovernmental organizations (NGOS) on states. Nonetheless, for all its insight, it misses a different but related dimension of activist work – the attempt by activists to shape public affairs by working within and across societies themselves.

Recent studies neglect the societal dimension of activists' efforts in part because they subscribe to a narrow understanding of politics. They see politics as a practice associated solely with government and thus understand activist efforts exclusively in terms of their influence upon government. Seen from this perspective, transnational activists are solely global pressure groups seeking to change states' policies or create conditions in the international system that enhance or diminish interstate cooperation. Other efforts directed toward societies at large are ignored or devalued because they are not considered to be genuinely political in character.

Such a narrow view of politics in turn limits research because it suggests that the conception and meaning of transnational activist groups is fixed and that scholarship therefore need only measure activist influence on states. This article asserts, by contrast, that the meaning of activist groups in a global context is not settled and will remain problematic as long as the strictly societal dimension of their work is left out of the analysis. Activist efforts within and across societies are a proper object of study and only by including them in transnational activist research can one render an accurate understanding of transnational activist groups and, by extension, of world politics.

This article focuses on activist society-oriented activities and demonstrates that activist organizations are not simply transnational pressure groups, but rather are political actors in their own right. The main argument is that the best way to think about transnational activist societal efforts is through the concept of "world civic politics." When activists work to change conditions without directly pressuring states, their activities take place in the civil dimension of world collective life or what is sometimes called global civil society. Civil society is that arena of social engagement which exists above the individual yet below the state. It is a complex network of economic, social, and cultural practices based on friendship, family, the market, and voluntary affiliation. Although the concept arose in the analysis of domestic societies, it is beginning to make sense on a global level. The interpenetration of markets, the intermeshing of symbolic meaning systems, and the proliferation of transnational collective endeavors signal the formation of a thin, but nevertheless present, public sphere where private individuals and groups interact for common purposes. Global civil society as such is that slice of associational life which exists above the individual and below the state, but also across national boundaries. When transnational activists direct their efforts beyond the state, they are politicizing global civil society.

[. . .]

Amnesty International, Friends of the Earth, Oxfam, and Greenpeace target governments and try to change state behavior to further their aims. When this route fails or proves less efficacious, they work through transnational economic, social, and cultural networks to achieve their ends. The emphasis on world civic politics stresses that while these latter efforts may not translate easily into state action, they should not be viewed as simply matters of cultural or social interest. Rather, they involve identifying and manipulating instruments of power for shaping collective life. Unfortunately, the conventional wisdom has taken them to be politically irrelevant.

In the following I analyze the character of world civic politics by focusing on one relatively new sector of this activity, transnational environmental activist groups (TEAGS). As environmental dangers have become part of the public consciousness and a matter of scholarly concern in recent years, much attention has been directed toward the transboundary and global dimensions of environmental degradation. Ozone depletion, global warming, and species extinction, for instance, have consequences that cross state boundaries and in the extreme threaten to change the organic infrastructure of life on earth. Responding in part to increased knowledge about these problems, transnational activist groups have emerged whose members are dedicated to "saving the planet." World Wildlife Fund, Friends of the Earth, Greenpeace, Conservation International, and Earth Island Institute are voluntary associations organized across state boundaries that work toward environmental protection at the global level. TEAGS have grown tremendously since the 1970s, with the budgets of the largest organizations greater than the amount spent by most countries on environmental issues and equal to, if not double, the annual expenditure of the United Nations Environment Program (UNEP). Furthermore, membership in these groups has grown throughout the 1980s and 1990s to a point where millions of people are currently members of TEAGS. This article demonstrates that, while TEAGS direct much effort toward state policies, their political activity does not stop there but extends into global civil society. In the following, I describe and analyze this type of activity and, in doing so, make explicit the dynamics and significance of world civic politics.

[. . .]

Disseminating an Ecological Sensibility

Few images capture the environmental age as well as the sight of Greenpeace activists positioning themselves between harpoons and whales in an effort to stop the slaughter of endangered sea mammals. Since 1972, with the formal organization of Greenpeace into a transnational environmental activist group, Greenpeace has emblazoned a host of such images onto the minds of people around the world. Greenpeace activists have climbed aboard whaling ships, parachuted from the top of smokestacks, plugged up industrial discharge pipes, and floated a hot air balloon into a nuclear test site. These direct actions are media stunts, exciting images orchestrated to convey a critical perspective toward environmental issues. Numerous other organizations, including the Sea Shepherds Conservation Society, Earth-First! and Rainforest Action Network, engage in similar efforts. The dramatic aspect attracts journalists and television crews to specific actions and makes it possible for the groups themselves to distribute their own media presentations. Greenpeace, for example, has its own media facilities; within hours it can provide photographs to newspapers and circulate scripted video news spots to television stations in eighty-eight countries. The overall intent is to use international mass communications to expose anti-ecological practices and thereby inspire audiences to change their views and behavior vis-à-vis the environment.

Direct action is based on two strategies. The first is simply to bring what are often hidden instances of environmental abuse to the attention of a wide audience: harpooners kill whales on the high seas; researchers abuse Antarctica; significant species extinction takes place in the heart of the rain forest; and nuclear weapons are tested in the most deserted areas of the planet. Through television, radio, newspapers, and magazines transnational activist groups bring these hidden spots of the globe into people's everyday lives, thus enabling vast numbers of people to "bear witness" to environmental abuse. Second, TEAGS engage in dangerous and dramatic actions that underline how serious they consider certain environmental threats to be. That activists take personal risks to draw attention to environmental issues highlights their indignation and the degree of their commitment to protecting the planet. Taken together, these two strategies aim to change the way vast numbers of people see the world – by dislodging traditional understandings of environmental degradation and substituting new interpretive frames.

[...]

Raising awareness through media stunts is not primarily about changing governmental policies, although this may of course happen as state officials bear witness or are pressured by constituents to codify into law shifts in public opinion or widespread sentiment. But this is only one dimension of TEAG direct action efforts. The new age envisioned by Hunter is more than passing environmental legislation or adopting new environmental policies. Additionally, it involves convincing all actors – from governments to corporations, private organizations, and ordinary citizens – to make decisions and act in deference to environmental awareness. Smitten with such ideas, governments will, activists hope, take measures to protect the environment. When the ideas have more resonance outside government, they will shift the standards of good conduct and persuade people to act differently even though governments are not requiring them to do so. In short, TEAGS work to disseminate an ecological sensibility to shift the governing ideas that animate societies, whether institutionalized within government or not, and count on this to reverberate throughout various institutions and collectivities.

[...]

Consider the following. In 1970 one in ten Canadians said the environment was worthy of being on the national agenda; twenty years later one in three felt not only that it should be on the agenda but that it was the most pressing issue facing Canada. In 1981, 45 percent of those polled in a U.S. survey said that protecting the environment was so important that "requirements and standards cannot be too high and continuing environmental improvements must be made regardless of cost"; in 1990, 74 percent supported the statement. This general trend is supported around the world. In a recent Gallup poll majorities in twenty countries gave priority to safeguarding the environment even at the cost of slowing economic growth; additionally, 71 percent of the people in sixteen countries, including India, Mexico, South Korea, and Brazil, said they were willing to pay higher prices for products if it would help to protect the environment.

These figures suggest a significant shift in awareness and concern about the environment over the past two decades. It is also worth noting that people have translated this sentiment into changes in behavior. In the 1960s the U.S. Navy and Air Force used whales for target practice. Twenty-five years later an international effort costing $5 million was mounted to save three whales trapped in the ice in Alaska. Two decades ago corporations produced products with little regard for their environmental impact. Today it is incumbent upon corporations to reduce negative environmental impact at the production, packaging, and distribution phases of industry. When multilateral development banks and other aid institutions were established after the Second World War, environmental impact assessments were unheard of; today they are commonplace. Finally, twenty years ago recycling as a concept barely existed. Today recycling is mandatory in many municipalities around the world, and in some areas voluntary recycling is a profit-making industry. (Between 1960 and 1990 the amount of municipal solid waste recovered by recycling in the United States more than quintupled.) In each of these instances people are voluntarily modifying their behavior in part because of the messages publicized by activists. If one looked solely at state behavior to account for this change, one would miss a tremendous amount of significant world political action.

A final, if controversial, example of the dissemination of an ecological sensibility is the now greatly reduced practice of killing harp seal pups in northern Canada. Throughout the 1960s the annual Canadian seal hunt took place without attracting much public attention or concern. In the late 1960s and throughout the 1970s and 1980s the International Fund for Animals, Greenpeace, the Sea Shepherds Conservation Society, and a host of smaller preservation groups saw this – in hindsight inaccurately, according to many – as a threat to the continued existence of harp seals in Canada. They brought the practice to the attention of the world, using, among other means, direct action. As a result, people around the globe, but especially in Europe, changed their buying habits and stopped purchasing products made out of the pelts. As a consequence, the market for such merchandise all but dried up with the price per skin plummeting. Then, in 1983, the European Economic Community (EEC) actually banned the importation of seal pelts. It is significant that the EEC did so only after consumer demand had already dropped dramatically. Governmental policy, that is, may have simply been an afterthought and ultimately unnecessary. People acted in response to the messages propagated by activist groups.

When Greenpeace and other TEAGS undertake direct action or follow other strategies to promote an ecological sensibility, these are the types of changes they are seeking. At times, governments respond with policy measures and changed behavior with respect to environmental issues. The failure of governments to respond, however, does not necessarily mean that the efforts of activists have been in vain. Rather, they influence understandings of good conduct throughout societies at large. They help set the boundaries of what is considered acceptable behavior.

When people change their buying habits, voluntarily recycle garbage, boycott certain products, and work to preserve species, it is not necessarily because governments are breathing down their necks. Rather, they are acting out of a belief that the environmental problems involved are severe, and they wish to contribute to alleviating them. They are being "stung," as it were, by an ecological sensibility. This sting is a type of governance. It represents a mechanism of authority that can shape widespread human behavior.

Multinational Corporate Politics

In 1991 the multinational McDonald's Corporation decided to stop producing its traditional clamshell hamburger box and switch to paper packaging in an attempt to cut back on the use of disposable foam and plastic. In 1990 Uniroyal Chemical Company, the sole manufacturer of the apple-ripening agent Alar, ceased to produce and market the chemical both in the United States and abroad. Alar, the trade name for daminozide, was used on most kinds of red apples and, according to some, found to cause cancer in laboratory animals. Finally, in 1990 Starkist and Chicken of the Sea, the two largest tuna companies, announced that they would cease purchasing tuna caught by setting nets on dolphins or by any use of drift nets; a year later Bumble Bee Tuna followed suit. Such action has contributed to protecting dolphin populations around the world.

In each of these instances environmental activist groups – both domestic and transnational – played an important role in convincing corporations to alter their practices. To be sure, each case raises controversial issues concerning the ecological wisdom of activist pressures, but it also nevertheless demonstrates the effects of TEAG efforts. In the case of McDonald's, the corporation decided to abandon its foam and plastic containers in response to prodding by a host of environmental groups. These organizations, which included the Citizens Clearinghouse for Hazardous Waste, Earth Action Network, and Kids against Pollution, organized a "send-back" campaign in which people mailed McDonald's packaging to the national headquarters. Additionally, Earth Action Network actually broke windows and scattered supplies at a McDonald's restaurant in San Francisco to protest the company's environmental policies. The Environmental Defense Fund (EDF) played a mediating role by organizing a six-month, joint task force to study ways to reduce solid waste in McDonald's eleven thousand restaurants worldwide. The task force provided McDonald's with feasible responses to activist demands. What is clear from most reports on the change is that officials at McDonalds did not believe it necessarily made ecological or economic sense to stop using clamshell packaging but that they bent to activist pressure.

Uniroyal Chemical Company ceased producing Alar after groups such as Ralph Nader's Public Interest Research Group (PIRG) and the Natural Resources Defense Council (NRDC) organized a massive public outcry about the use of the product on apples in the U.S. and abroad. In 1989 NRDC produced a study that found that Alar created cancer risks 240 times greater than those declared safe by the U.S. Environmental Protection Agency (EPA). This was publicized on CBS's *60 Minutes* and led to critical stories in numerous newspapers and magazines. Moreover, activists pressured supermarket chains to stop selling apples grown with Alar and pressured schools to stop serving Alar-sprayed apples. The effects were dramatic. The demand for apples in general shrank significantly because of the scare, lowering prices well below the break-even level. This led to a loss of $135 million for Washington State apple growers alone. Effects such as these and continued pressure by activist groups convinced Uniroyal to cease production of the substance not only in the U.S. but overseas as well. Like McDonalds, Uniroyal changed its practices not for economic reasons nor to increase business nor because it genuinely felt Alar was harmful. Rather, it capitulated to activist pressure. In fact, there is evidence from nonindustry sources suggesting that Alar did not pose the level of threat publicized by activists.

Finally, in the case of dolphin-free tuna, Earth Island Institute (EII) and other organizations launched an international campaign in 1985 to stop all drift-net and purse seine fishing by tuna fleets. For unknown reasons, tuna in the Eastern Tropical Pacific Ocean swim under schools of dolphins. For years tuna fleets have set their nets on dolphins or entangled dolphins in drift nets as a way to catch tuna. While some fleets still use these strategies, the three largest tuna companies have ceased doing so. TEAGS were at the heart of this change. Activists waged a boycott against all canned tuna, demonstrated at stockholders' meetings, and rallied on the docks of the Tuna Boat Association in San Diego. Furthermore, EII assisted in the production of the film *Where Have All the Dolphins Gone?* which was shown throughout the United States and abroad; it promoted the idea of "dolphin-safe" tuna labels to market environmentally sensitive brands; and it enlisted Heinz, the parent company of Starkist, to take an active role in stopping the slaughter of dolphins by all tuna companies. Its efforts, along with those of Greenpeace, Friends of the Earth, and others, were crucial to promoting dolphin-safe tuna fishing. One result of these efforts is that dolphin kills associated with tuna fishing in 1993 numbered fewer than 5,000. This represents one-third the mortality rate of 1992, when 15,470 dolphins died in nets, and less than one-twentieth of the number in 1989, when over 100,000 dolphins died at the hands of tuna fleets. These numbers represent the effects of activist efforts. Although governments did eventually adopt domestic dolphin conservation policies and negotiated partial international standards to reduce dolphin kills, the first such actions came into force only in late 1992 with the United Nations moratorium on drift nets. Moreover, the first significant actions against purse seine fishing, which more directly affects dolphins, came in June 1994 with the United States International Dolphin Conservation Act. As with the Canadian seal pup hunt, government action in the case of tuna fisheries largely codified changes that were already taking place.

In each instance, activist groups did not direct their efforts at governments. They did not target politicians; nor did they organize constituent pressuring. Rather, they focused on corporations themselves. Through protest, research, exposés, orchestrating public outcry, and organizing joint consultations, activists won corporate promises to bring their practices in line with environmental concerns. The levers of power in these instances were found in the economic realm of collective life rather than in the strictly governmental realm. Activists understand that the economic realm, while not the center of traditional notions of politics, nevertheless furnishes channels for effecting widespread changes in behavior; they recognize that the economic realm is a form of governance and can be manipulated to alter collective practices.

Perhaps the best example of how activist groups, especially transnational ones, enlist the economic dimensions of governance into their enterprises is the effort to establish environmental oversight of corporations. In September 1989 a coalition of environmental, investor, and church interests, known as the Coalition for Environmentally Responsible Economies (CERES), met in New York City to introduce a ten-point environmental code of conduct for corporations. One month later CERES, along with the Green Alliance, launched a similar effort in the United Kingdom. The aim was to establish criteria for auditing the environmental performance of large domestic and multinational industries. The code called on companies to, among other things, minimize the release of pollutants, conserve nonrenewable resources through efficient use and planning, utilize environmentally safe and sustainable energy sources, and consider demonstrated environmental commitment as a factor in appointing members to the board of directors. Fourteen environmental organizations, including TEAGS such as Friends of the Earth and the International Alliance for Sustainable Agriculture, publicize the CERES Principles (formerly known as the Valdez Principles, inspired by the Exxon *Valdez* oil spill) and enlist corporations to pledge compliance. What is significant from an international perspective is that signatories include at least one Fortune 500 company and a number of multinational corporations. Sun Company, General Motors, Polaroid, and a host of other MNCs have pledged compliance or are at least seriously considering doing so. Because these companies operate in numerous countries, their actions have transnational effects.

The CERES Principles are valuable for a number of reasons. In the case of pension funds, the code is being used to build shareholder pressure on companies to improve their environmental performance. Investors can use it as a guide to determine which companies practice socially responsible investment. Environmentalists use the code as a measuring device to praise or criticize corporate behavior. Finally, the Principles are used to alert college graduates on the job market about corporate compliance with the code and thus attempt to make environmental issues a factor in one's choice of a career. Taken together, these measures force some degree of corporate accountability by establishing mechanisms of governance to shape corporate behavior. To be sure, they have not turned businesses into champions of environmentalism, nor are they as effectual as mechanisms available to governments. At work, however, is activist discovery and manipulation of economic means of power.

Via the CERES Principles and other forms of pressure, activists thus influence corporate behavior. McDonald's, Uniroyal, and others have not been changing their behavior because governments are breathing down their necks. Rather, they are voluntarily adopting different ways of producing and distributing products. This is not to say that their actions are more environmentally sound than before they responded to activists or that their attempt to minimize environmental dangers is sincerely motivated. As mentioned, environmental activist groups do not have a monopoly on ecological wisdom, nor is corporate "greening" necessarily well intentioned. Nonetheless, the multinational corporate politics of transnational groups are having an effect on the way industries do business. And to the degree that these enterprises are involved in issues of widespread public concern that cross state boundaries, activist pressure must be understood as a form of world politics.

Empowering Local Communities

For decades TEAGs have worked to conserve wildlife in the developing world. Typically, this has involved people in the First World working in the Third World to restore and guard the environment. First World TEAGs – ones headquartered in the North – believed that Third World people could not appreciate the value of wildlife or were simply too strapped by economic pressures to conserve nature. Consequently, environmental organizations developed, financed, and operated programs in the field with little local participation or input.

While such efforts saved a number of species from extinction and set in motion greater concern for Third World environmental protection, on the whole they were unsuccessful at actually preserving species and their habitats from degradation and destruction. A key reason for this was that they attended more to the needs of plants and especially animals than to those of the nearby human communities. Many of the earth's most diverse and biologically rich areas are found in parts of the world where the poorest peoples draw their livelihood from the land. As demographic and economic constraints grow tighter, these people exploit otherwise renewable resources in an attempt merely to survive. Ecological sustainability in these regions, then, must involve improving the quality of life of the rural poor through projects that integrate the management of natural resources with grassroots economic development.

Often after having supported numerous failed projects, a number of TEAGs have come to subscribe to this understanding and undertake appropriate actions. World Wildlife Fund (WWF) or World Wide Fund for Nature, as it is known outside English-speaking countries, is an example of such an organization. WWF is a conservation group dedicated to protecting endangered wildlife and wildlands worldwide. It originated in 1961 as a small organization in Switzerland, making grants to finance conservation efforts in various countries. Over the past thirty years it has grown into a full-scale global environmental organization with offices in over twenty countries. Within the past decade, WWF has established a wildlands and human needs program, a method of conservation to be applied to all WWF projects linking human economic well-being with environmental protection. It structures a game management system in Zambia, for example, which involves local residents in antipoaching and conservation efforts, and the channeling of revenues from tourism and safaris back into the neighboring communities that surround the preserves. It informs a WWF-initiated Kilum Mountain project in the Cameroon that is developing nurseries for reforestation, reintroducing indigenous crops, and disseminating information about the long-term effects of environmentally harmful practices. Finally, it is operative in a project in St. Lucia, where WWF has lent technical assistance to set up sanitary communal waste disposal sites, improved marketing of fish to reduce overfishing, and protected mangroves from being used for fuel by planting fast-growing fuel-wood trees. WWF is not alone in these efforts. The New Forests Project, the Association for Research and Environmental Aid (AREA), the Ladakh Project, and others undertake similar actions.

In these kinds of efforts, TEAGS are not trying to galvanize public pressure aimed at changing governmental policy or directly lobbying state officials; indeed, their activity takes place far from the halls of congresses, parliaments, and executive offices. Rather, TEAGS work with ordinary people in diverse regions of the world to try to enhance local capability to carry out sustainable development projects. The guiding logic is that local people must be enlisted in protecting their own environments and that their efforts will then reverberate through wider circles of social interaction to affect broader aspects of world environmental affairs.
[...]

World Civic Politics

The predominant way to think about NGOS in world affairs is as transnational interest groups. They are politically relevant insofar as they affect state policies and interstate behavior. In this article I have argued that TEAGS, a particular type of NGO, have political relevance beyond this. They work to shape the way vast numbers of people throughout the world act toward the environment using modes of governance that are part of global civil society. [...]

I suggested that the best way to think about these activities is through the category of "world civic politics." When TEAGS work through transnational networks associated with cultural, social, and economic life, they are enlisting forms of governance that are civil as opposed to official or state constituted in character. Civil, in this regard, refers to the quality of interaction that takes place above the individual and below the state yet across national boundaries. The concept of world civic politics clarifies how the forms of governance in global civil society are distinct from the instrumentalities of state rule.

At the most foundational level, states govern through legal means that are supported by the threat or use of force. To be sure, all states enjoy a minimum of loyalty from their citizens and administrate through a variety of nonlegal and noncoercive means. Ultimately, however, the authority to govern per se rests on the claim to a monopoly over legitimate coercive power. By contrast, civic power has no legally sanctioned status and cannot be enforced through the legitimate use of violence. It rests on persuasion and more constitutive employment of power in which people change their practices because they have come to understand the world in a way that promotes certain actions over others or because they operate in an environment that induces them to do so. Put differently, civic power is the forging of voluntary and customary practices into mechanisms that govern public affairs. When TEAGS disseminate an ecological sensibility, pressure corporations, or empower local communities, they are exercising civic power across national boundaries.
[...]

19 Affinity Groups and the Movement Against Corporate Globalization

William Finnegan

For Juliette Beck, it began with the story of the Ittu Oromo, Ethiopian nomads whose lives were destroyed, in vast numbers, by a dam – a hydroelectric project sponsored by the World Bank. Beck was a sophomore at Berkeley, taking a class in international rural development. The daughter of an orthopedic surgeon, she had gone to college planning to do premed, but environmental science caught her interest, and the story of the Ittu Oromo precipitated a change of major. Beck was a brilliant student – "One of these new Renaissance people, so smart they could be almost anything," a former professor of hers recalls. [...] By her junior year, she was teaching a class on the North American Free Trade Agreement. "It was one of the most popular student-led classes we've had," her professor says. "I understand it's been cloned on other campuses."

Beck had found her strange grand passion – international trade rules – at an auspicious time. Besides the popularity of her class, there were the events last November in Seattle, where fifty thousand demonstrators shut down a major meeting of the World Trade Organization. Beck, who is twenty-seven, was a key organizer of the Seattle protests.

[...]

Zooming around the scruffy, loft-style offices of Global Exchange, the human-rights organization in San Francisco where she works, she seems conspicuously lacking the self-décor of the other young activists around the place – piercings, tattoos, dreadlocks. It may be that she's simply been too busy to get herself properly tatted up. While we were talking in her office on a recent evening, she tried to deal simultaneously with me and with a significant fraction of the seven hundred E-mail messages that had piled up in her in-box – reading, forwarding, filing, trashing, replying, sighing, grumbling, erupting in laughter.

[...]

> **Participatory Democracy**   In the early 1960s, the New Left promoted what it called participatory democracy (sometimes called "direct democracy"), as opposed to the regular channels of representative democracy. Instead of voting for those who would make the ultimate decisions, a basic goal was to allow people to make decisions directly. Participatory democracy was meant to involve everyone in discussions of an issue before voting on it as a group. Better yet, a consensus might emerge so that a formal vote would not be necessary. Needless to say, this approach, popular with social movements of the 1960s through the 1980s and beyond, works best with small groups, and no one has yet quite figured out how to extend the principle to national decisionmaking or link it to traditional representative democracy. Critics have pointed to the seemingly endless discussions it entails in practice, as well as to the possibility that golden-tongued informal leaders can dominate a group without the accountability they would face if they were formal leaders. Participatory democracy reveals some of the core values of the New Left, especially the idea that individuals should control the world around them by making decisions about issues that directly shape their lives.

After college, Beck went to work as an environmental engineer for a small Bay Area firm. The pay was good, and the work was interesting, but she found herself spending most of her time competing with other firms for contracts. "It made me realize I didn't want to be doing work that was all about money." So she made the downward financial leap into the non-profit sector (and was recently forced to move from chic, expensive San Francisco to cheaper, inconvenient Oakland, where she lives in a group house with no living room). It's a step she says she's never regretted. "I think a lot of people in my generation – not a majority, maybe, but a lot – feel this void," she told me. "We feel like capitalism and buying things are just not fulfilling. Period." She became an organizer for Public Citizen, Ralph Nader's consumer group, which was campaigning, along with labor unions and other allies, to stop the Clinton Administration's effort to get renewed "fast track" authority to negotiate trade agreements with limited congressional oversight. (The problem with such authority, according to its opponents, is its bias, in practice, in favor of industry.) The campaign was successful – the first major defeat in Congress for trade advocates in sixty years. "That was a great victory," Beck said happily. "We defeated some of the most powerful forces on the planet."

[. . .]

In her office at Global Exchange, still crashing through the underbrush of her in-box, she suddenly pulled up short. "Oh, check this out," she said, and pointed to her computer screen. "Have you seen this?"

I had. It was a report prepared by Burson-Marsteller, the Washington publicity firm, which had been leaked and was making the electronic rounds. It was titled "Guide to the Seattle Meltdown: A Compendium of Activists at the W.T.O. Ministerial." Burson-Marsteller's cover letter began, "Dear [Corporate Client]," and characterized the report "not so much as a retrospective on the past, but as an alarming window on the future." The report offered profiles of dozens of groups that had participated in the Seattle protests – from the Anarchist Action Collective to Consumers International to the A.F.L.-C.I.O. – naming leaders, giving Web-site addresses, and including brief descriptions,

usually lifted from the literature of the groups themselves. The cover letter mentioned possible "significant short-term ramifications for the business community" because of the "perceived success of these groups in disrupting Seattle" and, more portentously, warned of "the potential ability of the emerging coalition of these groups to seriously impact broader, longer-term corporate interests."

Burson-Marsteller was at least trying to reckon with what had been revealed in Seattle. The press, the Seattle authorities, the Clinton Administration, the W.T.O., and many other interested parties had largely been ignorant of the popular movement being built around them. Suddenly challenged, everyone had scrambled to respond, some (the police) attacking the protesters, others (Bill Clinton) rhetorically embracing them (while his negotiators continued to pursue in private the controversial policies he was renouncing in public), but all basically hoping that the problem – this nightmare of an aroused, mysteriously well-organized citizenry – would just go away. Burson-Marsteller knew better. Its "compendium" had even picked up on demonstrations being planned for April against the World Bank and the I.M.F. during meetings in Washington, D.C. This was before anything about those demonstrations had appeared in what movement activists insist on calling the corporate press.

I say "movement activists" because nobody has yet figured out what to call them. Sympathetic observers refer to them as "the Seattle coalition," but this title reflects little of the movement's international scope. In the United States, the movement is dramatically – even, one could say, deliberately – lacking in national leaders. It is largely coördinated on-line. I picked Juliette Beck almost at random as a bright thread to follow through this roiling fabric of rising, mostly youthful American resistance to corporate-led globalization.

[. . .]

The World Bank lends money to the governments of poor countries. It was founded, along with the International Monetary Fund, after the Second World War to help finance the reconstruction of Europe. When the Marshall Plan usurped its original purpose, the Bank had to reinvent itself, shifting its focus to Asia, Africa, and Latin America, where the elimination of poverty became its declared mission. This was the first in a long series of institutional costume changes. Today, the Bank, which is headquartered in Washington, D.C., has more than ten thousand employees, a hundred and eighty member states, and offices in sixty-seven of those countries, and lends nearly thirty billion dollars a year. It ventures into fields far beyond its original mandate, including conflict resolution – demobilizing troops in Uganda, clearing land mines in Bosnia. The I.M.F., whose founding purpose was to make short-term loans to stabilize currencies, has similarly had to shape-shift with the times. Also headquartered in Washington, it now makes long-term loans as well and tries to manage the economies of many of its poorer member states.

Both institutions have always been dominated by the world's rich countries, particularly the United States. During the Cold War, this meant that loans were often granted on a crudely political basis. Indeed, the World Bank's first loan – two hundred and fifty million dollars to France, in 1947 – was withheld until the French government purged its Cabinet of Communists. In the Third World, friendly dictators were propped up by loans. Robert McNamara, after presiding over the Vietnam War, became president of the World Bank in 1968, and he expanded its operations aggressively, pushing poor countries to transform their economies by promoting industrialized agriculture and export production. There were fundamental problems with this development model. By the time McNamara retired, in 1981, his legacy consisted largely of failed megaprojects, populations no longer able to feed themselves, devastated forests and watersheds, and a sea of hopeless debt.

Bank officials have consistently vowed to improve this record, to start funding projects that benefit not only big business and Third World élites but also the world's poor. Accordingly, projects with non-governmental organizations and other "civil society" groups, along with efforts to promote access to health care and education, have increased. But Bank contracts are worth millions, and multinational corporations have remained major beneficiaries. In 1995, Lawrence Summers, then an under-secretary at the Treasury Department – he is now its Secretary – told Congress that for each dollar the American government contributed to the World Bank, American corporations received $1.35 in procurement contracts. One of the Bank's major proposals at the moment is for the development of oilfields in Chad, in central Africa, and the construction of an oil pipeline running more than six hundred miles to the coast at Cameroon. The environmental impact of this pipeline is predicted by many to be dire, the benefits to the people in the area minimal. The big winners will, in all likelihood, be the Bank's major partners in the project – Exxon Mobil and Chevron.

More onerous than ill-advised projects, however, for the people of the global South has been the crushing accumulation of debt by their governments. This debt now totals more than two trillion dollars, and servicing it – simply paying the interest – has become the single largest budget item for scores of poor countries. About twenty years ago, the World Bank and the I.M.F. began attaching stricter conditions to the loans they made to debtor countries to help them avoid outright default. More than ninety countries have now been subjected to I.M.F.-imposed austerity schemes, also known as structural-adjustment programs. Typically, these force a nation to cut spending in health, education, and welfare programs; reduce or eliminate food, energy, and transport subsidies; devalue its local currency; raise interest rates to attract foreign capital; privatize state property; and lower barriers to foreign ownership of local industries, land, and assets.

This is where the World Trade Organization comes in – or, rather, where its agenda dovetails with the work of the Bank and the I.M.F. All three institutions have always sought to increase world trade. (The W.T.O. is the successor to the General Agreement on Tariffs and Trade, which began in 1947 and was folded into the W.T.O. in 1995.) But the W.T.O. is the spearhead of the present surge toward economic globalization. It is a huge bureaucracy that makes binding rules intended to remove obstacles to the expansion of commercial activity among the hundred and thirty-five countries that constitute its membership. This means, in practice, an incremental transfer of power from local and national governments (the bodies likely to erect such obstacles) to the W.T.O., which acts as a trade court, hearing, behind closed doors, disputes among members accusing one another of creating barriers to trade. These "barriers" may be health, safety, or environmental laws, and a W.T.O. ruling takes precedence over all other international agreements. A country found to be impeding trade must change the offending law or suffer harsh sanctions. The effect is to deregulate international commerce, freeing the largest corporations – which, measured as economic entities, already dwarf most of the world's countries – to enter any market, extract any resource, without constraint by citizenries. Speaking anonymously, a former W.T.O. official recently told the *Financial Times*, "This is the place where governments collude in private against their domestic pressure groups."

There is, in other words, little mystery about why the W.T.O. and its partners in free-trade promotion, the World Bank and the I.M.F., have become the protest targets of choice for environmentalists, labor unions, economic nationalists, small farmers and small-business people, and their allies. Trade rules among countries are obviously needed. The question is whom those rules will benefit, whose rights they will protect.

The fifty thousand people who took to the streets of Seattle chanting "No new round – turn around!" had clearly decided that the

W.T.O. was not on their side when it came to steering the direction of global trade. But even that might be too broad a statement – for the coalition that gathered there was wildly diverse, its collective critique nothing if not eclectic. Many of its members would probably not agree, for instance, that trade rules are "obviously" needed. [. . .]

The Direct Action Network (DAN) probably belongs in the deeply anticapitalist category. But the group is less than a year old and extremely loosely structured, so its ideology isn't easy to get a fix on. What does seem certain is that the shutdown (or "meltdown," as Burson-Marsteller has it) of the Seattle Ministerial would never have happened without the emergence and furious efforts of the Direct Action Network.

Juliette Beck was present at DAN's creation. Late last spring, a young organizer named David Solnit, who was well known in the movement for his dedication and ingenuity, and for his giant homemade puppets – Solnit's allegorical figures have appeared in demonstrations from coast to coast – approached Beck with a plan to shut down the Seattle meeting. Dozens of groups, including the A.F.L.-C.I.O. and Global Trade Watch, a leading branch of Nader's Public Citizen, were already planning for Seattle. But no one was talking shutdown. Solnit thought it could be done, and he figured that Global Exchange could help. Beck and Kevin Danaher called in the Rainforest Action Network and a Berkeley-based group called the Ruckus Society, which specializes in nonviolent guerrilla action, and DAN was hatched.

Solnit was the dynamo but not the leader. "DAN is lots of lieutenants, no generals," Danaher says. The word went out, largely over the Internet, about DAN's plans, and dozens of groups and countless individuals expressed interest. The DAN coalition developed along what is known as the "affinity-group model." Affinity groups are small, semi-independent units, pledged to coalition goals, tactics, and principles – including, in DAN's case, nonviolent action

– but free to make their own plans. Members look out for one another during protests, and some have designated roles: medic, legal support (avoids arrest), "spoke" (confers with other affinity groups through affinity "clusters"), "action elf" (looks after food, water, and people's spirits). Thousands signed up for training, and for "camps" organized by the Ruckus Society, where they could learn not only the techniques of classic civil disobedience but specialized skills like urban rappelling (for hanging banners on buildings), forming human blockades, and how to "lock down" in groups (arms linked through specially constructed plastic tubes). Solnit coördinated a road show that toured the West in the months before the W.T.O. Ministerial, presenting music and speakers and street theatre, urging people to get involved and come to Seattle.

They came, of course, and the combination of strict civil-disobedience discipline (the only way that the lines around the hotels and meeting places and across key intersections could have held, preventing W.T.O. delegates from gathering) and polymorphous protest (dancers on vans, hundreds of children dressed as sea turtles and monarch butterflies, Korean priests in white robes playing flutes and drums to protest genetically modified food) could never have been centrally planned.

The affinity-group model proved extremely effective in dealing with police actions. Downtown Seattle had been divided by a DAN "spokescouncil" into thirteen sectors, with an affinity cluster responsible for each sector. There were also flying squads – mobile affinity groups that could quickly take the place of groups that had been arrested or beaten or gassed from the positions they were trying to hold. The structure was flexible, and tactically powerful, and the police, trying to clear the streets, resorted to increasingly brutal methods, firing concussion grenades, mashing pepper spray into the eyes of protesters, shooting rubber bullets into bodies at short range. By the afternoon of November 30th (the first day of the meeting), the police had run

low on ammunition, and that evening the mayor of Seattle called out the National Guard.

There were hundreds of arrests. Beck, who was teargassed on a line blocking the entrance to the convention center, had credentials, through Global Exchange, to enter the theatre where the W.T.O. was supposed to be having its opening session. She went inside, found a few delegates milling, and an open microphone. She and Danaher and Medea Benjamin – another co-founder of Global Exchange – took the stage, uninvited, and suggested that delegates join them in a discussion. The interlopers were hustled off the stage. Beck elected not to go quietly. Marshals put her in a pain hold – her arm twisted behind her back – and dragged her through the theatre. A news camera recorded the event. "Then CNN kept showing it, over and over, them carrying me off, whenever they talked about the arrests," she says. "My claim to fame. Except I wasn't arrested! They just threw me out."

Ironically, the only protesters not following the nonviolence guidelines – a hundred or so "black bloc" anarchists, who started smashing shopwindows – were hardly bothered by the police. The black-bloc crews, whose graffiti and occasional "communiqués" run to nihilist slogans ("Civilization Is Collapsing – Let's Give It a Push!"), were masked, well organized, young and fleet of foot, and armed with crowbars and acid-filled eggs. The police in their heavy riot gear could not have caught them if they'd tried. The targeted shops belonged to big corporations: Nike, the Gap, Fidelity Investments, Starbucks, Levi's, Planet Hollywood. Still, other protesters chanted "Shame! Shame!" Some even tried to stop the attacks. There were scuffles, and suggestions that the black blocs contained police agents provocateurs – hence the masks. Medea Benjamin, who had helped produce the original exposé of Nike's sweatshops in Asia, found herself in the absurd position of siding with protesters who were defending a Niketown. And her fear (shared by many) that a few broken windows might snatch away the headlines in the national press proved justified.

The political spectrum represented in the protests was improbably wide, ranging from, on the right, James Hoffa's Teamsters and the A.F.L.-C.I.O. (who fielded tens of thousands of members for a march) to, on the left, a dozen or more anarchist factions (the black blocs were a rowdy minority within a generally less aggressive minority), including the ancient Industrial Workers of the World. All these groups had found, if not a common cause, at least a common foe. Some unlikely alliances were cemented. The United Steelworkers union and Earth First!, for example, had a common enemy in the Maxxam Corporation, which logs old-growth forests *and* owns steel mills, and the two groups are currently working together to end a bitter lockout at a Kaiser Aluminum plant in Tacoma.

Inside the besieged W.T.O. Ministerial, there was a rebellion among countries from the global South, which raised the possibility of another, truly formidable alliance with some of the forces out in the streets. The leaders of the poorer countries, though often depicted as pawns of the major powers, content to offer their countries' workers to the world market at the lowest possible wages – and to pollute their air and water and strip-mine their natural resources, in exchange for their own commissions on the innumerable deals that come with corporate globalization – in reality have to answer, in many cases, to complex constituencies at home, many of whom are alarmed about their own economic recolonization. In Seattle, delegations from Africa, Asia, the Caribbean, and Latin America – rattled by the total disruption of the Ministerial's schedule, and furious about being excluded from key meetings held privately by the rich countries – issued statements announcing their refusal to sign "agreements" produced at such meetings. In the end, no agreements were signed, no new round launched, and the Ministerial finished in disarray. This insurgency was often depicted in the American press as a refusal by the representatives of the poor countries to accept higher labor and environmental standards being imposed on them by the West, but that was not the gist of the revolt, which ran deeper and echoed the fundamental questions being asked outside in the streets about the mandate of the W.T.O.

"Coalition-building is hard," Juliette Beck said. "There's no doubt about it. But it's what we do." We were sitting in a deserted café in some sort of Latino community center one Sunday night in Berkeley, sipping beers. "At Global Exchange, we try to think of campaigns that will appeal to the average Joe on the street. We're really not interested in just organizing other leftists. Big corporations are a great target, because they do things that hurt virtually everybody. My dad, who's very right-wing, but libertarian, hates corporations. The H.M.O.s have practically ruined his medical practice, mainly because he insists on spending as much time with his patients as he thinks they need.

[...]

I asked Beck if she considered herself an anarchist.

She shrugged, as if the question were obtuse.

DAN seemed, at a glance, to be an anarchist organization, or at least organized on anarchist principles, I said.

"Sure," Beck said, still looking nonplussed. Finally, she said, "Well, I definitely respect anarchist ways of organizing. I guess I'm still learning what it means to be an anarchist. But the real question is: Can this anarchist model that's working so well now for organizing protests be applied on an international scale to create the democratic decision-making structures that we need to eliminate poverty?"

I took this opportunity to float a theory [...]. Anarchism, I said, first arose in Europe as a response to the disruptions of peasant and artisanal life caused by industrialization and the rapid concentration of power among new business élites. After a good long fight, anarchism basically lost out to socialism as an organizing vision among workers –

and lost again, after a heady late run, in Republican Spain, to Communism (which then lost to fascism). But anarchism was obviously enjoying some kind of small-time comeback, and, if today's Information Revolution was even half as significant as both its critics and its cheerleaders like to claim – the most important economic development since the Industrial Revolution, and so on – then perhaps the time was ripening, socialism having been disgraced as an alternative to capitalism, for another great wave of anarchist protest against this latest, alarmingly swift amassing of power in the hands of a few hundred billionaires. Did Beck know that the term "direct action" was used by anarcho-syndicalists in France at the turn of the last century?

She did. She also knew, it seemed, that anarchism has become wildly popular among Latin American students who are fed up with what they call *neoliberalismo* (their term for corporate-led globalization) but disenchanted, also, with the traditional left. And she knew that the students who went on strike and took over the National University in Mexico City for nine months recently were mostly anarchists. But did I know (I didn't) that it had been a structural-adjustment edict from the World Bank that led the Mexican government to raise student fees, which sparked the strike and the takeover?

Beck drained her beer. DAN, whatever its historical analogues, had been thriving since its triumph in Seattle, she said. The network was now directing most of its considerable energies toward the April action in Washington, D.C., which people were calling "A16," for April 16th, the day the I.M.F. planned to meet. She was going to Washington herself in a couple of days, and then joining a road show, which would start making its way up the East Coast, beating the drums for the big event.

"I Am Funkier Than You," the bumper sticker said, and it was almost certainly true. But the Mango Affinity Group, as the road-show crew had taken to calling themselves, had scored this big, extremely grubby van free from a woman in Virginia simply by asking for a vehicle on the A16 E-mail list serve, so they were not complaining. Liz Guy, an efficient DAN stalwart usually known as Sprout, had pulled together both the crew – eight or nine activists, aged nineteen to thirty-two, including Juliette Beck – and a tight, three-week, show-a-day itinerary that ran from Florida to Montreal before looping back to Washington. I found them in St. Petersburg, bivouacked under a shade tree on the campus of Eckerd College, working on a song.

Beck introduced me. They were a sweet-voiced, ragamuffin group, drawn from Connecticut, Atlanta, Seattle (Sprout), and the mountains of British Columbia. This afternoon was going to be their first performance together, and, judging from the situation as showtime approached and they began lugging their gear into a low-roofed, brutally air-conditioned hall, somebody had blown the publicity. There was virtually no one around except their hosts – two young DAN guys, Peter and Josh, who were hopefully laying out anarchist and vegan pamphlets and books on a table. Peter and Josh, embarrassed, said they had just returned from a Ruckus Society camp. Evidently, they had left arrangements in the wrong hands. "Let's do a skate-by, see where people are," one of them said, and both jumped on skateboards and shot off.

[...]

Beck had told me, back in San Francisco, "I get so tired of the Internet and E-mail. We couldn't do this work without it, but, really, it's not organizing. There's nothing like face to face."

Now in Florida, Beck, perhaps getting desperate for some F2F, approached two young women who had wandered into the frigid hall, possibly just to get out of the afternoon heat, and started regaling them with a spiel about how the World Bank and the I.M.F. are "partners in crime." The young women, who wore tank tops and looked as if they belonged on a beach somewhere, nodded politely but said nothing.

In the background, Damon, a tall, dark-skinned, curly-haired musician from British Columbia, strummed a guitar, and the rest of the Mango Affinity Group busied themselves making posters denouncing exploitation.

Blessedly, between the skate-by and Damon's guitar, people began to trickle into the hall. Soon there was an audience of thirty or so, and the show began. Damon disappeared inside a towering, black-suited puppet with a huge papier-mâché head, sloping skull, and cigar stuck between his lips, Beck slapped a "World Bank/I.M.F." sign on his chest, and he began to roar, "You are all under my power!" The crowd laughed, and he roared, "It's not funny, it's true!" They laughed harder. A political skit followed, with a series of fresh-faced young women getting thrashed by an I.M.F. henchman for demanding health and safety standards, then put to work in a Gap sweatshop. "Right to Organize" also got pounded. Afterward, Beck led a teach-in called Globalization 101, with pop quizzes on the meaning of various trade and finance acronyms, and Hershey's Kisses tossed to those who got the answers right. One middle-aged trio – Eckerd faculty, from the look of them – seemed well versed on the topic. Then the Mango members introduced themselves individually – Leigh, from an "intentional community" in Atlanta, Ricardo, from a Canadian "solar-powered coöperative" where people grew much of their own food. Sprout took the opportunity to encourage people to form affinity groups, explaining what they were and how they worked.

I was struck by Sprout's poise. Talking to dozens of strangers, she somehow made her presentation seem like an intimate conversation, with pauses, eye contact, murmurs back and forth, little encouraging interjections ("Awesome!" "Cool!") when she felt she'd been understood. Twenty-five, physically small, and dressed with utter simplicity – loose shirt, cargo pants, no shoes – she achieved, with no theatricality, an effect of tremendous presence. It occurred to me that Sprout, with her neighborly voice and unerr-

ing choice of words, could easily be very successful in a completely different arena. On another sort of road show, for instance – the sort that dot-com startups mount, touring and performing for investors and analysts, before taking their companies public. The same was true for Beck. And both women came from cities (Seattle, San Francisco) that were crawling with rich dot-commers more or less their age. What was it that made them choose this raggedy, low-status, activist's path instead? While the rest of the country obsessed over its stock portfolio, these brainy young people were working killer hours for little, if any, pay – quixotically trying, as they sometimes put it, to globalize the world from below.

Next on the program was a rousing folk song, with Damon on guitar and Sage, his regular bandmate from B.C., on drums. Their vocal harmonies sounded fairly polished. Then Sprout produced a viola, slipping without fanfare into the tune, and began improvising fiddle breaks of steadily increasing warmth and precision. I caught Beck's eye. Who *was* this woman? Beck could not stop grinning. The Mango group then ruined the soaring mood, as far as I was concerned, by leading the crowd in some mortifyingly corny chants – "Ain't no power like the power of the people, cuz the power of the people don't stop!"

Beck asked for a show of hands. How many people thought they might go to Washington for A16? Fifteen or twenty hands shot up, including those of the two women in tank tops. I was amazed that they had even stayed for the show. A signup sheet was circulated.

Next came nonviolence training, for which ten or twelve people stuck around. Leigh and Sprout led the training, which lasted into the evening and included a lot of "role-playing" – people pretending to be protesters, police, I.M.F. officials, workers trying to get to work. There were drills in quick decision-making among affinity groups: shall we stay locked down or move when threatened with arrest and felony charges? Group dynamics were dissected after each scene. Sprout demonstrated unthreatening body language. Hand signals for swift, clear communication were suggested. Peter and Josh, the two local DAN guys, joined in the training, and it was soon obvious that they had a lot of experience. Peter, who was wiry, bushy-bearded, and soft-spoken, firmly refused to be bullied by some of the bigger, more aggressive men in the group. It became clear that effective nonviolent protest needed a cool head, and that bluster wasn't helpful. Toward the end of the evening, Leigh presented a list of things to bring to an action. Most were commonsense items like food, water, and herbal remedies for tear gas. The rationale for others was less self-evident. Maxi pads?

Leigh and Sprout glanced at one another. "If the cops start using chemical warfare, some women start bleeding very heavily," Leigh said. There was a brief, shocked silence. "They're good as bandages, too," she added.

What about gas masks?

"They can become targets," Josh said. "In Seattle, the cops tried to tear them off, and if they couldn't reach them they fired rubber bullets, or wooden bullets, or these wooden dowel rods they had, at the masks. Some people got a lot of glass in their faces. Masks can be dangerous."

The trainees stared.

"One thing that's good to have is big toenail clippers," Peter said cheerfully. "Put 'em in your pocket, and if you're arrested, and just left in a cell or a paddy wagon, somebody can fish them out of your pocket and cut off your cuffs with 'em. They use cheap plastic cuffs when they arrest a lot of people, and if they leave you sitting for ten or fifteen hours it's a lot more comfortable if your hands aren't tied behind you."

Ten or fifteen hours?

"It happens. It happened to me in Seattle."

It had happened to Sprout, too – seventeen hours in an unheated cell alone, doing jumping jacks to try to stay warm.

The tone of the gathering was entirely sober now. Somebody asked about carrying I.D. during an action.

"It depends whether you want to practice jail solidarity," Beck said. "That's something you need to decide with your affinity group."

None of the trainees knew what jail solidarity was.

"Noncoöperation with the system," they were told. It might be widely used in Washington – to clog the jails and courts and try to force mass dismissals of charges.

But the details of jail solidarity could wait for another session, Beck said. It was late. People were tired. DAN would be offering more nonviolence training locally in the weeks ahead, and everybody going to Washington for A16 should get as much training as possible.

[...]

Part VII

What Do Movements Do?

Introduction

If you are in a social movement, the most pressing question you face is: what is to be done? How do you choose tactics that will help your cause? How do you recruit more people, attract the news media, favorably impress decision-makers? Tactical decisions are the real "stuff" of social movements. Yet, oddly, few scholars have taken a serious look at how these decisions are made, how or when protestors innovate in their tactics, or what the tradeoffs are between different kinds of tactics. Most of those who have written about issues like these have been practitioners rather than academics.

One reason scholars have avoided the question of tactical choice may be that movements have a hard enough time simply surviving. For researchers in the mobilization tradition, this was a serious accomplishment for movement organizations. As a result, they examined how these organizations raised funds, took advantage of tax laws, and recruited members. Similarly, process theorists concentrated on movements (workers, civil rights) that faced considerable repression from the state, so again simple survival was an accomplishment.

Scholars have also avoided questions of tactics because choices made in the heat of conflict are hard to explain in a rigorous fashion. Much depends on the instincts of movement leaders, who themselves may not always be able to explain why they made one choice rather than another. Decisions are sometimes made fast, and it

Civil Society   Civil society refers to the sphere of association and conversation which falls outside the direct control of the state and other authorities. Civil society encompasses the dialogues and interactions through which political views are formed and through which groups come to understand their interests vis- à-vis those of other groups and the state. Civil society includes voluntary associations, friendship networks, religious groups, independent newspapers, and the like. Social movements generally emerge out of civil society and often attempt to expand it, and movements are themselves an important component of civil society.

Repertoires of Protest   What do protestors do to further their cause? In any given society, there are a handful of routine ways in which people protest. In modern Western societies, for example, most social movements choose from a surprisingly small number of tactics, especially petitions, demonstrations, marches, vigils, and sit-ins (and similar forms of civil disobedience). This is our "repertoire of protest." Widespread knowledge of one or more of these routines both facilitates protest and constrains the tactical options available. At the same time, expectations about what protestors are likely to do may also help authorities contain or suppress protestors. A repertoire is learned, shared, and occasionally modified. Innovative forms of protest are not easy to invent, even when they would seem to be helpful or necessary. According to Charles Tilly, who first coined the term, a repertoire is shaped by a society's sense of justice (which a tactic must appeal to or at least not violate), the daily routines and social organization of the population (a tactic should fit with these), their prior experience with collective action (so they have the know-how), and the patterns and forms of repression they are likely to face (which a good tactic will minimize). Tactics endure because they are relatively successful and/or deeply meaningful to people.

may be difficult to reconstruct the process later – when being interviewed by researchers, for instance.

Tactical choices are usually made during the course of interaction with other decision-makers: with one's opponents, of course, but also with the police, the media, legislators, potential allies, and many others. To take just one example: before most rallies or marches today, leaders negotiate with the police over where they will go, what they will do, how many will be arrested, and so on. Leaders must also make tactical choices with regard to their own followers: how to placate disaffected factions, how to keep members coming back to future events, how to increase the membership. As a result, any given action will probably be designed for several different audiences at the same time. An action that satisfies one may not please another.

In regard to their opponents, protestors hope to change behavior through persuasion or intimidation, and to undermine their credibility with the public, media, and the state. With state agencies, protestors hope to change laws, policies, regulatory practices, administrative rules, and to avoid repression. From the courts protestors typically strive to have unfavorable laws struck down. With both courts and police, they hope for tolerance of their own protests. Social movements seek to use the news media to spread their message, and sometimes to undermine their opponents. Protestors may also approach professional groups, such as engineers, to change their standards. They may seek allies in other protest groups. And from the public at large, they may hope for sympathy, contributions, changes in awareness. Finally, they even have goals for their own members: personal transformations and continued fervor for the cause. In other words, movements have a lot of goals to balance in their tactics.

As a result of this complexity, scholars have usually dealt with strategy and tactics by trying to make them a structural issue. Charles Tilly developed the concept of a repertoire of collective action to explain the range of tactics available to protestors in any given society in a particular period. Most social movements in that society will then draw on the same repertoire, because it is largely structurally determined. But this concept says little about how any given leader applies the existing repertoire: why a march rather than a letter-writing campaign?; why wait a week before responding to your opponents' actions rather than acting immediately?; why choose one cultural frame rather than another for a speech?

But Tilly's instincts are solid: protestors adapt their tactics to their resources, opportunities, and daily life. James Scott (1985, 1990) has described what resistance looks like in slave and peasant societies, where there is close surveillance and few legal and political freedoms. He calls these tactics "weapons of the weak." Only with industrialization and urbanization did protestors have newspapers and later television at their disposal. Workers lived and worked more closely together, so planning and coordination were easier than they had been for peasants. Large numbers of people could be mobilized. A broad range of tactics – from the formation of national organizations to mass rallies – became available to movements in industrial society which had not been to peasants.

Protestors in different societies face different political structures within which they must operate, even controlling for level of economic development. In an article that helped define the process approach, Herbert Kitschelt (1986) argued that antinuclear protestors in Europe and the United States chose different strategies because their countries contained different kinds of political machinery. French protestors could not bring lawsuits as their American counterparts did, in part because they lacked the grounds on which to sue. French political parties are also less open to new grassroots issues, compared to American parties, and so French antinuclear protestors could not work through the electoral system either. As a result, they took to the streets more quickly than the Americans did, forced to work outside the system because that system lacked openings for input.

Our first reading is by one of the greatest community organizers of the twentieth century, Saul Alinsky. His tactical principles are not unlike those of theorists of war: try to take your opponents by surprise, try to make them think you are more powerful than you are. Try to use tactics your own followers enjoy and are familiar with. The idea of keeping the pressure on is important, because you never know where and when your opponent will be vulnerable or will make a blunder. The greater the pressure, the greater the chance you will trip them up. Alinsky also recognizes that it is usually necessary to portray your enemy as an utter villain, a real flesh-and-blood person who can be blamed, not an abstract principle. This can lead to strong emotions and polarization. Alinsky's rules are quite general, but they can be helpful reminders to social movement leaders.

If tactical choice is a difficult topic to model rigorously, that of tactical innovation is even more so. In describing civil-rights sit-ins, Aldon Morris exemplifies the resource-mobilization approach to tactics. He is not so much concerned with the origins of this tactic, or the strategic thinking behind its use. Rather, he is concerned to show the indigenous organizations and social networks through which it rapidly spread, primarily arguing against a view of protest as spontaneous eruptions. In this excerpt Morris also touches on another important issue: the emergence of "movement centers" with resources, social ties (especially preachers and NAACP activists), and regular meetings (usually at churches). Other theorists have called these "free spaces," places relatively free from surveillance where oppositional ideas and tactics can develop.

Mary Bernstein examines the use of identity claims as a form of strategy, inserting culture into a political process framework. She contrasts "identity deployment" that emphasizes the differences between a group and the majority with those that emphasize the similarities. The major determinants of which kind of identity rhetoric a group will favor are the group's political interactions with their opponents and with the state, as well as the group's own organizational structure. In the process tradition, her concentration is on external audiences, who may favor very different messages from the ones movement members prefer.

Mary Fainsod Katzenstein, in the excerpt from her book *Faithful and Fearless*, looks at how feminists have worked *within* religious institutions to pursue gains for women. She focuses on the kinds of language feminists use, the rhetorical claims they make, but at the same time she precisely describes the settings in which they make these claims. She calls these feminists' "habitats" in the institutions they hope to change. "Free spaces" *outside* normal organizations are not always necessary for movements to flourish; sometimes they can thrive *within* dominant institutions. Movement messages (in both words and actions) and the audiences they are aimed at remain the essence of what social movements do.

The choice of strategies and tactics is certainly an area in which additional research is needed. One limitation has been that most scholars have thought about movements as their unit of analysis: how each grows, operates, and affects the world around it. But tactical choices are made in close interaction with others in the same "field of conflict." Similarly, the internal structure of movements may affect their ability to innovate and choose the most effective courses of action. One recent step forward in this area is an article by Marshall Ganz, which we placed in part VIII because it is also a critique of process models. Ganz discusses why some protest groups are more innovative strategically than others, looking precisely at the sources of strategic choices.

Discussion Questions

1 Why do social movements in different societies and different periods of history have different repertoires of collective action available to them?
2 How and why do new tactics spread?
3 What roles do "movement centers" play in social movements?
4 In what ways can identity claims be seen as strategic?
5 What costs and benefits are there to working within the very organizations protestors hope to change? When does it make more sense to work from without?

20 Protest Tactics

Saul D. Alinsky

We will either find a way or make one.
— HANNIBAL

Tactics means doing what you can with what you have. Tactics are those consciously deliberate acts by which human beings live with each other and deal with the world around them. In the world of give and take, tactics is the art of how to take and how to give. Here our concern is with the tactic of taking; how the Have-Nots can take power away from the Haves.

For an elementary illustration of tactics, take parts of your face as the point of reference; your eyes, your ears, and your nose. First the eyes; if you have organized a vast, mass-based people's organization, you can parade it visibly before the enemy and openly show your power. Second the ears; if your organization is small in numbers, then do what Gideon did: conceal the members in the dark but raise a din and clamor that will make the listener believe that your organization numbers many more than it does. Third, the nose; if your organization is too tiny even for noise, stink up the place.

Always remember the first rule of power tactics:

Power is not only what you have but what the enemy thinks you have.

The second rule is: *Never go outside the experience of your people.* When an action or tactic is outside the experience of the people, the result is confusion, fear, and retreat. It also means a collapse of communication, as we have noted.

The third rule is: *Wherever possible go outside of the experience of the enemy.*

Here you want to cause confusion, fear, and retreat.

General William T. Sherman, whose name still causes a frenzied reaction throughout the South, provided a classic example of going outside the enemy's experience. Until Sherman, military tactics and strategies were based on standard patterns. All armies had fronts, rears, flanks, lines of communication, and lines of supply. Military campaigns were aimed at such standard objectives as rolling up the flanks of the enemy army or cutting the lines of supply or lines of communication, or moving around to attack from the rear. When Sherman cut loose on his famous March to the Sea, he had no front or rear lines of supplies or any other lines. He was on the loose and living on the land. The South, confronted with this new form of military invasion, reacted with confusion,

Weapons of the Weak   Today, social movements are one common way in which people protest against something they fear or dislike. But organized movements are rare in many other kinds of societies, especially where those in power are likely to repress any organized efforts. In most agricultural societies, like those of feudal Europe, peasants or slaves have been watched carefully by landlords or overseers. In situations of close surveillance, people find other ways to resist. They may work very slowly or poorly when doing tasks for their lord or master. They may do the wrong thing and "play dumb" when confronted by their bosses. They may subtly sabotage a construction project. At night they may poach or pilfer from local elites. They also tell jokes or spread gossip about their superiors as a way of undermining their power. For thousands of years, slaves and serfs have used "weapons of the weak" like these to get back at those exploiting them. See Scott (1985).

panic, terror, and collapse. Sherman swept on to inevitable victory. It was the same tactic that, years later in the early days of World War II, the Nazi Panzer tank divisions emulated in their far-flung sweeps into enemy territory, as did our own General Patton with the American Third Armored Division.

The fourth rule is: *Make the enemy live up to their own book of rules.* You can kill them with this, for they can no more obey their own rules than the Christian church can live up to Christianity.

The fourth rule carries within it the fifth rule: *Ridicule is man's most potent weapon.* It is almost impossible to counterattack ridicule. Also it infuriates the opposition, who then react to your advantage.

The sixth rule is: *A good tactic is one that your people enjoy.* If your people are not having a ball doing it, there is something very wrong with the tactic.

The seventh rule: *A tactic that drags on too long becomes a drag.* Man can sustain militant interest in any issue for only a limited time, after which it becomes a ritualistic commitment, like going to church on Sunday mornings. New issues and crises are always developing, and one's reaction becomes, "Well, my heart bleeds for those people and I'm all for the boycott, but after all there are other important things in life" – and there it goes.

The eighth rule: *Keep the pressure on,* with different tactics and actions, and utilize all events of the period for your purpose.

The ninth rule: *The threat is usually more terrifying than the thing itself.*

The tenth rule: *The major premise for tactics is the development of operations that will maintain a constant pressure upon the opposition.* It is this unceasing pressure that results in the reactions from the opposition that are essential for the success of the campaign. It should be remembered not only that the action is in the reaction but that action is itself the consequence of reaction and of reaction to the reaction, and infinitum. The pressure produces the reaction, and constant pressure sustains action.

The eleventh rule is: *If you push a negative hard and deep enough it will break through into its counterside;* this is based on the principle that every positive has its negative. We have already seen the conversion of the negative into the positive, in Mahatma Gandhi's development of the tactic of passive resistance.

One corporation we organized against responded to the continuous application of pressure by burglarizing my home, and then using the keys taken in the burglary to burglarize the offices of the Industrial Areas Foundation where I work. The panic in this corporation was clear from the nature of the burglaries, for nothing was taken in either burglary to make it seem that the thieves were interested in ordinary loot – they took only the records that applied to the corporation. Even the most amateurish burglar would have had more sense than to do what the private detective agency hired by that corporation did. The police departments in California and Chicago agreed that "the corporation might just as well have left its fingerprints all over the place."

In a fight almost anything goes. It almost reaches the point where you stop to apologize if a chance blow lands *above* the belt. When a corporation bungles like the one that burglarized my home and office, my visible public reaction is shock, horror, and moral outrage. In this case, we let it be known that sooner or later it would be confronted with this crime as well as with a whole series of other derelictions, before a United States Senate Subcommittee Investigation. Once sworn in, with congressional immunity, we would make these actions public. This threat, plus the fact that an attempt on my life had been made in Southern California, had the corporation on a spot where it would be publicly suspect in the event of assassination. At one point I found myself in a thirty-room motel in which every other room was occupied by their security men. This became another devil in the closet to haunt this corporation and to keep the pressure on.

The twelfth rule: *The price of a successful attack is a constructive alternative*. You cannot risk being trapped by the enemy in his sudden agreement with your demand and saying "You're right – we don't know what to do about this issue. Now you tell us."

The thirteenth rule: *Pick the target, freeze it, personalize it, and polarize it*.

In conflict tactics there are certain rules that the organizer should always regard as universalities. One is that the opposition must be singled out as the target and "frozen." By this I mean that in a complex, interrelated, urban society, it becomes increasingly difficult to single out who is to blame for any particular evil. There is a constant, and somewhat legitimate, passing of the buck. In these times of urbanization, complex metropolitan governments, the complexities of major interlocked corporations, and the interlocking of political life between cities and counties and metropolitan authorities, the problem that threatens to loom more and more is that of identifying the enemy. Obviously there is no point to tactics unless one has a target upon which to center the attacks. One big problem is a constant shifting of responsibility from one jurisdiction to another – individuals and bureaus one after another disclaim responsibility for particular conditions, attributing the authority for any change to some other force. In a corporation one gets the situation where the president of the corporation says that he does not have the responsibility, it is up to the board of trustees or the board of directors, the board of directors can shift it over to the stockholders, etc., etc. And the same thing goes, for example, on the Board of Education appointments in the city of Chicago, where an extra-legal committee is empowered to make selections of nominees for the board and the mayor then uses his legal powers to select names from that list. When the mayor is attacked for not having any blacks on the list, he shifts the responsibility over to the committee, pointing out that he has to select those names from a list submitted by the committee, and if the list is all white, then he has no responsibility. The committee can shift the responsibility back by pointing out that it is the mayor who has the authority to select the names, and so it goes in a comic (if it were not so tragic) routine of "who's on first" or "under which shell is the pea hidden?"

The same evasion of responsibility is to be found in all areas of life and other areas of City Hall Urban Renewal departments, who say the responsibility is over here, and somebody else says the responsibility is over there, the city says it is a state responsibility and the federal government passes it back to the local community, and on ad infinitum.

It should be borne in mind that the target is always trying to shift responsibility to get out of being the target. There is a constant squirming and moving and strategy – purposeful, and malicious at times, other times just for straight self-survival – on the part of the designated target. The forces for change must keep this in mind and pin that target down securely. If an organization permits responsibility to be diffused and distributed in a number of areas, attack becomes impossible.

[...]

One of the criteria in picking your target is the target's vulnerability – where do you have the power to start? Furthermore, any target can always say, "Why do you center on me when there are others to blame as well?" When you "freeze the target," you disregard these arguments and, for the moment, all the others to blame.

Then, as you zero in and freeze your target and carry out your attack, all of the "others" come out of the woodwork very soon. They become visible by their support of the target.

The other important point in the choosing of a target is that it must be a personification, not something general and abstract such as a community's segregated practices or a major corporation or City Hall. It is not possible to develop the necessary hostility against, say, City Hall, which after all is a concrete, physical, inanimate structure, or against a corporation, which has no soul or identity, or a public school administration, which again is an inanimate system.

John L. Lewis, the leader of the radical C.I.O. labor organization in the 1930s, was fully aware of this, and as a consequence the C.I.O. never attacked General Motors, they always attacked its president, Alfred "Ice-water-In-His-Veins" Sloan; they never attacked the Republic Steel Corporation but always its president, "Bloodied Hands" Tom Girdler, and so with us when we attacked the then-superintendent of the Chicago public school system, Benjamin Willis. Let nothing get you off your target.

With this focus comes a polarization. As we have indicated before, all issues must be polarized if action is to follow. The classic statement on polarization comes from Christ: "He that is not with me is against me" (Luke 11:23). He allowed no middle ground to the money-changers in the Temple. One acts decisively only in the conviction that all the angels are on one side and all the devils on the other. A leader may struggle toward a decision and weigh the merits and demerits of a situation which is 52 per cent positive and 48 per cent negative, but once the decision is reached he must assume that his cause is 100 per cent positive and the opposition 100 per cent negative. He can't toss forever in limbo, and avoid decision. He can't weigh arguments or reflect endlessly – he must decide and act. Otherwise there are Hamlet's words:

> And thus the native hue of resolution
> Is sicklied o'er with the pale cast of thought,
> And enterprises of great pith and moment
> With this regard their currents turn awry,
> And lose the name of action.

Many liberals, during our attack on the then-school superintendent, were pointing out that after all he wasn't a 100 per cent devil, he was a regular churchgoer, he was a good family man, and he was generous in his contributions to charity. Can you imagine in the arena of conflict charging that so-and-so is a racist bastard and then diluting the impact of the attack with qualifying remarks such as "He is a good churchgoing man, generous to charity, and a good husband"? This becomes political idiocy.

[...]

- *The real action is in the enemy's reaction.*
- *The enemy properly goaded and guided in his reaction will be your major strength.*
- *Tactics, like organization, like life, require that you move with the action.*

21 Tactical Innovation in the Civil Rights Movement

Aldon Morris

Roots of a Tactical Innovation: Sit-Ins

During the late 1950s activists associated with direct action organizations began experimenting with the sit-in tactic. The 1960 student sit-in movement followed naturally from the early efforts to mobilize for non-violent direct action that took place in black communities across the South. Analysis of sit-ins of the late 1950s will reveal the basic components of the internal organization that was necessary for the emergence of the massive sit-ins of 1960.

In earlier chapters it was demonstrated that the NAACP Youth Councils, CORE chapters, and the SCLC affiliates were the main forces organizing the black community to engage in nonviolent protest. It was emphasized that these groups were closely tied to the black church base. The adult advisers of the NAACP Youth Councils were often women, who supervised the activities of fifteen to twenty young people, but it was not

---

Tactical Innovation   Sometimes people may have intense grievances, they may be fairly well organized, and they may even believe that some authorities might be willing to listen to them, yet they do not protest because they are not quite sure how to do so effectively. The types of protest with which they are familiar may seem too difficult to carry out or may not strike them as likely to make a difference. However, certain tactical innovations – the discovery (or rediscovery) of new forms of protest – may spread very quickly and mobilize many people if these new tactics are relatively easy to adopt, resonate with people's moral views, and seem likely to succeed. The rapid spread of the sit-in tactic in 1960 is an example of how a tactical innovation can sometimes lead to an explosion of protest.

---

unusual to find men functioning as advisers also. Some of the Youth Councils felt a kinship with the direct action movement and were not rigidly locked into the legal approach of the NAACP.

The Southern CORE chapters, operating primarily in South Carolina and several border states, were organized by James McCain and Gordon Carey, were headed largely by local ministers, and had a disproportionate number of young people as members. These groups were preparing the way for the massive sit-ins of 1960 by conducting sit-ins between 1957 and 1960 at segregated facilities, including lunch counters.

Early Sit-ins: Forerunners

On February 1, 1960, four black college students initiated a sit-in at the segregated lunch counter of the local Woolworth store in Greensboro, North Carolina. That day has come to be known as the opening of the sit-in movement. Civil rights activists, however, had conducted sit-ins between 1957 and 1960 in at least sixteen cities: St. Louis, Missouri; Wichita and Kansas City, Kansas; Oklahoma City, Enid, Tulsa, and Stillwater, Oklahoma; Lexington and Louisville, Kentucky; Miami, Florida; Charleston, West Virginia; Sumter, South Carolina; East St. Louis, Illinois; Nashville, Tennessee; Atlanta, Georgia; and Durham, North Carolina. The Greensboro sit-ins are important as a unique link in a long chain of sit-ins. Although this book will concentrate on the uniqueness of the Greensboro link, there were important similarities in the entire chain. Previous studies have presented accounts of most of the earlier sit-ins, but without due appreciation of their scope, connections, and extensive organizational base.

The early sit-ins were initiated by direct action organizations. From interviews with participants in the early sit-ins and from published works, I found that civil rights organizations initiated sit-ins in fifteen of the sixteen cities I have identified. The NAACP, primarily its Youth Councils, either initiated or co-initiated sit-ins in nine of the fifteen cities. CORE, usually working with the NAACP, played an important initiating role in seven. The SCLC initiated one case and was involved in another with CORE and FOR. Finally, the Durham Committee on Negro Affairs, working with the NAACP, initiated sit-ins in Durham. From these data we can conclude that the early sit-ins were a result of a multifaceted organizational effort.

Those sit-ins received substantial backing from their respective communities. The black church was the chief institutional force behind the sit-ins; nearly all of the direct action organizations that initiated them were closely associated with the church. The church supplied those organizations with not only an established communication network but also leaders and organized masses, finances, and a safe environment in which to hold political meetings. Direct action organizations clung to the church because their survival depended on it.

Not all black churches supported the sit-ins, and many tried to keep their support "invisible." Clara Luper, the organizer of the 1958 Oklahoma City sit-ins, wrote that the black church did not want to get involved, but church leaders told organizers "we could meet in their churches. They would take up a collection for us and make announcements concerning our worthwhile activities." Interviewed activists revealed that clusters of churches were usually directly involved with the sit-ins. In addition to community support generated through the churches, the activists also received support from parents of those participating in demonstrations.

The early sit-ins were organized by established leaders of the black community. The leaders did not spontaneously emerge in response to a crisis but were organizational actors in the fullest sense. Some sit-in leaders were also church leaders, taught school, and headed the local direct action organization; their extensive organizational linkages gave them access to a pool of individuals to serve as demonstrators. Clara Luper wrote, "The fact that I was teaching American History at Dungee High School in Spencer, Oklahoma, and was a member of the First Street Baptist Church furnished me with an ample number of young people who would become the nucleus of the Youth Council." Mrs. Luper's case is not isolated. Leaders of the early sit-ins were enmeshed in organizational networks and were integral members of the black community.

Rational planning was evident in this early wave of sit-ins. As we have seen, during the late 1950s the Reverends James Lawson and Kelly Miller Smith, both leaders of Nashville Christian Leadership Council, formed what they called a "non-violent workshop." In them Lawson meticulously taught local college students the philosophy and tactics of nonviolent protest. In 1959 those students held "test" sit-ins in two department stores. Earlier, in 1957, members of the Oklahoma City NAACP Youth Council created what they called their "project," whose aim was to eliminate segregation in public accommodations. The project comprised various committees and groups that planned sit-in strategies. After a year of planning, the project group walked into the local Katz Drug Store and initiated a sit-in. In 1955 William Clay organized an NAACP Youth Council in St. Louis. Through careful planning and twelve months of demonstrations, its members were able to desegregate dining facilities at department stores. In Durham, North Carolina, in 1958 black activists of the Durham Committee on Negro Affairs conducted a survey of "five-and-dime" stores in Durham. It revealed that such stores were heavily dependent on black trade. Clearly, the sit-ins in Durham were based on rational planning.

Rational planning was evident in CORE's sit-ins during the late 1950s. CORE prepared for more direct action, including sit-ins, by conducting interracial workshops in Miami in September 1959 and January 1960. Dr. King assisted in the training of young people in one of the CORE workshops. In April 1959 a newly formed Miami CORE group began conducting sit-ins at downtown variety store lunch counters. In July 1959 James Robinson, writing to affiliated CORE groups and others, stated: "You have probably read in the newspaper about the dramatic all-day sit-ins which Miami CORE has conducted at a number of lunch counters. Up to 50 people have participated at many of these sit-ins." In early September 1959 CORE conducted a sixteen-day workshop on direct action in Miami, called the September Action Institute. Robinson wrote of it: "The discussion of the theory and techniques of nonviolent direct action will become understandable to all Institute members precisely because their actual participation in action projects will illuminate what otherwise might remain intangible." While the institute was in session, sit-ins were conducted at the lunch counters of Jackson's–Byrons Department Store. According to Gordon Carey of CORE, "Six days of continuous sit-ins caused the owners of the lunch counter concession to close temporarily while considering a change of policy." Immediately following that store's closing, CORE activists began sitting in at Grant's Department Store. Carey wrote: "We sat at the lunch counter from three to six hours daily until the 2–week Institute ended on September 20." On September 19, 1959, officials of the Jackson's–Byrons Store informed CORE that Negroes would be served as of September 21. Four black CORE members went to the store on September 21 but were refused service. Carey's account continues:

Miami CORE determined to return to Jackson's–Byrons every day. The lunch counter has about 40 seats: On September 23 we had 40 persons sitting-in. It is not easy to get 40 persons on a weekday to sit-in from 10 A.M. till 3 P.M., but we maintained the demonstrations throughout the week. One woman who sat with us daily, works nights from 10 P.M. to 6 A.M. Cab drivers and off-duty Negro policemen joined us at the counter.

On September 25, 1959, city officials in Miami began arresting CORE members, and local whites physically attacked the protesters. Carey was told to be "out of Miami by Monday." Yet, Carey reports, "That day we had 80 persons sitting-in – half of them at Grant's." The Grant's store closed rather than serve blacks. On November 12, 1959, CORE made plans to sit in at the "white" waiting room of the Greenville, South Carolina, airport. The action was planned to protest the fact that the black baseball star Jackie Robinson had been ordered to leave the "white" waiting room a few days earlier. On January 23, just ten days before the famous sit-in at Greensboro, North Carolina, the CORE organization in Sumter, South Carolina, reported that its teenage group was "testing counter service at dime store: manager says he plans to make a change." Again, the action in Sumter had long-range planning behind it: A year earlier, at CORE's National meeting of 1959, the Sumter group had reported that students were involved in its activities. The Sumter CORE organization also had expressed the opinion that "emphasis should be on students and children. In future projects [we] hope to attack employment in 10¢ stores, food stores and chain stores."

In the summer of 1959 the SCLC, CORE, and FOR jointly held a nonviolent workshop on the campus of Spelman College in Atlanta. When the conference ended, James Robinson, Executive Secretary of CORE, along with the Reverend Wyatt Walker, James McCain, Professor Guy Hershberger, and Elmer Newfield, headed for Dabbs, a segregated restaurant in Atlanta. This interracial group shocked everyone by sitting down and eating. In a CORE news release, James Robinson humorously wrote: "We all had agreed that it was the best coffee we had ever had – the extra tang of drinking your coffee interracially across the Georgia color bar is highly recommended!" Besides providing an example for the other workshop participants, these acts of defiance showed everyone how to protest. Marvin Rich of CORE explained: "They were being demonstrated in a public form, so people would just walk by and see it. And people who didn't think things were possible saw that they were possible, and six months later, in their own home town, they may try it out."

Finally, the early sit-ins were sponsored by indigenous resources of the black community; the leadership was black, the bulk of the demonstrators were black, the strategies and tactics were formulated by blacks, the finances came out of the pockets of blacks, and the psychological and spiritual support came from the black churches.

Most of the organizers of the early sit-ins knew each other and were well aware of each other's strategies of confrontation. Many of the activists belonged to the direct action wing of the NAACP. That group included such activists as Floyd McKissick, Daisy Bates, Ronald Walters, Hosea Williams, Barbara Posey, and Clara Luper, who thought of themselves as a distinct group because the national NAACP was usually disapproving or at best ambivalent about their direct action approach.

The NAACP activists built networks that bypassed the conservative channels and organizational positions of their superiors. At NAACP meetings and conferences they sought out situations where they could freely present their plans and desires to engage in confrontational politics and exchange information about strategies. Once acquainted, the activists remained in touch by phone and mail.

Thus it is no accident that sit-ins occurred between 1957 and 1960. Other instances of "direct action" also occurred during this period. Daisy Bates led black students affili-

ated with her NAACP Youth Council into the all-white Little Rock Central High School and forced President Eisenhower to send in federal troops. CORE, beginning to gain a foothold in the South, had the explicit goal of initiating direct action projects. We have already noted that CORE activists were in close contact with other activists of the period. Although the early sit-ins and related activities were not part of a grandiose scheme, they were tied together through organizational and personal networks.

The Sit-in Cluster of the Late 1950s

Organizational and personal networks produced the first cluster of sit-ins in Oklahoma in 1958. In August 1958 the NAACP Youth Council of Wichita, Kansas, headed by Ronald Walters, initiated sit-ins at the lunch counters of a local drug store. At the same time Clara Luper and the young people in her NAACP Youth Council were training to conduct sit-ins in Oklahoma City. The adult leaders of the two groups knew each other: They worked for the same organization, so several members of the two groups traded numerous phone calls to exchange information and discuss mutual support. Direct contact was important, because the local press often refused to cover the sit-ins. Less than a week after Wichita, Clara Luper's group in Oklahoma City initiated its planned sit-ins.

Shortly thereafter sit-ins were conducted in Tulsa, Enid, and Stillwater, Oklahoma. Working through CORE and the local NAACP Youth Council, Clara Luper's friend Shirley Scaggins organized the sit-ins in Tulsa. Mrs. Scaggins had recently lived in Oklahoma City and knew the details of Mrs. Luper's sit-in project. The two leaders worked in concert. At the same time the NAACP Youth Council in Enid began to conduct sit-ins. Mr. Mitchell, who led that group, knew Mrs. Luper well. He had visited the Oklahoma Youth Council at the outset of its sit-in and had discussed sit-in tactics and mutual support. The Stillwater sit-ins appear to have been conducted independently by black college students.

The network that operated in Wichita and several Oklahoma communities reached as far as East St. Louis, Illinois. Homer Randolph, who in late 1958 organized the East St. Louis sit-ins, had previously lived in Oklahoma City, knew Mrs. Luper well, and had young relatives who participated in the Oklahoma City sit-ins.

In short, the first sit-in cluster occurred in Oklahoma in 1958 and spread to cities within a 100-mile radius through established organizational and personal networks. The majority of these early sit-ins were (1) connected rather than isolated, (2) initiated through organizations and personal ties, (3) rationally planned and led by established leaders, and (4) supported by indigenous resources. Thus, the Greensboro sit-ins of February 1960 did not mark the movement's beginning but were a critical link in the chain, triggering sit-ins across the South at an incredible pace. What happened in the black community between the late 1950s and the early 1960s to produce such a movement?

In my view the early sit-ins did not give rise to a massive sit-in movement before 1960 because CORE and the NAACP Youth Council did not have a mass base. The SCLC, which did have a mass base, had not developed fully. Besides, direct action was just emerging as the dominant strategy during the late 1950s.

As the SCLC developed into a Southwide direct action organization between 1957 and 1960, it provided the mass base capable of sustaining a heavy volume of collective action. It augmented the activities of CORE and the NAACP Youth Councils, because they were closely tied to the church. Thus the SCLC, closely interlocked with NAACP Youth Councils and CORE chapters, had developed solid movement centers by late 1959. The centers usually had the following seven characteristics:

1. A cadre of social change-oriented ministers and their congregations. Often one minister would become the local leader of a given center, and his church would serve as the coordinating unit.

2. Direct action organizations of varied complexity. In many cities local churches served as quasi-direct action organizations, while in others ministers built complex church-related organizations (e.g. United Defense League of Baton Rouge, Montgomery Improvement Association, Alabama Christian Movement for Human Rights of Birmingham, Petersburg Improvement Association). NAACP Youth Councils and CORE affiliates also were components of the local centers.

3. Indigenous financing coordinated through the church.

4. Weekly mass meetings, which served as forums where local residents were informed of relevant information and strategies regarding the movement. These meetings also built solidarity among the participants.

5. Dissemination of nonviolent tactics and strategies. The leaders articulated to the black community the message that social change would occur only through nonviolent direct action carried out by masses.

6. Adaptation of a rich church culture to political purposes. The black spirituals, sermons, and prayers were used to deepen the participants' commitment to the struggle.

7. A mass-based orientation, rooted in the black community, through the church.

From the perspective of this study, the period between the 1950s bus boycotts and the 1960 sit-ins provided pivotal resources for the emerging civil rights movement. My analysis emphasizes that the organizational foundation of the civil rights movement was built during this period, and active local movement centers were created in numerous Southern black communities. The next chapter will demonstrate that those movement centers were the new force enabling the 1960 sit-ins to become a mass movement and a tactical innovation within the movement.

22 The Strategic Uses of Identity by the Lesbian and Gay Movement

Mary Bernstein

[The organizers of the 1993 lesbian and gay march on Washington] face a dilemma: how to put forward a set of unsettling demands for unconventional people in ways that will not make enemies of potential allies. They do so by playing down their differences before the media and the country while celebrating it in private.

(Tarrow 1994, p. 10)

Sidney Tarrow's portrayal of the 1993 lesbian and gay march on Washington highlights a central irony about identity politics and the decline of the Left: Critics of identity politics decry the celebration of difference within contemporary identity movements, charging them with limiting the potential for a "politics of commonality" between oppressed peoples that could have potential for radical social change (Gitlin 1995). On the other hand, the lesbian and gay movement seems largely to have abandoned its emphasis on *difference from* the straight majority in favor of a moderate politics that highlights *similarities to* the straight majority.

Over time, "identity" movements shift their emphasis between celebrating and suppressing differences from the majority. For example, the Civil Rights movement underscored similarities to the majority in order to achieve concrete policy reforms. At other times, movements that assert radical racial identities to build communities and challenge hegemonic American culture take center stage. The American feminist movement has alternately emphasized innate gender differences between men and women and denied that such differences exist or that they are socially relevant. Under what political conditions do activists celebrate or suppress differences from the majority? Why does the stress on difference or similarity change over time?

To answer these questions, this article draws on evidence from several campaigns for lesbian and gay rights ordinances. The lesbian and gay movement was chosen because it is considered the quintessential identity movement (Melucci 1989; Duyvendak 1995; Duyvendak and Giugni 1995). The cultural barriers to acceptance of homosexuality and the challenge of self-acceptance for lesbians and gay men require cultural struggle. However, the lesbian and gay movement has been altered from a movement for cultural transformation through sexual liberation to one that seeks achievement of political rights through a narrow, ethnic-like (Seidman 1993) interest-group politics. This well-documented transition has yet to be explained.

This research will show that celebration or suppression of differences within political campaigns depends on the structure of social movement organizations, access to the polity (Tilly 1978), and the type of opposition. By specifying the political conditions that explain variation in strategies within movements, one can better understand differences in forms of collective action across movements.

Identity and Movement Types

Attempts to classify social movements have typically centered around the distinction between "strategy-oriented" and "identity-oriented" movements (Touraine 1981). Abandoning this distinction, Duyvendak and Giugni argue instead that "the real difference is, however, the one between movements pursuing goals in the outside world, for which the action is instrumental for goal realization, and identity-oriented movements that realize their goals, at least partly, in their activities" (1995, pp. 277–78). Social movements, then, are classified on "their logic of action," whether they employ an identity or instrumental logic of action, and whether they are internally or externally oriented. Movements such as the lesbian and gay movement are internally oriented and follow an identity logic of action. Instrumental movements, by contrast, engage in instrumental action and are externally oriented (Duyvendak and Giugni 1995, pp. 84–85).

This mechanical bifurcation of movement types, reflected in the division between identity theory on the one hand and resource mobilization and political process theory on the other, has left the literature on contentious politics unable to explain changes in forms of collective action. First, the casual use of the term "identity" obscures fundamental distinctions in meaning (e.g., Gitlin 1995). Second, I argue that theorists must abandon the *essentialist* characterization of social movements as expressive or instrumental because it impairs the study of all social movements. This essentialist characterization stems from the conflation of goals and strategies (i.e., that instrumental strategies are irrelevant to cultural change, while expressions of identity cannot be externally directed) apparent in resource mobilization, political process, and new social movement theories. Finally, attempts to integrate these theories have been unsuccessful.

Subsumed under the rubric of new social movements, "identity movements" have been defined as much by the goals they seek, and the strategies they use, as by the fact that they are based on a shared characteristic such as ethnicity or sex. According to new social movement theorists, identity movements seek to transform dominant cultural patterns, or gain recognition for new social identities, by employing expressive strategies.

New social movement theory suggests that movements choose political strategies in order to facilitate the creation of organizational forms that encourage participation and empowerment. Thus strategies that privilege the creation of democratic, nonhierarchical organizations would be chosen over strategies narrowly tailored to produce policy change.

For resource mobilization and political process theorists, identity may play a role in mobilization through solidary incentives but once the "free rider" problem is overcome all other collective action is deemed instrumental, targeted solely at achieving concrete (i.e., measurable) goals. Resource mobilization and political process theorists have neglected the study of identity movements with their seemingly "nonpolitical," cultural goals. Even when culture is recognized as an integral part of sustaining activist communities, changing or challenging mainstream culture is rarely considered a goal of activism. Strategies are seen as rationally chosen to optimize the likelihood of policy success. Outcomes are measured as a combination of policy change ("new advantages") and access to the structure of political bargaining (Jenkins and Perrow 1977; Tilly 1978; McAdam 1982; Gamson 1990). Such a narrow framing of social movement goals can lead to erroneous assumptions about the reasons for collective action and for strategy choice (Turner and Killian 1972; Jenkins 1983). Where goals are cultural and therefore harder to operationalize, theorists assume collective action has no external dimension but is aimed simply at reproducing the identity on which the movement is based (see Duyvendak 1995; Duyvendak and Giugni 1995). This leaves theorists unable to explain social movement action that seems to be working at cross purposes to achieving policy change. Furthermore, it relegates "prefigurative" (Polletta 1994) politics—a politics that seeks to transform observers through the embodiment of alternative values and organizational forms – to the realm of the irrational.

Although political opportunity or political process models share resource mobilization's assumptions about the relationship between strategies and goals, they provide a more useful starting point for understanding how political strategies are chosen. According to Tilly (1978), forms of collective action will be affected by "political coalitions and...the means of actions built into the existing political organization" (p. 167). These short- and medium-term "volatile" (Gamson and Meyer 1996) elements of "political opportunity" include the opening of access to participation, shifts in ruling alignments, the availability of influential allies, and cleavages among elites. As the political context changes, strategies should also change. Yet political opportunity models lack specificity in analyzing why or under what political conditions movements choose particular forms of collective action.

Attempts to reconcile the disjuncture between new social movement and resource mobilization or political process theory center on the relationship between forms of collective action and the movement's life cycle. The emergent "new social movements" of the 1960s and 1970s seemed so striking because they utilized innovative, direct action tactics. According to Calhoun (1995):

> As Tarrow (1989) has remarked, this description confuses two senses of *new*: the characteristics of all movements when they are new, and the characteristics of a putatively new sort of movement.
>
> It is indeed generally true that any movement of or on behalf of those excluded from conventional politics starts out with a need to attract attention; movement activity is not just an instrumental attempt to achieve movement goals, but a means of recruitment and continuing mobilization of participants. (p. 193)

In this view, a lack of historical perspective has mistakenly led new social movement theorists to label behavior "distinctive" when it is simply behavior indicative of an emergent social movement.

This criticism of new social movement theory glosses over important empirical and theoretical distinctions. First, not every emergent social movement employs novel or dramatic tactics in order to gain new recruits. Religious right organizations that arose in the 1970s drew on the dense network of conservative churches as well as direct mail lists to mobilize; they did not employ innovative or novel tactics. Rather than misattributing certain forms of collective action to the newness of social movements, one should ask what accounts for different forms of mobilization. Furthermore, attributing certain forms of collective action to the newness of social movements precludes an understanding of why such forms of collective action may emerge at later points in a movement's protest cycle.

Second, the glib dismissal of the sorts of political action attributed to new social movements as simply expressive, or unrelated to political structure, ignores the external or instrumental dimensions of seemingly expressive action. If putatively new social movements do challenge dominant cultural patterns, then theorists must take seriously the political nature of such collective action. Social movement theory must examine the challenges all social movements present to dominant cultural patterns.

This research seeks to provide a more complete understanding of the role of identity in collective action. I build in part on political process theory, while incorporating new social movement theory's emphasis on the importance of cultural change to movement activism. I argue that the concept of "identity" has at least three distinct analytic levels, the first two of which have been developed in the social movement literature. First, a shared collective identity is necessary for mobilization of *any* social movement, including the classic labor movement (Calhoun 1995). Second, identity can be a goal of social movement activism, either gaining acceptance for a hitherto stigmatized identity or deconstructing categories of identities such as "man," "woman," "gay," "straight"

(Gamson 1995), "black," or "white." Finally, this research argues that expressions of identity can be deployed at the collective level as a political strategy, which can be aimed at cultural or instrumental goals.

Once the concept of identity is broken down into these three analytic dimensions, then one can explore the political conditions that produce certain identity strategies. [...]

Three Analytic Dimensions of Identity

The creation of communities and movement solidarity, which the bulk of research on collective identity examines (Williams 1995), is necessary for mobilization. I define *identity for empowerment* to mean the creation of collective identity and the feeling that political action is feasible (see table 22.1). In other words, some sort of identity is necessary to translate individual to group interests and individual to collective action. All social movements require such a "political consciousness" (Morris 1992) to create and mobilize a constituency (Taylor and Whittier 1992; Calhoun 1995).

Identity for empowerment is not necessarily a consciously chosen strategy, although it is a precursor to collective action. If a movement constituency has a shared collective identity and the institutions or social networks that provide a cultural space from which to act, then community building and empowerment will be forfeited to "instrumental" goals of policy attainment. In the absence of visibility or movement organizations, more work must be done to build organizations and recruit activists.

Collective identity can also have an external dimension in mobilization. Beckwith (1995) argues that an actor can use her or his identity to gain "political standing" (i.e., to legitimate participation) in a social movement in which she or he is not directly implicated. So, for example, women involved in coal mining strikes who are not miners can justify participation based on their relations to the miners, such as mother, sister, or wife. The choice of identity (e.g., wife of miner vs. working-class woman) can have implications for future activism.

Identity can also be a goal of collective action (*identity as goal*). Activists may challenge stigmatized identities, seek recognition for new identities, or deconstruct restrictive social categories. New Left organizations of the 1960s, for example, sought not only concrete policy reform, but thought that the creation of alternative cultural forms could foster structural change. Polletta (1994) asserts that "student-organizers of the Student Nonviolent Coordinating Committee (SNCC) saw their task as to mobilize and secure recognition for a new collective iden-

Table 22.1 The three analytic dimensions of "identity"

Dimension	Description
Identity for empowerment	Activists must draw on an existing identity or construct a new collective identity in order to create and mobilize a constituency. The particular identity chosen will have implications for future activism.
Identity as goal	Activists may challenge stigmatized identities, seek recognition for new identities, or deconstruct restrictive social categories as goals of collective action.
Identity as strategy	Identities may be deployed strategically as a form of collective action. *Identity deployment* is defined as expressing identity such that the terrain of conflict becomes the individual person so that the values, categories, and practices of individuals become subject to debate. *Identity for critique* confronts the values, categories, and practice of the dominant culture. *Identity for education* challenges the dominant culture's perception of the minority or is used strategically to gain legitimacy by playing on uncontroversial themes.

tity – poor, 'unqualified' southern blacks – in a way that would transform national and local politics by refashioning criteria of political leadership" (p. 85). Feminists influenced American culture by challenging and altering conventional usage of sexist terms in the English language. Gamson (1995) argues that social movement theory must take seriously the goal of contemporary "queer politics" to deconstruct social categories, including "man," "woman," "gay," and "straight." Without a broader understanding of the goals of collective action and their relationship to the structural location of the actors, social movement theory cannot adequately explain strategy choices made by activists.

In addition to influencing motivations and goals of collective action, "cultural resources also have an external, strategic dimension" (Williams 1995, p. 125). I define *identity deployment* to mean expressing identity such that the terrain of conflict becomes the individual person so that the values, categories, and practices of individuals become subject to debate. What does it mean to "deploy identity" strategically? Taylor and Raeburn (1995) view identity deployment as a way to contest stigmatized social identities for the purposes of institutional change. Yet contesting stigma to change institutions is not the only reason for identity deployment. The goal of identity deployment can be to transform mainstream culture, its categories and values (and perhaps by extension its policies and structures), by providing alternative organizational forms. Identity deployment can also transform participants or simply educate legislators or the public.

Identity deployment can be examined at both the individual and collective level along a continuum from education to critique. Activists either dress and act consistently with mainstream culture or behave in a critical way. *Identity for critique* confronts the values, categories, and practices of the dominant culture. *Identity for education* challenges the dominant culture's perception of the minority or is used strategically to gain legitimacy by playing on uncontroversial themes. Although the goals associated with

either identity strategy can be moderate or radical, identity for education generally limits the scope of conflict by not problematizing the morality or norms of the dominant culture.

Identity deployment should be understood dramaturgically as the collective portrayal of the group's identity in the political realm, whether that be in city council hearings or at sit-ins in segregated restaurants. The strategic deployment of identity may differ from the group's (or individuals') private understanding of that identity. In this research, I examine identity deployment at the collective level.

It is important not to conflate the goals of identity deployment with its form (i.e., critical or educational). Both can be part of a project of cultural challenge or a strategy to achieve policy reform. Whether these strategies are associated with organizational forms that encourage participation and empowerment by privileging the creation of democratic, nonhierarchical organizations, as new social movement theory would suggest, or with narrow interest group strategies designed to achieve policy change, as resource mobilization and political process perspectives would suggest, then becomes an empirical question, not an essentialist assumption based on movement types.

Understanding identity as a tool for mobilization, as a goal, and as a strategy will lead to a more comprehensive understanding of social movements. Instead of asking whether identity plays a role in a given movement, we can ask several questions: What role does identity play in mobilization? To what extent is identity a goal of collective action? Why or under what political conditions are identities that celebrate or suppress differences deployed strategically?

General Model

I argue that identity strategies will be determined by the configuration of political access, the structure of social movement organizations, and the type and extent of opposition. In addition to affecting political outcomes, the characteristics of movement organizations should also influence political strategies. I define *inclusive* movement organizations to be those groups whose strategies, in practice, seek to educate and mobilize a constituency or maximize involvement in political campaigns. *Exclusive* organizations actively discourage popular participation, choosing strategies unlikely to mobilize a movement constituency. Changes in the political context should also influence political strategies. I consider that a movement has *access* to the polity if candidates respond to movement inquiries, if elected officials or state agencies support and work toward the movement's goals, or if movement leaders have access to polity members (e.g., through business affiliations, personal contacts, or official positions in political parties). Organized opposition is also an important part of the political context. Most contemporary American social movements eventually face organized opposition to their goals, and this should influence the types of identities deployed. *Routine opposition* will refer to polity insiders (Tilly 1978); that is, those who by virtue of their institutional position (such as a cardinal of the Catholic Church) have the ear of policy makers. *Opposing movements* will refer to groups outside the polity mobilized around the issues of contention.

The role of identity in mobilization will differ across movements, but not because of some abstract essentialism of movement types. For example, identity for empowerment may play a smaller role in mobilizing movements sparked by a "moral shock" – such as the antiwar movement, the antinuclear movement, or the animal rights movement – than in mobilizing movements based on a shared characteristic or identity. But once a movement has emerged, I suggest that the same conditions that determine identity deployment should also apply to movements started by moral shocks.

In order to emerge, a social movement requires a base from which to organize and some sort of collective identity to translate individual into group interests. Movements with access to the structure of political bargaining *or* strong organizational infrastructures that have fostered a shared identity will tend to seek policy change, emphasize sameness rather than difference, and will use identity for education rather than identity for critique (see figure 22.1, paths 1, 2a). However, if the movement faces organized opposition from outside the political establishment, and if the movement is led by exclusive, narrowly focused groups uninterested in movement building, the movement may split, with some groups emphasizing differences and community building, while the exclusive groups continue to emphasize sameness and narrowly focused policy change (a mixed model; see figure 22.1, path 2b). In such cases, critical identities may be deployed as much in reaction to movement leadership as to the opposition.

When an emergent movement lacks both political access and an organizational infrastructure or collective identity, then an emphasis on difference will be needed to build solidarity and mobilize a constituency (figure 22.1, path 3). Such movements will tend to focus on building community and celebrating difference, as will those sectors of a movement marginalized by exclusive groups encountering nonroutine opposition (figure 22.1, path 4b).

Once a movement has been established – with constituency and organizational actors – then movement between the cells in figure 22.1 may take place as organized opposition emerges or declines, political coalitions shift, and the structures of movement organizations change over time.

After a movement's emergence, the types of identity deployment will be related to the structure of social movement organizations, access to the polity and whether opposition is routine, deriving from polity insiders, or external, arising from organized opposing movements. Changes in short- or medium-term elements of the political context should have a determining effect on forms of collective action such that greater access

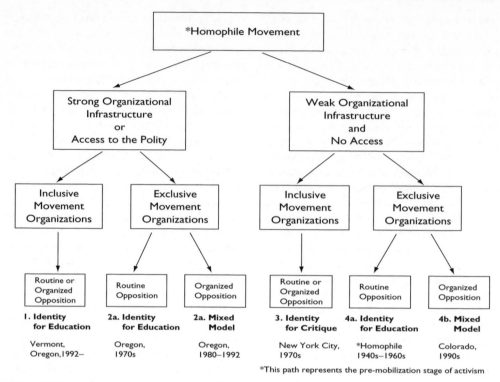

Figure 22.1   Identity deployment in the lesbian and gay movement

produces more moderate forms of collective action and identity for education strategies, while closing opportunities will lead to an emphasis on identity for critique. When the polity is relatively open and diverse segments of the activist community are represented in movement organizations or are included in political campaigns, there will be less emphasis on criticizing normative values. Because identity is deployed in the context of concrete interactions, the baseline against which activists define themselves will be influenced by opposing movements. Exclusive social movement organizations, the presence of a strong opposition, and negative interactions with the state will likely result in greater dissension within the community. That dissension will lead to factionalization and will produce moderates who will focus more on education and traditional lobbying tactics and radicals who will focus on criticizing dominant values (a "mixed model"). Radicalization in the movement can stem as much

from reaction to movement leaders as from reactions to the political context. In short, identity deployment in the political realm will depend on the structure of and relations among movement organizations, the extent of political access, and the type of opposition.
[...]
When lesbians and gay men deploy their identity strategically, debates may center around whether sexual orientation is immutable, what constitutes "homosexual practices," or whether pedophilia is the same as homosexuality. Lesbian and gay lives become the subject of conflict. Nothing about the lesbian and gay movement dictates the strategic use of identity at the collective level. For example, activists could draw attention to discriminatory employment practices, with a universal appeal to everyone's right to a job based on their skills. That is different than disclosing one's sexual orientation to legislators or neighbors, saying "Here I am, know me."

In the case of the lesbian and gay movement, identity for education challenges negative stereotypes about lesbians and gay men, such as having hundreds of sexual partners a year or struggling with uncontrollable sexual urges, while identity for critique challenges dominant cultural assumptions about the religious or biological "naturalness" of gender roles and the heterosexual nuclear family. Arguably the greatest success of the women's movement has been to break down the division between public and private through challenging traditional notions of gender. Both identity for critique and identity for education can be part of broader projects seeking cultural change or policy reform.

Although many have looked at the relationship between lesbian and gay culture and individual-level identity strategies, few have examined this phenomena empirically, as a collective, consciously chosen political strategy. The rest of this article explores identity strategies along the continuum from critique to education at the collective level. As Seidman (1993, pp. 135–36) argues, we must "relate the politics of representation to institutional dynamics" rather than reducing cultural codes to textual practices abstracted from institutional contexts. The lesbian and gay movement has challenged a variety of institutions in American society, but I will restrict my analysis to interactions with the state because, with the onslaught by the Religious Right, the state has become one of the central loci of identity deployment. Future research will have to determine the ways diverse institutional dynamics (e.g., the church or psychiatry) influence the creation and deployment of identities.

The Homophile Movement

A collective identity among lesbians and gay men emerged prior to the strategic recruitment of a constituency by organizational actors, as long-term structural changes brought increasing numbers of gay men and lesbians together in urban settings. The secretive nature of the early homophile organizations, however, precluded mass mobilization. The only public meeting places for lesbians and gay men – cruising places and Mafia-run bars – were ill-suited for mobilization. Cherry Grove, Fire Island, a visible lesbian and gay summer community, may have provided a more hospitable avenue for mobilization but was not linked to a broader organizational infrastructure.

The predominantly underground homophile movement of the 1940s and 1950s has been well documented. Groups such as the Daughters of Bilitis and the Mattachine Society had exclusive organizational structures, lacked access to the polity, and faced routine opposition from the state (see figure 22.1, path 4a). The goals of the homophile movement varied over the years as some sought assimilation while others thought homosexuality was a distinctive and positive trait that should not be subsumed by mainstream culture. Yet both sides agreed on strategies: homophile activists would educate professionals (in particular medical professionals) about the realities of homosexuality; those professionals would in turn advocate for changes in state policies on behalf of homosexuals.

As the social strictures against homosexuality loosened, the lesbian and gay movement became more public through the 1960s. Much of the emergent movement's activism appeared to be "expressive," aimed for and at lesbians and gay men. In part, that perception was strengthened by the connection of many activists in post-Stonewall organizations to the New Left (e.g., RadicaLesbians, the Furies, and the Gay Liberation Front)[1] who felt that alternative cultural forms would lead to a revolutionary restructuring of society. The visible and outspoken nature of 1960s and 1970s activists accounts for the perception by scholars that the lesbian and gay movement was fundamentally different from other social movements.

But this perception is misguided because it ignores the diversity within the lesbian and gay movement, even around the time of

Stonewall. The development of these local movements and the strategies they chose depended on their access to the polity, on their organizational structure, and on the type of opposition they faced. For example, where movement leaders had access to the polity, usually in smaller cities where gay white businessmen had contacts in government or where earlier movement activities had created political access, as in Washington, D.C., expressive action was minimal. In most cases, local movements lacked access to the polity and had to create a constituency. To do so, they had to locate others like themselves. The lack of lesbian and gay institutions, such as churches or bookstores, forced leaders to construct those spaces as well as to launch political campaigns.

When groups lack their own institutions and a political consciousness, they will concentrate on identity for empowerment and community growth. Over time, as institutions and opportunities to act develop, what was once seen as an expressive movement will come to be seen as instrumental as political representation increases and the emphasis on empowerment decreases. Once a movement has been established, forms of collective action will depend on access to decision makers, the extent of opposition, and the degree of inclusiveness of movement organizations.

New York City and Oregon

In 1971, New York City's Gay Activists Alliance (GAA) launched a campaign to add "sexual orientation" to the list of protected categories in the city's human rights ordinance. Although GAA engaged political authorities in the public realm, it emphasized identity for critique, seeking to increase publicity and refusing to compromise for the sake of policy change (Figure 22.1 path 3). Activists borrowed freely from the tactics of other contemporary movements, turning sit-ins into "kiss-ins" at straight bars to protest bans on same-sex displays of affection. They held peaceful demonstrations protest-ing police brutality and infiltrated local political clubs to "zap" public officials with questions about police raids on gay bars, entrapment, and support for antidiscrimination policies. Activists consistently refused to dress in accordance with mainstream culture, using their identity to criticize gender roles and heterosexual norms. In short, they used theatrical tactics that increased the scope of the conflict, demanding publicity, regardless of its potentially dilatory effect on achieving policy change. For example, Eleanor Holmes Norton, chair of New York City's Commission on Human Rights, offered GAA members the option of holding private hearings on the ordinance. GAA refused, declaring that it would only participate in open hearings, although that was less likely to achieve policy change. GAA finally secured public hearings after a demonstration – intended to be peaceful – outside General Welfare Committee chair Saul Sharison's apartment building turned bloody when Tactical Police Force officers taunted and then beat demonstrators with their clubs. Despite dissension within GAA, drag queens were ultimately allowed to participate in the hearings. City council members would subsequently exploit the confusion between transvestism and homosexuality to defeat the ordinance.

The fight for antidiscrimination legislation in Oregon contrasted sharply with the battle in New York City. Activists in Portland and Eugene in the 1970s – primarily gay white men – had easy access to the polity because of their status as business persons. The Portland Town Council (PTC), an informal coalition of gay-oriented businesses and organizations, was founded in 1970. Due largely to the lack of opposition and the semi-insider status of its members, the PTC won a series of incremental victories culminating in Portland's passage of a law to prohibit discrimination against city employees on the basis of sexual orientation. In Eugene, activists also capitalized on their insider status by choosing strategies that discouraged mass participation, including secret meetings with council members. In 1977,

Eugene passed a lesbian and gay rights ordinance.

The PTC also spearheaded efforts to add sexual orientation to the state's human rights statute. Despite agonizingly narrow defeats of statewide antidiscrimination bills (by one vote in 1975), activists continued to work with state officials. In 1976, at the PTC's request, Oregon Governor Straub created the Ad Hoc Task Force on Sexual Preference to conduct factual research and to make policy recommendations to the Oregon legislature. The PTC served as an advisory board, recommended areas for research, and facilitated interactions between lesbian and gay communities and the task force.

The strategies employed in New York City and Oregon contrasted sharply. When given the choice, New York City activists consistently privileged strategies that challenged dominant cultural values over those that would maximize the likelihood of policy success. By refusing to hold private hearings with the Human Rights Commission, activists increased the scope of conflict. Rather than allaying the fears of legislators and the public by reassuring them of the incremental nature of the policy reform, activists exacerbated those fears by having transvestites testify at public hearings. In Oregon, activists were content to hold secret meetings with lawmakers in order to gain legal change.

What accounts for these diverse approaches to political change? The early stage of New York City's lesbian and gay liberation movement appears to be consistent with a new social movement interpretation. At the time, movement theorists stated explicitly that the battle was over ending oppressive gender roles and the restrictive categories of heterosexuality and homosexuality that inhibited everyone's true bisexual nature. Thus activists chose strategies that highlighted differences from the straight majority, seeing themselves as the embodiment of the liberation potential. Uncompromising strategies that reproduced the identity on which the movement was based and created participatory organizations took priority over goals of achieving

policy reform. Creating a sense that gay was good and should be expressed publicly, with pride, would not come through secretive meetings with city officials or concealing drag queens.

In Oregon, on the other hand, little emphasis was placed on creating democratic organizations. The goals in Eugene, Portland, and at the state level were to obtain narrow legal protections. Rather than focus on mobilization, the PTC hired a lobbyist to advocate for the new antidiscrimination legislation. The comparison of Oregon to New York City suggests that newly emerging social movements will only emphasize differences through expressive tactics to the extent that they lack access to the polity and a strong organizational infrastructure.

Political access and differing resources explain in part the different orientations of the Oregon and New York City activists to cultural and legal change. In New York City, activists faced a closed polity. New York State retained an antisodomy statute, which effectively criminalized the status of being lesbian or gay and was used to justify police entrapment and bar raids. The New York City police routinely used violence to quell peaceful lesbian and gay demonstrations and were unresponsive to lesbians and gay men who were the victims of violence.

Lesbians and gay men needed to become a political minority. To do so, they had to increase visibility at the expense of losing short-term policy battles. Influenced as well by other contemporary movements (e.g., the Civil Rights, New Left, and feminist movements) activists had little to lose and much to gain by radical political action. Although deploying identity for critique may have had long-term political benefits, many saw the goal of a political battle in terms of empowering the lesbian and gay communities. In short, the political battle was an opportunity to create a cultural shift in sensibilities among lesbians and gay men (Marotta 1981).

Despite the importance of the political context, it was in interactions with the state that identities were formed and deployed.

Although activists' analysis of the relationship between political and cultural change – either that political campaigns served the purpose of empowering activists or that political reforms would enable cultural change – produced and reinforced critical identities, negative interactions with the state entrenched an oppositional dynamic. The New York City Council's initial refusal to hold public hearings, in addition to the police repression that included the attack on demonstrators outside Sharison's building, cemented the antagonistic relationship between activists and the state. Because organizations were inclusive and the lesbian and gay social movement sector was relatively undifferentiated, a cultural critique could only be expressed in the political realm. There was nothing about the movement per se that dictated the deployment of critical identities. Activists' interpretations of the relationship between culture and politics and the types of identities deployed were contingent on interactions with the state.

A second part of the formation of a critical identity was the absence of an organized opposition. Because opposition was routine, lesbians and gay men had only to define themselves against mainstream cultural views in order to criticize the dominant culture. Identities were constructed through interactions with the state, in the absence of organized third parties. In short, inclusive movement organizations, lack of access to the polity, negative interactions with the state, and routine opposition produced critical identities.

Activists in Oregon had greater resources than did activists in New York City, due in part to class and gender differences. The unique access to government officials facilitated by business connections enabled quick passage of local legislation and almost won passage of statewide legislation. Unlike GAA, the PTC had had mostly positive relations with state authorities in Portland, Eugene, and the state capitol. So after narrow losses in the state legislature, rather than respond in a critical way through dramatic demonstrations, the PTC approached Governor Robert Straub for redress. Had Governor Straub not been responsive to lesbian and gay demands, or, similarly, had the Eugene City Council initially rebuffed the gay activists, critical identities would have been deployed, as much in reaction to the elite gay leadership as to the state (which is what happened in Oregon more than a decade later).

Critical identities, however, were not deployed in Eugene, and success came easily as a result of political access and the low-key tactics of the gay activists. The elitist attitude and nonparticipatory stance of the gay leadership, however, created antagonisms between different lesbian and gay communities. But because interactions with the state had been positive, as shown by the bill's relatively quick passage, these tensions lay dormant. When newly organized religious right groups placed a referendum to repeal Eugene's lesbian and gay rights ordinance on the ballot, the dissension within the lesbian and gay communities made it difficult for them to present a united front, and the anti-lesbian and antigay referendum ultimately passed.

By the end of the 1970s, the lesbian and gay movement had undergone profound internal change. Activists no longer placed the same emphasis on challenging gender roles and the construction of heterosexuality in state-oriented lesbian and gay rights campaigns. As many have observed, an ethnic- or interest-group model that sought achievement of rights replaced the liberation model that sought freedom from constraining gender roles and sexual categories. Institutionalized, professionally led organizations often supplanted the grassroots groups of the early 1970s in leading campaigns directed at the state. The gay liberation fronts and the gay activists' alliances had all but disappeared. In addition to internal changes within the lesbian and gay movement, by the end of the 1970s the religious right emerged and worked to oppose all of the changes sought by lesbian and gay activists.

The next section explains why these changes within the lesbian and gay movement occurred and what accounts for the continued variation in forms of collective action across the United States. Access to political decision makers produced identity for education, as in Vermont (figure 22.1, path 1). However, where exclusive groups faced organized opposition, as in Colorado, a mixed model of identity deployment was produced as marginalized groups within the lesbian and gay movement reacted to the lesbian and gay leadership and to the opposition (path 4b). In Oregon, exclusive leadership and intense opposition would later produce a mixed model (path 2b). But as activists realized that sustaining a prolonged campaign against the religious opposition required cooperation among diverse lesbian and gay communities, organizations became more inclusive and an educational model prevailed (path 1).

[...]

Implications

This approach to understanding the strategic deployment of identity has potential applications to other movements based on a shared characteristic. For example, the Southern Civil Rights movement that emerged in the 1950s followed path 1 as shown in figure 22.2. The complex organizational infrastructure of the South, which included black colleges, black churches, and even beauty parlors, provided a locus from which to organize (Morris 1984). Thus when federal policies began to change, leaders were able to mobilize from an existing base. Emergent, inclusive civil rights organizations underscored sameness rather than difference and sought concrete policy goals.

Over time, the focus on identity for education often gave way to identity for critique as the black power movement gained momentum (figure 22.2, path 3). According to Robert Scheer (1970, p. 202), black power, or "black *revolution* [is] the statement of an alternative system of values, the move to

acquire power to assert those values, and the express willingness to respond with revolutionary violence to the violence inherent in established power." By fostering an identity based on differences from the majority, black nationalism was a way to challenge dominant cultural values, to build communities, and to create revolutionary change. Leaders hoped that deploying critical identities based on perceived cultural differences would be a crucial step toward economic independence and political power.

I suggest that local variations in political access and organizational infrastructures, as well as the degree of exclusivity of African-American leadership would also account, in part, for the relative stress placed on deploying critical or educational identities. In short, local conditions (political access and the type of opposition) as well as the relationships among African-American political organizations should help explain the vicissitudes in the deployment of radical racial identities on the one hand and educational identities on the other.

When the feminist movement began to emerge in the 1960s, two activist factions were identified. Older professional women appointed to state governmental commissions on the status of women created formal organizations and began to lobby (Evans 1979; Freeman 1984). What came to be known as the liberal wing of feminism stressed similarities to the majority, deployed identity for education (i.e., that there were no socially significant differences between men and women), and focused attention on gaining formal policy reforms (figure 22.2, path 1). Because of their political access, older feminists stressed similarities to men.

The other wing of the emergent feminist movement was dominated by college-age women. Lacking the political access of the older wing, and of course influenced by the New Left, these women stressed identity for critique and their activism followed a dramatically different path from that of the older wing (figure 22.2, path 3). The younger wing, which eventually became

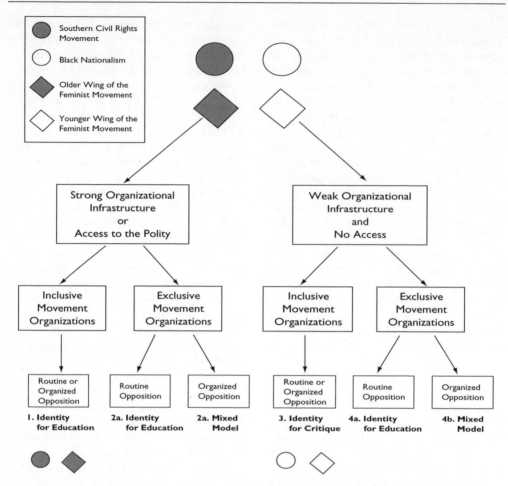

Figure 22.2   General model of identity deployment

identified with radical feminism, drew attention to "women's values" deriving from motherhood as a positive and distinct characteristic that set women apart from men in socially meaningful ways. Rather than devaluing these traits, critical female identities were deployed to criticize problematic manifestations of male dominance (such as violence and nuclear arms).

Reforming policy and challenging culture was a goal of both strategies. Suppressing differences to denaturalize categories such as "family" challenged the cultural underpinnings of existing policies based on an allegedly natural, gender-based public/private distinction. Stressing differences

was also a part of a broader project of normative challenge. Over time, the relative emphasis on stressing similarities or differences changed as local conditions varied.

This brief overview of the feminist and Civil Rights movements broadly suggests how the differing structural locations of the actors, the extent of political access, and the strength of the organizational base from which these movements could mobilize influenced the types of identities deployed. This cursory overview of the movements cannot (and is not meant to) capture their complexity, but only to suggest the importance of understanding identity deployment and *why* certain movements *appear to be* internally or externally directed, and why they seem to seek "instrumental" or "identity" goals.

[...]

Note

1 "Stonewall" refers to the 1969 riots that took place in New York City when patrons of the gay afterhours club, the Stonewall Inn, fought back during a police raid. The weekend of rioting that ensued sparked national publicity for the movement, and dozens of new gay liberationist organizations formed, accelerating the trend toward radicalism that had begun earlier in the 1960s.

References

Beckwith, Karen. 1995. "Women's Movements and Women in Movements: Political Opportunity in Context." Paper presented at the meetings of the American Political Science Association, August 31–September 3, Chicago.

Calhoun, Craig. 1994. "Social Theory and the Politics of Identity." Pp. 9–36 in *Social Theory and the Politics of Identity*, edited by Craig Calhoun. Cambridge, Mass.: Blackwell.

——. 1995. "'New Social Movements' of the Early Nineteenth Century." Pp. 173–215 in *Repertoires and Cycles of Collective Action*, edited by Mark Traugott. Durham, N.C.: Duke University Press.

Duyvendak, Jan Willem. 1995. "Gay Subcultures between Movement and Market." Pp. 165–80 in *New Social Movements in Western Europe: A Comparative Analysis*, edited by Hanspeter Kriesi, Ruud Koopmans, Jan Willem Duyvendak, and Marco G. Giugni. Minneapolis: University of Minnesota Press.

Duyvendak, Jan Willem, and Marco G. Giugni. 1995. "Social Movement Types and Policy Domains." Pp. 82–110 in *New Social Movements in Western Europe: A Comparative Analysis*, edited by Hanspeter Kriesi, Ruud Koopmans, Jan Willem Duyvendak, and Marco G. Giugni. Minneapolis: University of Minnesota Press.

Evans, Sara. 1979. *Personal Politics: The Roots of Women's Liberation in the Civil Rights Movement and the New Left*. New York: Vintage Books.

Freeman, Jo. 1984. "The Women's Liberation Movement: Its Origins, Structure, Activities, and Ideas." Pp. 543–56 in *Women: A Feminist Perspective*, edited by Jo Freeman. Palo Alto, Calif.: Mayfield.

Gamson, Joshua. 1995. "Must Identity Movements Self Destruct? A Queer Dilemma." *Social Problems* 42 (3): 390–407.

Gamson, William. 1990. *The Strategy of Social Protest*, 2d ed. Belmont, Calif.: Wadsworth.

Gamson, William A., and David S. Meyer. 1996. "The Framing of Political Opportunity." Pp. 275–90 in *Comparative Perspectives on Social Movements: Political Opportunities, Mobilizing Structures, and Cultural Framings*, edited by John McCarthy, Doug McAdam, and Meyer N. Zald. Cambridge: Cambridge University Press.

Gitlin, Todd. 1995. *The Twilight of Common Dreams: Why America Is Wracked by Culture Wars*. New York: Metropolitan Books.

Jenkins, J. Craig. 1983. "Resource Mobilization Theory and the Study of Social Movements." *Annual Review of Sociology* 9: 527–53.

Jenkins, J. Craig, and Charles Perrow. 1977. "Insurgency of the Powerless: Farm Worker Movements (1946–1972)." *American Sociological Review* 42 (2): 249–68.

Marotta, Toby. 1981. *The Politics of Homosexuality*. Boston: Houghton Mifflin.

McAdam, Doug. 1982. *Political Process and the Development of Black Insurgency, 1930–1970*. Chicago: University of Chicago Press.

Melucci, Alberto. 1989. *Nomads of the Present*. London: Hutchinson Radius.

Morris, Aldon D. 1984. *The Origins of the Civil Rights Movement: Black Communities Organizing for Change*. New York: Free Press.

——. 1992. "Political Consciousness and Collective Action." Pp. 351–73 in *Frontiers in Social Movement Theory*, edited by Aldon D. Morris and Carol McClurg Mueller. New Haven, Conn.: Yale University Press.

Polletta, Francesca. 1994. "Strategy and Identity in 1960s Black Protest." *Research in Social Movements, Conflicts and Change* 17: 85–114.

Scheer, Robert. 1970. "Editor's note to 'The Biography of Huey P. Newton' by Bobby Seale in *Ramparts*." Pp. 202–6 in *The Movement toward a New America: The Beginnings of a Long Revolution*, edited by Mitchell Goodman. New York: United Church Press and Alfred A. Knopf.

Seidman, Steven. 1993. "Identity and Politics in a 'Postmodern' Gay Culture: Some Historical and Conceptual Notes." Pp. 105–42 in *Fear of a Queer Planet: Queer Politics and Social Theory*, edited by Michael Warner. Minneapolis: University of Minnesota Press.

Tarrow, Sidney. 1989. *Struggle, Politics, and Reform: Collective Action, Social Movements and Cycles of Protest*. Ithaca, N.Y.: Cornell University Press.

——. 1994. *Power in Movement: Social Movements, Collective Action and Politics*. New York: Cambridge University Press.

Taylor, Verta, and Nicole C. Raeburn. 1995. "Identity Politics as High-Risk Activism: Career Consequences for Lesbian, Gay, and Bisexual Sociologists." *Social Problems* 42 (2): 252–73.

Taylor, Verta, and Nancy E. Whittier. 1992. "Collective Identity in Social Movement Communities; Lesbian Feminist Mobilization." Pp. 104–29 in *Frontiers in Social Movement Theory*, edited by Aldon D. Morris and Carol McClurg Mueller. New Haven, Conn.: Yale University Press.

Tilly, Charles. 1978. *From Mobilization to Revolution*. Reading, Mass.: Addison Wesley.

Touraine, Alain. 1981. *The Voice and the Eye: An Analysis of Social Movements*. Cambridge: Cambridge University Press.

Turner, Ralph, and L. Killian. 1972. *Collective Behavior*. Englewood Cliffs, N.J.: Prentice-Hall.

Whittier, Nancy. 1995. *Feminist Generations: The Persistence of the Radical Women's Movement*. Philadelphia: Temple University Press.

Williams, Rhys H. 1995. "Constructing the Public Good: Social Movements and Cultural Resources." *Social Problems* 42 (1): 124–44.

23 Discursive Activism by Catholic Feminists

Mary Fainsod Katzenstein

The Institutionalization of Feminism

The abundance of conferences and workshops reflected the existence, by the 1980s, of institutionalized feminist spaces within the church. Feminism in the church operated from five kinds of feminist habitats. Religious congregations themselves constituted one such habitat. From the late 1960s and to this day, many religious orders held discussions in their regular assembly meetings about gender and race issues. These discussions were general self-explorations as well as specific debates about matters of particular relevance to individual religious orders. Should the congregation support the ERA? What does racism mean in the everyday lives of sisters? How to think about the meaning of inclusive liturgy? Should a particular resolution on sanctuaries be adopted? In the case of particular orders (say, the Sisters of Mercy) there might be discussions, for instance, over the responsibilities of Sisters of Mercy-run hospitals for women's gynecological and reproductive health care. Smaller networks were also formed within a congregation. When particular subgroups within an order wished to address themselves to an issue not necessarily involving the whole congregation, measures were taken to constitute community-connected associations. Loretto Women's Network, formed by a group within the Loretto Sisters, and the network's newspaper, *couRAGE*, represent one example.

Church renewal and social justice organizations provided a second habitat for the development of a feminist voice within the church. Renewal organizations surfaced with the momentum driven by Vatican II and the women's movement. Women religious were the founders and core activists of many of these groups. One of the first organizations to be established was the National Assembly of Women Religious (NAWR), later to change its name to the National Assembly of Religious Women (NARW) to reflect the participation of laywomen. Founded in 1968, NARW endeavored to give voice to a more grassroots expression of views by women religious than was at that time possible in the Leadership Conference of Women Religious, and remained until its demise in 1995 one of the groups most actively involved in tackling class and race issues within the movement of Catholic feminism. The National Coalition of American Nuns (NCAN) was formed in 1969 with the intent of speaking out on a range of social justice and human rights issues. In 1971, the Conference of Major Superiors of Women changed its name to the Leadership Conference of Women Religious (LCWR), clearly signifying an effort to reconceptualize their view of authority within the church. Approval for the change in name was withheld by the Vatican for three years. In 1971 as well, Las Hermanas, an organization of Hispanic sisters and laywomen engaged in the struggle against poverty and discrimination, was also founded. The Women's Ordination Conference (WOC) was founded in 1974, the same year that Chicago Catholic Women (CCW) was established. In 1974, Catholics for a Free Choice (CFFC), directed by Frances Kissling, was founded to support the right to legal reproductive health care, including family planning and abortion; it was later declared by the Vatican not to be an official voice of the Catholic Church. Other multiple-issue groups also date from this period (the Quixote Center, the Eighth Day Center for Justice, Call to Action), all of which worked toward the advancement of gender equality as part of their broad agendas. In 1977, Sister Jeannine Gramick and Father Robert Nugent founded the New Ways ministry to work toward reconciliation of church teachings and gay/lesbian issues. In 1982, Mary Hunt and Diann Neu founded the Women's Alliance for Theology, Ethics, and Religion, which organizes workshops and resources for an ecumenical constituency. In 1987, Mary's Pence was established to raise and distribute money for women's causes. (Peter's Pence collections raise money for the papacy.) The feast of Teresa of Avila, 15 October, has been selected as Mary's Pence Day, but because many of the fund's donors are not churchgoers, much of the fund-raising occurs through other avenues. In 1995, the fund distributed sixty thousand dollars – a surprisingly high sum given that Mary's Pence has not been approved for entry in the *Kennedy Book*, which lists sanctioned Catholic charities.

These organizations gained a visibility that was striking in light of their tiny staffs and limited budgets. Skilled in the arts of communications and media, all the renewal organizations, no matter how small, produced quantities of literature – newsletters, resources for workshops, liturgies, and press releases. The spokeswomen/men for the organizations were also spending large amounts of time on the road, interacting with others in projects, conferences, and educational endeavors. From this brief inventory, two facts stand out: that the 1970s and 1980s propelled feminist thought into the contemporary affairs of the American Catholic Church, and that women religious were absolutely at the core of this development.

A third habitat for feminism within the church has been academic institutions housing feminist scholars. By the 1980s, feminist theologians, historians, and sociologists had secured, in fairly significant numbers, tenured places in American universities. These

positions have provided not-always-safe spaces from which feminist scholars have been able to produce hundreds of volumes about church teachings and church history. Feminist theologians have developed an array of new ideas about what church, spirituality, and ritual might look like in the context of a Catholic faith dedicated to equality and justice within its own institutional practices. This was not a smooth road. The obstacles were evident from the beginning, with the tenure battle over Mary Daly's promotion at Boston College, a Jesuit institution, and with the controversy over the promotion of Charles Curran at Catholic University in the late 1960s. By the 1980s, feminist theologians were being appointed in significant numbers to posts that were, unsurprisingly, as much in non-Catholic institutions as in Catholic colleges and universities, but it is not unexpected that some of the most vociferous and critical voices in feminist theology from the 1970s and 1980s came out of institutions where Rome's approval was not required.

It was of no small importance to feminism's institutionalization that feminist theological writings found outlets in prominent commercial presses (Harper and Row, Simon & Schuster, Beacon) in addition to the presses that produce largely religious publications. It is also telling that by the late 1980s, women were one-quarter of all students enrolled in American Roman Catholic theological schools.

A fourth habitat where feminist voices have found an albeit limited protected space within the church has been in the parishes themselves. The women who have become pastors in so-called priestless parishes bring feminist perspectives to much of their work almost by virtue, alone, of being on the frontier. Ruth Wallace estimates that there were about three hundred priestless parishes in the early 1990s (2 percent of all Catholic parishes in the United States) approximately three-quarters of which are "pastored" by women. The number of women who have assumed lay ministry positions (as pastoral associates, liturgists, in positions responsible for the elderly or the sick, among other roles) has certainly also increased. I know of no study that systematically explores the dissemination of feminism among lay ministers. But it seems to be the case that in numerous parishes male priests are under pressure from at least some parishioners to use more inclusive language, to allow female altar servers, to utilize women in liturgical ministries (as lectors, choir directors).

A fifth habitat that feminism came to occupy in the 1970s and 1980s was the liturgy groups and base communities that sprang up in numerous locations. Those who have become frustrated with the institutional church, with the Mass, or with a particular priest or parish have often gravitated to such communities. Groups meet in community centers, in parish basements, or in someone's living room. Many are feminist although most liturgy groups identify themselves in broad terms as endeavoring to constitute themselves as egalitarian communities. One member of a group that calls itself St. Harold ("because we meet in the Harold Washington apartments...we canonized Harold Washington") is constituted by members of a Chicago parish that began to meet separately after experiencing frustration with the constraints a newly assigned priest had begun to impose. The group includes a sympathetic priest but, as one member of the community explained, "We basically got to the point in our liturgies where we all preside together." One night at a party, this member explained, the priest turned to her and said, "'Lee Ann [not her real name], do you have mass tomorrow or do I?' I thought I was on another planet."

Discursive Acts

To say that contemporary Catholic feminism can be described through a narrative of conferences and workshops, an account of *ideas* rather than *policies*, is not to say that women (both lay and religious) in the church do not "act" in the "real world" to effect social change. Many nuns as well as many committed Catholic laywomen are engaged in direct social justice activism (in prisons, shelters, hospices, and sanctuaries), working to redress problems of poverty and racism as they affect both women and men. Others have sought positions in the church (as educators, pastoral assistants, chaplains, and in a range of different ministries) from which they hope to work toward a more just as well as faith-driven society. But much of the work women activists do when they come together is discursive: rewriting through texts and symbolic acts their own understanding of themselves in relationship to both church and society.

It may be helpful in specifying the character of feminist discursive politics if I say a little more about what it is not: For the most part feminist groups in the church do not lobby either the state or the church. Network, a sister-run organization with offices in Washington, is an exception. It explicitly monitors legislation on a range of social justice and peace issues, conducts letter-writing campaigns, and undertakes the requisite visits to congressional offices. Within the context of church politics, for a brief period in the 1980s, women's groups strategized in "interest-group" fashion, discussing who the sympathetic bishops might be, and how it might be best to frame an issue so as to be "heard" by the clerical hierarchy, but few feminist activists devote much time now to this form of strategizing. The LCWR probably does somewhat more of this kind of strategic thinking than other organizations. Because the LCWR sees itself as representing religious communities to Rome and thus makes an attempt if not to "lobby" at least not to alienate the papacy, they too spend time discussing acceptable approaches to voicing concerns with the Vatican. But in their efforts to engage with elite decision-makers in the government or in the church, both Network and the LCWR are more the exception than the rule among feminist activists.

What is more noticeable is how infrequent "protest acts" are used among the repertoire of feminist challenges to the church. Nuns have readily participated in civil disobedience (to protest nuclear missiles) or demonstrations to bring attention to the needs of migrant farmers or the poor, but comparable actions are rarely directed against the church. There have been some dramatic 1960s-style moments: The spontaneous action of women at Marjorie Tuite's funeral in 1986 was one such instance. As Ruth McDonough Fitzpatrick recounted it, the priest reminded those in the church that only Catholics were to come forward for Communion.

> At the consecration, the priest on the altar was surrounded with women. He was trying to elbow them back to give him his sacred space. But all of us extended our hands and said the words of consecration so loudly that you could hear it in this huge New York church. Now we've said consecration at many of our liturgies, in living rooms and smaller places. That's the first time in my life I've ever heard a consecration said from a parish church. Finally, we could really hear it. Before communion, Maureen Fiedler got out of the pew and went up and down the first seven rows saying, "Everybody, please come to communion; everybody is very welcome."

There have been other dramatic occasions as well: Drawing for inspiration on the blue-armbanded nuns who stood in protest during the pope's 1979 visit to the National Shrine of the Immaculate Conception in Washington, D.C., some Chicago nun-activists decided to take their protests inside the church. For a period in 1980–81, Chicago women chose to disrupt ordinations – "Franciscans, Benedictines, Jesuits, Dominicans and parlor-variety diocesan priests." Barbara Ferraro describes the occasions:

> The taking of Holy Orders is a sacrament in the Catholic Church. The ceremony itself is inserted into the ritual of the Mass. The men waiting to be ordained lie facedown on the floor before the altar rail, and the bishop comes down from the altar and calls them forward.

> "Joseph McGhee, come forth, you are called to be ordained," says the bishop. And the ordinate rises and replies, "I am ready and willing."
>
> The first time we had tried our new protest, no one suspected anything. I guess they thought we had settled for symbols when they saw our arm bands. So they were surprised when, after the last man was called to be ordained, we began popping up, one after the other, all over the church, and calling out, "I am ready and willing."

Women have also engaged in foot washing on Holy Thursday; in Ash Wednesday protests outside the church – in one case with ashes from a burned copy of the Vatican statement banning ordination; in the regular Chicago Mother's Day demonstrations outside the Holy Name Cathedral ("for a Eucharistic Celebration") protesting the ban on ordination. Recently, too, a small group of nuns, organized by NCAN, carried banners (one reading "They are meeting about us – without us") across the piazza outside St. Peter's during the Synod on the Consecrated Life in October 1994. The reporter for the *International Herald Tribune* commented that "the police who patrol St. Peter's Square could scarcely believe their eyes . . . [as] American nuns marched into the cavernous piazza. . . ." But on the whole, feminists in the church have mostly eschewed the kind of demonstrative "disobedience" engaged in by ACT UP on several occasions in the early 1990s both inside and on the steps of St. Patrick's Cathedral in New York City.

At the same time, few activists explicitly engage in parish politics. Of the many activist nuns and laywomen with whom I met, only a small handful regularly attend Sunday Mass. It is not unusual to hear activists speak of church services as "abusive" or "assaulting." As one sister asked me, rhetorically, "Why should I go to Sunday service every week and then have to spend all the time in between recovering from abuse?" The vehemence with which she appeared to feel punished by what she saw as the misogyny of regular church services was more typical than atypical of those with whom I talked. Recognizing that an activist can engage in parish politics only as a committed parish member, most activist sisters consider the route of direct parish mobilization to be foreclosed. Indeed, few groups aim at directly mobilizing women in the "pews." Parish politics, rather, is left to those feminists who are willing to take on ministry within the church (on necessarily conditional terms) and to those who seek change by engaging in liturgical rethinking and in the production of church language that is inclusive rather than male-centered. As Elizabeth Johnson, SSJ, explained, in discussing her motivation for writing her recent book, *She Who Is* (insisting that God is both male and female), "Language doesn't just reflect what we think, it shapes what we think and defines our world."

Sharing Johnson's premise, activists have spent much of their time in reflection and deliberation, fashioning new words and meanings to describe their changing understanding of women in society and church. But it would be a mistake to see these words as "simply" the literary or scholarly exercises of armchair radicals. Judging by the attempts of the church hierarchy to silence those who speak out (as described at length in the next chapter), words are believed by both feminists and the church clerical leadership to have very real consequences.

[...]

Part VIII

How Do the State and Mass Media Influence Movements?

Introduction

Any social movement group must deal with a range of other groups, individuals, and bureaucracies. Among them, the state is usually the most important. Many movements make demands directly of the state, primarily through demands for changes in policies or laws. Sometimes it is state actions that are the focus of the grievance. If nothing else, the state lays down the rules of the game within which protestors maneuver, and if they choose to break those rules they are likely to encounter punitive action from the police or armed forces. Another major institution with which social movements usually come into contact are the news media, which can be used to purvey a movement's message, portray opponents in an unfavorable light, and influence state decisions. In this section we examine these major players in a social movement's environment.

In the political process school, the state is the major influence on social movements, even to the extent of very often causing movements to arise in the first place. In part II we saw that, according to this theory, it is changes in the state ("political opportunities" like the lessening of repression, divisions among elites, etc.) which often allow movements to form.

There are different ways of understanding the term "opportunity." One is in a more structural fashion, in which large changes occur without much intervention by movements themselves. Sociologists Craig Jenkins and Charles Perrow represent this point of view in the excerpts below, from a 1977 article that helped define the process approach. For one thing, they argue that the same factors explain both the rise of farmworker insurgency and its outcomes. Those factors center squarely on political and economic elites. When they are divided, such that some of them provide resources and political support to a social movement, then that movement has a much better chance of both establishing itself and attaining its goals (we'll see in part X that these are both seen as forms of success in the process model). In another argument typical of the process approach, Jenkins and Perrow dismiss the explanatory importance of discontent, which they say "is ever-present for deprived groups." Jenkins and Perrow also exemplify the process school's focus on those social movements composed of people with little or no political and economic power, groups who normally face severe repression when they try to organize and make demands on the system.

Another way to understand opportunities is shorter term. During any conflict, there will be moments when quick action can have a big effect. The media suddenly notice your cause, perhaps because of a crisis or accident, or maybe because of an event you have organized. You must move quickly to use them to get your message across. Or there may be a crisis in government that gives your social movement room to maneuver and make the government concede to your demands just to keep the peace. Social movements are constantly looking for these openings in the state, as well as for sympathetic politicians. But many of these windows of opportunity can hurt as well as help, reshaping, curtailing, or channeling movement demands in the very process of recognizing them. "Opportunities" are also "constraints."

David Meyer, political scientist and former antinuclear activist, describes a perverse form of recognition by politicians in his discussion of the nuclear freeze movement of the early 1980s that was inspired by Reagan's rapid military buildup. This was perhaps the largest mobilization in the United States since the 1960s, with one million people attending a 1982 New York rally (possibly the largest group of protestors ever assembled in one place in the United States). Congressional Democrats were attracted to antinuclear positions as a way of attacking

> **Celebrities**   Most social movements try to publicize their cause by attracting media coverage. They seek to stage protest events that will be considered newsworthy, perhaps because they are flamboyant or represent a new twist on old tactics. But certain people are also newsworthy, attracting attention simply because they are celebrities. When they call a news conference, reporters come. Social movement groups often try to get well-known actors, musicians, singers, and athletes to support their causes, knowing they will get more publicity this way. This strategy can backfire, however, when a celebrity has her own view of a social issue which may be at odds with that of the protest group.

Reagan, but their "smothering embrace" deeply transformed and watered down the movement's program. Politicians are a form of celebrity – when Senator Ted Kennedy calls a press conference reporters come – and so were able to use that power to promote but also redefine antinuclear proposals. The effects of the media and of the political system overlap here. Politicians affect social movements not only in their official structural roles but also via their influence on the news media.

A third way to envision opportunities (or a third kind of opportunity) is as relatively permanent features of a country's political landscape. Administrative structures, legal systems, electoral rules, and constitutions all constrain what social movements can achieve. We might call these "horizons" of opportunity, since they define what is possible within that system, in contrast to "windows" of opportunity that open and shut quickly.

As a long-time activist, Marshall Ganz has thought more deeply about strategic choices and innovation than most academics. We could have placed his paper in part VII (on movement tactics), but decided to put it here because it so strongly criticizes Jenkins and Perrow by exploiting a flaw in their argument. Their argument is based on changes in the political environment over time, but Ganz points out that at any given time there was more than one group trying to organize California's farmworkers. These groups faced the same environment, yet only Cesar Chavez's UFW succeeded. What is it about his group, Ganz asks, that was different? Ganz is in a unique position to answer this question, as he worked for the UFW for many years before becoming a sociologist. Ganz especially examines the two factors that Jenkins and Perrow rejected as unimportant: the movement organization and its underlying social base.

We turn now to the effects of the media on social movements. Modern social movements can hardly be imagined without the media to amplify their messages. The cheap newspapers that appeared in the nineteenth century, for instance, helped larger, more national movements form for the first time in the industrialized countries. Today, hardly any movement can afford to ignore the media, which can reach much larger numbers than can the movement itself through personal networks or its own publications. These anonymous audiences can be especially important in contributing funds and in affecting state policies.

Movement activists devote considerable time to figuring out events that will attract news coverage, in other words, events which editors and reporters will consider "newsworthy" (Gans, 1979). Especially flamboyant marches and rallies, new twists on old themes, and clever incantations can all help events to get on the evening news. Abbie Hoffman was a genius at attracting this kind of attention, with events such as the "levitation" of the Pentagon. But social movements challenging the status quo often face media that are not entirely sympathetic, and which sometimes are hostile to the movement's message. What is more, movement's opponents often have better access to the news media. Movements have little control over how they are ultimately portrayed.

Perhaps the best analysis of the complex interaction between a movement and the media is Todd Gitlin's book about the New Left of the 1960s, *The Whole World Is Watching*, parts of which appear below. He first shows some of the ways that the media "framed" the protest at its height (in other words when it was most threatening to mainstream institutions) by concentrating on its more extreme ideas and actions and at the same time trivializing the threat it posed. At the same time, this loosely organized movement began thinking about itself in the terms laid out by the media! As the next part of Gitlin's excerpt shows, one hazard of media coverage is the creation of media stars from among movement leaders. These are not always the actual organizational or intellectual leaders, but usually people who are flamboyant and photogenic, in other words, with a talent for attracting media attention. This creation of spokespersons whose power comes from their ability to attract media coverage further distorts a movement's message. Many potential leaders simply abdicate this role in the face of media dynamics.

> **Moral Panics** Students of deviance, social problems, and politics have used the concept of a moral panic to describe sudden concern over a group or activity, accompanied by calls for control and suppression. Out of an infinite range of potential perceived threats, one – which may be neither new nor on the rise – suddenly receives considerable attention. Marijuana use, motorbikes, and rock and roll music are common examples. The news media, public officials, religious leaders, and private "moral entrepreneurs" are key in focusing public attention on the issue, typically by identifying some recognizable group as "folk devils" – usually young people, racial and ethnic minorities, or other relatively powerless groups – responsible for the menace. New political or legal policies are sometimes the result, as are new symbols and sensibilities (available as the raw materials for future panics). Some moral panics inspire grassroots protest groups, but others are manipulated by interested elites to undo the work of social movements. For instance, a series of moral panics over the "black underclass" in American cities – having to do with crime, teenage pregnancy, drugs, and so on – were used to scale back affirmative action programs in the 1980s.

It is clear from Gitlin's account that one effect of the media can be to give undue prominence to radical or illegal wings of movements, or to segments that are further outside mainstream culture: the "kooks" in a movement. Governments, too, often radicalize a movement by indiscriminately repressing moderates and radicals (in which case there is little incentive to be a moderate), or simply by repressing a movement too heavy-handedly. In the end, these interactions with media and the state deeply affect a movement's ability to change its society.

Discussion Questions

1   What kinds of "opportunities" affect the efficacy of social movements?
2   What are the benefits and risks of having allies among prominent politicians or other celebrities?
3   To what extent was the farmworkers' movement successful because of a shifting political environment? To what extent was its success a product of specific strategies (which not all farmworkers' groups employed)?
4   As a protestor, how would you go about getting media attention for your cause? What are some of the risks of that attention?
5   What factors shape how the media will portray a social movement and its ideas?

24 The "Smothering" Allies of the Nuclear Freeze Movement

David S. Meyer

Opponents played a critical role in defining the nuclear freeze, but allies were even more significant in shaping the scope of the movement's demands. As the freeze demonstrated popular appeal and the ability to mobilize support, organizations and individuals with a wide variety of purposes seized upon it, attempting to make some use of the support that had grown up around the freeze. Congressional supporters appropriated the movement's language and symbolism, turning the freeze proposal into something much more moderate and less threatening to the bipartisan tradition of arms control. By convincing freeze supporters that these modifications were in their best interest, purported allies convinced the movement to cooperate in its own demobilization. Apparent access to conventional channels of political participation cut into the legitimacy and intensity of extra-institutional protest. The redefined freeze was further diluted, as critics and supporters alike found ways to express both their shared concern and their unequivocal opposition to nuclear war.

Antinuclear Concerns

Perhaps the most striking example of this was President Reagan's decision to adopt General Daniel Graham's High Frontier project as his own. On March 23, 1983, Reagan gave a nationally televised address proposing a Strategic Defense Initiative (SDI), soon popularly known as Star Wars. In it, after criticizing the freeze as a reward to the Soviet Union, he questioned the morality of nuclear deterrence, arguing that defense would be better. Said Reagan, "Wouldn't it be better to save lives than to avenge them?" SDI "could pave the way for arms control measures to eliminate the weapons themselves. ...Our only purpose – one which all people share – is to search for ways to reduce the dangers of nuclear war." The televised address came just before the nuclear freeze resolution was scheduled for floor debate in the House of Representatives for the second time. At first Congressional freeze advocates viewed the Reagan initiative as an opportunity, for it enabled them to stop defending their hazy version of the freeze against its critics and take the offensive in a counterattack against the president and his military policies. Representatives Tom Downey and Ed Markey took to the House floor and railed against Reagan's attempt to find a deus ex machina ending not for the arms race but for the nuclear freeze.

Although the House later passed a nuclear freeze resolution, the Reagan speech demonstrated the movement's weaknesses in defining its own terms and goals. Star Wars enabled the president and all sorts of freeze opponents to sound like antinuclear activists, and this marked the beginning of the end for the movement. Star Wars became a cornerstone of the Republican campaign during the 1984 election, effectively preventing Democrats from claiming the peace issue. Randy Kehler remarked on this after watching a videotape about SDI shown at the Republican National Convention in 1984. "It was just like ours," he said. "It said how deterrence is folly and immoral, and economically the arms race is killing us, and there's no defense against nuclear weapons anyway." Certainly most freeze advocates were not convinced by the Reagan approach, and indeed opposition to Star Wars became a new and significant element in the disarmament movement. But by changing his rhetoric and looking toward the end of the nuclear arms race, the president was able to put his critics on the defensive and regain command of the language of debate and, in the process, dilute the perceived urgency of the antinuclear movement.

SDI was hardly the most subtle or even the most effective way in which politicians and arms controllers tried to coopt the freeze movement, putting to their own uses its high public profile and vast grassroots support. Indeed, opponents of the movement were far less effective and dangerous in this regard than apparent allies, who redefined the freeze to allow strategic nuclear modernization, for example, or to be nothing more than a plea for traditional arms control. The movement must bear some of the responsibility for failing to maintain control of its identity and goals, but this failure must be understood in the context of the assault it endured from friends and foes alike.

Given the context of Reagan's military and arms control policies, many arms control professionals initially welcomed the movement, the pressure it put on the administration, and the attention it brought to arms control. The movement and the resolution were seen as a way to force the Reagan administration to maintain an arms control regime. Representative Les Aspin (D-WI), who eventually and reluctantly came to support the freeze, frequently commented, "If we had a President who was genuinely interested in arms control...we would need no [freeze] resolution at all." He hoped that the resolution would keep the prospects for arms control alive during Reagan's term.

Similarly, Albert Carnesale, a SALT I negotiator and Harvard University dean, reported that arms control advocates initially viewed the freeze movement as a "godsend," believing it would bring attention to arms control and build support for subsequent agreements. At the same time, he cautioned, there was a concern that the movement, by seeking unrealistic goals and overselling the potential of a freeze, might pass without influence. Freeze activists were not always responsive to the attempts by arms control experts to remake the freeze into something experts thought would be more useful and achievable.

In addition to those who hoped to use the freeze to make political points for their causes, there was a larger number apparently interested in using the movement to make personal political gains. In his history of the freeze, Representative Markey's former legislative aide Doug Waller is candid about this:

> Peter Franchot, Markey's administrative assistant, was the first in the office to run across a copy of Randall Forsberg's *Call to Halt the Nuclear Arms Race*...Franchot immediately took to the freeze. He had done enough public interest work to become a fair judge of grass-roots campaigns and how they could catch fire – and of how a politician could ride the crest of a movement's wave, if he or she were willing to take a few chances. "The freeze is going to sweep this country," he told us time and again...."And there's no reason why we shouldn't be in the middle of it."

According to Waller, the freeze was exactly the vehicle Markey needed to broaden his base of support and increase his visibility. Waller supported Markey's interest in the proposal but insisted that the Congressman present the freeze as a nonbinding resolution expressing the sense of Congress, not as a bill with potential policy impact. "We should make it clear," he said, "that we are introducing a symbolic measure." This first of many qualifications incorporated, Markey sent a "Dear Colleague" letter around Congress on February 5, 1982, asking for support; within five days 28 Democrats responded with offers to cosponsor a nuclear freeze resolution.

The movement's leadership, however, was wary about jumping into the Congressional fray, and Markey was not its only alternative. By the end of 1981 a number of more prominent legislators, including Senators Claiborne Pell (D-RI), Mark Hatfield (R-OR), and Patrick Leahy (D-VT), and Markey's Massachusetts colleagues in the House, Representatives Silvio Conte (R), Nicholas Mavroules (D), and Gerry Studds (D), had signed on to the freeze. Several had already offered to introduce the resolution, but the campaign wanted to make sure that it had first built sufficient public support, referring to the original strategy paper that called for a wait of 2–5 years. A strategy paper written in February of 1982, just days after Markey's "Dear Colleague" letter, expressed this reluctance clearly: "Let us be careful about moving too rapidly into these other phases before we have a sufficiently large and broad base of support. While the issue is filled with urgency, we can do more harm than good by a premature attempt to win at the national level."

While movement leaders attempted to negotiate with Congressional supporters to develop a legislative strategy, Senator Edward Kennedy, whose unannounced (and ultimately unrealized) 1984 presidential campaign had been building for more than a year, seized upon the freeze. Kennedy's staff saw the freeze as an opportunity for the senator. Said one aide, "We could all see that the movement was on the verge of a breakthrough.... The Senator just wanted to get on top of it, harness all that energy, and bring it to Washington instead of just letting it go on." Although freeze leaders wanted to wait, Kennedy did not. He promised to introduce a freeze with or without the movement's support. The campaign worked with him because it did not really seem to have a choice. The freeze decided to work with Kennedy and other Congressional supporters rather than choosing the impossible task of trying to restrain them.

The Freeze in Congress

On March 10, 1982, with the support of the national freeze leadership, Kennedy and Representative Jonathan Bingham (D-NY) held a press conference at American University to announce their introduction of the nuclear freeze resolution into Congress. Kennedy introduced the freeze in the Senate with Mark Hatfield and 18 cosponsors; Bingham, Markey, and Conte presented the resolution in the House, with 115 cosponsors, including Speaker Tip O'Neill. Suddenly the movement was given massive national attention and a dramatic infusion of professional political support, much of it generated by Kennedy's office, including endorsements from well-respected establishment figures Frank Church, William Colby, Averell Harriman, Henry Cabot Lodge, Gerard Smith, and Paul Warnke.

The profile of the movement and the content of the resolution had changed. Kennedy deliberately wrote his freeze proposal in vague language to attract moderate support, perhaps considering the right wing of the Democratic Party. The nonbinding resolution called upon the president to "decide when and how to achieve a mutual verifiable freeze on the testing, production, and further deployment of nuclear warheads, missiles, and other delivery systems." Freeze leaders and early supporters were dubious about the new language. Said Randall Forsberg, "The resolution was watered down, it has so many minutes of caveats ... it represented virtually nothing." George Rathjens, Forsberg's thesis adviser at MIT and an early freeze supporter, reported that after reading the Kennedy-Hatfield resolution he almost "fell off the wagon." The number of qualifiers, including the "when and how" clause, made the resolution "a prescription for going nowhere," he said. The Reagan administration could have easily coopted the movement at that point by endorsing the freeze and beginning negotiations, simultaneously rejustifying its nuclear modernization programs as necessary "bargaining chips," Rathjens observed, "but they weren't smart enough to do that."

Kehler agreed but was characteristically more optimistic. Commenting on the wording of the Congressional freeze, he said,

> Here I think we have a problem and I hope it's not a problem that we can't correct soon. In fact, the original wording of the freeze proposal said "immediate freeze." For some reason that I don't understand myself, the word immediate was taken out at our founding convention. Then, to make matters worse...[Congressional sponsors] deliberately made it vague in order to win additional support.

Not only the vision of realpolitik, but also the goals of Congressional leaders, differed dramatically from those of the freeze initiators.

While Forsberg and the early freeze supporters saw the freeze as a first step toward ending the nuclear arms race, and as a radical departure from previous arms control efforts, Congressional activists viewed it as a vehicle to pressure the Reagan administration to return to the established arms control processes it had eschewed and to improve their own electoral prospects. Democratic presidential aspirant Walter Mondale endorsed this view on the eve of the resolution's introduction in Congress. Responding to a question about the freeze, he explained, "I think it is a very useful initiative as an expression of concern. This administration has broken with the bipartisan tradition that's existed since the bomb first went off by which our leaders have solemnly sought to restrain nuclear arms buildups."

While pushing the Reagan administration back to an arms control posture compatible with previous U.S. policy, Congressional supporters also reaped less policy-oriented benefits from their embrace of the freeze. Kennedy particularly was seen by many as a leader of the freeze movement, and he worked to encourage this perception. During 1982 he sponsored his own nuclear freeze rallies, at which he was the featured speaker. He also coauthored a book with Hatfield about the freeze. (It was actually drafted by aides Robert Shrum and Corey Parker.) Drafted in about a week, the book was initially published in a paperback run of 200,000 copies. Proceeds were to go to the Freeze Foundation, a conduit the senators had established ostensibly to gain Congressional backing for the freeze resolution. Markey also established his own antinuclear PAC, the U.S. Committee Against Nuclear War, which raised more than $1 million between 1982 and 1984. Other political action committees raised substantial sums of money by putting the freeze resolution on their agendas and in their appeals. Support for the freeze made good financial sense, and Democratic politicians were eager to politicize the freeze in a way that was profitable for them.

For Congressional advocates, however, endorsing the freeze entailed redefining the movement and the resolution into something they found easier to support; specifically, the freeze was an expression of discontent with the Reagan program, not an alternative. Unsurprisingly, movement leaders were not enthusiastic about this definition. Wanting to press their views more forcefully, freeze leaders proposed a coordinated campaign against appropriations bills for new nuclear weapons systems at their June 1982 national convention in Atlanta. Congressional allies, represented by aides from Markey's and Kennedy's offices, were able to dissuade the national campaign from adopting this strategy, arguing that it would harm chances for passing their freeze resolution. In a memo to Waller, Markey's aide Howard Homoroff acknowledged that "it seemed strange for our office to be a moderating influence on anything" and expressed concern about problems in the future should the campaign not be willing to adapt to Capitol Hill realities.

Congressional freeze supporters were themselves confronted by opponents who attempted to coopt their language to weaken the resolution and the movement. Within three weeks of the Kennedy-Hatfield freeze resolution's introduction, conservatives proposed a freeze of their own – to be negotiated *after* both sides had engaged in very substantial reductions like those President Reagan had proposed in his attempts to avoid arms control. The president strongly supported this version, introduced into the Senate by a bipartisan slate of conservatives, including Democrats Henry Jackson (WA), Robert Byrd (WV), Sam Nunn (GA), and Lloyd Bentsen (TX), and Republicans John Warner (VA), Howard Baker (TN), Richard Lugar (IN), and William Cohen (ME). The so-called Jackson-Warner freeze, or "phony freeze" to critics, was antithetical to the goals of the movement and even to the Kennedy-Hatfield version. By appropriating the language of the freeze and putting it in the service of the administration's plans, freeze opponents tried to confuse and diffuse the movement. In Washington it was widely assumed that the proposal had been written by top Reagan adviser Richard Perle, who had previously worked for Jackson. At least in the Senate, the strategy worked, winning 61 cosponsors, some supporting the proposal because, according to Elizabeth Drew, "they wanted to sign everything in sight that had the word 'freeze' in it and because they wanted, as they say in Washington, to 'buy political protection'."

This strategy, introducing substitutes for movement-backed legislation with freeze-style language, would be repeated throughout the nuclear freeze resolution's legislative life. Congressional politicians who opposed the freeze wanted alternatives to support instead. Gary Hart's STOP, William Cohen's build-down, "no first use" proposals, percentage reductions, test bans, and numerous other proposals appeared in Congress whenever the freeze was discussed, effectively muddying the issues; many legislators supported mutually contradictory pieces of legislation. In June of 1982 there were 32 pieces of legislation on arms control before Congress.

In 1982 at least, the basic debate in Congress was between the Kennedy-Hatfield and Jackson-Warner freezes. *Congressional Digest* described the nuclear freeze as the "current vehicle for debate over nuclear weapons policy," explaining the conflict as being between war avoidance and deterrence. "The controversy over the nuclear freeze proposal centers on whether to halt arms programs first and then reduce quantity, or reduce to an equitable level and then halt production." While both resolutions were filled with loopholes and loose language, in testimony before Congress Forsberg and Kehler argued that the Kennedy-Hatfield version was far preferable because, if implemented, it would end the modernization of nuclear forces; whereas it was unclear that Jackson-Warner would do anything. The Senate Foreign Relations Committee rejected the Kennedy-Hatfield freeze on July 12, 1982, by a vote of 12–5, supporting the Jackson-Warner resolution and Reagan's START proposals instead.

The real legislative fight was in the House. Jonathan Bingham effectively shepherded the resolution through the House Foreign Affairs Committee, which reported the resolution favorably on June 23, 1982, by a vote of 28–8. The freeze resolution reached the floor of the House on August 5, 1982, where Republican critics attacked the vague wording and ambiguity that supporters had deliberately built into it. Ultraconservative Henry Hyde (R-IL) asked movement supporters, for example, how they could call for a freeze first and concurrent negotiations to achieve that freeze. Representative William S. Broomfield (R-MI) offered an amendment based on the Jackson-Warner bill. The amendment was adopted by a vote of 204–202, before the resolution passed overwhelmingly. While the Broomfield amendment effectively killed the freeze in 1982, the extremely close vote made many freeze advocates optimistic and reinforced their faith in a Congressional strategy.

The entire legislative record on nuclear weapons and foreign policy issues provided much less evidence for optimism. The Coalition for a New Foreign and Military Policy tracked 11 key votes, noting defeats on nine.

The vote on the nuclear freeze resolution was close, but attempts to reduce the military budget and to delete funds for the B-1 bomber, Trident missiles, Pershing II missiles, civil defense planning for nuclear war, and airfield construction in Honduras all lost by large margins. For the most part, these bills were introduced by strong freeze supporters, including Markey, Tom Downey, Tom Harkin (D-IA), Nicholas Mavroules, and Ronald Dellums. Dellums also offered an amendment to the military budget to delete some $50 billion allocated for "first strike weapons," including many of the weapons listed above, as well as cruise missiles and nuclear-powered aircraft carriers. It was defeated 55–348, although certainly it more clearly expressed what Forsberg had in mind when she drafted the freeze. Ironically both victories, deleting funding for MX procurement and banning the production of binary nerve gas, were overturned by Congress the following year.

For activists, however, the year ended with several hopeful notes. Freeze referenda passed with large margins of support virtually everywhere they appeared on the ballot. The close vote on the Broomfield amendment led many activists and organizations to focus their efforts on the 1982 elections. Although the movement's direct impact on the elections is unclear, Democrats and freeze supporters gained 26 seats in the House of Representatives, virtually ensuring, or so it seemed, passage of the resolution in the House in 1983. As a result, many within the freeze coalition argued that the movement should look beyond passing the resolution to other objectives, particularly stopping the development and deployment of counterforce weapons and the Euromissiles. Pam Solo and Mike Jendrzejczyk wanted the movement to focus on the appropriations process, using its apparent strength, support in the House of Representatives, to prevent funding for particularly provocative programs. They argued that this could be done within the bilateral approach, making funding suspensions contingent upon reciprocal restraint by the Soviet Union. Funding for Pershing II and cruise missile deployment, for example, would be deleted as long as the Soviet Union suspended its own deployment of SS-20s. They also wanted to tighten the language in the freeze proposal, particularly to eliminate the "when and how" clause.

Doug Waller reports that he and Jan Kalicki, Kennedy's legislative aide, were shocked when activists discussed this more aggressive approach at their February 1983 national conference in San Francisco. They worked to convince freeze leaders that it would be hard enough to get the freeze adopted without the burden of new language. Jonathan Bingham's retirement had cost the movement a strong and respected legislative supporter, they contended, and House Foreign Affairs Committee Chairman Clement Zablocki (D-WI) had agreed to manage the resolution in committee only on the condition that the language be identical to the previous year's resolution. The Congressional aides were even more adamant that the freeze not be too closely connected with efforts to stop Euromissile deployment. There was no support in Congress for addressing this issue, Waller argued, "The missiles were a European problem to be settled by European governments, not the U.S. Congress." The national freeze agreed to support the older and more vaguely written resolution and endorsed compromise wording on the Pershing II and cruise missiles, criticizing both U.S. and Soviet intermediate-range missiles.

These compromises, although acceptable to Congressional freeze advocates, exacerbated already growing rifts within the national leadership of the movement. In a memo to Forsberg and Kehler, Jendrzejczyk and Solo discussed the importance of connecting the freeze movement to concrete achievements, raised questions about the willingness of staff members, particularly lobbyists, to adhere to the national committee's strategy, and questioned whether the freeze organization was becoming beholden to Kennedy and Markey. "Do we cater too much to what Jan Kalicki and Doug Waller think our priorities should be?" they asked. "Kalicki was a tough bargainer," Kehler later conceded, "and we didn't always realize when he said we can't budge, that it was a bargaining stance."

Along with Forsberg and Melinda Fine (NWFC's liaison with Western European disarmament groups), Solo and Jendrzejczyk pushed the freeze to take an unequivocal stand against Euromissile deployment. While the national committee adopted their proposal to endorse a one-year deployment delay, contingent upon Soviet cooperation, freeze lobbyists never emphasized the issue. The national freeze organization eventually endorsed antideployment demonstrations organized by AFSC, MfS, and other groups, but its influence was belated and barely visible.

Meanwhile, the freeze resolution's movement through the House in 1983 seemed to demonstrate activists' worst fears about the movement being coopted and trivialized.

[. . .]

25 Farmworkers' Movements in Changing Political Contexts

J. Craig Jenkins and Charles Perrow

Repression Armies and police are almost always better armed than social movements. If political leaders retain control over the military and police, accordingly, then they can suppress almost any social movement that they choose. Such repression will be constrained primarily by public opinion or by disagreements among elites. While repression generally works to dampen protest, however, it sometimes "backfires," provoking greater levels of protest, including armed resistance, by people who are angry and outraged by the repression, in addition to whatever grievances prompted them to protest in the first place. Even armed revolutionaries, however, rarely succeed against a unified state. But the likelihood that (or at least the speed with which) a state will move to suppress a social movement varies enormously. Movements aimed at seizing state power receive the fastest attention. Those that are disruptive or which challenge economic elites can also expect a powerful repressive response. But many moderate movements, asking for reforms within the existing political and economic order, may escape repression. In fact, this is usually a prerequisite for their survival, given the enormous imbalance in power between the state and most social movements.

From about 1964 until 1972, American society witnessed an unprecedented number of groups acting in insurgent fashion. By insurgency we mean organized attempts to bring about structural change by thrusting new interests into decision-making processes. Some of this insurgency, notably the civil rights and peace movements, had begun somewhat earlier, but after 1963 there were organized attempts to bring about structural changes from virtually all sides: ethnic minorities (Indians, Mexican-Americans, Puerto Ricans), welfare mothers, women, sexual liberation groups, teachers and even some blue-collar workers. The present study isolates and analyzes in detail one of these insurgent challenges – that of farmworkers – in an effort to throw light on the dynamics that made the 1960s a period of dramatic and stormy politics.

Our thesis is that the rise and dramatic success of farmworker insurgents in the late 1960s best can be explained by changes in the political environment the movement confronted, rather than by the internal characteristics of the movement organization and the social base upon which it drew. The salient environment consisted of the government, especially the federal government, and a coalition of liberal support organizations. We shall contrast the unsuccessful attempt to organize farmworkers by the National Farm Labor Union from 1946 to 1952 with the strikingly successful one of the United Farmworkers from 1965 to 1972.

The immediate goals of both movements were the same – to secure union contracts. They both used the same tactics, namely, mass agricultural strikes, boycotts aided by organized labor, and political demands supported by the liberal community of the day. Both groups encountered identical and virtually insurmountable obstacles, namely, a weak bargaining position, farmworker poverty and a culture of resignation, high rates of migrancy and weak social cohesion, and a perpetual oversupply of farm labor, insuring that growers could break any strike.

The difference between the two challenges was the societal response that insurgent demands received. During the first challenge, government policies strongly favored agribusiness; support from liberal organizations and organized labor was weak and vacillating. By the time the second challenge was mounted, the political environment had changed dramatically. Government now was divided over policies pertaining to farmworkers; liberals and organized labor had formed a reform coalition, attacking agribusiness privileges in public policy. The reform coalition then furnished the resources to launch the challenge. Once underway, the coalition continued to fend for the insurgents, providing additional resources and applying leverage to movement targets. The key changes, then, were in support organization and governmental actions. To demonstrate this, we will analyze macrolevel changes in the activities of these groups as reported in the *New York Times Annual Index* between 1946 and 1972.

The Classical Model

In taking this position, we are arguing that the standard literature on social movements fails to deal adequately with either of two central issues – the formation of insurgent organizations and the outcome of insurgent challenges. Drawing on Gusfield's (1968) summary statement, the classical literature holds in common the following line of argument.

Social movements arise because of deep and widespread discontent. First, there is a social change which makes prevailing social relations inappropriate, producing a strain between the new and the old. Strain then generates discontent within some social grouping. When discontent increases rapidly and is widely shared, collective efforts to alleviate discontent will occur. Though there is disagreement about how to formulate the link between strain and discontent,

e.g., subjective gaps between expectations and satisfactions versus emotional anxiety induced by anomie, the central thrust is consistent. Fluctuations in the level of discontent account for the rise of movements and major changes in movement participation.

Recent research, though, has cast doubt on the classic "discontent" formulations. Disorders do not arise from disorganized anomic masses, but from groups organizationally able to defend and advance their interests (Oberschall, 1973; Tilly et al., 1975). As for relative deprivation, Snyder and Tilly (1972) and Hibbs (1973) have failed to find it useful in accounting for a wide variety of collective disruptions. Nor is it clear that we can use the concept without falling into post hoc interpretations (cf. Wilson, 1973:73–9).[1]

In this study, we do not propose to test each of the various "discontent" formulations currently available. *A priori*, it is rather hard to believe that farmworkers' discontent was, for example, suddenly greater in 1965, when the Delano grape strike began, than throughout much of the 1950s when there was no movement or strike activity. Indeed, it seems more plausible to assume that farmworker discontent is relatively constant, a product of established economic relations rather than some social dislocation or dysfunction. We do not deny the existence of discontent but we question the usefulness of discontent formulations in accounting for either the emergence of insurgent organization or the level of participation by the social base. What increases, giving rise to insurgency, is the amount of social resources available to unorganized but aggrieved groups, making it possible to launch an organized demand for change.

As for the outcome of challenges, the importance of resources is obvious. Though the classical literature has rarely dealt with the issue directly, there has been an implicit position. The resources mobilized by movement organizations are assumed to derive from the aggrieved social base. The outcome of the challenge, then, whether or not one adopts a "natural history" model of movement development, should depend primarily upon internal considerations, e.g., leadership changes and communication dynamics among the membership.

However, are deprived groups like farm-workers able to sustain challenges, especially effective ones, on their own? We think not. Both of the movements studied were, from the outset, dependent upon external groups for critical organizational resources. Nor, as the history of agricultural strikes amply attests, have farmworker movements proven able to mobilize numbers sufficient to wring concessions from employers. For a success-ful outcome, movements by the "powerless" require strong and sustained outside sup-port.

If this line of argument is correct, we need to contest a second thesis frequently found in the classical literature – the assertion that the American polity operates in a pluralistic fashion (cf. Kornhauser, 1959; Smelser, 1962). A pluralistic polity is structurally open to demands for change. As Gamson (1968; 1975) has put it, the political system should be structurally "permeable," readily incorporating new groups and their interests into the decision-making process. Once or-ganized, groups redressing widely-shared grievances should be able to secure at least some part of their program through bargain-ing and compromise. Yet our evidence shows that farmworker challenges have failed, in part, because of the opposition of public officials, and that a successful challenge depended upon the intervention of estab-lished liberal organizations and the neutral-ity of political elites.

We can then summarize the classical model as follows. (1) Discontent, traced to structural dislocations, accounts for collect-ive attempts to bring about change. (2) The resources required to mount collective action and carry it through are broadly dis-tributed – shared by all sizeable social group-ings. (3) The political system is pluralistic and, therefore, responsive to all organized groups with grievances. (4) If insurgents suc-ceed, it is due to efforts on the part of the social base; if they do not, presumably they

lacked competent leaders, were unwilling to compromise, or behaved irrationally (e.g., used violence or broke laws).

In contrast, we will argue that (1) discon-tent is ever-present for deprived groups, but (2) collective action is rarely a viable option because of lack of resources and the threat of repression. (3) When deprived groups do mo-bilize, it is due to the interjection of external resources. (4) Challenges frequently fail be-cause of the lack of resources. Success comes when there is a combination of sustained out-side support and disunity and/or tolerance on the part of political elites. The important variables separating movement success from failure, then, pertain to the way the polity responds to insurgent demands.

Structural Powerlessness of Farmworkers

The major impediment to farmworker unionization has been the oversupply of farm labor, undercutting all attempted har-vest strikes. There are few barriers of habit or skill that restrict the entry of any appli-cant to work in the fields. The result is an "unstructured" labor market, offering little job stability and open to all comers. The fields of California and Texas are close enough to the poverty-stricken provinces of Mexico to insure a steady influx of workers, many of whom arrive by illegal routes. Con-tinuous immigration not only underwrites the oversupply of labor, but complicates mo-bilization by insuring the existence of cul-tural cleavages among workers.

Furthermore, there are reasons to believe that a significant number of workers have only a limited economic interest in the gains promised by unionization. The major-ity of farmworkers, both domestic and alien, are short-term seasonal workers. During the early 1960s, farm employment in California averaged less than three months of the year. This means that a major-ity of workers are interested primarily in the "quick dollar." Imposition of union restric-tions on easy access to jobs would conflict with that interest. And for the vast majority of farmworkers, regardless of job commitment or citizenship status, income is so low as to leave little economic reserve for risk-taking. Since a major portion of the year's income comes during the brief harvest period, workers are reluctant to risk their livelihood on a strike at that time.

In addition to these structural restraints on collective action, there were the very direct restraints of the growers and their political allies. The California Department of Employment and the U.S. Department of Labor have long operated farm placement services that furnish workers for strike-bound employers. Insurgent actions that directly threaten growers, like picket lines and mass rallies, consistently have been the target of official harassment. Though never returning to the scale of the "local fascism" of the 1930s grower vigilante actions are not uncommon.

Bringing these considerations to bear on the comparison of farmworker challenges, there is reason to believe that circumstances were slightly more conducive to the mobilization efforts of the UFW. Between 1946 and 1965 farm wage rates rose slightly and a few public welfare benefits were extended, at least within California. Presumably, farmworkers were slightly more secure economically by the mid-1960s. More significant, though, were changes in the social composition of the farm labor force. During the late 1940s farmworkers in California were either "dustbowlers" or Mexican *braceros* (government-imported contract workers); by the mid-1960s the California farm labor force was predominantly Mexican-descent, short-term workers, most of whom only recently had migrated across the border. Not only were linguistic-cultural cleavages somewhat less pronounced, but these new immigrants were more likely to settle and develop stable community ties than their "Okie" predecessors.

Also, the United Farmworkers pursued a mobilization strategy better designed than that of the NFLU to sustain the participation of farmworkers. From its inception, the UFW was an Alinsky-styled community organization. The primary advantage was that it offered a program of services and social activities that did not depend upon first securing a union contract. Members developed an attachment to the organization independent of the immediate gains that might derive from any strike. Though the National Farm Labor Union had taken limited steps in a similar direction, its program remained primarily that of the conventional "business" union, promising wage gains and better working conditions rather than social solidarity and community benefits.

But the critical issue is whether differences in either the structural position of farmworkers or the mobilization strategy adopted by the movements affected either dependent variable. As we shall see, the impetus for both of the challenges came from the interjection, into an otherwise placid situation, of a professionally-trained cadre backed by outside sponsors. Farmworker discontent remained unexpressed in any organized way until outside organizers arrived on the scene.

As for the question of challenge outcome, despite the UFW's advantages, it experienced no more success in strike efforts than did the NFLU. Where the NFLU had to contend with the semi-official use of *braceros* as strikebreakers, the UFW had to deal with vastly increased numbers of illegal aliens and short-term workers crossing the picket lines. The combination of structural constraints and direct controls insured that neither union was able to mobilize a sufficiently massive social base to be effective.

What separated the UFW success from the NFLU failure was the societal response to the challenges. The NFLU received weak and vacillating sponsorship; the UFW's backing was strong and sustained. Under the pressure of court injunctions and police harassment, the NFLU boycott collapsed when organized labor refused to cooperate. By contrast, the UFW boycotts became national "causes," receiving widespread support from organized labor and liberal organizations; though official harassment remained, the UFW did not deal with the same systematic repression confronted by the NFLU. The success of a "powerless" challenge depended upon sustained and widespread outside support coupled with the neutrality and/or tolerance from the national political elite.

[...]

Our analysis centers on the comparison of three time periods. The first, 1946–1955, spans the challenge of the National Farm Labor Union. Chartered to organize farmworkers at the 1946 American Federation of Labor convention, the NFLU launched a strike wave in the Central Valley of California that ended with the abortive Los Baños strike of 1952. The selection of 1955 as the end point of the period was somewhat arbitrary.

By comparison, the third period, 1965–1972, covers the sustained and successful challenge of the United Farmworkers. The 1965 Coachella and Delano strikes announced the UFW challenge; in 1970, after two years of nation-wide boycott efforts, the UFW brought table-grape growers to the bargaining table and began institutionalizing changes in the position of farmworkers. (The Teamster entry in 1973 is not dealt with in this paper.)

During the period intervening between the two challenges, 1956–1964, important changes took place in the political system that set the stage for a successful challenge. In the absence of a major "push" from insurgents, issues pertaining to farm labor received a different treatment in the hands of established liberal organizations and government officials. We will argue that these years constituted a period of germination and elite reform that made possible the success of the late 1960s.

[...]

Period I: The NFLU Conflict (1946–1955)

The first period illustrates in classical terms the obstacles to a sustained and successful farmworker challenge. In addition to the structural constraints restricting farmworker activity, the political environment confronting the insurgents was unfavorable. Government officials at all levels and branches came into the conflict predominantly on the side of the growers, despite the mandate of agencies such as the Department of Labor or the Education and Labor Committees in Congress to protect the interests of deprived groups like farmworkers. Though external support was decisive in launching the challenge, it was weak and frequently ill-focused, dealing with the consequences rather than the causes of farmworker grievances. When support was withdrawn, the challenge soon collapsed.

Chartered at the 1946 convention of the American Federation of Labor, the National Farm Labor Union set out to accomplish what predecessors had been unable to do – successfully organize the farmworkers of California's "industrialized" agriculture. The leadership cadre was experienced and resourceful. H. L. Mitchell, President of the NFLU, was former head of the Southern Tenant Farmers Union; the Director of Organizations, Henry Hasiwar, had been an effective organizer in several industrial union drives during the 1930s; Ernesto Galarza, who assumed prime responsibility for publicity efforts, had served as political liaison for Latin American unions and had a Ph.D. in economics from Columbia University.

Initially, the strategy was quite conventional: enlist as many workers as possible from a single employer, call a strike, demand wage increases and union recognition, and picket to keep "scabs" out of the fields. American Federation of Labor affiliates would then provide strike relief and political support to keep the picket line going. An occasional church or student group would furnish money and boost morale.

But the government-sponsored alien labor or *bracero* program provided growers with an effective strike-breaking weapon. According to provisions of the law, *braceros* were not to be employed except in instances of domestic labor shortage and *never* to be employed in fields where domestic workers had walked out on strike. Yet in the two major tests of union power, the DiGiorgio strike of 1948 and the Imperial Valley strike of 1951, the flood of *braceros* undermined the strike effort of domestic workers. In the Imperial strike, the NFLU used citizen's arrests to enforce statutes prohibiting employment of *braceros* in labor disputed areas. However, local courts ruled against the tactic and the Immigration Service refused to remove alien "scabs" from the fields. Nor were affairs changed when the *bracero* administration was transferred to the U.S. Department of Labor in 1951. Domestic workers were pushed out of crops by *braceros*, and *braceros* reappeared in the Los Baños strike of 1952 to break the challenge.

In response, the NFLU launched a two-pronged political challenge – a demand for termination of the *bracero* program and, to get around the problem of ineffective strikes, requests for organized labor's support of boycotts. Neither demand found a favorable audience. Lacking strong labor or liberal support, the demand for an end to the *bracero* traffic ended in minor reforms in the *bracero* administration. As for the boycott, despite initial success, it collapsed when a court injunction was issued (improperly) on the grounds that the NFLU was covered by the "hot cargo" provisions of the Taft-Hartley Act. The National Labor Relations Board initially concurred and reversed its position over a year later. By then the Union's resources were exhausted and organized-labor support had long since collapsed.

Figure 25.1 charts the level of favorable actions by selected groups, allowing us to gauge the societal response to insurgency. The curves delineating government, liberal, and farmworker activities move roughly in concert. (Organized labor, though, played little public role in this or the next period.) [. . .]

The main issue for the period was labor supply. [. . .] The union attempted, through court actions, lobby efforts and public protest, to pressure government to end the *bra-cero* program since it was so central to the control of the labor supply. The official response, however, was largely symbolic. Though government tended to respond to concrete insurgency with favorable concrete actions, the majority of favorable governmental actions were actually symbolic (58%). Nor did many of these concrete moves decisively aid the farmworker cause. Key actions, such as pulling strike-breaking *braceros* out of the fields, did not occur.

What, then, are we to make of the fact that 50% of reported governmental actions were coded as favorable to the interest of farmworkers? Was government responding to the conflict between insurgents and growers in some even-handed "pluralist" way? Here it is necessary to recall that we are using news media reportage on a social problem and efforts to redress that problem. The news media will be more sensitive to efforts attempting to define or solve that problem than to efforts to maintain the *status quo*. Consequently, unfavorable actions by government and growers are underrepresented in our data. If only 50% of news-reported government actions can be coded as favorable, then the full universe of governmental activities should, in the balance, be more favorable to growers.

The strength of this assertion is borne out by information on actions favorable to growers. Figure 25.2 charts these actions for government and growers. [. . .] In quantitative terms, government was more responsive to agribusiness interests. Clearly, in critical instances, e.g., leaving *braceros* in struck fields, government policies favored growers over workers.

In addition to the predominantly unfavorable response of government, the NFLU failed to receive sustained, solid support from the liberal community. The major problem was the type of activities in which liberals engaged. When they acted, liberals consistently supported farmworkers over growers but they rarely moved beyond symbolic proclamations. Only 24% of liberal actions during the period were concrete. By

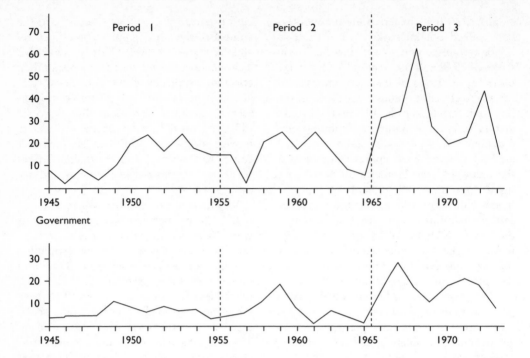

Government

Liberal Organizations

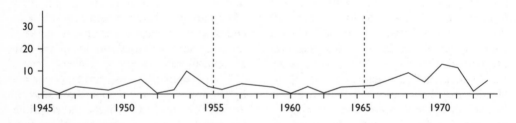

Organized Labor

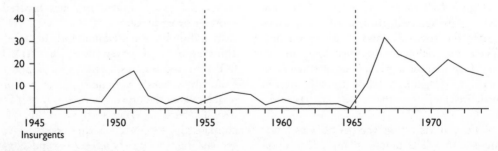

Insurgents

Figure 25.1   Actions favorable to insurgents

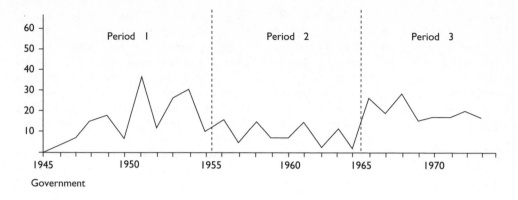

Government

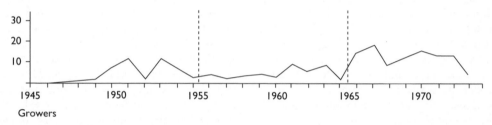

Growers

Figure 25.2   Actions favorable to growers

contrast, 38% during the UFW challenge were so. [...] Where the UFW experienced consistent and concrete support, the NFLU found itself relatively isolated.

Though liberals did not rush to the side of the NFLU, they did play a role in the pressure campaign. [...] Insofar as liberals did act alongside insurgents, apparently it was in the presence of public officials. But there were problems even with this limited-scale liberal support. Liberals focused almost exclusively on the working and living conditions of farmworkers. Following the lead of Progressive Party candidate Henry Wallace in 1948, several religious and "public interest" associations sponsored conferences and issued study reports publicizing deplorable camp conditions and child labor. In what might be considered a typical pattern of liberalism of the time, they were concerned with the plight of the workers rather than the fact of their powerlessness or the role of the *bracero* program in underwriting that

powerlessness. It was a humanitarian, non-political posture, easily dissipated by "red baiting" in Congressional investigations and "red scare" charges by growers and their political allies throughout the late 1940s and early 1950s. The two issues, poverty and the question of labor supply, were not to be linked by the liberal organizations until well into Period II.

Period II: Elite Reform and Realignment (1956–1964)

The late 1950s and the early 1960s, the second Eisenhower administration and the brief Kennedy period emerge from this and other studies in the larger project as a period of germination. Contrary to some interpretations, the remarkable insurgencies of the late 1960s did not originate with the Kennedy administration, but with developments that initially began to appear during

Eisenhower's second term. Nor did the Kennedy years witness a dramatic escalation of insurgent activity. Indeed, in the case of farmworkers, insurgency showed a decline (figure 25.1). For our purposes, the two presidential administrations can be treated as a single period, one that witnessed important realignments and shifts in political resources in the national polity, culminating in a supportive environment for insurgent activity.

Farmworker insurgency during the reform period was at a low ebb. Actions by farmworker insurgents dropped from 16% to 11% of all pro-worker activity. In 1956–1957 the NFLU, now renamed the National Agricultural Workers Union (NAWU), secured a small grant from the United Auto Workers, enabling it to hang on as a paper organization. Galarza, by then the only full-time cadre member, launched a publicity campaign to reveal maladministration and corruption within the *bracero* administration. Aside from a brief and ineffective organizing drive launched in 1959 by the Agricultural Workers Organizing Committee (AWOC), generating only one reported strike (in 1961), this was the sum of insurgent activity for the nine-year Period II (figure 25.1). Growers remained publicly inactive and seemingly secure in their position, aroused only at renewal time for the *bracero* program to lobby bills through Congress. Until the insurgency of Period III began, growers retained a low profile in the *Times* (figure 25.2).

With the direct adversaries largely retired from the public arena, affairs shifted into the hands of government and the liberals. Despite the absence of significant insurgency, the balance of forces in the national polity had begun to shift. Actions favorable to the interests of farmworkers increased from 50% to 73%, remaining on the same plane (75%) throughout the following UFW period. Beginning during the last years of the Eisenhower administration, three interrelated developments brought about this new supportive environment: (1) policy conflicts within the political elite that resulted in a more "balanced," neutral stance toward farmworkers; (2) the formation of a reform coalition composed of liberal pressure groups and organized labor that, in the midst of elite divisions, was able to exercise greater political influence; (3) the erosion of the Congressional power-base of conservative rural interests, stemming immediately from reapportionment.

The concern of liberal pressure groups initially was focused on the need to improve housing and educational conditions of migrant workers. In 1956, the Democratic National Convention included a plank for increased welfare aid to migrants. The next year, the National Council of Churches, already involved in the early civil rights movement in the South, began a study of migrant camp conditions and child labor. In early 1958, the Council brought public pressure to bear on Secretary of Labor James Mitchell to enforce existing laws regarding migrant camps throughout the nation. In late 1958, several liberal pressure groups were joined by the AFL-CIO in attacking the *bracero* program, scoring administrative laxity, and arguing that federal labor policies were the origin of social problems. The two as yet unrelated issues – poverty and labor policies – were now firmly linked in the public debate.

The fusion of these two issues was significant. Of course, economic conditions already had been linked with social deprivations in public parlance, but the concern of liberal groups in the past had been with inspection of housing, assurances of educational opportunity, and public health measures. To argue now that a public program of importing foreign labor perpetuated the list of conditions deplored by liberals was a substantial change. As later happened more generally with the New Left, the advocates of reform had begun to look at the source of problems in terms of a system.

About the same time, organized labor took a new interest in farmworkers. In 1959, the AFL-CIO Executive Council abolished the NAWU and created the Agricultural Workers Organizing Committee

(AWOC), headed by Norman Smith, a former UAW organizer. Despite strong financial backing, the AWOC produced little results. Concentrating on 4 a.m. "shake-ups" of day laborers, the AWOC managed to sponsor a number of "job actions" but only one major strike and little solid organization. Like the NFLU, the AWOC had to confront the problem of *braceros*. In the one reported strike, the Imperial Valley strike of February, 1961, the AWOC used violence to intimidate strikebreaking *braceros* and create an international incident over their presence. Officials quickly arrested the cadre, and the AWOC ceased to exist except on paper. Though the AWOC drive consumed over one million dollars of AFL-CIO funds, it produced neither contracts nor stable membership. Yet, and this indicates the shift, this type of financial support had never before been offered by organized labor.

The final element in the formation of a supportive environment was a shift in governmental actions. Actions favorable to farmworkers increased from the unfavorable 50% prevailing during Period I to a more "balanced" 68% of all governmental actions. Of these, the portion coded "concrete," and therefore more likely to have impact, increased from 40% in Period I to 65%. Indicative of the change taking place in official views, the focus of governmental attentions shifted from the labor supply issue (56% of favorable actions during Period I) to the question of farmworkers' living and working conditions (73% during Period II).

The change in official actions stemmed, in part, from internal conflicts within the national political elite. Secretary of Labor James Mitchell was a surprise Eisenhower appointee from the Eastern wing of the Republican Party, a former labor consultant for New York department stores and a future protege of Nelson Rockefeller. Mitchell took the Department of Labor in a more pro-union direction than was thought possible, at the time becoming a "strong man" in the cabinet because of his success

in mollifying unions. In 1958, an open fight between the Taft and Eastern wings of the Republican Party developed, with the conservatives favoring a national "right-to-work" law. Mitchell, as an advocate of unionism and apparently jockeying for position for the Republican Vice-Presidential nomination, became a figure of elite reform within Republican circles.

A second factor contributing to the shift in official actions was the pressure campaign launched by the reform coalition. [...]

Tangible effects of the pressure campaign appeared almost immediately. In 1957, under pressure from the liberal reform coalition, the Department of Labor under Mitchell's guidance carried out an internal review of farm labor policies. The upshot was a series of executive orders to tighten up enforcement of regulations covering migrant camps. When the economic recession of 1958–1959 arrived, sensitivity within the Administration to rising unemployment levels increased. In response, Mitchell vowed to enforce more fully the 1951 statutes requiring farm employment to be offered to domestic workers prior to importation of *braceros*. Growers, long accustomed to having their *bracero* requests met automatically, rebelled when asked to provide more justification. In February, 1959, Mitchell took an even stronger step, joining the liberal reformers in support of legislation to extend minimum-wage laws to agriculture and to impose new restrictions on the use of *braceros*.

The following year, the division within the Eisenhower Administration opened up into a full-scale, cabinet-level battle over renewal of the *bracero* program. The Farm Bureau and the state grower associations engaged that other administration "strong man," Secretary of Agriculture Ezra Taft Benson, to defend the program. In testimony before the House Committee on Agriculture, the White House took a neutral stance; Benson defended the program, while Mitchell argued that the program exerted demonstrable adverse effects upon domestic workers and should be abolished. Into this breach in the political elite stepped the liberal-labor support coalition. At the same time, the House Committee on Public Welfare opened hearings on health and camp conditions, giving the Cotton Council and the Meatcutters Union a chance to air opposing views.

Initially, the reform effort failed. In March, 1960, Secretary Mitchell withdrew his program, resolving the dispute on the cabinet level. The next month, agribusiness pushed a two-year renewal of the *bracero* program through Congress. But, for the first time, the issue had been debated seriously and a loose coalition of liberal pressure groups (e.g., National Council of Churches, National Advisory Committee of Farm Labor, NAACP) and organized labor had formed. Though the eventual termination of the *bracero* program did not undermine growers' ability to break strikes (there were other substitutes, e.g., "green card" commuters, illegal aliens), the fight against the program did refocus the concern of liberals and organized labor on the structural problem of farmworker powerlessness.

The reform coalition sustained the campaign over the next three years. In 1960, the Democratic platform condemned the *bracero* program. Once in office, the New Frontiersmen, though demanding no important statutory changes, did vow to enforce fully the laws restricting *bracero* use. By renewal time in 1963, the Kennedy Administration was in the pursuit of a public issue ("poverty") and courting minority-group votes. For the first time, the White House went formally on record against the program. Only at the last minute was a pressure campaign, mounted by Governor Pat Brown of California and the Department of State, responding to Mexican diplomatic pressure, able to save the program temporarily. Amid promises from Congressional farm bloc leaders that this was the last time the program would be renewed, a one-year extension was granted.

In addition to the efforts of the reform coalition, which played a critical role in other reforms of the same period, and the new elite-level neutrality, the fall of the *bracero* program stemmed from the narrowing power base of the Congressional farm bloc. Congressional reapportionment had visibly shaken the conservative farm bloc leaders. Searching for items in the farm program that could be scuttled without damaging the main planks, the farm bloc leaders fixed on the *bracero* program. The mechanization of the Texas cotton harvest had left California growers of specialty crops the main *bracero* users. When the test came, *bracero* users, as a narrow, special interest, could be sacrificed to keep the main planks of the farm program intact.

Period II, then, emerges from this analysis as a period of reform and political realignment that dramatically altered the prospective fortunes of insurgents. Reforms, stemming from elite-level conflicts and a pressure campaign conducted by liberal public-interest organizations and organized labor, came about in the virtual absence of activity by farmworker insurgents. The activism of several key liberal organizations depended, in turn, upon broad economic trends, especially the growth of middle-class disposable income that might be invested in worthy causes (McCarthy and Zald, 1973). Insurgents did not stimulate these changes in the national polity. Rather, they were to prove the beneficiaries and, if anything, were stimulated by them.

Period III: The UFW Success (1965–1972)

During the NFLU period, the number of insurgent actions reported totalled 44. Most of these were symbolic in character, only 27% being concrete. Insurgency was brief, concentrated in a four-year period (1948–1951). However, in the third period, insurgency became sustained. Insurgent actions reached a new peak and remained at a high level throughout the period. A total of 143 actions conducted by farmworker insurgents were recorded. Significantly, 71% of these were concrete in character. By the end of the period, the success of the United Farmworkers was unmistakable. Over a hundred contracts had been signed; wages had been raised by almost a third; union hiring halls were in operation in every major agricultural area in California; farmworkers, acting through ranch committees set up under each contract, were exercising a new set of powers.

The key to this dramatic success was the altered political environment within which the challenge operated. Though the potential for mobilizing a social base was slightly more favorable than before, the UFW never was able to launch effective strikes. Though the UFW cadre was experienced and talented, there is little reason to believe that they were markedly more so than the NFLU leadership; neither did the tactics of the challenge differ. The boycotts that secured success for the UFW also had been tried by the NFLU, but with quite different results. What had changed was the political environment – the liberal community now was willing to provide sustained, massive support for insurgency; the political elite had adopted a neutral stance toward farmworkers.

As before, external support played a critical role in launching the challenge. The initial base for the United Farmworkers was Cesar Chavez's National Farmworkers Association (NFWA) and remnants of the AWOC still receiving some support from the AFL-CIO. During the 1950s, Chavez had been director of the Community Service Organization, an Alinsky-styled urban community-organization with strong ties to civil rights groups, liberal churches and foundations. Frustrated by the refusal of the CSO Board of Directors to move beyond issues salient to upwardly-mobile urban Mexican-Americans, Chavez resigned his post in the winter of 1961 and set out to organize a community organization among farmworkers in the Central Valley of California. Drawing on his liberal contacts, Chavez was able to secure the backing of several liberal organizations which had developed a new concern with poverty and the problems of

minority groups. The main sponsor was the California Migrant Ministry, a domestic mission of the National Council of Churches servicing migrant farmworkers. During the late 1950s, the Migrant Ministry followed the prevailing policy change within the National Council, substituting community organization and social action programs for traditional evangelical ones. By 1964, the Migrant Ministry had teamed up with Chavez, merging its own community organization (the FWO) with the NFWA and sponsoring the Chavez-directed effort.

By summer, 1965, NFWA had over 500 active members and began shifting directions, expanding beyond economic benefit programs (e.g., a credit union, cooperative buying, etc.) to unionization. Several small "job actions" were sponsored. Operating nearby, the remaining active group of the AWOC, several Filipino work-crews, hoped to take advantage of grower uncertainty generated by termination of the *bracero* program. The AWOC launched a series of wage strikes, first in the Coachella Valley and then in the Delano-Arvin area of the San Joaquin Valley. With the AWOC out on strike, Chavez pressed the NFWA for a strike vote. On Mexican Independence Day, September 16th, the NFWA joined the picket lines.

Though dramatic, the strike soon collapsed. Growers refused to meet with union representatives; a sufficient number of workers crossed the picket lines to prevent a major harvest loss. Over the next six years, the same pattern recurred – a dramatic strike holding for a week, grower intransigence, police intimidation, gradual replacement of the work force by playing upon ethnic rivalries and recruiting illegal aliens. What proved different from the NFLU experience was the ability of the insurgents, acting in the new political environment, to secure outside support.

Political protest was the mechanism through which much of this support was garnered. By dramatic actions designed to capture the attention of a sympathetic public and highlight the "justice" of their cause, insurgents were able to sustain the movement organization and exercise suffi- cient indirect leverage against growers to secure contracts. The UFW's use of protest tactics departed from that of rent strikers analyzed by Lipsky (1968; 1970). Though the basic mechanism was the same (namely, securing the sympathy of third parties to the conflict so that they would use their superior resources to intervene in support of the powerless), the commitments of supporting organizations and the uses to which outside support was put differed. Lipsky found that protest provided unreliable resources, that the news media and sympathetic public might ignore protestors' demands and that, even when attentive they often were easily satisfied with symbolic palliatives. Though the UFW experienced these problems, the presence of sustained sponsorship on the part of the Migrant Ministry and organized labor guaranteed a stable resource base.

Nor were the uses of protest-acquired re- sources the same. Lipsky's rent-strikers sought liberal pressure on public officials. For the UFW, protest actions were used to secure contributions and, in the form of a boycott, to exercise power against growers. Marches, symbolic arrests of clergy, and public speeches captured public attention; contributions from labor unions, theater showings and "radical chic" cocktail parties with proceeds to "La Causa" supplemented the budget provided by sponsors and mem- bership dues.

Given the failure of strike actions, a suc- cessful outcome required indirect means of exercising power against growers. Sympa- thetic liberal organizations (e.g., churches, universities, etc.) refused to purchase "scab" grapes. More important, though, major grocery chains were pressured into refusing to handle "scab" products. To exer- cise that pressure, a combination of external resources had to be mobilized. Students had to contribute time to picketing grocery stores and shipping terminals; Catholic churches and labor unions had to donate office space for boycott houses; Railway Union members had to identify "scab" ship- ments for boycott pickets; Teamsters had to

refuse to handle "hot cargo"; Butchers' union members had to call sympathy strikes when grocery managers continued to stock "scab" products; political candidates and elected officials had to endorse the boycott. The effectiveness of the boycott depended little upon the resources of mobilized farm- workers; instead, they became a political symbol. It was the massive outpouring of support, especially from liberals and organ- ized labor, that made the boycott effective and, thereby, forced growers to the bargain- ing table.

The strength of liberal-labor support for the UFW is indicated by the high level of concomitant activity between insurgents and their supporters. [...] Given the fact that liberal activities rarely occurred jointly with pro-worker government activities, it is clear that liberals directed their efforts toward supporting insurgents rather than pressuring government.

The more "balanced," neutral posture of government that was the product of the reform period continued. Sixty-nine percent of all official actions were favorable to farm- workers (as against 50% and 68% in Periods I and II). Concretely, this meant that court rulings no longer routinely went against insurgents; federal poverty programs helped to "loosen" small town politics; hear- ings by the U.S. Civil Rights Commission and Congressional committees publicized "injustices" against farmworkers; welfare legislation gave farmworkers more eco- nomic security and afforded insurgents a legal basis to contest grower employment practices. National politicians, such as Sen- ators Kennedy and McGovern, lent their re- sources to the cause.

The most striking changes in official actions took place on the federal level. Actions favorable to farmworkers rose from 46% of federal level activity in the first period, to 63% in the second and 74% in the third. State and local government, more under the control of growers, followed a different pattern. In Period I, when growers had opposition only from insur- gents, only 26% of official actions were judged favorable to workers. In Period II, when farmworkers were acquiescent but the liberal-labor coalition was experiencing growing influence in national politics, 67% were favorable, slightly more than on the federal level. But when insurgency re-appeared in Period III, the percent favorable dropped to 45%, far lower than the federal level. Government divided on the question, federal actions tending to be neutral, if not supportive, of insurgents while state actions, still under grower dominance, continued to oppose insurgents.

Significantly little of the pro-worker trend in governmental actions during the UFW period is associated with either insurgent or liberal activities. [. . .] Only organized labor appeared to be performing a pressure function. [. . .] Official positions had already undergone important changes during the reform period. The termination of the *bracero* program had left government in a neu-tralized position. No longer a key player in the conflict, but still under the influence of the reform policies, government preserved its neutral stance despite less visible pressure from any of the partisans.

There was, of course, opposition on the part of growers and allied governmental actors. There were numerous instances of police harassment, large-scale purchases of boycotted products by the Department of Defense, and outspoken opposition from Governor Reagan and President Nixon.

However, growers had lost their en-trenched political position. Public officials no longer acted so consistently to enhance grower interests and to contain the chal-lenge. [. . .] By the time the United Farm-workers struck in 1965, agricultural employers were no longer able to rely upon government, especially at the federal level, to be fully responsive to their interest in blocking unionization.

Conclusion

The critical factor separating the National Farm Labor Union failure from the United Farmworker success was the societal response to insurgent demands. In most respects, the challenges were strikingly simi-lar. In both instances, the leadership cadre came from outside the farmworker commu-nity; external sponsorship played a critical role in launching both insurgent organiza-tions; both movements confronted similar obstacles to mobilizing a social base and mounting effective strikes; both resorted to political protest and boycotts. What pro-duced the sharp difference in outcome was the difference in political environment encountered. The NFLU received token contributions, vacillating support for its boy-cott and confronted major acts of resistance by public authorities. In contrast, the UFW received massive contributions, sustained support for its boycotts and encountered a more "balanced," neutral official response.

The dramatic turnabout in the political environment originated in economic trends and political realignments that took place quite independent of any "push" from insur-gents. During the reform period, conflicts erupted within the political elite over pol-icies pertaining to farmworkers. Elite div-isions provided the opening for reform measures then being pressed by a newly active coalition of established liberal and labor organizations. Though the reforms did not directly effect success, the process entailed by reform did result in a new polit-ical environment, one which made a success-ful challenge possible.

If this analysis is correct, then several assumptions found in the classic literature are misleading. Rather than focusing on fluc-tuations in discontent to account for the emergence of insurgency, it seems more fruit-ful to assume that grievances are relatively constant and pervasive. Especially for de-prived groups, lack of collective resources and controls exercised by superiors – not the absence of discontent – account for the relative infrequency of organized demands for change. For several of the movements of the 1960s, it was the interjection of resources from outside, not sharp increases in discontent, that led to insurgent efforts.

Nor does the political process centered around insurgency conform to the rules of a pluralist game. The American polity had not been uniformly permeable to all groups with significant grievances (cf. Gamson, 1975). Government does not act as a neutral agent, serving as umpire over the group contest. Public agencies and officials have interests of their own to protect, interests that often bring them into close alignment with well-organized private-interest groups. When insurgency arises threatening these private interests, public officials react by helping to contain insurgency and preserve the *status quo*. But if an opposing coalition of established organizations decides to sponsor an insurgent challenge, the normal bias in public policy can be checked. Sponsors then serve as protectors, insuring that the political elite remains neutral to the challenge.

The implications for other challenges are rather striking. If the support of the liberal community is necessary for the success of a challenge by a deprived group, then the liberal community is, in effect, able to determine the cutting edge for viable changes that conform to the interests of those groups still excluded from American politics. Moreover, there is the possibility of abandonment. Since liberal support can fade and political elites shift their stance, as has happened to the UFW since 1972, even the gains of the past may be endangered. The prospects for future insurgency, by this account, are dim. Until another major realignment takes place in American politics, we should not expect to see successful attempts to extend political citizenship to the excluded.

Note

1 Shifts in perceptions, treated as central by relative deprivation theorists, in our view would be secondary to the main process – changes in social resources.

References

Gamson, William 1968 "Stable unrepresentation in American society." *American Behavioral Scientist* 12:15–21.
——1975 *The Strategy of Social Protest*. Homewood, Il.: Dorsey.
Gusfield, Joseph 1968 "The study of social movements." Pp. 445–52 in David Sills (ed.), *International Encyclopedia of the Social Sciences*, Volume 14. New York: Macmillan.
Hibbs, Douglas 1973 *Mass Political Violence*. New York: Wiley.
Kornhauser, William 1959 *The Politics of Mass Society*. Glencoe, Il.: Free Press.
Lipsky, Michael 1968 "Protest as political resource." *American Political Science Review* 62:1144–58.
——1970 *Protest in City Politics*. Chicago: Rand McNally.
McCarthy, John and Mayer Zald 1973 *The Trend of Social Movements in America*. Morristown, N.J.: General Learning Corporation.
Oberschall, Anthony 1973 *Social Conflict and Social Movements*. Englewood Cliffs, N.J.: Prentice-Hall.
Smelser, Neil J. 1962 *The Theory of Collective Behavior*. New York: Free Press.
Snyder, David and Charles Tilly 1972 "Hardship and collective violence in France, 1830 to 1960." *American Sociological Review* 37:520–32.
Tilly, Charles, Louise Tilly and Richard Tilly 1975 *The Rebellious Century*. Cambridge, Ma.: Harvard University Press.
Wilson, John 1973 *Introduction to Social Movements*. New York: Basic Books.

Biography

A brief biography of Cesar Chavez, written by the editors of this volume, can be found on page 373.

26 Another Look at Farmworker Mobilization

Marshall Ganz

Until the success of the United Farm Workers (UFW) in the 1960s and 1970s, repeated efforts to unionize California's 400,000 farmworkers had failed.[1] Since 1900, three major attempts at labor organization had been made by four different unions: the Industrial Workers of the World (IWW) prior to World War I; the Cannery, Agricultural, and Industrial Workers Union (CAIWU) and United Cannery, Agricultural Packing, and Allied Workers CIO (UCA PAWA) in the 1930s; and the National Farm Labor Union AFL (NFLU) in the 1940s. By the spring of 1966, however, just four years after it had begun organizing and six months after calling its first strike, the UFW signed the first multiyear union contract to cover California farmworkers, established a new union, and launched a farmworker movement. By 1977, the UFW held over 100 contracts, had recruited a dues-paying membership of more than 50,000, and had secured enactment of the 1975 California Agricultural Labor Relations Act, the only legislative guarantee of collective bargaining rights for agricultural workers in the continental United States. The UFW had also played a major role in the emergence of a Chicano movement in the Southwest, had recruited and trained hundreds of community activists, and had become a significant player in California politics. In this article, I ask why the newly formed, uncertainly funded, and independent United Farm Workers succeeded, while the well-established union with which it found itself in competition failed – the AFL-CIO's Agricultural Workers Organizing Committee (AWOC).

Answering this question requires going beyond Jenkins and Perrow's (1977) classic of social movement theory, "Insurgency of the Powerless," which attributes the UFW's success, as compared with another effort in the late 1940s, to a more favorable political opportunity structure. Although the 1960s were an era of greater political responsiveness to groups like the UFW than the 1940s had been, this cannot explain why the UFW was more successful than its rival. Nor can scholars who rely on differences in resources to account for differences in outcomes (McCarthy and Zald 1977) explain why the resource-poor UFW succeeded while its resource-rich opponents did not. Those who attribute the UFW's success to the "charismatic leadership" of Cesar Chavez explain little of what that is, where it comes from, and why it works. And even those who acknowledge the unique effectiveness of the UFW's strategy do not explain why it was the UFW that developed this strategy and not its competitor. Drawing evidence from this case and insights from organization theory, social psychology, and cognitive sociology, I argue that consigning the influence of leadership and organization on strategy to a "black box" has created a serious deficit in social movement theory. As shown in figure 26.1, I argue that difference in the outcomes of AWOC and UFW efforts can be explained by differences in their strategy – the targeting, timing, and tactics through which they mobilized and deployed resources. Differences in their strategy, however, and the likelihood it would be effective in achieving desired goals, were due to differences in leaders' access to salient information about the environment, heuristic use they made of this information, and their motivation – what I call their "strategic capacity."

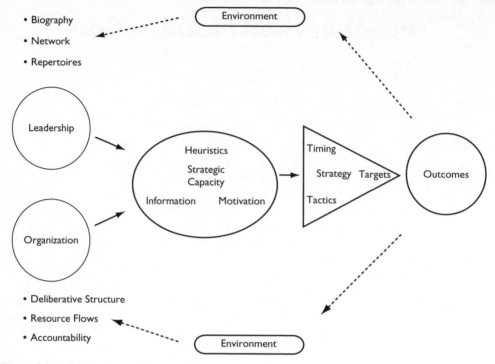

Figure 26.1   Strategic process model

Differences in strategic capacity, in turn, were due to differences in leaders' life experience, networks, and repertoires of collective action and the deliberative processes, resource flows, and accountability structures of their organizations. Strategic capacity is greater if a leadership team includes insiders and outsiders, strong and weak network ties, and access to diverse, yet salient, repertoires of collective action and also if an organization conducts regular, open, authoritative deliberation, draws resources from multiple constituencies, and roots accountability in those constituencies. I explain the UFW's success over its rivals by differences in its strategy, account for differences in strategy by the way in which it was developed, and explain how it was developed in the interaction of leadership and organization with environment.

Analysis of this case offers a way to specify conditions under which one organization is more likely than another to develop strategy that is effective in achieving its goals. I do not focus on why one kind of tactic is more effective than another – a topic dealt with extensively in political, military, and management literature – but rather on why one organization is more likely to develop a series of effective tactics than another – its strategic capacity. Although strategic capacity, strategy, and outcomes are distinct links in a probabilistic causal chain, I argue greater capacity is likely to yield better strategy, and better strategy is likely to yield better outcomes. Differences in strategic capacity can explain how resourcefulness compensates for lack of resources when insurgent social movements overcome more powerful opponents. Differences in strategic capacity can also explain why some new organizations overcome the "liability of newness" to succeed in domains in which old organizations fail, suffering from a "liability of senescence." Because of more recent selection, organizational flexibility, and closer articulation with the environment, leaders of new organizations may have greater access to salient information about current environments, heuristic opportunity, and motivation than leaders of old organizations. Attention to strategic capacity also helps explain why reconfigurations of leadership and organization at certain "focal moments" can produce dramatic strategic change, including the emergence of a social movement.

[...]

Theory

Strategy and Social Movements

Social movement scholars tell us little about the relationship of strategic leadership to social movement success. Explanations of the emergence, development, and outcomes of social movements are usually based on variation in resources, opportunities, and framing – concepts that stress the influence of environmental change on actors. In this view, social movements unfold as actors predictably respond to new political opportunities, newly available resources, or changes in cultural frames. Although students of tactics do offer accounts of their sources and their effect on outcomes they do not explain why one organization should devise tactics that turn out to be more or less strategically effective than those of another. Even in domains of management, military, and political studies in which strategic leadership receives far greater attention, the focus has been more on how leadership and strategy work than on explaining why some organizations devise more effective strategy than others.

Understanding social movements, however, requires accounting for the fact that different actors act in different ways, some of which influence the environment more than others. Some see political opportunities where others do not, mobilize resources in ways others do not, and frame their causes in ways others do not. And because it is based on the innovative, often guileful, exercise of agency, good strategy is often anything but obvious. It can thus be hard to deduce from "objective" configurations of resources and opportunities and is based rather on novel assessments of them. As a consequence, popular accounts of effective strategy attribute it to the charismatic gifts of particular leaders rather than offering systematic explanations of conditions under which leaders are more or less likely to devise effective strategy.

But neither is strategy purely subjective. Strategic thinking is reflexive and imaginative, based on how leaders have learned to reflect on the past, pay attention to the present, and anticipate the future. Leaders are influenced by life experience, relationships, and practical learning, which provide them with lenses through which they see the world, and by the organizational structures within which they work and through which they interact with their environment.

Failure to bring attention to the important influence of strategic leadership on social movements is an important theoretical shortcoming in general – and in scholarly efforts to explain the farmworker movement in particular. Students of the farmworker movement who focus on the changing environment or political opportunity structure correctly point to the importance of an emergent liberal coalition (Jenkins and Perrow 1977) and new politics of race, but do not explain why the UFW took advantage of these opportunities in ways its competitors did not. Scholars who rely on differences in resources to account for success and failure (Jenkins and Perrow 1977) cannot explain why the resource-rich AWOC failed, while the resource-poor UFW succeeded. Scholars who point to the UFW's strategy of redefining the arena of conflict by mobilizing dual constituencies of farmworkers and supporters, so they could "turn the moral tables" on the opposition with a grape boycott, fail to explain why only the UFW devised this strategy. And observers who attribute the UFW's success to the charismatic leadership of Cesar Chavez fail to explain what it is, where it came from, and how it worked.

Understanding Strategy

Strategy is the conceptual link we make between the places, the times and ways we mobilize and deploy our resources, and the goals we hope to achieve. Strategy is how we turn what we have into what we need – by translating our resources into the power to achieve purpose. Although we often do not act "rationally" and outcomes are often unintended, we do act purposefully. Strategy is effective when we realize our goals by means of it. Studying strategy is a way of discerning pattern in the relationship between intention, action, and outcome.

Strategy is a way of "framing" specific choices about targeting, timing, and tactics. As schema theory teaches us, we attribute meaning to specific events by locating them within broader frameworks of understanding. The strategic significance of choices we make about how to target our resources, time our initiatives, and employ tactics depends on how we frame them in relation to other choices in a path toward our goals. One reason it is difficult to study strategy is that, although choices about targeting, timing, and tactics can be directly observed, the strategic "frame" within which we make these choices – and provide them with their coherence – must often be inferred.

Since strategy is a way of orienting *current* action toward future goals, however, it develops in interaction with an ever-changing environment, especially the actions and reactions of other actors (Alinsky 1971). In fixed contexts in which rules, resources, and interests are given, strategy can to some extent be understood in the analytic terms of game theory. But in settings in which rules, resources, and interests are emergent – such as social movements – strategy has far more in common with creative thinking. Strategic thinking in these settings can best be understood as an ongoing creative or innovative process of understanding and adapting new conditions to one's goals.

My argument about the relationship of strategy to outcomes can be clarified by drawing on the distinction game theorists make between games of chance, skill, and strategy. In games of chance, winning depends on the luck of the draw. In games of skill, it depends on behavioral facility, like hitting a tennis ball. In games of strategy, it depends on cognitive discernment – in interaction with other players – of the best course of action, as in Go. In most games, all three elements come into play. In poker, for example, getting cards is a matter of chance; estimating probabilities, of skill; and betting, of strategy. Although chance may be dispositive in any one hand, or even one game, in the long run, skill and strategy distinguish excellent players – and their winnings – from others. Similarly, environmental developments can be seen as "chance," in so far as any one actor is concerned. But, in the long run, some actors are more likely to achieve their goals than others because they are better able to take advantage of these chances. Environmental changes may generate opportunities for social movements to emerge, but the outcomes and legacies of such movements have far more to do with strategies actors devise to turn these opportunities to their purposes – thus reshaping their environment.

Strategic Capacity

Organizations differ in the likelihood they will develop effective strategy – what I call their "strategic capacity." Viewing strategy as a kind of creative or innovative thinking, I build on the work of social psychologists, cognitive sociologists, and organization theorists by focusing on three key influences on creative output: salient knowledge, heuristic processes, and motivation (Amabile 1996). In this section, I link leadership and organizational variables with these elements to specify conditions under which one group is likely to develop more effective strategy than another (see table 26.1, below).

Salient knowledge. – When actors face routine problems, their familiarity with domain-specific algorithms – or action repertoires – facilitates effective problem

Table 26.1 Three elements of strategic capacity

	Motivation	Salient information	Heuristic processes
Dimensions of leadership:			
Biography (insiders and outsiders)	Personal, vocational commitment Intrinsic rewards	Diverse local knowledge	Broad contextualization
Networks (strong and weak ties)	Personal commitment Reputation	Diverse local knowledge Feedback	Broad contextualization
Repertoires (diverse salient repertoires)	Competence Feedback	Diverse local knowledge	Sources of bricolage or analogy
Organization:			
Deliberation (regular, open, and authoritative)	Commitment Autonomy	Diverse local knowledge	Heterogeneous perspectives Periodic assessment
Resource flows (multiple constituencies; reliance on people)	Commitment Autonomy Feedback	Feedback	Heterogeneous alternatives
Accountability (salient constituencies; entrepreneurial or democratic)	Commitment Intrinsic rewards Feedback	Diverse local knowledge Feedback	Heuristic skills

Note. The illustrated influences of leadership and organization on motivation, heuristics, and information are meant to be simultaneous, not sequential.

solving. The better one's information about a domain within which one is working, the better the "local" knowledge, the more likely one is to know how to deal effectively with problems that arise within that domain. Since environments change in response to actors' initiatives, however, regular feedback is especially important in evaluating responses to these initiatives. The test of salience I use is one of relevance to the environment in which leaders are trying to get results, or their "operating environment."

Heuristic processes. – When faced with novel problems – often the case for leaders of organizations operating within new or changing environments – heuristic processes permit actors to use salient knowledge to devise novel solutions by imaginatively recontextualizing their understanding of the data. This reframes understanding of the data so as to make alternative interpretations and pathways conceivable, facilitating analogic thinking and bricolage. At the most basic level, the more different ideas are generated, the greater the likelihood there will be good ones among them. Encounters with diverse points of view and ways of doing things thus facilitate innovation, whether based upon one's life experience or the experience of a group. Knowledge of diverse domains not only offers multiple routines from which to choose, but contributes to "mindfulness" that multiple solutions are possible and that most known solutions are "equivocal".

Motivation – Motivation is critical to creative output because of its effect on the focus actors bring to their work, their ability to concentrate for extended periods of time, their persistence, their willingness to take risks, and their ability to sustain high energy. Motivated actors are also more likely to do the work it takes to acquire needed domain-specific knowledge and skills than those who are less motivated. Perhaps the most important source of creative motivation is the "intrinsic reward" it brings to actors who love their work – for whom it is their "vocation" – in contrast with those motivated by "extrinsic rewards," which can actually inhibit creativity. Actors can also override "programmed" modes of thought to think more critically and reflexively if they are intensely interested in a problem, dissatisfied with the status quo, or experience a schema failure as a result of sharp breaches in expectations and outcomes. The influence of motivation on outcomes also helps explain the positive effect of affective or normative commitment on workplace performance. Finally, one reason successful leadership teams can become more successful over time is that success augments motivation, not only resources and opportunities. Organizational settings in which people enjoy autonomy, receive positive feedback from peers and superiors, and are part of a team competing with other teams enhance their motivation. It is diminished when they enjoy little autonomy, get no feedback or negative feedback from peers and superiors, and are competitive within a team.

Sources of Strategic Capacity

As illustrated in table 26.1 and explained in the text below, I argue that leadership variables of biography, networks, and repertoires, and organizational variables of deliberation, resource flows, and accountability, link in specific ways to each of the above three elements of an organization's "strategic capacity."

Leadership. – To identify sources of variation in strategic capacity, I compare the leaders of the AWOC and the UFW as to their biographies, sociocultural networks, and tactical repertoires – who they were, whom they knew, and what they knew. I define leaders as persons authorized to make strategic choices within an organization. I do not evaluate their qualities of leadership as such but rather their contribution to formulation of strategy. Although researchers have linked leaders' psychological, professional, organizational, and generational backgrounds to strategies they adopt, few have studied the relationship between leaders' backgrounds and the likelihood they will develop *effective* strategy.

Although strategy is more often described as the work of individual leaders than of formal or informal leadership teams, I argue that strategy is usually a product of the interaction among those persons who share responsibility for its formulation – what I call here a "leadership team." I recognize that the "person in charge" plays a uniquely important role in formulating strategy, particularly in the formation and maintenance of the leadership team itself. But I argue that strategy is more often the result of interaction among leaders than organizational myths acknowledge. I argue that leadership teams that combine insiders and outsiders, strong and weak ties to constituencies, and diverse yet salient repertoires of collective action have greater capacity to develop effective strategy than those that do not.

Because biographical experience is the primary source of a person's cognitive socialization, cultural perspective, and motivating interests, I first analyze leaders' biographies as to race, class, gender, generation, ethnicity, religious beliefs, family background, education, and professional training. As shown in the first row of table 26.1, I argue that leadership teams of "insiders" and "outsiders" combine diversity of salient local knowledge with an opportunity to heuristically recontextualize this knowledge. Persons with "borderland" experience of straddling cultural or institutional worlds may make innovative contributions for the same reasons. Insiders personally committed to constituencies with whom they identify or outsiders normatively committed to a vocation are likely to be more motivated than those whose interest is solely instrumental or professional – and they are more likely to find their work intrinsically rewarding.

As shown in the second row of table 26.1, teams that combine leaders with "strong" and "weak" ties will have greater strategic capacity than those that do not. Sociocultural networks are sources of ideas about what to do and how to do it, mechanisms through which social movements recruit, sources of social capital, and incubators of new collective identities. Leaders with "strong ties" to constituencies are more likely to possess salient information about where to find resources, whom to recruit, what tactics to use, and how to encourage these constituencies to identify with the organization. On the other hand, leaders with "weak ties" to diverse constituencies are more likely to know how to access the diversity of people, ideas, and routines that facilitate broad alliances. Combinations of strong and weak ties are associated with social movement recruitment because they link access with commitment, just as they are associated with innovation because they link information with influence. Informal and formal ties are also important means for feedback of salient information, especially on organizational initiatives. Diverse ties, like diverse life experience, facilitate heuristic "recontextualization" of strategic choices. Strong ties strengthen a leaders' motivation to the extent they have personal commitments to those whose lives are influenced by choices they make and from whom they acquire their reputations.

Finally, as shown in row three, leaders with knowledge of a diversity of salient collective action repertoires are more likely to develop effective strategy than those without such knowledge. Knowledge of collective action repertoires is valuable because of their practical (people know what to do), normative (people think they are right), and institutional (they attach to resources) utility in mobilizing people who are familiar with them. Repertoires known to one's constituency, but not to one's opposition, are particularly useful. Knowledge of multiple repertoires not only widens leaders' range of possible choices, but also affords them the opportunity to adapt to new situations by heuristic processes of bricolage or analogy. The motivation of leaders adept in these repertoires is enhanced by competence they experience in their use and by positive feedback from constituencies who find these repertoires familiar.

Organization. – Turning to the second major set of influences on strategic capacity, I argue that organizational structures that afford leaders venues for regular, open, and authoritative deliberation; draw resources from a diversity of salient constituencies; and hold leaders accountable to those constituencies – and to each other – are more likely to generate effective strategy than those that do not. Organizational structure is created by commitments among founders who enact ways to interact with each other and with their environment. It defines patterns of legitimacy, power, and deliberation. Although organizational form is a consequence of founders' strategic choices, once established, it has a profound influence on innovativeness and strategy.

As shown in row 4, leaders who take part in regular, open, and authoritative deliberation gain access to salient information, participate in a heuristic process by means of which they learn to use this information, and are motivated by commitment to choices they participated in making and upon which they have the autonomy to act. Regular deliberation facilitates initiative by encouraging periodic assessment of the organization's activities. Deliberation open to heterogeneous points of view enhances strategic capacity because "deviant" perspectives facilitate better decisions, encourage innovation, and develop group capacity to perform cognitive tasks more creatively and effectively. Authoritative deliberation – in the sense that it results in actionable decisions – motivates actors both to participate in decisions and to implement that which was decided upon.

As shown in row 5, organizations that mobilize resources from multiple constituencies enjoy greater strategic capacity than those that do not. First, leaders who must obtain resources from constituents must devise strategy to which constituents will respond. If membership dues are a major source of support, leaders learn to get members to pay "dues." However, reliance on resources drawn primarily from outside the operating environment – even when those resources are internal to their organizations – may dampen leaders' motivation to devise effective strategy. As long as they attend to the politics that keep the bills paid, they can keep doing the same thing "wrong." At the same time, leaders who draw resources from multiple constituencies gain strategic flexibility because they enjoy the autonomy of greater room to maneuver. Finally, a decision to rely more on people than on money encourages growth in strategic capacity when it encourages selection and development of more leaders who know how to strategize. The more strategists, the greater the flexibility with which an organization can pursue its objectives and the scale on which it can do so. Leaders' choices as to constituencies from whom to mobilize resources thus strongly influence their subsequent strategy.

Finally, as shown in row 6, accountability structures affect strategy by establishing routines for leadership selection and defining loci of responsiveness. Leaders accountable to those outside the operating environment may have been selected based on criteria that have little to do with knowledge of – or motivational connection with – constituencies within that environment. Leaders selected bureaucratically are more likely to possess skills and motivations compatible with bureaucratic success than with the creative work innovation requires. Leaders selected democratically are at least likely to have useful knowledge of the constituency that selected them and enough political skills to have been selected if that constituency is within one's operating environment. Entrepreneurial or self-selected leaders – in the sense that the undertaking is their initiative – are more likely to possess skills and intrinsic motivations associated with creative work. Although democratic and entrepreneurial leadership selections are in tension with one another, either may yield greater strategic capacity than bureaucratic leadership selection.

Liability of Senescence

It is a "given" of organization theory that the failure rate among new organizations is greater than that among old organizations – the "liability of newness". At the same time, scholars describe processes of organizational inertia that inhibit adaptation by old organizations to new environments, opening "niches" within which new organizations emerge – a liability of aging or "senescence." Differences in strategic capacity may explain why some new organizations do survive and at the same time account for less adaptive behavior by older organizations. Leaders of new organizations may have more strategic capacity because they were recently selected, have more organizational flexibility, and work in closer articulation with the environment. Leaders of old organizations often were selected in the past, are constrained by institutionalized routines, and may have the resources that allow them to operate in counterproductive insulation from the environment.

Focal Moments

Finally, because of the profound influence of leadership and organization on strategy, the choices leaders make at "focal moments," which reconfigure leadership and organization themselves, can create dramatically new strategic possibilities, including conditions for the emergence of a social movement. As I will show below, this is what took place with the UFW.

Summary

Returning to figure 26.1, this article argues that an organization is more likely to achieve positive outcomes if it develops effective strategy, and it is more likely to develop effective strategy if its leaders can access diverse sources of salient information, employ heuristic processes, and demonstrate deep motivation – their strategic capacity. Variation in strategic capacity, again, derives from differences in leaders' life experience, networks, and repertoires, and organizations' deliberative processes, resource flows, and accountability structures.

Organizing California's *Factories in the Field*

California's uniquely large-scale agricultural industry requires seasonal workers. It has also tried to protect itself from seasonal demands those workers make when organized. Growers solved this problem historically by employing workers who were politically, economically, and culturally disfranchised. Politically, their status as migrants, immigrants, or undocumented workers meant few farmworkers ever became voters. Economically, farmworkers were excluded from the 1935 National Labor Relations Act (NLRA), which conferred the right to organize on industrial workers. And culturally, the fact that farmworkers were most often recruited from communities of color placed them beyond the racially bounded concerns of many white Americans. As a result, local law enforcement usually stood ready to crush strikes through intimidation, injunctions, jailings, and violence, while state and federal officials could be counted upon to find alternative, usually immigrant, sources of labor.

Despite these challenges, since the 1880s, farmworkers made repeated attempts to organize. When ethnic minorities took the initiative, they usually formed ethnic labor associations. Chinese (1880s), Japanese (1900s), Mexican (1920s), and Filipino (1930s) farmworkers all tried one version or another, some of which were more successful than others, but all of which ultimately failed to yield the desired protection. Union attempts, on the other hand, with the exception of CAIWU, were usually made when or where Anglos constituted a major proportion of the workforce – such as IWW and AFL attempts to organize "fruit tramps" around 1910, CIO and Teamster attempts to organize "Okies" in the 1930s, and the AFL's National Farm Labor Union (NFLU) organizing attempt in the 1940s. None of these efforts succeeded in making lasting improvements in the lives of the workers, in building a stable membership base, or in getting union contracts.

In 1959, the year the AWOC was chartered, some 350,000 workers were employed in California agriculture, of whom some 90,000 were braceros – Mexican nationals imported as harvest hands under treaty between the United States and Mexico since 1942. The bracero program was at risk because of lobbying by farmworker advocacy groups, diminished demand for braceros outside California due to mechanization of cotton and tomato harvesting, opposition by Midwestern farmers to "privileges" afforded California agriculture, and concerns about domestic unemployment following the 1958 recession. In August, 1959, the Senate Subcommittee on Migratory Labor was formed, and on Thanksgiving day, 1960, Edward R. Murrow aired a graphic documentary on migrant farmworkers titled *Harvest of Shame*.

For these and other reasons, AFL-CIO President George Meany chartered the AWOC in February 1959 and shortly thereafter allocated it an organizing budget of $250,000 a year. Meany was influenced by the National Advisory Committee on Farm Labor, a citizen's group chaired by Eleanor Roosevelt with ties to church leaders, labor leaders, liberals, and Democratic politicians. Some labor leaders also believed that organizing agricultural workers could contribute to "curbing the political power of agribusiness" as "some of the most reactionary forces in the United States." Finally, because of their rivalry for leadership of the Federation, Meany hoped to avoid giving the "organizing issue" to Walter Reuther, president of the United Autoworkers and vice president of the AFL-CIO.

Early in 1961, as the AWOC seemed to be making progress, the Teamsters also declared an interest in farmworker organizing, signing a nominal contract with a lettuce grower whom the AWOC had struck. Then, in 1962, during a hiatus in AWOC

organizing, the independent National Farm Workers Association (NFWA), led by former community organizer Cesar Chavez, was founded and began organizing. By early 1966, however, it was the NFWA – not the AWOC or the Teamsters – that won the first genuine union contract in California agriculture. By 1970, as the United Farm Workers Organizing Committee (UFWOC, AFL-CIO), this union had brought the entire California table grape industry under contract, unionized some 70,000 workers, and achieved clearer success than any farm labor organizing effort in U.S. history.

The AWOC and the UFW, 1959–66

The following account compares choices made by AWOC and UFW leadership at three critical junctures: their organizational foundings (1959–65), the Delano Grape Strike (1965–66), and the Schenley Boycott (1966). After comparing their strategy – emphasizing differences in targeting, timing, and tactics – I contrast the leadership and organization of the two groups, demonstrating the difference in their strategic capacity.

Organizational Foundings, 1959–65

AWOC's strategy unfolded in two phases under two different directors. When chartered by the AFL-CIO in 1959, the AWOC was charged to organize farmworkers to improve their wages, hours, and working conditions and support efforts to repeal the bracero program. AWOC's strategy was to mobilize the workers, motivate them to pressure their employers, and get contracts. Although the struggle over the bracero program unfolded in a national, political, and long-term arena, AWOC's primary organizing mission was local, work centered, and short term.

The AWOC targeted workers based less on characteristics of the workers themselves than on workplace settings they deemed favorable for organizing. Although it operated for five years, AWOC's timing was short term and focused on visible results, quickly achieved. Its principal tactics – organizing at early morning pickup sites – or "shape-ups" – for wage strikes, exercising insider political pressure, and recruiting through labor contractors – extended a familiar repertoire of conventional labor union tactics that had served in quite different historical settings.

In contrast, during a brief volunteer phase in 1961 when it operated without "professional" leadership and found itself dependent for resources on its constituency, AWOC's strategy changed, anticipating that of the UFW by more than a year. AWOC activists targeted workers most likely to provide a long-term organizational base, rather than those whose workplaces seemed to offer short-term advantages. They took a longer-term time perspective, and their tactics mobilized around the broad range of farmworker needs, not only their work situation. As is shown below, this strategic consistency, the variation observed within it, and its ineffectiveness can be explained by changes in AWOC's leadership, the structure of its organization, and how these influenced its strategic capacity.

During the first phase (1959–61), under the direction of Norman Smith, the AWOC targeted workers who gathered daily for early morning shape-ups because they were "easier" to organize. These were mostly white single men, casual day laborers in very seasonal crops, a rapidly disappearing remnant of "dust bowlers" in an increasingly Mexican workforce. AWOC's tactics were to conduct leafleting campaigns among these workers and to call strikes to raise wages. During its first 18 months, the AWOC led more than 150 strikes, some of which yielded temporary wage increases, but it failed to produce stable membership or a union contract.

In early 1961, the AWOC shifted its tactics but continued targeting workers based on short-term political advantages and an "insider" political repertoire. AWOC leadership persuaded itself the new Democratic administration would enforce

bans against use of braceros as strike-breakers. Targeting lettuce growers who were major users of braceros, the AWOC mobilized unemployed domestic workers to picket them, persuaded the few domestic workers employed there to walk out, claimed the existence of a strike, and called on Labor Secretary Goldberg to order the braceros out. Despite costly contests in local courts, the effort met with initial success. It backfired, however, when organizers used violence to create a threat to the safety of the braceros so the Mexican consul would insist on their withdrawal. AWOC leaders were jailed and ended up with fines and legal bills approaching $50,000, which the AFL-CIO had to pay. When AFL-CIO auditors checked the books, they also found inflated membership reports. This offense, combined with a general lack of results and the existence of jurisdictional issues within the AFL-CIO, was enough for Meany to fire AWOC Director Smith, close down the AWOC, and transfer its members to other unions.

Significantly, however, during the nine months the AWOC was officially shut down – and a new leadership team emerged, operating within a different organizational structure – a new strategy also emerged based on mobilizing volunteer support among farmworkers, farmworker advocacy groups, and within the labor movement itself. Among farmworkers, AWOC volunteers targeted stable resident Mexican families, organizing them to create "area councils" around a number of community concerns including housing, health care, and so on. They convened farmworkers and supporters for a widely attended organizing conference in December 1961 and organized a very dramatic appeal at the national AFL-CIO meeting early in 1962. The ironic outcome was that the AFL-CIO refunded the AWOC – but also hired another "professional" director who returned to the old strategy.

The new director, A. C. Green, targeted labor contractors whom the AWOC could picket. Contractors were middlemen paid by growers to recruit workers, who often took advantage of their role as "brokers" to cheat workers and growers. When the picketing worked, contractors signed agreements making their workers AWOC members and deducted dues from the workers' pay. The intent was to produce immediate membership growth and, using contractors to control the labor supply, to get better terms from the growers. The membership grew, and the AWOC eventually signed 136 contractors. But there were hundreds more it could not sign up, the contractors had no control over what growers chose to pay, and workers learned an AWOC contract meant paying dues for nothing in return. The only positive, if unintended, result of the focus on contractors was that Green hired two Filipino labor organizers, including Larry Itliong, with ties to Filipino labor contractors or crew leaders. Filipino crew leaders had traditionally negotiated with growers on behalf of crews of skilled workers, serving as advocates as well as supervisors. The initiative of these crew leaders actually started the Delano Grape Strike (see below). By September 1965, on the eve of the grape strike, the AWOC had spent over $1,000,000 and had failed to create a genuine membership base or to sign a single contract with a grower.

The FWA, by contrast, which began organizing in 1962, developed a strategy of organizing a community of workers, developing mutual benefits to strengthen it, and then putting pressure on the employers to get contracts. The FWA leadership believed a critical error farmworker organizers had made in the past was in trying to strike and organize at the same time, the most recent evidence of which was the AWOC debacle in Imperial Valley the previous year. Unlike the AWOC, the NFWA saw its strategy unfolding in a community, statewide, and long-term arena.

The FWA targeted Mexican resident farmworker families who were the growing part of the workforce. A major center of this workforce was in Delano, the heart of the table grape industry, which provided one of the longest periods of employment in California agriculture. The FWA's tactics were to build a statewide association, blending community organizing techniques with a mutual benefit society and an ethnic labor association. Its timing extended over the five-year period the leaders believed would be required before they would be ready to confront the growers. The organizing began in the spring of 1962 with a statewide house meeting drive in farmworker communities, leading to a fall founding convention of the Association de Campesinos or Farm Workers Association. "Association" was selected to avoid turning away workers with negative experiences in earlier unionization attempts or provoking a premature reaction from the growers. "Campesino" was descriptive of the Mexican peasantry, whose movement since the Revolution was evocative of land, dignity, and resistance.

Within three years, the FWA had established a small death benefit, a social service program, credit union, newspaper (*El Malcriado*), its own flag, small treasury ($1,700), two paid staff, 1,500 members, and a capacity to engage in rent strikes, small work stoppages, and the like. Although largely self-sufficient to this point, in the summer of 1965, before the strike began, the NFWA applied for an Office of Economic Opportunity (OEO) grant of $500,000 to develop a range of cooperative community services for farmworkers. As we will see below, by the time the grant was awarded, circumstances had changed so dramatically that the NFWA decided to turn it down.

I now show how variation in the composition of the leadership and the organizational structure of the AWOC and the UFW not only yielded the difference in strategy described above, but a sharp difference in the underlying capacity to develop effective strategy – a point which becomes increasingly clear as events unfold.

Leadership

Salient differences among the leaders, staff, and volunteers of the two efforts become quite clear upon review of...biographical data including...age at the time participant undertook farmworker organizing; race or ethnicity; religion; regional background; position; family background; family status; education, work, and organizing experience; work commitment; network affiliation; and repertoires of collective action. [...]

AFL-CIO president George Meany, organizing director John Livingston, and AWOC directors Norman Smith and A. C. Green developed the AWOC strategy. All were white men, age 52 or over, with extensive union backgrounds and experience at "insider" politics. [...] [T]he men whom Meany and Livingston chose to lead the AWOC were of a generation of "union men" who valued "legitimate" ways to do union work and had little understanding of workers different from themselves or of a public whose support they would need. They had no biographical experience of the farmworker community, few sociocultural networks reaching beyond their milieu (much less into the farmworker community), and tactical repertoires learned by organizing people like themselves in circumstances far different from those they now faced. Smith, who had done no union organizing for 18 years, was chosen because of a relationship with Livingston going back to UAW organizing in Flint, Michigan, and because more likely candidates such as Ernesto Galarza or Clive Knowles were associated with rival international unions, neither of which Meany wanted to offend.

Among those who worked with the AWOC but remained outside the leadership circle, however, were the 17 organizers whom the AWOC hired, the farmworkers it was trying to organize, and community supporters. The life experience, networks, and tactical repertoires of many of these people – such as Father Tom McCullough, Henry Anderson, Dolores Huerta, Andy Arellano, Cipriano Delvo, Raul Aguilar, and Larry Itliong – linked them not only to the farmworker community, but to religious, student, and liberal groups as well. Most were younger, many were Mexican American or

Filipino, and a few were women. Dr. Ernesto Galarza, the Mexican academic who had worked with the NFLU since 1949, served as Smith's assistant for 6 months, until October 1959 when he resigned over jurisdictional concerns. His main role had been to instruct Smith and the organizers in how to document abuses of the bracero program, a mission he had pursued for the previous eight years. Since this staff was not party to AWOC decision making, however, no one making strategic choices had ties to the farmworker constituency or "local knowledge" of the conditions about which they were making choices. As a result, the organizing repertoires decision makers brought to this new situation constrained more than they enabled. The personal commitment motivating AWOC's leadership to find ways to make the effort successful was also very limited. Meany's commitment to the AWOC was minimal. His decisions about how much support to give were the result of political pressure from farmworker advocacy groups, their liberal allies, and his rival, Walter Reuther. For Livingston, Smith, and Green, organizing farmworkers was an assignment, not a mission.

The composition of the FWA leadership team was far different from that of the AWOC, combining insiders and outsiders, those with strong and weak ties, and a diversity of salient repertoires. The FWA strategy was developed by leaders who were Mexican and Mexican American men and women mostly under 35, whose lives were rooted in the farmworker community but extended well beyond it – such as Cesar Chavez, Dolores Huerta, and Gilbert Padilla. They worked in collaboration with two white clergymen affiliated with the California Migrant Ministry (CMM), Chris Hartmire and Jim Drake, both of whom were under 30 with middle-class backgrounds but who, as a result of their seminary experience, had come to share a vocation to improve the lives of farmworkers. FWA leaders thus drew on life experience that combined "local knowledge" of the farmworker world with experience in military service, college, small business, and professional organizing. The clergy brought "local knowledge" of religious groups and insight into the middle-class support constituency from which they themselves were drawn. Many of the leaders benefited from the insights of "borderland" experience as young Mexican Americans growing up in the 1940s. The leadership of the FWA also had a deep personal interest in finding ways to succeed at what was a personal mission. Not only had they come from farmworker backgrounds, they had given up secure jobs and other opportunities to risk building a new organization from the ground up. This combination of personal, vocational, and professional interests infused the effort with powerful motivation to develop a strategy that would make it work.

The range of sociocultural networks with which they were affiliated extended from the farmworker community into the worlds of community organizing, Mexican American activists, religious groups, and liberal circles throughout California. These networks combined strong ties to the farmworker community and the religious community with weak ties to many groups who would play important roles in the organizing.

Finally, their tactical repertoire grew out of their experience and training as professional community organizers, particularly within the Spanish-speaking community. But they also drew on some union experience (Huerta and Chavez), Catholic retreat training (Chavez), and electoral experience (Chavez, Huerta, Padilla). The house meeting drive and founding convention used to kick off the FWA, for example, was a tactic adapted from numerous local Community Service Organization (CSO) organizing drives to statewide purposes.

Neither the AWOC nor the FWA "had to" pursue the strategies they did – a fact demonstrated in AWOC's case by the alternate approach taken by volunteers during the organizational hiatus. To learn why the experience of its leaders imposed "limits" on the effectiveness of its strategy – and why the experience of FWA leaders was such a fruit-

ful source of strategy – we turn to the organizational setting within which strategy was developed.

Organization

While the FWA's deliberative structure was anchored in regular board meetings and inclusive strategy sessions, AWOC's deliberative structure provided no focal point for creative discussion. Within the AWOC, not only were there no advisory councils or farmworker committees, but staff meetings were irregular, lacked agendas, and were venues for announcements, not strategic reflection – especially after Galarza left. Either Director Smith or Director Green was in charge. They decided what to do. The organizers' job was to do what they were told. This severely limited opportunity for diverse perspectives to be heard, for reflection, and for learning. In the FWA, on the other hand, regular board meetings and strategy sessions anchored a deliberative process, which included a far wider leadership group (including Drake and Hartmire) in frequent discussion of the choices facing the organization.

Resources flowed from the top down within the AWOC, motivating the development of strategies that would satisfy those at the top, while the FWA's financial and human resources flowed upward, motivating the development of strategies that could yield the needed resources. For the AWOC, the main organizing resource was money to pay staff, cover organizing expenses, and maintain offices. The fact that dues were not a significant source of income meant there was limited motivation to create a financial base among workers. The AWOC also had little motivation to generate volunteer participation from farmworkers or supporters, relying on paid staff to do its work. The FWA's financial resources, on the other hand, were based on membership dues of $3.50/month per family, which were collected in cash by local representatives. Dues entitled member families to a small death benefit, social services, membership in the credit union, and a newspaper. Chavez's personal savings and individual contributions from supporters supplemented these resources. The UFW's human resources included one intermittently paid staff member (Chavez earned $50 a week), which grew to three staff members by 1965 (with the addition of Huerta and Bill Esher, newspaper editor). In addition, the CMM paid Padilla part time and offered the services of Drake and Hartmire as needed and available. Most of the organization's work, however, was done on a volunteer basis by board members, representatives, and other activists – resting on maintenance of the extraordinary level of motivation that underlay the whole undertaking.

The accountability structure of the AWOC was based on a chain of command that precluded input from those below the top levels at which strategy was discussed, while that of the FWA was based on responsiveness to the farmworker community and to those doing the daily work of the organization. AWOC's bureaucratic command structure was viewed as the only source of strategic legitimacy within the organization. As an organizing committee of the AFL-CIO, Meany appointed its directors, on the recommendation of Livingston, and the directors, in turn, hired the staff who reported to them. There was no advisory board of supporters, accountability mechanism to farmworkers, or role for farmworker leadership within this chain of command. Not even Livingston was permitted to sit in on Executive Council settings in which Meany formulated strategy. The FWA, on the other hand, was built around a six-person executive board (Chavez, Huerta, Padilla, Orendain, Terronez, and Hernandez) elected by farmworker delegates at the founding convention. It was led by a full-time president, part-time volunteer officers, and a network of appointed local representatives in each community. Chavez, Huerta, and the others had also "selected themselves" for this mission.

Strategic Capacity

Differences in deliberative processes, resource flows, and accountability structures interacted with differences in the composition of leadership teams to create far greater strategic capacity for the UFW than for the AWOC. AWOC's extremely narrow deliberative process limited the quality of leaders' thinking by excluding the diverse – and more salient – perspectives of others in and around the AWOC. The top-down resource flow meant not even AWOC directors had autonomy to develop strategy that assigned first priority to the mission of organizing farmworkers. This is illustrated when Meany shut down the AWOC in 1961 and assigned Green to do political work for the better part of 1962, his first year as AWOC director. The fact that AWOC's leadership was not accountable to farmworkers meant the concerns of Meany and Livingston would always carry the day. "Getting quick results" or "building up the membership numbers" had a far greater influence on Smith and Green than would have been the case if they had to deal with an organized farmworker constituency whose reactions they had to consider as well. Ironically, the top-down accountability structure and resource flows yielded little motivation to develop organizing strategies that could produce resources – financial resources through worker dues or contributions of supporters, or human resources such as volunteering by farmworkers and others. AWOC leaders had the resources to keep making the same mistakes, as long as the people at the top were satisfied.

FWA leadership, on the other hand, made the most of its capacity because of organizational arrangements it made. FWA's deliberative process assured extensive and diverse input. Inclusion of the clergy infused the conversation with input from those not in a direct chain of command and thus more likely to argue their own point of view. FWA leaders drew heavily – but not exclusively – on the farmworker community for both human and financial resources. Need for these resources motivated development of strategy that would successfully expand its membership and base. FWA's accountability structure also tied its leadership to those whose active support was needed if the enterprise was to succeed. Although it was based on election by a farmworker convention, on a day-to-day basis, as members of a "committed band," leaders were accountable to each other, including Chavez and the officers, through board meetings. The leaders were thus motivated to devise effective strategy and enjoyed the autonomy to act on strategy they devised – single-mindedly pursuing a farmworker organizing agenda. This had the consequence that the FWA would make its allies uncomfortable from time to time but never find itself so dependent upon any one of them that a supporter's priorities would supplant its own.

The contrast between AWOC and FWA leadership in terms of access to salient information, heuristic facility, and motivation could not have been greater. The diverse experience of FWA leadership, working in a productive organizational setting, allowed it to develop strategy more effectively than the AWOC. Although the AWOC had access to far richer leadership resources than it utilized, it structured itself to preclude their engagement in the development of strategy – which was developed by those least well equipped to do so. The differences in outcomes achieved by the two organizations during this founding period were more than the result of "mistakes" on the part of the AWOC and "brilliance" on the part of the UFW. As FWA leaders drew on their strategic capacity to devise the targeting, timing, and tactics with which it could achieve its goals, what emerged was something new: a combination ethnic labor association, mutual benefit society, and community organization. And, when these tactics did not work, the leaders had also developed the capacity to change.

[...]

Conclusions

This article began by posing the question of why organizing success came to the fledgling UFW and not to the well-established union with which it found itself in competition. Studying the influence of strategy reveals the role of resourcefulness in power – as mythically memorialized in tales of David and Goliath or Odysseus and the Trojans. One way groups compensate for a lack of material resources is through creative strategy, a function of access to a diversity of salient information, heuristic facility, and motivation – a result of the way the composition of leadership teams and organizational structures influence interaction with the environment. Changing environments generate new opportunities – and constraints – but the significance of those opportunities or constraints emerges from the hearts, heads, and hands of the actors who develop the means of acting upon them.

As summarized in table 26.2, the source of difference in the strategic capacity of the two groups was in observable differences in leadership and organization. The contrast in the biography, networks, and repertoires of the leadership and deliberative processes, resource flows, and accountability structures of the organizations could not have been greater. Because strategy unfolds as a process, it is important to pay attention to the mechanisms that generate it – not only to the role of specific strategies in specific outcomes. Since strategy is interactive, getting it "right" in a big way is likely to be evidence of having learned how to "get it right" in numerous small ways – and doing it time after time. This can only be studied by observing organizations over time.

The UFW's strategy thus turned out to be more effective than that of the AWOC because of the way in which it was developed. It drew on elements of an ethnic labor association (reminiscent of earlier organizing attempts by farmworkers of color), a union, and community organizing drives in a new synthesis that went far beyond its individual components as its founders engaged environmental challenges by adapting familiar repertoires to new uses. The UFW's response to the crisis precipitated by the grape strike was to draw on the Civil Rights movement to reframe its effort as a farmworker movement. This then led to development of a "dual strategy" based on mobilization of workers (without whom there would have been no people, no cause, and no movement) along with the mobilization of urban supporters (without whom there would have been no financial, political, and economic resources). By recontextualizing the arena of combat to reach beyond the fields to the cities, the UFW turned the moral tables on the growers, exposing what growers considered to be a legitimate exercise of their authority as illegitimate in the public domain (much as had occurred in the Civil Rights movement). The significance of this strategic stream for this article is not in its particulars – although it points to important

lessons about targeting, timing, and tactics – but in that it emerged from a strategic capacity that could have generated a different strategic stream in different circumstances.

[...]

Finally, this approach offers fresh ways to make intractable problems actionable by holding out the possibility of change. People can generate the power to resolve grievances not only if those with power decide to use it on their behalf, but also if they can develop the capacity to out-think and outlast their opponents – a matter of leadership and organization. As students of "street smarts" have long understood, "resourcefulness" can sometimes compensate for a lack of resources. While learning about how the environment influences actors is very important, learning more about how actors influence the environment is the first step not only to understanding the world, but to changing it.

[...]

Table 26.2 Comparison of AWOC and UFW strategic capacity

	AWOC	UFW
Leadership:		
Biography	Little diversity of experience	Diversity of experience
	No salient local knowledge	Salient local knowledge, broader context
	Professional commitment	Personal, vocational commitment
Networks	No strong ties to constituency	Strong ties to constituencies
	Few salient weak ties	Weak ties across constituencies
	Little diversity of ties	Diversity of ties
Repertoires	No salience to constituencies	Salience to constituencies
	Little diversity of repertoires	Diversity of repertoires
Organization:		
Deliberation	No regular meetings	Regular meetings
	No strategy sessions	Regular strategy sessions
	Closed to diverse perspectives	Open to diverse perspectives
	Not authoritative	Authoritative
Resource flows	Resources flow top down	Resources flow bottom up
	Resources flow from outside: single source	Resource flow inside and outside: multiple sources
	Resources depend on internal politics	Resources depend on task effectiveness
	Based on financial resources	Based on people resources
	Little strategic autonomy	Strategic autonomy
Accountability	No constituency accountability	Constituency accountability
	Hierarchical accountability	Mutual accountability
	Bureaucratic leadership selection	Democratic, entrepreneurial selection

Note

1 The union which has called itself the United Farm Workers (UFW) since 1972 called itself the Farm Workers Association (FWA) from 1962 to 1964, the National Farm Workers Association from 1964 to 1966 (NFWA), and the United Farm Workers Organizing Committee (UFWOC) from 1966 to 1972. When referring to the organization in general, I use the designation "UFW," but when referring to it in a specific historical context, as I do in most of this article, I use the name that was used at the time.

References

Alinsky, Saul. 1971. *Rules for Radicals*. New York: Watage.

Amabile, Theresa M. 1996. "A Theoretical Framework." Pp. 81–130 in *Creativity in Context*. Boulder, Colo.: Westview Press.

Jenkins, J. Craig, and Charles Perrow. 1977. "Insurgency of the Powerless: Farm Worker Movements in the U.S." *American Sociological Review* 42:429–68.

McCarthy, John D., and Meyer N. Zald. 1977. "Resource Mobilization and Social Movements: A Partial Theory." *American Journal of Sociology* 8(6): 1212–41.

Stinchcombe, Arthur. 1965. "Social Structure and Organizations." Pp. 143–53 in *Handbook of Organizations*, edited by James G. March. Chicago: Rand McNally.

27 The Media in the Unmaking of the New Left

Todd Gitlin

With the SDS March on Washington on April 17, 1965, student antiwar protest – and SDS activity in particular – became big news. Now reporters began to seek out SDS leaders and to cover protest events. That spring, major articles on the New Left appeared in news-magazines (*Newsweek, Time, U.S. News & World Report*), large-circulation weeklies (the *Saturday Evening Post*, the *New York Times Magazine*), and liberal weeklies (the *Nation*, the *New Republic*, the *Reporter*); and television news produced its own survey pieces. The movement was amplified.

But which movement? The observer changed the position of the observed. The amplification was already selective: it emphasized certain themes and scanted others. Deprecatory themes began to emerge, then to recur and reverberate. The earliest framing devices were these:

- *Trivialization* (making light of movement language, dress, age, style, and goals);
- *Polarization* (emphasizing *counter*demonstrations, and balancing the antiwar movement against ultra-Right and neo-Nazi groups as equivalent "extremists");
- *Emphasis on internal dissension*;
- *Marginalization* (showing demonstrators to be deviant or unrepresentative);
- *Disparagement by numbers* (undercounting); and
- *Disparagement of the movement's effectiveness*.

In the fall, as parts of the antiwar movement turned to more militant tactics, new themes and devices were added to the first group:

- *Reliance on statements by government officials and other authorities*;
- *Emphasis on the presence of Communists*;
- *Emphasis on the carrying of "Viet Cong" flags*;
- *Emphasis on violence in demonstrations*;
- *Delegitimizing use of quotation marks* around terms like "peace march"; and
- *Considerable attention to right-wing opposition to the movement*, especially from the administration and other politicians.

Some of this framing can be attributed to traditional assumptions in news treatment: news concerns the *event*, not the underlying condition; the *person*, not the group; *conflict*, not consensus; the fact that "*advances the story*," not the one that explains it. Some of this treatment descends from norms for the coverage of deviance in general: the archetypical news story is a crime story, and an opposition movement is ordinarily, routinely, and unthinkingly treated as a sort of crime. Some of the treatment follows from organizational and technical features of news coverage – which in turn are not ideologically neutral. Editors assign reporters to beats where news is routinely framed by officials; the stories then absorb the officials' definitions of the situation. And editors and reporters also adapt and reproduce the dominant ideological assumptions prevailing in the wider society. All these practices are anchored in organizational policy, in recruitment and promotion: that is to say, in the internal structure of institutional power and decision. And when all these sources are taken into account, some of the framing will still not be explained unequivocally; some must be understood as the product of specifically political transactions, cases of editorial judgment and the interventions of political elites. The proportion of a given frame that emanates from each of these sources varies from story to story; that is why stories have to be scrutinized one by one, as concretely as possible, before we can begin to compose general theories.

When we examine stories closely, we discover that there were exceptional moments of coverage within both the *Times* and CBS News. Not only was there – within the boundaries of the norms – some latitude for expressions of individual idiosyncrasy, for random perturbations within the general terms of the code; there were also larger conflicts within the news organizations about how to cover the movement, conflicts that were fought and resolved in different ways at different times. The overall effect of media coverage was blurred and contradictory; there was not a single voice. But increasingly the impression was conveyed that extremism was rampant and that the New Left was dangerous to the public good.

In short, the media were far from mirrors passively reflecting facts found in the real world. The facts reported were out there in the real world, true: out there *among others*. The media reflection was more the active, patterned remaking performed by mirrors in a fun house.

As media actively engaged the movement, an adversary symbiosis developed. Within the movement, arguments emerged about how best to cope with the new situation. Some groupings within the movement stayed on the defensive; others turned to the offense. In neither case was it possible to ignore the media spotlight, or to turn it at will to the movement's own uses.

Some movement organizers responded casually, at first, to the media's attentions. Their commitment to face-to-face organization remained primary; in their view, the press would play a secondary role in transmitting news and images to uncommitted publics. They were working within a pre-

spotlight organizational form; they were eager to maintain the movement's own distinct communication channels. But in the fall of 1965, media attention and right-wing attacks caught them by surprise. The strategy they improvised called for a sort of judo operation: using the weight of the adversary to bring him down. They would use the unsought media attention to amplify the antiwar message. They began to speak into the symbolic microphone.

Others, committed to an antiwar movement before all else, and operating mostly outside SDS, began to organize symbolic events deliberately to attract the media spotlight. Very small groups of draft-card burners could leap to national prominence. Three pacifists, trying to awaken a national conscience, immolated themselves and died. Some within SDS proposed attention-getting actions – later called "media events" – that would, they hoped, place the issue of the war at the focus of national politics. Galvanizing opposition, even repression, from the administration or from the political Right could be a means to that end.

As the spotlight kept on burning, media treatment entered into the movement's internal life. The media helped recruit into SDS new members and backers who expected to find there what they saw on television or read in the papers. The flood of new members tended to be different from the first SDS generation – less intellectual, more activist, more deeply estranged from the dominant institutions. Politically, many of them cared more about antiwar activity than about the broad-gauged, long-haul, multi-issued politics of the earlier SDS. They were only partially assimilated into the existing organization; they viewed the SDS leaders, the remnants of the founding generation, with suspicion. The newcomers overwhelmed SDS's fragile institutions, which had been created for a tiny organization, a network of so-called Old Guard elite clusters living in intense political and personal community. The fragile person-to-person net of organizational continuity was torn.

This new generation coursed into SDS in the wake of the April 1965 antiwar march, and by June 1966 they had moved into the key positions of leadership. They were known as the Prairie Power people, underscoring – and at times exaggerating – their non-Northeastern, non-elite origins. True, this generation *did* differ from the founders in many ways; the distinction cannot be laid purely and simply at the door of the media and their selectivities. For one thing, the Old Guard elite had already graduated from college, many from elite colleges at that; many had moved into Northern ghettoes as community organizers. Most of the new leaders, by contrast, were still students at state universities. Coming from more conservative regions, Texas and the Great Plains primarily, many of the new generation had become radical quickly, because even mild rebellion against right-wing authority – hair grown slightly long, language grown obscene, or the like – provoked repression. If one were to be punished for small things, it was only a small step to declaring oneself an outlaw in earnest, a communist, a revolutionary: as soon be hanged for a sheep as a goat. So, as cultural rebels, they tended to skip the stage of consciousness that marked the Old Guard generation and informed its politics: a *radical disappointment* with existing liberal institutions, liberal promises, and liberal hopes. In style, too, they declared their deep disaffection from the prevailing culture: many were shaggy in appearance, they smoked dope, they had read less, they went for broke. Even Northeastern members of the Prairie Power leadership shared the new style.

The media not only helped produce and characterize this sharp break within SDS, but they proceeded to play it up; in so doing, they magnified its importance – both to the outside world and inside the organization. When it happened that, as the former SDS National Secretary wrote in December 1965, "chapters, regional offices, and members find out what the organization is doing by reading the newspapers," mass-mediated images were fixing (in the photo-graphic sense) the terms for internal debate; they were helping define the organization's situation for it. Again, none of this happened in a vacuum. The drastic escalation in the war was at the same time pushing many people, both in and out of SDS, toward greater militancy, greater estrangement from dominant American values. The default of liberal forces isolated the whole generation of radical youth, pushing them toward the left. Larger cultural forces were nourishing the possibility of a deviant counterculture. But the media blitz, by amplifying and speeding all these processes, prevented SDS from assimilating them. The organization tried – and failed. Thus the internal frailties that were later to undo the organization were already built in at the moment of its greatest growth and vigor. In its beginning as a mass organization was its end.

[...]

Celebrity as Career: Performing

The career of Jerry Rubin personifies another course, another variant of pyramiding and a greater, typically American success: the slide toward inflated rhetoric that followed from the celebrity conferred by the mass media. Rubin had been involved in the Free Speech Movement of 1964 and had headed the Vietnam Day Committee of 1965; each had been made to appear both trivial and outlandish by the media. So when Rubin was subpoenaed by the House Un-American Activities Committee (HUAC) in the summer of 1966, he was inventive enough to try to devise a stratagem which would permit him to make a political critique of HUAC despite the interference of the image-transmitting process. He thus situated himself in the avant-garde artistic tradition of straining for effect.

R. G. Davis, then the director of the San Francisco Mime Troupe (and no relation to Rennie), remembers talking with Rubin in the Café Mediterraneum in Berkeley about tactics for his impending appearance before HUAC: "What image was good for him? We talked about the variable of what you could dress like. And we talked about it a lot. I suggested that he come up in an American Revolutionary costume....It seemed to me that *they might not report what he had to say, but they would take a picture of him*. It was unlikely that the press would have listened to his statement."

Experienced activists had learned that they could not determine which of their words, if any, would end up on the air. A twenty-minute interview or speech might be recorded, and a fifteen-second clip would end up on the evening news. So R. G. Davis and Rubin applied themselves to the judo tack: turning the unavoidable spotlight to some political advantage. Davis goes on:

> I think there was general agreement that if you had a long statement and you answered questions, they still would distort....I don't know how we got there, but I remember firmly saying, "The American Revolution was an easy [image] to get, and it would be a great statement about freedom of speech." Here was a solid image that everyone would recognize as a real contradiction. A House Committee that is investigating what people think and say! And the contradiction would be obvious if you could get it across that way. It felt to me like the dollar, you know, the straight image of America. He thought that was a good idea. He said he was going to do it.

Rubin did wear the American Revolutionary costume before HUAC, and his image was broadcast far and wide. Rubin's act of devout derision helped discredit the Committee on campuses. On top of the small fame of the Vietnam Day demonstrations of 1965, Rubin's appearance gave him a national reputation not only within the movement but outside it; it launched his career as a purveyor of conspicuous symbols. *Because of the media's procedures for identifying and confirming leaders, and his skill in manipulating them, and because of the weakness of the movement's organizations*, he was able to operate for years as a freelance broad-caster of symbols, outside any sizable organization, speaking for "youth," for "the movement," and for any action he thought represented his shadow Yippie group.

This made him a celebrity if not a leader; after he left Berkeley to organize the March on the Pentagon in 1967, he had no organized base. Many of his peers disliked what they saw as his egotism, and many resented him as a usurper of the spotlight; this resentment probably drove him still further toward flamboyance and unaccountability. His own desire for the spotlight, undoubtedly the product of several political and personal purposes, matched the media's need for quotable, eccentric, engagingly wacky personalities. Again, though, the issue is not simply personality but the structure of movement assumptions, tolerances, and vulnerabilities. One of Rubin's co-workers in the Berkeley antiwar movement, Michael P. Lerner, recalls a widespread feeling in the movement there that Rubin's "ego was so offensive they had to smash it." Lerner argues that this antagonism explains "not only why Jerry left Berkeley, but...why Jerry then moved toward the politics which he didn't really believe in. And he moved toward it for opportunistic reasons." By Lerner's account, only a few months before Jerry helped found the Youth International Party in 1967, "Jerry wasn't a Yippie":

> His reaction at first to the hip phenomenon was curiosity, interest, but not identification. So what was happening was that as the more straight-line political people were giving him less and less place to be a political person, presumably because of his great sin of wanting to have his name in the paper, or his face on TV, ... he began to move more and more to trying to find a politics that would give him a space for... getting some kind of personal recognition and allowing for him to be who he was.

Deprived by resentful constituents of the chance to use the media *legitimately* as political amplification, but still committed to that use of both media and themselves, Rubin and other such leaders were isolated.

As Lerner puts it, "they were driven to the media as their base when their own base abandoned them."

But sustained media performance requires a recognizable persona, an objectified quasi-identity like a newscaster's or a comedian's. Lerner's theory draws support from a notion proposed by the old Berkeley movement hand Michael Rossman: that Rubin's Yippie show was a willed fusion of hippie and politico styles for media consumption. In an open letter of March 1968, Rossman – himself an anti-leader partial to the styles and projects that for shorthand can be called "hippie" – wrote to Rubin: "Years ago I asked one of my students what she thought of Leary and his League of Spiritual Discovery, traveling pitchman selling the Way. 'Leary,' she said, 'is a Harvard professor who dropped acid.' Don't become known as a politico who dropped acid, Jerry."

Rubin acquired a *following* instead of a face-to-face political base. His following was organized precisely as a mass media audience: atomized, far-flung, episodic, not alive politically except when mobilized in behalf of centralized symbols of revolt. Among all the movement leader-celebrities of the late sixties, Rubin enjoyed the quintessential notoriety, moving from the leadership of one improvised, occasional organization to another: from the Berkeley mayoral race of April 1966 to the San Francisco Be-In of January 1967, to the March on the Pentagon in October 1967, to Yippie and the Chicago demonstrations of August 1968. By then, he and the rest of the Yippie handful were almost automatically news. He learned that he could make news by playing the role "Jerry Rubin." With Abbie Hoffman, Paul Krassner, and occasional others, he could call press conferences and infuse the Youth International Party with a solid reputation for size and significance. As Michael Rossman wrote to him, "In our developing theology of organizing, you're into the Leadership Heresy; Yippie is a hippy bureaucracy that decrees." Although his media-summoned constituency failed to descend on Chicago for the demonstrations in 1968,

Rubin's celebrity status remained untouched, for the Chicago city government, the police, and the national apparatus of repression took his media reputation at face value and thereby ratified it. In the fall of 1968, he dressed up again for the cameras in a confused uniform of Indian war paint, hippie beads, Vietnamese sandals, and a toy machine gun – a living emblem of the confusion of iconographic realms in the late days of the New Left, and of the counterculture's insensitive, mechanical appropriation of the insignia of oppressed peoples. The underground papers, themselves severed from day-to-day political life and growing wild with revolutionism, joined the national media in amplifying this mishmash.

And then the Chicago Conspiracy trial of 1969–70, which Rubin construed as a sort of reward for his rebellion and revelry, provided him an almost daily stage for his continuing show. Stanhope Gould, the field producer who supervised much of CBS's coverage of the trial, remembers accompanying Rubin and Abbie Hoffman with a camera crew on their speaking engagements. Why Rubin and Hoffman rather than, say, Rennie Davis, Tom Hayden, or Dave Dellinger? I asked Gould. "Because they were the most colorful and symbolic of the [Chicago] Seven," Gould said. By contrast, Gould had earlier produced and edited a takeout on Rennie Davis when Rennie had been subpoenaed by HUAC before the Nixon inauguration ("in-hog-uration") protest of January 1969. Replete with "lots of long-lens, artsy-craftsy stuff," by Gould's account, this "mood piece" of five or six minutes meant to explain how Rennie Davis, the son of one of President Truman's Council of Economic Advisors, had grown into a radical leader; and thus Gould intentionally omitted a balancing spokesman of the HUAC type. Because the piece wasn't balanced, Gould's superior, Russ Bensley, the top CBS News producer in charge of takeouts, canceled it. Over the ten years that Gould worked for the Cronkite News, this was one of the very few pieces he completed that was not aired; he had violated an outer limit which had not been drawn clearly until after the fact. But the standard that ruled out a respectful investigation of Rennie Davis's political evolution permitted coverage of more "colorful and symbolic" – and more easily dismissible – movement celebrities. Yippie avant-garde defiance was permissible as entertainment; sympathetic treatment of a would-be organizer of communities was not.

Rubin's performances were not devoid of method or strategy; rather, they were justified by an explicit theory of revolution. Rubin believed that his self-dramatizations, and the spectacular events they accompanied, mobilized oppositional consciousness and revolutionary action. His concept of mass organization mirrored the mass media's theory of itself. The mass media try to turn the audience into replicas of the ideal consumer; Jerry Rubin believed he could turn part of his audience, youth, into replicas of himself, and inspire them to reproduce the symbolic events he and the media could define as revolutionary actions. Ché Guevara had called for "two, three...many Vietnams" throughout the Third World; in the spring of 1968, Tom Hayden had called for "two, three...many Columbias." If "two, three...many Columbias," why not two, three...many Chicagos, Yippies, Rubins? In January 1970, on a day off from the Conspiracy trial in Chicago, R. G. Davis taped a discussion with Rubin in which Rubin articulated his theory of media effect:

> The year after Chicago, there were more demonstrations on college and high school campuses than any other year. And I would say it was directly and psychologically related to Chicago, the memory and myth of Chicago. People sang, "I miss Chicago." There was a riot in Berkeley the week after Chicago. Chicago reached people through the media. It became a myth in their own heads, it became exaggerated way out of proportion. And they tried to act it out in their own situation thanks to Chicago.

Rubin went on to argue that "FSM [the Free Speech Movement] created Columbia,

thanks to the media." Davis objected: "But Columbia was so many years after FSM." Rubin responded:

> But dig this: the kids who watched FSM were ten, eleven years old. Five years later, campuses were up all over the country. And it wasn't through traditional political organizing – reading books, and getting leaflets and hearing arguments. It was through being turned on by something they saw on television.

Rubin argued that mobilization through media "doesn't negate the micro" level of local organizing; "we were just on a macro level." But his contempt for the written word spoke more loudly. Rubin's confusion between image and reality was shared by much of his youthful audience, raised on television as it had been; Rubin's genius was to transpose that confusion into a theory of revolutionary mobilization. In his conception, the revolutionary mass was just that: a *mass*, to be "turned on" by media buttons. Since in this view the revolutionary task reduced itself to mobilizing that passive mass for a specific action – an assumption similar to conventional marketing assumptions – the problem of the mobilizer was simply instrumental: not whether or why to mobilize for a newsworthy action, but *how*?

Of course, Rubin could only have thrived as a celebrity if the media reported him. That he was "colorful and symbolic" *even when he explicitly violated approaches more legitimate in the movement* was the basis of his success as a celebrity. *It was precisely the isolated leader-celebrities, attached indirectly to unorganized constituencies reached only through mass media, unaccountable to rooted working groups, who were drawn toward extravagant, "incidental," expressive actions – actions which made "good copy" because they generated sensational pictures rich in symbolism.* They were repelled by the movement and attracted by the media at the same time. This logic of symbiosis was to reach one culmination, appropriately enough, in the Symbionese

Liberation Army of 1973: a tiny group with no actual political base kidnapped a newspaper heiress and hijacked the spotlight with a memorable hydra-headed logo, some extravagant rhetoric ("Death to the fascist insect!"), and a political program that, only a few years later, no one remembers.

Celebrity as Trap: Abdicating

One distinct alternative to the pyramiding process in the movement was to refuse leadership altogether. A leader abdicated if he or she was no longer willing or able to withstand the conflicting demands of the media world and the movement base, and was unwilling to step up the tension (double or nothing) by leaping further into the glittering, envy-provoking, fickle world of celebrity. Since the movement was not clear about the difference between legitimate leadership and authoritarianism, leaders were reluctant to lead; and at the same time, internal criticism veered into ad hominem attacks. The resulting binds stepped up the pressure on leaders who were already deeply unsure of the basis of their authority. And so abdication was a strikingly common way out. Staughton Lynd was one of the better-known leaders who chose that route; Mario Savio of the Berkeley Free Speech Movement was another; a third was Robert Moses of the Student Nonviolent Coordinating Committee.

Moses was perhaps the most inspiring of the early SNCC leaders, one of the first to organize in dangerous Mississippi, a man whose courage, clarity, and stature in the movement were extraordinary. But especially as SNCC formalized its structure, Bob Moses could not believe in the authority he exercised. At a tumultuous meeting of the SNCC staff in February 1965, Moses renounced not only his leadership but his very name. One SNCC worker wrote this account at the time:

> Bob Moses came in Monday night after the structure and the elections were done, drunk. He had been fighting all weekend, fairly or unfairly, rightly or wrongly, for the voice of the silent people – the Negroes in Mississippi, the quiet bewildered staff. He had been saying that "if you want to have slaves, you had better give them the vote and call them free men, because that's the only way the world will let you do it." So now he was drunk. First he shared cheese, bread, and an empty bottle of wine. Then he spoke....First he announced that he had changed his name – he was no longer Robert Parris Moses, but Robert Parris [his mother's name]. He didn't want to be, and he wasn't the myth we had created. He wanted to be a person again. No one had shouted him down in the past few days, because he was Robert Moses. Now he would be Robert Parris.

Bob Moses soon left SNCC altogether, worked in early antiwar projects, and then abandoned the United States for over a decade in Africa.

Mario Savio, the most visible FSM leader, also rejected his own leadership in the course of criticizing the movement's "excessively undemocratic character." His parting words were strikingly close to Bob Moses's: "If the action isn't organized by you," he told a noon rally on the steps of Sproul Hall, April 26, 1965, "it's not worth being organized." "Lest I feel deserving of the charge of 'Bonapartism' which even I sometimes have made against myself, I'd like to wish you good luck and goodbye." Not only did the media assign Savio a power that his own political base did not, to make matters worse, the same media which granted him celebrity also flayed him unmercifully. The status conferred by the media was an ambiguous gift – and for a sensitive person, wrenching.

Indeed, all the celebrated movement leaders suffered from an enormous breach between the status conferred by the media and the support they could not muster from co-leaders and constituents. Breach easily became tension, and the tension could be devastating. The abdicators refused to be the victims of the conflicting demands

made upon them; to save themselves from
the dissociation of the looking glass, they
removed themselves from leadership altogether. And then the movement suffered
from the loss of its more sensitive leaders;
the field was left to those less vulnerable to
peer criticism, less accountable to base.

Alternatives for Leadership

Between abdication and the pyramiding of
celebrity, there remained one slender choice:
to try to use the media straightforwardly to
broadcast ideas, without getting trapped in
celebrity's routines. Many counted this the
ideal choice; most spotlit leaders believed
this was, in fact, what they were doing, and
often they were making the attempt. But
resisting the temptation of converting celebrity to outright stardom – playing court jester
on the campus circuit or on talk shows,
trying to slip one's few sentences about
racism or war between commercials and
Hollywood gossip – took enormous self-
discipline. Experience was not sufficient
guide. The inconsistent anti-authoritarianism
of the white radical movement worked havoc
on Paul Booth, on Rennie Davis, on Mario
Savio, and on a good number of others.

The question arises then: in what circumstances could movements succeed in holding
their leaders accountable, keep them from
departing into the world of celebrity, and
encourage them instead to use the media
for political ends while minimizing damage
to leaders and movement both? For one
thing, a youth movement in a culture that
celebrates youth is probably especially prone
to the pressures and consequences of celebrity. Its leaders, lacking the adult rewards of
career and family, are more dependent on
the media for esteem; youth amidst the
mass culture market feels entitled to fame,
whether as rock star, athlete, or activist.
Each way, the personal importance of access
to media gets inflated. But more, a movement that could agree on goals and positions
would permit its leaders less discretion to
create policy in front of the cameras. The

New Left, again, refused the self-discipline
of explicit programmatic statement until too
late – until, that is, the Marxist-Leninist
sects filled the vacuum with dogmas, with
clarity on the cheap. And finally, a movement organization could agree on formal
procedures to review a leader's mass-
mediated presentations. The movement
would struggle to align its leaders with its
policies, while leaders and constituents
would agree on the prerogatives and obligations of each role. The issue, at bottom, is
whether a movement can develop clear
standards for what it expects from leaders,
standards which do not jam its leaders into
double binds; and whether leaders can avert
celebrity's traps without abandoning leadership altogether.

The New Left met none of these conditions; thus its peculiar vulnerability to the
spotlight. The pressure of political events
intensified the strain on its structural weaknesses. And so it was difficult for any leader
to maintain a plain, consistent, utilitarian
approach to the media: to use the spotlight
without getting burned up. Even more so
because on the seemingly revolutionary
wave of the late sixties, it seemed more and
more that the way to be assured of access to
that spotlight was to look and sound ever
more extravagant.

[. . .]

Implications for Movements

Straining to take advantage of the media's
interest in "exciting" or "important" news,
opposition movements step into this web of
conflicting yet interdependent corporate and
State powers. One core task of opposition
movements is to contest the prevailing definitions of things, the dominant frames. They
must "rectify names," they must change the
way people construe the world, they must
penetrate and unmask what they see as the
mystification sustained by the powers that
be. In this sense, all insurgent movements
must be empirical in their approach to the
conventional definitions of objective reality;

they must probe to discover *in practice* how far the principles of news "objectivity" can be severed both from the disparaging codes and from the corporate and State interests that sustain and delimit them.

Since the sixties, opposition movements have become still more sensitive to the impact of the media on their messages and their identities. At one extreme, the Symbionese Liberation Army learned how to manage an exercise in total manipulation, commandeering the media for a moment of spurious glory. At the other, the women's liberation movement, recognizing some of the destructive and self-destructive consequences of the spotlight, has learned from the experience of the New Left and worked with *some* success to decentralize leadership and "spokespersonship," avoiding *some* (not all) of the agonies of the single-focused spotlight. This is after much trial and much error. The results are uneven.

To what extent have the terms of hegemony been renegotiated? Hegemony exists in historical time, and its boundaries are adjustable as the media adjust to new social realities. *The more closely the concerns and values of social movements coincide with the concerns and values of elites in politics and in media, the more likely they are to become incorporated in the prevailing news frames.* Since the sixties, for example, consumer organizations have been elevated to the status of regular news makers; they and their concerns are reported with sympathy, sufficiently so as to inspire corporate complaints and counter-propaganda in the form of paid, issue-centered advertising. Ralph Nader and other public-interest lawyers have become respected celebrities, often interviewed for response statements, photographed in suits and ties and sitting squarely behind desks or in front of bookshelves, embodying solid expertise and mainstream reliability. They have learned to make the journalistic code work for them, while journalists have extended them the privilege of legitimacy. At times, environmentalist groups like the Sierra Club have been adept at using the media to publicize particular issues and to

campaign for particular reforms. In the seventies, the prestigious media policymakers have legitimized some political values of their ecologically-minded peers in class and culture. These concerns have been institutionalized in government agencies like the Environmental Protection Agency and the Council on Environmental Quality, which now serve as legitimate news sources. The more radical wings of the environmental movement – those which challenge the raison d'être of centralized mass production and try to join the concerns of labor and environmentalists – are scanted.

Indeed, the very concept of a *movement* has been certified; an *activist*, left or right, is now a stereotyped persona accorded a right to parade quickly through the pageant of the news. Consumer activists, environmentalists, gay activists, feminists, pro- and anti-busing people, as well as anti-abortionists, Jarvis-Gann supporters, Laetrile legalizers, angry loggers, farmers, and truck drivers – many movements which can be presented as working for (or against) concrete assimilable reforms have become regular, recognizable, even stock characters in newspapers and news broadcasts. The media spread the news that alternative opinions exist on virtually every issue. They create an impression that the society is full of political vitality, that opinions and interests contend freely – that the society, in a word, is pluralist. But in the process, they do extend the reach of movements that agree, at least for working purposes, to accept the same premise – and are willing to pay a price.

It is hard to know in advance what that price will be, hard to generalize about the susceptibilities of movements to the publicity process and its internal consequences. Of internal factors, two seem bound to increase a movement's *dependency* on the mass media: (1) the narrowness of its social base; and (2) its commitment to specific society-wide political goals. And then two other factors, when added onto the first two, seem to produce the most destructive *consequences* of media dependency: (3) the movement's turn toward revolutionary desire and rhetoric in a nonrevolutionary situation; and (4) its unacknowledged political uncertainties, especially about the legitimacy of its own leaders. Thus, in the case of the New Left: (1) It was contained within a relatively narrow social base: students and the young intelligentsia. (2) It had a specific political purpose, to end the war. These two factors in combination were decisive in forcing the movement into dependency on the media, although they did not by themselves generate destructive consequences. Proceeding into national reform politics from its narrow social base, the movement could hope to end the war only by mobilizing wider constituencies. Attempting to affect government policy in a hurry, it was forced to rely upon the mass media to broadcast the simple fact that opposition existed. And then the other factors came into play. (3) The New Left, in its revolutionary moment, allowed itself to believe it was in a revolutionary situation. In this mood, which flowed from (though it also contradicted!) the reformist antiwar moment, much of the New Left determined to muscle its way through to a political transformation so far beyond its means that it hurled itself into a politics of spurious amplification. Now mass-mediated images, and metaphors borrowed from the histories of previous revolutions, were dragooned into the Leninist role of vanguard organization – with consequences predictably ludicrous and self-destructive. And at the same time, (4) the New Left's ambivalence about criteria for leadership, especially when coupled with its inability to engender a coherent political ideology and organization, left all parties damaged: leaders were vulnerable to the temptations of celebrity, while the rank and file were stranded without means of keeping their leaders accountable. On the face of it, the black movement of the sixties and seventies shared these vulnerabilities, and for the same reasons. For the black movement also began with a narrow social base, the black population and students; it campaigned for the specific purpose of ending de jure segregation; it failed to give clear

signals to its leaders; and a significant portion ended up committed to a revolutionary project within a nonrevolutionary situation.

But each factor is powerful insofar as it reinforces the previous factor or factors. If the chain can be broken, then the consequences of the previous factors can be minimized. If a movement is committed to working for specific political goals but refuses to devote itself to revolutionary politics, it may avoid the most severe dependency on the media; it is more likely, too, to be able to control the content of its publicity. The United Farm Workers, for example, are entrenched within a narrow social base and are committed to specific goals; but they have an undisputed leader whose media presence is (I am told) heralded with pride rather than envy; and by avoiding revolutionism, they have been able to occupy the media spotlight without subjecting themselves to its most destructive glare.

Reformist movements, then, are less vulnerable to structural deformation in the publicity process than are revolutionary ones. Reformists can achieve media standing by getting *their* experts legitimated; the standard frames are equipped to show them – and their class – to relatively good advantage. Revolutionaries, by contrast, can achieve media standing only as deviants; they become "good copy" as they become susceptible to derogatory framing devices; and past a certain point, precisely what made them "good copy" may make them dangerous to the State and subject, directly or indirectly, to blackout. But to say that reformist movements are less vulnerable to disparagement is not to say that they are immune. They, too, must confront the spotlight's tendency to convert leadership to celebrity, to highlight extravagant rhetoric (if not action), and to help induce transitional crises of generations. Likewise, the standard journalistic frames persist in marginalizing the most radical aspects of movements and setting them against the more moderate. They cover single-issue movements, but frame them in opposition to others: feminists against blacks, blacks against chicanos. *The routine frames that I examined earlier endure for reformist as well as deeply oppositional movements.* Even reformist movements must work industriously to broadcast their messages without having them discounted, trivialized, fragmented, rendered incoherent. Awareness of the media's routines and frames is no guarantee that a movement will be able to achieve publicity for its analysis and program on its own terms; the frames remain powerful, processing opposition into hegemonic order. But surely ignorance of the media's codes condemns a movement to marginality.

Biography

A brief biography of Abbie Hoffman, written by the editors of this volume, can be found on page 374.

Part IX

Why Do Movements Decline?

Introduction

Not surprisingly, scholars have had much more to say about why social movements arise than why they decline, enter a period of "abeyance," or disappear altogether. Nonetheless, several hypotheses about movement decline have attained some notoriety. Most explanations for decline focus on the surrounding political environment, which may of course constrain as well as facilitate movements. Of course, the very success of a movement in changing laws or government policies may undermine the motivations that many people had for participating in that movement. Movement organizations may also be legally recognized by the government, leading to their "institutionalization" and declining reliance upon disruptive protest. Government concessions of this type, even if they do not redress all the grievances and concerns of movement participants, may nevertheless be sufficient to satisfy or placate many people, who will then drift away from the movement or from protest tactics. Social movements, in short, may become victims of their own success.

> **Movements in Abeyance** Some political causes go through long periods of relative inactivity, disappearing from the public eye, before springing back to life. While in abeyance, they are kept alive by small groups or networks of people who remember previous mobilizations and remain committed to ideals that are generally out of favor among the broader public. Such "abeyance structures" also include formal organizations that continue to work for social change even when there is no evidence of a surrounding movement. For instance, the small and largely obscure National Woman's Party (NWP) led by Alice Paul agitated for the Equal Rights Amendment (ERA) during the 1940s and 1950s, until that cause was picked up again by the women's movement of the 1960s and 1970s. The persistence of such networks and organizations helps to explain why certain movements, ideas, and tactics can sometimes reappear quickly after decades of dormancy. See Taylor (1989).

The "political opportunities" that may have helped give rise to a movement may also begin to contract or disappear. Elite divisions may be resolved or (perhaps because of elite unity) elites may decide to harshly repress a movement. Both of these factors are usually invoked to explain the violent demise of the democracy movement in China in 1989. In the excerpt below, Patricia Cayo Sexton also emphasizes repression as a key factor in the decline of the U.S. labor movement since the 1950s. More specifically, Sexton argues that union decline in America is largely explained by aggressive employer opposition to unions, which is in turn facilitated by laws and policies that favor employers over workers. One does not see the same type of employer resistance in Canada, Sexton points out, mainly because laws discourage it. As a result, unions have become stronger in Canada. American unions have also been hurt by factory closings in recent years; many businesses have transferred their operations to parts of the country (mainly the South) or other countries where unions are weak and wages relatively low.

A primary reason for the existence of a legal framework in the United States which encourages business opposition to unions is the historic *political* weakness of the American labor movement. Unlike all other developed capitalist countries, Sexton points out, the United States has never had a strong labor or leftist political party (although some scholars have suggested that the Democratic Party briefly functioned like one during the 1930s and 1940s). Scholars refer to the historical weakness of labor and socialist parties in the United States as "American exceptionalism." The precise reasons for this exceptionalism continue to be debated, with factors such as the two-party system, racial and ethnic antagonisms among workers, and the American creed of individualism receiving considerable emphasis.

Movements may also decline as a result of their own internal dynamics and evolution. In her account of the decline of the women's movement in America, Barbara Epstein stresses how the movement gradually lost its radical élan and vision. This was a result in part of intense ideological conflicts among radical feminists within the movement, who had provided much of the movement's activist core and ideological inspiration. Gradually, and partly because of its own success in opening up new professional careers for women, the women's movement as a whole took on a middle-class outlook. It became more concerned with the career opportunities and material success of individual women than with the group solidarity of women or addressing the concerns of poor and working-class women. A remarkably wide range of women's organizations have now been successfully institutionalized, Epstein points out, but they have not been able, and most have not been concerned, to bring about gender equality within the larger society.

The excerpt by Joshua Gamson emphasizes yet another way in which a movement's internal dynamics may lead to schism, if not decline. Movements typically require – or themselves attempt to create – clear and stable collective identities. How can we make claims and demands upon others, after all, if we do not know who "we" and "they" are? Many recent movements have been centrally concerned with establishing, recasting, and/ or defending collective identities, including previously stigmatized identities. But collective identities, sociologists argue, are not "natural" or given once and for all; they are culturally constructed and continually reconstructed. Some identities, moreover, may obscure or devalue others. As a result, people have often attempted to blur, reconfigure, or deconstruct certain identities. Hence, Gamson's question: must identity movements self-destruct?

Gamson shows how the gay and lesbian movement has been shaken in recent years by "queer" theorists and activists who have challenged fixed sexual identities like "gay," "lesbian," and "straight." Queer activists have also challenged the "assimilationist" goals of mainstream (and generally older) gay and lesbian activists, some of whom object to the very use of a stigmatized label like "queer." To some extent, Gamson points out, queer activism developed out of the growing organization of bisexual and transgendered people, whose very existence challenges the notion of fixed sexual and gender identities.

In the end, then, the gay and lesbian movement and indeed all identity movements face a dilemma: to be politically effective they may feel a need to emphasize exclusive and secure collective identities, but this may paper over and effectively ignore important differences among movement participants – differences that may later erupt in a way that weakens the movement. How movements handle this dilemma in order to avoid self-destruction – how they weigh and balance competing and potentially disruptive identity claims – is an important question for future research.

Discussion Questions

1   How might a social movement become a victim of its own success? Could this be said of the women's movement?
2   Why has the labor movement in the United States declined over the past several decades? Do you think this decline is irreversible?
3   Why has the women's movement declined in recent years? Do you think this decline is permanent or is the movement simply in "abeyance," with the possibility of springing back to life under the right conditions?
4   How have "queer" activists challenged the gay and lesbian movement? Is this challenge simply destructive or potentially beneficial to that movement?

28 The Decline of the Labor Movement

Patricia Cayo Sexton

The war on the labor-left has been waged with relentless vigor for well over a century. The New Deal era did transform and empower labor for a time, but starting in the mid-1950s and accelerating rapidly in the 1970s and 1980s, the war drove labor into retreat and even turned its sights on the most conservative trade unions and their moderate politics. The calculated result of this effort has been a steady decline in union "density" (the unionized share of the work force) and a parallel loss of labor's political influence and bargaining power.

In the mid-1950s, union members were some 36 percent of the labor force; by 1989, that figure had dropped to about 16 percent, the lowest density of any developed democracy with the possible exception of France. But even at its peak in the 1950s, union density was lower in the United States than in almost all comparable countries. By the 1990s, it was much lower, about 16 percent compared with over 95 percent in Sweden and Denmark, 85 percent in Finland, over 60 percent in Norway and Austria, over 50 percent in Australia, Ireland, and the United Kingdom, and over 40 percent in West Germany and Italy. Unions almost everywhere were on the defensive, but only U.S. union density had declined sharply in the 1970s and 1980s. In 1987, U.S. union density was 37 points below the average of seventeen countries surveyed, down from 17 points below average in 1970, and it was less than half the Canadian density, down from rough equality in 1970. During the same period, density declined in only three other countries: in Austria by 3 percent, Japan 7 percent, and the Netherlands 4 percent. In the United States, it declined by 14 percent.

Density losses have been greatest in the most unionized sectors of the economy – in manufacturing, down from 42 percent in 1953 to 25 percent in the late 1980s; in transportation, from 80 percent to 37 percent; in mining, from 65 percent to 15 percent; and in construction, from 84 percent to 22 percent. Losses in the private sector (42 percent) greatly exceeded those in the public sector (10 percent) from 1971 to 1985. The U.S. private sector loss of 42 percent was significantly greater than in other developed democracies: 2 percent in Canada, 3 percent in Norway, 6 percent in West Germany, 7 percent in Switzerland, 9 percent in Austria, 14 percent in the United Kingdom, 15 percent in Italy – and zero in Sweden. U.S. unions were disadvantaged by the relatively small size of U.S. public sector employment – only 16 percent of total employment (public and private), compared with 33 percent in Sweden, 30 percent in Canada, 27 percent in the United Kingdom and Germany – and by the lower degree of U.S. union penetration of the public sector.

The war's escalation contrasts with the experiences of other developed democracies, where labor has also been subjected to considerable repression but nowhere on so massive a scale as in the United States. Aside from Britain, in other developed democracies neither employers nor the state has joined in equivalent hostilities to labor, despite more serious economic problems in some cases. Even British employers have generally abstained from heightened hostilities to unions, despite antiunion campaigns and legislation sponsored by the Thatcher government.

Causes of Union Decline

Explaining contemporary union decline (historical declines are dealt with later) is complicated by the need to consider not only why U.S. unionism has declined but also, for our purposes here, why it has declined so much more than unionism in other countries – or its "relative decline." Among the most popular explanations of the decline are public disapproval of unions and the behavior of the unions themselves.

Public approval of unions, however, explains nothing about the U.S. union decline, since approval has actually improved over the period of the decline. Between 1981 and 1988, for instance, public approval of U.S. unions climbed 6 percentage points, with 61 percent of Americans approving of unions in 1988, 25 percent disapproving, and 14 percent having no opinion—approval being lowest among those aged thirty-five to forty-four. Moreover, polls show little difference in public "confidence" in unions between nations with declining density and those with stable or rising density: 33 percent confidence in the United States, 26 percent in Britain, 32 percent in Italy, 36 percent in Germany and France, and a less favorable attitude in Canada, where unions have grown.

As for union behavior, some critics claim that "sellouts" by union leaders have been the major cause of union decline. They blame contract concessions on union bureaucrats and "business unionism" and urge strikes against the give-backs demanded by employers. Yet almost all concession strikes in the 1980s ended in defeat, and in some cases the unions themselves were broken. In a context of weakened unions, reduced political influence, the use of replacement workers, and employer threats to close plants, the success rates of strikes and other union tactics have plunged.

Other observers claim that U.S. unions excite employer hostility by their bargaining tactics and by making too many wage demands. Although the allure of cheaper labor may be greatly responsible for U.S.

employer responses and union decline, high wages do not explain the *relative* decline of U.S. unions. In 1987, average hourly labor costs as measured in U.S. dollars were, in fact, higher in eight Western European countries than in the United States: the United States $13.44, Norway $17.39, Switzerland $17.14, West Germany $16.87, Netherlands $15.46, Sweden $15.12, Belgium $15.02, Denmark $14.56, Finland $13.52. Private sector unions in almost all those countries had declined somewhat between 1971 and 1985, but none so sharply as in the United States.

Employers, Government, Repression   *explanation*

Almost all theories of the contemporary U.S. union decline fall finally under the rubric "repression," typically originated by employers and sustained by government. I deal briefly with only four of the theories: those based on (1) the "wage gap"; (2) public sector penetration; (3) closings and cutbacks; and (4) labor relations and labor law.

The Wage Gap.   The decline of U.S. union density is explained by economists David Blanchflower and Richard Freeman largely in terms of the gap between union and nonunion wages, which is greater in the United States than in comparable countries. This gap, they say, stimulates employers to oppose unions in order to hire cheaper nonunion labor.

Yet in Canada, despite a union/nonunion wage gap second only to that in the United States, and an equal stress by unions on wage demands, union density has nonetheless risen. This deviation is attributed to the fact that labor law in Canada seriously limits the antiunion activity of employers. In the end, then, union decline is caused, not by excessive wage demands, but by employer efforts to repress unionism and employer inspired labor laws that allow them to do so.

Public Sector Penetration.   According to comparisons of U.S. and Canadian unionism made by economist Leo Troy, the size and union penetration of the public sector, rather than employer opposition, account for the stronger position of Canadian unions. The Canadian public sector is proportionately much larger than the U.S. sector, and Canadian unions grew rapidly in that sector, to a density of 66 percent by 1985, when U.S. unions had a density in a smaller public sector of only 36 percent. In the final analysis, however, the U.S. public sector and union penetration of it are small compared to Canada because the growth of both have been far more vigorously opposed by American than by Canadian economic elites and more vigorously supported by Canada's labor party.

Closings and Cutbacks. Deindustrialization and the closings and cutbacks of unionized plants account for much of contemporary U.S. union decline, some economists say more than 70 percent. According to an International Labor Office (ILO) study of seven countries, laws sharply restricted such closings during the 1980s in Japan, West Germany, France, the United Kingdom, and Italy, but in the United States and Canada, employers could generally cut back the work force without notice, in the absence of contrary agreements. Again, employer opposition to laws restricting closings and the political power to enforce such opposition account for much of U.S. job and union density loss.

In Japan, for example, workers through their union sued their American employer, Procter and Gamble, when it closed the plant where they worked, even though all workers were offered job transfers to a nearby Procter and Gamble plant and jobs elsewhere were in plentiful supply. Other U.S. employers, because of habits permitted by U.S. law, have run into similar problems in Japan with layoffs and closings. Japanese law permits such suits, and tradition encourages them. Japanese plants rarely close or even lay off workers permanently; deeply troubled companies are usually taken over by affiliates, or workers are transferred to other companies.

Labor Relations and Labor Law. Richard Freeman's study shows that management opposition to unions in the workplace best explains the relative decline of U.S. unions. U.S. labor relations, he says, exemplify what aggressive management can do to unionism. In the 1970s and 1980s, U.S. management "turned against unions and collective bargaining to a degree not seen anywhere else in the free world." Almost all U.S. firms facing union elections conducted "expensive aggressive campaigns to persuade/pressure workers to reject unions," unfair labor practices rose to five and six times the rates of earlier decades and included the firing of more than 1,000 union activists in a year, and some 45 percent of the relatively moderate members of the Conference Board's Personnel Forum (a prestigious business group) claimed in 1983 that their main labor goal was to be union free. Even when workers voted to unionize, management refused a first contract in a third of the cases.

Freeman says that a militant, market-oriented ideology has developed that excuses almost all antiunion activities on the grounds that they give management more flexibility. Because Canadian laws prohibit most such activities, many of the same employers who have fought U.S. unions have accepted them in Canada. If present trends continue, Freeman concludes, nations will be divided between those with strong unions functioning in a neocorporatist setting, such as in Scandinavia, and those with ghetto unions restricted to a small segment of the work force, as is happening in the United States.

Political Contexts

Canadian and U.S. Law

Comparisons of American and Canadian unions are instructive. The union structures are similar, and in some cases unions in both countries can even be part of the same "international" union, but one twin, the Canadian, has grown to a density almost twice that of the American. The difference is not in the unions but in the nature of the "class forces" they confront, the laws and their enforcement, and the general political context of unionism.

The main source of divergence between the twins has been that Canadian laws (federal and provincial) encourage public sector unionism and seriously limit the antiunion practices of employers. In 1967, the Canadian Parliament passed a law that gave almost all federal employees the right to organize, bargain, and strike, and most provinces promptly passed similar laws. Moreover, the Canadian government, especially in the major provinces of Ontario and Quebec, prohibits the kind of warfare waged on labor by U.S. employers. Ontario provides for first-contract arbitration; U.S. employers are free to refuse a contract even when employees vote for a union. In British Columbia, when a first contract cannot be agreed on, one is imposed by law. In Quebec, where union density has risen most, the provincial Ministry of Labor extends contracts negotiated by unions in a given industry to the whole of the industry. Other provincial laws regulate strikebreaking, union membership for some professions, and other matters.

Most important, under Canadian law, unions usually only need to submit membership cards signed by a majority of employees in order to be considered a certified bargaining agent. Such a provision is a far cry from the costly and prolonged election procedures to which American unions seeking National Labor Relations Board (NLRB) certification are subjected. Because of such laws, the union certification rate in highly industrialized Ontario was 76 percent in 1982, for example, compared with less than 50 percent in the United States. Canadian law is more hospitable to unions because the political system has facilitated the rise of a potent labor party, the New Democratic Party, which in 1991 came to power in Canada's most populated and industrialized province, Ontario.

Neocorporatism and Tripartitism

Even before the enactment of prolabor laws, union growth and influence were stronger in Canada than in the United States. This fact can be attributed to Canada's history of having tripartite boards (labor, employers, government) to deal with labor disputes, greater government involvement in economic life, a parliamentary rather than a congressional system of government, and the participation of democratic socialist parties in both provincial and state elections.

In most developed democracies, unions function in neocorporatist settings characterized by strong labor parties and strong unions, in which bargaining tends to be more centralized and more attention is paid to reducing wage inequalities for comparable work and adjusting wages in keeping with national income policies. Richard Freeman concludes that unions fare best in these neocorporatist settings.

After World War II, tripartite boards in many developed democracies formulated policy on a broad range of issues, including economic policy, the framework for collective bargaining, minimum wages, occupational health and safety, and equal opportunity. In some cases, unions became disenchanted when the boards ignored their views, but the union position generally remained strong because the unions themselves and their parties remained strong. As a result, public policy was likely to support favorable labor laws, include unions in the delivery of social services, and provide a climate for union stability or growth. In many countries, unions also won seats on governing boards of corporations and pension funds, though in some cases the resistance of conservative governments and employers during the 1980s slowed this trend.

In West Germany, a neocorporatist state and the leading European economy of the postwar era, union density has risen in recent decades. Work hours in the metal industry have declined, shift work has disappeared, union codetermination has grown, manipulative labor relations programs have declined, and unions have made few wage or other concessions. Few plant closings or takeovers have occurred, and laws limit worker layoffs and restrain deregulation of industry. Such improvements are largely attributable to the fact that West Germany has had relatively strong unions, a strong Social Democratic Party, codetermination in industry, and an economic elite that is not all that hostile to labor.

U.S. labor, on the other hand, has lacked the essential political influence to enter as a full partner into such arrangements, so tripartitism has not fared well in the United States. Even joint labor-management efforts to define policy have often failed. In 1978, as an example, Douglas Fraser, then president of the United Automobile Workers (UAW), resigned from the high-level Labor-Management Group formed to reduce workplace conflict, charging that business leaders, with few exceptions, had discarded the unwritten contract of coexistence and had chosen to "wage a one-sided class war in this country – a war against working people, the unemployed, the poor, the minorities, the very young and the very old, and even many in the middle class of our society." Moreover, he said, the two major parties have no "clear-cut ideological differences" and, because of business domination, are ineffective in protecting the victims of this class war.

The Unique Absence of Labor Parties

Labor's strength obviously depends on the success of its politics and on government policy; at the same time, its politics depend on its success in collective bargaining. The two are mutually dependent, and both are the object of repression.

Most of what is said about America's unique conservatism deals with politics rather than unionism, especially with the singular absence in the United States of a mass labor or democratic socialist party. Usually the conservatism of U.S. politics is

attributed to the attitudes of labor itself, and when militant union struggles are referred to, they are usually considered as a puzzling aberration from these assumptions about labor conservatism. The failure to connect the history of unionism and politics is indeed a major deficit in these assumptions, for one cannot be understood except in the context of the other, and in the larger social and comparative context.

Although the United States has no labor (or social democratic or democratic socialist) party, in almost all other democracies – including those in Western Europe, Japan, Israel, Australia, New Zealand, Canada, India, and many third world nations – parties of the democratic left have flourished and often exercised dominant power. By the 1990s, these parties included almost fifty full-member affiliates of the democratic Socialist International (SI) based in some forty-five countries around the world. Even in Japan, the seat of corporate giants, a self-identified democratic socialist party has won enough votes to challenge the undefeated conservative party. These various parties of the democratic left are usually associated with organized labor and with the International Confederation of Free Trade Unions (ICFTU) and its secretariats, and all identify with the label "democratic socialist."

Americans may be the only people in developed democracies who are generally unaware of the successes and profoundly democratic nature of these labor, social democratic, and democratic socialist parties. This unawareness and the general disrepute in the United States of the word "socialism," even in association with the word "democratic," would suggest that a euphemism should be used, but that would only defeat a major purpose of any inquiry into America's unique conservatism: explaining how the word came to be so unfairly stigmatized in the first place.

It is said that socialism itself gave "socialism" a bad name, as Westerners legitimately came to fear what the communist world called "socialism." But that does not explain why so many Western Europeans and others who are politically aware obviously regard "democratic socialism" as good, clearly distinguish it from Stalinist brands of communism and Soviet command economies, and vote heavily for democratic socialist parties at election time. Nor does it explain why the communist world's adoption of the word "democratic" (as in "democratic peoples' republics") did not also vilify *it* in the American lexicon.

[...]

The policies of labor-left parties are not wholly unfamiliar in the United States. Most have sought, but far more avidly and fruitfully than American parties, to support decent levels of social welfare, distribute opportunity and wealth more equitably, extend democracy into economic policy making, and through public interventions stimulate and direct economic growth. Pragmatic rather than doctrinaire, labor-left parties hold sacred neither public nor private ownership of industry and are inclined to favor whatever competitive mixture of the two leads to best results. They support regulation of the private sector as required by the public interest, cooperative or public ownership when the need is indicated, social planning to stabilize and stimulate the economy, full employment, and public action to control the disastrous business cycles that figure so prominently in world depressions and wars.

Above all, these parties insist that a government belongs to its citizens, not to an oligarchy of wealth and institutional power, and that it is possible, as Bogdan Denitch writes, "for ordinary men and women to make effective changes in their societies" and for those "traditionally excluded from power, the so-called objects of history, to become its subjects." This belief, rather than advocacy of social ownership of industry, or high growth rates, or a centrally planned economy, is now central to democratic socialist belief.

German unions, for example, have won key legislative gains, including codetermination, through their support of the German Social Democratic Party (SPD), which alter-nates between first and second place in German politics and is a leading party of the Socialist International. The SPD is far from "communistic." It is essentially a labor party opposed to a command or a nationalized economy or one controlled by a wealthy elite. Like other labor and social democratic parties, it favors a mixed economy guided by an elected government, equitably shared, and democratized at all levels. The SPD has not won all it wants, but it has won a major role in German politics.

One indication of the economic stability promoted by the policies of these parties is the fact that three of the five countries least affected by the economic recession starting in the 1970s were Sweden, Norway, and Austria, all of which have strong social democratic governments; the other two countries, Japan and Switzerland, are conservative with respect to the welfare state but have also been committed to full employment sustained by government initiatives. Because of the influence of labor-left parties, some Western nations have rivaled or exceeded the American standard of living, and many have achieved degrees of social justice, stability, tranquillity, cultural maturity, and economic democracy that reach well beyond the American standard.

Most labor parties and governments have had their own problems in recent years, but from 1945 to the 1990s their voter support has been extremely stable. Some European parties have gained (mainly in southern Europe) while others have declined somewhat; some have formed majority governments while many others have played a dominant role in coalition governments. All have favored market economies over command economies and, where indicated, a competitive mixture of private, public, and cooperative enterprises.

The recessions of the 1970s and early 1980s put the social democratic agenda on hold for a time in many places, and governments cut back on social welfare programs, sold state-owned properties in order to reduce national debts, and made regulatory, tax, and other concessions to attract investment capital. But the expedient "move to the right" first slowed, then largely halted in the mid-1980s, and is likely to be reversed in the 1990s. Even with those cutbacks, however, the social democracies have remained well to the left of American politics – though S. M. Lipset and others see them as having joined the true path of conservatism and as proof that no "third way" is possible.

Many third world countries have also "moved to the right" and made free-market concessions to investors and lenders, but here the pattern is clearer. In Latin America, for example, many of the changes have been required by the policies of the World Bank and other foreign lending institutions or enforced by military and economic intervention. In the developed democracies, the pressures for change have been more subtle.

Some people are convinced, perhaps too optimistically, that the Europe of 1992 and beyond is likely to be more self-contained, more independent and freer of pressures to attract investment capital – domestic or foreign – and is likely to be dominated by labor and social democratic parties, as their plurality in the European Parliament suggests. Most likely, then, the cold war will have been lost, not to capitalism, but to social democracy and to policies that humanize, moderate, and discipline the raw forces of capitalism. Although it is believed that democratic left parties in Europe need a clearer sense of identity, a stronger vision of their future, and longer-term goals, they have "done more for humanity in the past century," as Michael Harrington puts it, than any other social movement, both morally and materially, and these "bewildered half-exhausted democratic-socialist parties continue to be the major hope for freedom and justice."

Relations between democratic left parties and labor unions have not always been as supportive as they might be, and once in power, the parties have not always dealt fairly with labor. The parties of southern Europe that came to power in the 1970s and 1980s, sometimes unsupported by strong democratic unions, have often been heavily influenced by middle-class technocrats. In some cases, they have adopted more conservative programs than those promised, and sometimes they have even broken legitimate strikes. Even in those cases, however, the contrast with the American conservative agenda has been conspicuous. The parties of northern Europe have been more closely tied to established union movements and therefore have been less susceptible to technocratic influence. As for the priority of party versus union, European unionist Dan Gallin writes that it is difficult but not impossible "to imagine social-democratic objectives achieved without the help of a party; it is impossible to imagine such objectives achieved without workers organized into unions, whose class interests require the achievement of a human, just and sustainable society for all."

Of major importance, European social democrats worked closely with progressive Catholics in the 1970s and 1980s, and they came to agree on the principles of an extended welfare state (which reduces class conflict), the defense of workers and unions, government intervention in critical economic decisions, and aid to the third world. Progressives in the Catholic church, sociologist Bogdan Denitch notes, have become important in the European left, entering into coalitions with social democrats (as in Germany), often voting for democratic socialist parties, and rejecting the "cult of the market as the supreme regulator of what is socially desirable." Similarly, many Catholic unions moved toward the left and secularism in the 1970s, and their programs are indistinct from those of democratic socialists.

Consequences of U.S. Union Decline

Is the United States better off without unions and striking workers? Not at all. By almost any measure, it is worse off. For instance, labor has played a key role in enacting and defending legislation of general public benefit, including social security, medicare and medicaid, education funding, unemployment compensation, occupational safety and health laws, mine safety and health laws, black lung disability funds, the National Labor Relations Act, minimum wage laws, civil rights legislation, and all progressive tax law. In effect, labor in the United States, as elsewhere, has led in developing the nation's entire social welfare system and in pursuing a stable full-employment economy. In countries with weak unions, unemployment rates have generally been higher than in countries with strong unions, social welfare spending has been meager, and income inequality has been greater.

Economists Richard Freeman and James Medoff have found that productivity is generally higher in unionized firms than in comparable nonunion firms, that American unionism reduces inequality, that union wage gains are not a major factor in inflation, and that unions provide members with both material benefits and a voice in decisions affecting their lives. In a study of 1,000 metal-working companies, all of which had employee involvement committees, Bennett Harrison and others found that the labor relations arrangement that made the biggest productivity difference was "an organizational form that many people believe has outlived its usefulness and only stands in the way of progress: the trade unions" and that at corporate branch plants, the average production time per unit of output was 35 percent greater in nonunion than in union plants.

Based on an extensive study of electoral politics, journalist Thomas Edsall claims that there is no broad-based institution in American society other than unions that can "represent the interests of those in the working and lower-middle classes in the formulation of economic policy" and that in no Western democracy is any other organization able to cut across racial and ethnic lines in defending a more equitable distribution of taxes and spending. Economist Robert Kuttner claims that unions have

served as a "prime constituency for a social democratic conception of society" and embodied a broad "moral authority as the advocate of society's nonrich, as the constituency for universalistic social insurance, full employment policies, and distributive justice." They have given the most loyal backing to liberal-left politics and served as an "ideological counterweight to both the claims of the market and the influence of capital in a political democracy whose economic institutions remained fiercely capitalist." It is only when unions are weakened and defensive, he notes, that they take on the appearance of narrow interest groups.

Unions, then, seek equality of opportunity, a fair sharing of income and wealth, strong safety nets, economic democracy, full employment, and a robust economy. They provide members (potentially some 90 percent of the labor force) a voice and a vote in setting the terms of employment and, increasingly, the governing policies of the workplace. More important, they help people to organize for political action and to press toward such goals as national health insurance, a goal long ago achieved by almost all other developed democracies.

Almost alone, unions have denounced the massive flight of industry, capital, and industrial jobs; the damage to society of corporate raids and junk bonds; the excessive deregulation of industry; the environmental and work hazards of corporate pollution; and the privatization of key government functions. They have also protested the massive sale of U.S. resources, land, and industry to foreigners, but they have lacked the bargaining power to prevent these transactions.

If unions are good riddance, as some say, and if they cripple business, why is it that West Germany, the leading economy in Europe, also has one of the strongest labor movements in the world? In fact, unions, fallible as they are, provide an essential check on the runaway powers of economic elites – whether capitalist, communist, or monarchical – and in many cases, such as in the Scandinavian countries, they dominate humane, responsible, thriving economies.

It is predicted that union density in the private sector will fall to below 5 percent by the turn of the century. This prediction resembles the observations of George E. Barnett, president of the American Economic Association, who noted in 1932, on the eve of the organization of the CIO, that the past decade had seen a change of "amazing magnitude" – "the lessening of trade unionism in American economic organization."

American conservatism and union decline have had serious consequences for the society, including the decline in real wages of American workers since the 1970s, the displacement of millions of workers from jobs and communities, and the growing gap between the rich and others. Union decline has even been associated with losses by the Democratic Party and other liberal forces. As just one example, in the nine states where union decline has been greatest – California, Colorado, Idaho, Nevada, Oregon, South Carolina, Texas, Utah, and Virginia – the number of Democratic senators dropped from ten out of eighteen in 1970 to only one in the mid-1980s.

The average weekly earnings of nonsupervisory workers in the private sector, adjusted for inflation, fell 15.3 percent from 1972 to 1988. And largely because of this real wage decline, the U.S. standard of living in that period rose only 8 percent, or a fourth of the average gain in West Germany, France, Italy, Britain, and Canada and a seventh as much as in Japan.

In the 1980s, the U.S. jobless rate was two and three times higher than the Japanese, and although U.S. job creation rates were often high, 85 percent of the new jobs added were in low wage industries, mainly in service and retail trade.

Between 1979 and 1984 alone, some 11.5 million U.S. workers were displaced from their jobs because of plant shutdowns or the abolition of jobs – or about 10 percent of the total labor force. For blue-collar workers who found other jobs, the average income loss was 16 percent, but the loss was more than 25 percent for more than a third of the displaced, and in the late 1980s, some 5 million workers who wanted full-time work had to accept part-time jobs. The eligible jobless receiving unemployment benefits declined to 31 percent in 1987 from 72 percent in 1975.

In 1979, income *in*equality was greater in the United States than in West Germany, Japan, and many other countries. In the 1980s, the after-tax income of the top 5 percent of U.S. households rose 51 percent, and for the top 1 percent it rose 87 percent, while that of the poorest fifth declined 5 percent. As for the wealth gap, in 1983 the richest 10 percent of families controlled 86 percent of all financial assets, and more than half of all families had zero or negative assets.

Taxes on the rich have fallen, and those on people of modest income have risen. Consumer debt has escalated, the national debt has climbed to the highest in the world, and the ability and willingness of citizens to pay higher taxes for needed public services have fallen. Meanwhile, conservative policies have increased the need for public spending.

The American welfare system, as Fred Block and his coauthors point out, is "a flawed and fragmented creation" that is "notorious among Western democracies for the narrow and niggardly protections it provides." The flaws appear even in the health of the nation's citizens. In 1985, infant mortality rates were higher in the United States than in seventeen other countries, and by 1988, it was higher than in twenty other countries – despite being second among all nations in per capita income. In 1988, Japan had the lowest infant mortality rate, Taiwan was sixth, Hong Kong seventh, Singapore seventeenth, and the United States twenty-first. Life expectancy, even removing the effects of infant mortality, was lower in the United States than in almost every other developed democracy, and for males it was only a fraction above that in mainland China (70.5 and 70.1, respectively). In 1991, an infant born in Shanghai, China, had a better chance of surviving than an infant born in New York City, and life expectancy at birth was at least three years longer in the former than in the latter.

In 1989, some 37 million Americans lacked health insurance, and South Africa was the only other industrialized nation without some form of national health insurance, a situation that has tended in the United States to shift such costs to the workplace and put both employers and labor at a competitive disadvantage. The Ford Motor Company in 1989, for instance, spent $49.80 per vehicle on employee health care in Canada (which has a highly successful, quality, low-cost health plan), but a half-hour away in its Michigan headquarters, the cost per vehicle was $311 – more than six times greater.

Of seven major countries (the United States, Japan, Canada, Italy, France, the United Kingdom, and West Germany), the United States had the lowest adult literacy rate in 1985 (96 percent), the lowest proportion of scientists and technicians (55 per 1,000 in 1970–1986, compared to Japan's high of 317), the lowest gross domestic savings as a percentage of the gross domestic product (GDP) in 1987 (13 percent compared with Japan's high of 34 percent), and the highest military expenditure as a percentage of GNP in 1986 (6.7 percent compared to Japan's low of 1.0 percent).

29 The Decline of the Women's Movement

Barbara Epstein

From the late sixties into the eighties there was a vibrant women's movement in the United States. Culturally influential and politically powerful, on its liberal side this movement included national organizations and campaigns for reproductive rights, the Equal Rights Amendment (ERA), and other reforms. On its radical side it included women's liberation and consciousness raising groups, as well as cultural and grassroots projects. The women's movement was also made up of innumerable caucuses and organizing projects in the professions, unions, government bureaucracies, and other institutions. The movement brought about major changes in the lives of many women, and also in everyday life in the United States. It opened to women professions and blue-collar jobs that previously had been reserved for men. It transformed the portrayal of women by the media. It introduced the demand for women's equality into politics, organized religion, sports, and innumerable other arenas and institutions, and as a result the gender balance of participation and leadership began to change. By framing inequality and oppression in family and personal relations as a political question, the women's movement opened up public discussion of issues previously seen as private, and therefore beyond public scrutiny. The women's movement changed the way we talk, and the way we think. As a result, arguably most young women now believe that their options are or at least should be as open as men's.

Despite the dramatic accomplishments of the women's movement, and the acceptance of women's equality as a goal in most sectors of U.S. society, gender equality has not yet been achieved. Many more women work outside the home but most continue to be concentrated in low-paying jobs; women earn, on the average, considerably less than men; women are much more likely than men to be poor. Violence against women is still widespread. Responsibility for childcare remains largely the responsibility of women; despite the fact that most women work outside the home, nowhere is it seen as a societal rather than a familial responsibility. In the sixties and seventies feminists protested the imbalance in power between men and women in family and personal relations. But these continue to exist.

Worst of all, there is no longer a mass women's movement. There are many organizations working for women's equality in the public arena and in private institutions; these include specifically women's organizations such as the National Organization for Women, and in environmental, health care, social justice and other areas that address women's issues. But, where there were once women's organizations with large participatory memberships there are now bureaucratic structures run by paid staff. Feminist theory, once provocative and freewheeling, has lost concern with the conditions of women's lives and has become pretentious and tired. This raises two questions. Why is there so little discussion of the near-disappearance of a movement that not so long ago was strong enough to bring about major changes in the social and cultural landscape? What are the causes of the movement's decline?

Why the Silence?

[...] It is my impression that the real reason for avoiding or suppressing criticisms within the movement is fear that discussing the movement's problems will hasten a process of unraveling that is already well underway. Movements are fragile; the glue that holds them together consists not only in belief in the causes that they represent, but also confidence in their own growing strength. Especially when a movement is in decline it is tempting to silence criticism and turn to whistling in the dark, in the hope that no one will notice that something has gone wrong. But problems that are not acknowledged or discussed are not likely to go away; it is more likely that they will worsen. Understanding why a movement has declined may not lead to the revival of that movement as it was in the past, but it may help in finding new directions.

Reluctance to look at the weaknesses of the current women's movement may also have to do with the fear that second wave, or contemporary, feminism could disappear, sharing the fate of first wave feminism. The first women's movement in the United States, which took place in the latter part of the nineteenth and the early twentieth century, was almost wiped from historical memory during the four-decade interlude between the two waves of feminist activism. It was the weaknesses of first wave feminism, most of which have not been shared by feminism's second wave, that made this possible. First wave feminism was largely confined to white, middle and upper-middle class women. First wave feminism also moved, over the course of its history, toward a narrowness of vision that isolated it from other progressive movements. The first feminist movement in the United States originated in the abolitionist movement. In its early years feminism's alliance with the anti-slavery movement, and its association with other protest movements of the pre-Civil War decades, gave it a radical cast. But when the Civil War ended and suffrage was extended to former slaves but not to women, much of the women's movement abandoned its alliance with blacks. In the decades between the Civil War and the turn of the twentieth cen-

tury, racist and anti-immigrant sentiment spread within the middle class. In the last decades of the nineteenth century and the first two decades of the twentieth the women's movement narrowed its focus to winning woman's suffrage, and leading feminists turned to racist and anti-immigrant arguments on behalf of that goal. Other currents in the women's movement, such as the women's trade union movement, avoided racism and continued to link feminism with a radical perspective. But by the late nineteenth century the mainstream woman's suffrage organizations dominated the women's movement. By the time woman's suffrage was won, first wave feminism had abandoned any broader agenda and had distanced itself from other progressive movements. Feminism was easily pushed aside by the conservative forces that became dominant in the twenties.

The impact of second wave feminism has been broader and deeper than that of the first wave. Whatever direction U.S. politics may take it is hard to imagine feminism being wiped off the slate as it was in the thirties, forties and fifties. In the last three decades feminism has changed women's lives and thinking in ways that are not likely to be reversed. Where first wave feminism collapsed into a single-issue focus, second wave feminism has in many respects broadened. Second wave feminism had its limitations in its early years. Though participants included women of color and of working class backgrounds, their route into the movement was through the same student and professional circles through which white middle class women found feminism. The presence of women of color and working class women did not mean that feminism was being adopted within these communities. Second wave feminists, especially in the intoxicating early years of the movement, tended to believe that they could speak for all women. Such claims contained a small grain of truth, but ignored the composition of the movement, which was overwhelmingly young, white, college educated, heterosexual, and drawn from the post-Second World War middle class.

Unlike first wave feminism, the second wave broadened over time, in its composition and, in important respects, in its perspective. In the seventies and eighties, lesbian feminism emerged as a current within the movement. Women of color began to articulate their own versions of feminism, and working class women, who had not been part of the movement's early constituency of students and professionals, began to organize around demands for equal treatment at the workplace and in unions, for childcare, and for reproductive rights. Where first wave feminism pulled back, over time, from its early alliances with the black movement and other radical currents, second wave feminism increasingly allied itself with progressive movements, especially with movements of people of color and with the gay and lesbian movement. Second wave feminists also developed increasing sensitivity to racial differences, and differences of sexual orientation, within the women's movement.

From a Movement to an Idea

The heyday of the women's movement was in the late sixties and early seventies. During the eighties and nineties a feminist perspective, or identity, spread widely and a diffuse feminist consciousness is now found nearly everywhere. There are now countless activist groups and social and cultural projects whose goals and approaches are informed by feminism. There are women's organizations with diverse, grassroots constituencies focusing on issues of concern to working class women and women of color. There is the National Congress of Neighborhood Women, dealing with the problems of working class women and women of color. There are many local groups with similar concerns; an example from California is the Mothers of East Los Angeles, which has played an important role in environmental justice struggles. There is Women's Action

for New Directions (previously Women's Action for Nuclear Disarmament), bringing women of color and white women together around issues of health and the environment. There are many others. Nevertheless, grassroots activism is not the dominant, or most visible, sector of the women's movement. Public perception of feminism is shaped by the staff-run organizations whose concerns are those of their upper middle class constituencies and by the publications of feminists in the academy. The mass diffusion of feminist consciousness, the bureaucratization of leading women's organizations, and the high visibility of academic feminism are all consequences of the acceptance of feminism by major sectors of society. But these changes have not necessarily been good for the movement. Feminism has simultaneously become institutionalized and marginalized. It has been rhetorically accepted, but the wind has gone out of its sails.

Feminist activism has not ceased, nor have the numbers of women engaged in feminist activity or discussion declined. Millions of U.S. women talk to each other about women's concerns, using the vocabulary of feminism. There are countless organized feminist projects, focusing on domestic violence, reproductive rights and women's health. There are international networks of women continuing efforts begun at the international meeting of women at Beijing in 1995. Young feminist writers are publishing books addressed to, or speaking for, their generation.

The proliferation of feminist activism is part of a broader pattern. The numbers of people involved in community, social justice, and progressive activism generally appear to have increased since the seventies (though there is no way of counting the numbers of people involved). Feminist activism is not an exception to this trend, especially if one includes in this category women's involvement in the environmental and public health movements, addressing women's issues among others. The fact that feminist perspectives have been adopted by movements outside the women's movement, by organizations that also include men, is itself an achievement. Women play a role in leadership of the environmental and anti-corporate movements that is at least equal to men's; feminism is understood by most of these groups to be a major element in their outlook. But these activist projects do not shape the public image of feminism. The organizations and academic networks that shape public perceptions of feminism have become distant from the constituencies that once invigorated them, and have lost focus and dynamism.

Feminism has become more an idea than a movement, and one that often lacks the visionary quality that it once had. The same could be said about progressive movements, or the left, generally: we now have a fairly large and respectable arena in which feminist and progressive ideas are taken for granted. And yet we seem to have little influence on the direction of politics in the United States as a whole, and a kind of "low-grade depression" seems to have settled over the feminist/progressive arena. This is both result and cause of the weakness of the left in recent decades, a response to the widespread acceptance of the view that there is no alternative to capitalism. The women's movement has been weakened along with other progressive movements by this loss in confidence in the possibility that collective action can bring about social change.

Why the Decline of the Women's Movement?

In the sixties and early seventies the dominant tendency in the women's movement was radical feminism. At that time the women's movement included two more or less distinct tendencies. One of these called itself Socialist Feminism (or, at times, Marxist Feminism) and understood the oppression of women as intertwined with other forms of oppression, especially race and class, and tried to develop a politics that would challenge all of these simultaneously. The other tendency called itself Radical Feminism. Large-R Rad-

ical Feminists argued that the oppression of women was primary, that all other forms of oppression flowed from gender inequality.

Feminist radicals of both stripes insisted that the inequality of the sexes in the public sphere was inseparable from that in private life; radical feminism demanded equality for women in both spheres. And despite disagreements among themselves about the relationship between the oppression of women and other forms of oppression, radical feminists agreed that equality between women and men could not exist by itself, in a society otherwise divided by inequalities of wealth and power. The goal of radical feminism was an egalitarian society, and new kinds of community, based on equality.

During the sixties and seventies the radical current within the women's movement propelled the whole movement forward, but it was the demand for women's entry into the workplace, on equal terms with men, that gained most ground. The more radical feminist demands for an egalitarian society and new kinds of community could not be won so easily. Though the liberal and radical wings of the women's movement differed in their priorities, their demands were not sharply divided. Radical feminists wanted gender equality in the workplace, and most liberal feminists wanted a more egalitarian society. Affirmative action was not only a tool of privileged women. In an article in the Spring 1999 issue of *Feminist Studies*, Nancy McLean points out that working women used this policy to struggle for equality at the workplace, both opening up traditionally male jobs for women and creating a working class component of the women's movement. As long as the women's movement was growing and was gaining influence, demands for equal access to the workplace and for broad social equality complemented one another.

But a movement's demands, once won, can have different consequences than intended. Affirmative action campaigns were on the whole more effective in the professions than elsewhere, and it was educated, overwhelmingly white, women who were poised to take advantage of these opportunities. This was in large part due to the failure of the labor movement to organize women and people of color. The class and racial tilt of affirmative action was also a result of the accelerating stratification of U.S. society in the seventies, eighties, and nineties, the growing gap between the lower and higher rungs of the economy. The gains made by working women for access to higher-paid jobs could not offset the effects of widening class divisions. From the early seventies on, the standard of living of workers generally declined. Women, who were poorer to begin with, suffered the worst consequences.

The radical feminist vision became stalled, torn apart by factionalism and by intense sectarian ideological conflicts. By the latter part of the seventies, a cultural feminism, aimed more at creating a feminist subculture than at changing social relations generally, had taken the place formerly occupied by radical feminism. Alice Echols' book *Daring to Be Bad: Radical Feminism in America 1967–1975* describes these developments accurately and empathetically. Ruth Rosen's recent survey of the women's movement, *The World Split Open: How the Modern Women's Movement Changed America*, includes a clear-eyed account of the impact of these developments on the women's movement generally. Ordinarily, such sectarianism occurs in movements that are failing, but the women's movement, at the time, was strong and growing. The problem was the very large gap between the social transformation that radical feminists wanted and the possibility of bringing it about, at least in the short run. The movement itself became the terrain for the construction of, if not a new society, at least a new woman. The degree of purity that feminists demanded of one another was bound to lead to disappointment and recriminations.

I think that radical feminism became somewhat crazed for the same reasons that much of the radical movement did during the same period. In the late sixties and early seventies many radicals not only adopted revolution as their aim but also

thought that revolution was within reach in the United States. Different groups had different visions of revolution. There were feminist, black, anarchist, Marxist-Leninist, and other versions of revolutionary politics, but the belief that revolution of one sort or another was around the corner cut across these divisions. The turn toward revolution was not in itself a bad thing; it showed an understanding of the depth of the problems that the movement confronted. But the idea that revolution was within reach in the United States in these years was unrealistic. The war in Vietnam had produced a major crisis in U.S. society. Protest against the war, combined with protest against racism and sexism, led some to think that it had become possible to create a new society. In fact, the constituency for revolution, however conceived, was limited mostly to students and other young people, and this was not enough for a revolution. When the war ended the broad constituency of the protest movement evaporated, isolating its radical core. Radical feminism lasted longer than other insurgencies due to the continuing strength of the women's movement as a whole, and the ongoing receptivity of many feminists to radical ideas. But by the eighties radical feminism, at least as an activist movement with a coherent agenda, also became marginal to politics in the United States.

Affirmative action for women constituted an effort toward gender equality in the workplace, a goal not yet achieved. But the success of the women's movement in opening up the professions to women, ironically, has had the effect of narrowing the movement's perspective and goals. When it was mostly made up up of young people, and infused with radical ideas, feminism was able to develop a perspective that was in many ways independent of, and critical of, the class from which most feminists were drawn. Now, although there are important new, younger feminist voices, the largest part of the organized women's movement consists of women of my generation, the generation that initiated second wave feminism. I am not suggesting that people necessarily become less radical as they get older. I think that what happens to people's politics depends as much on the times, and the political activity that they engage in, as it does on their age. In a period when radicalism has been made to seem irrelevant even for the young, it is easy for a movement whose leadership is mostly made up of middle aged, middle class professionals to drift into something like complacency.

This of course does not describe the whole women's movement. What we now have is a women's movement composed on the one hand of relatively cautious organizations such as the National Organization for Women, the National Women's Political Caucus, and others, as well as more daring but also less visible organizations concerned with specific issue grassroots organizing. What we do not have is a sector of the women's movement that does what radical feminism once did, that addresses the issue of women's subordination generally, and places it within a critique of society as a whole. Liberal feminism lost the ERA, but it did accomplish many things. Largely due to liberal feminist organizing efforts, young women and girls now have opportunities that did not exist a few decades ago, and expectations that would have seemed wildly unrealistic to earlier generations.

Radical versions of feminism still exist, but more in the academy and among intellectuals than among organizers. Some feminists have continued to work at bridging this gap, both in their intellectual work and in engagement with grassroots movements. The growing numbers of women, including feminists, in the academy, has meant that many students have been introduced to feminist and progressive ideas, and feminist and progressive writings have influenced the thinking of a wide audience. But on the whole, feminists in the academy, along with the progressive wing of academics generally, lack a clear political agenda, and have often become caught up in the logic and values of the university. In the arena of high theory, and to some extent cultural studies, both of which are closely associated with feminism,

the pursuit of status, prestige, and stardom has turned feminist and progressive values on their head. Instead of the sixties' radical feminist critique of hierarchy, we have a kind of reveling in hierarchy and in the benefits that come with rising to the top of it.

Though the contemporary women's movement has avoided the racial and ethnic biases, and the single-issue focus, that plagued the early feminist movement, it resembles first-wave feminism in having gradually lost its critical distance from its own middle and upper middle class position. First wave feminism narrowed, over the course of its history, not only in relation to the issue of race but also in relation to the issues of capital and class. In the pre-Civil War years, first wave feminism was part of a loose coalition of movements within which radical ideas circulated, including critical views of industrial capitalism. In the late nineteenth century, as the structures of industrial capitalism hardened and class conflict intensified, feminists played important roles in the reform movements that championed poor and working class people, and some sections of the women's movement criticized capitalism and reached out to labor. The Women's Christian Temperance Union, for instance, criticized the exploitation of labor by capital and entertained support for "gospel socialism" as "Christianity in action." In the early years of the twentieth century the alliance between feminism and socialism continued within the Socialist Party. But after the turn of the century mainstream feminists moved away from any critique of capitalism, instead identifying women's interests and values with those of the upper middle class. By the time first wave feminism disappeared it had lost any critical perspective on capitalism or on its own class origins.

Feminism Has Absorbed the Perspective of the Middle Class

Like first wave feminism, contemporary feminism has over time tended to absorb the perspective of the middle class from which it is largely drawn. Meanwhile the perspective of that class has changed. Over the last several decades, under the impact of increasing economic insecurity and widening inequalities, the pursuit of individual advancement has become an increasingly important focus within the middle class. Community engagement has weakened for many, perhaps most, middle class people. For many people, especially professionals, work has become something of a religion; work is the only remaining source of identity that seems valid. Meanwhile the workplace has become, for many, more competitive and more stressful. This is not just a problem of the workplace, but of the culture as a whole. This country has become increasingly individualistic, cold, and selfish. And feminism has not noticeably challenged this. The feminist demand for equal workplace access was and remains important; for most women this demand has not been achieved. But the most visible sector of the women's movement appears to have substituted aspirations toward material success for the demand for social equality and community. This evolution, from the radical and transforming values of its early years, has been so gradual that it has been easy for those involved not to notice it. But it is a reflection of the shifting perspectives of women who were once part of a radical movement and now find themselves in settings governed by a different set of values.

In the seventies and eighties, many feminists thought that if only we could get more women into the universities, the universities would be transformed and would become less elitist, less competitive, more humane, and more concerned with addressing social problems. We now have a lot of women in the universities, and it is not clear that the universities have changed for the better. Indeed, in many respects the universities are worse, especially in regard to the growing pursuit of corporate funds and the resultant spread of the market ethos. But so far neither women in general nor feminists in particular have been especially prominent in challenging these trends and demanding a more humane, less competitive, or less hierarchical university. Feminist academics have not in recent years been particularly notable for their adherence to such values. There are some areas of academic feminism where there is open discussion, where people treat each other with respect, and where everyone involved is treated as an equal participant toward a common purpose. But in too much of feminist academia this is not the case. In the arena of high theory, the most prestigious sector of academic feminism, competition and the pursuit of status are all too often uppermost.

The shift in values that has taken place in the women's movement has been part of a broader trend. In a period of sharpening economic and social divisions, characterized by corporate demand for greater and greater profits and the canonizing of greed, a whole generation has been seized by the desire to rise to the top. Feminists are no exception to this. The image of the feminist as careerist is not merely a fantasy promulgated by hostile media. Put differently, feminists, at least those in academia and in the professions, have been no more overtaken by these values than other members of the middle class. But to say this is to admit that feminists have lost their grip on a vision of a better world.

[...]

30 The Dilemmas of Identity Politics

Joshua Gamson

Focused passion and vitriol erupt periodically in the letters columns of San Francisco's lesbian and gay newspapers. When the *San Francisco Bay Times* announced to "the community" that the 1993 Freedom Day Parade would be called "The Year of the Queer," missives fired for weeks. The parade was what it always is: a huge empowerment party. But the letters continue to be telling. "Queer" elicits familiar arguments: over assimilation, over generational differences, over who is considered "us" and who gets to decide.

New Social Movements Since the 1960s, a cluster of social movements have swept through Europe and the United States which are not pursuing the economic or class interests of their members. Instead, they are pursuing issues such as the quality of life or democratic procedures. The antinuclear movement, ecology, the animal-rights and peace movements, and the women's and student movements are examples. Many theorists argued that these movements were to "postindustrial" society what the labor movement – the quintessential "old" social movement – had been to "industrial" society: the central social conflict whose outcome would determine the direction of social change. These new movements were thought to be resisting corporate and government "technocrats" who make a range of decisions that, without being publicly debated, profoundly shape everyone's lives. Other scholars have argued that these movements are not so new, especially in the United States, which had non-class movements such as temperance or "anti-vice" in the nineteenth century. While these "post-class" movements use many of the same tactics as more traditional movements, they may also pay more attention to the manipulation of images on television and in other media.

On this level, it resembles similar arguments in ethnic communities in which "boundaries, identities, and cultures, are negotiated, defined, and produced" (Nagel 1994:152). Dig deeper into debates over queerness, however, and something more interesting and significant emerges. Queerness in its most distinctive forms shakes the ground on which gay and lesbian politics has been built, taking apart the ideas of a "sexual minority" and a "gay community," indeed of "gay" and "lesbian" and even "man" and "woman." It builds on central difficulties of identity-based organizing: the instability of identities both individual and collective, their made-up yet necessary character. It exaggerates and explodes these troubles, haphazardly attempting to build a politics from the rubble of deconstructed collective categories. This debate, and other related debates in lesbian and gay politics, is not only over the *content* of collective identity (whose definition of "gay" counts?), but over the everyday *viability* and political *usefulness* of sexual identities (is there and should there be such a thing as "gay," "lesbian," "man," "woman"?).

This paper, using internal debates from lesbian and gay politics as illustration, brings to the fore a key dilemma in contemporary identity politics and traces out its implications for social movement theory and research. As I will show in greater detail, in these sorts of debates – which crop up in other communities as well – two different political impulses, and two different forms of organizing, can be seen facing off. The logic and political utility of deconstructing collective categories vie with that of shoring them up; each logic is true, and neither is fully tenable.

On the one hand, lesbians and gay men have made themselves an effective force in this country over the past several decades largely by giving themselves what civil rights movements had: a public collective identity. Gay and lesbian social movements have built a quasiethnicity, complete with its own political and cultural institutions, festivals, neighborhoods, even its own flag. Underlying that ethnicity is typically the notion that what gays and lesbians share – the anchor of minority status and minority rights claims – is the same fixed, natural essence, a self with same-sex desires. The shared oppression, these movements have forcefully claimed, is the denial of the freedoms and opportunities to actualize this self. In this *ethnic/essentialist* politic, clear categories of collective identity are necessary for successful resistance and political gain.

Yet this impulse to build a collective identity with distinct group boundaries has been met by a directly opposing logic, often contained in queer activism (and in the newly anointed "queer theory"): to take apart the identity categories and blur group boundaries. This alternative angle, influenced by academic "constructionist" thinking, holds that sexual identities are historical and social products, not natural or intrapsychic ones. It is socially-produced binaries (gay/straight, man/woman) that are the basis of oppression; fluid, unstable experiences of self become fixed primarily in the service of social control. Disrupting those categories, refusing rather than embracing ethnic minority status, is the key to liberation. In this *deconstructionist* politic, clear collective categories are an obstacle to resistance and change.

The challenge for analysts, I argue, is not to determine which position is accurate, but to cope with the fact that both logics make sense. Queerness spotlights a dilemma shared by other identity movements (racial, ethnic, and gender movements, for example): Fixed identity categories are both the basis for oppression and the basis for political power. This raises questions for political strategizing and, more importantly for the purposes here, for social movement analysis. If identities are indeed much more

unstable, fluid, and constructed than movements have tended to assume – if one takes the queer challenge seriously, that is – what happens to identity-based social movements such as gay and lesbian rights? Must sociopolitical struggles articulated through identity eventually undermine themselves?

Social movement theory, a logical place to turn for help in working through the impasse between deconstructive cultural strategies and category-supportive political strategies, is hard pressed in its current state to cope with these questions. The case of queerness, I will argue, calls for a more developed theory of collective identity formation and its relationship to both institutions and meanings, an understanding that *includes the impulse to take apart that identity from within*.

[...]

Social Movements and Collective Identity

Social movements researchers have only recently begun treating collective identity construction as an important and problematic movement activity and a significant subject of study. Before the late 1980s, when rational-actor models came under increased critical scrutiny, "not much direct thought [had] been given to the general sociological problem of what collective identity is and how it is constituted" (Schlesinger 1987: 236). As Alberto Melucci (1989:73) has argued, social movement models focusing on instrumental action tend to treat collective identity as the nonrational expressive residue of the individual, rational pursuit of political gain. And "even in more sophisticated rational actor models that postulate a *collective* actor making strategic judgments of cost and benefit about collective action," William Gamson points out, "the existence of an *established* collective identity is assumed" (1992:58, emphasis in original). Identities, in such models, are typically conceived as existing before movements, which then make them visible through organizing and deploy them politically; feminism wields, but does not create, the collective identity of "women."

Melucci and other theorists of "new social movements" argue more strongly that collective identity is not only necessary for successful collective action, but that it is often an end in itself, as the self-conscious reflexivity of many contemporary movements seems to demonstrate. Collective identity, in this model, is conceptualized as "a continual process of recomposition rather than a given," and "as a dynamic, *emergent* aspect of collective action" (Schlesinger 1987:237). Research on ethnicity has developed along similar lines, emphasizing, for example, the degree to which "people's conceptions of themselves along ethnic lines, especially their ethnic identity, [are] situational and changeable" (Nagel 1994:154). "An American Indian might be 'mixed-blood' on the reservation," as Joane Nagel describes one example, "'Pine Ridge' when speaking to someone from another reservation, a 'Sioux' or 'Lakota' when responding to the U.S. census, and 'Native American' when interacting with non-Indians" (1994:155).

How exactly collective identities emerge and change has been the subject of a growing body of work in the study of social movements. For example, Verta Taylor and Nancy Whittier, analyzing lesbian-feminist communities, point to the creation of politicized identity communities through boundary-construction (establishing "differences between a challenging group and dominant groups"), the development of consciousness (or "interpretive frameworks") and negotiation ("symbols and everyday actions subordinate groups use to resist and restructure existing systems of domination") (1992:100–111). Other researchers, working from the similar notion that "the location and meaning of particular ethnic boundaries are continuously negotiated, revised, and revitalized," demonstrate the ways in which collective identity is constructed not only from within, but is also shaped and limited by "political policies and institutions, immigra-

tion policies, by ethnically linked resource policies, and by political access structured along ethnic lines" (Nagel 1994:152, 157).

When we turn to the disputes over queerness, it is useful to see them in light of this recent work. We are certainly witnessing a process of boundary-construction and identity negotiation: As contests over membership and over naming, these debates are part of an ongoing project of delineating the "we" whose rights and freedoms are at stake in the movements. Yet as I track through the queer debates, I will demonstrate a movement propensity that current work on collective identity fails to take into account: the drive to blur and deconstruct group categories, and to keep them forever unstable. It is that tendency that poses a significant new push to social movement analysis.

Queer Politics and Queer Theory

Since the late 1980s, "queer" has served to mark first a loose but distinguishable set of political movements and mobilizations, and second a somewhat parallel set of academy bound intellectual endeavors (now calling itself "queer theory"). Queer politics, although given organized body in the activist group Queer Nation, operates largely through the decentralized, local, and often anti-organizational cultural activism of street postering, parodic and non-conformist self-presentation, and underground alternative magazines ("zines") (Berlant and Freeman 1993; Duggan 1992; Williams 1993); it has defined itself largely against conventional lesbian and gay politics. The emergence of queer politics, although it cannot be treated here in detail, can be traced to the early 1980s backlash against gay and lesbian movement gains, which "punctured illusions of a coming era of tolerance and sexual pluralism;" to the AIDS crisis, which "underscored the limits of a politics of minority rights and inclusion;" and to the eruption of "long-simmering internal differences" around race and sex, and criticism of political organizing as "reflecting a white, middle-class experience or standpoint" (Seidman 1994:172).

Queer theory, with roots in constructionist history and sociology, feminist theory, and post-structuralist philosophy, took shape through several late 1980s academic conferences and continues to operate primarily in elite academic institutions through highly abstract language; it has defined itself largely against conventional lesbian and gay studies (Stein and Plummer 1994). Stein and Plummer have recently delineated the major theoretical departures of queer theory: a conceptualization of sexual power as embodied "in different levels of social life, expressed discursively and enforced through boundaries and binary divides;" a problematization of sexual and gender categories, and identities in general; a rejection of civil rights strategies "in favor of a politics of carnival, transgression, and parody, which leads to deconstruction, decentering, revisionist readings, and an anti-assimilationist politics;" and a "willingness to interrogate areas which would not normally be seen as the terrain of sexuality, and conduct queer 'readings' of ostensibly heterosexual or non-sexualized texts" (1994: 181–182).

[...]

My discussion of this and the two debates that follow is based on an analysis of 75 letters in the weekly *San Francisco Bay Times*, supplemented by related editorials from national lesbian and gay publications. The letters were clustered: The debates on the word "queer" ran in the *San Francisco Bay Times* from December 1992 through April 1993; the disputes over bisexuality ran from April 1991 through May 1991; clashes over transsexual inclusion ran from October 1992 through December 1992. Although anecdotal evidence suggests that these disputes are widespread, it should be noted that I use them here not to provide conclusive data, but to provide a grounded means for conceptualizing the queer challenge.

The controversy over Queerness: Continuities with existing lesbian and gay activism

In the discussion of the "Year of the Queer" theme for the 1993 lesbian and gay pride celebration, the venom hits first. "All those dumb closeted people who don't like the Q-word," the *Bay Times* quotes Peggy Sue suggesting, "can go fuck themselves and go to somebody else's parade." A man named Patrick argues along the same lines, asserting that the men opposing the theme are "not particularly thrilled with their attraction to other men," are "cranky and upset," yet willing to benefit "from the stuff queer activists do." A few weeks later, a letter writer shoots back that "this new generation assumes we were too busy in the '70s lining up at Macy's to purchase sweaters to find time for the revolution – as if their piercings and tattoos were any cheaper." Another sarcastically asks, "How did you ever miss out on 'Faggot' or 'Cocksucker'?" On this level, the dispute reads like a sibling sandbox spat.

Although the curses fly sometimes within generations, many letter writers frame the differences as generational. The queer linguistic tactic, the attempt to defang, embrace and resignify a stigma term, is loudly rejected by many older gay men and lesbians. "I am sure he isn't old enough to have experienced that feeling of cringing when the word 'queer' was said," says Roy of an earlier letter writer. Another writer asserts that 35 is the age that marks off those accepting the queer label from those rejecting it. Younger people, many point out, can "reclaim" the word only because they have not felt as strongly the sting, ostracism, police batons, and baseball bats that accompanied it one generation earlier. For older people, its oppressive meaning can never be lifted, can never be turned from overpowering to empowering.

Consider "old" as code for "conservative," and the dispute takes on another familiar, overlapping frame: the debate between assimilationists and separatists, with a long history in American homophile, homosexual, lesbian, and gay politics. Internal political struggle over agendas of assimilation (emphasizing sameness) and separation (emphasizing difference) has been present since the inception of these movements, as it has in other movements. The "homophile" movement of the 1950s, for example, began with a Marxist-influenced agenda of sex-class struggle, and was quickly overtaken by accommodationist tactics: gaining expert support; men demonstrating in suits, women in dresses. Queer marks a contemporary anti-assimilationist stance, in opposition to the mainstream inclusionary goals of the dominant gay rights movement.

"They want to work from within," says Peggy Sue elsewhere (Berube and Escoffier 1991), "and I just want to crash in from the outside and say, 'Hey! Hello, I'm queer. I can make out with my girlfriend. Ha ha. Live with it. Deal with it.' That kind of stuff." In a zine called *Rant & Rave*, co-editor Miss Rant argues that:

> I don't want to be gay, which means assimilationist, normal, homosexual. . . . I don't want my personality, behavior, beliefs, and desires to be cut up like a pie into neat little categories from which I'm not supposed to stray (1993:15).

Queer politics, as Michael Warner puts it, "opposes society itself," protesting "not just the normal behavior of the social but the *idea* of normal behavior" (1993:xxvii). It embraces the label of perversity, using it to call attention to the "norm" in "normal," be it hetero or homo.

Queer thus asserts in-your-face difference, with an edge of defiant separatism: "We're here, we're queer, get used to it," goes the chant. We are different, that is, free from convention, odd and out there and proud of it, and your response is either your problem or your wake-up call. Queer does not so much rebel against outsider status as revel in it. Queer confrontational difference, moreover, is scary, writes Alex Chee (1991), and thus politically useful:

> Now that I call myself queer, know myself as a queer, nothing will keep [queer-haters] safe. If I tell them I am queer, they give me room. Politically, I can think of little better. I do not want to be one of them. They only need to give me room.

This goes against the grain of civil rights strategists, of course, for whom at least the appearance of normality is central to gaining political "room." Rights are gained, according to this logic, by demonstrating similarity (to heterosexual people, to other minority groups) in a nonthreatening manner. "We are everywhere," goes the refrain from this camp. We are your sons and daughters and co-workers and soldiers, and once you see that lesbians and gays are just like you, you will recognize the injustices to which we are subject. "I am not queer," writes a letter writer named Tony. "I am normal, and if tomorrow I choose to run down the middle of Market Street in a big floppy hat and skirt I will still be normal." In the national gay weekly *10 Percent* – for which *Rant & Rave* can be seen as a proud evil twin – Eric Marcus (1993:14) writes that "I'd rather emphasize what I have in common with other people than focus on the differences," and "the last thing I want to do is institutionalize that difference by defining myself with a word and a political philosophy that set me outside the mainstream." The point is to be not-different, not-odd, not-scary. "We have a lot going for us," Phyllis Lyon says simply in the *Bay Times*. "Let's not blow it" – blow it, that is, by alienating each other and our straight allies with words like "queer."

Debates over assimilation are hardly new, however; but neither do they exhaust the letters column disputes. The metaphors in queerness are striking. Queer is a "psychic tattoo," says writer Alex Chee, shared by outsiders; those similarly tattooed make up the Queer Nation. "It's the land of lost boys and lost girls," says historian Gerard Koskovich (in Berube and Escoffier 1991:23), "who woke up one day and realized that not to have heterosexual privilege was in fact the highest privilege." A mark on the skin, a land, a nation: These are the metaphors of tribe and family. Queer is being used not just to connote and glorify differentness, but to revise the criteria of membership in the family, "to affirm sameness by defining a common identity on the fringes" (Berube and Escoffier 1991:12; see also Duggan 1992).

In the hands of many letter writers, in fact, queer becomes simply a shorthand for "gay, lesbian, bisexual, and transgender," much like "people of color" becomes an inclusive and difference-erasing shorthand for a long list of ethnic, national, and racial groups. And as some letter writers point out, as a quasi-national shorthand "queer" is just a slight shift in the boundaries of tribal membership with no attendant shifts in power; as some lesbian writers point out, it is as likely to become synonymous with "white gay male" (perhaps now with a nose ring and tattoos) as it is to describe a new community formation. Even in its less nationalist versions, queer can easily be difference without change, can subsume and hide the internal differences it attempts to incorporate. The queer tribe attempts to be a multicultural, multigendered, multisexual, hodge-podge of outsiders; as Steven Seidman points out, it ironically ends up

> denying differences by either submerging them in an undifferentiated oppositional mass or by blocking the development of individual and social differences through the disciplining compulsory imperative to remain undifferentiated (1993:133).

Queer as an identity category often restates tensions between sameness and difference in a different language.

Debates Over Bisexuality and Transgender: Queer Deconstructionist Politics

Despite the aura of newness, then, not much appears new in recent queerness debate; the fault lines on which they are built are old ones in lesbian and gay (and other identity-based) movements. Yet letter writers agree on one puzzling point: Right now, it matters what we are called and what we call ourselves. That a word takes so prominent a place is a clue that this is more than another in an ongoing series of tired assimilationist-liberationist debates. The controversy of queerness is not just strategic (what works), nor only a power-struggle (who gets to call the shots); it is those, but not only those. At their most basic, queer controversies are battles over identity and naming (who I am, who we are). Which words capture us and when do words fail us? Words, and the "us" they name, seem to be in critical flux.

But even identity battles are not especially new. In fact, within lesbian-feminist and gay male organizing, the meanings of "lesbian" and "gay" were contested almost as soon as they began to have political currency as quasi-ethnic statuses. Women of color and sex radicals loudly challenged lesbian feminism of the late 1970s, for example, pointing out that the "womansculture" being advocated (and actively created) was based in white, middle-class experience and promoted a bland, desexualized lesbianism. Working-class lesbians and gay men of color have consistently challenged "gay" as a term reflecting the middle-class, white homosexual men who established its usage (Stein 1992; Phelan 1993; Seidman 1993, 1994). They have challenged, that is, the definitions.

The ultimate challenge of queerness, however, is not just the questioning of the content of collective identities, but the *questioning of the unity, stability, viability, and political utility of sexual identities* – even as they are used and assumed. The radical provocation from queer politics, one which many pushing queerness seem only remotely aware of, is not to resolve that difficulty, but to exaggerate and build on it. It is an odd endeavor, much like pulling the rug out from under one's own feet, not knowing how and where one will land.

To zero in on the distinctive deconstructionist politics of queerness, turn again to the letters columns. It is no coincidence that two other major *Bay Times* letters column controversies of the early 1990s concerned bisexual and transgender people, the two groups included in the revised queer category. Indeed, in his anti-queer polemic in the magazine *10 Percent* (a title firmly ethnic/essentialist in its reference to a fixed homosexual population), it is precisely these sorts of people, along with some "queer straights," from whom Eric Marcus seeks to distinguish himself:

> Queer is not my word because it does not define who I am or represent what I believe in.... I'm a man who feels sexually attracted to people of the same gender. I don't feel attracted to both genders. I'm not a woman trapped in a man's body, nor a man trapped in a woman's body. I'm not someone who enjoys or feels compelled to dress up in clothing of the opposite gender. And I'm not a "queer straight," a heterosexual who feels confined by the conventions of straight sexual expression.... I don't want to be grouped under the all-encompassing umbrella of queer... because we have different lives, face different challenges, and don't necessarily share the same aspirations (1993:14).

The letters columns, written usually from a different political angle (by lesbian separatists, for example), cover similar terrain. "It is not empowering to go to a Queer Nation meeting and see men and women slamming their tongues down each other's throats," says one letter arguing over bisexuals. "Men expect access to women," asserts one from the transgender debate. "Some men decide that they want access to lesbians any way they can and decide they will become lesbians."

Strikingly, nearly all the letters are written by, to, and about women – a point to which I will later return. "A woman's willingness to sleep with men allows her access to jobs, money, power, status," writes one group of women. "This access does not disappear just because a woman sleeps with women 'too'... That's not bisexuality, that's compulsory heterosexuality." You are not invited; you will leave and betray us. We are already here, other women respond, and it is you who betray us with your back-stabbing and your silencing. "Why have so many bisexual women felt compelled to call themselves lesbians for so long? Do you think biphobic attitudes like yours might have something to do with it?" asks a woman named Kristen. "It is our community, too; we've worked in it, we've suffered for it, we belong in it. We will not accept the role of the poor relation." Kristen ends her letter tellingly, deploying a familiar phrase: "We're here. We're queer. Get used to it."

The letters run back and forth similarly over transgender issues, in particular over transsexual lesbians who want to participate in lesbian organizing. "'Transsexuals' don't want to just be lesbians," Bev Jo writes, triggering a massive round of letters, "but insist, with all the arrogance and presumption of power that men have, on going where they are not wanted and trying to destroy lesbian gatherings." There are surely easier ways to oppress a woman, other women shoot back, than to risk physical pain and social isolation. You are doing exactly what anti-female and anti-gay oppressors do to us, others add. "Must we all bring our birth certificates and two witnesses to women's events in the future?" asks a woman named Karen. "If you feel threatened by the mere existence of a type of person, and wish to exclude them for your comfort, you are a bigot, by every definition of the term."

These "border skirmishes" over membership conditions and group boundaries have histories preceding the letters (Stein 1992; see also Taylor and Whittier 1992), and also reflect the growing power of transgender and bisexual organizing. Although they are partly battles of position, more fundamentally the debates make concrete the anxiety queerness can provoke. They spotlight the possibility that sexual and gender identities are not the solid political ground they have been thought to be – which perhaps accounts for the particularly frantic tone of the letters.

Many arguing for exclusion write like a besieged border patrol. "Live your lives the way you want and spread your hatred of women while you're at it, if you must," writes a participant in the transgender letter spree, "but the fact is we're here, we're dykes and you're not. Deal with it." The Revolting Lesbians argue similarly in their contribution to the *Bay Times* bisexuality debate: "Bisexuals are not lesbians – they are bisexuals. Why isn't that obvious to everyone? Sleeping with women 'too' does not make you a lesbian. We must hang onto the identity and visibility we've struggled so hard to obtain." A letter from a woman named Caryatis sums up the perceived danger of queerness:

> This whole transsexual/bisexual assault on lesbian identity has only one end, to render lesbians completely invisible and obsolete. If a woman who sleeps with both females and males is a lesbian; and if a man who submits to surgical procedure to bring his body in line with his acceptance of sex role stereotypes is a lesbian; and if a straight woman whose spiritual bonds are with other females is a lesbian, then what is a female-born female who loves only other females? Soon there will be no logical answer to that question.

Exactly: In lesbian (and gay) politics, as in other identity movements, a logical answer is crucial. An inclusive queerness threatens to turn identity to nonsense, messing with the idea that identities (man, woman, gay, straight) are fixed, natural, core phenomena, and therefore solid political ground. Many arguments in the letters columns, in fact, echo the critiques of identity politics found in queer theory. "There is a growing consciousness that a person's sexual identity (and gender identity) need not be etched in stone," write Andy and Selena in the bisexuality debate, "that it can be fluid rather than static, that one has the right to PLAY with whomever one wishes to play with (as long as it is consensual), that the either/or dichotomy ('you're either gay or straight' is only one example of this) is oppressive no matter

who's pushing it." Identities are fluid and changing; binary categories (man/woman, gay/straight) are distortions. "Humans are not organized by nature into distinct groups," Cris writes. "We are placed in any number of continuums. Few people are 100 percent gay or straight, or totally masculine or feminine." Differences are not distinct, categories are social and historical rather than natural phenomena, selves are ambiguous. "Perhaps it is time the lesbian community re-examined its criteria of what constitutes a woman (or man)," writes Francis. "And does it really matter?" Transsexual performer and writer Kate Bornstein, in a *Bay Times* column triggered by the letters, voices the same basic challenge. Are a woman and a man distinguished by anatomy? "I know several women in San Francisco who have penises," she says. "Many wonderful men in my life have vaginas" (1992:4). Gender chromosomes, she continues, are known to come in more than two sets ("could this mean there are more than two genders?"); testosterone and estrogen don't answer it ("you could buy your gender over the counter"); neither childbearing nor sperm capacities nails down the difference ("does a necessary hysterectomy equal a sex change?"). Gender is socially assigned; binary categories (man/woman, gay/straight) are inaccurate and oppressive; nature provides no rock-bottom definitions. The opposite sex, Bornstein proposes, is neither.

Indeed, it is no coincidence that bisexuality, transsexualism, and gender crossing are exactly the kind of boundary-disrupting phenomena embraced by much post-structuralist sexual theory. Sandy Stone, for example, argues that "the transsexual currently occupies a position which is nowhere, which is outside the binary oppositions of gendered discourse" (1991:295). Steven Seidman suggests that bisexual critiques challenge "sexual object-choice as a master category of sexual and social identity" (1993:123). [...]

The point, often buried in over-abstracted jargon, is well taken: The presence of visibly transgendered people, people who do not quite fit, potentially subverts the notion of two naturally fixed genders; the presence of people with ambiguous sexual desires potentially subverts the notion of naturally fixed sexual orientations. (I say "potentially" because the more common route has continued to be in the other direction: the reification of bisexuality into a third orientation, or the retention of male-female boundaries through the notion of transgendered people as "trapped in the wrong body," which is then fixed.) Genuine inclusion of transgender and bisexual people can require not simply an expansion of an identity, but a subversion of it. This is the deepest difficulty queerness raises, and the heat behind the letters: If gay (and man) and lesbian (and woman) are unstable categories, "simultaneously possible and impossible" (Fuss 1989:102), what happens to sexuality-based politics?

The question is easily answered by those securely on either side of these debates. On the one side, activists and theorists suggest that collective identities with exclusive and secure boundaries are politically effective. Even those agreeing that identities are mainly fictions may take this position, advocating what Gayatri Spivak has called an "operational essentialism" (cited in Butler 1990; see also Vance 1988). On the other side, activists and theorists suggest that identity production "is purchased at the price of hierarchy, normalization, and exclusion" and therefore advocate "the deconstruction of a hetero/homo code that structures the 'social text' of daily life" (Seidman 1993:130).

The Queer Dilemma

The problem, of course, is that both the boundary-strippers and the boundary-defenders are right. The gay and lesbian civil rights strategy, for all its gains, does little to attack the political culture that itself makes the denial of and struggle for civil rights necessary and possible. Marches on Washington, equal protection pursuits, media-image monitoring, and so on, are guided by the attempt to build and prove quasi-national and quasi-ethnic claims. By constructing gays and lesbians as a single community (united by fixed erotic fates), they simplify complex internal differences and complex sexual identities. They also avoid challenging the system of meanings that underlies the political oppression: the division of the world into man/woman and gay/straight. On the contrary, they ratify and reinforce these categories. They therefore build distorted and incomplete political challenges, neglecting the political impact of cultural meanings, and do not do justice to the subversive and liberating aspects of loosened collective boundaries.

[. . .]

References

Berlant, Lauren, and Elizabeth Freeman 1993 "Queer nationality." In *Fear of a Queer Planet*, ed. Michael Warner, 193–229. Minneapolis: University of Minnesota Press.

Berube, Allan, and Jeffrey Escoffier 1991 "Queer/Nation." *Out/Look* (Winter): 12–23.

Bornstein, Kate 1992 "A plan for peace." *San Francisco Bay Times*, December 3:4.

Butler, Judith 1990 "Gender trouble, feminist theory, and psychoanalytic discourse." In *Feminism/Postmodernism*, ed. Linda J. Nicholson, 324–340. New York: Routledge.

Chee, Alexander 1991 "A queer nationalism." *Out/Look* (Winter):15–19.

Duggan, Lisa 1992 "Making it perfectly queer." *Socialist Review* 22:11–32.

Fuss, Diana 1989 *Essentially Speaking: Feminism, Nature, and Difference*. New York: Routledge.

Gamson, William A. 1992 "The social psychology of collective action." In *Frontiers in Social Movement Theory*, eds. Aldon Morris and Carol McClurg Mueller, 53–76. New Haven: Yale University Press.

Marcus, Eric 1993 "What's in a name." *10 Percent*:14–15.

Melucci, Alberto 1989 *Nomads of the Present: Social Movements and Individual Needs in Contemporary Society*. Philadelphia: Temple University Press.

Nagel, Joane 1994 "Constructing ethnicity: Creating and recreating ethnic identity and culture." *Social Problems* 41:152–176.

Phelan, Shane 1993 "(Be)coming out: Lesbian identity and politics." *Signs* 18:765–790.

Rant, Miss 1993 "Queer is not a substitute for gay." *Rant & Rave* 1:15.

Schlesinger, Philip 1987 "On national identity: Some conceptions and misconceptions criticized." *Social Science Information* 26:219–264.

Seidman, Steven 1993 "Identity politics in a 'postmodern' gay culture: Some historical and conceptual notes." In *Fear of a Queer Planet*, ed. Michael Warner, 105–142. Minneapolis: University of Minnesota Press.

——1994 "Symposium: Queer theory/sociology: A dialogue." *Sociological Theory* 12:166–177.

Stein, Arlene 1992 "Sisters and queers: The decentering of lesbian feminism." *Socialist Review* 22:33–55.

Stein, Arlene, and Ken Plummer 1994 "'I can't even think straight': 'Queer' theory and the missing sexual revolution in sociology." *Sociological Theory* 12:178–187.

Stone, Sandy 1991 "The empire strikes back: A posttranssexual manifesto." In *Body Guards*, eds. Julia Epstein and Kristina Straub, 280–304. New York: Routledge.

Taylor, Verta, and Nancy Whittier 1992 "Collective identity in social movement communities." In *Frontiers in Social Movement Theory*, eds. Aldon Morris and Carol McClurg Mueller, 104–129. New Haven: Yale University Press.

Vance, Carole S. 1988 "Social construction theory: Problems in the history of sexuality." In *Homosexuality? Which Homosexuality?*, eds. Dennis Altman et al., 13–34. London: GMP Publishers.

Warner, Michael, ed. 1993 *Fear of a Queer Planet: Queer Politics and Social Theory.* Minneapolis: University of Minnesota Press.

Williams, Andrea 1993 "Queers in the Castro." Unpublished paper, Department of Anthropology, Yale University.

Part X

What Changes Do Movements Bring About?

Introduction

Social movements have a number of effects on their societies, some of them intended and others quite unintended. A few movements attain many or all of their goals, others at least manage to gain recognition or longevity in the form of protest organizations, and many if not most are suppressed or ignored. But whereas scholars used to talk about the success or failure of movements, today they are more likely to talk about movement "outcomes," in recognition of the unintended consequences. Some movements affect the broader culture and public attitudes, perhaps paving the way for future efforts. Others leave behind social networks, tactical innovations, and organizational forms that other movements can use. At the extreme, some movements may simply arouse such a backlash against them that they lose ground. (The far-right mobilization against the U.S. government which led to the Oklahoma City bombing probably inspired closer surveillance and repression of their groups than had previously existed.)

Even if we concentrate on movement goals and success for a moment, we see that most movements have a range of large and small goals. They may try at the same time to change corporate or state policy, transform public attitudes and sensibilities, and bring about personal transformations in protestors themselves. What is more, within a given movement different participants may have different goals, or at least a different ranking of priorities. And these goals may shift during the course of a conflict. Goals may expand in response to initial successes, or contract in the face of failures. When a movement faces severe repression, mere survival (of the group or the literal survival of members) may begin to take precedence over other goals. We have seen that movements have different audiences for their words and actions, and we can now add that they have different goals they hope to accomplish with each of these different audiences. A group may launch a campaign designed to prove its

> **Radical Flank Effects** Most social movements consist of diverse organizations and networks that disagree on strategy and ideology. Often, a more radical wing emerges that is more likely to use disruptive or illegal tactics and which develops a more pure (and less compromising) distillation of the movement's guiding ideas. The existence of a "radical flank" – more threatening to authorities – can have diverse effects on a movement. In some cases, it undermines public tolerance for the movement as a whole, making it easier for its enemies to portray it as undesirable. Authorities may decide to repress the entire movement, not just its radical wing. In other cases, the radical flank is threatening enough that the forces of order take the movement more seriously, often making concessions. The moderate flank can present itself as a reasonable compromise partner, so that authorities give it power in order to undercut the radicals (although the moderates must distance themselves from the radicals to garner these benefits). If nothing else, radical flanks, by creating a perception of crisis, often focus public attention on a new set of issues and a new movement. In many cases, radical flanks have a combination of negative and positive effects on the broader movement. See Haines (1988).

effectiveness to its financial backers, its disruptive capacity to state officials, and its willingness to compromise to members of the general public. It may not be possible to succeed on all these fronts at once; there may be tradeoffs among goals.

Even a movement's goals with regard to the state and its many agencies can conflict with one another. Burstein, Einwohner, and Hollander (1995) contrast six types or stages of policy effects alone: access to legislators and policymakers, agenda-setting for legislators, official policies, implementation and enforcement of those policies, achievement of the policies' intended impact, and finally deeper structural changes to the political system. And this does not even include effects on repression, in other words, a movement's relationship with the police or armed forces.

Success in the short and the long term may not coincide. In some cases, these even conflict with each other, as when a movement's initial successes inspire strong counter-mobilization on the part of those under attack. This happened to both the antinuclear and the animal-protection movements (Jasper and Poulsen, 1993). Efforts that are quite unsuccessful in the short run may have big effects in the long, as in the case of martyrs who inspire outrage and additional mobilization.

Overall, researchers have managed to demonstrate relatively few effects of social movements on their societies. In part this is due to their concentration on direct policy effects of benefits for constituencies. A large number of movements have met with considerable repression. Others have attained some acceptance for their own organizations without obtaining tangible benefits for those they represent. Still others have found government ready to establish a new agency or regulator in response to their demands, only to conclude later that this agency was ineffectual or unduly influenced by the movement's opponents. Scholars of social movements would like to believe that the mobilizations they study affect the course of history, but usually they have had to assert this without much good evidence.

A brief excerpt from William Gamson's classic, *The Strategy of Social Protest*, is an important statement of the meaning of success, reflecting a combination of mobilization and process perspectives. The stability and institutionalization of the protest group is as important as the benefits it achieves for its constituency. The assumption behind this approach seems to be that there is a pre-defined group ready to benefit, a group whose spokespersons have been excluded in some way from full participation in politics. In a later part of the same chapter, not included here, Gamson lists consultation, negotiation, formal recognition, and inclusion as signs of the protest group's acceptance. In the fifty-three groups he studied, twenty received a full response and twenty-two collapsed, while only five were subject to co-optation and only six preemption (Gamson, 1975:37).

Many movements are at least partially successful when they inspire government to act upon their grievances – often as a means of defusing the movement. In a version of process theory they call "political mediation" theory, Edwin Amenta and his collaborators examine the effects of Huey Long's "Share Our Wealth" movement on the Roosevelt administration in the 1930s. They place equal explanatory weight on conditions the movement can control, such as its level of mobilization and its strategies, and on political conditions it cannot always control. These latter include both abiding structural factors such as electoral systems and shorter-term opportunities such as favorable election results and coalitions. By concentrating on movement outcomes, these authors distinguish themselves from other process theorists, who aim to explain both a movement's emergence and its effects as the result of political opportunities.

Perhaps the hardest movement impacts to study are their cultural effects, yet these may be some of the most profound and longest-lasting outcomes. Many movements help articulate new ways of thinking and feeling about the world. Thus animal protectionists developed widespread sympathy for nonhuman species into an explicit ideology of outrage. Other movements raise issues for public debate, forcing informed citizens to think about a topic and decide how they feel about it. A majority may reject the movement's perspective, but it can still cause them to think more deeply about their own values and attitudes. Even those who disagree with anti-abortionists have still had to decide *why* they disagreed. Still other social movements inspire scientific research or technological change, as the environmental movement has.

Ron Eyerman and Andrew Jamison address some of these cultural effects in the excerpt below. It is taken from the conclusion to their book on the role of music in social movements, and it largely envisions culture as the arts. Art affects a society's collective memory and traditions, its "common sense" of how the world works. Culture is thus a bearer of truth, as they put it. They are keen to insist on the independent effects of culture in political life, on how our beliefs about the world affect our sense of what is possible and desirable.

One of the effects that Eyerman and Jamison mention is that movements create the raw materials for future movements. In their case, these are songs that movements may share with one another; the civil rights movement for instance generated a number of songs now associated generally with protest. Movements also create new tactics and other political know-how that future protestors can use. They also leave behind social ties that can be used to ignite new efforts in the future. The women's movement of the early twentieth century, for example, left a legacy of personal networks and organizations (as well as values and ideas) that the new women's movement of the 1960s could draw upon (Rupp and Taylor, 1987; Taylor, 1989).

There may be even broader cultural effects of social movements. On the one hand, they give people moral voice, helping them to articulate values and intuitions that they do not have time to think about in their daily lives. This is extremely satisfying for most participants. On the other hand, social movements can also generate extremely technical, scientific, and practical knowledge. They engage people in politics in an exciting way – rare enough in modern society. Unfortunately, some movements may go too far, when instead of trying to be artists they try to be engineers, telling others what is good for them rather than trying to persuade them.

Discussion Questions

1   What kinds of effects do social movements have on their societies?
2   What are the main institutional arenas in which protestors hope to have an impact?
3   Under what circumstances, or in what kind of movements, should we consider it a form of success for movement organizations to gain recognition, simply to survive?
4   How can movements contribute to a society's culture or knowledge, including its self-knowledge?
5   What kinds of unintended effects can a movement have?

31 Defining Movement "Success"

William A. Gamson

Success is an elusive idea. What of the group whose leaders are honored or rewarded while their supposed beneficiaries linger in the same cheerless state as before? Is such a group more or less successful than another challenger whose leaders are vilified and imprisoned even as their program is eagerly implemented by their oppressor? Is a group a failure if it collapses with no legacy save inspiration to a generation that will soon take up the same cause with more tangible results? And what do we conclude about a group that accomplishes exactly what it set out to achieve and then finds its victory empty of real meaning for its presumed beneficiaries? Finally, we must add to these questions the further complications of groups with multiple antagonists and multiple areas of concern. They may achieve some results with some targets and little or nothing with others.

It is useful to think of success as a set of outcomes, recognizing that a given challenging group may receive different scores on equally valid, different measures of outcome. These outcomes fall into two basic clusters: one concerned with the fate of the challenging group as an organization and one with the distribution of new advantages to the group's beneficiary. The central issue in the first cluster focuses on the *acceptance* of a challenging group by its antagonists as a

valid spokesman for a legitimate set of interests. The central issue in the second cluster focuses on whether the group's beneficiary gains *new advantages* during the challenge and its aftermath.

Both of these outcome clusters require elaboration, but, for the moment, consider each as if it were a single, dichotomous variable. Assume a group that has a single antagonist and a single act which they wish this antagonist to perform – for example, a reform group which desires a particular piece of national legislation. We ask of such a group, did its antagonist accept it as a valid spokesman for the constituency that it was attempting to mobilize or did it deny such acceptance? Secondly, did the group gain the advantages it sought – for example, the passage of the legislation that it desired?

By combining these two questions, as in figure 31.1, we acquire four possible outcomes: full response, co-optation, preemption, and collapse. The full response and collapse categories are relatively unambiguous successes and failures – in the one case the achievement of both acceptance and new advantages, in the other, the achievement of neither. The remainder are mixed categories: co-optation is the term used for acceptance without new advantages and preemption for new advantages without acceptance.

		Acceptance	
		Full	None
New advantages	Many	Full response	Preemption
	None	Co-optation	Collapse

Figure 31.1 Outcome of resolved challenges

Figure 31.1 is the paradigm for handling outcomes of challenging groups, but it requires additional complexity before it can be used to handle as diverse a set of groups as the 53 represented here. Acceptance must be given a special meaning for revolutionary groups, for example, which seek not a nod of recognition from an antagonist but its destruction and replacement. Similarly, new "advantages" are not always easy to define. We must deal with cases in which a group seeks, for example, relatively intangible value changes, shifts in the scope of authority, or a change in procedures as well as the simpler case of material benefits for a well-defined group.

The Endpoint of a Challenge

The outcome measures used refer to "ultimate" outcome, to the state of the group at the end of its challenge. A given group might achieve significant new advantages at one point without receiving acceptance, but we would not consider that preemption had occurred as long as it continued to press an active challenge. Only when it eventually collapsed or ceased activity would we classify its outcome as preemption. Or, if it eventually won acceptance, its outcome would be full response instead. Similarly, the new advantages might be withdrawn and the group brutally crushed, making "collapse" the appropriate outcome. Thus, during its period of challenge, a group might appear to be in one or another cell of figure 31.1 at different times, but the outcome measures only consider its location at the end.

A challenge period is considered over when one of the following occurs:

1. *The challenging group ceases to exist as a formal entity.* It may officially dissolve, declaring itself no longer in existence. Or, it may merge with another group, ceasing to maintain a separate identity. Note, however, that a group does not cease to exist by merely changing its name to refurbish its public image. Operationally, we consider that two names represent the same challenging group if and only if:

  a. The major goals, purposes, and functions of the two groups are the same.
  b. The constituency remains the same.
  c. The average challenging group member and potential member would agree that the new-name group is essentially the old group relabeled.

2. *The challenging group, while not formally dissolving, ceases mobilization and influence activity.* A five-year period of inactivity is considered sufficient to specify the end of the challenge. If, after such a dormant period, the group becomes active again, it is considered a new challenging group in spite of its organizational continuity with the old challenger. This occurred, in fact, with two of the 53 challengers in the sample. In each case the period of dormancy was quite a bit longer than the required five years, and, in one case, the geographical location of activity was different as well.

Marking the end of a challenge is more difficult with groups that continue to exist and be active. The line between being a challenging group and an established interest group is not always sharp. The essential difference lies in how institutionalized a conflict relationship exists between the group and its antagonists. When this conflict becomes regulated and waged under some standard operating procedures, the challenge period is over. Operationally, this can be dated from the point at which the group is accepted. Hence, for continuing groups, the challenge period is over when:

3. *The challenging group's major antagonists accept the group as a valid spokesman for its constituency and deal with it as such.* In the case of unions, this is indicated by formal recognition of the union as a bargaining agent for the employees. In other cases, the act of acceptance is less clear, and, even in the case of unions, different companies extend recognition at different times. Issues such as

these are dealt with in the discussion of measures of acceptance below.

With continuing groups, then, there is some inevitable arbitrariness in dating the end of a challenge. The compiler was instructed to err, in ambiguous cases, on the side of a later date. Thus, where acute conflict continues to exist between the group and important antagonists, the challenge is not considered over even when some other antagonists may have begun to deal with the challenger in a routinized way. Furthermore, by extending the challenge period, we include new benefits that might be excluded by using a premature termination date.

32 The Case of Huey Long and the New Deal

Edwin Amenta, Kathleen Dunleavy, and Mary Bernstein

In 1935, the New Deal of President Franklin D. Roosevelt was at a crossroads. The programs of his "first 100 days" in 1933 had failed to end the Great Depression, and criticism was mounting. From the left, Senator Huey P. Long of Louisiana promoted a plan to "Share Our Wealth"; by February he claimed that 7.7 million had joined more than 27,000 Share Our Wealth societies or clubs. In April 1935, the Democratic National Committee conducted a secret poll, and, to the Committee's chairman, James Farley, the results suggested that Long might hold the balance of power in the 1936 Presidential contest. The summer of 1935 saw the beginning of Roosevelt's "second hundred days." In June, Roosevelt demanded the passage of four liberal bills and added a "soak-the-rich" tax proposal to his "must" list of indispensable legislation. Could Long have upset Roosevelt's bid for reelection? Was the second New Deal, or parts of it, devised to "steal Long's thunder," as Roosevelt supposedly put it to one of his advisors?

These questions engage the wider issues of what success means for such social protest movements and assessing their impacts on social policy and the welfare state. [...] We are concerned with what we call state-oriented challengers: people or organizations bidding for collective benefits through changes in state policies. If Share Our Wealth influenced the Second New Deal, it would have been an impressive legacy for an organization that died so young, soon after its leader was assassinated in September 1935. Moreover, Long's organization had

displacement goals – the aspiration to replace its opponents – which typically doom a challenger to failure. Roosevelt may have offered concessions in the hope of wooing away Long's supporters. However, that an advisor to Roosevelt recalled the President saying that he wanted to "steal Long's thunder" is no smoking gun. For Roosevelt publicly ignored Long's insurgency, and the President's programs may have been ones that he would have proposed anyway. Generally speaking, researchers must consider other plausible paths to changes in policy to avoid overstating the influence of a challenger. Even if Share Our Wealth's impact can be established, questions still remain. What was it about the insurgency or the circumstances surrounding it, or both, that made Share Our Wealth effective or ineffective?

We argue that success for a state-oriented challenger means winning collective benefits for its beneficiary group. We also elaborate a "political mediation" theory, which holds that political openings not only aid the mobilization of challengers, but also influence the relationship between a collective action and its outcomes. Mobilization and collective action are necessary, but not sufficient for protest groups to win collective benefits by way of the state. Political circumstances must also be auspicious. We compare this theory to two alternatives: (1) the prevailing view in the social movement literature (e.g., Gamson 1990), that the characteristics of challengers determine their fates; and (2) an argument that resonates with the welfare state literature, that economic or political conditions determine policy changes that challengers seek and perhaps also determine the rise of challengers themselves.

Our investigation focuses on the politics and policies of the Second New Deal and on the Roosevelt Administration's poll. We compare the plans and actions of Share Our Wealth with the plans and policymaking of the Administration, to ascertain the influence of Share Our Wealth. We also compare the consequences of Share Our Wealth with those of Father Charles E. Coughlin's National Union of Social Justice (NUSJ) and Dr. Francis E. Townsend's Old Age and Revolving Pensions (OARP) – the two other principal national challengers in Depression-era "neopopulism," a movement espousing community control and safeguards against capitalism. Similar in ideology, these three organizations differed in their plans, forms of organization, collective actions, and achievements. Finally, we examine national spending in the 48 states by the Works Progress Administration (WPA). We employ this quantitative analysis to ascertain whether Share Our Wealth had an impact on social spending, net of standard determinants – including state-centered, social democratic, and pluralist factors. We also ascertain whether this impact was politically mediated.

Huey Long's "Share Our Wealth" and Depression-Era Neopopulism

Share Our Wealth, the name of the program as well as the organization, had several goals. It would end the Depression by breaking the power of the rich, whose greed, in Long's estimation, caused the slump. The Long Plan (as the program was also known) limited the wealth of individuals to $3 million through direct taxation. At the same time every family would be provided with what Long called a "homestead": $4,000 or $5,000 to purchase a house, car, and radio – the necessities of middle-class life as redefined by the 1920s. Long also would guarantee an annual income of

$2,000 to $3,000. The Long Plan reached out to certain mobilizing groups. Those 65 years and older would receive pensions of $30 a month or more, and World War I veterans' adjusted compensation certificates (or "bonuses") due in 1945 would be paid immediately. For workers, the Long Plan called for a minimum wage and hours limitations and for the purchase and storage of the agricultural goods produced by farmers. To bring equality of opportunity, educational scholarships would be granted to those scoring well on standardized tests.

Like the "Townsend Plan," an old-age pension program, and the National Union's "16 Principles," which were centered on monetary and banking reforms, Share Our Wealth included measures that benefited some groups and punished others, and in so doing it was supposed to end the Depression. Like the plans of the other neopopulist organizations, the Long Plan was simple and envisioned no need for extensive bureaucracies, such as the National Recovery Administration and the Federal Emergency Relief Administration, to bring recovery and relief. Share Our Wealth was more radical in its fiscal program than was Roosevelt's New Deal, but eschewed administrative power for the national state. Politically, Long was to the left of Dr. Townsend, whose expensive $200 per month pensions would be financed by regressive taxes; Townsend was to the left of Father Coughlin, who attacked private banking, but did not call for fiscal redistribution.

Share Our Wealth, the organization, was dualistic. Its home base was in Louisiana, where Long had gained almost total political control by 1931 promoting a program that favored corporate taxes, free school books, road building, and public works. Share Our Wealth was funded by Long's Louisiana political organization, which relied on "deductions" from state employees' paychecks and kickbacks from contractors: The Louisiana societies constituted perhaps as many as one-fourth of all Share Our Wealth clubs. Outside Louisiana, Share Our Wealth was organized differently. Any two people could begin a Share Our Wealth society, and members were not required to pay dues. Long followed up his speeches on NBC radio with mailings from Capitol Hill, especially with pamphlets on the Long Plan and on how to start a club. Requests for pamphlets were handled by Long's Washington staff, most of whom were on the Louisiana payroll. To supplement these efforts, Long, or more often his lieutenant, the Reverend Gerald L. K. Smith, would visit a town to drum up support.

Share Our Wealth worked on the fringes of institutional politics, mobilizing those who were economically harmed by the Depression and dissatisfied with the slow pace of the "first" New Deal. Although many of Share Our Wealth's supporters may have voted in the past, the organization urged a somewhat more profound political commitment than casting a vote. The activities of the clubs centered on spreading the Share Our Wealth message and supporting local groups and local leaders who espoused like-minded policies. In cities, clubs were often initiated and run by dissidents who hoped to disrupt normal patterns of local politics by injecting the issue of redistribution or other Share Our Wealth themes. For instance, in California, Share Our Wealth vied with other groups to pick up the pieces of "End Poverty in California" (EPIC) after Upton Sinclair's failed bid for governor in 1934. Clubs mobilized voters to aid such dissident progressives. Members and supporters also wrote to the President and other Administration officials, urging them to line up behind the Long Plan.

The Share Our Wealth organization was also the vehicle for Long's national political ambitions. Although he claimed that if his plan were enacted he would disband Share Our Wealth, Long hoped to ride it to the Presidency. The clubs were centers of protest and potential levers to install Share Our Wealth planks in the Democratic platform, bases to support progressive congressional candidates or the nucleus of a Presidential campaign. Long hinted that in 1936 he might enter the Democratic primaries or run at the head of a third party. But many, including Farley, thought Long would support a surrogate that year.

Share Our Wealth had a defiant edge uncharacteristic of "third" or new parties. Roosevelt considered Long one of the two most dangerous men in America and not only because of his electoral menace. Long's unorthodox deployment of the Louisiana National Guard, declaring martial law in New Orleans to rout political enemies, and his restrictions on debate in the Louisiana legislature made many doubt his commitment to democratic principles. What is more, Share Our Wealth allied with and appealed to groups with reputations for unruliness. Notably, Share Our Wealth championed the veterans' bonus and was closely associated with veterans' organizations, which had marched on Washington twice in the 1930s. Long participated in and encouraged demonstrations of veterans and their supporters on behalf of the bonus.

Share Our Wealth was the key organization in a larger neopopulist insurgency in the 1930s. It had a greater following and was better organized than Coughlin's NUSJ, Townsend's OARP, and Sinclair's EPIC, all of which lacked the national reach of Share Our Wealth. There is no standard definition of a "social movement" or a social movement organization. All the same, Share Our Wealth meets most definitions of a social movement organization, whether these definitions are based on political involvement (Gamson 1990), the political standing of the group the organization represents (Tilly 1985), or the organization's means of political action (McAdam 1982). Share Our Wealth mobilized people who were not previously mobilized or were undermobilized around the issue of economic redistribution – an issue that had been "organized out" of politics in the 1920s. Thus, Share Our Wealth fits a participation-based definition (Gamson 1990), which would count as well all third-party challengers. Moreover, Share Our Wealth made claims on behalf of the long-standing poor and Americans who were economically devastated by the

Depression – groups with little organized standing in U.S. politics. In addition, Share Our Wealth employed some noninstitutional means, such as boycotts and demonstrations, thus falling under stricter definitions based on political activity (McAdam 1982).

The Meaning of Success and the Social Politics of "Stealing Thunder"

Anyone analyzing movement outcomes must address Gamson's ([1975] 1990) landmark study of 53 randomly chosen U.S. "challenging groups." He argued that "success" has two dimensions – a movement organization might achieve "acceptance," or it might win "new advantages" for its constituency. Achieving both goals was called a "full response," or what Tilly (1978) has called "membership in the polity." A challenger winning neither movement recognition nor new benefits for its constituency was expected to "collapse." The other two combinations were viewed by Gamson as partly successful.

We contend, however, that Gamson advanced a conceptualization of success that is deficient in three ways. First, his definition is not focused enough on new advantages or, more precisely, collective benefits for beneficiary groups. Second, his definition does not take a broad enough view of these collective benefits. Finally, and most important, Gamson's definition may be too loose, impeding causal analysis by discounting beforehand the potential influences of other actors on the achievement of collective benefits. In short, we argue that a challenger cannot be considered successful unless it *wins some collective goods that aid its beneficiary group*.

We focus solely on what Gamson calls "new advantages." Gamson thought political access was as important as winning collective goods, and, though this is partly a matter of differences in interests, other researchers, such as Ragin (1989) and Frey et al. (1992), have converged on new advantages as a more meaningful outcome than

acceptance. This emphasis is shared by those who study collective action and collective goods – those benefits that cannot be easily denied to group members regardless of whether they participated in achieving them.

More important, our way of assessing new advantages does not rely entirely on the perspective of the movement organization. Although, like Gamson, we start by analyzing the benefits inherent in the organization's program, our criteria oblige us to consider the larger group's interests. Unlike Gamson, however, we consider outcomes outside the challenger's program that might promote the interests of the beneficiary group in conceptualizing success. For example, a social movement organization may be considered at least partly successful if its opponent or the state provided tangible collective benefits not specified by the challenger's program. Indeed, we expect that concessions granted by the state will appear often in forms unanticipated by the challenger.

Our conceptualization of partial success is based on collective goods won by the challenger. In the best case a social movement organization might gain the benefits specified in its program and other unanticipated collective benefits as well – a scenario as happy as it is unlikely. In the worst case, the challenger's agenda and beneficiary group may be completely ignored. More likely, a movement organization will gain some collective goods. We count this situation as a partial success. Following Ragin (1989), we consider acceptance of the organization significant only in that it may increase the chances of a challenger's winning collective benefits. We consider it to be closer to failure than to success when challengers win symbolic victories or token benefits, such as highly publicized benefits to prominent individuals, rather than benefits provided automatically to groups. Although Gamson conceptualized and coded "partial or peripheral" new advantages, in the end he categorized challengers as either having won new advantages or not. Instead, we conceptualize and analyze collective benefits along a continuum.

Our most important advance beyond Gamson concerns agency and causality, and, in our view, these issues are central to analyses of social movement outcomes. Unlike Gamson, we are able to investigate whether the organization itself *wins* the benefits. Gamson counted a challenger as having achieved new advantages merely if its agenda was mainly fulfilled (within 15 years of the challenger's demise) – and regardless of whether the movement organization had effected the realization of its goals. Calling a realized agenda a victory without the organization having made it happen, however, overstates the influence of a challenger. Such a premature declaration of success disregards theories that hold that political and economic conditions that influence social protest can also bring about programs that address protestors' grievances. One needs instead to ascertain the unique influence of the movement organization on changes in policy that yield collective benefits. And determining whether and to what degree a challenger effects policy changes is a necessary step in assessing the conditions behind the successes and failures.

Theories of Public Spending and Social Movements and the Political Mediation Theory

For those studying social movements, to explain outcomes of collective action often means to focus on organizations and participants (Gamson 1990; Piven and Cloward 1977; McAdam 1982). In contrast, theorists focusing on "political opportunity structures" see the impact of movement organizations and their collective action on policy outcomes as less significant (Kitschelt 1986); in their view, opportunity structures may determine both challenger formation and policy outcomes. For instance, to augment its coalition a member of the polity may aid movement organizations, perhaps by introducing spending programs favoring the challenger. Some theories of public social provision see matters similarly, focusing on the stimulant effects of left or center political

regimes, the labor movement, or state actors on the adoption and expansion of state spending policies. Left or center political parties, labor movements, or state actors may also encourage the mobilization of protest groups. Similarly, economic theories of public policy argue that crises lead to policy change; others argue that economic crises generate social movements. Because of the similarities in the determinants of social protest movements and in the determinants of public social spending, demonstrating the effectiveness of a state-oriented challenger requires that we show the challenger to be influential beyond the standard economic and political influences on spending policies.

Political mediation theory holds that to achieve gains challengers must be strong organizationally and must also engage in collective action, but all in the context of favorable political circumstances (Amenta, Carruthers, and Zylan 1992). This formulation builds on social science theorizing and research on welfare states and social movements. Research on the determinants of welfare state policies indicates that institutional political activity as well as economic factors have a crucial influence. Research on social movement organizations indicates that such organizations emerge out of pre-existing networks and organizations that are not primarily political. In short, we expect that state policy changes are often effected by institutional political actors. Yet challengers do not result completely from economic or political conditions, and they have some autonomy in their choice of tactics. Moreover, some studies of the determinants of public policy have found that strikes and protest have an impact, but other studies have found that such actions have little impact, or worse, result in "backlash" effects. The uneven results of research on the impact of social protest on public spending suggest that the outcomes of such collective actions are conditional.

According to political mediation theory, the ability of a social movement to win collective benefits depends partly on conditions it can control – its ability to mobilize its membership, its goals and program, its form of organization, its strategies for collective action. However, the success of well mobilized challengers also depends on the political context. This theory holds that political conditions not only influence the mobilization of a protest group, but also the *relationship* between its mobilization and collective actions taken, on the one hand, and policy outcomes, on the other. Unlike standard arguments about the influence of challengers, this mediation thesis holds that mobilization and collective action alone are usually insufficient to effect changes in public policy. We argue that favorable political conditions are crucial for success, not, however, that political opportunity structures determine both movements and policy outcomes.

Two key long-term aspects of the political context are the political system and the party system. First, an undemocratic political system – characterized by restricted voting rights, limited political participation, and a lack of choices among parties – discourages both challenges and public spending policies. Even if challengers do form in such polities, they are unlikely to achieve collective benefits. Second, traditional or patronage-oriented parties regard social movement organizations as menacing contenders and consider programmatic spending policies to be a threat to the individualistic rewards on which such parties thrive. Such structural impediments also thwart the efforts of state actors and insurgents in the party system to enact or enhance programmatic public spending policies.

Medium-range and short-term political conditions can also improve the prospects of mobilized groups that hope to gain leverage in the political system. Two key political actors are favorable regimes in power and sympathetic bureaucrats. A new regime hoping to add to its coalition may aid social movements by proposing spending or other legislation that favors a group. Bureaucrats whose missions are similar to those proposed by challengers may provide favorable administrative rulings, enforce laws favorably, or propose favorable new legislation.

These sympathetic regimes and bureaucrats may advance such legislation further than they had intended if a challenger summons a show of strength.

Regardless of the numbers of their supporters and their degree of commitment, challengers are likely to do better in closely contested political situations: that is, when the addition of a new group to existing coalitions members may change the balance of power. Close elections or alignments in a legislature can provide leverage. Newcomers holding the balance of power is a common occurrence in parliamentary systems, where small parties can decide which established party or parties may form a government. Even in the U.S. political system, where third parties are rare, similar conditions may hold. Political candidates may attempt to appeal to newly mobilized groups with coherent agendas. All the same, the presence of a closely contested polity relies in part on structural conditions. Elections are not likely to be closely contested when few can vote and other democratic rights are restricted. Parties oriented toward patronage may conspire to keep insurgent issues off the political agenda.

Success and the "Displacement" Challenger

One finding stands out in Gamson's study and in its reanalyses: challengers with displacement goals are destined to fail. Such "displacement" challengers are unlikely to be accepted by members of the polity, and only six of Gamson's challengers gained new advantages without first being accepted – a situation Gamson calls "preemption," because the purpose in granting benefits is often to check the insurgency. A benefit without acceptance is more properly considered a "concession," however. This is because the opponent or the state recognizes the need to respond, and protest leaders typically take credit. The social politics of "stealing thunder" – granting a new benefit to a constituency group to stop a challenger from making claims on its own behalf – is always charged, and those attempting to do so can be burned.

We argue that displacement challengers are more likely to be effective when they are electorally oriented or when they call for the replacement of groups that are not extremely powerful. Moreover, the often multi-issue nature of displacement groups should not be defined as being inimical to success. If a movement organization with far-reaching, multiple goals succeeds on some of them, it might be considered as successful as challengers that "thought small" and sought and realized a limited agenda. In addition, a challenger striving unsuccessfully to replace its opponents might bring collective benefits for its supporters, despite its ultimate political failure. Generally speaking, the typical displacement challenger in Gamson's sample wanted to replace *capitalism*. Displacement goals were confounded with what Gamson refers to as "systemic" goals, and anti-system groups face formidable obstacles in affluent democracies.

Of course, challengers bent on replacement might be ignored or repressed – sometimes this occurs even while politicians are granting concessions. All the same, to win concessions a number of key factors are outside the control of the challenger: that the challenger enjoys basic democratic rights, that its officials are concerned with or are constrained by the potential beneficiaries of the movement, and that its officials are not opposed to the challenger's goals. For instance, in democratic societies officials seeking office typically cannot afford to alienate large groups of people. In democratic political systems challengers with far-reaching goals are likely to be harassed by investigations and campaigns of disinformation aimed at discrediting them.

Analyzing the prospects of "unacceptable" challengers like Share Our Wealth presents certain methodological difficulties. If politicians grant benefits because of the pressure from a protest mobilization, the politicians will be unlikely to admit the benefits are being granted for that reason. For in-

stance, if Roosevelt was making concessions to the constituency of Share Our Wealth to woo away its supporters and keep the allegiance of potential converts to the challenger, he did so without announcing his intentions. Similarly, challenger leaders might claim that changes in policy unprovoked by movement activity are actually concessions, thus gaining new supporters and invigorating the commitment of current ones. These possibilities place a premium on comparing the plans of the Roosevelt Administration with its subsequent actions and on examining the historical evidence and data concerning the Administration's responses to Share Our Wealth.

Did Long's "Share Our Wealth" Influence the Second New Deal?

Contemporaries of Long and historians disagree on Share Our Wealth's impact on the Second New Deal, and the short life of the insurgency complicates the issue. Attributing "success" to Share Our Wealth is also complicated by the fact that two key determinants of social movements – economic grievances and political opportunities – could account for what Share Our Wealth leaders might claim were successes. Economic theories of policy posit that economic decline itself provokes public spending; political theories maintain that powerful state reformers or left-center regimes enact public policies of redistribution. Either type of theory might predict the emergence of the policies of Second New Deal, even in the absence of Share Our Wealth.

To ascertain the influence of this challenger, we examine outcomes from the perspective of Share Our Wealth's constituency, which might have won new benefits had Long become president. One road was mapped in Sinclair Lewis's ([1935] 1970) novel *It Can't Happen Here*. A character modeled on Long, Senator Buzz Windrip, challenges Roosevelt for the 1936 Democratic nomination and forms an alliance with a character based on Coughlin, the

Methodist Bishop Peter Paul Prang, and his "League of Forgotten Men." With the convention deadlocked, Prang (Coughlin) appears at the head of a band of Forgotten Men and stampedes the assembly for Windrip (Long), who goes on to defeat the Republican Walt Trowbridge, a character based on the former President Herbert Hoover. A second scenario in the novel was based on events in 1912, when Theodore Roosevelt, running as a Progressive, induced the defeat of the Republican President, William Taft, and the election of the Democrat Woodrow Wilson. Long might have similarly prevented the reelection of Franklin Roosevelt by leading or backing a left-wing third party. After "throwing" the election to a Republican, Long would, presumably, watch the Depression deepen, bide his time, contest the Democratic nomination in 1940, and then ascend to the Presidency. President Long would then implement his Plan, as he outlined in his fanciful *My First Days in the White House*.

This did not happen, but Share Our Wealth still may have won collective benefits for its supporters. To check the organization, the President may have adopted some parts of the Long Plan or similarly redistributive programs – stiff taxes on income and wealth, bonuses for veterans, pensions for the aged, aid for farmers, wages and hours legislation for workers. Did the President and Congress act on this agenda, and to what degree were they influenced by Share Our Wealth?

Roosevelt's Plans, the Neopopulists, and the Second New Deal

Many have noted that Roosevelt's "second hundred days" – a wave of reform that began in June 1935 – coincided with the crest of Share Our Wealth's mobilization. The four initial measures of the President's "must" legislation included a public utility holding company bill, a banking bill, a bill by Senator Robert Wagner guaranteeing rights of labor, and the bill that became the Social Security Act. A "soak-the-rich" tax bill was

soon added to the list. To determine whether Share Our Wealth influenced the construction or adoption of these proposals, we ask: What was the Roosevelt Administration expecting to do, and did it fear Long and alter its goals and priorities to counter him. If the Administration advanced proposals that it had already devised and planned to enact, Share Our Wealth would have to be judged irrelevant. If the Administration, however, went out of its way to appease this challenger, Share Our Wealth may be judged influential. Like Gamson, we rely in part on historians and historiography to answer these questions, but we were also able to examine some primary historical information about Long and the Second New Deal.

All indications are that Share Our Wealth had little influence on the *planning* of bills in the Second New Deal. The Social Security Act and the National Labor Relations Act were laid out before 1935. The Social Security Act was designed by experts on the President's Committee on Economic Security; its social insurance provisions were based on proposals developed by reform organizations inside and outside the state. The National Labor Relations Act was designed mainly by Wagner and his staff and ran somewhat outside the redistributive concerns of Share Our Wealth.

[...]

Winning concessions implies that new programs must confer collective benefits on the challenger's constituents. The tax legislation was expected to yield only about $400 million in new revenues and may have been partly a symbolic reform. Although this so-called "soak-the-rich" tax measure did not threaten the truly wealthy and the revenues from it could not finance Long's ambitious program, the measure broke the pattern of regressive New Deal taxation initiatives, such as the payroll taxes for social insurance. And although "broadening the base" of the personal income tax, as championed by Senator Robert LaFollette, Jr., the Wisconsin Progressive, might have resulted in greater redistribution, the soak the-rich taxation legislation was a good start.

Another plank from the Share Our Wealth platform – the early payment of veterans' bonuses – had to wait. In May 1935, Congress passed such a bill, but Roosevelt took the unprecedented step of delivering his veto message before Congress and over radio. He apparently felt that keeping the budget closer to balanced mattered more. He allowed the bill to pass, but not until 1936. To pay for the bonus, Roosevelt called for new taxes: a stiffer corporation income tax and an undistributed corporate profits tax, taxes that provided $800 million per year, much more than the previous soak-the-rich taxes. These moves were made after Long's death, but the Roosevelt Administration may have been motivated in part to prevent the regrouping of Long's supporters for a third-party run in 1936 behind a new leader. That summer Coughlin broke with Roosevelt and led a third-party bid against him, joining forces with Townsend and Smith.

In summary, then, Share Our Wealth's influence on the Second New Deal was more than negligible. Although none of the Second New Deal legislative proposals resembled closely the Long Plan and most were devised by others, Roosevelt did propose something unexpected – the tax message of June 1935. This tax program was not going to result in the leveling of incomes and wealth envisioned by Long, but the program did break a pattern of regressive taxation. And when the Administration agreed to pay the veterans' bonus in 1936, it also passed a more productive and progressive tax on corporations.

The Roosevelt Administration also attempted to undermine Long and other neopopulist leaders. In Louisiana Roosevelt denied Long federal patronage and used such patronage to promote his enemies. In 1934, the Administration reopened a Treasury Department investigation into Long's tax returns and those of his political allies. No doubt this harassment would have intensified had Long lived longer. The Administration began investigating Coughlin in

1934, and even the mild-mannered Townsend was the target of an April 1936 congressional investigation.

Share Our Wealth's impact during this period was doubtless greater than that of other neopopulist groups, such as Coughlin's National Union of Social Justice or Townsend's Old Age and Revolving Pensions. Although the Townsend Movement may have put pressure on politicians to do something to aid the elderly, old-age assistance – the Social Security Act's most significant spending program – had passed Congress the previous year, and the Townsendites opposed old-age insurance, but were powerless to defeat or change it. Western members of Congress avoided voting on the alternative Townsend bill, knowing colleagues from elsewhere would kill it. The banking bill of the second hundred days was dismissed by Coughlin as worthless, and Coughlin's monetary reforms probably would have done little to reduce unemployment had they been enacted. Share Our Wealth's agenda was advanced further, and the parts of the Long Plan that were enacted conferred some real collective benefits on the organization's constituents. Because the Roosevelt Administration clearly went somewhat out of its way to respond to Long, Share Our Wealth was responsible in part for these advantages. Yet what components of these benefits were due to other influences? And why was this insurgency relatively successful?

Political Mediation, the Influence of Share Our Wealth, and the Secret Poll

To analyze outcomes of interest to challengers it is best to start with what they wanted and how they attempted to get it. The three movement organizations of Long, Townsend, and Coughlin had displacement goals, but of different sorts. Of the three, Share Our Wealth's goals were the most profound, as they called for the replacement of the New Deal and of the President. The Townsend Movement mainly wanted to replace the Roosevelt Administration's old-age bureaucracies and programs. In 1935 Coughlin's National Union for Social Justice could not decide whether to influence the President or topple him. In addition, Share Our Wealth was a "multiple-issue" challenger, and Long's influence in 1935 means that displacement goals did not automatically rule out winning policy victories.

More important, Share Our Wealth's mobilization was the largest and most widespread of the three challengers. Share Our Wealth was inaugurated in February 1934, one month after Townsend's organization was incorporated. According to the incredibly precise Christenberry, Long's secretary, after one year Share Our Wealth had 27,431 clubs with 7,682,768 members, a number that had supposedly doubled since November 1934. And the organization also flourished afterwards, as Smith, Long's lieutenant, visited half the U.S. states, and as Long delivered his message over the radio. In contrast, by February 1935 the Townsend Movement included about 450,000 fee-paying elderly who were mainly located in the West. Both groups had far more members and more extensive operations than Coughlin's National Union, which was inaugurated only in November 1934 and whose organizational efforts in 1935 went little beyond radio broadcasts.

Share Our Wealth also had the simplest strategy – to create loosely organized local groups committed to Long's brand of economic democracy and willing to support him against the President. Townsend's strategy was more involved and time-consuming: organize clubs in every Congressional district across the country and induce candidates of both parties to endorse the plan. By 1935 it had only begun. To the extent that Coughlin had a plan of action in 1935, it was to implore his radio listeners to write letters to the President to convince him to back Coughlin's banking reforms. All in all, in 1935 Share Our Wealth had the largest following and a collective action program that had achieved some measurable success. Because of its greater mobilization and the simplicity of its early collective action pro-

gram, it is not surprising that Long's organization enjoyed the greatest success of the three in 1935.

Long and Share Our Wealth stimulated the first scientific public opinion poll on a Presidential race: Emil Hurja, the chief statistician and an executive director of the Democratic National Committee, mailed straw ballots and a cover letter on April 30, 1935 to about 150,000 people in the U.S. states. He made the poll appear as if it were being conducted by a magazine, the nonexistent *National Inquirer*. All the information was to be received from a three-by-five inch card – the two-cents postage was prepaid. (Farley, the chairman of the Democratic National Committee, was also Postmaster General.) Emphasizing that it was a "Secret Ballot," the postcard and letter asked the voter, "If an election were held today, who would be your choice for President of the United States" and encouraged him or her to mark an "X" in one of four boxes: for Franklin D. Roosevelt, a Republican Candidate, Huey P. Long, and a dotted line for a write-in alternative. The ballot also asked for the respondent's state and for whom the respondent voted in 1932.

Hurja employed a two-tier sampling process. One sample was apparently drawn from telephone owners – a group containing mainly employed people. Exactly 100,000 were polled, with ballots on white cards, in the 48 states. He polled separately people who received unemployment aid, or in common parlance, "relief recipients." They were sent ballots printed on blue cards. Some 49,742 relief recipients in 32 states were sampled. Ballots were sent mainly to men, but also to some women. About 21 percent (30,924 of the 150,000) ballots were returned. Overall Roosevelt was selected by 54.2 percent, the Republican by 29.6 percent, and Long by 10.9 percent. The strongest write-in candidate was Father Coughlin, who received about 1 percent. Other candidates were categorized as "miscellaneous left" and "miscellaneous right." Among the employed, however, the race was close: Roosevelt was selected by 47.2

percent of the telephone-owning respondents, the Republican by about 40 percent, and Long by 7.8 percent. Although Long's best states were Louisiana and ones nearby, his support was nationwide and not limited to the South or rural areas.

In reviewing this polling effort, Farley (1948) wrote that Long might have captured between 3 to 4 million votes – including "100,000 in New York State" – and "his third party movement might constitute a balance of power in the 1936 election" (p. 51). In his final tallies, Hurja discounted the "blue" ballots from relief recipients and relied on the "white" ballots from telephone owners. To adjust the results for the fact that the white ballot sample did not represent the voting public at large, Hurja relied on information on the candidate for whom the respondent had voted in 1932 and compared the poll responses to the actual results of the 1932 election. Because the white ballot responses concerning the 1932 Presidential vote matched the actual results, his adjustments were minimal, and the "official" poll results indicated a tight race: Roosevelt with 49.3 percent of the vote, the Republican 42.5 percent, Long 7.4 percent, and Coughlin .8 percent. Roosevelt would win in 33 states with 305 electoral votes, and the Republican would win in 15 states with 226 electoral votes.

The official results show that Long was on the verge of delivering the election to the Republicans. If Long was drawing support only from the left, the poll indicated that he would transfer five states, including New York, and 122 electoral votes to the unknown Republican candidate. According to these results, it would take only the defection of Michigan, Iowa, and Minnesota – where Roosevelt held a lead of 7 percentage points or less – to swing the election. Because the official results indicated that Long might have made the outcome close, it is plausible that Roosevelt would act on the Share Our Wealth agenda. Still, Hurja's analyses, based greatly on the preferences of Roosevelt's supporters in 1932, found that Roosevelt was losing voters not only to Long and the left,

but also to the Republicans and the right. Hurja found only 10 states where Roosevelt's 1932 voters were moving more to the left than to the right. It is possible to infer from this result that Roosevelt should also have been shoring up his right flank – a kind of political tacking.

However one reads the poll results, the desire of Roosevelt to win over the supporters of Share Our Wealth depended on specific political opportunities. The first was the perceived closeness of the contest between the Democratic and the Republican candidates. Roosevelt's chances were expected to be harmed not where Share Our Wealth was strongest, but where the challenger might tip elections in electorally important states. This result depended on the mobilization of voters behind Long and the closeness in support between Roosevelt and the Republican. Long had strong backing in Louisiana and in some of the nearby nondemocratic states, but in none of these was he within 20 percentage points of tipping these Democratic bastions to the Republican. In contrast, the five states expected to be "thrown" by Long averaged about 8 percent support for him, his overall average. To have an impact, Share Our Wealth required not only a minimum level of mobilization, but also secure voting rights and tight competition for electoral votes. Had Roosevelt's advisors viewed his lead as more solid, Long would not have seemed as threatening.

Another political precondition of Share Our Wealth's influence was the existence of a reform administration and a left-center coalition in Congress – characteristics often claimed to be important for the passage of programs of economic redistribution. Under most circumstances, the President might have neither the inclination nor the power to preempt a challenger bidding for redistribution. Had a Republican been President, as was the case in 1932 when Long presented his first taxation program to no avail in the Senate, Share Our Wealth would not have affected the Administration's agenda. And without a strongly Democratic Congress, Roosevelt's taxation and other proposals would not have resulted in new laws. The Democratic majority in Congress reached an all-time high after the elections in 1934, during which Democrats benefited from the activism of Roosevelt's first New Deal. Though they might stall or modify legislation, Republicans and southern and conservative Democrats could not veto reforms. Share Our Wealth required an already left-leaning administration and Congress to be able to make an impact, and in 1935 these conditions were met.

The movement organization's form and rhetoric may have limited its support and its possibilities for coalition-building. The apparent impracticality of central elements of the Long Plan alienated many on the left and made cooperation difficult with the Wisconsin Progressives and the Minnesota Farmer-Labor party. Although the Roosevelt Administration was not averse to the skillful use of patronage and ignored the blatant fund-raising tactics of some of its allies (such as the Edward J. Kelly machine of Chicago), the fact that Long so ruthlessly employed patronage made him and Share Our Wealth suspect among the progressive radical parties of the Midwest and left him open to attack.

Moreover, like these other third parties, the viability of Long's Share Our Wealth was based on controlling politics in one state. When Long was assassinated, Share Our Wealth died with him, only in part because he had embodied the insurgency. It was as crucial that the Louisiana Democratic party no longer backed it. Rev. Smith tried to pick up the pieces, but was exiled by Long's Louisiana successors, who had made peace with Roosevelt in what was soon labeled by Share Our Wealth supporters as the Second Louisiana Purchase.

[...]

Conclusion

This study's implications range from the methodological to the historical to the theoretical. Our *methodological* suggestions in

studying the impact of collective action are for researchers to examine and compare how specific challengers are organized, what they want, how they are trying to get it, with what resources, strategies, and tactics, under what conditions, and to what degree they gain collective benefits. Researchers should go beyond the strategy of Gamson and others, who focus solely on the agenda of the movement organization's leaders. This is usually possible because most scholars, who examine one or a few movements at a time, are not operating under the same constraints as did Gamson, whose path-breaking research encompassed the gamut of social movement organizations, with their sundry goals, structures, and strategies ranging across the expanse of American history. Other investigators can and should attend to the interests of a movement organization's potential beneficiaries. Protest groups with far-reaching demands that achieve gains on only some demands might actually be more successful than groups that think small and win most of what they request. Moreover, researchers should pay attention to alternative causal routes to what social movement organizations may claim as victories won. To count favorable outcomes as victories, one needs to build a case that things happened differently from what would have occurred in the absence of the challenger. This task can be approached by examining closely the responses to the movement, ranging from historical information on changes in plans by the movement's targets to systematic statistical data about policy outcomes.

As for the *historical* question of influence, Share Our Wealth doubtless had an impact on some policymaking in the Second New Deal. Share Our Wealth pressed the Roosevelt Administration to propose progressive taxation, and partly because of Share Our Wealth the Administration began to change the face of U.S. tax policy. Regression analyses indicate that Share Our Wealth may have also influenced the distribution of unemployment relief. Although other neopopulists, like Townsend and Coughlin, made bids for influence and for economic redistribution during the mid-1930s, Share Our Wealth had the most immediate effect. This is not to say that standard determinants of public policy had no impact or that Share Our Wealth accounted for the bulk of the Second New Deal.

More important, our results suggest that the impact of the collective action of challengers on policy is conditional. Specifically, this historical episode supports the *political mediation theory*, according to which outcomes depend not only on mobilization and action, but also on political opportunities. It was not merely Share Our Wealth's ability to mobilize supporters around a program of redistribution that led to its influence. The creation and adoption of the soak-the-rich tax plan required other political conditions outside the control of Share Our Wealth. The movement organization had to become a plausible threat to the President's reelection by drawing enough support to give a Republican candidate a chance to win. But this possibility depended crucially on the character of the race between the two major-party candidates. Share Our Wealth had an impact not because of states like Louisiana and its neighbors where Long was strongest, but because of electorally important states where Long's candidacy may have tightened close races. In addition, the influence of the insurgency depended on the existence of a regime and a Congress actually sympathetic to its goals. Without the reformer Roosevelt in office, a program of redistribution might never have been proposed. Without an overwhelmingly Democratic Congress, initiatives proposed by the President might not have become laws. The evidence on relief spending suggests that Share Our Wealth had an impact, not where it had the greatest following, but where Long's candidacy had the greatest expected electoral effect on the race. Needless to say, the evidence on WPA spending also supports theories of the welfare state based on institutional politics.

Our study also has implications for understanding the impact of a challenger's goals and structure on outcomes. We find that the displacement goals of Share Our Wealth did not sentence it to failure. A social movement organization, like Share Our Wealth, that seeks to displace established representatives of political parties or state bureaucrats in charge of policies can win victories. Moreover Share Our Wealth's kind of insurgency – based both on a program and one person's Presidential ambitions – has certain advantages. One is that the challenger's program can come to the fore quickly, without an extensive collective action program. Share Our Wealth merely had to win a following and wait for the Roosevelt Administration to take note. A personal political challenger that is issue-based may help to put the movement organization's issue on the political agenda. The displacement goals of a challenger based simultaneously on leader and program minimizes conflicts of interest between the organization's leadership and its supporters. Share Our Wealth, the program, was unlikely to be bartered for favors from the Administration, as Long had irrevocably broken with Roosevelt. The fact that Share Our Wealth championed so many issues had a double-edged effect, however. Pressing different concerns probably increased the chances that the Administration would take action on *something*, but *which* proposals would be addressed was in the Administration's hands; it chose tax increases rather than veterans' bonuses. Displacement groups and other groups with far-reaching demands might win a lot for their supporters and beneficiaries, even when the target is not replaced.

The anxiety of Roosevelt's men over Long and Share Our Wealth was marked by the Administration's unprecedented polling effort to ascertain Long's strength. Roosevelt also sought to discredit Long, to undermine his organization in Louisiana, and in part to steal his thunder: making appeals over the heads of Share Our Wealth's leaders to win over their followers. All of this probably would have been enough to deflect this challenger in 1936 had Long lived to run for President, but who can say for sure? What seems more certain is that Long's insurgency did have an impact on the New Deal, in part because of the support that Long had accumulated, but also because of other political circumstances that worked to the advantage of Share Our Wealth.

References

Amenta, Edwin, Bruce G. Carruthers, and Yvonne Zylan. 1992. "A Hero For the Aged? The Townsend Movement, the Political Mediation Model, and U.S. Old-Age Policy, 1934–1950." *American Journal of Sociology* 98:308–39.

Farley, James A. 1938. *Behind the Ballots: The Personal History of a Politician*. New York: Harcourt, Brace.

——1948. *Jim Farley's Story: The Roosevelt Years*. New York: McGraw Hill.

Frey, R. Scott, Thomas Dietz, and Linda Kalof. 1992. "Characteristics of Successful Protest Groups: Another Look at Gamson's *Strategy of Social Protest*." *American Journal of Sociology* 98:368–87.

Gamson, William A. [1975] 1990. *The Strategy of Social Protest*. Belmont, CA: Wadsworth.

Kitschelt, Herbert P. 1986. "Political Opportunity Structures and Political Protest: Anti-Nuclear Movements in Four Democracies." *British Journal of Political Science* 16:57–85.

Lewis, Sinclair. [1935] 1970. *It Can't Happen Here*. New York: New American Library.

McAdam, Doug. 1982. *Political Process and the Development of Black Insurgency*. Chicago, IL: University of Chicago Press.

Piven, Frances Fox and Richard A. Cloward. 1977. *Poor People's Movements*. New York: Random House.

Ragin, Charles C. 1989. "The Logic of the Comparative Method and the Algebra of Logic." *Journal of Quantitative Anthropology* 1:373–98.

Tilly, Charles. 1978. *From Mobilization to Revolution*. Reading, MA: Addison-Wesley.

——1985. "Models and Realities of Popular Collective Action." *Social Research* 52: 717–47.

33 Movements and Cultural Change

Ron Eyerman and Andrew Jamison

Structures of Feeling and Cultural Transformation

We have discussed social movements [. . .] as articulators and transformers of culture. As forms of collective action emerging in social and historical contexts, social movements presuppose and make use of preexisting forms of social solidarity and communication: culture, that is, at its most basic. In the process, they draw upon and revitalize traditions at the same time as they transform them. As cultural as well as political actors, social movements reinterpret established and shared frameworks of meaning which make communication and coordinated action possible. This "common culture" comprises many levels and dimensions and takes on many specific forms, which can be broadly specified as national, regional, religious, class- and age-related, ethnic, and ideological. [. . .] [W]e have sought to show how common cultures change through the catalytic intervention of social movements.

Social movements also open spaces in which particular movement cultures – rituals, traditions, forms of artistic expression – can emerge. While such cultures are related to and dependent upon the deeper social structures from which they emerge, they are also capable of producing something new and different. Social movements produce innovative forms of understanding – what we have called exemplary action – which impact upon and are capable of transforming wider, established cultures. Even if such transformation is minimal or indirect, in the case of short-lived or violently re-pressed movements – or movements, like that of the 1960s, that have inspired waves of reaction and counter-movement – social movements can help to reinvent and reproduce traditions of protest and rebellion, "alternative" cultures, which live on in the collective memory and which may influence and affect the emergence of future social movements. We have used music and musical traditions to illustrate these processes. Our discussions of African-American and American folk musics, as well as the Swedish progressive music movement, were meant to illustrate how social movements have influenced and developed distinct musical genres and how music and movements together have affected the wider popular culture.

The kinds of cultural processes that we have been exploring resemble what Raymond Williams termed "structures of feeling." Our argument has been that those structures of feeling are more than merely emotive – that they contain a rational or logical core, a truth-bearing significance, as well. The construction of meaning through music and song is, we claim, a central aspect of collective identity formation, and our examples have been meant to illustrate and exemplify how collective structures of feeling are actually made and reorganized, in part, through song. The structures of feeling that Williams talked about are difficult to grasp by reading individual literary texts or analyzing individual artistic creations. Rather, we would contend that they can be read more easily through the songs that are sung in movements, that songs and music give us access to both feelings and thoughts that are shared by larger collectivities and that make better claim, perhaps, for cultural representativity. Structures of feeling, like emergent cultural formations, need to be conceptualized in relation to real social actors.

There is another side to our argument that is even more important. Not only are songs significant and largely untapped resources for the academic observer; they are also channels of communication for activists – within movements, but also between different movements, and, indeed, between movement generations. Music enters into what we have called the collective memory, and songs can conjure up long-lost movements from extinction as well as reawakening forgotten structures of feeling. In this respect, the songs of social movements affect the dynamics of cultural transformations, the historical relations between dominant, residual, and emergent cultural formations.

Tradition, the past in the present, is vital to our understanding and interpretation of who we are and what we are meant to do. As such, it is a powerful source of inspiration for social movements and emergent cultural formations. These include most obviously traditions of protest and rebellion, but also, more subtly, forms of living and underlying sensibilities, which are at a remove from those currently available, but which still exist in the residues and margins of society. Such structures of feeling can be embodied and preserved in and through music, which is partly why music is such a powerful force in social movements and in social life generally. Music in a sense *is* a structure of feeling. It creates mood – bringing it all back home, as Dylan once said – and in this way can communicate a feeling of common purpose, even amongst actors who have no previous historical connections with one another. While such a sense may be fleeting and situational, it can be recorded and reproduced, and enter into memory, individual as well as collective, to such an extent that it can be recalled or remembered at other times and places. In such a fashion, music can recall not only the shared situationally bound experiences, but also a more general commitment to common cause and to collective action. For the musician or songwriter as "movement intellectual," the spirit of his or her work can live on even when they're gone, to paraphrase an old Phil Ochs song.

In its broadest and deepest sense, culture is about meaning and identity, aspects of human life which are not instrumental, but basic and fundamental. In our understanding, social movements help articulate meaning and identity, and engender strong emotional commitment, even if they are also instrumental and strategic. Within social movements actors reinterpret their relation to the world and to others in it. They experiment with identities, individual and collective, by restating them in conscious ways, as authentic and/or traditional, for instance. By singing together at the lunch counter in Mississippi, "We shall not be moved," civil rights activists became moral witnesses, practitioners of civil disobedience. As such, they altered their identities through exemplary action. To ignore this or to see it as of secondary importance to the more strategic aspects of social movement activity is to trivialize social movements, and the motivations and understandings of activists, as well as to define far too narrowly the boundaries of culture and of collective identity. Those who would reduce social movements to instrumental actors engaged in power struggles on a battlefield called a "political opportunity structure" have made an ontological choice. They have chosen to see the world in terms of structures and processes which exist outside the meanings actors themselves attach to them. For them the world consists of causal connections between dependent and independent variables, not the struggles of real human beings meaningfully engaged in constructing their world in conflict and cooperation with others. Culture from this instrumentalist perspective must be "operationalized" as a dependent variable, as a weapon in strategic battle, which can be taken on and discarded more or less at will. In this book, we have clearly made another ontological choice, namely to view culture as the independent variable, as the seedbed of social change, supplying actors with the sources of meaning and identity out of which they collectively construct social action and interaction. In social movements, new collective meanings are consciously made and remade by creatively working with these cultural materials: this is what we have called the mobilization of tradition.

In a narrower but no less emotionally powerful sense, culture can be understood as symbolic representation and expression. Here music and art generally come into the picture as cultural expressions which represent the past in the present. We have attempted to illustrate the role social movements play in this process of tradition-making and -transforming, as well as acknowledging the more instrumental and strategic functions of art and music to social movement mobilization. Further, we have suggested ways in which the musical traditions reinterpreted within social movements have spread into and transformed the wider culture, in both the broad and the narrow understandings of the term. The musical traditions reinterpreted through social movements have helped transform popular music in the United States, as they have affected the way Americans, and others, understand themselves and their society. In making this clear we have reinstated the ancient understanding of music, and art generally, as truth-bearing cognitive forces. We have unified the two generally accepted notions of culture, as a way of life and as representation and record of that way of life in symbolic form as art. At the same time, we have brought together the two sites or repositories that have divided sociological discussions of culture: the subjective and the objective. Music as experienced and performed within social movements is at once subjective and objective, individual and collective in its forms and in its effects. Through its ritualized performance and through the memories it invokes, the music of social movements transcends the boundaries of the self and binds the individual to a collective consciousness. This is what we have identified as the "truth-bearing" message, or the rationality, of movement music, where individual and collective identity fuse and where past and future are reconnected to the present in a meaningful way.

[...]

Biographies

Martin Luther King, Jr.: Prophet of Nonviolence

In the days following Rosa Parks' arrest for refusing to yield her bus seat to a white man, leaders of the African-American community in Montgomery, Alabama, scrambled to organize a city-wide bus boycott. It was a challenge to reach the 45,000 African-Americans in this city of 120,000, and the social networks of the black churches were the only way to do it. Unfortunately, there were longstanding tensions among them, and several different preachers probably felt they should be chosen to lead the new Montgomery Improvement Association. Perhaps for this very reason, a young, 26-year-old preacher, who had been in Montgomery only two years and had not yet become embroiled in the infighting, was selected. Few outside his own Dexter Avenue Baptist Church knew who he was.

That night, Martin Luther King, Jr., delivered his first big speech to an audience of thousands. He spoke for only a few minutes. He began awkwardly, fumbling for images that would stir the crowd, most of whom could not fit in the church and were listening to loudspeakers outside. Then King said, "And you know, my friends, there comes a time when people get tired of being trampled over by the iron feet of oppression." The line was a winner, and occasional "yeses" and "Amens" combined into a great sustained cheer. King had the audience now, surprising himself and the members of his own congregation who were present. His rhetoric would only improve during his remaining twelve, remarkable years.

King was born to the African-American elite, son of an Atlanta preacher and educated at Morehouse College, Crozer Theological Seminary, and Boston University, where he earned his Ph.D. in 1955. He was ordained at age 19. But stardom was thrust upon him, through his rather accidental choice to lead the Montgomery bus boycott. His charisma was, some have argued, created by his structural position. At the same time, he more than lived up to expectations. King had a resonant voice, a good store of Biblical allusions, a keen sense of what would rouse his audience, and a mastery of the theory and art of civil disobedience. Not everyone would have played the role so well.

The Montgomery boycott, which succeeded after a grueling year, helped bring national attention to the Southern civil rights movement, even landing King on the cover of *Time* magazine. He helped form, and was selected leader of, a new organization that would apply Montgomery's lessons elsewhere in the South, the Southern Christian Leadership Conference (SCLC). Black preachers, familiar figures in their dark blue suits, were respected leaders of the African-American community. They brought to the civil rights movement important resources such as places to meet and organize, a flow of funds from African-American churches in northern cities, and social networks that helped spread the word about successful tactics.

King's SCLC simply was the civil rights movement in the late 1950s. It eclipsed the older National Association for the Advancement of Colored People (NAACP), which pursued legal solutions to the problems of segregation, discrimination, and disenfranchisement. In 1960 the SCLC was joined by a more radical organization, composed of students, which grew out of lunch-counter sit-ins, the Student Nonviolent Coordinating Committee (SNCC). Later, the Nation of Islam, the Black Panther Party, and other radicals and black "nationalists" would create a more separatist movement and pugnacious brand of protest. Inspired by Gandhi's philosophy of nonviolence, however, King continued to favor large rallies, marches, and arrests for civil disobedience. His style of civil rights protest reached its apogee with the 1963 March on Washington, attended by a quarter million people. With "I Have a Dream," King delivered one of the most famous speeches in history. He was awarded the Nobel Prize for Peace the following year. But King continued to evolve.

After the passage of the Civil Rights Act of 1964 and the Voting Rights Act of 1965, King increasingly turned his attention to states outside the South. He came to see poverty as the key problem of black Americans, and of America generally, and he hoped to forge a broad antipoverty coalition. King's rhetoric became increasingly radical in his last years, calling for a "radical revolution of values." "You can't talk about solving the economic problem of the Negro without talking about billions of dollars," King proclaimed in 1966. "Now this means that we are treading in difficult waters, because it really means that we are saying that something is wrong...with capitalism.... There must be a better distribution of wealth and maybe America must move toward a Democratic Socialism." In 1967 King initiated a "Poor People's Campaign" which focused on providing jobs for the poor of all races. He began planning a new March on Washington, which he did not live to see, which would demand an Economic Bill of Rights guaranteeing employment for able-bodied individuals, incomes for those unable to work, and an end to housing discrimination.

King was also an early and vocal opponent of the Vietnam War, at a time when most liberals as well as conservatives supported the war. He encouraged young men to become conscientious objectors. King viewed the war as a grotesque waste of life and resources. He suggested that "A nation that continues year after year to spend more money on military defense than on programs of social uplift is approaching spiritual death."

King was assassinated on April 4, 1968, while supporting a strike of black sanitation workers in Memphis, Tennessee. In 1986 the third Monday of January was designated a federal holiday in his honor.

Betty Friedan and *The Feminine Mystique*

Ideas are crucial to social movements, and in the literate modern world those ideas are often expressed in books. The volume that did the most to revive the women's movement in the 1960s was packaged as a critique of housewives written by one: *The Feminine Mystique*. Its author, Betty Friedan, was born in Peoria, Illinois, in 1921, only one year after the Nineteenth Amendment had given women the right to vote. Her father was an ambitious immigrant who had put himself through medical school. Her mother was a housewife who, when young, had wanted to go to Smith College, something her parents did not allow.

From childhood, Friedan was known to have a brilliant mind and a quick temper, two things girls were not supposed to have in Peoria. Having skipped a grade, she felt like an outsider, a status probably exacerbated by local anti-Semitism and her lack of traditional good looks. At Smith College she developed, despite her own affluent background, radical sympathies as well as a rabble-rousing reputation as editor of the school news-paper. She supported, for instance, a strike by the maids who cleaned students' rooms and served them in the dining halls. Between her junior and senior years she spent several weeks at the Highlander Folk School in Tennessee, a training ground for leftist labor organizers.

After graduating in 1942, Friedan went to Berkeley to study psychology. She shone there as well, and was soon offered a lucrative fellowship that would have supported her through finishing her Ph.D. She panicked when a boyfriend implied that his envy would ruin their relationship if she took the scholarship, and – feeling torn between love and career – she left the university. For the next nine years she would work for a left-wing news service, then the newspaper of a leftist union, the United Electrical, Radio and Machine Workers of America.

At the age of 26, Friedan met a veteran named Carl Friedman and fell in love. He was a college drop-out, and no intellectual, but he loved the theater and seemed to love Betty. Despite misgivings on each side, they soon married. Their first child was born in late 1948, and Betty was given a maternity leave by the union (which was later cut short, however). She became pregnant again in 1952, during a crisis for the union, which had lost two thirds of its members in the face of redbaiting by the government and the Congress of Industrial Organizations (CIO). The four-person newspaper staff, two men and two women, had to be cut in half, and both the women left (how voluntarily is not altogether clear). Brilliant, radical Betty became a housewife in Queens.

Sort of. She continued to write articles, now for women's magazines, in which any political and economic analysis, or anything that implied that women might be more satisfied working than raising children, was assiduously edited out. A serious debate was raging over whether women should go to college at all, or instead be schooled in the skills of managing a home, since that is what they were going to do. Many otherwise sensible scholars argued that college was wasted on women. Friedan wrote an article arguing the opposite, only to see it rejected by *McCall's* and published by the *Ladies' Home Journal* only after it was edited to make the opposite point. At the same time, she also helped organize community groups for various causes, from a rent strike to sex education in the schools. Friedan was not your typical housewife.

In 1957, Friedan and two of her Smith classmates wrote a lengthy questionnaire to distribute at their fifteenth reunion that spring. Inspired by their own experiences in therapy, and a sense from the tenth reunion that most of the women were overwhelmed with childrearing, they asked a number of proto-feminist questions, like "What problems have you had working out your role as a woman?" Friedan did other research on women's issues, and realized that she might be able to publish her ideas as a book, since they were too controversial for most magazines. W. W. Norton gave her an advance, and in 1963 she published *The Feminine Mystique*.

Her book became a bestseller, in part due to her own ferocious self-promotion (she replaced her agent, forced Norton to hire an outside publicist for the book, and went on her own publicity tour). Even more, it touched a nerve among millions of women, and by 1970 it had sold 1.5 million copies. It described and analyzed the dissatisfaction felt by so many American housewives and mothers, each locked up in her own "comfortable concentration camp": "Each suburban wife struggled with it alone. As she made the beds, shopped for groceries, matched slipcover material, ate peanut butter sandwiches with her children, chauffeured Cub Scouts and Brownies, lay beside her husband at night – she was afraid to ask even of herself the silent question – 'Is this all?'" Friedan had packaged the ideas of Simone de Beauvoir and Margaret Mead for middle-class house-wives. She had also carefully avoided linking her analysis to Marxism, and suppressed any mention of her own years in the Left, now discredited by years of McCarthyism. The plight of women, it seemed, was distinct. To help sell her book, Friedan shrewdly but inaccurately presented herself as a simple suburban housewife who just couldn't take it any more.

The Feminine Mystique helped the women's movement coalesce in the mid-1960s, providing an ideology for the networks that had formed around the National Commission on the Status of Women (and state-level equivalents). Many of these women (and some men) were active in forming the National Organization for Women (NOW) in 1966. Its goal was to integrate women into the mainstream of American society and institutions, and it would remain the central organization of the liberal, reformist wing of the women's movement. Friedan, now a celebrity, was elected its first president. She would remain active in the cause the rest of her life. But her foremost contribution was her writing, her ability to articulate discontent, to provide a rationale for what would become one of the most successful social movements of the twentieth century.

Cesar Chavez and the UFW

Cesar Estrada Chavez, born in Yuma, Arizona, in 1927, led the most successful union of farmworkers in U.S. history. Chavez himself worked as a migrant farmworker from the age of ten, after his family lost their land during the Great Depression. Cesar, who was forced to attend dozens of elementary schools as his family moved about, quit school after the eighth grade to help support his family. After serving in the navy during World War II, Chavez married and settled in the San Jose, California, *barrio* called *Sal Si Puedes* ("Get out if you can").

While working in the orchards outside San Jose, Chavez met Fred Ross, an Anglo organizer for the Community Service Organization (CSO), which was sponsored by the Chicago-based Industrial Areas Foundation led by the famous community organizer, Saul Alinsky (see chapter 20). Chavez was soon working full time for the CSO, register-ing farmworkers to vote and organizing chapters of the CSO across California and Arizona. He once registered more than two thousand voters in just two months.

Chavez's wife, Helen, worked in the fields to support her husband and family during these years. (During his lifetime, Chavez never earned more than five thousand dollars a year.) In 1962 Chavez decided to leave the CSO to organize a union of farmworkers, the National Farm Workers Association (NFWA), later renamed the United FarmWorkers of America (UFW). Farmworkers had tried to organize unions before, but none had been successful, even though most farmworkers earned little more than a dollar an hour during this time.

Chavez roamed from one migrant camp to the next during the mid-1960s, tirelessly organizing a few followers in each. By 1964 the NFWA had about one thousand members in fifty locals. Chavez once said that "A movement with some lasting organiza-tion is a lot less dramatic than a movement with a lot of demonstrations and a lot of marching and so forth. The more dramatic organization does catch attention quicker. Over the long haul, however, it's a lot more difficult to keep together because you're not building solid.... A lasting organization is one in which people will continue to build, develop and move when you are not there."

In 1965, the NFWA joined in a strike against California grape growers, who brought in scabs and thugs who beat up the strikers. The strikers took a pledge of nonviolence, and Chavez himself conducted a 25-day fast in 1968 (a tactic he utilized often, like his hero Mahatma Gandhi) which attracted national media attention. Senator Robert Kennedy was at his side when he broke his fast, calling Chavez "one of the heroic figures of our time." Chavez also organized a nationwide boycott of grapes, forging a broad support coalition that included other unions, churches, and student and civil rights groups. Most of the major growers finally signed contracts with the union by 1970, and in 1975 the Agricultural Labor Relations Act was passed in California, which provided for secret-ballot elections, guaranteed the right to boycott, and oversaw collective bargaining between growers and farmworkers. Tens of thousands of farmworkers covered by UFW contracts enjoyed better wages, health insurance, and pension benefits.

The UFW lost much of its momentum during the early 1980s, confronting a new conservative state government in California. Chavez announced a new grape boycott in 1984, emphasizing how pesticides were harming both farmworkers and consumers. In 1988 Chavez conducted a 36-day "Fast for Life" to protest growers' use of harmful pesticides.

Chavez was president of the UFW when he died on April 23, 1993. Tens of thousands of mourners attended his funeral. The following year, President Bill Clinton posthumously awarded him the Presidential Medal of Freedom, the highest civilian honor.

Abbie Hoffman: "Marx with Flowers in his Hair"

Born in Worcester, Massachusetts, in 1936, Abbie Hoffman became one of the most famous revolutionaries of the 1960s, embodying the playful side of the period better than anyone else. He graduated from Brandeis in 1959 with a B.A. in psychology, but soon embarked on a lifetime of political and cultural activism. He became a civil rights organizer, then moved to Manhattan's Lower East Side to market the products of Mississippi cooperatives. When black nationalism came to dominate Student Nonviolent Coordinating Committee (SNCC) in the mid-1960s, he turned to the antiwar movement. He later said that he had tried "to bring the hippie movement into a broader protest," in other words to combine cultural expression with political protest. The "Yippies," which he founded with Jerry Rubin, were an effort to do just that.

Media events were Hoffman's specialty, based on his belief that "a modern revolutionary heads for the television station, not for the factory." In April 1967, Hoffman and a handful of companions threw dollar bills from the visitors' gallery of the New York Stock Exchange, causing a pause in trading while brokers scrambled for the money. That fall he organized an "exorcism" of the Pentagon, using incantations to try to levitate the building. (It did not work.) He and his friends planted a soot bomb at Con Edison headquarters, mailed joints to three thousand people selected randomly from the phone book. In 1968 he traveled around with a pig, which he tried to nominate for President. Abbie later explained his approach: "Recognizing the limited time span of someone staring at a lighted square in their living room, I trained for the one-liner, the retort jab, or sudden knockout put-ons."

Hoffman's fame peaked in the aftermath of the Chicago Democratic convention in 1968, when he and seven other defendants went on trial for conspiracy in organizing the protests. (The "Chicago Eight" became the "Chicago Seven" when Black Panther Bobby Seale was bound and gagged and imprisoned for contempt of court.) Hoffman especially turned the trial into a form of guerilla theater to express the ideas of the left. He even claimed, at one point, to be the illegitimate son of the judge presiding over the trial.

Hoffman had his critics. He had begun by using the media to get his message across, but the media in turn had made him a star. This came with a cost, as he and a handful of other celebrity-protestors came more and more to define the whole movement. Egalitarian efforts to avoid formal leaders had left a vacuum in which the media could place their own favorite spokespersons, inevitably those who were the most flamboyant.

Many protestors of the 1960s continued political activity alongside later jobs, but Hoffman devoted his adult life to full-time activism. He went underground in 1973 after being arrested in the sale of cocaine to undercover police, for which he faced a mandatory fifteen-year sentence. Using the name Barry Freed, he was active in environmental protest even while in hiding. In 1980 he turned himself in to authorities and served one year in prison. After that, he was a popular campus speaker and returned to writing. (*Steal This Book*, 1971, was his most memorable title.) He continued his political activities until 1989, when he committed suicide. In pain from an automobile accident the previous year, and on drugs for manic depression, he took a large dose of alcohol and phenobarbital on April 12. "Marx with flowers in his hair," one of Hoffman's phrases, described him well.

Lois Gibbs, Housewife Warrior

Compared to many social movements, the American environmental movement has created few nationally prominent leaders. Much of the movement's work is not flamboyant enough to attract media attention, but many groups have consciously tried to avoid the kind of celebrity leaders who rose to fame in the 1960s, like Abbie Hoffman. What is more, most environmental groups since the 1980s have been local, not national, efforts. Lois Gibbs is an exception, thanks to the intense media attention that came her way. She lived in a housing development called Love Canal.

Love Canal was a neighborhood in the town of Niagara Falls, in upstate New York. The land had been owned by the Hooker Chemical Company from 1946 until 1953, when it sold it to the Niagara Falls Board of Education for one dollar. The condition was that the company not be held liable for the chemical wastes (22,000 tons) it had buried there. The city built an elementary school on the site, then sold the remainder to real estate developers.

In the mid-1970s, Lois Gibbs' attention was focused on raising a family. She had a normal suburban existence, amidst tree-lined streets and weekend do-it-yourselfers. She and her husband, a chemical worker, had high-school degrees. When she was 26, they had bought their own modest three-bedroom house. They had two children, and Lois stopped working when they were born. Neither she nor her husband were interested in politics or active in any community organizations. Lois thought of herself as painfully shy, incapable of public speaking.

Gibbs began to see articles about Love Canal's health hazards in the *Niagara Falls Gazette*; at first she didn't realize it was her neighborhood. When she did, she grew alarmed, as her son Michael had just completed kindergarten in the school built right on top of the old canal. Could this, she wondered, explain the seizures he had begun having right after he started school, or the sudden drop in his white blood count during the winter? She turned to her brother-in-law, a biologist at the Buffalo campus of the State University of New York, who confirmed what the articles said: many of the chemicals buried in Love Canal are known to damage the central nervous system. They decided Michael should no longer go to the 99th Street School.

Concern for her own children quickly developed into a moral shock. The superintendent of schools for the district refused to allow Michael to attend a different elementary school, despite two doctor's letters pointing to his special sensitivities. The president of the PTA seemed uninterested as well. Shy Lois Gibbs began carrying a petition door to door, beginning with her own friends and acquaintances. She was surprised to hear about so many mysterious illnesses, crib deaths, and other cases of children suffering. When the New York Department of Health held a meeting in June 1978, she heard more: a pet dog had burned its nose just sniffing the ground, a toddler could not walk in her own backyard without burning her feet, basements with chemicals oozing through the walls. By now, she had the courage to ask questions, although she did not get serious answers.

Lois Gibbs was soon testifying before government hearings, addressing rallies of local residents, and leading a surging movement angry with the government for not doing enough to help. The Love Canal Homeowners Association, which she helped found, was a major reason that government eventually did respond, paying to relocate those residents who wished to move. It was their frequent, and frustrating, interactions with government bureaucrats which helped the Love Canal residents coalesce as a group, with considerable collective spirit and identity.

The New York State Health Department declared a health emergency, recommending that pregnant women and children under two leave the area closest to the old dump site. Eventually President Jimmy Carter declared it a federal disaster area. The state and federal government would spend nearly $300 million over the next twelve years studying and cleaning up the land, before declaring it safe again in 1990. Many homes in the most affected areas were purchased by the government. Love Canal helped inspire Congress to pass the Superfund cleanup program for toxic waste in 1980.

The battle also propelled Gibbs into an activist career. She left Love Canal, and her husband, moving to the Washington, D.C. area to establish the Citizens' Clearinghouse for Hazardous Waste. Its purpose was to provide information and advice to other local groups facing toxic waste and other hazards, just as the Love Canal neighbors had. Within a few years, there were thousands of groups associated with Gibb's new organization, forming one of the most vital wings of the environmental movement in the 1980s.

Joan Andrews, Living Martyr

Social movements get an enormous boost from martyrs who give their lives for the cause. They testify to the importance of the issue, as important to them as life itself. Plus they demonstrate how viciously repressive and brutal the other side, or the police, are. Death raises deep emotions, and forces people to ask what their deepest values are, what they might consider dying for. Short of these literal martyrs are figurative martyrs whose sacrifices fall somewhat this side of death, but are severe enough to earn them wide recognition in their social movement. In the anti-abortion movement, Joan Andrews was a person like this.

An anti-abortion protestor for some years, Andrews was convicted of third-degree burglary for entering the Ladies Center clinic in Pensacola, Florida in 1986 and damaging abortion equipment she found there. She was sentenced to five years in Florida state prisons. She protested her sentence by refusing to stand at her sentencing or to cooperate with the guards, who had to carry her out. She spent twenty months in a small cell in solitary confinement, with no church services and few visitors.

Despite her own plea to "focus on the babies," Andrews became a rallying cry for the anti-abortion movement, living proof of how the government ignored and repressed the movement. She also helped to bring the abortion issue, until then mostly of concern to Catholics, to Protestant fundamentalists, as her situation became a regular topic on Christian radio and television. Although she herself was Catholic, she was from the rural South, and mostly she was a victim of the evils of secular America – a threat to both Catholics and Protestants. She helped join these two wings of the anti-abortion movement.

Joan had an unusual religious background. Her mother was fervidly Catholic and raised her six children that way – the only Catholics in their part of rural Tennessee. Born in 1948, Joan grew up getting into fights in defense of her religious beliefs. An even more memorable event, when Joan was twelve, was her mother's miscarriage three or four months into another pregnancy. Mrs. Andrews put the tiny fetus in holy water, had it blessed by the local priest, and let her children see and hold it before they named and buried it (along with a lock of hair from each child). The image of her tiny brother, wrapped up in Catholic ceremony, strongly shaped Joan's view of the world.

Like many others who would flood into the anti-abortion movement, Andrews was shocked by the *Roe v. Wade* decision in January 1973. Outraged at how widespread the practice was as well as its legitimation by the Supreme Court, she decided to devote her life to the anti-abortion cause. She was soon available for any anti-abortion protest, anywhere, anytime. She never had a job, and only needed bus fare. She and a handful of others also pushed the movement into more radical tactics, spray-painting clinic walls, putting superglue in their locks, and pouring foul-smelling liquids in their waiting rooms. Andrews' nomadic activism was an inspiration to the growing movement, and at the same time she helped link local networks with each other. She also brought plenty of practical know-how to each city she visited. The conflict over abortion escalated in the mid-1980s, with shouting and pushing in front of clinics, vandalism and bombings of clinics, and lawsuits against the movement for a national conspiracy to shut down the clinics.

In Pensacola in March 1986, Andrews managed to sneak in the back entrance of a clinic while a large confrontation was unfolding in front. Before police could stop her, she had destroyed some machinery. As soon as she was out of jail on bond, she went right back to the same clinic. But her timing was bad; the protest occurred several months after three local abortion clinics had been bombed. Public and judicial opinion were not favorable. Yet even after her conviction in a nonjury trial in July, she was offered probation in exchange for agreeing to stay away from that same clinic. She refused, on the theory that total noncooperation with the justice system would bring more attention and gum up the works more than additional protest. The judge sentenced her to five years in prison.

She perfected noncooperation in jail. She slept on the floor and refused blankets. She stopped taking showers or exercising. She went limp and forced guards to carry her whenever she was supposed to leave her cell. She ate only the bare minimum amount of food she thought necessary to keep herself alive. She refused to accept the voluminous mail, tens of thousands of letters, that were sent her. Because everyone in the anti-abortion movement knew her, and had prayed and protested beside her, they rallied to her defense. She became an issue almost as prominent as that of abortion!

Most anti-abortionists are conservatives who favor prisons, and often think not enough is being done to fight crime. So the image of Joan Andrews in jail, while – they were convinced – most real felons were not, was shocking. Said one televangelist, "For nine months, she's been in solitary confinement. It seems it's a worse crime today to save a life than it is to take one." Florida's new law-and-order governor Bob Martinez couldn't simply grant Andrews clemency, but Florida decided to ship her out to Pennsylvania, where she had an outstanding warrant. She was released on probation after serving more than two years in prison. By then, October 1988, the anti-abortion movement was solidly fundamentalist, with the spotlight on Randall Terry and Operation Rescue. Andrews did not feel comfortable in this milieu and quickly dropped out of sight. But it was a movement that she, through her conscientious objection, had helped to create.

References
from part introductions/key concepts

Adorno, Theodor W. et al. 1950. *The Authoritarian Personality*. New York: Harper.

Breines, Wini. 1982. *Community and Organization in the New Left, 1962–1968: The Great Refusal*. South Hadley, MA: J. F. Bergin.

Burstein, Paul, Rachel L. Einwohner, and Jocelyn A. Hollander. 1995. "The Success of Social Movements." In J. Craig Jenkins and Bert Klandermans, eds., *The Politics of Social Protest*. Minneapolis: University of Minnesota Press.

Davies, James C. 1962. "Toward a Theory of Revolution." *American Sociological Review* 27:5–19.

Evans, Sara M., and Harry C. Boyte. 1986. *Free Spaces: The Sources of Democratic Change in America*. New York: Harper and Row.

Gamson, William A. 1990. *The Strategy of Social Protest*, 2nd edn. Homewood, IL: Dorsey.

Gans, Herbert J. 1979. *Deciding What's News*. New York: Random House.

Gerlach, Luther P., and Virginia H. Hine. 1970. *People, Power, and Change: Movements of Social Transformation*. Indianapolis: Bobbs-Merrill.

Goode, Erich, and Nachman Ben-Yehuda. 1994. *Moral Panics: The Social Construction of Deviance*. Oxford: Blackwell.

Goodwin, Jeff. 1997. "The Libidinal Constitution of a High-Risk Social Movement: Affectual Ties and Solidarity in the Huk Rebellion, 1946 to 1954." *American Sociological Review* 62:53–69.

Goodwin, Jeff, and James M. Jasper, eds. 2003. *Rethinking Social Movements: Structure, Meaning, and Emotion*. Lanham, MD: Rowman and Littlefield.

Goodwin, Jeff, James M. Jasper, and Francesca Polletta, eds. 2001. *Passionate Politics: Emotions and Social Movements*. Chicago: University of Chicago Press.

Gurney, Joan M. and Kathleen J. Tierney. 1982. "Relative Deprivation and Social Movements: A Critical Look at Twenty Years of Theory and Research." *Sociological Quarterly* 23:33–47.

Gurr, Ted. 1970. *Why Men Rebel*. Princeton: Princeton University Press.

Hall, John R. 1988. "Social Organization and Pathways to Commitment: Types of Communal Groups, Rational Choice Theory, and the Kanter Thesis." *American Sociological Review* 53:679–92.

Hoffer, Eric. 1951. *The True Believer*. New York: Harper and Row.

Isaacs, Harold R. 1963. *The New World of Negro Americans*. London: Phoenix House.

Jasper, James M. 1990. *Nuclear Politics: Energy and the State in the United States, Sweden, and France*. Princeton: Princeton University Press.

——. 1997. *The Art of Moral Protest: Culture, Biography, and Creativity in Social Movements*. Chicago: University of Chicago Press.

Jasper, James M., and Dorothy Nelkin. 1992. *The Animal Rights Crusade: The Growth of a Moral Protest*. New York: Free Press.

Jasper, James, and Jane Poulsen. 1993. "Fighting Back: Vulnerabilities, Blunders, and Countermobilization by the Targets in Three Animal Rights Campaigns." *Sociological Forum* 8:639–57.

Jasper, James M., and Jane Poulsen. 1995. "Recruiting Strangers and Friends: Moral Shocks and Social Networks in Animal Rights and Animal Protest." *Social Problems* 42:493–512.

Jenkins, J. Craig, and Charles Perrow. 1977. "Insurgency of the Powerless: Farm Worker Movements (1946–1972)." *American Sociological Review* 42:249–68.

Kanter, Rosabeth Moss. 1972. *Commitment and Community: Communes and Utopias in Sociological Perspective*. Cambridge, MA: Harvard University Press.

Keck, Margaret E., and Kathryn Sikkink. 1998. *Activists Beyond Borders: Advocacy Networks in International Politics*. Ithaca, NY: Cornell University Press.

Kitschelt, Herbert. 1986. "Political Opportunity Structures and Political Protest: Anti-Nuclear Movements in Four Democracies." *British Journal of Political Science* 16:57–85.

Klandermans, Bert. 1983. "Locus of Control and Socio-political Action-taking: The Balance of Twenty Years of Research." *European Journal of Social Psychology* 13:399–415.

——. 1989. "Grievance Interpretation and Success Expectations: The Social Construction of Protest." *Social Behaviour* 4:113–25.

Klandermans, Bert, and Dirk Oegema. 1987. "Potentials, Networks, Motivations and Barriers: Steps toward Participation in Social Movements." *American Sociological Review* 52:519–31.

Kornhauser, William. 1959. *The Politics of Mass Society.* Glencoe, IL: The Free Press.

LeBon, Gustave. 1960 [1895]. *The Crowd: A Study of the Popular Mind.* New York: Viking.

Mansbridge, Jane J. 1986. *Why We Lost the ERA.* Chicago: University of Chicago Press. Excerpted in this volume.

McAdam, Doug. 1982. *Political Process and the Development of Black Insurgency, 1930–1970.* Chicago: University of Chicago Press.

——. 1986. "Recruitment to High-Risk Activism: The Case of Freedom Summer." *American Journal of Sociology* 92:64–90.

——. 1988. *Freedom Summer.* New York: Oxford University Press.

McAdam, Doug, John D. McCarthy, and Mayer N. Zald. 1988. "Social Movements." In Neil J. Smelser, ed., *Handbook of Sociology.* Beverly Hills, CA: Sage.

McCarthy, John D., and Mayer N. Zald. 1973. *The Trend of Social Movements in America: Professionalization and Resource Mobilization.* Morristown, NJ: General Learning Press.

——. 1977. "Resource Mobilization and Social Movements: A Partial Theory." *American Journal of Sociology* 82:1212–41.

Melucci, Alberto. 1996. *Challenging Codes.* Cambridge: Cambridge University Press.

Morris, Aldon D. 1984. *The Origins of the Civil Rights Movement: Black Communities Organizing for Change.* New York: Free Press.

Oberschall, Anthony. 1973. *Social Conflict and Social Movements.* Englewood Cliffs, NJ: Prentice-Hall.

Olson, Mancur. 1965. *The Logic of Collective Action: Public Goods and the Theory of Groups.* Cambridge, MA: Harvard University Press.

Piven, Frances Fox, and Richard A. Cloward. 1979. *Poor People's Movements: Why They Succeed, How They Fail.* New York: Vintage.

Polletta, Francesca. 2002. *Freedom Is an Endless Meeting: Democracy in American Social Movements.* Chicago: University of Chicago Press.

Rothschild, Joyce, and J. Allen Whitt. 1986. *The Cooperative Workplace: Potentials and Dilemmas of Organizational Democracy and Participation.* Cambridge: Cambridge University Press.

Rupp, Leila J., and Verta Taylor. 1987. *Survival in the Doldrums.* New York: Oxford University Press.

Scott, James C. 1985. *Weapons of the Weak: Everyday Forms of Peasant Resistance.* New Haven: Yale University Press.

——. 1990. *Domination and the Arts of Resistance.* New Haven: Yale University Press.

Skocpol, Theda. 1979. *States and Social Revolutions: A Comparative Analysis of France, Russia, and China.* Cambridge: Cambridge University Press.

Smelser, Neil J. 1968. "Social and Psychological Dimensions of Collective Behavior." In Smelser, *Essays in Sociological Explanation.* Englewood Cliffs, NJ: Prentice-Hall.

Snow, David A., and Robert D. Benford. 1988. "Ideology, Frame Resonance, and Participant Mobilization." *International Social Movement Research* 1:197–217.

Snow, David A., and Susan Marshall. 1984. "Cultural Imperialism, Social Movements, and the Islamic Revival." Pp. 131–52 in *Social Movements, Conflicts, and Change*, Vol. 7, edited by Louis Kriesberg. Greenwich, CT: JAI Press.

Snow, David A., Louis A. Zurcher, and Sheldon Ekland-Olson. 1980. "Social Networks and Social Movements: A Microstructural Approach to Differential Recruitment." *American Sociological Review* 45:787–801.

Snow, David A., E. Burke Rochford, Jr., Steven K. Worden, and Robert D. Benford. 1986. "Frame Alignment Processes, Micromobilization, and Movement Participation." *American Sociological Review* 51:464–81.

Tarrow, Sidney. 1998. *Power in Movement*, 2nd edn. Cambridge: Cambridge University Press.

Taylor, Verta. 1989. "Social Movement Continuity: The Women's Movement in Abeyance." *American Sociological Review* 54:761–75.

Tilly, Charles. 1978. *From Mobilization to Revolution*. Reading, MA: Addison-Wesley.

Touraine, Alain. 1977. *The Self-Production of Society*. Chicago: University of Chicago Press.

Useem, Bert. 1980. "Solidarity Model, Breakdown Model, and the Boston Anti-Busing Movement." *American Sociological Review* 45:357–69.

Walsh, Edward J. 1981. "Resource Mobilization and Citizen Protest in Communities around Three Mile Island." *Social Problems* 29:1–21.

Woodward, C. Vann. 1974. *The Strange Career of Jim Crow*, 3rd edn. New York: Oxford University Press.

Index

Note: page numbers in italics refer to key concepts or figures